THE G3N3S1S DEBATE

CruXpress
books that matter

three views on the days of creation

THE G3N3S1S DEBATE

Edited by David G. Hagopian

CONTRIBUTORS

J. Ligon Duncan III & David W. Hall

The 24-Hour View

Hugh Ross & Gleason L. Archer

The Day-Age View

Lee Irons with Meredith G. Kline

The Framework View

CruXpress
books that matter

MISSION VIEJO, CALIFORNIA

The Genesis Debate: Three Views on the Days of Creation

Published by
Crux Press, Inc.
28715 Los Alisos Blvd., #7-418
Mission Viejo, California 92692

Cover design by Dwayne Cogdill, Cognition Design

Printed in the United States of America

Unless otherwise indicated, Scripture quotations are from the following translations:

J. Ligon Duncan III and David W. Hall, Hugh Ross and Gleason L. Archer—*The Holy Bible, New International Version*, © 1973, 1978, 1984 by International Bible Society. Used by permission of Zondervan Publishing House. All rights reserved.

Lee Irons and Meredith G. Kline—the *New American Standard Bible* (Updated Edition), © 1960, 1962, 1963, 1968, 1971, 1972, 1973, 1975, 1977, 1995 by The Lockman Foundation. Used by permission.

Scripture quotations designated NKJ are from the New King James Version, © 1979, 1980, 1982 by Thomas Nelson Inc., Publishers, Nashville, Tennessee

Italics in Scripture quotations indicate emphasis added.

Excerpts from *The Genesis Question* and *Creation and Time* are used and adapted with permission of NavPress, Colorado Springs, Colorado.

Library of Congress Catalog Number BT695-749

ISBN 0-9702245-0-8

To my precious daughter,

Kirstin Amber Hagopian,

lover of Scripture and nature,
dreamer of big dreams

CONTENTS
THE GENESIS DEBATE

ACKNOWLEDGMENTS

THE GENESIS DEBATE

No book, much less one as weighty as this one, could successfully make its way into print without the careful eye and attention to detail of good editors. Joette Whims and Lynn Copeland are to be thanked for their superb editorial skill and their willingness to work under difficult deadlines.

I also am grateful to Courtney Huntington for taking documents produced in the bland world of word processing and bringing them to life by typesetting them with great finesse. He loves words and pursues typesetting as a calling, and it shows.

Dwayne Cogdill of Cognition Design made us all look good by creating a brilliant cover and overseeing the design and print production of this book, bringing it from the computer to the shelf. He is a man of tremendous talent who is too humble to accept praise. So I thought it only appropriate to embarrass him in print.

I appreciate the valuable time Norman Geisler, R. C. Sproul, Jr., Marvin Olasky, and John Armstrong spent reviewing the manuscript, offering their helpful comments, and lending their stature by graciously endorsing the manuscript. They are men of integrity whose hands never tire serving the Christian community.

Of course, there could be no book without authors. J. Ligon Duncan III, David W. Hall, Hugh Ross, Gleason L. Archer, and Lee Irons in consultation with Meredith G. Kline not only are to be commended for cogently presenting their respective views of the Genesis creation days, but also for their patience, given that this debate spanned some 18 months.

I also thank Keith Nobriga and Don Buskirk of Crux Press for their friendship and collaboration in making this dream a reality.

My wife, Jamie, was gracious enough to allow me to pass too many nights staring at a monitor, and my four children—Brandon, Kirstin, Anallyce, and Alden—allowed Dad to miss more than a few games of checkers creating a book they won't be able to enjoy for many years to come!

Finally, I thank the One who demonstrated His splendor in the work of creation and His grace in the work of redemption. He gave us a good thing when He blessed us with books. Any good in this book comes from His hand, and any foibles come from mine.

Norman L. Geisler

FOREWORD
THE GENESIS DEBATE

he Genesis Debate is an example of the venerable adage, "In essentials, unity; in non-essentials, liberty; and in all things, charity." All the participants—J. Ligon Duncan III, David W. Hall, Hugh Ross, Gleason L. Archer, Lee Irons, and Meredith G. Kline—hold a high view of Scripture, affirming both the infallibility and inerrancy of Holy Writ. Within this context, the participants carry on a civil and scholarly interchange on a topic of considerable interest: whether the Genesis creation days are 24 hours long, ages of time, or merely a literary framework. The participants shed light on the importance of this debate and where it fits into an orthodox understanding of the faith.

The Genesis Debate teaches us several important lessons. First, the creation-day debate is not over the *inspiration* of the Bible, but over its *interpretation*. Each participant holds firmly to the full inspiration of Scripture. No one holding any of the views should be charged with unorthodoxy for the position he espouses in this volume.

Second, at best the creation-day debate is not one of evangelical *authenticity* but of evangelical *consistency*. That is, the maximum charge that

11

should be leveled by one proponent against another is that his view is not consistent with Scripture or the facts of nature, not that it is unorthodox.

Third, the *time* of creation is not as important as the *fact* of creation. That is, it is far more important to defend the biblical position that God created the universe, all basic kinds of life, and man in His image than it is to argue about how long it took God to do so.

Fourth, the Church needs to shift its focus to the real enemy—*evolutionism*—not to other forms of *creationism* that remain true to the historicity of the events recorded in Genesis. Our foe is liberalism, not different stripes of conservatism. Evangelicals need to start turning their cannons on *naturalists*, not on other *supernaturalists*.

Fifth, just as the issue is not one of *orthodoxy*, so it also is not one of *morality*. Good and godly people are found on all sides of the creation-day debate. No one should impugn another's faith or character simply because he holds one of the views represented in this volume.

Sixth, *popularity* should not dictate *orthodoxy*. In the long history of the Church, several views of the creation-day debate emanating from those who hold to the infallibility and inerrancy of Scripture have been within the pale of orthodoxy. Indeed, many of the greatest champions of the highest view of Scripture have held divergent views regarding the age of the earth.

Nonetheless, a warning is in order. We must not sacrifice our orthodox understanding of Genesis 1 and 2. The Church must uphold the historical nature of the creation account, for on it rest other important doctrines of Scripture (see Romans 5:12 and Matthew 19:4–6). In addition, we must uphold the factual nature of the record as important to orthodoxy. We should reject all attempts to reduce the creation record to fable as opposed to fact, or to mythology as opposed to history. Finally, we must preserve the literal sense of Scripture, no matter what literary devices biblical authors employ. We must preserve at all costs the historical-grammatical method of interpreting the Bible, since denying it undermines other important doctrines. If we deny the historical-grammatical method when interpreting the first few chapters of Genesis regarding creation, why not do so when interpreting the last chapters of the Gospels regarding the resurrection? Our understanding of creation affects our understanding of the rest of Scripture.

Since Scripture contains the very words of God, Christians must respect it and must treat one another charitably when they arrive at different interpretations about important issues, like the creation days in Genesis. *The Genesis Debate* paves the way for the Christian community to work toward consensus regarding the creation account in Genesis 1 and 2. Regardless of whether you hold to the 24-hour, day-age, or framework view,

The Genesis Debate is a worthwhile volume that will help you better understand the biblical doctrine of creation.

David G. Hagopian

INTRODUCTION
THE GENESIS DEBATE

hilosopher George Edward Moore wrote that "the difficulties and disagreements, of which history is full, are mainly due to a very simple cause: namely to the attempt to answer questions, without first discovering precisely *what* question it is which you desire to answer."

So it is with the creation controversy. As we enter the third millennium and witness scientific paradigms about cosmic, life, and human origins shifting yet again, can it be that much of the controversy that has roiled the Church for the past 150 years has arisen because we failed to heed Moore's sage advice? Can it be that we have spent far too much time answering questions about creation without first discovering precisely *what* question we desire to answer?

We could ask and answer several questions about creation: Is macroevolutionary theory unorthodox? Does nature reveal intelligent design? What is the proper relationship between natural revelation and special revelation? As important as it may be to address these questions, the primary question for Christians committed to the truth of Scripture always must be: *What does Scripture itself say about the Genesis creation days?* Even more precisely: *Are the creation days 24 hours, ages, or a literary framework?*

The Structure of the Debate

For some time, the Christian community has needed to have committed evangelicals charitably discuss their divergent views about the creation days in a single volume. That need has given birth to this book, *The Genesis Debate: Three Views on the Days of Creation.*

As the title indicates, this volume gives proponents of three evangelical schools of thought the opportunity to explain their respective views and to interact directly and meaningfully with one another. The three views presented are known, respectively, as the 24-hour, day-age, and framework views.

The *24-hour view* holds that God created the universe and all life in six sequential natural days marked by evenings and mornings. According to this view, God created the universe and all life in approximately 144 hours and in the sequence presented in Genesis 1. Defending this view are J. Ligon Duncan III and David W. Hall.

The *day-age view*, defended by Hugh Ross and Gleason L. Archer, agrees with the 24-hour view that the events recorded in Genesis 1 are sequential. The day-age view, however, parts company with the 24-hour view regarding the length of the creation days. According to the day-age view, God did not create the universe and all life in six 24-hour days, but in six sequential ages of unspecified, though finite, duration.

The *framework view* holds that the days of Genesis form a figurative framework in which the divine works of creation are narrated in a topical, rather than sequential, order. This view holds that the picture of God completing His work of creation in six days and resting on the seventh was not intended to reveal the sequence or duration of creation, but to proclaim an eschatological theology of creation. Lee Irons defends this view in consultation with Meredith G. Kline.

The debate started with each author team preparing its opening essay. Those essays were circulated to the other two teams, and each team prepared response essays that interacted with the opposing views. After the responses were circulated, each team concluded the debate by preparing a reply essay that addressed the points raised in the response essays.

The debate is presented in three parts, corresponding to each of the three views. Part One focuses on the 24-hour view, presenting the 24-hour opening essay, followed by the day-age and framework responses, and closing with the 24-hour reply. Part Two repeats this pattern with the day-age view, and Part Three presents the framework view.

Other views of the creation days that compete in the marketplace of ideas are not featured in this volume. One previously popular view, known as the gap theory, posits long ages between the initial creation *ex nihilo* (Gen. 1:1) and the formation of the habitable earth, which took place in six 24-hour days. The restitution theory modifies the gap theory by holding that the chaos of Genesis 1:2 was caused by Satan's fall from heaven. Augustine argued that God created the universe in an instant, while P. J. Wiseman argued that when ancient literary forms are applied to Genesis 1, the six creation days refer to the time occupied by God in revealing the origins of the universe to man.

These views, however, have not been embraced by large numbers of evangelicals. More important, there is little, if any, scriptural evidence to support them, making a sustained exegetical discussion like this one somewhat difficult.

One exception on the exegetical front is the anthropomorphic days view espoused by C. John Collins of Covenant Theological Seminary. Because this view bears similarities to the framework view and shares other features with the day-age view, it has not been included here. The same could be said of the age-separated, 24-hour-days view, which shares features with both the 24-hour and day-age views. According to this view, the six days of creation each occurred in 24 hours, but are punctuated by intervening ages of unspecified, though finite, duration. While these two views are important, multi-view volumes unfortunately must limit the discussion to avoid becoming unwieldy, and other recent volumes have incorporated them. Therefore, this book restricts discussion to the 24-hour, day-age, and framework views.

The Uniqueness of the Debate

If other volumes exist, why this one? First, this volume attempts to avoid addressing tangential questions and goes to the *crux* of the matter by focusing on what Scripture teaches about the length of the creation days. All the comments are driven first and foremost by biblical considerations.

Second, while single-author volumes are helpful, the debate format is even more helpful by presenting the views of three teams of authors. At the same time, this book avoids the flaw of some multiple-author volumes which present a series of essays, with each author presenting his own view but never responding directly to opposing views. The format used in this debate is also richer than multi-view volumes where authors explain their views, only to have other authors come in from the side as "color commentators" to reply. This volume, by contrast, allows the authors to defend their respective views throughout. As you will see, this makes the debate more coherent, and promotes a most meaningful and interesting dialogue.

Third, this volume stays within the parameters of evangelical ortho-doxy and Christian charity. Each author is wholeheartedly committed to the infallibility and inerrancy of Scripture from Genesis to Revelation. Each author rejects the macroevolutionary theory of human origins as incom-patible with Scripture. And each author extends the principle of charity to his counterparts. When the stakes are high, emotions run high, and we need to be all the more vigilant to avoid the temptation to argue by epi-thet. While the emotions of the creation debate come through here in appropriate places, the authors admirably avoid the mudslinging that sadly characterizes many Christian discussions of creation.

Although the author teams vigorously argue that their own view is more biblical than the views of their counterparts, they do not accuse each other of denying the gospel. Difficult passages of Scripture may allow dif-fering interpretations without necessarily threatening the gospel. Those who make such accusations serve neither the peace nor the purity of the Church, especially when they fail to meaningfully discuss the views they attack. The modern Church also needs to learn that declaring a view as unorthodox is *not* a matter of private judgment; it is a matter for the Church *as the Church* to decide.

The Importance of the Debate

This debate has important ramifications for how we interpret Scripture, proclaim the faith, embrace science, and stand on the shoulders of those who have preceded us in the faith. We all would do well to remember that we agree on far more than we disagree, but we also must remember that we gain nothing by ignoring our differences or sweeping them under the rug. In fact, we stand to gain quite a bit by discussing our differences openly, honestly, and charitably.

The Genesis Debate does precisely that. It gives evangelicals who are committed to the infallibility and inerrancy of Scripture an opportunity to defend their respective views in a lively, yet friendly, forum. Whether you are new to the creation debate or have followed it for years, *The Gen-esis Debate* will deepen your understanding and strengthen your faith. Praise be to God—our Creator and Redeemer—both now and forever!

The 24-Hour View

PART
ONE
THE GENESIS DEBATE

J. Ligon Duncan III & David W. Hall

THE 24-HOUR VIEW

he debate over the Genesis creation days involves issues of enduring significance to the evangelical Christian community. It involves our doctrine of knowledge (epistemology), doctrine of man
(anthropology), defense of the faith (apologetics), and method of interpreting Scripture (hermeneutics), all of which are intertwined with the
Genesis creation account. While the creation debate should not become a
preoccupation, nonetheless, it is far too important to be dismissed as un-
worthy of our best thought, study, and biblical interpretation. The stakes
are too high.

The ongoing discussion of the creation days is an obvious part of what
has been perhaps the most important sustained theological controversy in
the Western world over the last century—resolving the conflicting truth
claims between historic Christianity and modern evolutionary science. That
reason alone warrants a sane, less trendy, and restrained discussion of the
creation days. We hope that our discussion benefits the Christian community as we seek to "take captive every thought" (2 Cor. 10:5) and prepare ourselves to "give an answer [*apologia*] . . . for the hope that [we] have"
(1 Pet. 3:15).

21

From the outset, let us state that our defense of the historic Judeo-Christian view does not imply that we agree or disagree with various "creationist" positions on the age of the universe. The age of the universe is a matter of inference and sometimes speculation, whereas the interpretation of scriptural references to *day* is a distinct issue. We purposefully limit our discussion to the meaning of *day* in Scripture and the history of interpretation. We decline to speculate about unbiblical theories; nor do we believe that detailed knowledge of certain scientific fields is a prerequisite for believers—past or present—to understand God's word on this limited subject. In short, we take no position on the age of the universe precisely because that question is not directly addressed by the canon. The use of *day*, by contrast, *is* addressed and, thus, is our focal point.

THE BIG PICTURE

Objective historians, theologians, and interpreters should admit that the debate over the creation days and their nature and length is strictly recent. While one may find in the record of historical theology a small smattering of orthodox theologians who approached the days of Genesis as something other than normal days, he will not find detailed debate over this matter until the sixteenth century and will seldom find debates between orthodox divines arguing for and against the days as long ages until the nineteenth century.[1]

What are we to make of this undeniable fact? Simply this: The historic Christian tradition, which is rooted in a cumulative history of interpretation, has viewed these days mainly as normal days because it has viewed the Genesis account as historical. No significant debate existed on the matter before the nineteenth century because the plainest and most straightforward reading of the text had no sustained challengers. For example, when a revived form of Augustine's instantaneous creation view made its appearance among select guild theologians in the Western Church in the sixteenth and seventeenth centuries, John Calvin and the later Puritan divines dealt it a swift death blow. Not until certain theories in modern geology, biology, paleontology, anthropology, and physics gained wide acceptance in various Western intellectual communities in the nineteenth and twentieth centuries did debates about the Genesis days begin to roil the Church.

AN EXEGETICAL DEBATE?

Let us state the matter boldly: *The debate over the nature of the creation days is not a purely exegetical or interpretive debate*. It is also a hermeneutical and theological debate. Why? Because compelling exegetical evidence for reading the creation days as anything other than normal days is lacking. Few even attempt to approach this text on purely exegetical grounds and then claim that the text alone drives them from a literal toward a figurative understanding. Rather, the concerns surrounding this text that bedevil modern interpreters and theologians are hermeneutical and theological, not textual and exegetical. As we shall see, the intent of the author of Genesis 1–2 as to the nature of the creation days is so apparent that it is, frankly, beyond dispute. We will prove that this intent was not only understood and accepted throughout the whole of the Old Testament canon, but also in the New Testament canon and the history of orthodox interpretation until the nineteenth century. Developments external to the canon that arose after (and in support of) revolutionary shifts in science animated hermeneutical changes in how some Christians approached the Genesis creation days.

Even those who are not normally viewed as friends of the historic Christian view of creation concur. James Barr, for example, comments:

> So far as I know there is no professor of Hebrew or Old Testament at any world-class university who does not believe that the writer(s) of Genesis 1–11 intended to convey to their readers . . . that creation took place in a series of six days which were the same as the days of 24 hours we now experience.[2]

An earlier adversary of the orthodox view of creation, Andrew White, admitted, despite his wish to the contrary, that Calvin had a "strict" interpretation of Genesis as teaching creation *ex nihilo*, and that

> down to a period almost within living memory [1896], it was held, virtually "always, everywhere, and by all," that the universe, as we now see it, was created literally and directly by the voice or hands of the Almighty, or by both—out of nothing—in an instant or in six days.[3]

Even though ardent opponents of the orthodox view of creation find it difficult to challenge the biblical record, sadly, some friends of the orthodox faith have done so in recent years.[4]

This debate, then, is not only about interpretation, but also systematic theology. It is not only about biblical theology, but also historical theology. It is not only about reflecting on present formulations, but also deeper historical realities. In short, it is not only about *text*, but also *context*.

First we will turn our attention to the divine texts themselves. We also will bring in previous voices who may know as much as, if not more than, commentators from our own enfeebled century, especially those who seem to be driven to accommodate transient academic norms and conclusions. Then we will answer major objections to our views, and finally, emphasize why this debate is not only worthwhile, but also why it demands our clearest thinking.

Throughout our discussion, we will demonstrate that the Scriptures themselves teach that the creation days are normal days consisting of 24 hours and that the history of Christian interpretation prior to the modern era—now outfitted with its acquired biases—maintained this understanding. We also will demonstrate that extrabiblical considerations are insufficient to convince us to depart from the faith handed down. Indeed, departing from that faith with less reason than we have been provided to date endangers the very future of the Church. Thus, our position is based on the fundamentally conservative methodological premise that we ought to preserve well-founded teachings of antiquity until superior exegesis (interpretation) definitively repudiates those teachings. Mere claims to novel interpretations that conform to fluctuating scientific theories are inadequate to justify a departure from sound interpretation.

We do not believe that Christians of the past, who lacked the scientific expertise of our day, were less capable of interpreting the Genesis texts. We remain unconvinced that the Hebrew language itself, knowledge of Semitic syntax, confirmation of the Genesis texts by other biblical texts, or authorial intent have so changed as to require us to opt for a different interpretation of Genesis 1–2. To us, the words and meaning of Scripture are little changed from the interpretations of Basil, Ambrose, or Calvin. The only things that have changed are the extrabiblical and secular cosmological theories of the past two centuries.[5] Therefore, we believe that the burden rests upon our counterparts to prove conclusively that the intention of Scripture, particularly Genesis 1–2, somehow has been altered with age or with the "progress" of scientific knowledge.

In other words, we are not convinced that secular theories are so certain that they require us to alter the classical interpretation of Scripture. History may prove us wrong, but to date, we assign higher enduring status to the interpretations of Scripture from 2000 B.C.–A.D. 1800, than we do to those influenced by evolution from A.D. 1800–2000.

Rather than succumb to the temptation to side with modern science, we would be far better off to side with an earlier scientist, Sir Isaac Newton, who, in 1681, commented on whether the days in Genesis 1 were fictitious: "Methinks one of the Ten Commandments given by God on Mount Sinai, pressed by divers of the prophets, observed by our Savior, his Apostles, and [the] first Christians . . . should not be grounded on a fiction."[6] Clearly, Newton did not agree with viewing the creation days as "fictional" or "metaphorical," but viewed them as normal days.

Throughout this discussion, we hope to sound a ringing affirmation *for* the classical Christian view of creation. Believers need not be bullied into embracing more recent schemes. Even though we appreciate the long-standing tradition of taking the Genesis days as normal days, we do not consider the opinions of others to be primary. *What is primary is what God intended to communicate about the creation days to Moses and his original audience and whether the rest of Scripture corroborates such original intent.* Accordingly, we will spend the bulk of our time interpreting the Scriptures because they provide clear answers to the question of the days' duration.

THE CREATION NARRATIVES AND NORMAL CREATION DAYS

In this section, we will prove that the creation narratives themselves, far from being ambiguous, clearly teach that the creation days were normal days. We will do so by setting forth the straightforward and clear meaning of Genesis 1–2 concerning the creation days, indicating some of the "exegetical markers" to which proponents of nonliteral views frequently appeal and explaining why none of these markers can justify a nonliteral rendering of the Genesis days.

God as the Author of Creation
The very opening words of Genesis thrust upon us the issue of our "origin" or "beginning"—"In the beginning God created the heavens and the earth. Now the earth was formless and empty, darkness was over the surface of the deep, and the Spirit of God was hovering over the waters" (Gen. 1:1–2). This language is important because several esteemed theologians (Meredith G. Kline, Henri Blocher, Mark Futato, C. John Collins, and others) argue that Moses was not trying to give us a detailed or technical discourse on the origins of the universe, but rather was propounding a sustained apologetic argument against the pagan worldviews of the day. For this reason, we should not press certain details of the narrative—including the length of the creation days—as though they reflect a divinely inspired cosmogony.

This conclusion, however, does not follow from its premise. The mere presence of an apologetic in the narrative does not compromise the cosmogony it contains. Indeed, the cosmogony is the apologetic! In other words, we may agree with nonliteralists that cosmogony *per se* is not the main thrust of the text. Nonetheless, if the cosmogony or aspects of it are merely a literary framework or a didactic tool, then the theology as a whole loses its force in countering pagan opinion. Ironically, we end up compromising the apologetic function of the text.

Throughout the narrative, the God-revealed and real cosmogony (as opposed to merely literary, analogous, anthropomorphic, or didactic cosmogony) is the vehicle by which Moses wages war against the heathen worldviews of the day while buttressing the convictions of the Hebrew people. If we analyze the text fairly, we cannot ignore or relegate to a secondary status the cosmogony it contains. Cosmogony is central in every way.

Thus, the book of Genesis, and especially its first section, is designed (at the very least) to teach us several great truths:

- God created the world and is distinct from it (but not unconcerned about it).

- God shaped His creation from formlessness into order and filled it from emptiness into fullness.

- God's world was originally good and, therefore, different from the corrupted world in which we now live.

- Man's sin is entirely responsible for corrupting original creation.

- God's character (justice and mercy) is revealed as He responds to the three "low points" of primeval history: the Fall, the Flood, and Babel.

Evangelicals acknowledge these theological truths, none of which require us to question the literal reality and historicity of the specific details of the creation account.

The first two verses of Genesis bring us face to face with the ultimate reality: the one true God. It is that reality which ought to be the conscious arena of our experience.[7] These verses present the author, source, and cause of the creation: God—In the beginning God! As Matthew Henry puts it:

> The first verse of the Bible gives us a surer and better, a more satisfying and useful, knowledge of the origin of the universe, than all the volumes of the philosophers. The lively faith of humble Christians understands this matter better than the elevated fancy of the greatest wits.[8]

Henry's wisdom acutely applies to our current discussion.[9] After introducing us to the sovereign, self-revealed, personal God of heaven and earth, Moses' account shows us the effect of God's work in producing the heavens and the earth. God's immediate creation of the universe is the very basis of its teleology. Again, Henry says:

> The foundation of all religion being laid in our relation to God as our Creator, it was fit that the book of divine revelations which was intended

to be the guide, support, and rule, of religion in the world, should begin as it does, with a plain and full account of the creation of the world.[10]

Genesis 1:1 asserts the comprehensiveness of God's creation. He made everything. But the text also hints at the manner or method of this work: creation *ex nihilo*—out of nothing. The phrase "In the beginning God . . ." manifests the truth that nothing existed prior to God's speaking (Heb. 11:3). This Christian view of creation is under assault in our time by historians who allege that it is a late, Greek philosophical doctrine annexed to patristic Christian doctrine. Creation *ex nihilo* is also under attack by scientific skeptics who refuse to seriously consider the relevance of Christian truth claims to the space-time universe that they study. But, as Donald Macleod has observed, the Christian view is not as vulnerable as some might wish it to be:

> The impression has got abroad not only that the Christian doctrine of the creation has been disproved but that scholars have agreed on an alternative. Neither of these assumptions is correct. There is no agreed alternative to the Christian position. Those which are affirmed are beset with enormous difficulties. The Christian doctrine, on the other hand, seems to have no particular difficulty of its own, is supported by a great body of argument, philosophical and scientific, and is confirmed by the whole process of special revelation in which God both asserts and describes Himself.[11]

Macleod correctly observes that there are only three options in the marketplace of ideas on this issue. The first option is the Christian doctrine of creation *ex nihilo*, which Macleod writes is the view that "before creation, God alone existed and His existence is the reason for the coming into being of all else."[12]

The second option represents one possible pagan view, *ex nihilo nihil fit* (out of nothing, nothing was made). According to this view, "before Creation *nothing* existed—not God, not matter, not mass, not energy, not potential, not a protoplasm, but nothing."[13] Needless to say, this pagan view requires a high degree of faith or unsubstantiated leaps. The fact that something now exists drives us to the conclusion that something always existed.

The third option is another pagan view: "Before Creation an impersonal something existed—some protoplasm or primary particle in which all the potentialities later realised in the universe were latent."[14] But as Macleod observes:

> Surely, however, the existence of such an impersonal something is no less of a mystery and no less of a stumbling block to the radically sceptical intellect than the existence of God Himself. Such a something already possesses some of the characteristics of deity, being eternal, self-existent,

and omnipotent. Moreover, this theory of origins is burdened with all the difficulties that face consistent materialism. The nature of the universe itself is against it. It is difficult to believe that the complexity of familiar life forms is the result of unprogrammed molecular and genetic change; and even more difficult to convince ourselves that *Paradise Lost*, *Hamlet*, and the Sermon on the Mount are derived through an inexorable sequence of cause and effect from a primitive protein.[15]

The movement from the impersonal to the personal in the second and third options is an insurmountable philosophical barrier to both, which commends the Christian view.

Genesis 1:1 sets forth the sovereign God who created all things, in opposition to modern naturalism and ancient paganism. This one verse establishes the sovereign Lord's rights and interest in all things because He created them.

Moses then begins to recount the specific productive and ordering acts of the Lord's grand creative design. He does so after noting in Genesis 1:2 that "the earth was formless and empty, darkness was over the surface of the deep, and the Spirit of God was hovering over the waters." We see here the chaos of the first created matter and God's method of crafting the world from formlessness and emptiness to the order and fullness which we now experience, even in this fallen world. Moses shows us how God's Spirit works in creation, providence, and grace. Three characteristics of the original creation are addressed in God's work during creation. The earth is (1) formless (Heb., *tohu*): without form, a trackless waste, chaos, that which is futile; (2) empty (*bohu*): void, barren, vacuous, vacant; and (3) dark (*hasek*): unlit, obscure, murky.[16] In six days, God turns this formless mass into something well-formed and ordered. This ordering of the original chaotic creation is depicted in Genesis 1:3–2:3.

The structure of the creation week addresses these three qualities. God takes up the challenge of form in Days 1–3, which speak of God's shaping the world, ordering it out of formlessness (Gen. 1:3–10). Then He deals with fullness in Days 4–6, which speak of God's filling the world, bringing fullness to emptiness (vv. 11–13, 14–31). He creates light on both Days 1 and 4 (the first of the parallel triads), rolling back darkness. God thus impresses His creation with the stamp of His character. The heavens declare His glory: the glory of order, fullness, and light.

While recent studies of this great passage cause us to increasingly appreciate its intricacy and structure, we are not inclined to deduce that the account is therefore artificial or metaphorical. Nor should the overt theological and apologetic purposes of the narrative lead us to assume that the details of the narrative are contrived or immaterial.

A Few Observations

Before we look at the creation days themselves, we will pause to make a few observations. First, as we stated earlier, most of the great interpreters of the Church have construed the creation days as normal days. We mention this fact again to buttress the conclusion that the most straightforward reading of the text, including the issue of the length of the days, is that these are normal days. Further, this straightforward understanding is not restricted to unlearned readers of the English Bible, rabid fundamentalists, Seventh-Day Adventists, and conservative Lutherans, but is, in fact, the consensus of the greatest minds in the history of Christianity. We increasingly hear people claim that a literal reading of the days may reflect the naïve reader's initial understanding of the text, but that a more diligent wrestling with the text will uncover more and more problems for the literal view and will naturally lead the astute interpreter to some kind of figurative interpretation. While that claim may appeal to many modern evangelical interpreters, it finds no support in the witness of history. In light of this fact, advocates of nonliteral views need to address themselves humbly to, and not with imperious contempt for, the legitimate concerns of the conservative Christian community. These people see in nonliteral views another illustration of the long history of revisionism when it comes to understanding Genesis 1–2.

Second, our traditional understanding of the creation days contains a wonderful observation about God's goodness in the way He went about the work of creation. Calvin insists that the creation week was not merely a didactic tool or framework the Lord employed to reveal Himself intelligibly to His finite creatures. Rather, God actually performed His work of creation in an ordinary week out of love for His people, who could identify with the cycle of days. Hence, Calvin emphatically holds to the 24-hour-day view and vehemently rejects any suggestion that the structure of the creation narrative is merely a didactic device. For Calvin, God not only accommodated Himself to His people in the way He *explained* His creative work; He actually accommodated Himself in the way He *performed* His creative work. Calvin replied to advocates of an analogical, anthropomorphic, revelatory, or framework view of the creation days four hundred years before the idea was in vogue:

> It is too violent a cavil to contend that Moses distributes the work which God perfected at once into six days, for the mere purpose of conveying instruction. Let us rather conclude that God himself took the space of six days, for the purpose of accommodating his works to the capacity of men.[17]

Calvin rejects Augustine's "instantaneous creation" interpretation. Augustine's view was neither born of a mastery of the original Hebrew nor motivated by considerations internal to the text; rather, his concern was for theological harmonization with a statement in the apocryphal book Ecclesiasticus (18:1). But Calvin's point is also apropos for modern evangelicals. He maintains that in the structure of the creation account, our Lord accommodated Himself to our capacities, not merely in His words but in His very works. To accommodate in word only would be to employ a pedagogical device familiar to all of us: using the known to explain the unknown. To accommodate in His very works, however, singularly expresses such divine condescension as to flood the heart with praise to the One who would go so far to reveal a true and saving knowledge of Himself to His people. What can we do in response but bow the knee?

Third, as we approach Genesis 1–2, we should be wary of those who accommodate Scripture to current scientific theory, because he who marries the spirit of the age will be a widower in the next. In addition, even the most intrepid defender of harmonizing the Bible and science faces insurmountable difficulties finding in the creation narrative an original authorial intent that foreshadowed the opinions of modern geology, biology, and physics.

Fourth, any view that undercuts the historical character of the creation story opens the door to more thoroughgoing reinterpretations. Who, after all, is the arbiter fit to determine what is structure and what is *kerygma* (the essence of the message)? Conservative literary views, for example, hold that literary devices in the Genesis creation account teach us that man is the apex of God's creation. But if we admit that part of the creation account is figurative, why stop there? To press the logic of the figurative view, why couldn't we say that Adam's creation in Genesis 1:27 is the climax of the discourse? We would then be able to stress man's role in God's created order while finding no reason to press Christian anthropologists into holding to the special creation of Adam. If the scientist, as Kline has argued elsewhere, may be "left free of constraints when hypothesizing about cosmic origins"[18] by a literary approach to the meaning of the days, why shouldn't he also be left free of constraints when hypothesizing about human origins? No figurative view can provide a sturdy answer to prevent its adherents from sliding down this slippery slope.

Fifth, we look back into the creation days through several imposing barriers, such as the Noahic Flood. In the Mosaic account, the post-Flood world seems to have changed in basic ways from the pre-Flood world, thus raising significant questions about assumptions of uniformity. The Fall of Adam is no small barrier either. We barely can estimate its impact on our intellect in general and our knowledge of the original order in particular. The sixth day of creation is a formidable barrier as well. Whatever one's view may be of sequence, chronology, and duration, much of the creation was completed before man arrived. In Genesis 12, for example, Moses tells us what Abraham himself heard from God, but in Genesis 1, prior to the sixth day, Moses describes what no man ever saw! At this point, some may reasonably argue that if the Genesis days are not normal days, then we do not know what they are. Thus, we are down to two and only two views of the creation days: (1) normal days or (2) *days* unknown to us.

Sixth, as we approach the creation narratives, two overriding factors influence us to read the days as normal days. To begin with, the simplest explanation of the text, as we argued above, is that Moses intended the days to be thought of in the most common sense of that term. Both Ockham's razor and the history of interpretation confirm the primacy of this reading. Furthermore, many of those who adhere to figurative views admit that the Hebrew word *yôm*, accompanied by the phrase "and there was evening and there was morning," is set in the context of a week and is employed as a Sabbath argument by Moses. Thus, we have no reason to doubt what the author intended regarding the nature of the creation days. The precise denotation of the phrase "and there was evening and there was morning" is immaterial to the argument. Whether that phrase describes/ defines creation days (as the older commentators preferred), or provides a boundary between the divine worker's creative activity establishing a rhythm of work and rest (as many modern commentators prefer), or is a mere transitional clause of no great theological import, it clearly is language that is intimately associated with normal days in the experience of readers from every age and culture. As such, this phrase strengthens one's predilection toward understanding the creation days as normal days.

The Role of the Days in the Narrative

Now we will briefly consider the role of the days in the larger structure of the narrative.

The First Day. By all accounts, God's sheer power is expressed in creation by fiat:

> Then God said, "Let there be light"; and there was light. And God saw that the light was good; and God separated the light from the darkness. And God called the light day, and the darkness He called night. And there was evening and there was morning, one day. (Gen. 1:3–5)

This pattern is apparent from the first to the sixth day—by eight simple commands, God spoke the world into reality. As Kidner notes: "[This] leaves no room for notions of a universe that is self-existent, or struggled for, or random, or a divine emanation; and the absence of any intermediary implies an extremely rich content for the word 'said.'"[19] We ourselves know what it means to order things to happen, but God does so cosmically and effectually.

The Second Day. Note the immediate emphasis on "dividing" day and night. Differentiation is the divine way of ordering: God separated light from the darkness (see also vv. 6–7, 14, 18, and Lev. 20:25). Modern philosophy may have difficulty making absolute distinctions, but God transforms chaos into order by differentiation, division, and distinction (1:6–8), as He does on the second day. This day recounts the creation of sky (the expanse, heaven) and the separation of the heavenly waters from the terrestrial. Note already a six-part formula for each day: (1) introductory word ("Then God said"); (2) creative word ("let there be"); (3) fulfillment word ("and it was so"); (4) lordship word ("God called"); (5) commending word ("it was good," beginning on Day 3); and (6) concluding word ("and there was evening . . .").

The Third Day. On the third day, God is ultimately responsible for the earth's productive powers (vv. 9–13). Beginning on that day, the emphasis of creation shifts from formation/ordering to filling/bearing. Here we see that even mediate creation comes from the hand of God and depends upon Him entirely for its procreational powers. Thus, Moses delivers a bold strike against earth worship, ancient and modern.

The Fourth Day. When we arrive at the fourth day, we stumble upon one of the main arguments for understanding the creation days as figurative or anthropomorphic. The theological message of this passage is that God is sovereign over the markers that order our lives (vv. 14–19). Opponents of the 24-hour view often point out with glee that the sun and moon were not created until the fourth day, thereby presenting a seemingly insurmountable obstacle to the 24-hour view and a strong argument in favor of a nonliteral view.

Aside from the fact that Calvin answered this objection almost half a millennium ago, it misses Moses' brilliant and ironic polemic against those who worshiped various astral bodies. The sun, moon, and stars were gods to many, but Moses' God is so independent of creation that He did not hasten to create those grand luminaries until the halfway point in His work. Hence, not only are they products of His creative dominion, but they are—as vast and awesome as they may be—not even the focal point of the account, standing at neither the beginning nor the end of the discourse on creation. Thus, the sun and moon are not gods to be worshiped, but God's gifts to order our lives and structure our time. The Lord's awesome power is also manifest in the almost afterthought, "He made the stars also." As Kidner says: "In a few sentences the lie is given to a superstition as old as Babylon and as modern as a newspaper horoscope."

The Fifth Day. The fifth day reveals God as sovereign over the most powerful of earthly forces: sea and sea monsters (vv. 20–23). The powerful sea creatures clearly are God's creation, not rival gods, much less pre-existing forces! We detect here an anti-Babylonian apologetic.

The Sixth Day. On the sixth day, God indicates that man is the pinnacle of His creation and vests him with His own image (vv. 24–31). In this bold declaration, we cannot help but notice the striking contrast that the creatures are made "after their kind," but man is made "in Our image." Nigel Cameron expresses the sense of this contrast forcefully and provocatively, but with all due reverence and regard for the Creator-creature distinction: "Moses is telling us that man is of the genus of God." Obviously, creation in the image of God disposes of the idea that matter and body are evil and, at the same time, dispenses with all forms of racism, which essentially deny the *imago Dei* to some portion of the human race.

The Seventh Day. The seventh day marked the completion of God's special creative work, but it does not imply inactivity: "Thus the heavens and the earth were completed, and all their hosts" (Gen. 2:1). In this phrase, God proclaims that He has completed His work of creating the entire organized world. It was finished. "Finished" here is the same word used in Exodus 40:33 when Moses completed the tabernacle and in 2 Chronicles 7:11 when Solomon completed the temple. Also note two other completions: Jesus' work of redemption is "finished" (John 19:30), and the old creation is finished (Rev. 21:5–6). Although God's work of creation is done, He continues His work of providence—preserving and governing His creation. Calvin says, "Inasmuch as God sustains the world by His power, governs it by His providence, cherishes and even propagates all creatures, he is constantly at work."[20]

Many proponents of a figurative reading of the days of creation appeal to the seventh day as yet another "exegetical marker" indicative of a figurative meaning of yôm in Genesis. They do so in at least two ways. First, they claim that there is no end to the seventh day, indicated by the text's omission of the phrase "and there was evening and there was morning." Second, they claim that Psalm 95 and Hebrews 4 confirm this nonliteral reading. (We will respond to this view in detail later.) This novel interpretation of Hebrews 4 ignores the connective function of the phrase "and there was evening and there was morning" in the creation week. Of course, the phrase is not appended to the seventh day. Why? Because the whole of the Sabbath day is God's rest from His creative labor for the sake of man, not just the restful nights between each of the days of creation! Thus, this passage states twice that God rested from His creational labors on the seventh day (Gen. 2:2–3). God's finished work of creation is sealed with the words, "He rested." Although this text implies that God ceased from His special creational activity, it does not mean that God is inactive. He continues to nurture.

First, we find this truth affirmed in our Lord's constructive use of the Sabbath in John 5:15–17:

> The man went away and told the Jews that it was Jesus who had made him well. So, because Jesus was doing these things on the Sabbath, the Jews persecuted him. Jesus said to them, "My Father is always at his work to this very day, and I, too, am working."

Second, we also find this truth in the way Jesus preserved the creational pattern of the Sabbath as blessed and hallowed. Mark 2:27–28 tells us, "[Jesus] said to them, 'The Sabbath was made for man, not man for the Sabbath. So the Son of Man is Lord even of the Sabbath.'" Thus, the point of the seventh day and Jesus' commentary on it is that God's Sabbath is a gift to man and a promise for believers, which is precisely the point of Hebrews 3:7–4:11, not that the day described in Genesis 2:1–3 is eternal.

God set apart and specially favored the seventh day because He rested from creation (Gen. 2:3). Because of His resting for our benefit, God favored (blessed) and sanctified (set apart) the Sabbath. "He blessed it" means that He made it an effectual means of blessing to those who, by faith, observe it by rest, worship, and service. "He sanctified it" means that He consecrated and set it apart for holy use, as a day unto Himself as Lord. We must not forget that those who first heard Genesis already had a Sabbath. Moses merely tells them where it came from to encourage them to observe it.

A Summary of the Markers for Various Figurative Views

Those who hold to figurative interpretations of the Genesis creation days point to several "exegetical markers" when arguing that the Genesis days should not be taken as normal days. Following is a summary of those markers and our response to them.

- *The narrative is generally geocentric and phenomenological, and contains other acknowledged anthropomorphisms, which suggest that the days themselves may be phenomenological or analogous.* Calvin and other 24-hour proponents acknowledge certain anthropomorphic elements, but they do not see that these elements pose any fundamental problem for the 24-hour view.

- *The separation of light from darkness on the first day and the creation of the sun and moon on the fourth day seem to pose problems for the 24-*

hour-day view. The better view, however, steers clear of this marker simply because it calls into question God's capacity to work with or without, above or against, secondary causes.

- *Because the cosmogony of the narrative is general rather than detailed and is not the purpose of the account, we need not press the specific meaning of the days.* We stress once again that the cosmogony is the apologetic, the vehicle of Moses' theological agenda.

- *The highly stylized nature of the creation account and its literary nuance are unlike eyewitness testimony, leading to the conclusion that there is no reason to assume that the author meant to convey literal days to his readers.* While the whole protological section of Genesis bears some of these markers, it nevertheless is written with many other markers typical of later historical accounts. Moreover, it is consistently taken as historical throughout Scripture. If we determine that the structure, including the days, is didactic, why not some or all of the *kerygma?*

- *Since the focus of the narrative is on the sixth day (especially Gen. 1:27), details regarding the days are secondary.* Those who make this argument erroneously assume that the genre of Genesis 1–2 is radically different from other historical genres. Advocates of figurative views simply have not proven that the conclusion follows from the premise. For instance, Gospel literature is both unique and historical. The authors are perfectly free to be selective. But it is one thing to say that a historical account is selective, and quite another to deduce that because something is secondary, it is only a literary device.

- *The alleged non-termination of the Sabbath day in Genesis 2:1–3 raises questions about the nature of the other six days.* By contrast, this interpretation is wholly novel and eccentric. The traditional interpretation of Genesis 2 and Hebrews 4 suffers from no difficulties aided by this new approach and is, in fact, superior to it in many respects.

- *The busyness of the sixth day, in view of the recapitulation of Genesis 2:5–25, raises the possibility of a nonliteral reading of the passage.* By contrast, imposing the limitations of fallen humanity on the unfallen Adam transgresses the barrier of wisdom. To paraphrase: "Aristotle was but the rubbish of unfallen Adam."

- *Because yôm has at least three meanings in Genesis 1–2, the days can be understood figuratively.* By contrast, competent exegetes and philologists will be slow to agree with this broad claim. The issue is not whether yôm can ever mean something else; it is whether there are any positive indications that it means something other than a normal day in this particular context, in connection with each of the seven days. We have heard no compelling internal exegetical evidence to prove that yôm means anything other than a normal day.

THE PENTATEUCH AND NORMAL CREATION DAYS

Being divine history, the Pentateuch picks up where the creation narratives leave off by presenting the creation days as normal days. As with Genesis 1–2, the rest of the Pentateuch—indeed, the rest of Scripture—affirms creation by the unmediated word of God, as opposed to natural providence over long periods of time. At no time does the Pentateuch even hint at anything other than creation in six 24-hour days.

Genesis

Genesis 5:1–2 summarizes the earlier narratives and asserts, "In the day when God created man, He made him in the likeness of God. He created them male and female, . . . and named them Man in the day when they were created" (NASB). This passage does not suggest that creation occurred over millions of years; rather, like Genesis 1–2, it teaches that God created humans. Genesis 5:1 does not refer to any other extra-divine agency involved in creation. Nowhere does the Genesis record itself suggest that the creation days were long or that creation came about by any method other than directly from God.[21]

Throughout Genesis, whether overtly or covertly, creation is consistently treated as God's direct activity, in which He does not depend on other forces or agencies. Before the Flood, God's stated intent was to eliminate from the earth "men and animals, and creatures that move along the ground, and birds of the air" (6:7). Even though this passage describes events centuries later, it is similar to the description of the works of God during creation. This similarity reveals an understanding that the creatures of God just prior to the Flood[22] were created by the same process used during the creation week described in Genesis 1. In Genesis 6:7, the language of Scripture clearly reveals that God will eliminate those "whom I have created, from the face of the earth." Had God wished to hint at developmental processes employed over a long period as the mode of creation, He certainly could have revealed this fact and still been understood by Old Testament people. However, even in the face of pressure to conform the certain words of Scripture to the less certain theories of an age, none of the Genesis texts, short of hermeneutical re-engineering, actually teach that God created either slowly or over a lengthy period. Instead, every verse omits any such claim, each one affirming *prima facie* that God simply created and is powerful enough to do so instantly and without assistance from other forces.

Even those outside Israel praised God as Creator. Melchizedek, the priest of God Most High, worshiped with Abram and blessed God as the "Creator of heaven and earth" (14:19). In response, Abram tells of a covenantal oath that he swore in the name of "God Most High, Creator of heaven and earth" (14:22). Those who hold to figurative views must prove that either Melchizedek's audience of the nineteenth century B.C. or the readers in Moses' time, or any other Old Testament interpreters understood this description as anything other than a reference to God as Creator who created all things in the space of six normal days, just as Genesis 1 provides. Nowhere does Holy Writ correct or elongate that understanding. Nor did exegetes do so until after the recent ascent of certain secular theories.

Exodus

Exodus harkens back to the Genesis creation account without expanding the creational period. *The history of commentary on the Fourth Commandment in Exodus 20 and elsewhere corroborates yet again that the Old Testament writers understood the creation days as normal days.*

When the Fourth Commandment enjoins God's people "six days you shall labor and do all your work" (Exo. 20:9), it does not suggest that those days are anything other than 24-hour days. God gave no modifiers or extenuating qualifiers in the text to indicate anything other than a normal day. The commandment certainly does not require labor for six thousand years or six million years prior to Sabbath observance. Both the original audience and an unbroken stream of interpreters before the nineteenth century correctly understood the commandment to refer to normal days.

In a sermon on Exodus 20:11, a leading Old Testament scholar called the six days "natural days," a term that meant 24-hour days. Bishop John Lightfoot asked and answered as follows:

> But let us consider of the second thing, as it tends to the end of this command, the setting forth the reason of the institution of the Sabbath; that he created all things 'in six days.' And what needed he take six days, that could have done all in a moment? He had as little need to take time for his work, as he had of the world, he being Lord of all. What reason can we give? But that he, by his own proceeding and acting would set the clock of time, and measure out days, and a week, by which all time is measured,—by his own

standard, evening and morning, to make a *natural day*, i.e., day and night; and seven natural days to make a week; six days of labour, the seventh for rest. . . . That the world was made at equinox, *all grant*,[23]—but differ at which, whether about the eleventh of March, or twelfth of September; to me in September, without all doubt. All things were created in their ripeness and maturity; apples ripe, and ready to eat, as is too sadly plain in Adam and Eve's eating the forbidden fruit. . . . So that look at the first day of the creation, God made heaven and earth in a moment. The heaven, as soon as created, moved, and the wheel of time began to go; and thus, for *twelve hours*, there was universal darkness. This is called the 'evening' (night). Then God said, 'Let there be light,' and light arose in the east, and, in twelve hours more, was carried over the hemisphere; and this is called, 'morning,' or 'day.' And the evening and morning made the *first natural day; twelve hours, darkness,—and twelve, light.*[24]

Zacharias Ursinus commented similarly on the Fourth Commandment: "That by the example of himself resting on the seventh day, he might exhort men, as by a most effectual and constraining argument, to imitate him and so abstain on the seventh day, from the labors to which they were accustomed *during the other six days* of the week."[25] The consistent literary presence of the phrase "within six days" amid historical commentaries is a thorn in the flesh to those who wish that history was not so specific on this issue.

When the Sabbath commandment is reiterated in Exodus 31:12–18, it takes on heightened importance because the tablets of stone were "inscribed by the finger of God" (v. 18). The divine inscription does not contain misleading or ambiguous information. To the contrary, when God spoke and wrote to an audience in approximately 1400 B.C. and said that the Sabbath was to be a lasting sign, He meant exactly what He said. The clear intent in verse 17 ("for in six days the Lord made the heavens and the earth, and on the seventh day he abstained from work and rested") is that God created in six days and desired to be understood for perpetuity as having done so. Any contrary understanding must be based on hermeneutical theories foreign to conventional rules of interpreting Scripture. The scriptural evidence itself is clear.

Deuteronomy

The testimony of the Pentateuch is rounded out with two references from Deuteronomy. In Deuteronomy 4:32, Moses challenges his listeners to compare the true God to false religions. Amid this comparison, his listeners in the fourteenth century B.C. were reminded of the length of the creation days. They were told that "from the day God created man on the earth," nothing so astounding has happened. Note that the text does not speak of the age, eon, or era in which God created man on the earth, but of the *day* of man's creation.

Later, Deuteronomy 32:6 contains lyrics that praise God as "your Father, your Creator, who made you and formed you." The Hebrew words and audience demanded no other theories of interpretation besides the normal meaning of the creation language. Again, there is no evidence that Israelite worshipers injected or permitted vastly different explanations for these words.

OLD TESTAMENT POETIC LITERATURE AND NORMAL CREATION DAYS

Old Testament poetic literature and worship also reinforce the fact that the days of creation were normal days.

Job

The Book of Job refers numerous times to unmediated creation. When the Lord begins to rebuke Job (Job 38–41), He first corrects Job by pointing to His powerful creation. God asked Job, "Where were you when I laid the earth's foundation? . . . Who marked off its dimensions? . . . Who stretched a measuring line across it? On what were its footings set, or who laid its cornerstone . . . ?" (38:4–6). The point is not only to show Job his smallness in comparison to God, but also to reveal God's creative activity as praiseworthy because it is an unassisted work among the Trinity (*opera ad intra dei*). We may diminish an attribute of God if we insist that this passage permits a long period of evolutionary unfolding.

Moreover, when God grills Job about shutting "up the sea behind doors when it burst forth from the womb, . . . when I fixed limits for it and set its doors and bars in place" (vv. 8–10), the very nature of seas and their boundaries seem to defy gradual development or a long span of creation. Instead, the Book of Job teaches creation of the cosmos (including a "morning" with a "dawn," as in Job 38:12, much like the morning and evening of creation, as in Gen. 1:5) as occurring dramatically, without mediation, and in a brief period. short of injecting an extrabiblical cosmology, nothing in the text itself suggests a long period of evolutionary beginnings.

Job 38:19 parallels the Genesis account by discussing light that may arise from other than normal sources. Celestial constellations were known and catalogued as early as 2000 B.C., when Job ascribed praise to God for creating them. Indeed, much of this section, which predates Moses' composition of Genesis, neither was written in response to later deities nor suggests that God used slow ordinary providence to effect creation.

Psalms

The Psalter also contains many praises of God's mighty and immediate creation. Beginning with Psalm 8, God is praised as majestic for creating the earth. He "set" His glory in the heavens (Psa. 8:2); He did not slowly develop His glory in the heavens. As David considers the heavens and the celestial bodies, he thinks of them as having been "set in place" by God, his Creator. His praise might be significantly less if it were only praise for God, the Starter of Creation, who subsequently retired to permit normal forces to finish the creation process. David views all created life (8:6–8) that was made on Days 5 and 6 as having been created by God's word, not by impersonal forces. Thus is God's majesty ascribed.

In Psalm 19, the heavens declare God's glory and the firmament shows His handiwork. Had they evolved from earlier forms or matter, it might have been appropriate to express *some* praise for those forces. Interestingly, no praise occurs in the Psalter for a *process of creation*—only for a powerful Creator who created by unmediated means. David believed that God's creation bore a universal testimony (19:2).

A little later, David joins Job's earlier testimony to praise God for founding and establishing His creation of the world and all of its component parts (24:1–2).[26] Rather than the parts of creation competing with each other, as some forms of the framework interpretation imply, here in the Old Testament canon, God founds and establishes "the earth . . . and everything in it," without implying the use of intermediate agencies.

Psalm 33 contains bold statements about God's creational activity. The "word of the Lord" that is right and true (33:4) is also the word that is the agent by which the heavens were made. Consistent with the Old Testament message, the psalmist does not praise any agencies except the word of God. The same psalm clarifies: "For he spoke, and it came to be; he commanded, and it stood firm" (33:9). This Hebrew parallelism reiterates the same concept twice, each time using the *waw*-consecutive. Nothing occurs between God's speaking (commanding) and the coming into existence of creation (its standing firm). The completed creation seems to be in view. Thus, Psalm 33 affirms that God's completed creation is accomplished as quickly as words are spoken or commands are given. There is no hint of long intervening ages or of interposed agents: "By the word of the Lord were the heavens made, their starry host by the breath of his mouth" (v. 6).

Psalm 136:5–6 affirms the same unmediated creation by God. The temple worshipers would greet the One "who by his understanding made the heavens" with the refrain "his love endures forever," just as they would respond to "who spread out the earth upon the waters" with the same refrain, "his love endures forever." Furthermore, the "great lights" of Day 4 (Gen. 1:16), with the sun governing the day and the moon and stars governing the night, were also tokens of His enduring love. Nowhere are these tokens of God's enduring love explicitly described as coming about in any fashion other than by His understanding or by His unmediated word. That teaching can be suggested only when extrabiblical theories are imposed on the texts, for the texts themselves suggest no such thing. All these created objects are to praise God (Psa. 148), for God "set them in place for ever and ever." Scripture does not teach that they evolved in place over long periods of time.

Psalm 148:5 affirms God's creation in a short span of time, taking only as long as it takes for Deity to speak. Amid the lyrical praise of Israel, God is praised, "for he commanded and they [heavens, angels, celestial lights, vv. 1–4] were created." Thus, with regularity ancient Israel and psalm singers throughout the centuries have affirmed that the things created in Genesis 1 were created by God's mere command. Such musical repetition may partially account for the longevity of the interpretation of God's creation as having occurred on normal days. Indeed, to sing Psalm 148 with a different meaning requires hermeneutical gymnastics that ancients were loathe to perform—especially in the context of worship.

Proverbs

Proverbs 3:19 echoes similar themes when it says that the earth's foundations were laid by God, who employed His own understanding and wisdom to set the heavens in place. Personified wisdom is praised for setting the heavens in place (Prov. 8:27) and settling the mountains into their places (v. 25), but no long periods or natural processes are extolled.[27]

Thus far in the progress of revelation, we cannot legitimately interpret any of the Old Testament Scriptures to support *mediated* creation (i.e., creation that depends on normal providence and secondary agents). Instead, the consistent Old Testament view is that creation is *unmediated*, "by the word of his power."[28]

OLD TESTAMENT PROPHECY AND NORMAL CREATION DAYS

The prophecies of the Old Testament teach nothing but normal creation days. This fact is true of both the major and minor prophets.

The Major Prophets

Isaiah repeatedly affirms direct and quick creation by God's word, not by normal providence. The concentrated section from Isaiah 40–45 contains no fewer than 10 distinct affirmations of God's creation. None of them suggest long days. God created all things, including the heavenly lights (Isa. 40:26); He is the "Creator of the ends of the earth" (40:28). There is no reference to His creation occurring by providence or evolutionary unfolding. According to the Holy Spirit's revelation to an eighth-century B.C. audience that had no reason to expect God to create over long ages, Isaiah revealed God as the One "who created heavens and stretched them out . . . who gives breath to its people" (42:5). God is not only the Creator of Jacob and Israel (43:1), but is revealed as the One who created for His own glory (43:7). This same God is the One who created light and darkness (45:7), the earth and mankind (45:12), and by His "own hands stretched out the heavens [and] marshaled their starry hosts" (45:12). The recent suggestion that such creation took place over long periods is foreign to these texts. If God's people are capable of understanding them only after Darwin, then all who came before either were deceived into believing that *day* meant a normal day or were hopelessly uninformed by the God who purports to reveal Himself in these verses. It remains for adherents of the figurative views to explain how and why these texts refer to creation *days* longer than 24 hours.

God is also the Creator, not developer, of breath (57:16), and subsequent to Isaiah's day, He will "create" the new heavens and a new earth (65:17–18). Again, these verses contain no hint that creation was—or will be—anything other than quick, instantaneous, declarative (by God's speaking), and independent of gradually unfolding naturalistic processes.

Jeremiah also alluded to the fact that God created by speaking creation into existence. Following the announcement of God's covenant with Israel, Jeremiah describes Him as the One "who appoints the sun to shine by day, who decrees the moon and the stars to shine by night" (Jer. 31:35). God's decrees and the celestial lights shine in what can only refer to a short span of creation. Jeremiah also affirmed that God "made the earth by his power; he founded the world by his wisdom and stretched out the heavens by his understanding" (10:12).

Ezekiel 28:13 refers to Eden as a historic "garden of God." In that verse, Ezekiel speaks of precious stones that were prepared "the day you were created." He does not refer to a long span of creation, but to a *day*. Later, he reiterates that the spiritual being depicted in these verses was created in a day, not in an age (Ezek. 28:15).

The Minor Prophets
The prophet Amos described the God "who forms the mountains" as the One who "creates the wind" and who also without lengthy ages "turns dawn to darkness" (Amos 4:13).

Late into the Old Testament period, Nehemiah affirmed that God "made the heavens . . . and all their starry host, the earth and all that is on it" (Neh. 9:6), never mentioning intermediaries or lengthy processes.

Malachi affirms that God is the Father of all humans by creation: "Have we not all one Father? Did not one God create us?" (Mal. 2:10). There is no hint that God created by any means other than special, divine fiat. Therefore, no need for framework or day-age interpretations existed for the original audience of Holy Writ. Those interpretations have arisen only as certain scientific theories dominated the landscape.

Summary

The Old Testament Law, the Psalms, and the Prophets manifest a consistent view of creation. The authors give no evidence or awareness of creation occurring over long periods. The only justifications for re-exegeting these passages are extra-scriptural. The reconsiderations of cosmology by modern contemporaries occurs only in or after the nineteenth century and never occurred to interpreters "unenlightened" by modern secular theories.

CHRIST, THE GOSPELS,
AND NORMAL CREATION DAYS

The same view of creation consistent throughout the Old Testament—with no evidence that it occurred over long periods—of course continues in the New Testament. In his prologue, John speaks of the *Logos* as present in the beginning with the Father. Through (dative of means) this *Logos*—not through nature nor awaiting assistance from either naturalistic evolutionary process or divine providence—"all things were made; without him nothing was made that has been made" (John 1:3).

John does not seek to explain away divine fiat; rather, he continues the Old Testament teaching and assumes creation *ex nihilo*. If creation was by God's word (instead of by secondary agencies), and if creation was revealed in the Old Testament as having occurred in normal days (instead of various modern interpretations unknown before the nineteenth century), then the New Testament itself, beginning with the Gospels, must correct this understanding to convince us to believe otherwise. The Gospels, however, do not require, let alone hint, that we need to revise the Old Testament view of the process, agency, extent, or span of creation. Nor does the rest of the New Testament. At every mention, the New Testament corroborates rather than corrects the Old Testament understanding of creation as by God, from nothing, in the space of six days as we know them, and all very good.

Christ Himself places His imprimatur on the hermeneutic of continuity. He approves the normal understanding that the Creator made male and female at the beginning (Matt. 19:4). Nowhere in His words does our Lord try to anticipate evolutionary theory; nor does He stretch syntax to make room for such, even though, as the omniscient God of the universe, He foresaw nineteenth- and twentieth-century developments. Modern interpreters face a rather daunting challenge to show exactly where Jesus ever sought to correct the normal understanding of the process and duration of creation. In both Mark 10:6 and 13:19, Jesus concurred with Mosaic interpretations of creation; He never expressed any disagreement with or sought to clarify Moses' intent regarding any aspect of creation. On one occasion, Jesus even spoke of God's creation of the world in the context of *days* (Mark 13:19). In other words, He had the perfect opportunity to revise the Mosaic understanding of days had He wished to do so. Jesus, however, never parted company with Moses or the rest of the Old Testament writers on creation.

THE EPISTLES, THE APOCALYPSE,
AND NORMAL CREATION DAYS

The Epistles and the Apocalypse introduce no theory other than normal creation days. Suggesting other theories would require us to impose extrabiblical theories on the text of Scripture itself.

Acts 17:24 affirms that God "made the world and everything in it." Romans 1:20 continues the New Testament thread of interpretation, which ascribes praise to God as Creator (see also Rom. 1:25). He is nowhere depicted as Developer, Grand-Watchmaker, or First Cause alone. Romans 4:17 contains another stunning affirmation of God's creation *ex nihilo*. While describing the miraculous conception that God performed for Abraham and Sarah (which is not attributed to natural processes), this text also describes God as the One who "gives life to the dead and calls things that are not as though they were." The history of orthodox interpretation has recognized that this text subtly but powerfully acknowledges that God is the Creator who calls things into existence when they do not exist.[29]

In 1 Corinthians 11:9, Paul joins this chorus. He affirms that Adam (man) was created before Eve.[30] In 2 Corinthians 4:6, Paul compares the unmediated impartation of God's light into our hearts at redemption to His powerful, unmediated creation of light out of darkness at creation. Neither act implies nor requires agency or extent of time more than a normal creation day. In Ephesians 3:9, Paul affirms that God created all things. He does not attempt to modify, clarify, or correct the Mosaic creation account. In addition, Colossians 1:16–17 depicts Jesus as the One through whom "all things were created." Whether in heaven (which is certainly not subject to evolutionary development) or on earth, whether visible or invisible, "all things were created by him and for him." He is not only the Creator but the Sustainer of creation: "in Him all things hold together" (v. 17). The New Testament credits the totality of the created order to God (1 Tim. 4:3–4), and the normal Mosaic understanding of the Sabbath and creation days is endorsed by the New Testament (Heb. 4:3–4).

Furthermore, Hebrews 11:3 equates faith with a particular view of creation.[31] Since without this faith it is impossible to please God (Heb. 11:6), believers are required to come up to the divine expectations set forth in this verse. Specifically, faithfulness to God requires us to "understand that the universe was formed at God's command, so that what is seen was not made out of what was visible." This understanding parallels what Moses taught in Genesis 1–2 and what is taught throughout the rest of Scripture. There is no scriptural reason to believe anything other than the fact that the days of creation were 24 hours long. Only extrabiblical hermeneutical considerations lead to any other conclusion.

Hebrews 11:3 affirms at least three things: (1) The universe is not self-existent or self-developed; it was formed (passive voice) by an Agency outside of itself. (2) The means or mechanism by which this non-self-existent universe was created was God's command, not natural process, evolutionary development, or even deistically guided providence. (3) This created universe that came about from God's unmediated command consists of things that were created *ex nihilo*, rather than molded or evolved from pre-existing substances.

According to Hebrews 11:3, this is an essential doctrine that is known "by faith." The author does not indicate that he is revising earlier Mosaic testimony at all, but speaks of this doctrine in connection with numerous other Old Testament passages (mostly from Genesis) that were understood by normal rules of grammar and vocabulary. It is not the Revealer who requires *ex post facto* hermeneutical and linguistic rules that would confound the original audience. For centuries, Hebrews 11:3 was understood to corroborate the same teachings about creation held by Jesus and Moses.[32] Nowhere do the New Testament Epistles seek to alter the normal understanding of the agency, mechanism, or span of creation—all propositions that must be proven, according to modern revisionists.

Peter further confirms that "long ago by God's word the heavens existed and the earth was formed out of water and by water" (2 Pet. 3:5). This passage proclaims that the cosmos was created "by God's word," not by other processes nor unfolded by indirect means. Verse 7 indicates that the very same miraculous word also preserves the cosmos. In neither case does Peter attribute the effect or event to normal providence, but to divine power.

The New Testament concludes with several powerful testimonies to the received teachings on creation. Revelation 4 provides affirmation hymns about the doctrine of creation without correcting Mosaic nuances or intents. Amid the attributes of holiness, worthiness, and omniscience, God is praised as Creator. Since God's work as Creator is specifically singled out for praise, evidently that is an essential part of His being. His work as Creator is not differentiated from His other attributes. Not only is He the originator of creation, but by His will all things were created and have their existence (v. 11). It is not by processes or time or chemical sparks that God created, but by His will. All things owe their existence to God, the Creator. God's creation, therefore, extends to all areas. Creation is not something that is important only in Genesis; it continues to be important as long as there is song.

Further, the "phrases since the creation of the world" and "before the foundation of the world" occur in numerous contexts (Matt. 13:35; 25:34; John 17:24; Eph. 1:4; 1 Pet. 1:20; Rev. 13:8; 17:8). None of these occurrences imply that the creation/foundation was evolutionary, gradual, or lengthy.

Nowhere does the New Testament alter or reinterpret the Genesis narratives in any fashion other than as received or use anything other than normal vocabulary. The uniform testimony of Scripture attests to divine creation out of nothing by God's word in the space of six normal days. There simply is no contrary evidence *within* the canonical Scriptures. It requires the imposition of extrabiblical concepts to reinterpret the texts in other ways. Unfortunately, the drive to be reconciled to fluctuating secular theories has animated most departures from these classical interpretations, for the Scriptures themselves do not call for such re-imagining, nor did such re-imagining occur to interpreters prior to a certain worldview shift.

To present a compelling case, advocates of long days will have to address two key hermeneutical questions by giving more persuasive answers than they have until now:

- Why do the Old Testament and New Testament fail to allude to long days or slow, developmental creation? In other words, where in Scripture is the affirmative statement to prove that the days of creation refer to anything other than normal days?

- Why didn't any interpreters discover long days or slow, developmental creation until after certain scientific revolutions? If these interpretations are contrary to the history of exegesis, how can Christians be so convinced that these interpretations are not additional illustrations of conforming Christ to culture?

THE HISTORY OF INTERPRETATION AND NORMAL CREATION DAYS

The history of interpretation confirms that the cumulative testimony of the Church favored normal creation days until the onslaught of certain scientific theories.

Basil

In his exposition of Genesis 1:5, Basil (329–379) indicates his position on the length of the creation days when he writes: "And there was evening and morning, one day. Why did he say 'one' and not 'first'? . . . He said 'one' because he was defining the measure of day and night . . . since *the twenty-four hours* fill up the interval of one day."[33]

Ambrose

Ambrose of Milan (339–397) was one of the first theologians to explicate a mature view of creation. In his *Hexameron*, Ambrose affirmed, "God created day and night at the same time. Since that time, day and night continue their daily succession and renewal."[34] In his fullest discussion of the lengths of the creation days, Ambrose commented:

> The end of day is the evening. Now, the succeeding day follows after the termination of night. The thought of God is clear. First He called light "day" and next He called darkness "night." In notable fashion has Scripture spoken of a "day," not the "first day." Because a second, then a third day, and finally the remaining days were to follow, a "first day" could have been mentioned, following in this way the natural order. But Scripture established a law that *twenty-four* hours, including both day and night, should be given the name of day only, as if one were to say the length of one day is *twenty-four hours* in extent.[35]

Augustine, Anselm, and Lombard

Some allege that Augustine (354–430), Anselm (1033–1109), and Lombard (1100–1160) opted for long creation days. C. John Collins, however, confirms, "Augustine and Anselm do not actually discuss the length of the creation days. . . . Certainly Augustine and Anselm cannot be called as witnesses in favor of a day-age theory."[36] Attempts to enlist Augustine as a pre-supporter of long creation periods are contradicted by Augustine's own clear and persistent statements to the contrary. He believed that all creation, rather than occurring in 144 hours, occurred in a nanosecond.

Aquinas

Aquinas (1224–1274) did not consistently or explicitly advocate "long days."[37] He believed, "The words *one day* are used when day is first instituted, to denote that one day is made up of *twenty-four hours*."[38] Moreover, he commented elsewhere: "But it [the cosmos] was not made from something; otherwise the matter of the world would have preceded the world. . . . Therefore, it must be said that the world was made from nothing."[39]

Recently, Hugh Ross has asserted, "Many of the early Church fathers and other biblical scholars interpreted the creation days of Genesis 1 as long periods of time." However, he errs when he claims that "the list includes . . . Irenaeus, . . . Basil, . . . Augustine, and later Aquinas to name a few."[40] Ross includes an argument for long days of creation[41] and blames fundamentalism for the origin of creationism. Despite Ross' assertion, the views of Augustine and Calvin merely demonstrate that earlier commentaries appreciate symbolic language.[42] It is an overreach to infer that these authors repudiate traditional (pre-Darwinian) creationism from their use of a symbolic hermeneutic.[43] Furthermore, it certainly is not true that "many" Church fathers believed in long days.

Calvin

Interestingly, had Calvin (1509–1564) wanted to lobby for "long days," two ideal verses presented themselves: Psalm 90:4 and 2 Peter 3:8. Yet, while commenting on both of them, Calvin refrained from injecting the idea that the first days of creation could be as long as millennia. Calvin did not interpret these verses to satisfy certain scientific theories but rather to teach that God is above time. Calvin never suggests that creation occurred over a long period, and he never entertains even the possibility that creation came about by mediating processes other than God's word. Such modern suggestions were made significantly later than Calvin.

In his commentary on Genesis, Calvin even uses the phrase "in the space of six days" (Gen. 1:5), which was later adopted by the Westminster Assembly, consistent with Calvin's view. He also classified the rubric "evening and morning" as "according to the custom of his nation . . . [Moses] accommodated his discourse to the received custom." The accommodation from the context is not to secular science but to the Hebrew "mode of reckoning." It is in this sense, therefore, that Calvin refers to accommodation when he later notes regarding Genesis 1:5 that God "accommodat[ed] his works to the capacity of men." Regarding the fourth day, Calvin refers parenthetically but clearly of his intent to "the natural day (which he mentions above)."[44]

Luther

Martin Luther's (1483–1546) view is largely uncontested.[45] Those who make their case for long creation days seldom refer to Luther[46] (and others), thus illustrating how selective they are in finding sources molded to fit their modern biases. A search for the mainstream of orthodox interpretation on this subject should not omit Luther, even if he mitigated the propositions ardently maintained by modern revisionism.

Robert Bishop concurs: "Neither the original audience of that book [Genesis] nor anyone else until about two hundred years ago would have understood a 'geological era' to be a meaningful concept."[47] Earlier exegetes considered no such option. There is scant evidence, if any, that prior to the nineteenth century any view of creation that accorded with macroevolution was anything but aberrant.[48]

Ussher

Within a century of Calvin, the orthodox consensus was attained by simultaneously repudiating Augustine and explaining that creation occurred "in the space of six days." Ussher (1581–1656) affirmed, "In the beginning of time, when no creature had any being, God by his word alone, in the space of six days, created all things, and afterwards, by his providence, doth continue, propagate, and order them according to his own will."[49] Ussher's phrase "by his word alone" agreed with the intent of Moses, and it did not mean long ages. Between Luther and Ussher, most others defined the creation days in similar fashion.

Babington

Gervase Babington (1550–1610), Bishop of Worcester, commented on Genesis 1:7 that God created "not in one moment, but in *six days* space" (*non uno momento, sed sex dierum spatio*), thereby exhibiting an early use of the phrase "in the space of six days" to refer to actual days.[50] Later Babington noted that God rested on the seventh day, following "*six days* creating." There was certainly no hint of an expansive period of creation at that time.

Lightfoot

Far from originating his chronology, Ussher may have been concurring with the premier Old Testament scholar of England, John Lightfoot (1602–1675). Lightfoot, like Ussher and many others living long before Darwin, did not dream of the interpretations modern interpreters suggest. Lightfoot was the leading Hebraist of his day and treated, as did Ussher, each of the creation days as natural days and of limited duration.[51] He was so specific as to affirm that the heavens moved in darkness "twelve hours" before God commanded the creation of light,[52] and also that all six creation days were 24-hour days and natural days.[53] Of the second day, he claimed that "in *four and twenty hours* it was accomplished."[54] Lightfoot stated that Moses presented "the seven days, or the first week of the world, altogether without interposition."[55] Rather than imagining a long period of evolution, Lightfoot commented on Genesis 1:9 that "the earth instantly brought forth trees and plants in their several kinds."[56]

In at least five other works, Lightfoot stated the same opinions. In his "Chronicle of the Times," his understanding of 24-hour days is clear: "*Twelve hours* was there universal darkness through all the world; and then was light created in the upper horizon, and there it enlightened twelve hours more." Similarly, in his "Rules for a Student of the Holy Scriptures," he affirmed that day and night were each twelve hours, "And in *four and twenty hours* the command is accomplished."[57] In his *De Creatione*, the Old Testament expert wrote that the days were natural days, consisting of *24 hours*.[58]

Ley, Gouge, and Featly

Several Puritans lent their hand to the *1645 Annotations upon All the Books of the Old and New Testament* (London, 1645). Among the Westminster divines[60] appointed to draft these "study notes" were John Ley (1583–1662), William Gouge (1575–1653), and Daniel Featly (1582–1645). Ley composed the annotations on the Pentateuch in which he expressed that "the word *Day* is taken for the natural day consisting of *twenty-four hours*, which is measured most usually from the Sun-rising to the Sun-rising; or from the Sun-setting to the Sun-setting." Ley noted that such sense was also used in Exodus 12:29, Numbers 3:13 and 8:17.[61]

In these *Annotations*, Ley reiterated: "This first day consisting of *twenty-four hours*" and "the Sabbath being as large a day as any of the rest, and so containing *twenty-four hours* is measured from even to even." Ley and other divines also publicly commented on Genesis 1:14 that each creation day was a "*day natural* consisting of *twenty-four hours*."[62]

We find similar contemporary testimony in the *Dutch Annotations upon the Whole Bible* ordered by the Synod of Dort. This commentary observes the following on Genesis 1:5: "The meaning of these words [day/night] is that night and day had made up one natural day together, which with the Hebrews began with the evening and ended with the approach of the next evening, comprehending *twenty-four hours*."[63]

Turretin

Writing later, Francis Turretin (1623–1687) was quick to note, "Augustine thought that creation took place not during an interval of six days, but in a single moment."[64] Turretin then rejected Augustine's view, and sided with Ussher: "Nor does the sacred history written by Moses cover any more than six thousand years. . . . Greek history scarcely contains the history of two thousand years."[65] Turretin went so far as to commend Ussher and others for specifying that creation happened in autumn, not in spring.[66]

Ussher, not Augustine, dominated the seventeenth- and eighteenth-century interpretation of the days of creation. In the Victorian period, no exegetical change was in the offing, as evidenced by scanning the King James Version (1611), which contains no hints of Augustinian influence or any view that holds to a long geologic period of creation. Reflecting the consensus of the day, this version used the phrase "the space" only to indicate definite time (e.g., Gen. 29:14; Lev. 25:8; Deut. 2:14; Acts 5:7, 34; 15:33; 19:8; Rev. 2:21; 8:1). However, it never uses the phrase "in the space of" in the creation narratives or in references to the length of creation. Had the translators wished to, they could have done so, but these Elizabethan wordsmiths were careful to follow Scripture and translate yôm as a day in creational contexts.

In light of the consistent testimony of Scripture regarding the days of creation and the long tradition of interpreting it as teaching 24-hour creation days, we concur with those who suspect that modern deviations from that interpretation stem from accommodation. And accommodation may be driving the train away from these clear biblical teachings, especially in light of the exegetical history we have presented.

In other works, we discuss how exemplary thinkers like Charles Hodge, B. B. Warfield, Alexander Mitchell, and John MacPherson were examples of such accommodation.[67] Even fine theologians (usually post-Darwinian) have succumbed to the spirit of the age. When a fine theologian like Hodge pledges to alter his cosmology "with the utmost alacrity" to accord with the current state of science, or when Warfield asserts that John Calvin was a precursor to theistic evolution, accommodation or revision of some type is afoot.[68]

If we admit that something drastic changed about a century and a half ago in the way some Christians interpret Scripture, perhaps we can prevent it from happening again. Some very fine evangelicals were not as guarded as we might prefer. Even good men err. Excellent men like Hodge, Warfield, and others may be wrong on the issue of creation and still worthy of great respect in other areas.[69] Thus, we need to acknowledge that these men are exceptions to what the catholic and apostolic Church has held on this matter. At the same time, we should not compromise with this pattern of deviation, unless we find an equal or greater number of earlier pre-Darwinian theologians who held to long, geological periods of creation.

OBJECTIONS ANSWERED

Having established what the Scriptures teach about the days of creation and presented the cloud of witnesses through the centuries, we now conclude by briefly responding to several common objections.

If the sun and moon did not appear until the fourth day, how could there be a "literal" evening and morning during the first three days? One simple solution to this objection is to understand that God, the Creator, may have employed nonsolar sources of light before creating the sun. Since God is light and in Him is no darkness, He certainly does not depend on the sun for light. Light could well have emanated from nonsolar sources before the creation of the sun and moon. Consistent with this response, the final chapters of Scripture present a future time during which light will come from nonsolar sources (Rev. 21:23; 22:5). Both of these eschatological texts provide the analogy for protological texts to teach that light is not confined to the sun. To interpret the creation narrative in a manner that makes the created sun absolute is to permit an aspect of creation to rival the Creator. Bishop Joseph Hall (1574–1656) addressed this concern by affirming the earlier tradition:

> Thou madest the sun; madest the light without the sun, before the sun, so that light might depend upon thee, and not upon thy creature. Thy power will not be limited to means. It was easy to thee to make an heaven without sun, light without an heaven, day without a sun, time without a day. It is good reason thou shouldst be the Lord of thine own works. . . . One day we shall have light again without the sun: . . . Now this light, which for three days was thus dispersed through the whole heavens, it pleased thee, at last, to gather and unite into one body of the sun. The whole heaven was our sun, before the sun was created.[70]

If the only remaining challenge is how God could do something so different from our normal observation and expectations, the answer is that it was a miracle in a week saturated with the miraculous. Admittedly, what happened was quite different from our normal experience or observation, but our normal experience or observations are not the standard.

When commenting on Genesis 1:3, Calvin said that the presence of light before the sun, far from being problematic, was actually a cause for praising God:

To nothing are we more prone than to tie down the power of God to those instruments the agency of which he employs. The sun and moon supply us with light: And, according to our notions we so include this power to give light in them, that if they were taken away from the world, it would seem impossible for any light to remain. Therefore the Lord, by the very order of the creation, bears witness that he holds in his hand the light, which he is able to impart to us without the sun and moon. Further, it is certain from the context, that the light was so created as to be interchanged with darkness. But it may be asked, whether light and darkness succeeded each other in turn through the whole circuit of the world; or whether the darkness occupied one half of the circle, while light shone in the other. There is, however, no doubt that the order of their succession was alternate, but whether it was everywhere day at the same time, and everywhere night also, I would rather leave undecided; nor is it very necessary to be known.[71]

If we take the words of Genesis 1:12 and 2:9 in their plain sense, don't they present us with instances of plants growing gradually over a period of time? This objection is not well-founded. We are not compelled to take the words in the sense of what we observe after creation. If the events described were supernatural, then obviously, the text does not refer to the natural process of growth. As construed for thousands of years,[72] creation begins *atypically*, as compared to our own experience. Thus, to impose what we denominate as "normalcy" on the text is to distort the text itself. Frequently, those who approach the texts confuse the normal operation of providence after creation's completion with distinct acts of creation, which, because they are by nature miraculous, did not operate under normal providence.

How could all the events described in Genesis 2:5–25 have occurred on the sixth day? Most orthodox interpreters of Scripture respond to the critic of Scripture who wishes to find contradiction within Genesis 1 and 2 by explaining that following the overview of the seven creation days (Gen. 1:1–2:4), Genesis 2:5–25 recapitulates and focuses on a single day—the sixth day of creation. Indeed, the only other interpretive option is to assume contradiction within the biblical narratives.

But the question before us presents no real problem, especially if we assume the miraculous. This interpretation is not new. The chief theologian of the Westminster Assembly, William Twisse, reflected the earlier consensus by endorsing a short creation period when he asserted that Adam fell on the seventh day, following a 24-hour sixth day: "And surely Adam's naming of them cost him no study; and undoubtedly all this was done before noon, and space enough allowed for the Devil's conference with Eve."[73] Even if one differs with other parts of these original formulations or considers this view old-fashioned, earlier commentators clearly had a definite and presumed view of the meaning of "six days." This supposed difficulty was no real challenge, unless those who voice it wish to deny the miraculous or impose a contradiction on Scripture. Again, the Church hardly noticed the "problem" before Darwin.

Because the Hebrew word for day *is used in at least three different ways in Genesis 1:1–2:4, shouldn't we be cautious when we interpret it?* This objection begs the question, as we will demonstrate in our answer to the next objection. Proponents of longer creation days, in fact, have no reason—apart from assuming their unproven conclusions—to understand *yôm* in Genesis 1:1–2:4 as anything other than a normal day. Besides, this objection is factually mistaken since, at most, *yôm* bears one other nuance (not a different meaning) when it refers to the fraction of a normal day that is characterized by light (1:5, 14, 16, 18). One should simply interpret day/light in the same fashion as he interprets night/darkness in the same verse (1:10 is another parallel). Moreover, were we to take *day* in 1:14 in other than its literal sense, consistency also would require us to bracket as nonliteral the terms "seasons" and "years," which, in the context, is nonsensical. Those who voice this objection have no reason, other than cosmological assumptions, for construing *yôm* to mean anything other than a normal day, the way that passage was understood by audiences from the time of Moses to Jesus. Moreover, millennia of interpreters have understood the seventh *day* in Genesis 2:1–3 as of the same duration as *day* in Genesis 1.

Why are the events in Genesis 2 mentioned in a different order than those in Genesis 1? This objection is related to the preceding objection. Briefly put, there is no inherent discrepancy between Genesis 1 and 2 unless we impose it on the texts. We offer the following reading of the two chapters without any contradiction:

- Genesis 1:1–2 provides an overview of the pre-creation state, devoid of internal suggestion that time references need a special set of definitions.

- Genesis 1:3–5 describes in ordinary terms the creation of light (not necessarily solar) on the first day, which is framed by an evening and a morning in the Hebrew chronology of the day.

- Genesis 1:6–8 describes in ordinary terms the creation of an expanse and the seas on the second day, which is framed by an evening and a morning according to the normal Hebrew reckoning of the day.

- Genesis 1:9–13 describes in ordinary terms the creation of land masses and vegetation (which would reproduce after their kind) on the third day, which is framed by a normal Hebrew evening and morning.

- Genesis 1:10–19 describes in ordinary terms the creation of celestial bodies on the fourth day, which is framed by a normal Hebrew evening and morning.

- Genesis 1:20–24 describes the creation of sea and air animals (which would reproduce after their kind) on the fifth day, framed by a normal Hebrew evening and morning.

- Genesis 1:25–31 describes in ordinary terms the creation of land animals (which would reproduce after their kind) and humans on the sixth day, which is framed by a normal Hebrew evening and morning. The placement of humankind following animal life in Genesis 1:25–31 preserves the literary accent on the uniqueness of man as the crown of God's creation. The phrase "then God said" in Genesis 1:26 does not need to be interpreted as strictly sequential. All the events of the sixth day of creation are pointing toward, and are subservient to, the creation of mankind. Thus, we see the emphasis that the created work of that day is "very good" (1:31), as distinguished from "good." Genesis 1:3–2:4 provides an overview of creation.

- Genesis 2:1–4 describes in ordinary terms God's rest on the seventh day. Since there is no additional creation, the frame using the normal Hebrew chronology of evening and morning is not needed. The creation overview is completed.

- Genesis 2:5–25 does not return to Day 1 or Day 5, but according to verse 7, attends only to the formation of man from the dust of the ground. Like a zoom lens, these verses neither contradict nor provide a sequential description of Genesis 1:25–2:4. Rather, Genesis 2:5–25 devotes itself to one fraction of the creation, the sixth day, and more specifically to the creation and role of humans among the other creations of God. Genesis 2:8–14 provides pre-Fall historical details about the Garden and where it was located. Genesis 2:15–17 contains the original covenant between God and Adam, and Genesis 2:18–25 describes Adam's relation to other animals and the first woman. Unless some philosophy is imposed on the texts, they indicate that many significant events occurred on this sixth day, but there is no internal teaching of Scripture to suggest that the sixth day allowed for evolution or took place over millennia. While this text may call for faith, surely such faith is better than transitory human theories.

Thus, Genesis 1–2 may be interpreted, and has been for centuries, in a harmonious fashion. Only of late and under duress from hostile cosmologies have harmonies been viewed as problematic. One wonders if exegetes are on as solid ground as they expect if they depart from centuries of pious insight merely to flock to the changing landscape of scientific theories that may be fading.

Shouldn't we favor modern interpreters over ancient interpreters? We do not think that modern interpreters have a monopoly on truth; neither are we convinced that contemporary theologians are decidedly superior to their predecessors. While some may presuppose that modernity is superior, they need to prove, not merely accept, this unquestioned article of faith. We may differ with our fathers in the faith, but to do so requires good reason and more than imitation of scientific fads.

We would hate to see an interpretative effort presuppose—apart from compelling proof—that modern biases and studies are automatically superior to those studies and biases of the Church in Early, Medieval, Reformation, and Puritan days. Neither is it necessarily prudent to disenfranchise all commentators before 1800, as if they were theological dunderheads. Moreover, it remains methodologically unproven that today's ministers and theologians are inherently more capable or perceptive than Augustine, Luther, Calvin, Twisse, Ussher, and others.[74] Our belief in the one holy, universal, and apostolic Church precludes us from assuming that recent conclusions are automatically advances in doctrine.

For example, simply because a modern theologian presents a coherent case explaining the creation narratives differently than the long history of orthodoxy on the subject, it does not logically follow that he has presented the *only* coherent case. Often, knowledgeable theologians can weave an interesting tale or create an ingenious explanation (never before suspected) of a text that conforms more closely to the scientific theories of the day. However, that interesting explanation may not be necessary, and it may not endure as the shifting sands of science recede.[75]

In fact, if current theologians present studies that exhibit superior exegetical merit, we would join any reasonable person in weighing their merit. This process, however, implies that the believing community will also evaluate *which* studies and findings are most consistent with biblical teaching. If modern theologians can disprove the interpretation of the earlier biblical commentators and show where their predecessors are in error based on biblical interpretation, not scientifically driven eisegesis, then we can afford to be open-minded. Merely claiming that our fathers in the faith were hopelessly "prescientific" is inadequate. We find that in many respects, our fathers in the faith demonstrate superior piety and clarity of thought. We must prove them to be deficient in this area before this objection can withstand scrutiny.

Briefly put, we should not presuppose that we know more than they did, simply because we live and have been educated under post-Darwinian paradigms. If those scientific paradigms are correct, then we could benefit from them. If they are erroneous at any point, however, then theological formulations based even incidentally upon them will collapse like a house of cards. Specifically, we are not sure that modern interpreters are superior in exegetical ability or more sanitized from cultural bias than earlier theologians. Prove that modernity has fostered interpretation that is freer from bias or superior to ancient interpretation, and we will happily listen. But assumption is not the same as proof. Assuming something is so doesn't make it so.

Moreover, Solomon's maxim that there is nothing new under the sun seems to require a bias in favor of antiquity. We do not agree to assume any presupposition that elevates modern scholarship above the long history of the Church's interpretation, particularly on an issue that is primarily an exegetical one. In the face of the tidal wave of modernity, we must ask repeatedly, "Why have our spiritual ancestors held strongly to views of sexuality, ethics, worship, or cosmology for hundreds of years, and what theory has changed to demand different interpretation of the inspired texts? Is a modern theory so certain as to require us to change?" Modern secular theories are not so compelling that they require the Church to alter its exegetical conclusions.

We remain unwilling to assume accommodation, especially if those who make this assumption suggest that the Church's theology must fit with the world's theorizing. Not only would that method be unfaithful to the authority of Scripture, but it also would fail to conform to what the best of secular science says about itself. The best of secular science is self-consciously provisional; its theories are only tentative, changing, and always subject to retesting and reconceptualization.

One of the more potent analyses of the progress of science has been provided in Thomas Kuhn's *The Structure of Scientific Revolutions*. While this work itself is worthy of criticism, still its central tenet is accepted by most historians. Kuhn's thesis is that scientific worldviews ("paradigms") are constantly formed, amended, and disregarded. He documents an ongoing process in which a revolution may occur in the paradigm of scientists (normally over a span of time, not instantaneously). When a sufficient number of anomalies are found and the paradigm cannot be amended to account for them, eventually a new paradigm will form.

While mid-nineteenth-century Darwinian evolution was one such scientific revolution, it appears that soon it will be replaced by a superior paradigm. While we do not yet know what that forthcoming paradigm will be, the anomalies of mid-nineteenth century Darwinian evolutionary schemes are mounting, and a Kuhnian crisis appears imminent—even as that crisis is dogmatically resisted by adherents of fading evolutionary orthodoxies. It would be unseemly, to say the least, for evangelicals to defend an orthodoxy that even anti-theists have come to reject.

Our 24-hour interpretation will be successful if it encourages other evangelicals not to board the train driven by a secular engine just as the engineers themselves are disembarking. If evangelicals fine-tune their message to fit a waning scientific cosmology just as secularists themselves are beginning to realize its indefensibility, we will not provide the best possible testimony of eternal truth to a lost generation.

There is, in other words, good and sufficient reason to hold to the classical view. Those who wish to move us from the view of insightful fathers in the faith must do a better job—not only exegetically, but also theologically, historically, and practically—to persuade us to depart from the truths understood by Moses' and Jesus' audiences. We would rather expect fluctuating theories to change.

Scientific revolutions, after all, occur with regularity. Twentieth century science is changing, and twenty-first century conclusions might make certain views, if tailored to fit a retrograde horizon, look foolishly out of touch in a few years.

Because science, by its very nature, is provisional, the Church must remain critical of theories that conform to science. Proven truth should prevail until those who question it can demonstrate, if ever, that their conclusions are based on superior exegesis. Therefore, until assured exegetical results are repudiated by superior exegesis, the Church should prefer continuity.

What is the relationship of special revelation to natural revelation? Our case for the 24-hour view implies a corollary that we should make explicit: We should not grant natural revelation (which is always filtered by the interpreter) a status equal to, or greater than, special revelation as it has been interpreted by the community of the faithful and circumscribed by the analogy of faith.

While there certainly is a "light of nature"—and Protestant theology has embraced a range of understandings about the role of natural revelation—the evangelical tradition has not assigned the same epistemological authority to natural revelation as to special revelation rightly interpreted. When forced to choose between conflicting sources of authority, we join the chorus begun by the apostle Paul, "Let God be true, and every man a liar" (Rom. 3:4).

CONCLUSION

Unless someone is tempted to dismiss the classical interpretation we have summarized above as trivial or lacking in pragmatic value, we respond by pointing out that the God who inspired Scripture did not seem to agree. One's view of creation affects many other areas: principles of hermeneutics, cosmology, apologetic method, the nurture of the young, and the trustworthiness of Scriptures in both the Old and the New Testaments. In short, because one's view of creation is part of one's worldview, it affects every glance.

Perhaps earlier theologians were more sensitive to this. Ussher explained in detail why these creation questions were so important for both faith and practice. He affirmed the classical view and argued that one of the reasons he did so was "to convince all heathen, that either thought that the world was without beginning, or that it began millions of years before it did."[76] "And though," asserted Ussher, "[God] could have perfected all the creatures at once and in a moment [contra Augustine]; yet he was six days and six nights in creating the world."[77] Another reason that Ussher cited was "that we might observe, that many of the creatures were made before those which are ordinarily their causes; and thereby learn, that the Lord is not bound to any creature, or to any means; thus the sun was not created before the fourth day, and yet days, which now are caused by the rising of the sun, were before that."[78] Thus, Ussher saw great value in miraculous creation by divine fiat. His explanation of what else is at stake is still useful today.

Neither Ussher nor his predecessors believed that God created mediately, using ordinary providence in the first week. Instead, God created immediately (not to be confused with "in an instant"), and He did not need any forces or agents outside of His word to create.

Herman Witsius subsequently explained that any view of creation which allowed natural processes excessive credit invariably would permit Job to answer God's questions ("Where were you?") or explain creation apart from the miraculous. That would be to "boldly contradict the prophets and God Himself; for since they expressly declare, that God stretcheth forth the heavens *alone*, they exclude every other cause of every sort; and since it is added that God spreadeth abroad the earth by *Himself*, we are taught that this is an immediate act, in which no cause, not even one that is instrumental operates."[79]

Witsius, perhaps with greater insight than modernity-biased contemporaries, had the perspective to observe that

> the act of creating is so peculiar to God that no creature can be admitted to any share in it. . . . If, therefore, we imagine that God communicates this privilege to any creature, that at his (the creature's) command, a certain other thing may exist, that thing would either exist without any co-operation on the part of God for the effecting its existence . . . and would be wholly indebted for its existence to the fiat of the commanding creature; or it would exist in consequence of God's willing and commanding in existence, in concert with the creature which is supposed to create. Now, each of these ideas is most dishonouring to God, and involves a manifest contradiction.[80]

We side with what the Scriptures teach about the days of creation. We side with the Law and the Prophets. We side with the apostles. We side with the consensus of the Church fathers. We side with the Reformation and Puritan divines. We side with the uniform testimony of the Church until recently. We can do no other. Future generations may scoff at the once-prevailing Darwinian paradigm of the nineteenth and twentieth centuries and realize that the interpretations of Witsius, Ussher, and the cloud of witnesses we have cited will long outlast the short half-life of interpretations held hostage to Darwinism's fling. Indeed, the heavens and the earth as we know them will eventually perish, but God's word will last forever.

NOTES

1. Alan Hayward, who disagrees with our interpretation, is honest enough to admit that "the idea of long days of creation was introduced" in "the early nineteenth century" (*Creation and Evolution: Facts and Fallacies* [London: Triangle, 1985], p. 161). Of course, since the 24-hour view was held by rabbinic commentators and the Old Testament itself, we disagree with those who attempt to demonize creationists for holding to the plain sense of "day," as if they were introducing novel theological notions.

2. James Barr to David C. C. Watson, personal letter, April 23, 1984.

3. Andrew D. White, *A History of the Warfare of Science with Theology in Christendom* (New York: D. Appleton & Co., 1896), p. 60. Edward D. Morris added: "But the language of the [Westminster] Confession, in the space of six days, must be interpreted literally, because this was the exact view pronounced by the Assembly" (*Theology of the Westminster Symbols* [Columbus, OH: 1900], p. 202).

4. Modern liberal theologians ranging from Marcus Dods to James Barr support the fact that only very recent formulations twist the original intent on this issue. Regrettably, many of these recent innovations have flowed from evangelical pens more interested in swiftly

conforming to the ideas of passing scientific trends than in defending classical orthodoxy.

5. Indeed, the recent demise of certain cosmological and evolutionary paradigms permits us the luxury to dissent more readily from modern theories that no longer dominate the landscape, a luxury our immediat predecessors did not have.

6. H. S. Thayer, ed., *Newton's Philosophy of Nature: Selections from His Writings* (New York: Hafner Publishing Co., 1953), pp. 64–5.

7. Derek Kidner observes: "It is no accident that God is the subject of the first sentence of the Bible, for this word dominates the whole chapter and catches the eye at every point of the page: it is used some thirty-five times in as many verses of the story" (*Genesis: An Introduction and Commentary*, Tyndale Old Testament Commentaries [Downers Grove, IL: InterVarsity Press, 1967], p. 43).

8. Matthew Henry, *A Commentary on the Whole Bible*, vol. 1 (Old Tappan, NJ: Revell, n.d.), p. 2.

9. Henry also astutely observes that Moses' creation account serves to confirm what is already apparent in the book of nature but is not readily acknowledged by fallen man because of the effects of sin: "The holy Scripture therefore, designing by revealed religion to maintain and improve natural religion, to repair the decays of it and supply the defects of it, since the Fall, for the reviving of the precepts of the law of nature, lays down, at first, this principle of the unclouded light of nature, that this world was, in the beginning of time, created by a Being of infinite wisdom and power, who was himself before all time and all worlds" (*A Commentary on the Whole Bible*, vol. 1, p. 2).

10. Ibid.

11. Donald Macleod, *Behold Your God* (Scotland: Christian Focus Publications Ltd., 1995 [1990]), p. 63.

12. Ibid.

13. Ibid.

14. Ibid.

15. Ibid.

16. Many commentators note that in visions of judgment, all or part of this trilogy of chaos, emptiness, and darkness come back: "'My people are fools; they do not know me. They are senseless children; they have no understanding. They are skilled in doing evil; they know not how to do good.' I looked at the earth, and it was *formless and empty*; and at the heavens, and their *light was gone*" (Jer. 4:22–23); and "Throw that worthless servant outside into the *darkness*, where there will be weeping and gnashing of teeth" (Matt. 25:30).

17. John Calvin, *Commentaries on the First Book of Moses Called Genesis*, vol. 1, trans. John King (Grand Rapids, MI: Baker Book House, 1981), p. 78.

18. Meredith G. Kline, "Space and Time in the Genesis Cosmogony," *Perspectives on Science and Christian Faith*, vol. 48, no. 1 (April 1996), p. 2.

19. Kidner, *Genesis: An Introduction and Commentary*, p. 46.

20. Calvin, *Commentaries on the First Book of Moses Called Genesis*, p. 103.

21. Louis Berkhof, among others, indicated that the Hebrew word for "create" (*bara*) only referred to creational activity out of nothing (*Systematic Theology* [Grand Rapids, MI: Wm. B. Eerdmans Publishing Co., 1941], pp. 132–3). Other Hebrew phrases could mean "form" or "develop," but *bara* was reserved for creation instead of shaping. Berkhof also affirms the universality of the Church's interpretation of normal days until recent times, and that "The Reformers . . . regarded the days of creation as six literal days" (ibid., p. 127). See also Calvin's commentary on Genesis 1; Robert L. Dabney, *Lectures in Systematic Theology* (Edinburgh, UK: The Banner of Truth Trust, 1985 [1871]), pp. 247–9; and Francis Turretin, *Institutes of Elenctic Theology*, vol. 1, ed. James T. Dennison, Jr. (Phillipsburg, PA: Presbyterian & Reformed, 1992 [1679–85]), p. 431.

22. Interestingly, interpretations of the Flood, in contrast to creation, rarely seek to treat those days (e.g., Gen. 8:10) in a nonliteral fashion. It seems that for the sake of consistency, interpretations of Noah waiting "seven more days" might extend to long eras to reconcile Scripture to geology, but we are not aware of such interpretations.

23. Lightfoot's claim that "all grant" this metascheme is highly significant, indicating that at the height of British Puritanism, this matter was settled, and settled decisively in favor of the classical view. Augustine, who was far from advocating a long creation period, had been repudiated. This consensus held until the scientific revolutions of the nineteenth century.

24. *The Whole Works of the Rev. John Lightfoot, D.D.*, vol. 11, ed. J. R. Pitman (London: Printed by J. F. Dove, 1822).

25. Zacharias Ursinus, *Commentary on the Heidelberg Catechism* (Columbus, OH: Scott and Bascom Printers, 1852 [1616]), p. 531; emphasis added to show the basis of comparison.

26. Psalm 89:12 affirms that God created "the north and the south," no small feat. Creation of such poles appears to be instantaneous, not gradual. Similarly, toward the end of the Old Testament, Amos affirms God's creation as effortless (Amos 4:13). We find it difficult to conceive of the formation of mountains or the creation of the wind as necessitating or comporting with long evolutionary unfolding.

27. In desperation, some have sought to enlist Athanasius to support long ages, based on his comments on personified wisdom in Proverbs 8. Rather than affirming long days, all Athanasius asserted was that wisdom existed "before his deeds of old" (Prov. 8:22), hardly a support for day-age views.

28. Westminster Shorter Catechism, Q. 9.

29. Numerous commentators apply this verse as a text supporting *ex nihilo* and unmediated creation. Among them are William Hendriksen, who interpreted this verse as applying "during the week of creation."

30. Elsewhere, the historicity of Adam and Eve, as normally understood, is taught in Acts 17:26; Rom. 5:12–14; 1 Cor. 15:22, 45; 1 Tim. 2:13–14; and Jude 14.

31. John Owen commented on Hebrews 11:3: "All the things we now behold in their order, glory, and beauty were made by the power of God out of that chaos, or confused mass of substance, which was itself fire made and produced out of nothing, having no cause but the efficiency of divine power" (*Hebrews: The Epistle of Warning*, ed. Herbert Lockyer, Sr. (Grand Rapids: MI: Kregel, 1953), p. 216.

32. John Calvin's disciple, Theodore Beza, also affirmed that Hebrews 11:3 taught creation *ex nihilo*. Beza explained: "The world is formed *ex nihilo*. We are not able to comprehend how from this which is not made, is that which is [made]." See also Theodore de Beze, *Cours Sur les Epitres aux Romains et aux Hebreaux (1564–1566), Travaux d'Humanism et Renaissance*, vol. 226 (Geneva, Switzerland: Library Droz, 1988), p. 311. Further, in his *Confession de Foi du Chretien* (1558), Beza affirmed that God the Father "has created all out of nothing" (2.2), and "we believe that he has not only created the visible world, the heaven and the earth and all that they contain, but also invisible spirits" (2.3; see also the English translation, *The Christian Faith*, trans. James Clark [East Sussex, UK: Christian Focus Ministries Trust, 1992], p. 3). Puritan leader William Perkins taught similarly in his lengthy *Commentary on Hebrews 11* (Boston, MA: Pilgrim Press, 1992).

33. *On the Hexameron*, 2.8. Lancelot Andrewes would later assert that the creation days should be measured as follows: "from Sunne to Sunne is counted a day" (*Lectures Preached in St. Paul's Church* [London: 1657], p. 661). Andrews affirmed: "Therefore we say a day hath *twenty-four hours*. . . . This was a day by itself, as the other six days were by themselves" (ibid., p. 662). Citing Basil, Andrews commented that the word *yôm* "had a meaning for our natural use that we should esteem *twenty-four hours* one day. . . . The first day is an example to the days after" (ibid., p. 663).

34. Ambrose, *Hexameron*, vol. 42, trans. John J. Savage (New York: Fathers of the Church, Inc., 1961), p. 72.

35. Ibid., pp. 42–3.

36. C. John Collins, "How Old is the Earth: Anthropomorphic Days in Genesis 1:1–2:3," *Presbuterion* (Fall 1994), vol. 20, no. 2, pp. 113–4.

37. Collins admits that Hugh Ross's claim that Aquinas held to long days is mistaken, even though in other ways Aquinas did follow Augustine (ibid., pp. 125–6).

38. Aquinas, *Summa Theologica* (London: Burns Oates & Washbourne, 1921), Q. 74, art. 3, p. 274.

39. Ibid., Q. 46, art. 2, pp. 248–9.

40. Hugh Ross, *The Fingerprint of God*, 2d edition (Orange, CA: Promise Publishers, 1991), p. 141. For support, particularly of Augustine's view, Ross cites the following: *The Literal Meaning of Genesis*, bks. 4 and 5; *The Confessions*, bk. 13, chaps. 48–52 (a mistake); and *The City of God*, bk. 11, chaps. 7–8, 30–1.

41. Ross, *The Fingerprint of God*, pp. 146–58. See also Hugh Ross, *Creation and Time* (Colorado Springs, CO: NavPress, 1994), pp. 45–71.

42. It is not necessary to assert that God intended the biblical narratives on creation to be literal in every aspect. Nonliteral or symbolic hermeneutical conclusions are different from the assertion that earlier exegetes maintained notions compatible with modern theories.

43. Collins helpfully notes the distinction between allegory and anthropomorphism ("How Old is the Earth," p. 120, n. 48). While someone might argue that ancient evangelicals used an anthropomorphic interpretation in numerous places, he could not necessarily conclude that they lobbied for long days in this instance.

44. Calvin, *Commentaries on the First Book of Moses Called Genesis*, p. 84.

45. See Martin Luther, *Luther's Works*, vol. 17 (St. Louis, MO: Concordia, 1972), pp. 29, 118.

46. Francis Pieper notes, "The time in which creation was completed was six days, as Gen. 1:31 and Gen. 2:2 expressly state (*hexameron*). These six days are neither to be shortened, for pious reasons (to set forth God's omnipotence), to a moment (Athanasius, Augustine, Hilary), nor are they to be extended, for impious reasons (to bring Scripture into agreement with the 'assured results' of science), to six periods of indefinite length (thus almost all modern theologians). Scripture forbids us to interpret the days as periods, for it divides these days into evening and morning. That forces us to accept the days as days of twenty-four hours" (*Christian Dogmatics*, vol. 1 [St. Louis, MO: Concordia, 1950], p. 468). In a related footnote, Pieper quotes Luther as follows: "Hilary and Augustine, two great lights in the Church, believed that the world was made all of a sudden and all at once (*subito et simul*), not successively during the space of six days. Augustine plays with these six days in a marvelous manner. He considers them to be mystical days of knowledge in the angels and not six natural days. . . . As Moses is not instructing us concerning allegorical creatures or an allegorical world, but concerning natural creatures and a world visible and capable of being apprehended by the senses, he calls, as we say in the proverb, 'a post a post,' he calls the thing by the right name, day and evening; his meaning is the same as ours when we use those terms, without any allegory whatever." Vilmar, too, admits: "The manner in which these 'six days' in Gen. 2:2–3 and later in the Law are used shows that days of twenty-four hours are meant, and the wording used seems to speak in favor of it" (ibid., p. 469).

47. Robert C. Bishop, "Science and Theology: A Methodological Comparison," *Journal of Interdisciplinary Studies*, vol. 5, no. 1/2 (1993), p. 155.

48. Similarly, C. S. Lewis noted that many ancient scientists knew many of the concepts that are considered quite modern. However, historical discrimination often occurs, as Lewis

noted: "Here is a simple historical falsehood. Ptolemy (*Almagest*, bk. 1, chap. 5) knew just as well as Eddington that the earth was infinitesimal in comparison with the whole content of space. There is no question here of knowledge having grown until the frame of archaic thought is no longer able to contain it. The real question is why the spatial insignificance of the earth, after being known for centuries, should suddenly in the last century have become an argument against Christianity. I do not know why this has happened; but I am sure it does not mark an increased clarity of thought, for the argument from size is, in my opinion, very feeble" (C. S. Lewis, "Dogma and the Universe," *God in the Dock* [Grand Rapids, MI: Wm. B. Eerdmans Publishing Co., 1970], p. 39. See also pp. 74, 99).

49. *The Irish Articles of Religion* (1615) quoted in Philip Schaff, *The Creeds of Christendom*, vol. 3 (Grand Rapids, MI: Baker Book House, 1983), p. 529.

50. *The Workes of Gervase Babington* (London: 1622), p. 6.

51. *The Whole Works of the Rev. John Lightfoot, D.D.*, vol. 2, ed. J. R. Pitman (London: Printed by J. F. Dove, 1822), p. 333.

52. Ibid., pp. 334–5.

53. Ibid., p. 334.

54. Ibid., p. 336.

55. Ibid., p. 337.

56. Ibid., p. 334.

57. *Works*, vol. 2, p. 71.

58. Ibid., pp. 10–1.

59. See the Appendix to "The Westminster View of Creation Days," (http://capo.org/creation.html), which contains a modern translation of *De Creatione* by Wesley Baker.

60. Most of the theological exemplars in this section are from Protestant or Reformed churches. Similar collections of testimony could equally be drawn, however, from Anglican, Methodist, Baptist, and Independent communions.

61. We wish to express our deepest gratitude for the research assistance of Christopher Coldwell, who uncovered much that entire faculties have not been able to unearth, and has made an irrefutable contribution to this discussion.

62. For more evidence that the Westminster divines held to the 24-hour view and that it was the dominant view of the day, see David W. Hall, "The Westminster View of Creation Days," *Premise*, vol. 5, no. 3, July 1998 (http://capo.org/creation.html). See also the revision at http://capo.org/creationRevise.html.

63. Patrick Symon, Bishop of Ely, commented similarly that the evening and the morning of the first day spanned "*twenty-four hours*" and that "God made all things at the first, which did not appear together, but in the space of six Days" (Patrick Symon, *A Commentary upon the First Book of Moses called Genesis* [London: 1698], p. 11).

64. Turretin, *Institutes of Elenctic Theology*, p. 444.

65. Ibid., p. 438.

66. Ibid., p. 442. Similarly, Simeon Ashe endorsed the following: "When was the world created? It is betwixt five and six thousand years since the world was created. If it be asked at what time of year, the most judicious answer [is] in the spring time; if in what time, in the space of six days (Gen. 1:31 compared with 2:1 and Exo. 20:11)." *The Good Old Way (or Perkins Improved): A Plain Exposition and Sound Application* (London: 1653), p. 26.

67. See J. Ligon Duncan III, "Animadversions on Alexander Mitchell and the Days of Creation," *The Presbyterian Witness*, vol. 12, no. 2 (Spring 1998), and David W. Hall, "The Westminster View of Creation Days: A Choice between Non-Ambiguity or Historical Revisionism," *The Presbyterian Witness*, vol. 12, no. 3 (Summer 1998). Both of these articles are also found at http://capo.org/premise/98/july/toc.html.

68. Warfield may prove far more than our friends wish to claim. One marvels at Warfield's

hermeneutical gymnastics in a 1915 work entitled "Calvin's Doctrine of Creation," where Warfield actually tried to mold Calvin into a proto-evolutionist. Warfield unequivocally asserted, "Calvin doubtless had no theory of evolution; but he teaches a doctrine of evolution." Warfield even speculated that had certain preconditions come about, "Calvin would have been a precursor of the modern evolutionary theorist." In a footnote responding to Herman Bavinck, Warfield concluded, "Calvin accordingly very naturally thought along the lines of a theistic evolutionism" (B. B. Warfield, "Calvin's Doctrine of Creation," *The Works of Benjamin B. Warfield*, vol. 5 (Grand Rapids, MI: Baker Book House, 1872), p. 306). That claim is as stunning as it is erroneous. The possibility that Calvin might have been an evolutionist is quite remote.

69. C. John Collins suggests that to label as the "path to compromise" the thought of the likes of Hodge, Shedd, and Schaeffer is to cast reproach on them. However, we can retain high regard for these men in general, while disagreeing with some particulars in their thinking. Our respect for fathers in the faith does not require us to hold them to be infallible (as Collins notes), nor that we grant their conclusions immunity from revision. Rather, we best maintain high respect for their work by honestly criticizing their weak points.

70. Joseph Hall, *Contemplations on the Historical Passages of the Old and New Testaments* (London: 1854 [orig. 1661]), p. 2. Similarly, John Diodati understood: "It is likely that the light was at first imprinted in some part of the heaven, whose revolution distinguished the first three days, and the fourth it was restrained into the body of the Sun, or of all the other Stars, but in a different degree" (*Pious and Learned Annotations upon the Holy Bible* [London: 1651]).

71. Calvin, *Commentaries on the First Book of Moses Called Genesis*, pp. 76–7.

72. Orthodox rabbinical commentaries, for example, lend sparse support for interpreting *day* as anything other than a normal day. On the specific question of plant growth, Diodati clarifies the earlier consensus (commenting on Genesis 1:5: "The meaning is that the first plants were immediately brought forth by God; the order of nature being as yet not established" [*Pious and Learned Annotations upon the Holy Bible*]). Moreover, Herman Witsius repeatedly affirms creation by God's word alone "by a mere command and volition," devoid of other intermediaries (*Sacred Dissertation on the Apostles' Creed*, vol. 1 [Phillipsburg, NJ]: Presbyterian & Reformed Publishing Co., 1993 (1681)], p. 197). He embraced the language we use, namely, "that this is an immediate act, in which no cause, not even one that is instrumental . . . has any place" (ibid., p. 198). He cites rabbinical tradition favorably, that creation was "immediately, and without any concatenation of causes" (ibid.). Others from within the orthodox rabbinical school agree. Rabbi Y. Chesner, in private correspondence, has written, "Judaism has always reckoned a 24-hour day, as written in the Torah in Genesis: 'And there was evening and there was morning, one day,' i.e., the evening [meaning night which starts in the evening] and morning [meaning day which starts in the morning] together constitute one day [of 24 hours]. The same goes for the other five days of the creation, as by all of them we find this expression: 'And there was evening and there was morning.' The Talmud also reckons a 24-hour day. All the accepted commentaries on the Torah understand the creation days as a normal day of 24 hours. There are some modern thinkers who wish to explain them as eons of time . . . in order to fit the story of the creation with modern scientific opinion, but this is not the accepted position." Rabbi Yaakov Spivak confirmed: "The medieval scholar and kabbalist Nachmanides (The Ramban) held to a literal interpretation as to the time of Creation—he believed that it took place in six, twenty-four-hour days."

73. Twisse, *Morality*, p. 51.

74. Collins ("How Old is the Earth," p. 110) agrees that the framework hypothesis as set forth by Kline is ruled out on exegetical grounds (ibid., p. 116, n. 29). Moreover, he confirms that much of the argumentation for long days based on idiomatic considerations in Genesis 2:4 "give[s] us no information on the range of meanings of *yôm* outside this bound form" and that "the day-age theorists have not been able to say by what criteria we

may discern an extended sense of *yôm* as 'age,' or what contextual clues seem to tip us off. This seems to be a fatal weakness."

75. With the rapidity of scientific revolutions in the information age, it is not difficult to imagine textbooks a century from now (perhaps the rough equivalent of a millennium of previous theological literature) documenting how quickly some segments of the evangelical community were to alter their interpretation in the face of secular constructs. Unless one sees twentieth-century cosmologies (which have assumed evolutionary dogma) as immune from revision or more certain than the history of biblical interpretation, we more cautiously expect that evolutionary cosmologies will pass away sooner than biblical teaching rightly understood. Some caution about the possibility of future embarrassment after the collapse of reigning scientific paradigms should temper one's interpretation or willingness to jump on a particular bandwagon.

76. James Ussher, *Sum and Substance of Christian Religion*, ed. Hastings Robinson (London: 1841), p. 118.

77. Ibid.

78. Ibid.

89. Herman Witsius, *Sacred Dissertation on the Apostles' Creed*, p. 198.

90. Ibid., pp. 199–200.

Hugh Ross & Gleason L. Archer

THE DAY-AGE RESPONSE

*I*n our debate over Genesis 1, Duncan and Hall correctly observe that "the stakes are high"—high enough to demand our best efforts in careful scholarship. Their studies and ours lead us to agree on some important particulars, such as the singularity of the creation event, the transcendence of the Creator, and the adequacy of scientific evidence to support these conclusions (e.g., the space-time theorem of general relativity[1] and the proven reliability of general relativity[2]). We see, as they do, a clear biblical case and a growing scientific basis for the recent, special creation of Adam and Eve and for the literal descent of all humanity from Adam and Eve.[3]

On most other points, however, our respective studies lead us to different conclusions, and we believe careful scholarship is, indeed, the key to resolving our differences. Ironically, such scholarship is hindered by the height of the "stakes" on one side of this debate. For Duncan and Hall, it seems that only one interpretation of the data is acceptable. Any other view represents the unthinkable—a perceived acquiescence to the tenets of atheistic or deistic naturalism.

67

Most scientists, on the other hand, spend a lifetime proving themselves and others wrong to refine understanding and dig deeper into truth. It is their job. Arrogance can get in the way, but many scientists take pride in making any progress toward truth, whether that progress took the direction they expected or not.

In the following pages, we address only a few of the major difficulties we see in Duncan and Hall's argument, difficulties that may result from a "need" for Duncan and Hall to see things a particular way. While our treatment of these major difficulties must be limited in this particular forum, we have prepared a more detailed response for those who want one.[4]

REVISITING CHURCH HISTORY

Duncan and Hall cite numerous sources to support their 24-hour interpretation. Unfortunately, they fail to prove their case, mostly because of faulty scholarship.

Sir Isaac Newton

Duncan and Hall, for example, quote Sir Isaac Newton to "support" their case for a 24-hour interpretation of the Genesis days. The quotation they cite is a brief excerpt of a six-page letter written in 1680 or 1681.[5] Apparently, Duncan and Hall did not peruse the entire letter or Newton's other writings to determine what he meant. They assert that "clearly Newton viewed [the creation days] as normal days." In the same paragraph from which they quote, however, Newton writes, "Now for ye number and length of ye six days: by what is said above you may make ye first day as long as you please, and ye second day too."[6] Also in that same paragraph, Newton goes on to suggest that Earth's first rotation, occurring he thought on the third creation day, took at least one year to complete.

In the following paragraph, Newton attributes the generation of the hills and mountains to gradual, natural processes. He also acknowledges that his contemporaries employ Proverbs 8:25, Job 15:7, and Psalm 90:2 to establish the antiquity of the earth,[7] but he apparently sees little need for such proof texts because the fact is so obvious. In this letter and other writings,[8] Newton expresses his "day-age" view and indicates that others in his peer group shared it.

The Church Fathers

Just as we dispute Duncan and Hall's reliance upon Newton, so we dispute their reliance upon earlier Church history. Duncan and Hall depict the creation-day debate as an artifact of Darwinian theory, specifically of the attempt of theologians to accommodate it. Actually, as we mention when we establish our interpretive case for the day-age view later in this volume, the 24-hour interpreters ironically rest far more heavily than Darwinists ever have on Darwinian theory to explain hypothesized speciation in the eras since the Fall of man and the Genesis Flood.

The 24-hour creationists repeatedly and emphatically identify their view as uniquely "traditional," "orthodox," "literal," and "classical." Duncan and Hall begin their argument by stating that scientific issues *only*, not exegetical ones, drive the day-age interpretation.

Ample documentation supports our claim that the early Church fathers did indeed discuss the *when* of creation (in addition to the Who, the how, and the order).[9] Justin Martyr, Irenaeus, Lactantius, Victorinus of Pettau, and Methodius of Olympus all explicitly endorse six consecutive thousand-year periods for the Genesis creation days.[10] According to Ambrose, so did Hippolytus. Though uncertain about the duration of the creation week, Clement of Alexandria, Origen, and Augustine explicitly rejected the 144-hour notion.[11]

As they did with Newton, Duncan and Hall quote selectively from Basil and Ambrose. They choose words that seem to show unequivocal support for their interpretation. However, further research into the writings of Basil and Ambrose reveals that they wrestled with the issue and struggled with ambiguity. In the same passages, they wrote of "ages" for creation.[12]

Duncan and Hall also cast Luther, Calvin, and the framers of *The Westminster Confession* as dogmatic, 24-hour creationists. While many of these men espoused a 24-hour-day view, they focused their certainty on the *Who*, the *how*, and the *what* of creation. As detailed as it is on the subject of creation, for example, *The Westminster Confession* never specifies the length of the creation days. While it teaches that God created in the space of six days, it simply mirrors the language of Scripture at that point. Thus, Duncan and Hall beg the question by assuming that the days necessarily are 24 hours long. The key question is, What does Scripture mean when it says that God made the heavens and the earth in six days?

It seems reasonable to conclude that the *timing* of creation had little doctrinal or apologetic significance until scientists uncovered evidence for the antiquity of the universe, earth, and life. Only after these discoveries does the *when* of creation become an important evangelistic issue, one worthy of in-depth analysis.

James Barr

Duncan and Hall try to get mileage out of quoting James Barr, who stated that no credible Old Testament scholar at "any world-class university" construes the days of creation as anything other than literal 24-hour days.

The irony is that Barr's statement comes from his attempts to *discount*, rather than support, biblical inerrancy and the integration of scientific fact with scriptural truth. But the statement was wrong when made because Gleason Archer and Walter Kaiser, among many other highly reputable Bible scholars,[13] did and do support the long-day interpretation.

REVISITING NATURE'S HISTORY

In their first footnote, Duncan and Hall claim that an ancient date for the universe's creation poses no threat to their view. If it doesn't, we see no rationale for them insisting that all stars are recently formed and that ongoing star formation is a false inference. We have difficulty imagining their failure to recognize the inseparability of the age of the universe from the ages of the stars.[14]

Duncan and Hall repeatedly assert that cosmic creation *ex nihilo* (that is, God's transcendent, miraculous creation of all matter, energy, space, and time) rules out natural star formation and subsequent stellar development. In truth, the creation of the universe *ex nihilo*[15] does not biblically or scientifically imply that matter, energy, space, and time can never interact according to God's prescribed physical laws after the creation event.

Duncan and Hall repeatedly assert creation *ex nihilo* where Genesis 1 does not. For example, in the case of the "light" in Genesis 1:3, the word for God's creative activity is *haya*, not *bara*. This verb choice suggests that the light "appeared," that it broke through to earth's surface for the first time, not that it came into existence on that day. Scientific findings demonstrate that God orchestrated a precise and intricate transformation of earth's early atmosphere from opaque to translucent, so that light could penetrate to the surface.[16]

Likewise, Genesis 1 records that atmospheric water, continental land masses, and "the great lights" came to be or showed up on Days 2, 3, and 4, respectively. The text does not mandate that they were manufactured *ex nihilo* on those days.[17] It does indicate, however, that birds, mammals, and human beings, at least in some respect, were created *ex nihilo* on Days 5 and 6.[18]

Duncan and Hall misrepresent the physics of stellar burning as uncertain and widely disputed. On that erroneous basis, they claim that Christians need not worry about astronomical research. They seem to link stellar burning with Darwinian evolution. Biblically and scientifically, the differences between them are enormous. When the great lights become visible on earth's surface for the first time, the writer uses the Hebrew verb *haya* ("let there be"), but when birds, mammals, and the first man and woman are introduced, the writer uses *bara* ("make what did not previously exist").

While the fossil record is discontinuous, the stellar record is strictly continuous. Whereas biological history must be inferred, astronomical history can be directly observed.[19] While complete animal speciation is limited to the past (previous to Adam), all the processes of stellar formation, development, and extinction are observed in the very recent past (up to eight minutes ago) as well as the distant past. Whereas biological evolution deals with incredibly complex, ill-defined systems, stellar burning addresses very simple, exhaustively defined systems.[20]

While the cessation of biological speciation requires no change in even a single law of physics, the cessation of star formation and stellar development demands the overthrow of *all* the laws of physics.[21] Scientific discoveries in the last two years have essentially toppled the case for biological naturalism and Darwinian evolution—even in the eyes of nontheistic scientists.[22] At the same time, recent discoveries have so strengthened the case for a singular *ex nihilo* cosmic creation event and a universe exquisitely fine-tuned for life as to persuade even nontheistic astronomers that a Designer must exist.[23]

If the evidence for ongoing raindrop formation does not disturb us, we see no reason to be disturbed by star formation. The processes by which stars coalesce and ignite are simpler, more straightforward, and more continuous than the processes that generate raindrops. Thanks to the Hubble Space Telescope, as well as millimeter and infrared wavelength telescopes, astronomers now have obtained images and detailed measurements of the entire star formation process.[24]

ASSESSING SIN'S IMPACT

Duncan and Hall, however, downplay the book of nature, based on their understanding of the impact of the Fall on physics and the mind.

Changed Laws of Physics?
Duncan and Hall maintain that pre-Adamic and/or pre-Noahic physics has no bearing on anything we observe today. We challenge this conclusion on both biblical and scientific grounds.

According to Genesis 1, stars were created before Adam was created. Stars rely upon the constancy of all four fundamental forces of physics (gravity, electromagnetism, the strong nuclear force, and the weak nuclear force), the gas laws, the first and second laws of thermodynamics, relativity, and quantum mechanics. Any change or discontinuity in any of these laws would destroy the possibility of their existence. The development of a wa-

ter cycle, continents, and the survival of plants on earth also require—
and thus demonstrate—the operation of all these laws. According to Genesis 2 and 3, Adam and Eve were moving, breathing, working, and eating
before the Fall. Such activities require the same set of physical laws.

Romans 8:20–22 tells us that the "whole creation" is subject to the
"bondage to decay"—i.e., to the second law of thermodynamics. Why? This
universe is temporary and is the site God has chosen to conquer evil, which
began with Lucifer's rebellion and came to earth through Adam and Eve's
rebellion. When God's redemptive work on earth is done, when the salvation made possible by Jesus' life, death, and resurrection has accomplished
all that God intends, when all evil and evildoers have been judged, God
will create an entirely new universe. Its description in Revelation 21–22
establishes that this new universe will operate by new and different physical laws.[25]

The Impact of Sin on the Mind

Duncan and Hall also ignore evidence because they believe that sin cata-
strophically impacts a person's capacity to interpret the record of nature,
to discern truth from error, especially since nature is so unclear compared
to the words of the Bible. If they followed this view to its logical conclusion, neither civilization nor any form of technology would be possible,
and their view implies that everyone exposed to the words of Scripture
would agree on (most) every point.

In reality, we see that believers and unbelievers alike have contributed to the body of knowledge about the universe, earth, and life—knowledge which enables us, in fact, to bring the gospel to even the remotest
parts of the world. In some disciplines of mathematics and physics, such
as Newtonian mechanics, statistical mechanics, and linear differential cal-
culus, all scholars agree on virtually all points.[26] We have difficulty even
imagining "deconstructionist" or "post-modern" mathematicians or physicists. We only wish we could say the same of theologians and Bible scholars.

Duncan and Hall declare that our understanding of nature's record is
in all respects inferior to our understanding of the Bible. Psalm 19:1–4,
however, emphatically states that God "speaks" through what He has created. Nature is God's "expression" as much as the Bible. According to many
of David's psalms, that expression is "perfect."[27] In nature's record we see
neither capriciousness nor inconsistency. In Scripture we see neither capriciousness nor inconsistency. We read in both accounts that God does
not and cannot lie[28] and that He is truth and delights to reveal truth to
anyone who, by the work of His Holy Spirit, desires it and seeks it.

Therefore, the record of nature can never contradict the words of the

Bible. If our reading of nature's record conflicts with our understanding of the Bible's words, we know we have erred in our interpretation of either or both. To ignore what the record of nature tells us about gravity or stars or creation dates would be just as foolish as ignoring what Romans tells us about propitiation or justification.

Downplaying the Book of Nature

Sadly, we see that Duncan and Hall's approach to Scripture leaves them with little appreciation for the growth in extent, quantity, variety, and accuracy of nature's "canon." Our understanding of the Creator's revelation in nature continues to expand exponentially, especially in astronomy. The evidence for divine attributes and divine design has been doubling every four years in this discipline alone.[29] We need humble hearts to respond to this evidence with faith (which is what we do in accepting the words of the Bible), but when we ignore it, we miss out on both a theological treasure and an evangelistic gold mine.

Extrabiblical evidences are not inconsequential. They are vital. Christianity's uniqueness resides not only in its gospel message, but also in its testability. Paul exhorts Christ's followers to "test everything,"[30] and Moses appeals to fulfilled prophecy.[31] Just as the fulfillment of biblical prophecy can attest and clarify biblical texts, so, too, the fulfillment of biblically predicated scientific discoveries help attest and elucidate Bible passages. The *Proceedings of the International Council on Biblical Inerrancy*, Summit II (1982), express our point:

> It is sometimes argued that our exegesis should not be influenced by scientific observations. We believe this view is mistaken. While the Bible clearly gives more specific information about our relationship to God than one can possibly deduce from natural revelation, it does not necessarily follow that our understanding of the physical world, its origin, etc., will also be more clearly deduced from God's revelation in His word than His revelation in His world. Since both are revelations from God, and therefore, give a unified story, it seems quite permissible to consider all of the evidence (scientific as well as biblical) to be significant to the degree that each revelation can be clearly interpreted.[32]

This conclusion led to the ICBI's 20th article, which we wholeheartedly endorse:

> WE AFFIRM that since God is the author of all truth, all truths, biblical and extrabiblical, are consistent and cohere, and that the Bible speaks truth when it touches on matters pertaining to nature, history, or anything else. We further affirm that in some cases extrabiblical data have value for clarifying what Scripture teaches, and for prompting correction of faulty

interpretations. WE DENY that extrabiblical views ever disprove the teaching of Scripture or hold priority over it.[33]

MORE EXEGETICAL DIFFICULTIES

The failure of Duncan and Hall to consider the physical consequences of their Genesis interpretation leads them inadvertently toward some strange exegetical twists.

Nonsolar Light Source?

Duncan and Hall, for example, hold that plants created on the third creation day survived not by sunlight but by some other divinely-provided light source. Of course, plants on the land need much more than light to survive. They need all that God provided on the first three creation days—a stable planet, day-night cycle, water cycle, and continental land masses—plus the effective temperature, spectral response, luminosity, mass, distance, and other characteristics of the sun. In other words, plants would need a surrogate sun identical to the sun we now orbit.

Plant life would also need virtually all the effective characteristics of the moon as well.[34] For example, it takes a single massive body as distant as the moon to stabilize the tilt of Earth's rotation axis, which is essential for a life-sustaining water cycle and, thus, for plants on the land. To force a two-sun, two-moon model into the language of Genesis 1 seems exegetically bizarre, if not impossible. Nor can science explain such a scenario in a way that would avoid the destruction of Earth. Appealing to divine action under radically altered physical conditions cannot be justified, for both the biblical text and astronomical observations affirm the operation of the present laws of physics throughout the six creation days.

Duncan and Hall's appeal to Revelation 21 and 22 for nonstellar light sources is invalid. The new creation is governed by different laws of physics, even a different set of dimensions. Gravity, electromagnetism, and thermodynamics do not exist in the new creation as the Bible describes it,[35] though they certainly operate throughout the six Genesis creation days. Therefore, while stars are impossible in the new creation, they are mandatory throughout the six Genesis creation days.

The Tasks of Adam on the Sixth Day

Another example is Duncan and Hall's claim that a sinless Adam achieved his sixth day tasks in just a few hours or less. In presenting our interpretive case for the day-age view later in this volume, we give five reasons why a sinless Adam could not finish his sixth-day duties and experiences as quickly as Duncan and Hall maintain. We point out, too, that "all kinds of trees [grew] out of the ground" on the sixth day. Duncan and Hall's claim demands not just a sinless Adam, but a supernatural Adam and supernatural trees, as well.

We are equally concerned, however, that Duncan and Hall seem to ignore the deeper message of Genesis 2. As God introduces Adam to the three levels of His creation—the physical, the soulish, and the spiritual— He teaches and prepares Adam for life on earth and for the care and keeping of the land, the plants, and the animals. He teaches Adam the value and blessings of a wife. He trains both Adam and Eve in resource management (Gen. 1:28–30), training in which experience plays a crucial role. Throughout Scripture we see that God offers no shortcuts to experience, knowledge, discipline, and maturity. For a secular example, we note that science professors insist that even their most gifted and best performing students take laboratory courses to supplement their classroom studies. For a biblical example, we observe that the incarnate Christ took thirty years to prepare Himself for ministry.

A Long Seventh Day

Finally, just as Duncan and Hall's view disregards the implicit evidence for a long sixth day, so it overlooks the explicit evidence for a long—in fact, ongoing—seventh day. God's current work, described in John 5:15–17, differs from His creation week work and does not prove that His creation Sabbath has ended. Jesus repeatedly declared that the Sabbath is not a cessation from all activity, and certainly not from spiritual activity, but rather, from physical rigors of work (Matt. 12:1–4; Mark 2:23–3:6; Luke 6:1–11; 13:10–17; John 5:1–19; 9:1–16). God worked at creating a habitat for humanity and then created and placed Adam and Eve in it. Since then, according to the scientific and biblical record, He has ceased from work on the habitat, including the introduction of new life forms. He invites us, present tense, to join Him in His Sabbath rest. We can directly observe, in nature, that God's creation rest (the seventh day) continues. We also observe, however, that His spiritual work is ongoing. According to Revelation 20–21, His Sabbath will continue until evil is conquered completely.

Duncan and Hall misapply the Fourth Commandment in their argument for 24-hour creation days. They stake much of their case on a preposition that does not appear in the original text. In most English Bibles, Exodus 20:11 reads "in six days" or "within six days." The Hebrew text contains no such preposition. We do not claim that the days in Exodus 20:9 are long periods. We hold, rather, that verse 9 addresses the workweek of humans (seven 24-hour days), verse 11 addresses the workweek of God (seven long periods), and Leviticus 25:4 addresses the workweek of farm lands (seven years).

Duncan and Hall's List of Verses

Much of Duncan and Hall's list of Bible verses supporting their position reads as follows: "[Passage X] does not suggest that creation occurred over millions of years" or "does not suggest the creation days are anything other than 24-hour days." But none of the verses they cite prove their point. The appellation "Creator of heavens and earth," for example, does not prove the 24-hour interpretation or immediate creation.

Duncan and Hall's handling of Proverbs 8 attempts to turn an old-earth reference in the opposite direction. Proverbs 8:22–31 presents us with a unified theme and a striking word picture. In verse 22, God's creation deeds are termed "old." In verse 23, the writer draws an analogy between God's eternity and the world's beginning. Verses 24–29 extend the analogy to the antiquity of the oceans, springs, mountains, hills, fields, dust, stars, and clouds. The analogy has no force and no significance, if the creation is just a few thousand years old.

We agree that Isaiah "repeatedly affirms direct and quick creation by God's word," but this wording presents no problem for our view. Isaiah 42:5 speaks not only about the creation of the universe, but also about the stretching out of the heavens. We affirm that God instantly brought into existence "out of nothing" all the matter, energy, and space-time dimensions of the universe. Then He remained involved, orchestrating formation of the stars, galaxies, planets, gas, dust, etc., that make up the heavens we now see.

The "stretching out" is wonderfully concordant with the exquisitely fine-tuned expansion rate of the universe. Physicists now recognize that stable planetary orbits and stable electron orbits around atomic nuclei (essential for physical life) are possible only in three large and slowly expanding dimensions of space. Astrophysicist Lawrence Krauss has determined that if the expansion rate of the universe were faster or slower by just one part in 10^{60}, physical life could not exist at any time in the universe's history.[36] (This degree of accuracy exceeds the best human engineering achievement by ten trillion trillion trillion times.[37])

The Big Bang, and consequently a cosmic creation date in the 12- to 15-billion-year range, can no longer be written off as an "opinion" or "passing scientific trend." Though the model continues to undergo refinements, it has been repeatedly and increasingly substantiated through the past several decades. In fact, today we can see that a universe of this age and with dozens of other observed characteristics is crucial to the existence of physical life.[38]

Duncan and Hall's treatment of Ezekiel 28 makes no sense. They seem to identify "the king of Tyre" as Adam, though the text refers to him as "a guardian cherub. . . on the holy mount of God," who was thrown to the earth by God. In this context, the king of Tyre must be a reference to Satan. Thus, Duncan and Hall's point evaporates, for the only Bible text dealing with Satan's creation date (Job 38:7) places it some (unspecified) time before God laid earth's foundations.

Duncan and Hall also inappropriately quote Jesus to support their view. When Jesus said, "At the beginning the Creator 'made them male and female'" (Matt. 19:4), we can surmise from the context that the "beginning" to which He referred was the beginning of human existence, not the beginning of the entire physical universe or of the planet.

THE QUESTION OF RECONCILIATION

Duncan and Hall state that "even the most intrepid defender of harmonizing the Bible and science faces insurmountable difficulties finding in the creation narrative an original authorial intent that foreshadowed the opinions of modern geology, biology, and physics." We strongly disagree, and we offer a much more thorough, detailed case for harmony and reconciliation in one of our books.[39] The case is simple. Only a misidentification of the frame of reference and initial conditions for the six creation days makes the task insurmountable. One of us recognized the possibility of concordance in 1955 without any formal training in the sciences. The other recognized the concordance in 1963 without any formal training in biblical languages. Each of us made predictions about the progress of scientific research based on our understanding of Genesis 1, predictions that later proved correct. We remain confident that the remainder of our predictions will be borne out by future scientific advances.

We make no claim to uniqueness or brilliance in harmonizing Genesis 1 with advances in astronomy, physics, geology, biology, and anthropology. Published accounts of others' success in harmonizing Genesis 1 with emerging scientific discovery date as far back as 1894[40] and 1729.[41]

Scripture leads us to expect an unequivocal consistency between God's written word and creation's facts. Moreover, we are exhorted to use such concordance as a tool for spreading our faith in Christ. Of all the world's religions, only Christianity can back its claims with established historical and scientific facts. It is the only faith that withstands objective testing and successfully predicts the future, including future scientific discovery.

Our interpretation of Genesis 1 must meet the same standard. We must embrace only those interpretations that survive the tests of consistency with God's general revelation and the whole of special revelation. We must hold to interpretations that successfully predict scientific discovery and enhance our understanding of other Bible passages. The day-age interpretation meets these interpretive criteria, as may other interpretations of Genesis 1. The six consecutive 24-hour creation day interpretation of Genesis 1 does not.

NOTES

1. Stephen Hawking and Roger Penrose, "Singularities of Gravitational Collapse and Cosmology," *Proceedings of the Royal Society of London*, Series A, 314 (1970), pp. 529–48.

2. Hugh Ross, *Beyond the Cosmos*, 2d edition (Colorado Springs, CO: NavPress, 1999), pp. 28–34.

3. Hugh Ross, *The Genesis Question* (Colorado Springs, CO: NavPress, 1998), pp. 53–5, 107–14, 173–6.

4. This detailed response is available from Reasons To Believe, P.O. Box 5978, Pasadena, CA 91117 and takes the form of notes appended to Duncan and Hall's original opening essay and a series of articles prepared by RTB's team of research theologians.

5. *The Correspondence of Isaac Newton*, vol. 2, 1676–1687, letter #247, Newton to Burnet, January 1680–1, ed. H. W. Turnbull (Cambridge, UK: Cambridge University Press, 1960), p. 334.

6. Ibid., p. 333.

7. Ibid., p. 334.

8. Ibid., letter #244, Newton to Burnet, December 24, 1680, p. 319; *The Correspondence of Isaac Newton*, vol. 3, 1688–1694 (Cambridge, UK: Cambridge University Press, 1961), letter #398, Newton to Bentley (December 10, 1692), pp. 234–5.

9. Hugh Ross, *Creation and Time* (Colorado Springs, CO: NavPress, 1994), pp. 16–24.

10. Justin Martyr, "Dialogue With Trypho," chap. 81, *Writings of Saint Justin Martyr*, in *The Fathers of the Church*, vol. 6, ed. Ludwig Schopp (New York: Christian Heritage, 1948), pp. 277–8; Irenaeus, "Against Heresies," bk. 5, chap. 23, sec. 2, *The Ante-Nicene Fathers*, vol. 1, ed. Alexander Roberts and James Donaldson (Peabody, MA: Hendrickson Publishers, 1995), pp. 551–2; Lactantius, "The Divine Institutes," bk. 7, chap. 14, *The Ante-Nicene Fathers*, vol. 7, p. 211; Victorinus of Pettau, "The Created World," bk. 6, *The Ante-Nicene Fathers*, vol. 7, p. 342; Methodius of Olympus, "Fragment," *The Ante-Nicene Fathers*, vol. 6, p. 310; Ross, *Creation and Time*, pp. 17–9.

11. Clement of Alexandria, "The Stromata," bk. 6, *Clement of Alexandria: A Study in Christian Platonism and Gnosticism*, ed. Salvatore R. C. Lilla (Oxford: Oxford University Press, 1971), pp. 198–9; Clement of Alexandria, "The Stromata," bk. 6, chap. 16, *The Ante-Nicene Fathers*, vol. 2, pp. 512–4; Origen, *Origen on First Principles*, bk. 4, chaps. 1–3, trans. G. W. Butterworth (New York: Harper Torchbooks, Harper and Row, 1966), pp. 277–8, 288; Origen, "Against Celsus," bk. 6, chap. 61, *The Ante-Nicene Fathers*, vol. 4, ed. Alexander Roberts and James Donaldson (Grand Rapids, MI: Wm. B. Eerdmans Publishing Co., 1979), pp. 600–1; Origen, "Homilies on Genesis and Exodus," trans. Ronald E. Heine, *The Fathers of the Church*, vol. 71, ed. Hermigild Dressler (Washington, DC: Catholic University of America Press, 1982), p. 48; Augustine, "The City of God," bk. 11, chap. 6, *The Fathers of the Church*, vol. 14, ed. Roy Joseph Deferrari (New York: Fathers of the Church, Inc., 1952), p. 196; Augustine, "The Literal Meaning of Genesis," bk. 4, chap. 27, bk. 5, chap. 2, *Ancient Christian Writers: The Works of the Fathers in Translation*, ed. Johannes Quasten, et al., no. 41; Augustine, *The Literal Meaning of Genesis*, trans. John Hammond Taylor, vol. 1, bks. 1–6 (New York: Newman Press, 1982), pp. 135–6, 148; Augustine,

"The Confessions," bk. 13, sec. 51, *The Fathers of the Church*, vol. 21, trans. Vernon J. Bourke (New York: Fathers of the Church, Inc., 1953), p. 455; Ross, *Creation and Time*, pp. 18–20.

12. Basil, "The Hexaemeron," *A Select Library of Nicene and Post-Nicene Fathers of the Christian Church*, 2d edition, ed. Philip Schaff and Henry Wace, vol. 8; *St. Basil: Letters and Select Works; The Nine Homilies of the Hexaemeron and the Letters of Saint Basil the Great, Archbishop of Caesarea*, trans. Blomfield Jackson (Grand Rapids, MI: Wm. B. Eerdmans Publishing Co., 1955), p. 64; Ambrose, "Saint Ambrose: Hexameron," trans. John J. Savage, *The Fathers of the Church, A New Translation*, vol. 42, ed. Roy Joseph Deferrari, et al. (New York: Fathers of the Church, Inc., 1961), p. 43; Hugh Ross, *Creation and Time*, pp. 21–3.

13. For example, when the International Council on Biblical Inerrancy deliberated on the subject of the duration of the Genesis 1 creation days at their second summit held in Chicago in 1982, *none* of the Hebrew and Old Testament professors who participated concluded that the Genesis creation accounts mandated six consecutive 24-hour creation days. The proceedings of this summit can be found in *Hermeneutics, Inerrancy, and the Bible: Proceedings from the International Council on Biblical Inerrancy*, ed. Earl D. Radmacher and Robert D. Preus (Grand Rapids, MI: Zondervan Publishing House, 1984), pp. 285–348, 900–3. The only possible defense for Barr's statement is that he takes such a biased definition of "world-class university" that only institutions hostile to evangelical Christianity are included.

14. Hugh Ross, *The Fingerprint of God*, 2d edition (Orange, CA: Promise Publishing, 1991), pp. 79–94; Bernard E. J. Pagel, *Nucleosynthesis and Chemical Evolution of Galaxies* (New York: Cambridge University Press, 1997).

15. "Out of nothing" can take on different meanings. Currently, physicists employ five different definitions of nothing: (1) lack of matter; (2) lack of matter and energy; (3) lack of matter, energy, and the dimensions of length, width, height, and time; (4) lack of matter, energy, and all ten space-time dimensions of the universe; and (5) lack of any entity, being, existence, or dimensionality whatever.

16. Ross, *The Genesis Question*, pp. 30–3.

17. Ibid., pp. 30–44, 193–6.

18. Ibid., pp. 49–54.

19. Because light takes time to travel from the stars, galaxies, quasars, etc., to us, we are directly observing these objects as they were in the past.

20. Normal burning stars are 100% gas, where more than 97% of the gas is made up of hydrogen and helium. Thus, the gas laws and Newtonian mechanics is adequate to describe all the gross features of burning stars. Despite the exponential increase in our understanding of stellar physics over the past 40 years, the following two books written 40 years apart do not differ in any significant manner in their conclusions about stellar burning: Martin Schwarzschild, *Structure of the Stars* (New York: Dover, 1958), pp. 30–94; Rudolf Kippenhahn and Alfred Weigert, *Stellar Structure and Evolution* (New York: Springer-Verlag, 1994), pp. 6–246.

21. Stars are extremely sensitive to even very tiny changes in the physical laws. In some cases, changing a physical constant by as little as one part in ten thousand trillion trillion trillion implies that solar-type stars can never form or that stars will instantly explode. See Kippenhahn and Weigert, *Stellar Structure and Evolution*, pp. 36–45, 234–55; Hugh Ross, *The Creator and the Cosmos*, 2d edition (Colorado Springs, CO: NavPress, 1995), pp. 111–21.

22. Ross, *The Genesis Question*, pp. 39–42, 51–2, 55–7, 110–4, 149–50.

23. Ross, *The Creator and the Cosmos*, pp. 121–4.

24. John Bally, et al., "Disk Mass Limits and Lifetimes of Externally Irradiated Young Stellar Objects Embedded in the Orion Nebula," *Astronomical Journal*, vol. 116 (1998), pp. 854–9; J. S. Greaves, et al., "A Dust Ring Around e Eridani: Analog to the Young Solar

System," *Astrophysical Journal*, vol. 506 (1998), pp. L133–L137; Klauss-Werner Hodapp, "The Protostar in B335: Near-Infrared Observations of the Class 0 Outflow," *Astrophysical Journal*, vol. 500 (1998), pp. L183–L187; K. L. Luhman, et al., "A Young Star Near the Hydrogen-Burning Limit," *Astrophysical Journal*, vol. 493 (1998), pp. 909–13; P. C. Myers, F. C. Adams, H. Chen, and E. Schaff, "Evolution of the Bolometric Temperature and Luminosity of Young Stellar Objects," *Astrophysical Journal*, vol. 492 (1998), pp. 703–26; Ayano Obayashi, et al., "Star Formation in the L1333 Molecular Cloud in Cassiopeia," *Astronomical Journal*, vol. 115 (1998), pp. 274–85; M. S. Oey and Shona A. Smedley, "Shell Formation and Star Formation in Superbubble DEM 192," *Astronomical Journal*, vol. 116 (1998), pp. 1263–74; N. C. Santos, J. L. Yun, C. A. Santos, and R. G. Marreiros, "Star Formation in Bok Globules: Near-Infrared Survey of a Southern Sample," *Astronomical Journal*, vol. 116 (1998), pp. 1376–87; Qizhou Zhang, Todd R. Hunter, and T. K. Sridharan, "A Rotating Disk Around a High-Mass Young Star," *Astrophysical Journal*, vol. 505 (1998), pp. L151–L154; Hans Zinnecker, Mark J. McCaughrean, and John T. Rayner, "A Symmetrically Pulsed Jet of Gas from an Invisible Protostar in Orion," *Nature*, vol. 394 (1998), pp. 862–5; Brian W. Casey, et al., "The Pre-Main-Sequence Eclipsing Binary TY Coronae Australis: Precise Stellar Dimensions and Tests of Evolutionary Models," *Astronomical Journal*, vol. 115 (1998), pp. 1617–33; Eric E. Mamajek, Warrick A. Lawson, and Eric D. Feigelson, "The h Chamaeleontis Cluster: A Remarkable New Nearby Young Open Cluster," *Astrophysical Journal*, vol. 516 (1999), pp. L77–L80.

25. Ross, *Beyond the Cosmos*, pp. 218–23.

26. Herbert Goldstein, *Classical Mechanics* (Reading, MA: Addison-Wesley, 1950), pp. 1–55, 93–178, 273–314; D. K. C. MacDonald, *Introductory Statistical Mechanics for Physicists* (New York: John Wiley, 1963), pp. 1–36, 114–36; Ralph Palmer Agnew, *Differential Equations* (New York: McGraw-Hill, 1960), pp. 1–101, 153–246.

27. Psa. 12:6; 19:7; 33:4; 119:86, 96, 142–4, 160.

28. Num. 23:19; 1 Sam. 15:29; Psa. 18:30; 19:7–9; 145:17; John 10:35; 2 Tim. 2:13; Titus 1:2.

29. For example, in the second edition of *The Creator and the Cosmos* published in 1995, Hugh Ross listed 41 different characteristics of the solar system that must be fine-tuned for physical life to be possible. Four years later the list stands at 110 different characteristics, with the odds of finding a planet anywhere in the universe capable of supporting life now calculated as 10^{82} times more remote.

30. 1 Thess. 5:21.

31. Deut. 18:21–2.

32. Walter L. Bradley, "The Trustworthiness of Scripture in Areas Relating to Natural Science," *Hermeneutics, Inerrancy, and the Bible*, p. 287.

33. Radmacher and Preus, *Hermeneutics, Inerrancy, and the Bible*, p. 901.

34. Ross, *The Genesis Question*, pp. 31–3; Ross, "The Heavens Resound With a Message for Mankind," *Connections*, vol. 1, no. 1 (1999), p. 2; Kimmo Innanen, Sippo Mikkola, and Paul Wiegert, "The Earth-Moon System and the Dynamical Stability of the Inner Solar System," *Astronomical Journal*, vol. 116 (1998), pp. 2055–7.

35. Ross, *Beyond the Cosmos*, pp. 218–20.

36. Lawrence M. Krauss, "The End of the Age Problem, and the Case for a Cosmological Constant Revisited," *Astrophysical Journal*, vol. 501 (1998), pp. 461–6.

37. Ross, *The Creator and the Cosmos*, p. 118.

38. For example, stable orbits of planets about stars and of electrons about the nuclei of atoms are possible only in a universe described by three large expanding dimensions of space. Also, the only possible explanation for the extremely high entropy we observe in the universe is that the cosmos had a near infinitely hot and near infinitely dense origin. Without this extremely high entropy, it would be impossible for stars, planets, and hence physical life to form.

39. Ross, *The Genesis Question*.

40. Sir J. Willian Dawson, *The Meeting-Place of Geology and History* (New York: Fleming H. Revell, 1894).

41. Thomas Burnet, *Archaelogia Philosophica or the Ancient Doctrine Concerning the Originals of Things* (London: E. Curll in the Strand, 1729).

Lee Irons with Meredith G. Kline

THE FRAMEWORK RESPONSE

he key issue before us in this debate is whether careful, contextual investigation of the Hebrew text of Genesis 1–2 demands that we interpret the total picture of the creation week—with its six-fold evening-morning refrain—literally or figuratively. Duncan and Hall, however, have added another dimension to the debate by arguing that any view other than the 24-hour view departs from the historic tradition of the Church and is motivated not by sound exegesis but by accommodation to modern evolutionary thought. We are disappointed that this argument, which is based on utterly erroneous assumptions and is tangential to this debate, appears to be Duncan and Hall's dominant concern, thus requiring us to devote much of our limited space to respond to it. But since we believe that the exegetical issues are of primary importance, we will begin with the exegetical debate, and then we will turn our attention to the dominant thesis of the Duncan-Hall essay.

THE EXEGETICAL DEBATE

While Duncan and Hall correctly observe that the important issue before us deserves "our best thought, study, and biblical interpretation," their essay does not evidence such superior exegetical engagement for at least three reasons.

Straw Man Arguments

The first element of Duncan and Hall's exegetical argument is an attempt to show that none of the arguments allegedly adduced in support of the framework interpretation can justify a nonliteral reading of the Genesis days. In theory, this tactic is valid, and if properly executed, it can enhance the plausibility of the alternative thesis, *but only if the challenger accurately represents the opposing arguments.* Otherwise, such arguments only end up erecting and knocking down a straw man.

Duncan and Hall's acquaintance with the literature of the framework interpretation appears to be cursory at best. For whatever reason, Duncan and Hall neither cite the published defenses of the framework interpretation nor represent our arguments fairly. They never mention or cite Noordtzij, who pioneered the two-triad scheme in 1924, or N. H. Ridderbos, whose popularization of Noordtzij was made available to the American audience in 1957. Kline's original 1958 article, "Because It Had Not Rained," is never cited, and his 1996 article, "Space and Time in the Genesis Cosmogony"—the most comprehensive defense of the framework interpretation in print—is (mis)quoted only once, not to engage his exegesis, but to ask whether he can avoid the slippery slope to human evolution.[1] Although Duncan and Hall mention the names of Henri Blocher and Mark Futato, they do not cite or discuss their scholarship.[2]

As would be expected, then, Duncan and Hall's attempts to critique the framework interpretation reflect an inadequate grasp of our position. For example, they assert, without any proof, that framework scholars hold that because Genesis 1 is "a sustained apologetic argument against pagan worldviews of the day, we should not press certain details of the narrative . . . as though they reflect a divinely inspired cosmogony." One framework scholar, Futato, has indeed argued that the first two chapters of Genesis contain a polemic against paganism. But he never argues that this is *a* reason, much less *the* reason, for taking the picture of the week of days figuratively. Nor does he, or any other abovementioned advocate of the framework interpretation, claim that Genesis 1 gives us something other than "a divinely inspired cosmogony." Duncan and Hall do not seem to have taken the time necessary to understand the arguments of their opponents or to present those arguments accurately.

This lack of understanding becomes evident when Duncan and Hall give "A Summary of the Markers for Various Figurative Views." Of the eight "exegetical markers" Duncan and Hall attribute to those who hold to figurative interpretations, only two are actually employed by defenders of the framework interpretation: (1) the problem posed by the separation of light from darkness on the first day and the creation of the luminaries on the fourth day, and (2) the eternal nature of the seventh day.

Duncan and Hall imply that those who question their 24-hour interpretation—including those who subscribe to the framework interpretations—defend their views by arguing that: (1) the phenomenological nature of the narrative suggests that the days themselves may be phenomenological; (2) the busyness of the sixth day argues against a literal reading of the passage; and (3) the three meanings of yôm in Genesis 1–2 suggest that the days can be understood figuratively. Because those arguments are not made by framework interpreters but by day-age interpreters, we need not address them.

Duncan and Hall present three other exegetical markers: (1) the general rather than detailed nature of the narrative as not requiring us to press the specific meaning of the days; (2) the highly stylized nature of the creation account as an argument against literal days; and (3) the focus of the narrative on the sixth day as rendering details about the days themselves to be of secondary concern. Because Duncan and Hall do not support these alleged markers with citations to specific authors, we cannot tell if they consider them to represent the framework position. In any event, all three are straw men. What framework scholar has argued that the narrative is "general rather than detailed," or that "the focus . . . is on the sixth day," and that *therefore* "we need not press the specific meaning of the days"? Certainly none of the major framework adherents mentioned above. They all believe that the days, with their evening-morning refrain, have a very specific meaning as part of the picture of a divine workweek of six days followed by a seventh day of rest. Furthermore, they argue for this interpretation, not on the shaky grounds Duncan and Hall allege, but on the grounds of several prominent features of the text that we explain in more detail in our opening essay later in this volume: (1) the two-triad structure of the account; (2) the temporal recapitulation of Day 1 at Day 4; (3) the evidence from Genesis 2:5–6; (4) the eternal nature of the seventh day; and (5) in Kline's case, the two-register cosmology that constitutes both the literary and theological marrow of the creation account.

Problems for the 24-Hour View

Strangely, when Duncan and Hall finally do come close to citing our actual arguments, they still do not understand them properly and fail to give anything approaching a satisfying response.

The Day One/Day Four Problem. One exegetical marker suggesting a figurative meaning for the days is that the creation of the luminaries on Day 4 is a temporal recapitulation of the creation of daylight on Day 1.[3] Duncan and Hall respond without any exegesis, asserting only that this argument "calls into question God's capacity to work with or without, above or against, second causes." But how? Our argument is that Genesis 2:5–6 informs us that the mode of divine providence during the creation period was *ordinary* rather than *extraordinary*. This rules out the possibility that the daylight was caused by a supernatural or nonsolar light source for the first three days, thus forcing us to view the fourth day as a temporal recapitulation and the days in general as being nonsequential. Observe, however, that this possibility is not ruled out on *a priori*, but exegetical, grounds. Certainly God has the capacity to work without, above, or against second causes, but the text reveals that God employed ordinary means in His providential sustaining of His creatures during the creation period. To argue that the framework interpretation calls God's omnipotence into question begs the question and betrays an inadequate familiarity with the published arguments.

Duncan and Hall have not wrestled sufficiently with the problem of the relationship between the first and fourth days. When attempting to explain how there could be a literal evening and morning during the first three days, they hypothesize that God "may have employed nonsolar sources of light before creating the sun." But what internal, exegetical justification can they provide for this arbitrary speculation? On the contrary, the text makes clear that when God created daylight on the first day, He created the physical reality with which Moses' audience was familiar; namely, a normal day divided into alternating periods of light and darkness (Gen. 1:5). Doesn't the plain meaning of Genesis 1:3–5 contradict Duncan and Hall's hypothetical nonsolar light source? And shouldn't this fact suggest that the fourth day is not to be taken sequentially and so is separated from the first day? Doesn't this fact strongly suggest instead that the author of Genesis presents us with a two-triad framework in which each triad is headed by a parallel (nonsequential) treatment of the creation of light/luminaries?

The Eternal Sabbath. The other exegetical argument Duncan and Hall cite is the eternal nature of the Sabbath. The unending character of the seventh day is supported by several exegetical factors. First, the seventh day lacks the concluding evening-morning formula, thus suggesting that it is still ongoing.

Second, as Kline has argued, since the seventh day consists of God taking His throne in the completed cosmic temple as the eternal King of Glory, and since that royal Sabbath rest is, in the very nature of the case, unending, the seventh day must be unending as well. Otherwise, if the seventh day is a finite day, God would be pictured as returning to another week of creative work after the close of the seventh day.[4]

Third, the New Testament interprets the seventh day as an ongoing reality on two separate occasions. In John 5:17, Jesus justifies His healing on the Sabbath day by appealing to His Father's example: "My Father is working until now, and I Myself am working." The argument presupposes that the Father's work occurs on His Sabbath. Thus, if the Father is working on the Sabbath "until now," then His Sabbath rest must also continue "until now." Similarly, in Hebrews 4:3–5, *the seventh day itself*, not just the divine rest which began on that day, is equated with God's rest referred to in Psalm 95:11, the eschatological rest which the people of God of all ages—the wilderness generation (Heb. 3:16–19), Israel in the time of David (Heb. 4:7), and the New Covenant Church (Heb. 4:1–2, 11)—are continually called to enter by faith. If the seventh day is eternal, clearly we are not to take it literally, and thus, neither are we to take literally the total picture of the divine creation week.

Again, Duncan and Hall simply brush this argument aside as "novel and eccentric," without even attempting to provide an alternative explanation of the exegetical data.

Advocates of the 24-hour interpretation seem unaware of the profound difficulties that accompany their position and assume that their reading is the only natural reading of the text. But we cannot allow this assumption to go unchallenged, for in reality the 24-hour interpretation engages in highly disputable exegesis at numerous points. The two outstanding instances of this have been discussed above: (1) its speculative hypothesis that the first three days were governed by a nonsolar light source, which is contrary to the text's affirmation that these days were ordinary solar days;[5] and (2) its dogmatism concerning the finite nature of the seventh day, which arbitrarily brushes aside the teaching of Scripture that it is a heavenly, unending reality. The Day 1/Day 4 problem and the unending nature of the seventh day, therefore, constitute major exegetical problems that decisively refute the 24-hour interpretation.

An Irrelevant Argument

Next, Duncan and Hall go through the entire canon of Scripture in an attempt to demonstrate that the days are literal, 24-hour days. The reader is treated to page after page of scriptural citations, which teach that God is the Creator of all things. None of those texts, however, address the question of the nature or length of the days; they simply teach that the world was brought into existence by the sovereign exercise of the divine will. But all three positions represented in this book presuppose the orthodox doctrine of divine creation *ex nihilo*. There is no debate on this point.

Furthermore, Duncan and Hall attempt to argue that subsequent canonical revelation regards the creative fiats of the six days—the acts of divine shaping and forming the "formless and void" into an orderly cosmos—as *unmediated acts of instantaneous creation*. That this is one of the principal points of their extensive survey of both testaments is made clear halfway through the exercise. They write,

> Thus far in the progress of revelation, we cannot legitimately interpret any of the Old Testament Scriptures to support *mediated* creation (i.e., creation that depends on normal providence and secondary agents). Instead, the consistent Old Testament view is that creation is *unmediated*, "by the word of his power."

A major shift has taken place. Duncan and Hall are surveying the totality of biblical teaching to demonstrate, not that the days are 24 hours long, but that after the initial *ex nihilo* event, God's subsequent cosmos-forming acts were, like His calling the several creatures into existence, instances of *direct, instantaneous* divine activity unmediated by secondary causes. They assert this conclusion, even though none of the texts they cite—from Genesis to Revelation—say this. All these passages teach is that the heavens and the earth, and all that is in them, were brought into existence by the powerful word of God. Psalm 33:9 is representative of the sort of passages they adduce: "He spoke, and it came to be; he commanded, and it stood firm" (NIV). But this text does not teach that God's sovereign, irresistible command was *invariably* fulfilled instantaneously, apart from the use of secondary causes. We emphasize "invariably," for while the several acts of creating the living creatures, including man, appear to have been supernatural acts,[6] we cannot gratuitously assume that the fiats concerning the cosmos-shaping processes of the first four days were fulfilled instantaneously apart from God's employing secondary causes.

Theoretically, one could take the position that all of the creative fiats were instantaneous, unmediated creative acts in which secondary causes played no role, yet deny that the days are literal, 24-hour days. The two issues are analytically distinct. So even if Duncan and Hall's reading of the eight creative fiats were valid, it would not demonstrate that we are to take the picture of the divine workweek literally.

Duncan and Hall's exegetical case for the 24-hour view thus contains mistakes of various sorts. First, their cursory acquaintance with the published arguments for the framework interpretation renders useless their critique of the various exegetical markers allegedly adduced in support of that interpretation.

Second, the 24-hour interpretation is decisively refuted by several exegetical problems—especially the Day 1/Day 4 problem and the unending nature of Day 7—to which Duncan and Hall give scant attention.

Third, Duncan and Hall's positive case, based on a survey of scriptural teaching on creation, flounders as it slips into the independent question concerning the mediated or unmediated nature of the eight creative fiats. In the final analysis, this question is irrelevant for determining whether we are to take the days of creation literally.

DUNCAN AND HALL'S DOMINANT THESIS

Having examined the shortcomings of Duncan and Hall's exegesis, we now turn to their dominant concern. Duncan and Hall maintain that the unanimous historic Christian tradition of literal days has been set aside in favor of nonliteral approaches only in the last two centuries. They contend that since "the nature of the creation days is so apparent that it is, frankly, beyond dispute," this departure from the tradition has occurred for other than purely exegetical reasons, namely, to accommodate biblical revelation to a naturalistic, evolutionary worldview. This thesis falters because it is based on an erroneous reading of Church history and an equally erroneous understanding of the role of tradition.

An Erroneous Reading of Church History
We question whether the Christian tradition is as monolithic as Duncan and Hall maintain. For one thing, Duncan and Hall have modified the question to stack the deck in their favor. They do not ask, "Does the Christian exegetical tradition approach the picture of the week, with its evening-morning refrain, literally or figuratively?" but, "Does the Christian exegetical tradition affirm long periods of time or unmediated, rapid creation?" Asking the latter question yields an answer that suits their purposes: No notable theologian taught long periods until the rise of evolution in the nineteenth century. But the question before us in this forum is whether the creation week is literal or figurative. When we survey the annals of Church history with *this* question in mind, two things stand out, both of which undercut Duncan and Hall's thesis.

First, both literal and figurative approaches to the days are attested throughout Church history. This shows that the Christian tradition does not "uniformly favor normal creation days," as Duncan and Hall would have it. Though not the first to advocate a figurative understanding of the days of creation, Augustine influenced subsequent theologians such as Anselm, Lombard, and the early Aquinas. Others, such as Basil of Caesarea, Gregory of Nyssa, Ambrose, and Chrysostom took a more literal approach, while some Church fathers attempted to reconcile the two positions by taking a *via media*. Incontestably, the debate over the creation days is not "strictly recent."[7]

Second, the Augustinian figurative interpretation of the days was unmotivated by a concern to accommodate modern evolutionary thought. This is true not only because Augustine predated the rise of modern evolution by fourteen centuries, but also because his professed reasons for taking the days nonliterally were strictly exegetical. He argued that the text itself contains features which suggest or require that the week of days is a literary framework describing the divine creative activity, rather than a literal statement of the progression of earthly time reckoned by the course of the sun. Two such textual features stood out in his mind: (1) Days 1–3 are mentioned before the creation of the sun, and hence, they, at least, were not to be taken literally; and (2) Augustine read Genesis 2:4 as stating that God made the heavens and the earth and all their hosts in one day.[8] On the basis of these textual considerations, he concluded that the six days were actually the one day of creation repeated six times to indicate the steps in which God accomplished His creative work.[9] It is safe to conclude that Duncan and Hall have fundamentally misread the evidence of Church history in their misguided effort to charge figurative views with Darwinian compromise.

The Role of Church Tradition
Furthermore, Duncan and Hall's thesis gives undue weight to ecclesiastical tradition. The authors state that their position is "based on the fundamentally conservative methodological premise that we ought to preserve well-founded teachings of antiquity until superior exegesis (interpretation) definitively repudiates those teachings." Of course, we claim that the framework interpretation *has* offered superior exegesis, demonstrating that the picture of the divine workweek is figurative. More to the point, Duncan and Hall have such a heavy bias toward tradition that it is difficult to see how the Church might ever be led to examine traditional views critically in the light of fresh scriptural exegesis. Ironically, Duncan and Hall, who have accused us of engaging in exegesis motivated by outside factors (what they call "scientific eisegesis"), themselves engage in a type of exegesis driven by the outside factor of Church tradition. Certainly, we must accord the

exegetical traditions of the Church due respect and should not flippantly set them aside. But as we have seen, there was no exegetical consensus on the days of Genesis, nor was the issue elevated to creedal status until relatively recently.[10]

We must also ask whether the authors are consistent with their own principles. Do they believe that the modern Church has offered a definitive repudiation of the "well-founded" exegetical tradition which maintained that the earth is immobile (Josh. 10:12–13; Psa. 104:5)? Why didn't any interpreters discover alternative explanations of the relevant texts "until after certain scientific revolutions"? On this score, nonliteral interpretations of the creation days seem to have an advantage over nongeocentric interpretations of the biblical data, since figurative views of the days arose independently and predated modern geology, whereas heliocentric interpretations arose only after Galileo's observational confirmation of the Copernican theory and in direct response to it. Presumably Duncan and Hall acknowledge that the traditional geocentric exegesis has rightly been replaced by one that does not conflict with modern astronomy. If this is so, then judged by their own principles, they must be guilty of "scientific eisegesis" and "accommodation" to science.

"Left Free of Biblical Constraints"

Duncan and Hall's dominant thesis not only is flawed in its appeal to Church history, but one of the key pieces of "evidence" they cite to support their claim that the framework interpretation implicitly accommodates an evolutionary worldview is based on a misquotation of Kline's 1996 article, "Space and Time in the Genesis Cosmogony." The third sentence in that article reads:

> The conclusion is that as far as the time frame is concerned, with respect to both the duration and sequence of events, the scientist is left free of biblical constraints in hypothesizing about cosmic origins.

Duncan and Hall snip off the first and most important part of the sentence, leaving only a fragment, which they misquote to allege that evolutionary compromise is inherent in the framework interpretation. They ask:

> If the scientist, as Kline has argued elsewhere, may be "left free of constraints when hypothesizing about cosmic origins" by a literary approach to the meaning of the days, why shouldn't he also be left free of constraints when hypothesizing about human origins?[11]

Notice the flagrant omission of the all-important qualifying phrase at the beginning of the sentence: " . . . as far as the time frame is concerned, with respect to both the duration and sequence of events. . . ." With these words, Kline has specifically restricted the sphere of the scientist's freedom when hypothesizing about cosmic origins to "the time frame," specifically "the *duration* and *sequence* of events." Thus, according to Kline, a Bible-believing Christian engaged in the scientific study of cosmic origins is not required, on the authority of Scripture, to promote only those scientific theories that posit a creation period of exactly 144 hours (duration), or an order of creation events that corresponds at every point to the narrative order of Genesis 1 (sequence).

Claiming that the Christian scientist has liberty in the areas of duration and sequence in no way grants him carte blanche autonomy to engage in any conceivable speculation apart from the authority of Scripture. It simply means that on these two points, God has chosen not to give a definitive revelation in Scripture, thus allowing the scientist to seek answers to these questions via the study of general revelation. While Duncan and Hall obviously disagree with Kline's conclusion that Scripture is silent on the duration and sequence of the creation events, they nevertheless should be able to see the validity of his overall point: We must speak where Scripture speaks and be silent where Scripture is silent. Duncan and Hall recognize the validity of this procedure in principle, for they state in their first endnote that "we take no position on the age of the universe precisely because that question is not directly addressed by the canon." In effect, they themselves are saying that with respect to the age of the universe, the scientist is left free of biblical constraints in hypothesizing about cosmic origins.[12]

It is not scientific accommodation, then, that motivates the framework interpretation, but the conviction that the sacred text should not be manipulated by an alien agenda to bind the conscience of the Church with extrabiblical, manmade constraints. Believing as we do that scriptural teaching rules out any theory of human origins that would posit biological ancestry for man, we firmly maintain that all Christians must submit to this teaching of Scripture in spite of contrary views claiming to be scientific.[13] Rejecting evolutionary origins for man is a scripturally mandated constraint on modern anthropology that has the sanction of divine authority. On the other hand, if scriptural teaching does not require believers to hold a particular view of the age of the universe or of the duration or sequence of the creation events, we are equally concerned to insist that their conscience is not bound by Scripture at this point, and that in these areas, believing scientists should follow the data of general revelation to whatever conclusions they may lead.

The dominant thesis of Duncan and Hall, then, fares no better than their handling of the exegetical debate. First, since figurative views were present long before the rise of evolution, their thesis that the motive be-hind figurative views is accommodation with evolution fails on factual grounds. Second, their approach is warped by an unacceptable view of the role of Church tradition in exegesis. And third, their attempt to convict the framework interpretation of an accommodationist hermeneutic hangs on an inexcusable misquotation of Kline's words.

CONCLUSION

Thus flawed, both in its scholarship in the exegetical arena and in its larger concerns regarding Church history and the specter of evolutionary com-promise, the Duncan-Hall essay fails to provide a viable case for the 24-hour view.

NOTES

1. For our response, see the following section entitled "Left Free of Biblical Constraints."

2. Arie Noordtzij, *Gods Woord en der Eeuwen Getuigenis* (Kampen, 1924); N. H. Ridderbos, *Is There a Conflict Between Genesis 1 and Natural Science?* (Grand Rapids, MI: Wm. B. Eerdmans Publishing Co., 1957); Meredith G. Kline, "Because It Had Not Rained," *Westminster Theological Journal*, vol. 20, no. 2 (May 1958), pp. 146–57; Meredith G. Kline, "Space and Time in the Genesis Cosmogony," *Perspectives on Science and Christian Faith*, vol. 48, no. 1 (April 1996), pp. 2–15; Henri Blocher, *In the Beginning: The Opening Chapters of Genesis*, trans. David G. Preston (Downers Grove, IL: InterVarsity Press, 1984); Mark D. Futato, "Because It Had Rained: A Study of Gen 2:5–7 with Implications for Gen 2:4–25 and Gen 1:1–2:3," *Westminster Theological Journal*, vol. 60 (Spring 1998), pp. 1–21.

3. See our essay, "The Framework View," for a fuller explanation of this argument.

4. Kline, "Space and Time in the Genesis Cosmogony," p. 10.

5. We affirm with the 24-hour interpretation that on the literal level yôm in Genesis 1 denotes an ordinary solar day of daylight and night (not an extended period or age), but we maintain that the *total picture* of the divine workweek is to be taken figuratively. See "The Framework Response to the Day-Age View.'"

6. The language of creation for both living creatures and man is remarkably similar: "The LORD God formed man of dust from the ground" (Gen. 2:7), and "out of the ground the LORD God formed every beast of the field and every bird of the sky" (Gen. 2:19). This parallel language suggests that man and the animals alike are products of supernatural, special creation.

7. For the evidence, see Jack P. Lewis, "The Days of Creation: An Historical Survey of Interpretation," *Journal of the Evangelical Theological Society*, vol. 32, no. 4 (December 1989), pp. 433–55; C. John Collins, "How Old is the Earth? Anthropomorphic Days in Genesis 1:1–2:3," *Presbyterion*, vol. 20, no. 2 (1994), pp. 109–30; and Robert Letham, "'In the Space of Six Days': The Days of Creation from Origen to the Westminster Assembly," *Westminster Theological Journal*, vol. 61, no. 2 (1999), pp. 149–74.

8. This reading seemed to be reinforced by the Vulgate's rendering of Ecclesiasticus (Sirach) 18:1, "He who lives forever created all things at once." However, unbeknown to Augustine, our most reliable ancient witnesses read either, "He who lives forever created the whole universe" (Greek), or, more likely, "The Eternal is the judge of all alike" (Syriac). In any case, Duncan and Hall badly misunderstand Augustine when they claim that his

figurative view was not "motivated by considerations internal to the text, but rather by his concern for theological harmonization with a statement in the aprocryphal book Ecclesiasticus." In fact, Augustine appealed to the two textual considerations noted above and challenged his readers to "propose an interpretation that is clearer and more in keeping with the text" of Genesis.

9. Augustine, "The Literal Meaning of Genesis," vol. 41, *Ancient Christian Writers*, ed. J. Quasten, et al. (New York: Newman Press, 1982), pp. 134–5, 155–7.

10. The first creed to explicitly affirm that God created the world "in the space of six days" was the Irish Articles of Archbishop Ussher (1615).

11. Duncan and Hall misquote Kline by omitting the word "biblical" and by changing "in hypothesizing" to "when hypothesizing."

12. We would have to question, however, whether Duncan and Hall are entitled to this disclaimer. It would appear that on their 24-hour view, the upper limit for the age of the universe would be set by the maximum amount of time allowed by the genealogies of Genesis 5 and 11 (unless they are ready to adopt some form of the gap theory). Even the most generous reading of the genealogies would limit the maximum time to somewhere around 100,000 years from Adam to Abraham, and most young-earth creationists argue for a much smaller figure. A logical implication of the 24-hour view, then, is that the billions of years proposed by modern geology and astronomy for the ages of the earth and the universe must be flatly rejected.

13. John Murray, "The Origin of Man," *Collected Writings of John Murray*, vol. 2 (Edinburgh, UK: The Banner of Truth Trust, 1977), pp. 3–13.

J. Ligon Duncan III & David W. Hall

THE 24-HOUR REPLY

We appreciate much of what the day-age and framework teams have said in response to our essay. It also appears that this debate has produced a vital clarification since its inception. From the responses and their own essays later in this volume, it appears that either the framework team has nearly convinced the day-age team of its position or vice versa. Marriage invitations may go out soon, announcing the formal union of these two views, both of which reject the classical biblical interpretation of key texts. After this debate is over, these two recent views may ultimately find marital union in this: a commitment to elevate the findings of various modern authorities over the ancient word of God.

We thank the day-age team for: (1) correctly noting that Augustine did not teach a long "duration of the creation week"; (2) admitting that "[Luther, Calvin, and many of the Westminster divines] espoused a 24-hour day"; (3) agreeing that no metaphorical markers in Genesis 1 support the complex framework conjecture; (4) noting the many scientific problems with various evolutionary schemes; and (5) pointing out that deconstructionist theologians are dangerous to the Church.

We also thank the framework team for: (1) identifying both "unbridled concordism" and Kantian fideism as extremes to avoid (since our view falls into neither camp); (2) rejecting the "experimental testability" posited by the day-age team as a measure of exegetical accuracy; (3) recognizing that Genesis 1 describes "an ordinary day composed of a period of daylight and a period of darkness"; (4) acknowledging that, comparatively speaking, "the 24-hour advocates are closer to the truth" than their day-age counterparts; and (5) making other generally sound criticisms of the day-age method.[1]

Nevertheless, the day-age and framework response essays do not interact with our compelling challenges or refute the massive weight of hundreds of previous commentators who loved Scripture. Neither do they present a comprehensive biblical theology, surveying biblical texts from Genesis to Revelation, as we have. Instead, they largely reassert answered or erroneous conjectures without accepting many fine insights by those who were not so isolated by the cultural context of American evangelicalism. Furthermore, to agree with our esteemed counterparts would require us to disagree with Solomon; for if they are right, they have discovered—where others have not—something new under the sun.

Indeed, we anticipate that our view, the Christian interpretation from previous ages, will continue to face fierce opposition from the framework and day-age teams, as they view our advocacy of the universal Church's position as outmoded and anachronistic. Perhaps we can save time and plead guilty to that charge so that they can interact with our substantive arguments instead of caricaturing our position. We merely hold to the interpretation of the vast majority of the Christian Church since its inception. These and other rival theories are welcome to join forces against that or attack it individually. We have every confidence that the classical view of creation will stand, while framework, day-age, gap, and numerous other theories will rise, fall, and face retirement.

In the end, two positions remain: (1) the classical, historic exegesis of Genesis 1, and (2) a plethora of modern varieties that, wittingly or unwittingly, tailor biblical interpretation to some contemporary form of rationalism or naturalism. We see the day-age and framework views as recent innovations, possessing far too much novelty and idiosyncrasy, unconvincing to most outside of our particular Western scientific paradigm, and indeed foreign to the Early, Medieval, Reformation, and post-Reformation Church. Instead of approximating the standard held by the one holy, universal Church, these views are new and most likely spawned in reaction to certain intellectual torrents.

The Ross-Archer team almost admits this point by asserting that the "timing of creation had little doctrinal significance" until the advent of modern science. That admission supports our insistence that the day-age view did not occur to people until recently; much less was it held by theologians who did not live in an age of scientism. When pressed, the earliest evidence Ross and Archer can produce for this type of harmonic convergence is an 1894 work or a 1729 work that, even if carrying weight among scientists, certainly is not by a recognized theologian and is an eccentric work at best. The Irons-Kline team seems to sense this vulnerability as well when they admit that their view lacks abundant published advocates prior to 1924 or 1957 (in English) and is "moderate concordism" (while they describe the Ross-Archer view as "strong concordism"). Regardless of the label, both the framework and day-age views are conformist, and both are quite modern.

The day-age response implies that we have a psychological "need" to see things a certain way or that we "fear" opposing views. Of course, we could assert that those who espouse views different from orthodoxy have a strong "need" to conform to the scientific rationality of the day, or perhaps a subconscious "fear" that orthodoxy's view might increasingly land them in positions contrary to their peers. However, rather than resorting to psychological labels which are inaccurate, we prefer to interact with the views our friends have articulated without attributing paranoia, psychological affect, or motives to them.

We do not so much "fear" the slippery slope arguments of our counterparts as we view their positions as needlessly conceding to modernity in many ways. The variety of modern concessions to philosophically hostile worldviews, more than threatening a future domino effect in the collapse of orthodoxy (like an avalanche), portends simultaneous aspects of thought already dangling on the brink (more like an earthquake fault line).

THE EXEGETICAL CONTEXT

Although we have provided the most comprehensive exegetical argument in this debate (including commentaries on the key creation passages by numerous Bible interpreters throughout Church history), we begin by summarizing the exegetical arguments supporting the 24-hour view.

First, the predominant use of the word *day* in Scripture is for a known, normal period of time. Lacking compelling reasons from the text itself (not from second order interpretations) to read in some meaning other than the normal one, good exegesis will preserve the normal meanings of words. It also will not require the original audience or the uneducated to possess a literary sophistication that has only been ingeniously "discovered" in the past two centuries—and that only after considerable mental gymnastics have been performed, hoping to conform Scripture to science.

Second, the use of the "evening and morning" formula is a hard brake for those views that propose nonliteral readings. Taking those words as they were intended to be taken leads to only one sound conclusion on the length of the days and repudiates all rivals.

Third, the use of ordinals (first, second, third, etc.) to indicate an ordered sequence underscores the literal reading and adds to the burden of those who argue that *day* does not mean "day," especially when God had the ability to choose other words to communicate a poetic structure or a long age. He chose, howeverr, to employ sequential numbers, the "evening and morning" refrain, and the customary term for day.

Fourth, we have yet to see internally compelling reasons for why *yôm* in Genesis 1 means an extended or undefined period. Though *yôm* may have that meaning in some passages, that does not necessarily indicate that it has that meaning in this passage in particular. While some may wish to fabricate an objection based on Genesis 2, and then call for reinventing Genesis 1 upon that supposed basis, our initial essay has shown that this objection is specious.

Fifth, when Genesis 1 declares the formula "God said . . . and it was so," the text does not indicate that it means "God said . . . and it took a while." To the contrary, direct creation in a short time magnifies the miraculous creative work of God, as Scripture consistently holds elsewhere. God's "saying" is not separated from "and it was so" in the authoritative text, even if some readers wish to interject long periods between those two acts.

Sixth, the flow of redemptive history after Genesis gives no indication that the creation days are anything other than ordinary days. No other Scripture writer encourages readers to reinterpret Genesis 1 as do our counterparts in this debate. Consistency within the scriptural texts is certainly in agreement with our view.

While our day-age and framework counterparts attempt to take aim at our list of key biblical passages on creation, they remain unable to show that those passages hint at anything but a literal interpretation of the creation days. They also are unable to show that those passages support the idea that God used only ordinary providence when He created the heavens, the earth, the sea, and all that is in them. Our view *is* more dependent on the miraculous in Genesis 1 than the day-age and framework views.

All these purely exegetical considerations taken together compel the 24-hour interpretation. The biblical record is clear—and was known to be so for centuries: God created the universe "by the Word of His power," He did it "in the space of six days," and it was all "very good."[2]

THE HISTORICAL CONTEXT

Scripture plainly teaches the 24-hour view, and the Church has for that reason perennially clung to this view. Not only did our counterparts fail to interact meaningfully with our exegetical arguments for the 24-hour view, but they also fail to interact meaningfully with the original sources we have cited. Since historical exegesis of the key texts rests at the center of our argument, for them to refuse our case, they not only must refute Scripture, but they also must show that all premodern exegetes were blind. What our historical exegesis demonstrates is the contrast between the long-held view of the Church and the adolescent novelty of the day-age and framework views.

We may express the matter this way: *The day-age view first arose when jazz was on the rise in America, while the framework view only surfaced in English just before the Beatles!* Conversely, the 24-hour view has been the consensus of the Church since the earliest hymns, chants, and doxologies, and long before Bach and Handel. If ever the Church agreed on anything, it has been on the days of creation. The paradigm shift occurred only recently when naturalistic and/or rationalistic paradigms were enthroned and Scripture was made subservient to them. Not willing to acknowledge this undeniable fact, our counterparts zealously impose views of relative obscurity throughout Church history, even if their views enjoy some level of prominence today within certain evangelical circles.

Moreover, the day-age team, attempting to make its view more palatable to modern readers, makes many embarrassing historical blunders along the way. Those who want to make room for modern views need to avoid citing famous theologians out of context when making their cases.

The Early Church
Ross and Archer, for example, strip many early Church fathers from their context in a desperate attempt to find ancient testimony for their modern view, which is contrary to what the ancients themselves actually wrote and taught.[3]

Justin Martyr. Ross and Archer claim that Justin Martyr and others explicitly endorse "six consecutive thousand-year periods for the Genesis creation days." This claim is false. In Martyr's *Dialogue With Trypho* (LXXX), far from espousing what Ross and Archer claim, Justin argued about the "reign of a thousand years." The following chapter (LXXXI) reveals that Martyr was not "wrestling" with the length of creation days, but the length of world history, which he and many other patristics expected to *total* 7,000 years. Accordingly, they believed in a rather recent creation and would probably be criticized today as young-earth creationists.

Irenaeus. Ross and Archer equally misappropriate Irenaeus as endorsing "six consecutive thousand-year periods for the Genesis creation days." In the Irenaeus text that Ross and Archer cite in their footnote, which supposedly shows that Irenaeus agreed with old-earth views or long creation days, Irenaeus actually says: "Thus, then, in the day that they did eat, in the *same* did they die, and became death's debtors, since it was one day of the creation. For it is said, 'There was made in the evening, and there was made in the morning, one day.'"[4] The days, according to Irenaeus, progress according to regular cycles. He believed that the Lord "recapitulated" the six days of creation, suffering Himself in the sixth millennium. Irenaeus, when read in context, was not arguing for the creation days lasting a thousand years each. Instead, he believed that creation was not more than 6,000 years old at his time.

Lactantius. Contrary to what Ross and Archer allege, Lactantius actually argued against a very old universe, as maintained by Plato and other philosophers. Lactantius wrote: "Therefore let the philosophers, who enumerate thousands of ages from the beginning of the world, know that *the six thousandth year is not yet completed*, and that when this number is completed the *consummation* must take place. . . ."[5] Lactantius then wrote: "God completed the world and this admirable work of nature *in the space of six days* [perhaps the earliest occurrence of that phrase which clarifies that it refers to duration], as is contained in the secrets of Holy Scripture."[6] Contrary to what Ross and Archer represent, one may read a few more sentences to see what Lactantius affirmed: "Therefore, since all the works of God were completed in six days, the world must continue in its present state through six ages, that is six thousand years."[7] Lactantius may be mocked as a young-earth creationist, as a literalist, or as explicitly opposed to a long period of creation, but he assuredly did *not* explicitly endorse "six consecutive thousand-year periods for the Genesis creation days" as Ross and Archer mistakenly claim.

Victorinus. One can see the early Church's view of the whole scope of history in Victorinus, another patristic author misrepresented by Ross and Archer. Victorinus did not teach that the creation days were a thousand years in length, but merely followed the scheme above by correlating the total length of world history to 6,000 years. In addition, on the pages preceding *and* following the non-contextualized Ross-Archer citation, he actually stated:

> In the beginning God made the light, and divided it in the exact measure of twelve hours by day and by night. . . . The day, as I have above related, is divided into two parts by the number twelve—by the twelve hours of day and night; and by these hours too, months, and years, and seasons, and

ages are computed. Therefore, doubtless, there are appointed also twelve angels of the day and twelve angels of the night, in accordance, to wit, with the number of hours.[8]

That passage is pretty literal and fairly clear.

Methodius. Ross and Archer also allege that Methodius explicitly endorses "six consecutive thousand-year periods for the Genesis creation days." But their citation does not prove their point, unless they find more in his discourse on "The Difficulty and Excellence of Virginity" than most do.[9] Even assuming, however, that they had another reference in mind, Methodius simply echoes the view of Irenaeus, Lantantius, and Victorinus that world history from the time of Adam to the patristics totaled six millennia and that the Second Coming/Resurrection would be consummated within 7,000 years.[10]

Clement of Alexandria. If Ross and Archer believe that Clement of Alexandria explicitly endorses "six consecutive thousand-year periods for the Genesis creation days," we urge them to read Clement's bizarre numerology aloud in its entirety to an audience.[11] Clement is more like Augustine, viewing creation as occurring "at once," not over a long period of time or needing gradual processes. In fact, Clement begins this section (a commentary on the Fourth Commandment, not Genesis 1) by stating: "And the fourth word is that which intimates that the world was created by God, and that He gave us the seventh day as a rest."

Basil. Contrary to Ross and Archer, Basil did not endorse "six consecutive thousand-year periods for the Genesis creation days" or "wrestle with the issue" when he commented on Genesis 1:7 (one page before the Ross-Archer reference): "So, with a single word and *in one instant*, the Creator of all things gave the boon of light to the world."[12] Ross and Archer cannot have read the next page of Basil to allege that he "struggled with ambiguity" and "wrote of 'ages' for creation." Basil explicitly denies that the creation days were to be confused with "ages" used elsewhere in Scripture. Here is what Basil thought about the length of days ("to determine the measure of day and night") when he commented on Genesis 1:8:

> Now twenty-four hours fill up the space of one day—we mean of a day and of a night; and if, at the time of the solstices, they have not both an equal length, the time marked by Scripture does not the less circumscribe their duration. It is as though it said: twenty-four hours measure the space of a day, or that, in reality a day is the time that the heavens starting from one point take to return there. Thus, every time that, in the revolution of the sun, evening and morning occupy the world, their periodical succession never exceeds the space of one day. . . . God who made the nature of time measured it out and determined it by interval of days, and wishing to give

it a week as a measure, he ordered the week to revolve from period to period upon itself, to count the movement of time, forming the week of one
day revolving seven times upon itself.[13]

This text is anything but ambiguous. Similarly, the Church's view has been
anything but agnostic.

Ambrose. While Ross and Archer assert that Ambrose agrees with
them, we refer readers to the pertinent claim of Ambrose, one of the first
theologians to adopt a mature view of creation. In his fullest discussion of
the lengths of the creation days—in his *Hexameron* (note that the title
itself refers to six days, not six eons)—Ambrose commented unambigu-
ously: "But Scripture established a law that twenty-four hours, including
both day and night, should be given the name of day only, as if one were
to say the length of one day is twenty-four hours in extent."[14] The Ross-
Archer claim that Ambrose "wrestled" with the issue or used "ages" as though
he somehow concurred with their recent day-age view is gratuitous, incompatible with Ambrose's context, and assumes far more than what
Ambrose actually wrote. Instead of being ambiguous, Ambrose is as definite as any Church father on the subject! Moreover, Augustine and others never repudiated Ambrose's quite literal scheme. That attempt would
not come until the twentieth century—a significant fact for anyone wish-
ing to side with timeless biblical interpretation.

Ross and Archer might want to explain why *so much* of the Church
got it *so wrong* for *so long*.[15] Indeed, not only must Ross and Archer explain away the actual sayings of Basil, Ambrose, and others who explicitly
asserted their views in favor of 24-hour days, but they must explain why
later commentators understood the early Church to favor 24-hour days.
To make a convincing argument, Ross and Archer must show *where* the
Church fathers went wrong and *why* later commentators understood them
to affirm what we assert. Neither the Ross-Archer team nor the Irons-
Kline team has done this.

The Middle Ages, the Reformation, and Beyond
In addition, the dominant commentators[16] from the Middle Ages, Refor-
mation, and post-Reformation eras support our interpretation of Basil,
Ambrose, and others such as Chrysostom.

Luther. Luther's view is clear, uncontested, and only ignored if scholarship selectively seeks to prove its own preconceptions.

Calvin. Although they rightly admit in one place that Calvin believed
the days of Genesis to be normal days, Ross and Archer wrongly imply
that Calvin was ambiguous on this subject.[17] Calvin affirmed in his commentary on Genesis (1:5) that creation was of the duration of "the space

of six days," a phrase later adopted by the Westminster Assembly consistent with Calvin's view.[18] In that same commentary, Calvin classified the rubric "evening and morning" as "according to the custom of his nation . . . [Moses] accommodated his discourse to the received custom." From Calvin's context, that accommodation is not to secular science, but to the Hebrew "mode of reckoning." Regarding the fourth day, Calvin refers parenthetically but clearly to "the natural day."

To understand how long the tradition of interpreting Basil and Ambrose remained intact, one should consider one of the fullest Reformation treatises on Genesis by Wolfgang Musculus (1497–1563). While commenting on the fourth day of creation[19] in his 1554 treatise, *In Genesim Moses Commentarii Plenissimi*, Musculus wrote:

> There were days before the sun, just as also there was night before the moon and stars. . . . At that time the days had an inexplicable light, with no observable sign of their stage, or even of their midpoint, which are governed (with regard to our experience) by the sun's course, as it is ordered and noted [by us]. Therefore it is rightly attributed to the sun because I do not say that it constitutes, but rather that it orders and arranges the day. However, I have not been inconsistent with the point in this place, understanding the work not as artificial but as natural days: and not only of the sun, but also of the moon and the stars. . . . In the space of a year there are twelve revolutions of the moon: i.e., twelve months are completed. And a solar year is when the sun returns to the end of its own circuit whence it began.

Concurring with Basil, other Church fathers, and Lombard, Musculus's commentary on the text—the fullest of the period (almost 800 octavo pages)—noted that the reckoning of time for the Hebrews was from the beginning hour (*horae*). Musculus—who also referred to Chrysostom's *Fourth Homily on Genesis* as concurring with his view—apparently thought the orthodox Church was of the same opinion, did not cite any dissenting voices, and added the voice of Lombard, who also confirmed that "morning" is not the first of the day.

Musculus further adds that the whole world was created by the sixth day: "Thus the days are numbered (*dies numerantur*) as time is (*tempus est*)." The days, he wrote, were *in tempora*, and "just as the entire world was constituted in the revolution of 6 days (*sex dierum revolutionibus*), so it continues." Musculus's massive commentary, certainly a theological paradigm of its day, does not seem to distinguish between the length and quality of the days, as if the fourth day began a new or different chronology. Musculus saw no reason to interpose an artificially long period in the creation days, and long before modern theories, he was aware of light prior to solar light. We did not invent this interpretation; it has had numerous other advocates before our century. Musculus and others knew that any difficulty presented by observation was ultimately resolvable by this simple proposition: "The sun is not the origin of light" (*Sol non est origo lucis*).

Do the Ross-Archer and Irons-Kline teams consider Musculus uninformed or just plain wrong? Calvin and the Protestant Reformers thought him neither.

The Geneva Study Bible. The 1562 *Annotations from the Geneva Bible* was one of the most authoritative commentaries during the Reformation era. While Calvin was still living and at the peak of his international prestige, Genevan annotators recorded one of the earliest English interpretations of the creation narratives. On Genesis 1:3 they write, "The light was made before either sunne or moone was created; therefore we must not attribute that to the creatures that are God's instruments which only appertaineth to God."

Evidently, Calvin and his fellow exegetes realized early that the sun was not created until the fourth day and that, in and of itself, this fact was not an insurmountable exegetical hurdle for the classical view. Believers such as Calvin have affirmed for centuries that light was created prior to the sun. Faithful biblical interpreters asserted that sunlight which occurred only on the fourth day should not be confused with this earlier nonsolar light and that creaturely/created light of the fourth day should not be attributed to that light on Day 1 "which only appertaineth to God."

The question asked in this volume that some consider so perplexing today—How could there be light without a sun?—did not perplex earlier commentators, who positively answered that question by distinguishing between solar light following the fourth ordinary day and that light which proceeded from a nonsolar source on Days 1–3. These commentators did not appeal to ordinary providence as the sole force in the creation days.[20] More of the miraculous was embraced by earlier biblical Christians, who commented on Genesis 1:8: "So that we see it is the only [exclusive] power of God's word that maketh the earth fruitful, which is naturally barren." If ever a study Bible's notes were widespread and orthodox, such annotations in the Geneva Bible were archetypical.

Other Reformers and Their Successors. Thus, at the time of the Reformation, the leading commentaries interpreted Genesis 1 in the same fashion as we have—and differently from the other views presented in this volume. All the major Reformers, including the towering biblical exegetes who succeeded Calvin—Beza, Diodati, Polyander, and the Puritans—held to the same interpretation we have espoused. In fact, the view held by Calvin prevailed without interruption until (and after) the Westminster Assembly (1643–1648) and was articulated by many. Other post-Reformation giants, such as Ursinus, Melancthon, Lightfoot, Baxter, and Perkins, affirmed a similar consensus.[21]

We continue to ask our friends to answer this question: How did all these godly commentators miss the point—and with such remarkable consistency? To answer that question, modern interpretations not only must put forward their hypotheses, but they also must show where and how this near-universal consensus was wrong and on such a grandiose scale. The only response modern interpreters can offer is that their predecessors were ignorant of the *science* we now think we know. That response is not an argument based on Scripture; it is an argument based on naturalism and/or rationalism.

If we are to take seriously advocates of modern interpretations like the day-age and framework views, they must come forward with centuries of exegetes who "saw" the same things that their modern eyes "see" in Genesis 1. We all would profit should such advocates refer us to where the major Reformers and others advocated post-Darwinian era cosmologies or interpretations. Earlier commentators (to whom these concepts never occurred) did not seem so quick to experiment as commentators in our modern era. Thus, the historical record indicts modern views as innovations manufactured only after, or in response to, the wide acceptance of certain scientific revolutions. Rather than deriving these modern interpretations from the Bible alone, these new views have been carefully devised to fit presupposed concepts more in keeping with the altered landscapes of scientific dogma. There was no "alternative view" until the nineteenth century, after the beginning of the warfare between science and Christianity.[22]

Despite the failure of some modern interpreters to embrace the demonstrable truth—that is, that earlier believers held to such a strong view of creation so definitely—this fact is clear: Not only did our fathers in the faith have fixed views that the creation *days* were ordinary, but their view was so universal that as time progressed, they easily codified these views in creeds and confessions *without objection*. Earlier orthodoxy was so undisputed that they set these items in creeds and found little or no opposition to enshrining as creedal the views of Ussher (the Irish Articles), Calvin (*The Westminster Confession*), Luther, Perkins,[23] and many others.

These earlier commentators and the creeds which developed after them were not merely concerned with the "Who" or "what" of creation. They went out of their way to affirm the "when" and the "how" as well. The burden rests on novel interpretations to convince us that the "how long"— since God reveals it—is unimportant.

The Westminster Divines. Ross and Archer again are wrong to allege that the Westminster divines did not endorse the 24-hour view. We have

proven elsewhere that any Westminster divine who wrote on the subject
of creation adopted the 24-hour view. There are no exceptions in the literature. Based on our ongoing historical research, we can correct the Ross-
Archer claim regarding the view of the Westminster Assembly by observing
that no Westminster divine held to a long age of creation or the framework interpretation. On the other hand, every Westminster divine who
wrote on the subject adopted the 24-hour view, a fairly short period between creation and Christ's birth, and a rejection of Augustine's instantaneous creation position.[24] In light of the overwhelming historical evidence,
we may reasonably and fairly require those advocating modern views to
present substantial evidence before we take them seriously.

Ross and Archer wrongly assert that *The Westminster Confession* "simply mirrors the language of Scripture at this point." *The Westminster Confession* contains the wording "in *the space of* six days." However, no major
English versions of the Bible within a century of the Westminster Assembly used that exact wording in Genesis 1. Moreover, a creed does not merely
parrot biblical phrases but seeks to apply biblical teaching to its day, and
the Westminster divines—to the man—affirmed 24-hour days when they
spoke to this issue. They meant real days (no deconstructionist word trick-
ery), and they confessed that it all happened "in the space of six days."
Energetic efforts to disqualify some divines may be undertaken, but the
important number here is *zero*. *No Westminster authors held to the day-age or
framework view.*

Both the day-age and framework teams claim that Protestant confessions are ambiguous on the length of the creation days. But we have taken
great pains to prove that the long history of biblical interpretation, and
specifically the written comments of the Westminster divines, endorse only
the 24-hour view. According to their interpretation, creation happened
neither in an instant nor over a long period, but in the space of six normally understood days. Moderns living after certain scientific revolutions
may wish to retreat from that history or even change their views, but the
historical record is abundantly clear, and it should not be distorted. Further, to wrongly distort the testimony of past theologians is to beg for readers
to question the credibility of research and to challenge the experimental
exegesis offered as well.

With a growing list of explicit testimonies for 24-hour days—and it is
more likely that that number will increase than that other modern views
will find superior support—our exegesis fits with the Church's previous history on this question.[25] The other views do not.

THE THEOLOGICAL AND APOLOGETIC CONTEXT

Natural and Special Revelation

When Ross and Archer later speak of natural revelation and special revelation as having equal footing, they have a view of natural revelation that is ill-conceived. If that were the case, any unbeliever could "claim" knowledge and elevate it to parity with God's revelation—on any subject! Ross and Archer claim, for example, that "to ignore what the record of nature tells us about gravity or stars or creation dates would be just as foolish as ignoring what Romans tells us about propitiation or justification." This is an extreme claim, indeed. Scripture is the only "unnormed norm"—the only ultimate rule for everything we believe and do as Christians. Nothing is on par with Scripture. We are to interpret nature in light of Scripture, not vice versa.

The day-age team also seems to be overly optimistic about science by claiming that it not only gives new information, but also yields a doubling of knowledge for the evidence of divine attributes and divine design every four years. Ross himself, however, is the only scientist cited in support of this claim,[26] one which would astound David and other biblical authors (not to mention many modern cosmologists), who knew that God clearly revealed Himself and His attributes.

Ross and Archer seem intent to put natural revelation on a par with the authority of Scripture. To illustrate, when they refer to Psalm 19, they describe nature as "God's 'expression' as much as the Bible." But they base this conclusion on the first part of Psalm 19 without noting the change of subject from the "heavens declaring" (v. 1) to "the law of the Lord is perfect" (v. 7). The Ross-Archer hermeneutic confuses the law, statutes, and precepts of the Lord, on the one hand, with natural revelation, on the other hand. The two often are harmonious, but sinful observers frequently misinterpret natural revelation. Special revelation, with its own Scripture-interpreting-Scripture hermeneutic, has a corrective built into it that nature is lacking.

For those inclined to permit science to trump Scripture or to put it on a par with Scripture, consider this: What if, for example, one presented the following argument while appealing to the assured results of natural revelation? Suppose someone claimed that more adulterers were reached with the gospel because the Christian Church began to say, "The current state of science tells us that adulterers have certain sexual proclivities due to genetics and due to no fault of their own. It is like eye-color. We also don't want to offend the community of adulterers by calling their alternative lifestyle 'sinful,' and we think the Church needs to catch up with the American Psychological Association categories for sexual addiction. Anyone who reverts to old classical morality has a latent 'need,' or 'fears' that one domino leads to another."

Both the day-age and framework teams would likely leap to denounce that view. They would not permit the natural theology of pro-adultery lobbies to trump clear biblical revelation—even if those advocates string verses together and create a new "framework." Nor would they say that God merely affirms that some sexual acts are wrong, treating "abomination" (Lev. 18) as nonspecific, triadic, or of long duration.

The same could be said of our friendly debaters on many other subjects. Hence, it mystifies us—on a methodological level—why they genuflect so deeply to other areas of the "assured results of science."

Unwarranted Dogmatism

We also note that the Ross-Archer essay is unduly confident about several supposed truths. Ross and Archer require a date of 12–15 billion years for cosmic creation as a dogma. This claim is quite troublesome, manifesting a confidence surpassing even the most zealous 24-hour advocates. When science inevitably changes, do we force Scripture to fit fluctuating science again? How many times can we do so without sacrificing the credibility of Scripture or our Christian testimony?

Ross and Archer also are unduly dogmatic about their interpretation of several biblical passages such as Psalm 19, Revelation 21–22, and John 5. The reader should know that their interpretations neither are compelling nor are they consistent with the best exegetes. Moreover, the Ross-Archer interpretation of Proverbs 8 is highly questionable. Further, the Creator intimately shapes the foundations of the earth in Proverbs 3, a passage which, like Proverbs 8, gives no indication that God helplessly waited for eons of development to run their course or passively depended on ordinary forces outside His powerful word.

The compelling burden for the day-age view, as well as the framework view, is to show that it had more orthodox (not eccentric) commentaries that teach day-age or framework speculations prior to, say, 1854. One cannot merely invent a theory, fine-tune it to fit with parts of Christian truth and parts of unbelieving naturalism,[27] insist that everyone else hold to it, and castigate those who refuse to hold to it. The day-age and framework views depart from an earlier unity, and they presume their departures to be equal with other views.

Compatibility Between the Day-Age and Framework Views

It appears to us that this debate has produced a vital union. Based on the response essays, the day-age and framework teams may have come close to convincing each other. While the framework team does not embrace the sequential view of Ross-Archer, they nevertheless describe the day-age essay as "interesting," "persuasive," and "most compelling," and "heartily agree with many of the points" in the day-age essay and "accept [Ross's] proposed model in broad outline," going so far as to appreciate the day-age attempt to harmonize Scripture with the Big Bang.

For their part, the day-age team hints later in this volume that one can hold both the day-age and framework views, which is true to a large extent. The day-age team also speaks glowingly of the framework view, asserts that the framework view has merit, suggests that it demonstrates "beauty and grandeur" of prose, and claims that it is "more compelling" for apologetic purposes than the 24-hour view. The day-age team is uncharacteristically gentle when critiquing one of the framework view's foundational assumptions regarding the upper-register hermeneutic. Indeed, since the framework view takes no stand on the age of the universe, the only apparent barrier separating the two views is the sequential reading of the text.

However, both the day-age and framework views depart from the clear and obvious meaning of the text, the meaning held by biblical writers and maintained throughout Church history until the last 150 years. The entire Judeo-Christian tradition—the Church transcending all denominational groupings and the orthodox Jewish tradition—has concurred with our view on the length of days, not for centuries, but for millennia. (The reckoning of the Jewish Calendar dates this year as 5760!) The only explanation for the paradigm shift is conformity with modern science.

While we remain in the embrace of theologians such as Calvin, Luther, Lombard, Ambrose, and Basil, we suggest that our brethren who are influenced by modernism recognize the obscurity of their views and return to the ancient paths. We appreciate the Ross-Archer insistence on sequentialism and sincerely hope that they will not abandon it. We also appreciate the Irons-Kline insistence that special revelation trumps natural revelation, and we sincerely hope that they continue to resist naturalism.

Familiarity with Framework Sources

Irons and Kline fault us because we did not cite recent literature defending their position. We have several responses to this criticism. First, we are familiar with the major framework sources but simply find them to be exegetically unconvincing and historically novel. The more we read them, the less persuasive they appear. When measured against the long history of the one holy, universal, and apostolic Church and the excellent exegetes who preceded us, we view the framework hypothesis as a literary fad, much like the once-hip Documentary Hypothesis that has since been found wanting and discarded (i.e., the view that the Pentateuch had multiple authors).

It is not that we failed to read the sources of the framework view, but that we simply do not agree with them.

Second, we have no obligation to cite every opposing source. We leave that task in the capable hands of the framework team, just as they chose not to cite every 24-hour source in their essays. To argue for a position that conforms to the historic consensus of the Church, as we have, does not require us to rehash every source advancing theories we believe to be erroneous. The number of citations we have made to framework theorists since 1957 has no compelling force for this debate.

We merely disagree with both modern views and find them quite lacking in longevity and exegetical compulsion. Furthermore, no logic whatsoever requires their position. While we are awed by the great energy and intellectual creativity that contributed to the framework view, it should be seen as an elaborate exercise to try to force a square peg into a round hole. It is a square peg, and it does not fit. Rather than citing that view, we think it better to retire it. It would be arduous to demonstrate that the body of Christ either has missed much before being informed that this intricate scaffold is so essential or has improved during the view's specious tenure of experimentation.

Our conclusion is that the framework view is incorrect. Irons and Kline are simply wrong in this matter, and therefore we are free to disagree with them. Neither are we under obligation to cite their sources exhaustively, especially when we find ourselves surrounded by such good company as the concurring saints we have cited. Indeed, we stand with the venerable view of the Church and with earlier historic commentators, and we still are not persuaded to follow these new interpretations.

Other Miscellaneous Matters

Our Dominant Thesis. The framework team senses but misstates our dominant thesis. It is not that tradition determines the truth. Rather, it is that there is a long practice of biblical interpretation, and those interpreters are more correct than the modern scientifically-biased tradition of Western evangelicalism on-the-run. Church tradition does not so much determine as it informs, and we retain a profound respect for earlier biblical interpreters. Rather than holding our view out of "fear," "need," or traditionalism, we hold our position for one reason only, the reason sung by many children: the Bible tells us so.

Augustine Not a Framework Triadist. The framework essay errs by citing Augustine as a witness. Our previous discussions about Augustine, Basil, and Lombard discount the Irons-Kline claim that Augustine's view of creation days led to something like the framework view. Certainly,

Augustine advocated a quicker span for creation than most (and he was later repudiated), but whatever figurative hermeneutic he employed never suggested anything as urbane as the framework triads. We strongly disagree with any caricature of Augustine that suggests he held to a literary framework as do Irons and Kline. Neither can we forget Augustine's dalliance with Platonism or attempt to morph him posthumously into a proto-framework triadist.

Exegetical Consensus on the Creation Days. Irons and Kline claim that "there was no exegetical consensus on the days of Genesis." This claim is wrong. There was only one view following the repudiation of Augustine's view, and seldom (if ever) before the nineteenth century was the day-age or the framework view advocated. This also is the reason why no creed prior to 1615 addressed the length of creation days (although paper-forests of sermons and commentaries did), and when "the space of six days" became a creedal item, *no one objected.* That is how consensual the Church was on this question, and how long she was monolithic.

Binding the Conscience. Irons-Kline criticize us for imposing our views and binding the conscience. Our view no more binds consciences than did the uniform view of Ambrose, Basil, Chrysostom, Lombard, Aquinas, Luther, Calvin, Perkins, Ames, a Brakel, Edwards, and the rest of the cloud of witnesses we have cited in this volume. The framework-view claim that the classical view is "an alien agenda to bind the conscience of the Church with extrabiblical, manmade constraints" harshly condemns all other interpreters before the last century. In the end, the framework theory itself may prove to be an attempt to bind consciences with its own idiosyncratic view.

Baseless Objections. Of course, we could give you many other responses, but space forbids. Some responses, such as the Ross-Archer dogmatism about the age of the stars, we consider immaterial (and they require no reply). We simply have no biblical information on this subject, and we refuse to speculate or let the state of scientific orthodoxy call into question the accuracy of Genesis.

We also think that one of the most specious arguments is the one that tries to erect a strict wall of separation between *haya* and *bara*, as if those words alone somehow prove that the celestial lights only "appeared" on the fourth day.

Moreover, we caution readers that several other arguments are not nearly as insuperable as often claimed. We have shown in our earlier exegesis that the text, as understood by prenaturalist believers, does not require that the tasks of Adam on Day 6 consumed eons. The supernatural, not the natural, saturates the whole creation narrative. Only if one is dogmatic about ordinary providence need the activity of the sixth day be viewed as problematic.

In addition, the appeal to the different formula for the seventh day need not mean that the seventh day of creation is millennia long—a conclusion that never occurred to earlier commentators and one that they would have considered absurd.

We also have shown that orthodox exegetes knew that the source of light for Days 1–3 is independent of ordinary providence. Since Christ will provide light for the new, eternal creation (Rev. 22), there is no logical reason why He could not have done so for the original creation in Genesis. In short, the greatly overrated objections to the classical view are all answerable, and those answers provide a better theological matrix than denying the plain language of Scripture and creating absurd ideas.

Finally, we wish to respond to the Irons-Kline suggestion that we beg the question by asking, "Does the Christian exegetical tradition affirm long periods of time or unmediated, rapid creation?" According to them, the question should be: "Does the Christian tradition approach the creation week literally or figuratively?"

We have three responses. First, the allegation that we beg the question seems like an admission that its answer is exactly what we propose. If the framework team should view the obvious answer as such (that the Christian exegetical tradition did not affirm long periods of time but unmediated, rapid creation), we would thank them for saying so.

Second, this debate was never cast only as a literal versus figurative discussion. When the text raises the issue of days, complete with order and "evening and morning," it is impossible to avoid its claim with integrity. We simply agree with the normal meaning of *day* in those verses; our counterparts do not.

Third, as our exegesis and review of history shows, the other views represented in this volume are outside the Christian consensus and were introduced very recently. To the contrary, of all the verses we cite, none require that God needed a long or indeterminate period to perform His creation. His strong power and rapid creation is indicated by the repetition of the powerful and profound phrase "and it was so." The Christian Church has taken such language literally, not figuratively. Even a child or the uneducated can understand this important truth.

No Prevailing Figurative Views before the Rise of Evolution. The framework team asserts that "figurative views [on the length of days] were present long before the rise of evolution."[28] One will look in vain for creeds or commentaries supporting this claim regarding yôm. Show us figurative views on the length of the days before the rise of evolution in the nineteenth century. Even if a few were produced, that fact would not prove the truth of the day-age or framework case. But until that is done, our case is not weakened. To attack the near-unanimous consensus of the Church through two millennia, the day-age and framework teams need to either marshal significant citations to buttress their views or admit the novelty of their respective views and confess what drives the alterations they propose.

The questions that remain for our friends to answer are: Did Bible-believing theologians before 1800 differ with, reject, or revolt against the pre-existing consensus of the Church regarding the days of creation? If so, where did they express their revolt? Until the age of Darwin, these modern ideas occurred to few Christians. Moreover, average readers of Scripture, either in biblical periods or in later ages, did not "see" the interpretations posited by the day-age and framework views. We still cannot imagine peasants in third-world countries (or many others besides cloistered academic elites) performing discourse analysis, and we do not think it realistic to imagine that pre-Christian Hebrews did. Neither do we believe that God's word requires extraordinary literary sophistication to read it correctly.

No one before the rise of modern evolution posited that creation occurred in anything other than six ordinary days by the special operation of God's miraculous fiat. Modern advocates who wish to show that day-age or framework views have longevity on their side will also need to explain away the following:

- Jonathan Edwards believed that creation occurred near an autumnal equinox, much like Archbishop James Ussher.

- Samuel Davies, in his 1756 "The Mediatorial Kingdom and Glories of Jesus Christ," stated that the "space between the creation and the flood" was "about 1600 years," indicating that he adopted the scheme held by Ussher, Calvin, Ames, Perkins, and Lightfoot, and expressed by the Westminster Assembly.

- Jedidiah Morse, one of America's first geographers, adopted Ussher's chronology in his 1796 *American Universal Geography*, dating the creation of the world and Adam and Eve to 4004 B.C.[29]

- John Adams, certainly a progressive in his day, affirmed as late as 1813 that the common notion was that God benevolently created the universe "six thousand years ago."

- Charles Spurgeon in 1885 still thought that God's omniscience not only recalled all the transactions of this world, but "of all the worlds in the universe—not only the events of the *six thousand years which have passed since the earth was created*, but of a duration without beginning."[30]

- Andrew White in 1896 claimed that Calvin had a "strict" interpretation of Genesis and that "down to a period almost within living memory, it was held, virtually 'always, everywhere, and by all,' that the universe, as we now see it, was created literally and directly by the voice or hands of the Almighty, or by both—out of nothing—in an instant or in six days."[31]

It is almost as if someone changed the theory of creation and forgot to mention it. The turning point occurred after Adams' comment (1813). Some avant-garde theologians were assimilating such views by the 1850s, while many—friend (Spurgeon) and foe (White) alike—were not aware of the cutting-edge switch. Likely, the 1894 source cited by Ross and Archer is one of the earliest conformist interpretations.

Rather than presenting compelling information supporting modern views or refuting evidence of the classical hermeneutic, it seems that the more one studies this issue, two things become clearer: (1) before nineteenth-century scientific revolutions, orthodox theology had answers for the questions posed today; and (2) changes in evangelical exegesis followed and reacted to secular scientific theories after 1800.

If those post-1800 theories are correct, the entire Church may need to alter its theology, and it might be candid to explain that those alterations arise from scientific theories, not the history of biblical interpretation. If, by contrast, those scientific theories are incorrect, as they are proving to be, it would be highly imprudent to try to make Scripture conform to them.

In light of the historical facts, mere humility should lead those who discuss these issues to refrain from ridiculing the sincere belief that Genesis 1 teaches what its words plainly say. The least we ask of our friends is that if they adopt experimental readings of the text, they refrain from besmirching the good name of the millions who have taken and who continue to take Genesis 1 at face value. The classical view of creation is not a second-class view, so believers in historic orthodoxy should be freed from those who try to bully them into believing otherwise.

CONCLUSION

We are certain that other discussions will follow and that this volume will not answer all questions. But we believe that we have presented a compelling exegetical, historical, and theological/apologetical case for the classical view that God miraculously created the universe in six ordinary days. In the process, we have proven that the day-age and framework views are lacking in exegetical, historical, and theological/apologetical weight. We have found that the day-age and framework theories are foreign to Scripture and are of recent origin. Those theories alone may not lead to a collapse of orthodoxy per se, but they already manifest multiple inadequacies. Thus, we do not recommend them to the Church. We cannot find that the Church has taught them in the past; we do not find that most evangelistic churches teach them today.

After all the ink dries, it appears that there are really two major interpretive options (not three) for the Genesis narratives: conformist and non-conformist. By that, we mean that the day-age and framework views share one thing in common: they both seek to appeal to the current state of knowledge. They have reinterpreted Scripture and have developed models that conform to the information of our age. This method will require the Church to constantly revise its doctrine of creation. Should conformism of either type prevail, the Church's doctrine of creation will always be evolving, whether it embraces evolution or not.

In contrast, the non-conformist model does not alter biblical interpretations, refusing to tailor them to the ever-changing horizons of knowledge, whether knowledge doubles in four years or four millennia. It also provides the Church with a fixed view of a very important doctrine.

Since the time of Darwin, evangelicals have been defensive, reactionary, conformist, or greatly cowed by science. In the process, the last century and a half has witnessed wholesale surrender of truth after critical truth, sacrificed on the altar of naturalism or its twin deity, rationalism. It is time for the Church to stop following secular culture and to start leading it again. For too long, evangelicalism has honored secular rationalism and natural theology too much. It is time to return to "thus saith the Lord." We are willing to offer argumentation for a new tradition, one that calls into question the claims of secularists. It is time for a new and bolder posture by Christians. Ironically, we have found that such new posture is uncannily similar to that held by the greatest Christian thinkers in the past, who were not as intimidated by the "claims" or "theories" of secular science as many moderns.

That new posture does not call for a diminution of intellect, and we are happy to reiterate that our counterparts are great intellects, as well as sincere Christians. Since we favor academic freedom, we wish them the best as they experiment with whatever new theories they wish to explore and test. What we hope our debate shows, however, is that there is a vital difference between contriving new theories and holding to sound biblical interpretation. Let the new theories—no doubt many more will be raised in the future—be seen as exactly that: theological experiments with Bunsen burners. However, the mere casting of an experiment is severely inadequate to displace the enormous thought of many esteemed thinkers and many simple believers who view the day-age and framework views as more like a sulfur poof in a lab than proof that we should reject the ideas of virtually every Christian before 1854, 1924, or 1957. We are happy to let our brothers experiment in the lab, as long as they admit when their conclusions differ with solid exegesis, and as long as the Church is free to require that their experimentation be subjected to the strictest scrutiny for an extended period before changing its views.

The *Wall Street Journal* recently published an editorial by Julia Vitullo-Martin entitled "Columbus' Circle." In that piece commemorating Columbus Day, Vitullo-Martin showed how distortions creep into scientific discussions and quickly become scientific dogma. She exposes the largely post-1896 myth that Columbus gnawed his nails as he approached America, wondering if he might at any moment fall off a flat earth. She points out that he never worried because the sphericity of the earth, contrary to hostile and uninformed caricatures of previous Christian theology, had long been proven before he ever set sail.

Indeed, the Greeks, Bede, and Aquinas all had their own calculations and proofs for the roundness of our globe. It was only after a hostile Andrew White (and a few others) miscast everyone before them as flat-earth crazies that the Columbus myth began to emerge and later became dogma. The Columbus myth (which did not appear in textbooks before the 1870s) has, no doubt, been repeated by well-intentioned but misinformed theologians about as frequently as the Ambrose, Augustine, Aquinas, and Calvin myths reiterated by our counterparts in this debate.

We hope that, if anything, some of the unfounded myths about what past commentators taught will be retired. Columbus didn't believe the earth was flat; that was the propaganda of White and other ideologues. It is equally preposterous to teach that the early church believed the day-age or framework views or prototypes thereof. Interestingly, secular mythology about Columbus began about the same time as some theologians and Bible commentators began molding their interpretations of creation to the growing popularity of Darwinism.

We don't wish to repeat that episode. We would rather maintain a heavily miraculous creation and call on science to conform to that truth than to dilute the faith, imagining somehow that scientists finally will give us their affection after we have sacrificed much of the virtue of our Christian worldview on the altar of secular naturalism or rationalism.

Further, we suspect that we are not the only parties rendezvousing with our spouses in this regard: the more we look at these tortured explanations, the sounder the classical view appears. We probably will find our-selves at the altar with many others who find these contrived views want-ing or implausible.

The Genesis text is and always has been clear. The record of Church history is and always has been clear. The theological and apologetical con-sequences of succumbing to secularism are now clear. Let God be found true!

NOTES

1. We reiterate, however, our disagreement with framework interpreters who view Gen-esis as primarily *eschatological* and covenantal. Genesis has long been correctly understood as *protological* and covenantal. To illustrate the point, consider Revelation. Merely asserting or citing a few journal articles claiming that Revelation is protological instead of eschatolog-ical (as the Church has read for years) does not make it so.

2. Westminster Shorter Catechism, Q. 9.

3. We refer the reader to our collection of relevant patristic citations at http://capo.org/patristics.html.

4. *The Ante-Nicene Fathers*, vol. 1, ed. Alexander Roberts and James Donaldson (Pea-body, MA: Hendrickson Publishers, 1995), p. 551 (emphasis added).

5. Ibid., vol. 7, p. 211 (emphasis added).

6. Ibid. (emphasis added).

7. Ibid.

8. Ibid., vol. 7, p. 341, 343.

9. See http://capo.org/patristics.html for the full context of the views of Methodius.

10. For an excellent survey of "The Early Church & the Age of the Earth," see http://www.robibrad.demon.co.uk/Chapter3.htm. That document indicates that few orthodox patristics (other than Philo and Origen, who were deemed heretical) believed anything other than the 24-hour view.

11. *The Ante-Nicene Fathers*, vol. 2, pp. 512–3.

12. *Nicene and Post-Nicene Fathers*, vol. 8, ed. Philip Schaff and Henry Wace (Peabody, MA: Hendrickson Publishers, 1995), p. 63 (emphasis added).

13. Ibid., p. 64.

14. *Hexameron*, vol. 42, trans. John J. Savage (New York: Fathers of the Church, Inc., 1961), pp. 42–3; see our initial essay for the context.

15. Ross consistently makes assertions (such as "According to Ambrose so did Hip-polytus") that either cannot be verified, are not supported by documentation, or are sim-ply incorrect if compared to the context. Unfortunately, seeking to enlist Hippolytus for their view is another assertion without proof. That is why we refer the reader to our web site (http://capo.org/patristics.html) for the original texts, which are so prone to misappro-priation.

16. One commentator a generation prior to Newton, Bishop Lancelot Andrewes, as-serted that the creation days should be measured as follows: "from Sunne to Sunne is counted a day." Later, he affirmed: "Therefore we say a day hath twenty four hours. . . . This was a day by itself, as the other six days were by themselves." What is particularly germane, how-ever, is that Andrewes explicitly cited and agreed with Basil, commenting that the word yôm "had a meaning for our natural use that we should esteem twenty-four hours one day. . . . The first day is an example to the days after" (Lancelot Andrewes, *Lectures Preached in St. Paul's Church* [London, 1657], pp. 661–3).

17. We believe Ross-Archer misrepresent our position when suggesting that the classical view, which was held for centuries, somehow "out-Darwins" Darwin, simply by believing what the Bible actually says.

18. For more on the views of Anselm, Lombard, Luther, and Calvin, see David W. Hall, "The Evolution of Mythology: Classic Creation Survives as the Fittest Among Its Critics and Revisers," *Did God Create in Six Days?*, ed. Joseph A. Pipa, Jr. and David W. Hall (Taylors, SC: Southern Presbyterian Press, Greenville Presbyterian Theological Seminary; and Oak Ridge, TN: The Covenant Foundation, 1999), pp. 279–82.

19. We include this example because it also speaks to the Irons-Kline concern that the fourth day necessitates a framework contrivance.

20. As our interpretation shows, the framework presumption that only ordinary providence was at work during the creation period is the *a priori* assumption that is never stated or demanded by the text itself. It drives their exegetical train. The text most certainly does not "reveal" that God "employed ordinary means" for creation. To the contrary, for centuries sanctified interpreters have considered creation to be by supernatural fiat. Rather than an exegetical conclusion, the Irons-Kline *philosophy* is showing through as they cling to this premise. Or perhaps they need to argue their *a priori* more extensively to prove it from Scripture, because orthodox interpreters prior to the nineteenth century certainly did not dogmatize about ordinary providence.

21. For more of our study on the history of interpretation of these issues spanning 1540–1740, see http://capo.org/1540-1740.html.

22. Thanks to the work of Rev. Mark Herzer and Dr. Kathy Thiessen, the following have been identified as additional adherents to the 24-hour day view: Jonathan Edwards (*A History of the Work of Redemption*); Richard Baxter (*The Practical Works of Richard Baxter* [vol. 4, p. 87]); Samuel Willard (*A Compleat Body of Divinity*, Sermon 35 [1690]); and Thomas Manton (*Works*, vol. 13, pp. 431–2). Many other names (e.g., William Perkins, Robert Baillie, John Lightfoot) are being added with regularity, while no one seems to be able to locate a sixteenth- or seventeenth-century Puritan who advocated in writing either the day-age or the framework view. See http://capo.org/thiessen.html for a presentation of Edwards' view.

23. Since he is frequently misrepresented, William Perkins, who lived shortly before that Assembly, should be allowed to speak for himself. Citing the agreement of many others, he wrote: "The sixth shall be touching the time of the beginning of the world, which is between five thousand and six thousand years ago. For Moses hath set down exactly the computation of time from the making of the world to his own days: and the Prophets after him have with diligence set down the continuance of the same to the very birth of Christ. . . . Some say there be 3929 from the creation to Christs birth as Beroaldus: some 3952 as Hierome and Bede: some 3960 as Luther and I. Lucidus: some 3963 as Melancton in his *Chronicle*, and Functius: some 3970 as Bullinger and Tremelius: some towards 4000 as Buntingus." [This obviously shows that they all took the days literally.] Then, arguing against instantaneous creation (*contra* Augustine), Perkins wrote: "Seventhly, some may ask in what space of time did God make the world? I answer, God could have made the world, and all things in it one moment: but he began and finished the whole work in six distinct days." As to why God took these days to make the creation, Perkins argued: "In six distinct days, to teach us, what wonderful power and liberty he had over all his creatures: for he made the light when there was neither Sun nor Moon, nor Stars; to show, that in giving light to the world, he is not bound to the Sun, to any creature, or to any means: for the light was made the first day: but the Sun, the Moon, and the Stars were not created before the fourth day (*An Exposition of the Creede*, vol. 1, p. 143).

24. See David W. Hall, "What Was the View of the Westminster Assembly Divines on Creation Days?" *Did God Create in Six Days?*, pp. 41–52. See http://capo.org/creationRevise.html.

25. Ross and Archer think we misinterpreted Newton. We still believe that our Newton quote is accurate in context. For Newton was speaking of "diurnal motion" when he

said, "You may make the first day as long as you please." In that context, he argued that the times were in relation to actual revolutions, and more importantly Newton disagreed with naturalism. If we are wrong, however, we sincerely repent, will make that correction in every venue possible, and thank our brothers for correcting us. Newton's view in the 1680s seems to repudiate the Irons-Kline idea that ordinary providence is the sole process during the creation period.

26. Danny Faulkner, Ph.D., describes Ross as treating nature as the 67th book of Scripture. See his critique of Ross, primarily on scientific grounds, at: http://www. answersingenesis.org/docs/4149.asp. Faulkner documents errors of calculation and theory, as well as theological and methodological problems with the work of Ross. Faulkner also refers to this as a *Scripture sub scientia* approach. His conclusion is quite telling, and we should seriously consider his criticisms of Ross. Jonathan Sarfati also analyzes Ross's errors—which he categorizes as canonization of nature, ignorance of Hebrew, fanciful exegesis, historical, and theological—in a book review at http://www.answersingenesis.org/docs/4128.asp. [Editor's Note: Ross's "self citation" represents a shorthand reference to an extensive bibliography on design evidence. With respect to the dissenting scientists cited, each is directly linked to a young-earth organization that publicly opposes Ross and his ministry.]

27. The heavy reliance of Ross and Archer on a secular cosmology, in this case the Big Bang theory, dies a natural death with the collapse of that theory. For interesting studies on this, see the recent publications: "A New Redshift Interpretation," by Robert V. Gentry (*Modern Physics A*, vol. 12, no. 37 (1997), pp. 2919–25; web posted at: http://arXiv.org/PS_cache/astro-ph/pdf/9806/9806280.pdf. In addition, Gentry's rebuttals of other Big Bang theorists are contained in his "The Genuine Cosmic Rosetta" (http://xxx.lanl.gov/gr-qc/9806061 or http://arXiv.org/PS_cache/gr-qc/pdf/9806/9806061.pdf) and "The New Redshift Interpretation Affirmed" (http://xxx.lanl.gov/physics/9810051 or http://arXiv.org/PS_cache/physics/pdf/9810/9810051.pdf).

28. The framework team believes that our unintentional shortening of the Kline quote is malicious and central to our argument. We assure readers that the quote is an unimportant point, hardly central to our position. But as with Newton, we never intended to take an author out of context (we shortened the quotation simply due to space considerations). We admit that fact and extend our apologies. Of course, we would expect the framework team to do the same regarding its appeals to Augustine, Anselm, Lombard, and "the early Aquinas." (Our citations from Aquinas about his 24-hour day view are from his final work, discontinued a year before his death due to illness.)

29. James H. Smylie, "America's Political Covenants, the Bible, and Calvinists," *Journal of Presbyterian History*, vol. 75, no. 3 (Fall 1997), p. 154.

30. *Treasury of David*, vol. 7, p. 238, commenting on Psa. 139:6 (emphasis added).

31. Andrew D. White, *A History of the Warfare of Science with Theology in Christendom* (New York: D. Appleton & Co., 1896), p. 60.

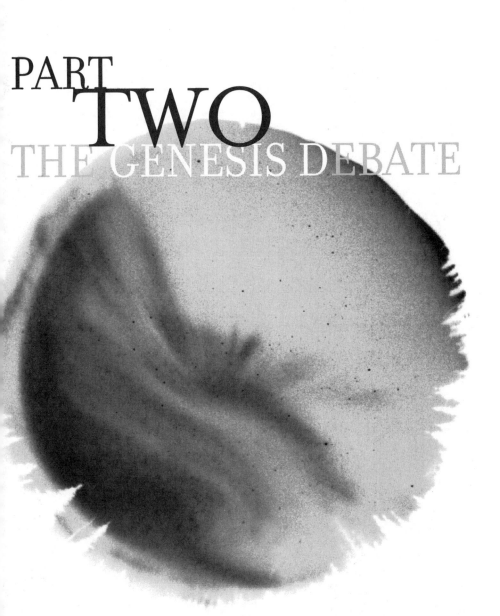

The Day-Age View

PART TWO

THE GENESIS DEBATE

Hugh Ross & Gleason L. Archer

THE DAY-AGE VIEW

he first chapter of Genesis has yielded many different day-age interpretations.[1] Our intent is to discuss and defend only one of them, in contrast with the 24-hour and framework views.

We build our day-age interpretation upon the conviction that we can trust God's revelation as truth in both the words of the Bible and the works of creation—including the entire physical universe. This conviction presupposes that truth is knowable, consistent, and, although sometimes paradoxical, never contradictory. Our day-age interpretation treats the creation days literally as six sequential, long periods of time. Integrating biblical and scientific data, we assert that the physical creation events reported in Genesis appear in correct sequence and in scientifically defensible terms.

The seventh day of God's creation week continues still. From the words of Scripture, we can infer that this seventh day will continue until God permanently conquers evil at the final judgment.[2] During this seventh day, God has ceased to miraculously intervene to prepare the planet for human habitation and to place human life upon it. His spiritual creation continues, however, and He intervenes in human affairs (before, during, and after the time of Jesus' earthly ministry) as He sees fit to fulfill His divine purposes.

Both Scripture and science suggest that the creation days begin in earth's primordial past. The creation of humanity at the end of the sixth creation day appears to be a relatively recent event. Both the biblical texts and scientific inquiry lead us to conclude that all humankind, *homo sapiens*, descended from Adam and Eve, who suddenly appeared no more than a few tens of thousands of years ago.

WHY THE CREATION-DAY CONTROVERSY?

Exegetical discussion of the Genesis creation account, and particularly of the meaning of *day*, abounds. Several authors, including us,[3] have presented the case for a day-age interpretation in some depth and detail. Obviously, we believe it to be a convincing case, one that uniquely upholds biblical inerrancy and answers the intractable problems we see in both the 24-hour and the framework views.[4] Evangelical support for the various interpretations has changed significantly,[5] however, since the time of our writings and the writings of others.[6] Despite these changes, the creation controversy persists. Why? We are convinced that many are hindered from resolving this controversy by nonexegetical issues.

The overarching hindrance is fear. People are afraid to integrate science and Scripture—some because they fear that science will shatter their confidence in Scripture, and others because they fear that science might shatter their excuse for ignoring Scripture. Who wants to talk about this fear? Most people would rather deny its existence or drown it out in noisy debate. But it lurks nonetheless, and its stranglehold keeps us from reasoning clearly and dialoguing calmly.

The salvo from one side says that the day-age view denies a literal reading of the Genesis text, disparages the character of God (by suggesting that He approves nature's "cruelty"), allows too much room for naturalism, and negates Christ's atoning sacrifice. The salvo from the other side says that the day-age view forces a literal reading of the Genesis text, allowing too little room for either literary license or scientific facts, particularly the facts of biological evolution. Meanwhile, secularists attack all who seek to defend the biblical creation account for their lack of a coherent, testable creation model.

We can only make progress toward resolving this controversy—both among ourselves as evangelicals[7] and between us and the secularists around us—as we face our fears and work through them. We must address these crucial concerns. Therefore, we begin our presentation by responding to the fears we have encountered initially, by demonstrating how the day-age view alone provides a coherent testable creation model,[8] and then, by proving our exegetical case for the day-age interpretation.

MULTIPLE LITERAL DEFINITIONS

Dispassionate discussion of the Genesis creation days often ends with the charge that the 24-hour interpretation alone is based on the one and only literal reading of the Genesis text. Those who advocate the 24-hour interpretation characterize competing views as neither plain nor literal. We contend, however, that the day-age interpretation is literal, and we support that contention with linguistic data. More importantly, we see the controversy in a wider frame of reference: the evangelical challenge is to discern which of the literal interpretations permits an internally and externally consistent reading of God's word—from Genesis to Revelation.

From the outset, we note that at least some of the acrimony over the interpretation of the Genesis days arises from language differences. Turning biblical Hebrew into English prose and poetry presents some enormous difficulties. Whereas biblical Hebrew has a vocabulary of under 3,100 words (not including proper nouns),[9] English words number over 4,000,000.[10] The disparity is even greater for nouns. Therefore, we should not be surprised that Hebrew nouns have multiple literal definitions.

The English word *day* most often refers either to the daylight hours or to a period of 24 hours. As in "the day of the Romans," it is also used for a longer time period. English speakers and writers, however, have many words for an extended period—age, era, epoch, and eon, just to name a few. The Hebrew word *yôm* similarly refers to daylight hours, 24 hours, and a long (but finite) time period.[11] Unlike English, however, biblical Hebrew has no word other than *yôm* to denote a long timespan.[12]

The word *yôm* appears repeatedly in the Hebrew Scriptures with reference to a period longer than 12 or 24 hours. The Hebrew terms *yôm* (singular) and *yamin* (plural) often refer to an extended time frame. Perhaps the most familiar passages are those referring to God's "day of wrath."

Before English translations were available, animosity over the length of the Genesis days did not exist, at least not as far as anyone can tell from the extant theological literature. Prior to the Nicene Council, the early Church fathers wrote two thousand pages of commentary on the Genesis creation days, yet did not devote a word to disparaging each other's viewpoints on the creation time scale.[13] All these early scholars accepted that *yôm* could mean "a long time period."[14] The majority explicitly taught that the Genesis creation days were extended time periods (something like a thousand years per yôm).[15] Not one Ante-Nicene Father explicitly endorsed the 24-hour interpretation. Ambrose, who came the closest to doing so, apparently vacillated on the issue.[16]

We certainly cannot charge the Church fathers with "scientific bias" in their interpretations. They wrote long before astronomical, geological, and paleontological evidences for the antiquity of the universe, the earth, and life became available. Nor had biological evolution yet been proposed. Lamarck, Darwin, and Huxley came along some 1,400 years later.

THE EVOLUTION FACTOR

The emergence of evolutionary theory gave impetus to the creation-day controversy. Late nineteenth- and early twentieth-century Darwinists, influenced by both science and philosophy, assumed that the seemingly endless expanse of the universe allowed an infinite or a nearly infinite time for life to "happen." They began to consider that all life on the earth (and perhaps elsewhere in the cosmos) could be explained by the operation of natural processes without *supernatural* involvement. Some scoffed at the biblical assertion that life was manufactured by God Himself.[17]

Tremendous animosity arose between naturalists and supernaturalists, and unfortunately, both sides mistakenly assumed that the origin time scale was the watershed issue. As astronomical advances proved the universe to be finite in time (only some ten to fifteen billion years old, in fact) many on both sides mistakenly assumed that billions of years would be ample time to account for naturalistic origin scenarios. This error has been costly to both sides. Biologists have spent years building models on wrong assumptions about the boundary conditions. A recent discovery of a much more limiting time boundary effectively negates naturalism, even for secular biologists.[18]

Young-earth creationists, on the other hand, have invested their efforts in fighting the wrong battle. What's worse, they have been battling their ally: scientific advance on virtually all fronts, which increasingly supports a theistic, interventionist (that is, miraculous) view of life's origin and development. Perhaps the most stunning irony of this decades-long controversy lies buried—but alive—in the creationist literature. Those who have leveled some of the most stinging criticism at old-earth creationists,[19] accusing them of being theistic evolutionists (those who believe God did not supernaturally intervene but merely initiated and controlled the outcome of natural process evolution), are actually forced by their own interpretation to be hyperevolutionists. Their apparent faith in the efficiency of natural-process biological evolution actually exceeds that of nontheists.

ANTI-EVOLUTIONISTS EMBRACE EVOLUTIONISM

Let us explain how the views of the young-earth creationists on the Fall (Adam and Eve's original sin) and the Flood drive them—knowingly or not—into this surprising corner. The first chapter of Genesis and other Bible passages state that after the sixth creation day, God ceased to introduce new life forms on the earth.[20] On this point, most interpreters agree. However, the young-earth creationists' understanding of the Fall and the Flood requires that a huge number of new species of animal life appear on the earth in just a few hundreds to thousands of years.

As they see it, animals ate only plants until the moment Adam and Eve rebelled against God's authority.[21] Because carnivorous activity involves animal death, they assume it must be one of the evil results of human sin. Therefore, they propose, all meat-eating creatures alive now and evident in the fossil record must have evolved rapidly from plant-eating creatures, and since God is no longer "creating," they must have evolved strictly by natural processes.[22]

The young-earth interpretation of the Flood account presents an equally serious problem. Young-earth advocates give themselves only thousands of years of earth's history to account for all the fossils and geological features, and hence, must invoke a global, extremely catastrophic Flood. Yet, even if all the animals aboard Noah's ark hibernated for the duration of the Flood, the ark's maximum carrying capacity, by their own estimates, would be about 30,000 pairs of land animals.[23] The fossil record, however, indicates the existence of at least a half billion species.[24] At least five million species are alive on the earth today,[25] and two million more lived in the era immediately after the Flood, as these interpreters date it. The problem grows worse. Shortly after the Flood, they say, a large proportion of the 30,000 species on board—dinosaurs, trilobites, etc.—became extinct. So, the remaining few thousand species must have evolved by rapid and efficient natural processes into four million or more land-dwelling species.

Thus, young-earth creationists propose an efficiency of natural biological speciation[26] greater than the most optimistic Darwinist has ever dared to suggest. They do so despite overwhelming physical evidence that denies the possibility for such rapid change. If naturalistic evolutionary processes actually did proceed with such speed, they would, of course, be observable in real time, in our time.

FEAR OF THE MILLIONS

This confidence in the superefficiency of biological evolution makes the young-earth creationists' extreme dogmatism on the time-scale issue more comprehensible. If Darwinian processes did work as smoothly and rapidly as young-earth creationists believe, a millions- or billions-of-years-old earth would seem to remove any need for God's involvement in the creation and diversification of life, the conclusion opposite to the one they whole-heartedly seek to defend.

From the perspective of young-earth creationists, any concession that the earth or universe may be more than about 10,000 years old attacks the very foundation of their faith, the veracity of the Scripture. Is it any wonder, then, that they vehemently and incessantly oppose anyone, even fellow evangelicals, who propose an ancient universe and earth?[27] The risks involved preclude their open-minded investigation of the scientific and biblical evidences for the earth's antiquity.[28]

Although young-earth creationists call themselves anti-evolutionists, their anti-evolutionism rests not on the inadequacy of naturalistic pro-cesses, regardless of time scale, but rather on their belief that these Dar-winian processes do not have sufficient time to produce nearly *all* the life forms we see on the face of the earth.

THE GNOSTIC FACTOR

The young-universe interpretation gives rise to a more subtle problem: it forces a gnostic-like theology—a belief that the physical realm is illusory and that only the spiritual realm is real. The universe by its sheer vast-ness testifies of a beginning much earlier than just a few or even several hundreds of thousands or millions of years ago. That testimony comes from light, which takes a certain amount of time to travel a given distance. For example, a galaxy measured to be about 13 billion light-years away must have existed about 13 billion years ago. That's when the light from that galaxy started on its way toward Earth's telescopes.

If its light had existed for only a few thousand years, the visible uni-verse would be very small indeed. The visible stars would be less numer-ous than is the observed case, and most of the Milky Way galaxy (as well as every other galaxy) would be invisible, since they are too far away for their light to have yet reached Earth. Adam wouldn't have seen any stars, Noah only a few, and Moses, thousands fewer than either Augustine or Aquinas.

Many seem to have forgotten a lesson from elementary science. Light travel time gives astronomers a direct window to the past. Because of light travel time, we can observe in the present moment what God did to the cosmos in the past. Astronomers need only select a heavenly body the ap-propriate distance away to see how it looked in the past. Even as we look at the moon, we see it not as it is this second, but rather as it was 1.5 seconds ago when the sun's light bounced off it on its way to us.

A few young-earth creationists explicitly concede that their view denies the reality of light travel. In his commentary on Genesis, for example, Gary North says,

> The Bible's account of the chronology of creation points to an illusion. . . . The seeming age of the stars is an illusion. . . . Either the constancy of the speed of light is an illusion, or the size of the universe is an illusion, or else the physical events that we hypothesize to explain the visible changes in light or radiation are false inferences.[29]

Others see light travel time as part of a myth concocted and disseminated by the astrophysical community, a deliberate lie religiously embraced and zealously perpetrated on others. In addressing the 1982 Annual Creation Convention, Russell Akridge made the following statement:

> Astrophysicists and astronomers have become the high priests of this decades-old cult. . . . [As] persuasive speakers [they] have deceived an unsuspecting public.[30]

Most young-earth/young-universe creationists, however, simply charge astronomers with collective naiveté and incompetence.[31] In their talks and writings, these creationists cite all the possible loopholes to the light-travel-time problem. They see six:

1. Astronomers are simply wrong about the distances.
2. God created the light already in transit.
3. Light traveled much faster in the past.
4. Light takes a shortcut through space.
5. The universe has the equivalent of more than one time dimension.
6. Distant "clocks" run at different rates.

The scientific impossibility and biblical implausibility of the first five loopholes is explained in considerable detail in three books, *Creation and Time*, *The Creator and the Cosmos*, and *Beyond the Cosmos*.[32] Little has been written in response to the sixth loophole for two reasons. First, it contradicts so much astronomical data[33] that it scarcely deserves to be taken seriously. Second, published articles by a number of scientists did a thorough (though somewhat technical) job of exposing its fatal mathematical flaws.[34] In a nutshell, God scattered astronomical "clocks" (time-indicating astronomical phenomena such as cosmic expansion rates, background radiation cooling times, supernovae, Cepheid variable stars, neutron stars, and black holes) throughout the universe, and they all agree. They reflect no differ-ences of time rate or dimensionality anywhere in the cosmos and thus at any epoch in cosmic history.

In embracing any of these supposed loopholes, the 24-hour creation-ists inadvertently and ultimately suggest that God, rather than the astro-nomical community, deceives us. Their interpretation implies that all the distant galaxies astronomers observe—nearly one trillion of them—are part of an elaborate mirage or a misconstrued "mural" painted on a nearby back-ground, which becomes visible nightly. On their view, stellar explosions such as the 1987 supernova eruption in our companion galaxy, the Large Magellanic Cloud, did not really occur; they just appear to have occurred. According to 24-hour day creationists, what astronomers observe in the heavens must be a detailed history of events that never happened.

Supposed biblical support for the "appearance of age" rests primarily on Adam's adult shoulders. Adam's adult body seems, at first glance, to argue for appearance of age. But does it? An adult body speaks of age only if we incorrectly assume that this body entered the world through the womb of a woman. We must go on to ask whether or not Adam carried memo-ries of his nonexistent childhood. To assume that he did would be to as-sume that God implanted falsehoods, a notion that virtually all believers would repudiate as a violation of God's revealed character.[35] The connec-tion with the day-age interpretation is this: The universe carries a kind of "memory" of the past. That memory is the light emitted long ago by dis-tant objects. This light shows us what was happening at those objects in the past, at the time the light was emitted. From the astronomer's per-spective, "appearance of age" implies that God filled the universe with the physical equivalent of false memories.

From the logician's standpoint, appearance of age represents a "non-falsifiable proposition," an assertion that cannot be proved or disproved. Taken to its inevitable conclusion, the hypothesis implies that we cannot be sure of our own or anyone else's past existence. We could have been created just a few hours ago with implanted scars, memories, progeny, pho-tographs, material possessions, liver spots, and hardening of the arteries to make us appear, feel, and believe ourselves older than we really are. In this case, even biblical history would be an illusion.

Although young-earth/young-universe creationists assume that they truly seek to defend the truth of God's word and lead people to Jesus Christ, they fail to realize that these theological implications flow from their po-sition. We think that they would repudiate the gnostic notion that "there is no life, truth, or substance in matter,"[36] though unfortunately that's the direction in which their view leans. According to Scripture, it's a potentially dangerous direction since God calls all of His creation "good," and since, after the Fall, all of us sin in the physical realm. Even more significantly, the assertion that matter is devoid of life and truth is then falsified by the fact that our Lord became a man—took on matter as the way, the truth, and the life—to save us from our sin.[37] To deny life, truth, and substance to matter is, at a minimum, to deny the biblical doctrines of creation, sin, Christ, and salvation. Ultimately, this view denies the Bible itself.

DEATH AND EXTINCTION BEFORE ADAM

Another emotion-packed issue hindering civil discussion of the creation controversy is that of death, including the extinction of entire species, before the moment of Adam and Eve's original sin. Many Christians associate death of any kind with evil. To think otherwise shakes their conception of a kind and loving God. They see multiplied generations of death and extinction as inconsistent with God's character and with His description of the creation as "very good." The death and extinction we see in history must result, they conclude, from humanity's Fall.

We can infer from Genesis 2, however, that the death of at least plants or plant parts and insects must have occurred before Adam and Eve sinned. Animals moved about and ate. Adam and Eve also walked and ate. Try to imagine an elephant's moving or eating without crushing an ant or two along with some grass and leaves. While several young-earth creationists argue that the Bible never attributes life and death to plants and lower animals,[38] many Scripture passages explicitly state that they do indeed experience life and death.[39]

Many Christians seem to forget that Adam and Eve were not the first creatures to sin. According to Scripture, Satan committed the first sin. When Satan sinned, he brought about his own spiritual death and the spiritual death of all the angels who joined him in his rebellion against God. Through Adam and Eve, Satan infected the human race with sin, but even that seeming disaster fits into God's plan for conquering evil and revealing His grace and glory.

Several more assumptions pour fuel on the fire of this controversy. First, young-earth advocates assume that a "very good" creation means a "perfect" creation in every sense of the word. Contrary to this assumption, Revelation 21 and 22 declare that a superior creation is yet to come, and it will follow God's "wrapping up" of the present creation. In Romans 8 and Revelation 20–21, we read that one purpose of our present cosmos is to provide a just-right setting for God's rapid and permanent conquest of evil. While the characteristics of the universe and the earth are ideal for this conquest of evil, they are less than perfect for glorified creatures, that is, for humans and angels who have been permanently delivered from the presence, power, and penalty of sin. God is preparing to move us into a far superior realm, the new creation.[40]

Second, young-earth advocates assume that Adam's sin is responsible for all manner of death. Two passages of Scripture refute this assumption by identifying the kind of death introduced by Adam's sin: Romans 5:12 and 1 Corinthians 15:21. Both passages explicitly state that Adam brought death to himself and to all human beings born of him by ordinary generation (i.e., all human beings other than Christ). We find no exegetical basis for including plants and animals in that introduction of death. More specifically, the death Adam introduced was "death through sin." Only humans among all the earth's creatures are capable of sinning, of violating God's moral code, hence, of experiencing the death that comes through sin. As Romans 5 and Genesis 3 tell us, Adam's sin brought about immediate spiritual consequences—spiritual death—which was followed later by physical death.[41] Wonderfully, God's grace provided for spiritual regeneration, making physical death an eternal blessing, setting human beings free from their mortal bodies to live forever in imperishable ones in the very presence of God.

Third, young-earth advocates assume that carnivorous activity is bad. Responding to this assumption requires us to compare several Bible passages. When we hold Genesis 1:29, 1:30, and 9:2–3 side by side, we see that God gave humanity some specific dietary guidelines appropriate to their circumstances. At first, humans lived for thousands of years, and a vegetarian diet was essential for their long-term health. Later, God shortened human life spans to about 120 years.[42] Within that time context, He changed the guidelines and permitted His human creatures to consume animals. Meat consumption poses no significant health risk within that shorter life span. With reference to animals, who rely on instinct rather than on choice in their eating habits, His comments were aimed at human managers and reflect no change from one passage and time frame to the next. He simply states and reiterates the importance of green plants. We know that both animals and humans ingest some non-green plants, such as mushrooms; but green plants are the foundation of the food chain. It seems likely that to assist Adam and Eve and all subsequent generations in their management of the planet's resources for the benefit of all life, God emphasizes to them (and to us) that all life depends ultimately on green plants for survival.

Fourth, young-earth advocates assume that death and extinction are bad in all contexts. Understanding a basic physical principle helps over-turn this assumption. That principle, known as the second law of thermo-dynamics, is familiar to most people as "the law of decay." This law states that heat flows from hot bodies to cold. Young-earth creationists deny that this thermodynamic law operated before Adam's sin.[43] They see it as some-thing bad primarily because death, extinction, and disorder are its inevi-table consequences. Both Scripture and science say otherwise. Romans 8:19–21 explains that God, not Satan, subjected the creation to this law, not in punishment but in hope and promise of the freedom that lies ahead. No stars would shed light (stars are near-perfect expressions of the second law[44]) nor would any creature be able to digest food, work, or physically move about apart from the operation of this thermodynamic law.[45] These conclusions are consistent with the observations of astronomers who, as they look back in time, see no interruptions in the operation of the sec-ond thermodynamic law.[46] Genesis certainly makes clear that the physical realities of starlight, eating, working, and physical movement preceded Adam and Eve's sin.[47]

While death and extinction from a human perspective seem horrible, they also bring certain benefits. By creating humans after millions of gen-erations of other creatures lived and died, God gave us rich resources of top soil, coal, oil, gas, limestone, marble, and kerogen, among other things.[48] The civilization that enables us to carry out a rapid completion of the Great Commission is based on the abundance of these resources.

Another benefit is the unique relationship we humans enjoy with car-nivorous birds and mammals. During the sixth creation day, God created easy-to-tame "soulish" animals (herbivorous birds and mammals) and difficult-to-tame "soulish" animals (carnivorous birds and mammals). The former make excellent farm animals, but because eating and digestion domi-nate their lives and limit their physical capabilities, they make poor pets. Carnivores, on the other hand, are more active, are easy to feed and house-break, and can be trained to live with us, even inside our homes. We can enjoy a deeper relationship with them because their lives are not so domi-nated by eating and digestion. In this context, carnivores are not "bad." They are animals God created to enrich our lives. It can even be said, though it takes more explanation, that carnivores benefit the populations of herbivores on which they feed.[49]

From a biblical standpoint alone, apart from our knowledge of science, we have reasons to reject the assumptions made by young-earth advocates and outlined above.

WHY NO VIABLE CREATION MODEL?

While all our fears and defenses have been significant stumbling blocks, we see a more significant hindrance to the impact of the Christian worldview on our society, especially among academics and intellectuals. That hindrance actually represents a momentous opportunity. The gauntlet has been thrown, and we are guaranteed the victory if we have the courage, integrity, and vigor to pick it up. The gauntlet is this: Don't simply bash biological evolution. Give us a creation model that can withstand scientific testing. The halls of higher learning echo with the accusation that we Christians preach Genesis without accepting the responsibility to present a viable creation model. We are perceived by many scholars, and thus by the society they influence, as either negative or cowardly. They see us blasting away at naturalism while ducking the challenge to present a specific, verifiable origins scenario. We must take up this challenge. Our effectiveness in fulfilling our God-given assignment on the earth depends upon it. Many thinking people, well-educated or not, will be helped toward committing their lives to Christ when they see a creation model that successfully predicts future discoveries and withstands the assaults of skeptics.

Perhaps the greatest factor preventing us from developing such a model is a pervasive defeatism among evangelicals. Many Christians see no possibility for integrating the record of nature with the words of Genesis. Writing nearly a hundred years ago, German theologian Friedrich Delitzsch described the schism in words that few would care to dispute to this day:

> How absolutely futile all attempts are and will forever remain to harmonize our biblical story of the creation with the results of natural science.[50]

This defeatism is understandable given the widespread failure to apply the scientific method to the interpretation of Genesis. The great irony here is that the scientific method comes from the Bible and from biblical theology.[51] The core of this method is an appeal to the interpreter to delay drawing conclusions until both the frame of reference and the initial conditions have been established. If we approach Genesis in this way, we discover that we can discern an account of creation that is scientifically plausible and defensible.

A MODEL EMERGES

The frame of reference in Genesis 1:1 is the cosmos, the beginning of space, time, matter, and energy. God declares through His spokesman, Moses, that He brought into existence the entire physical cosmos. The Bible successfully predicts what has been called "the discovery of the century," the observation of remnants from that initial creative burst.[52] Einstein's equations told us early in this century that the universe had a beginning in the finite past, but scientists subjected that notion to every test imaginable before acknowledging certainty about it. Einstein's equations now tell us that the *Cause* of the universe created it independently of all matter, energy, and even the ten space-time dimensions along which all the matter and energy are distributed.[53] The work on which the 1994 Nobel physics prize was based establishes this conclusion to better than 14-decimal-point precision.[54] All this testing has done the Christian community a great service, providing support for our confidence in biblical revelation.

Genesis 1:2 explicitly shifts the frame of reference, the narrator's vantage point, to the surface of the earth. That verse describes the initial conditions of primordial earth. Its surface was dark, covered with water, empty of life, and unfit for life.[55] With the frame of reference and the initial conditions for the six creation days thus established, a straightforward chronology for the creation days' events unfolds.[56] That chronology is as follows:

1. Creation of the entire physical universe (ten space-time dimensions, matter, energy, galaxies, stars, planets, etc.) by God's fiat miracle.

2. Singling out the earth for a sequence of creation miracles. At its beginning, it is empty of life and unfit for life; the earth's primordial atmosphere and the solar system's interplanetary debris prevent the light of the Sun, Moon, and stars from reaching the surface of the earth's ocean.

3. Clearing of the interplanetary debris and partial transformation of the earth's atmosphere so that light from the heavenly bodies now penetrates to the surface of earth's ocean.

4. Formation of water vapor in the troposphere under conditions that establish a stable water cycle.

5. Formation of continental land masses and ocean basins.

6. Creation of plants on the continental land masses.

7. Transformation of the atmosphere from perpetually translucent to occasionally transparent. Sun, moon, planets, and stars now can be seen from the vantage point of the earth's surface as distinct objects.

8. Creation of swarms of small sea animals.

9. Creation of sea mammals and birds by God's fiat miracles

10. Creation by God of three specialized kinds of land mammals, all specifically designed to cohabit with humans: (1) short-legged land mammals, (2) long-legged land mammals that are easy to tame, and (3) long-legged land mammals that are difficult to tame.

11. Creation of the human species by God's fiat miracle.

This biblical chronology allows one to turn the tables on the evolutionists (those seeking a naturalistic explanation for the changes in life forms over earth's history). For several decades now, evolutionists have pointed to "transitional forms" in the fossil record for proof that their explanation for life's history is correct.[57] The fact that the bone structures of certain large land-dwelling mammals (the mesonychids),[58] ancient fresh-water-drinking whales, ancient salt-water-drinking whales, and modern whales exhibit an apparent progression persuades them that modern whales naturally evolved from land-dwelling mammals. Evolutionists often cite this progression as their best demonstration of Darwinian evolution.

In reality, the evolutionists' "best example" is their worst. No animal is less efficient at evolving than the whales. No animal has a higher probability for extinction than the whales. Many factors severely limit their capacity for natural-process change and greatly enhance their probability for rapid extinction. The six most significant are:

- Relatively small population levels
- Long generation spans (the time between birth and the ability to procreate)
- Low numbers of progeny produced per adult
- High complexity of morphology and biochemistry
- Enormous sizes
- Specialized food supplies

These factors limit not only the whales' capacity to change through natural selection and mutations, but even their ability to adapt to change. Because of these six factors, small environmental changes would tend to drive whales rapidly to extinction.

The same conclusions can be drawn for the so-called descent of horses. The factors affecting whales also severely restrict the capacity of horses to survive internal and external changes. Indeed, ecologists have observed several extinctions of horse and whale species during human history, *never* a significant change within a species, much less the appearance of a new one.

Genesis offers this explanation: God created the first sea mammals on the fifth creation day. As the fossil record documents, sea mammals have

persisted on the earth from that epoch until now, though not without interruption. The multiple extinctions of sea mammals imply that God repeatedly replaced extinct species with new ones. In most cases, the new
species were different from the previous ones because God was changing
earth's geology, biodeposits, and biology, step by step, to prepare for His
ultimate creation on the earth—the human race.

The many "transitional" forms of whales and horses suggest that God
did more than just perform a few creative acts here and there, letting natural
evolution fill in the rest. Rather, God was involved and active in creating
new species.

For both secularists and many believers, God's replacement of species
of whales, horses, and bipedal primates that have just experienced extinction with new species of whales, horses, and bipedal primates seems counter
to the character and attributes of the God of the Bible. For them, an all-
powerful, all-loving Creator should only need to create life at one time.
Progressive creation appears to connote a bumbling, stupid, wasteful, or
cruel Creator.

What these secularists and believers fail to appreciate is that God created the universe and all life in the universe not just for the benefit of
humanity, but for the benefit of His angelic and future creations as well.
As already stated, the Bible reveals that Satan and his followers (demons)
introduced evil before Adam and Eve rebelled in Eden. We can infer from
Romans 8 and Revelation 20–22 that God created the universe for the
purpose of conquering all evil once and for all.[59] These same chapters help
us understand that gravity, electromagnetism, thermodynamics, and consequently a universe characterized by three large expanding dimensions of
space and a finite dimension of time,[60] all play a part in evil's conquest.
These necessary factors require that the physical conditions of the universe and the earth change dramatically over time. For example, even during its most stable burning phase, the sun brightens by about 8 percent
per billion years. Also, Earth's rotation rate lengthens by about four hours
per day per billion years. These conditions imply that Earth, the solar system, and the universe must fit within a narrowly constrained set of characteristics for physical life to survive.[60]

These conditions also lead to some deductions. For humanity to be
provided with an abundance of limestone, marble, ozone, oxygen, water,
top soil, coal, oil, gas, salt, phosphate, gypsum, etc., millions of generations of life would need to predate us. Because the physical realm changes
with time, God apparently created different species at different times to
suit the changing environment. For instance, only the most primitive and
tiny forms of life could survive the eight-hour-per-day rotation period of

early earth.[61] Because highly advanced life requires a more delicately balanced set of characteristics for survival than primitive life, such life forms are much more vulnerable to extinction. But when such species became extinct, God created new ones, sometimes the same, and more often different (according to environmental and ecological conditions and divine timing) to replace them.

The step-by-step approach to bipedal primate creation we see in the recent fossil record[62] may reasonably reflect God's understanding of the difficulty other life forms would encounter in adapting to sinful humans. The eco-crises we see in so many places of the world provide abundant testimony to that difficulty. Given this context, we can see that the bipedal primates predating Adam and Eve reflect care rather than waste. Their presence and activities helped prepare the other animals for future shock, the human beings' arrival.

The changing physical conditions on the earth imply, too, that relatively little time remains for humanity. Soon (within about 50 million years) the silicate-carbonate cycle will no longer be able to compensate for the ongoing brightening of the sun.[63] Soon (within about a million years) a supernova will explode too close. Soon (within about 10 million years) a large asteroid or comet will crash. Soon (within about 20 million years) the earth will rotate too slowly and manifest too little plate tectonics, volcanism, nitrogen fixation, etc., for the support of human life.[64] Like the whales, we are such poor evolvers that even before any of these environmental catastrophes strike, we could find ourselves biologically degenerating into extinction. The fastest path to our demise may be our sin.

What we can deduce from all this is that God created humanity at the end of the window of time for life on the earth so that we can be blessed and equipped with the maximum possible resources. He has mandated us to use these rich resources effectively and quickly to fulfill His purpose before the window of time completely closes. In so doing, we humans need spend only the briefest possible moment in this creation to prepare for eternity in the far superior new creation to come.

Although we could reflect on many more reasons why God created in this step-by-step fashion, Hugh Ross has discussed some of these reasons in detail elsewhere.[65] In any event, the reasons we have discussed above are sufficient to trace the contours of a creation model true to the words of the Bible and the record of nature.

TESTING THE DAY-AGE CREATION MODELS

The unique beauty of the day-age creation model is its ability to accurately predict advancing scientific discovery. This ability to predict is the hallmark of any reliable theory. By contrast, Darwinian evolution,[66] chaos theory,[67] and six consecutive 24-hour-day creationism fail to predict and, in fact, contradict the growing body of data. The framework interpretation offers no model for life's history and, therefore, cannot be tested. For purposes of this discussion, we limit ourselves to describing briefly seven successful predictions made by our day-age creation model.

Missing Horizontal Branches in the Fossil Record

Most biology textbooks depict the fossil record as a tree. All the various life forms branch off from a single trunk. The root represents the first life form that appeared on the earth. As the fossil data accumulates, it offers less and less support to this popular notion that life forms gradually and continuously drift from one morphological type to another and eventually to radically different ones. What the growing database does show is that many life forms persisted through several millennia without significant morphological change, then became extinct.

The extinct species or a similar species sometimes reappears after a long gap. But the appearance of these new species occurs suddenly without any natural mechanism to explain it. This fossil pattern contradicts naturalism, but it precisely fits what the day-age creation model predicts. According to that model, God supernaturally introduced new species, sometimes with little change, sometimes with significant change, replacing those that became extinct.

The day-age creation model predicts that future paleontological research will reveal more of these extinction-and-replacement episodes in earth's history. We also expect to see stronger evidence for stasis in long-existing species. For the more advanced life forms, the lack of evidence for missing links (the horizontal branches) and the stability of evidence for vertical branches in the fossil record should become even more pronounced than they already are.

Fossil Record Reversal

Again, most biology textbooks show the fossil record as a tree with a single trunk from which more and more branches grow throughout the millennia. According to the standard diagram, species continually become more numerous, more diverse, and more complExo. This pattern is at least partially accurate (especially if we remove the arbitrarily introduced horizontal branches), but only until the appearance of humanity. Then the pattern becomes demonstrably incorrect. Since the advent of human beings, the branching-tree pattern has essentially reversed. As time advances, fewer and fewer species remain on the earth, and the most advanced species show the fastest extinction rates. Naturalism has yet to offer a plausible explanation for this change.

This reversal is perfectly consistent, however, with the day-age creation model. According to this model, for six epochs God continues creating new species and replacing certain extinct ones. Then, with the creation of humans on the sixth day (age), His physical creation is complete. Throughout the six extended creation periods, God designs and introduces millions of new species of life. With the last creative act of the sixth day, the creation of Adam and Eve, God's activity in creating new species ends. Before Adam and Eve, the history of life was shaped predominantly by supernatural interventions. Since the introduction of humans, any changes we observe reflect natural processes.

Speciation and Extinction Rates

While researchers observe some limited speciation in the plant kingdom, virtually none is observed among animals. Many books and articles address this concern, and despite intense investigative efforts in this decade, they can only reiterate this succinct statement by Paul and Anne Ehrlich in their book *Extinctions*:

> The production of a new animal species in nature has yet to be documented. Biologists have not been able to observe the entire sequence of one animal species being transformed into two or more. . . . In the vast majority of cases, the rate of change is so slow that it has not even been possible to detect an increase in the amount of differentiation.[68]

We must contrast this finding with the exceptionally high speciation rate (an average of approximately one new species per year) observed from the time known as the Cambrian explosion (543 million years ago) until the appearance of humanity.[69]

Based on current observations of natural processes, nontheistic science can offer no plausible explanation for the Cambrian explosion with its burgeoning of life forms which continued so persistently, stopped, then reversed. What we see in real time is that natural speciation occurs only within those species with huge populations, short generation times, large numbers of progeny per adult, etc. given the ratio of harmful mutations to beneficial mutations (estimates range from 10,000:1 to 10,000,000:1), the only life forms with the possibility for mutational advance are those with high populations (about a quadrillion or more) and short generation times (period from birth to reproductive maturity of about three months or less).[70]

Viruses and bacteria serve as our best examples. Species with fewer individuals and longer generation times typically become extinct before any significant, survivable morphological or genetic changes can occur. This conclusion is entirely consistent with real-time field observations.[71]

The day-age creation model again predicts the observation. Speciation is abundant before the advent of humanity since, according to Genesis 1, that was the era during which God supernaturally created large numbers of new phyla, families, orders, genera, and species. Speciation is limited to natural-process advance after the advent of humanity, for this is the era of God's rest, His cessation from His work of creating new species, genera, etc. The very limited speciation we do see during God's rest era is consistent with the words used to describe God's creative activity during the six creation days.[72]

Recent Origin of Humanity

While the biblical genealogies offer no help in determining creation dates for the universe and the earth, they do assist interpreters' efforts to estimate the date of Day 6's culminating event, the creation of Adam and Eve. When we consider that the Hebrew words translated into English as "father" and "son" literally mean "progenitor" and "progeny," we discover that the Genesis genealogies, as well as those elsewhere in Scripture, are both accurate and adequate but certainly incomplete.[73] We see enough overlap, however, among the genealogies to set some realistic boundaries on the time line for humanity.[74] Conservative estimates among biblical scholars for the creation of Adam and Eve range from about 10,000 to 60,000 years ago.[75]

The opportunity to test this part of the day-age model has arisen very recently. It has come through advances in molecular biology, specifically in the instrumentation and techniques for research. With the capacity to study mitochondrial DNA and y-chromosomes has come the ability to study humanity's "genetic clock." We can expect more refinements in this area, but today's best understanding of this DNA research data places the first woman at about 50,000 years ago[76] and the most recent common ancestor of men (which would be Noah, rather than Adam, according to the biblical record) at 37,000–49,000 years ago.[77]

The potential impact of this new research capability and of the data it provides is enormous, but it will take some time to trickle down to the popular media and even longer to textbooks and educators. Already it is producing some profound earthquakes in the territory of evolutionary gradualists. For example, as investigators examine the mitochondrial DNA of Neanderthals (the only nonhuman bipedal primate species known to live during the past half million years), they find it so different from the mitochondrial DNA of homo sapiens that the "descent of man" theory becomes wholly implausible.[78] Similar studies comparing the y-chromosomes of humans, chimpanzees, gorillas, and orangutans demonstrate that these different species cannot have arisen naturally from a common ancestor.[79] Yet again, the biblical account fits the accumulating data, which nontheistic theory contradicts.

The relatively recent advent of humankind also finds support in the growing body of anthropological, astronomical, and geological research. The most ancient remnant of advanced art has been dated as 32,000 years old.[80] The Vela supernova, which showered the earth with life-shortening radiation, erupted 20,000–30,000 years ago.[81] Land bridges that made possible human migration to Australia and the Americas formed 12,000–30,000 years ago and 11,000–14,500 years ago, respectively.[82] The most ancient artifacts of religious expression, such as idols and altars, have been dated at 8,000–24,000 years ago.[83] All these findings support the biblical day-age creation scenario and the subsequent chapters of Genesis, as well.

Huge Biodeposits

The earth's crust contains an abundance of biological resources essential for advanced life such as top soil, coal, oil, gas, kerogen (including tar sands and oil-rich shales), limestone, and marble. The day-age model predicts that these resources would be laid down in the systematic course of creation events occurring over the few billion years of earth's history. These resources are orders of magnitude beyond anything possible in a young-earth creation paradigm.[84] In addition to fitting the scientific data, their existence also fits what we can project as the best-possible scenario for humanity: God created primitive life at the first possible opportunity afforded by the earth's changing environment,[85] and He created human life at the last possible opportunity.[86] As a result of this timing, we humans have at our disposal the greatest possible biodeposits for quickly developing civilization and ultimately for disseminating the Good News of salvation in Jesus Christ.

Rapid Origin of Life

The day-age model predicts that some forms of life would be abundant on the earth from very early in the planet's history. Again, this finding has been corroborated in well-established research data. Such data shows that life has been plentiful on the earth for the past 3.86 billion years.[87] This early date, however, overlaps the era of intense asteroidal bombardment by some 400 million years.[88] Astronomers estimate that the earth was literally "sterilized" (cleansed of all living species) at least several dozen times during that era. If we average the number of sterilizations over the timespan in which they occurred, we are forced to conclude that life must have "revived" at least once, if not more often, in a period of less than five million years.

If life did originate by spontaneous self-assembly in less than five million years under natural (and, we might add, "adverse") conditions, then to make it in the lab would be a trivial matter for today's richly endowed biochemists. In reality, though, our best efforts cannot succeed in even the simplest step, the task of selecting out the necessary right-handed nucleotide sugars and the left-handed amino acids. Mathematical biologist Harold Morowitz calculated that the much more difficult assembly process would require at least $10^{100,000,000,000}$ years.[89] (Note: The universe has existed for only 10^{10} years by astronomers' reliable measurements.)

Supernatural creation by a transcendent Creator is the only possible explanation for life's origin. Repeated origins of life during earth's early history shows God's intent to ensure that humans possess the maximum biodeposits.

The Perfect Fit of Genesis with the Fossil Record

Virtually every human culture tells its own story of beginnings. Creation stories express the values, the religious beliefs, and the worldview of a culture. To study them is to learn important truths about the people whose lives they both reflect and shape—and to discover common threads binding all peoples together. From a Western, objective-reality-based perspective, they belong to the genre we call "myth." They are imaginary or unverifiable narratives, in this case explaining origins. The Genesis creation story as interpreted by both the 24-hour creationists and framework proponents would be placed in the category of myth. The former defy the established data, suggesting that science is "imaginary," while the latter suggest that science is irrelevant.

Day-age creationists, however, see the Genesis creation narrative as an artistically exquisite *and objectively provable* account passed along by the Creator Himself to a human author by the agency of the Holy Spirit. In defiance of all the laws of probability, this ancient spokesperson described the initial creation event (commonly referred to as the Big Bang), the scientifically-verified initial conditions of the earth, and the scientifically verified sequence of events leading up to, and including, the appearance of modern man and the progress of civilization.[90] The march of scientific knowledge has never really threatened the accuracy and authority of this account. Instead, it offers progressively greater proof for divine inspiration and inerrancy.[91]

Uniqueness of the Day-Age Interpretation

Much has been written on the exegetical evidences for our day-age interpretation of Genesis 1.[92] A central thrust of such writing is to establish
the day-age view as both literal and consistent. Biblical consistency, which
we feel has been undervalued[93] in the interpretation debate, remains a pil-
lar of our day-age model. The unique feature of this view, compared to the
24-hour and framework views, is its ability to yield an internally, as well
as externally, consistent reading of all 66 books of the Bible.

Once we remove the emotional barriers, the exegetical clouds will clear,
and we can make progress toward unity and cooperation. The evangelistic
impact of such a resolution will be enormous. Opposition to the gospel
will remain, but it will be focused on the central figure, Jesus Christ, rather
than on peripheral, distracting controversies.

BIBLICAL EVIDENCES FOR LONG CREATION DAYS

We conclude that the Genesis days are literal, chronologically sequenced
long days or epochs. In addition to the biblical arguments we have made
already, several other arguments compel us to adopt the day-age interpretation.

The Long Time Required by the End of the Sixth Day

Genesis 1 tells us that three different kinds of specialized land mammals
and *both* Adam and Eve were created on the sixth day. Genesis 2 provides
further amplification, listing events between Adam's creation and Eve's.
First, God planted a garden in Eden, making "all kinds of trees to grow
out of the ground." The wording indicates that these trees were permitted
to grow and mature from seeds. Then Adam, after receiving instructions
from God, worked and cared for the Garden of Eden. The passage implies
that Adam was diligently occupied with his assigned tasks of pruning, har-
vesting, and keeping the ground free of brush and undergrowth, and, according to Genesis 2:18, for a long enough period to lose his initial
excitement and thrill at this wonderful occupation in the beautiful paradise of Eden.

Next, Adam carried out his assignment from God to name all the
soulish animals (the *nephesh* creatures—those endowed by God with mind,
will, and emotions, including all the birds and mammals). It must have
taken a good deal of study for Adam to examine each specimen thoroughly
and decide on a suitable name, especially since he had absolutely no tradition in nomenclature behind him. In the process Adam discovered that
though the animals offered much more fulfillment for him than the merely

physical plants, none of these soulish creatures was a suitable helper and companion for him.

Apparently, Adam had sufficient interaction and time with both the plants and *nephesh* animals of the garden to realize that something was still missing from his life. Next, God put Adam into a deep sleep, performed an operation, and after Adam awoke, introduced him to the newly created Eve.

Adam's exclamation on seeing Eve is recorded in Genesis 2:23 as *happa'am*. This expression is usually translated as "now at length" (see also Gen. 29:34–35; 30:20; 46:30; Judges 15:3), roughly equivalent to our English expression "at last."

Still later on the sixth day, Adam and Eve received instructions from God concerning their responsibilities and strategic plans for managing all the resources of the planet for the benefit of all life—a lengthy communication, one can imagine. Altogether, many weeks', months', or even years' worth of activities took place in this latter portion of the sixth day.

Some 24-hour creation day proponents argue that Adam's intelligence was so much higher before he sinned that he could do all these tasks at superhuman speed. This argument fails to account for Adam's response to Eve and, just as important, for the following five facts:

- No biblical basis can be found for suggesting that Adam functioned at superhuman speed before he sinned.

- The Bible never claims that intellect (as opposed to wisdom) is correlated with the degree of sin in one's life. Intellect is not a reliable measure of freedom from sin.

- Greater intellect would not significantly impact Adam's sixth-day tasks and experiences.

- In his perfect state, Adam would be more meticulous in performing his God-assigned tasks.

- Jesus, though He was perfect in every way, did not perform His carpentry work and other everyday activities at a much faster than normal rate.

The Continuation of the Seventh Day

Moses wrote of the first six creation days, "There was evening, and there was morning—the [X]th day." This wording provides a pattern, a framework (to borrow a word), for the events of each of the first six creation days. Each had a starting time and an ending time. However, no such wording is attached to the seventh day, neither in Genesis nor anywhere else in the Bible. Given the parallel structure marking the creation days, this distinct change in the pattern for narrating the seventh day strongly suggests that this day had (or has) not yet ended.

Further information about the seventh day is given in Psalm 95 and Hebrews 4. In these passages, we learn that God's day of rest continues. The Hebrews writer describes it thus:

> For somewhere [God] has spoken about the seventh day in these words: "And on the seventh day God rested from all his work." . . . It still remains that some will enter that rest. . . . There remains, then, a Sabbath-rest for the people of God; for anyone who enters God's rest also rests from his own work, just as God did from his. Let us, therefore, make every effort to enter that rest. (4:4–11)

According to this passage, the seventh day of the creation week carries on through the centuries from Adam and Eve, through Israel's development as a nation, through the time of Christ's earthly ministry, through the early days of the apostolic Church, and on into future years. In Psalm 95:7–11, King David also refers to God's seventh day of rest as ongoing.

From these passages, we gather that the seventh day of Genesis 1–2 represents a minimum of several thousand years and a maximum that is open-ended (but finite). Given the parallelism of the Genesis creation account, it seems reasonable to conclude that the first six days may also have been long time periods.

Supporting evidence for the seventh day as an ongoing period of rest from creating comes from John 5:16–18. Here Jesus defended His act of healing on the Sabbath by saying that God, His Father, "is always at his work to this very day, and I, too, am working." Jesus' appeal is that He is honoring the Sabbath in the same way as is His Father. That is, His Father works "to this very day" even though this very day is part of His Sabbath rest period. God—both the Son and Father—honors His Sabbath by ceasing from the work of creating. The Sabbath does not preclude healing people any more than it precludes a man from changing his baby's diaper. As already mentioned, a seventh day ongoing from Eve's creation answers the problem of observing abundant speciation in the fossil record but virtually none under real-time investigations.

The Rest (Cessation) from Creating and Future Re-creation
According to Revelation 21, once God permanently conquers evil, He will replace this present universe with an entirely new one. Though God has not physically created since He formed Eve, His Sabbath day of rest is scheduled to end. With evil no longer a factor, the purpose for our universe will have been fulfilled. Therefore, God will "roll up" this universe, with its

laws of physics and its space-time dimensions.[94] He will replace it with something He identifies as the new heavens, a new earth, and a new Jerusalem, with laws of physics and dimensionality or supra-dimensionality designed to make possible our eternal life and rewards in His presence.[95]

The creation week described in Genesis 1 is only the beginning. God will create again. His period of rest or cessation from creating has a definite beginning point in the past (right after the creation of Eve) and an ending point in the future (when God creates the new heavens and earth). Thousands of years are passing between this beginning and ending. The parallel structure in the description of the seven Genesis creation days suggests, then, that the other days are also longer than 24 hours.

God's Days Not Necessarily the Same as Our Days
The same author of Genesis (Moses) wrote in Psalm 90:4, "For a thousand years in your sight are like a day that has just gone by, or like a watch [four hours] in the night." Moses seems to state that just as God's ways are not our ways (Isa. 55:9), God's days are not our days.

The Wording of Genesis 2:4 for the Creation Week
A summary statement for the creation account, this verse in the literal Hebrew reads, "These are the generations of the heavens and the earth when they were created in the day of their making. . . ." Here the word *day* refers to all six creation days (and the creation events prior to the first creative day). Obviously, then, it refers to a period longer than 24 hours.

Explicit Biblical Statements of Earth's Antiquity
Habakkuk 3:6 directly declares that the mountains are "ancient" and the hills are "age-old." In 2 Peter 3:5, Peter tells us that the heavens (the stars and the universe) existed "long ago." Such descriptions of certain aspects of creation would have little impact if the earth and its hills were literally only a few days older than humankind. The point of the contrast would be lost.

God's Eternal Existence and Aspects of Creation
The figures of speech used in Psalm 90:2–6, Proverbs 8:22–31, Ecclesiastes 1:3–11, and Micah 6:2 all depict the immeasurable antiquity of God's presence and plans. Young-earth advocates postulate an earth of about 3,000 years when these passages were written. The brief span of about a 3,000-year terrestrial history, however, seems to be an inadequate metaphor to express God's eternality. The fact that the Bible does consider the antiq-

uity of the founding of the earth a suitable metaphor for God's eternality supports the case for an ancient earth.

The Hebrew Words *'ereb* and *boqer*

The Hebrew word *'ereb*, translated "evening," also means "sunset," "night," or "ending of the day."[96] The word *boqer*, translated "morning," also means "sunrise," "coming of light," "beginning of day," "break of day," or "dawning," with possible metaphoric usage.[97] In other words, "evening" and "morning" refer to the beginning and ending components of "day," however *day* is used.

Numbered Days Not Necessarily 24-Hour Days

Young-earth creationists have argued for 24-hour days on the basis that *yôm*, when attached to an ordinal (second, third, fourth, etc.) always refers to a 24-hour period. This argument can be challenged on several counts. For one, it is true only for passages describing days of human activity rather than days of divine activity. For another, nowhere else does the Bible enumerate sequential epochs. More important, the rules of Hebrew grammar do not require that *yôm* must refer to 24 hours, even when attached to an ordinal. Hosea 6:2, for example, prophesies that "after two days [God] will revive [Israel]; on the third day he will restore us." For centuries Bible commentators have noted that the term *days* in this passage (where the ordinal is used) refers to a year, years, a thousand years, or maybe more.[98]

The Hebrew Word *'olam* as Substitute for *yôm* in Genesis 1

Young-earth creationists also claim that the Hebrew word *'olam* (as opposed to *yôm*) would have been used if God had intended to indicate a long period. However, Hebrew lexicons show that only in postbiblical writings did *'olam* refer to a long age or epoch. In biblical times it meant "forever," "perpetual," "lasting," "always," "of olden times," or "the remote past, future, or both." But the range of its usage did not include a set period of time.[99]

Biblical Chronologies Intended to be Time-Discernable

When we study other chronologies in the Bible, we learn that they all share at least one common characteristic: They record sequences that are significant and that the reader can discern. The timing and order are important because they show the careful unfolding of God's plans and affirm His control. The discernability provides a tool for validating the message of God's spokesmen. Examples would include: Jeremiah 31:38–40 (a prediction, now fulfilled, of the location and construction sequence of Jerusalem's nine suburbs during the second rebirth of Israel as a nation);

Daniel 9:24–27 (a timetable for the rebuilding of Jerusalem, the Messiah's coming and death, the destruction of Jerusalem, years of desolation, and final restoration); and Daniel 11:2–35 (a prediction, since fulfilled, of the sequence of victories, defeats, and intrigues of various kings and kingdoms of the Greek and Roman eras). The supernatural accuracy of such chronologies not only proves their inspiration, but also gives assurance for today and hope for tomorrow.

Recorded events not intended to be time-discernible to the reader are presented without the use of sequence markers. For example, in Acts 6, Luke does not indicate the order in which the first seven deacons of the Church were chosen. He lists the names randomly because there was no special significance to the order of their selection.

For the creation days, long periods during which increasingly complex life-forms were created are verifiable and useful for validating the supernatural accuracy of the writer's statements. But if all creation were completed in six 24-hour days, the most sophisticated measuring techniques available, or even foreseeably available, would be totally incapable of discerning the sequence of events. Thus, a major use of the chronology would be thwarted.

The Unusual Syntax Regarding Specific Creation Days

Looking at the word-for-word translation of the Hebrew text, one finds this phraseology: "and was evening and was morning day X." The *New International Version* phrases the time markers this way: "And there was evening, and there was morning—the Xth day." The word arrangement in both cases is clearly a departure from simple and ordinary expression. It creates a kind of ambiguity for modern translators. If "day X" were intended as the noun complement for the one evening and morning together, the linking verb should appear just once, in plural form (as the *King James Version* renders it): "And the evening and the morning were the Xth day." We would expect the literal Hebrew to say, "and were evening and morning day X." But it does not. While this syntactic observation does not constitute a "proof," it does strongly suggest that we should understand the term *day* in Genesis 1 as something other than its most common literal definition.

Biblical Statements about the Vastness of the Universe

Three Scripture passages (Gen. 22:17; Jer. 33:22; Heb. 11:12) metaphorically compare the number of God's children with the number of stars in the sky and the number of grains of sand on the seashore—a "countless" number. (The Hebrews and Greeks had no words for numbers beyond the hundreds of millions.)

This metaphor for a vast number is significant for two reasons. First, it contradicted the popularly held notion in biblical times that the stars numbered six or seven thousand—definitely a countable number. Thus, the metaphor expresses truth which the author could not have known apart from inspiration.

Second, the great abundance of stars, which does approximate the abundance of sand grains on the earth's beaches, translates into a statement about size, which, in turn, indicates age. Hebrew and Greek included words for numbers up to (but not including) the billions. "Countless" would indicate a number in the billions or perhaps one or two orders of magnitude greater than billions: tens of billions or hundreds of billions. Given tens of billions of stars (up to 100 billion) as a minimum number, given that stars are separated by huge distances (an average of about ten light-years within a galaxy, many more light-years between galaxies), we can easily understand that a universe with so many stars must be truly huge, and if huge, then old, since matter can travel no faster than light speed.[100]

While God certainly has the power to construct the universe at a more rapid rate than the velocity of light, the physical evidence (via astronomers' observations of the past) indicates that He did not do so. A consistent pattern in God's revelation in both Scripture and nature is that when He does perform miracles, He does not intentionally hide the evidence of the miracles from us.

The Sabbath Day for Man and Sabbath Year for the Land

The Fourth Commandment says that the seventh day of each week is to be honored as holy: "For in six days the LORD made the heavens and the earth . . . but he rested on the seventh day" (Exo. 20:11). This passage has often been cited as proof positive for the 24-hour interpretation. However, this statement cannot be taken so definitively. Does the eight-day celebration of the Feast of Tabernacles prove that the wilderness wanderings under Moses occupied only eight days?[101]

Sometimes the *Sabbath* refers to a full year (Lev. 25:4). The wisdom of God for human well-being dictates one day of rest out of every seven days plus special holidays. He provided one year of rest out of every seven years for the well-being of crop land. Since God is not subject to biological cycles, His rest period is completely flexible. Clearly, the emphasis in Exodus 20 is on the pattern of work and rest, a ratio of six to one, not on the length of the creation days. The analogy of our Sabbath to God's Sabbath does not demand seven 24-hour days. Age-long creation days fit the analogy just as well, if not better.

Bloodshed before Adam's Sin and the Atonement

Hebrews 9:22 tells us that "the law requires that nearly everything be cleansed with blood, and without the shedding of blood there is no for-Giveness." Some young-earth creationists go so far as to claim that "the basis of the Gospel message is that God brought in death and bloodshed because of sin,"[102] and that "if death and bloodshed of animals (or man) existed before Adam sinned, then the whole basis of atonement—the basis of redemption—is destroyed."[103]

While we would never disagree with the biblical teaching that the shedding of Christ's blood is the one and only acceptable payment for our sin, we cannot agree that *all* bloodshed goes toward the remission of sin. (To say that there could have been no bloodshed before sin is to make the same exegetical error as made by those who claim that there were no rainstorms or rainbows before the Genesis Flood.)

Hebrews 10:1–4 explains that the blood of animal sacrifices *will not take away sin.* The sacrificial killing of animals was a physical picture of the spiritual death caused by sin, which necessitated the death of a substitute to make atonement as well as a foreshadowing of the ultimate, efficacious sacrifice that God Himself would one day provide. Since the penalty for sin is spiritual death, no animal sacrifice could ever atone for sin. The crime is spiritual. Thus, atonement had to be made by a spiritual Being.

The spilling of animal blood before Adam's sin in no way affects or detracts from the doctrine of the atonement. Upholding that central doctrine in no way demands a creation scenario in which none of God's creatures received a scratch or other blood-letting wound before Adam and Eve sinned. Incidentally, experiencing no bloodshed is just as big a problem for animal life existing for 48 hours as it would be for animal life existing for millions of years. Even in an ideal natural environment, animals would be constantly scratched, pricked, bruised, and even killed by accidental events and each other.

No Compromise of the Power of God

Some creationists have expressed the idea that a cosmic creation date of billions of years ago denies or diminishes the omnipotence of God. Just as the runner who covers a mile in four minutes must be stronger than the one who requires ten minutes, some creationists presume that a God who takes billions of years to create must necessarily be weaker than a God who takes only six 24-hour days.

Two fallacies underlie this line of reasoning. One is the assumption that God's creating in six 24-hour days proves Him all-powerful. Not so. Even that time frame is too long. For that matter, six nanoseconds would be too long. If time were a measure of His power, God would have created everything in one immeasurable instant. The second fallacy is that an all-powerful God must exercise all His power all the time. Just as a man capable of running a four-minute mile has the option to take more time, so God can choose whatever time frame He pleases for whatever He does.

God's deliberate action is emphasized by the apostle Peter in 2 Peter 3:9—"The Lord is not slow in keeping his promise, as some understand slowness." The rushing and hyperactivity characteristic of modern society in no way reflect the Creator. He is never anxious, always patient, and always willing to trade the temporal for the eternal.

Throughout the biblical narratives, we see God restraining His full power. This restraint is clearly visible in the actions of Jesus Christ. He steadfastly resisted pressure to unleash the full force of His divine power, choosing instead to achieve a higher goal.

Certainly God has His reasons for the time scale He chose. If we cannot comprehend all His reasons, we still have no basis for second-guessing Him. He is God, and His ways and thoughts are above ours. Perhaps the time scale He chose fits into His strategy for conquering evil. Perhaps He is using a certain time scale to teach something to human beings or to the angels. No matter how much we learn, we will never know the totality of God's mind.

No Condemnation of an Entire *Ethnos*

Jesus commands His followers to make disciples of all nations.[104] The Greek word for nation, *ethnos*, refers to a group of people associated with each other by some common characteristics or experiences.[105] The host of the redeemed pictured in Revelation 7:9 comes from "every nation, tribe, people, and language." In 1 Corinthians 1:26, Paul says that not many believers are from the group considered "wise" and "influential" by the standards of the world. He says "not many" rather than "not any."

We see the community of scientists, including astronomers and astrophysicists, as an *ethnos* of sorts. God calls us to reach out to them as He does to every other group on the planet. And though He warns that the childlike simplicity of trusting in Jesus will be a stumbling block for many, we have unwittingly placed another barrier in the path of scientists: the dogma of a young earth and universe. We cannot imagine a notion more offensive to this group. Since all their research convinces them that the universe and the earth they are studying are real and significant, they understandably resist embracing the unsupported assertion that it is all a mirage.

When oung-earth creationists claim (as do Akridge and others) that the worldwide community of secular astrophysicists and astronomers are banded together in a God-hating conspiracy to deceive the public about the creation date, the offense is driven deeper. Given the tendency toward independence and nonconformity among them, it's absurd to suggest that tens of thousands of them would or could unanimously carry out a plot through four decades to bamboozle the public. Another explanation must exist for their strong and united confidence in the creation date (as billions of years ago) for the universe and the earth.

BIBLICAL EVIDENCES FOR CHRONOLOGICAL CREATION DAYS

The day-age view we advocate not only holds that the days of creation are long periods of time or epochs, but also that they are sequential; that is, that the six epochs revealed in Genesis 1 occurred in the order revealed. This conclusion is based upon several arguments.

Genesis 1 and the Use of the Scientific Method

We all need to remind ourselves that the scientific method traces its origins to the Bible.[106] This method still serves as the appropriate tool for investigating and describing physical phenomena. Nowhere else in the Bible is the pattern we now formalize as the scientific method more evident than it is in Genesis 1.

The explicit use of this distinct pattern in describing the events of the six Genesis creation days implies that the creation events are to be taken chronologically (and literally). If we recognize the pattern and take it seriously, we find no difficulty in harmonizing the scientific data with the biblical narrative. The framework interpretation gives ground to no purpose. If, however, we fail to recognize and apply the scientific method, we will misidentify the frame of reference, misunderstand the initial conditions, and distort the sequence of events. In that case and only in that case can Delitzsch argue that all attempts "to harmonize our biblical story of the creation with the results of natural science" will prove absolutely futile, a case for resorting to the framework interpretation.

Genesis 2 and the Repetitive Use of bara in Genesis 1

In Genesis 1 the Hebrew word to create something brand new which did not exist before (bara) is used just three times. It is used first for the creation of the universe, second for the creation of soulish animals, and last for the creation of spirit species, mankind.

In Genesis 2, Adam is first made to interact with just the physical creation (working the Garden). Then God has him interact with the soulish creation (naming birds and mammals). Last of all, Adam finds fulfillment in a creature that like him is body, soul, and spirit.

The chronology of Adam in Genesis 2 being introduced first to that which is just physical, second to that which is both physical and soulish, and third to that which is physical, soulish, and spiritual is an interpretation accepted by all evangelical scholars. The fact that this chronology exactly parallels the three occurrences of *bara* in Genesis 1 supports the conclusion that the Genesis 1 creation events also are chronologically stated.

The Extensive Use of Chronological Terms in Genesis 1
A simple listing of a few physical creation events appears near the beginning of Genesis 2.[107] This list does not refer to time or sequence markers. We find nothing in the context to suggest that the list is chronological. By contrast, Genesis 1 employs *all* manner of rhetorical devices to indicate chronological relationships.

The word *yôm* certainly denotes a period of time. The creation events are allotted to six different days numbered first, second, third, fourth, fifth, and sixth. Measured pauses appear between creation events, insertions such as "God said," "God saw," "God blessed," and "God called." Each of the six creation days has a "morning" (or beginning) and an "evening" (or ending). Transitional terms such as "then," "so," "thus," and "now" are abundant. After each creation day, the narrator interjects "and it was so," "it was good," or sometimes both. Occasionally, such comments are inserted in the midst of a creation day's description.

It seems impossible to explain such prolific use of chronological terminology unless Genesis 1 is intended to be read as a chronology. Nowhere else in the Bible do we find such a density of chronological terms.

The Work-Rest Pattern
In Exodus 20 and Leviticus 25, God establishes a work-rest schedule for humans and for their agricultural lands. Humans are to engage in various types of gainful employment (for the purpose of planet management) for six consecutive 24-hour days followed by a day of rest. Work then rest, with work coming first. Likewise, agricultural lands are to be worked for six consecutive years then left fallow for a year, then worked again and rested again. Since the work-rest pattern is clearly sequential, it seems reasonable to conclude that the day-by-day events of creation also appear in sequence.

The Distinctness of Genesis 1

Those who gloss over the abundant chronological terminology of Genesis 1 usually attempt to do so by claiming Genesis 1 is no more than a poetic ballad designed to communicate the beauty and harmony of God's creation. The claim is that Genesis 1 is a metaphorical device to express God's enjoyment of nature and His exhortation to humanity to join Him in appreciating His created wonders.

While no one would deny the compelling artistry in the composition of Genesis 1, we challenge the notion that beauty denotes fantasy. We deny the assertion that elegant prose is indistinguishable from poetry.

Poetic accounts of creation do exist in the Bible. Their style and structure stand in marked contrast to Genesis 1. The most famous, Psalm 104, is a song about the majesty, power, and wisdom of God in creating and shaping the heavens and the earth for humanity. That song clearly implies that God performed mighty works in nature in an orderly, planned fashion. For the composer of Psalm 104, Genesis 1 was not devoid of scientific content or order. He makes reference to the Genesis account in concrete, scientific terms. So did King Solomon. In Proverbs 8:22–31, Solomon crafted powerfully evocative metaphors to describe God's attributes using material from the Genesis creation account. Other poetic accounts of creation in the Bible such as Job 36–41 and Psalms 8, 19, 33, and 148 reflect on Genesis 1 events in artistically beautiful and non-sequential terms. However, the authors of these passages clearly treat Genesis 1 as a nonfictitious, literally true record of events. Were they naïve or inspired? Scientific developments point to the latter.

Independent Creation Items Followed by Dependent Ones

From a scientific perspective, several of the Genesis creation day events cannot occur until others are set in place first. An obvious example is that continents must form (Gen. 1:9–10) before land vegetation (vv. 11–12) does. A less obvious example is that light diffusing through the clouds (vv. 3–5) and establishing an abundant, stable water cycle (vv. 6–8) must precede the production of land vegetation. Further, the animals mentioned on Days 5 and 6 (and not the life forms that precede them) need the visibility of the sun, moon, and stars (Day 4 events) to regulate their complex biological clocks. The fact that creation events requiring other creation events to have occurred first always appear in the right sequence mentioned in Genesis 1 supports the conclusion that the Genesis creation day events are stated chronologically and that the Genesis creation account is divinely inspired.

Genesis 1 as an Obvious Chronology

We have observed over the past fifty years that those who feel no motiva-tion to defend the Genesis text as the word of God always interpret Gen-esis 1 as a chronological account of creation events. Neither of us has ever met or heard of any secularist who, independent of any Christian influ-ence, has ever denied that Genesis 1 is a chronology of creation events. Evidently, the only motivation for interpreting Genesis 1 nonchrono-logically is to escape the dilemma posed by Delitzsch. If one concurs with Delitzsch that it is impossible to reconcile Genesis 1 with the creation chronology revealed in the record of nature, then the only way to main-tain Genesis as the inerrant word of God is to insist that Genesis 1 is not a chronology. However, such an escape hatch is bound to engender ridi-cule from secularists. How can we escape the charge that whenever objec-tive evidences contradict the Bible, Christians always will claim the Bible's content is less than what it appears? None of this maneuvering is neces-sary. Given that Delitzsch is wrong, as we maintain, the motivation or "need" to interpret Genesis 1 nonchronologically evaporates.

CONCLUSION

One doctrine on which evangelicals agree is that God inspired all 66 books of the Bible. Another is that God created the universe and life. Accord-ing to Psalm 19, God's word is written upon the heavens for everyone to read. The Bible also testifies that God is truthful and does not lie. Taken together, these truths lead us to conclude that the record of nature and the words of the Bible must completely agree. Only the day-age interpre-tation of Genesis 1 embraces that conclusion. Only the day-age interpre-tation provides a straightforward reconciliation of the established scientific record and a literal reading of Genesis 1.

The day-age interpretation provides a compelling defense of biblical inerrancy. By contrast, the six consecutive 24-hour-creation-day view forces different books of the Bible and even different chapters of Genesis into contradiction. While the framework interpretation avoids biblical contra-diction, it does so by robbing the text of significant testable content. By making Genesis 1 largely scientifically vacuous, the framework interpreta-tion avoids the issue of biblical accuracy.

The day-age interpretation we have presented here is uniquely consis-tent with Christ's evangelistic mandate. Why did God reveal Himself in a written document, the Bible, if not to draw people into the eternal rela-tionship for which He paid the supreme price? The faith that makes such a relationship possible can only be as strong as the conviction on which it rests, the conviction that the biblical texts are true.

According to the apostle Paul, we are responsible to test what we are taught and hold fast to that which proves true and good.[108] When we test the assertions of the 24-hour-creation-day interpretation, we find that they do not hold true,[109] either biblically or scientifically. Unfortunately, because of this failure to withstand rigorous testing, young-earth creationism has become a frequent excuse for rejecting the Christian gospel and worldview.[110]

The framework interpretation, of course, offers very little for the Christian or non-Christian to test. Hence, it offers no significant reason to either believe or disbelieve Scripture. By contrast, the day-age interpretation yields a long list of verifiable events and initial conditions as well as a testable sequence of events.

When the tests are applied, the account proves trustworthy to a degree that can only be described as "supernatural." The odds that an ancient, uninspired writer's descriptions and chronology of creation would be demonstrably accurate through thousands of years fall far below one in a trillion trillion. Thus, Genesis 1 by itself provides adequate proof that the Bible is the divinely inspired, inerrant word of God.

Finally, our day-age interpretation uniquely demonstrates the capacity to predict. Since our earliest attempts to document the scientific accuracy of Genesis 1 a few decades ago, at a time when advancing technology facilitated an exponential increase in knowledge about the universe, each year's research has served to strengthen the case for the biblical doctrine of a divine, personal, purposeful Designer—the God of the Bible—and for the complete scientific accuracy of both the Genesis creation events and their chronology.[111] Thus, we can reasonably expect that objective evidence for the inerrancy of Scripture, and of Genesis 1 in particular, will continue to mount. As it does, so will the importance of unity among Christians, as we challenge secularists to reconsider their views, as we invite skeptics to lay their doubts to rest on the solid ground of facts where saving faith can grow roots.

NOTES

1. H. Donald Daae, *Bridging the Gap: The First 6 Days* (Calgary, AlBerta: Genesis International Research Publishers, 1989); Robert C. Newman and Herman J. Eckelmann, Jr., *Genesis One and the Origin of the Earth* (Hatfield, PA: Interdisciplinary Biblical Research Institute, 1977); E. K. Victor Pearce, *Who Was Adam?* (Walkerville, South Africa: Africa Centre for World Mission, 1987); Howard J. Van Till, *The Fourth Day* (Grand Rapids, MI: Wm. B. Eerdmans Publishing Co., 1986); John Weister, *The Genesis Connection* (Nashville, TN: Thomas Nelson, 1983).

2. Hugh Ross, *Creation and Time* (Colorado Springs, CO: NavPress, 1994), pp. 69–70;

Hugh Ross, *Beyond the Cosmos* (Colorado Springs, CO: NavPress, 1996), pp. 195–205.

3. Gleason L. Archer, *Encyclopedia of Bible Difficulties* (Grand Rapids, MI: Zondervan Publishing House, 1982), pp. 58–65; Gleason L. Archer, "A Response to the Trustworthiness of Scripture in Areas Relating to Natural Science," *Hermeneutics, Inerrancy, and the Bible*, ed. Earl D. Radmacher and Robert D. Preus (Grand Rapids, MI: Zondervan Publishing House, 1984), pp. 321–34; Hugh Ross, *Genesis One: A Scientific Perspective* (Pasadena, CA: Reasons To Believe, 1983); *The Fingerprint of God*, 2d edition (Orange, CA: Promise Publishers, 1991), pp. 141–69; Ross, *Creation and Time*; Hugh Ross, *The Genesis Question* (Colorado Springs, CO: NavPress, 1998), pp. 13–92.

4. Ross, *The Genesis Question*, pp. 13–92, 183–96, 199–202; Ross, *Creation and Time*, pp. 45–158; Gleason L. Archer, "A Response to the Trustworthiness of Scripture," pp. 321–34.

5. We have observed a dramatic drop in support of the framework interpretation and young-earth creationism among the more than 50 university and seminary audiences we and our ministry teams have addressed over the past five years. The loss of support for these two positions is most pronounced for the faculty. We have observed a similar drop in support among more than 100 church audiences over the past two years.

6. Ronald L. Numbers, *The Creationists: The Evolution of Scientific Creationism* (New York: Alfred A. Knopf, 1992); Alan Hayward, *Creation and Evolution* (Minneapolis: Bethany House, 1995); Ronald Youngblood, *How It All Began* (Ventura, CA: Regal Books, 1980); Don Stoner, *A New Look at an Old Earth* (Paramount, CA: Schroeder, 1992).

7. Discussions we have had on Genesis 1 with theologians at conferences of The Evangelical Theological Society have been dominated by far with these concerns, as opposed to exegetical issues.

8. Ross, *The Genesis Question*, pp. 13–18, 39–57, 63–66, 81–100, 183–91; "Creation on the 'Firing Line,'" *Facts & Faith*, vol. 12, no. 1 (1998), pp. 6–7.

9. R. Laird Harris, Gleason L. Archer, Bruce Waltke, *Theological Wordbook of the Old Testament* (Chicago: Moody Press, 1980).

10. *The Compact Edition of the Oxford English Dictionary*, ed. J. Amphlett, et al. (Oxford, UK: Oxford University Press, 1971) contains about 500,000 words. The names of various chemicals and different species of plants and animals add several million more words.

11. Harris, et al., *Theological Wordbook of the Old Testament*, pp. 370–71; William Wilson, *Old Testament Word Studies* (Grand Rapids, MI: Kregel Publications, 1978), p. 109.

12. Ross, *Creation and Time*, p. 47; Harris, et al., *Theological Wordbook of the Old Testament*, pp. 672–3; Samuel P. Tregelles, *Gesenius' Hebrew-Chaldee Lexicon to the Old Testament* (Grand Rapids, MI: Baker Book House, 1979), pp. 612–3.

13. Ross, *Creation and Time*, pp. 16–24.

14. Ibid.

15. Ibid., pp. 17–23; Justin Martyr, "Dialogue With Trypho," chap. 81, *Writings of Saint Justin Martyr*, in *The Fathers of the Church*, vol. 6, ed. Ludwig Schopp (New York: Christian Heritage, 1948), pp. 277–8; Irenaeus, "Against Heresies," bk. 5, chap. 23, sec. 2, *The Ante-Nicene Fathers*, vol. 1, ed. Alexander Roberts and James Donaldson (Grand Rapids, MI: Wm. B. Eerdmans Publishing Co., 1981), pp. 551–2; Origen, "Against Celsus," bk. 6, chap. 61, *The Ante-Nicene Fathers*, vol. 4, p. 601; Lactantius, "The Divine Institutes," bk. 7, chap. 14, *The Ante-Nicene Fathers*, vol. 7, p. 211; Victorinus of Pettau, "The Created World," bk. 6, *The Ante-Nicene Fathers*, vol. 7, p. 342; Methodius of Olympus, "Fragment," *The Ante-Nicene Fathers*, vol. 6, p. 310; Augustine, "The Literal Meaning of Genesis," bk. 4, chap. 27 and bk. 5, chap. 2, *Ancient Christian Writers: The Works of the Fathers in Translation*, no. 41, ed. Johannes Quasten, Walter J. Burghardt, and Thomas C. Lawler; Augustine, *The Literal Meaning of Genesis*, trans. John Hammond Taylor, vol. 1, bks. 1–6 (New York: Newman Press, 1982), p. 148; Augustine, "The Literal Meaning of Genesis, bk. 4, chap. 27, *Ancient*

Christian Writers: The Works of the Fathers in Translation, no. 41, *The Literal Meaning of Genesis,* pp. 135–6; Augustine, "The Confessions," bk. 13, sec. 51, *The Fathers of the Church,* vol. 21, trans. Vernon J. Bourke (New York: Fathers of the Church, Inc., 1953), p. 455; Basil, "The Hexaemeron," *A Select Library of Nicene and Post-Nicene Fathers of the Christian Church,* 2d edition, ed. Philip Schaff and Henry Wace, vol. 8; *St. Basil: Letters and Select Works; The Nine Homilies of the Hexaemeron and the Letters of Saint Basil the Great,* trans. Blomfield Jackson (Grand Rapids, MI: Wm. B. Eerdmans Publishing Co., 1955), p. 64.

16. Ross, *Creation and Time,* pp. 22–3; Ambrose, "Saint Ambrose: Hexameron," trans. John J. Savage, *The Fathers of the Church, A New Translation,* vol. 42, ed. Roy Joseph Deferrari, et al. (New York: Fathers of the Church, Inc., 1961), pp. 42–3.

17. Gen. 1:21, 25–7; Ross, *The Genesis Question,* pp. 49–54.

18. Hugh Ross, "New Evidence of Old Life," *Facts & Faith,* vol. 11, no. 1 (1997), pp. 3–4; S. J. Mojzsis, et al., "Evidence for Life on Earth Before 3,800 Million Years Ago," *Nature,* vol. 384 (1996), pp. 55–9; John M. Hayes, "The Earliest Memories of Life on Earth," *Nature,* vol. 384 (1996), pp. 21–2; Verne R. Oberbeck and Guy Fogleman, "Impacts and the Origin of Life," *Nature,* vol. 339 (1989), p. 434; Christopher Chyba and Carl Sagan, "Endogenous Production, Exogenous Delivery and Impact-Shock Synthesis of Organic Molecules: An Inventory for the Origins of Life," *Nature,* vol. 355 (1992), pp. 125–32; Robert Shapiro, *Origins: A Skeptic's Guide to the Creation of Life on Earth* (New York: Summit Books, 1986), p. 128.

19. Henry M. Morris and John D. Morris, *Science, Scripture, and the Young Earth* (El Cajon, CA: Institute for Creation Research, 1989), p. 67; Russell Akridge, "A Recent Creation Interpretation of the Big Bang and Expanding Universe," *Bible-Science Newsletter* (May 1982), pp. 1, 4; Henry Morris, "The Compromise Road," *Impact,* vol. 177, March 1988 (El Cajon, CA: Institute for Creation Research), p. iv; "Recent Creation Is a Vital Doctrine," *Impact,* vol. 132 (June 1984), p. iv; John Morris, "How Can a Geology Professor Believe That the Earth Is Young?" *Back to Genesis,* vol. 29 (May 1991), p. d; Henry M. Morris, *The Long War Against God* (Grand Rapids, MI: Baker Book House, 1992), pp. 105, 134; "Old-Earth Creationism," *Back to Genesis,* vol. 100 (April 1997), pp. a–c.

20. Gen. 2:1–3; Psa. 95:11; Heb. 4:1–11.

21. John C. Whitcomb, Jr., and Henry M. Morris, *The Genesis Flood* (Phillipsburg, NJ: Presbyterian & Reformed Publishing Co., 1961), pp. 461–6; James S. Stambaugh, "Death Before Sin," *Impact,* vol. 191, May 1989, pp. i–iv; John D. Morris, "If All Animals Were Created As Plant Eaters, Why Do Some Have Sharp Teeth?" *Back to Genesis,* vol. 100 (April 1997), p. d.

22. John D. Morris, "If All Animals," p. d.

23. Whitcomb and Morris, *The Genesis Flood,* pp. 66–9.

24. Paul R. Ehrlich and Anne H. Ehrlich, *Extinction: The Causes and Consequences of the Disappearance of Species* (New York: Ballantine, 1981), p. 33.

25. Gary K. Meffe, C. Ronald Carroll, and Contributors, *Principles of Conservation Biology,* 2d edition (Sunderland, MA: Sinauer Associates, 1997), pp. 91–3.

26. Whitcomb and Morris, *The Genesis Flood,* pp. 66–9 (in particular figure 4 on p. 67 shows, for example, zebras and horses evolving from a single horse kind pair on board Noah's ark) and pp. 80–7; John D. Morris, "Did God Create the Earth in Its Present Condition?" *Back to Genesis,* vol. 113 (May 1998), p. d.

27. Morris and Morris, *Science, Scripture, and the Young Earth,* p. 67; Ken Ham, "What Is a Creationist?" *Back to Genesis,* vol. 30 (June 1991), p. b; Mark Van Bebber and Paul S. Taylor, *Creation and Time: A Report on the Progressive Creationist Book by Hugh Ross* (Mesa, AZ: Eden Productions, 1994).

28. Ross, *Creation and Time,* pp. 81–125.

29. Gary North, *The Dominion Covenant: Genesis* (Tyler, TX: Institute for Christian Economics, 1987), pp. 254–5.

30. Russell Akridge, "A Recent Creation Interpretation of the Big Bang and Expanding Universe," *Bible-Science Newsletter*, pp. 1, 4.

31. Ross, *Creation and Time*, pp. 117–8.

32. Ibid., pp. 95–102, 118, 122–23; Hugh Ross, *The Creator and the Cosmos*, 2d edition (Colorado Springs, CO: NavPress, 1995), pp. 63–93; Ross, *Beyond the Cosmos*, pp. 21–33. A more extensive and updated proof will be available in the third chapter of the second edition.

33. Ross, "Avoiding a Dangerous Trap," *Facts & Faith*, vol. 12, no. 4 (1998), pp. 10–1.

34. Samuel R. Conner and Don N. Page, *The Big Bang Cosmology of Starlight and Time* (Pasadena, CA: Reasons To Believe, 1997); Samuel R. Conner and Don N. Page, "Starlight and Time Is the Big Bang," *Creation Ex Nihilo Technical Journal*, vol. 12, no. 3 (August 1998), pp. 195–212; Samuel R. Conner and Hugh N. Ross, *The Unravelling of "Starlight and Time"* (Pasadena, CA: Reasons To Believe, 1998).

35. Ross, *Creation and Time*, pp. 53–5.

36. This statement by the founder of the modern-day gnostic cult, Christian Science, is recited during every worship service held in every Christian Science Church.

37. Col. 1:9–3:17; 1 John 1:8–4:6.

38. James S. Stambaugh, "Death Before Sin," *Impact*, vol. 191, p. ii.

39. Exo. 7:18; 8:13; 10:17; Job 14:8–10; Psa. 37:2; 105:29; Prov. 30:25–28; Eccl. 10:1; Isa. 50:2; Matt. 6:28, 30; Hugh Ross, *Scriptural Evidences for Plants and Primitive Animals Experiencing Life and Death* (Pasadena, CA: Reasons To Believe, 1996).

40. Ross, *Beyond the Cosmos*, pp. 178–84, 195–205.

41. Ross, *Creation and Time*, pp. 60–9.

42. Gen. 6:3.

43. Scott M. Huse, *The Collapse of Evolution*, 2d edition (Grand Rapids, MI: Baker Book House, 1993), p. 78; Ian T. Taylor, *In the Minds of Men: Darwin and the New World Order* (Toronto, Canada: TFE Publishing, 1984), p. 294; Henry M. Morris, "The Logic of Biblical Creation," *Impact*, vol. 205 (July 1990), pp. iii–iv.

44. John P. Cox and R. Thomas Guili, *Principles of Stellar Structure, Volume II: Applications to Stars* (New York: Gordon and Breach, 1968), pp. 804–73; R. Kippenhahn and A. Weigert, *Stellar Structure and Evolution* (New York: Springer-Verlag, 1994), pp. 25–35, 129–34; David Arnett, *Supernovae and Nucleosynthesis* (Princeton, NJ: Princeton University Press, 1996), pp. 182–275.

45. Ross, *Creation and Time*, pp. 65–9; Ross, *The Genesis Question*, pp. 94–7; Mark W. Zemansky, *Heat and Thermodynamics* (New York: McGraw-Hill, 1957), pp. 42–60, 157–94.

46. For example, astronomers observe that stars burn at the same rates and the same intensities everywhere throughout the cosmos.

47. Ross, *The Genesis Question*, pp. 39–45, 47–57.

48. Ibid., pp. 52, 55–7, 151–4.

49. Ibid., p. 98.

50. Friedrich Delitzsch, *Babel und Bible*, trans. Thomas J. McCormack and W. H. Carruth (Chicago: The Open Court Publishing, 1903), p. 45.

51. Ross, *The Genesis Question*, pp. 21–4, 189–91; Thomas F. Torrance, *Theology in Reconstruction* (Grand Rapids, MI: Wm. B. Eerdmans Publishing Co., 1965); Thomas F. Torrance, *Reality and Scientific Theology* (Edinburgh, UK: Scottish Academic Press, 1985); Thomas, F. Torrance, "Ultimate and Penultimate Beliefs in Science," *Facets of Faith & Science, Volume I: Historiography and Modes of Interaction*, ed. Jitse M. van der Meer (New York: University Press of America, 1996), pp. 151–76.

52. Ross, *The Creator and the Cosmos*, pp. 19–29.

53. Ross, *Beyond the Cosmos*, pp. 21–4, 30–2.

54. Roger Penrose, *Shadows of the Mind* (New York: Oxford University Press, 1994), pp. 229–31.

55. Ross, *The Genesis Question*, pp. 23, 26–7.

56. Ibid., pp. 29–57.

57. Carl Zimmer, *At the Water's Edge: Macroevolution and the Transformation of Life* (New York: Free Press, 1998); Michael Behe, David Berlinkski, William F. Buckley, Jr., Phillip Johnson, Barry Lynn, Kenneth Miller, Michael Ruse, Eugenie Scott, *Firing Line, PBS Debate on Creation and Evolution*, December 19, 1997.

58. Annalisa Berta, "What Is a Whale?" *Science*, vol. 263 (1994), pp. 180–1.

59. Ross, *The Genesis Question*, pp. 95–7; Ross, *Beyond the Cosmos*, pp. 133–4, 178–205.

60. Ross, *The Creator and the Cosmos*, pp. 111–56; Ross, *Big Bang Refined by Fire* (Pasadena, CA: Reasons To Believe, 1998), pp. 11–30.

61. For a fast-rotating earth, the wind velocity will rise exponentially from the surface. With an eight-hour-per-day rotation period, the wind velocity would be zero at the surface, several hundred miles per hour an inch above the surface, and over a thousand miles per hour a few feet above the surface. The precise surface would not be a safe environment. It would be pelted by debris kicked up by the winds. Thus, only the tiniest life forms could avoid being destroyed or sheared.

62. Ross, *The Genesis Question*, pp. 110–4; Guillermo Gonzalez, "Circumstellar Habitable Zones," *Facts & Faith*, vol. 12, no. 4 (1998), pp. 4–5.

63. K. L. Moulton and R. A. Berner, "Quantification of the Effect of Plants on Weathering: Studies in Iceland," *Geology 26* (1998), pp. 895–8; W. R. Kuhn, J. C. G. Walker, and H. G. Marshall, "The Effect on Earth's Surface Temperature from Variations in Rotation Rate, Continent Formation, Solar Luminosity, and Carbon Dioxide," *Journal of Geophysical Research*, vol. 94 (1989), pp. 11, 129–31, 136.

64. Kuhn, et al., "The Effect on Earth's Surface Temperature," pp. 11, 129–31, 136; Ross, *The Genesis Question*, pp. 27, 33–6; P. Jonathan Patchett, "Scum of the Earth After All," *Nature*, vol. 382 (1996), p. 758; R. Monastersky, "Speedy Spin Kept Early Earth From Freezing," *Science News*, vol. 143 (1993), p. 373.

65. Ross, *The Genesis Question*, pp. 26–57, 70–80, 93–100, 110–4.

66. Richard Dawkins, *The Blind Watchmaker* (New York: W. W. Norton, 1987); *Climbing Mount Improbable* (New York: W. W. Norton, 1996).

67. Stuart Kauffman, *At Home in the Universe: The Search for the Laws of Self-Organization and Complexity* (New York: Oxford University Press, 1995); Ilya Prigogine, *The End of Certainty: Time, Chaos, and the New Laws of Nature* (New York: Free Press, 1997).

68. Paul R. Ehrlich and Anne H. Ehrlich, *Extinction: The Causes and Consequences of the Disappearance of Species*, p. 23.

69. Ibid., pp. 32–3.

70. These numbers come from mathematical models. The largest uncertainties arise from estimates of environmental constraints on the relevant species.

71. Significant Darwinian-type changes are most easily seen in real time with viruses. To a much lesser extent, it also is observed for bacteria. A subject of ongoing debate is whether or not any differentiation at all is observable for species with as few individuals and as long a generation time as ants and termites. The largest ant and termite species' populations number a quadrillion; their generation time is three months.

72. Gen. 1:11–2, 20–7.

73. Ross, *The Genesis Question*, pp. 107–9.

74. Ibid., pp. 109–10.

75. Ibid., p. 110.

76. Hugh Ross and Sam Conner, "Eve's Secret to Growing Younger," *Facts & Faith*, vol. 12, no. 1 (1998), p. 2; Ann Gibbons, "Calibrating the Mitochondrial Clock," *Science*, vol. 279 (1998), p. 29.

77. Simon I. Whitfield, John E. Sulston, and Peter N. Goodfellow, "Sequence Variation of the Human Y Chromosome," *Nature*, vol. 378 (1995), pp. 379–80.

78. Patricia Kahn and Ann Gibbons, "DNA From an Extinct Human," *Science*, vol. 277 (1997), pp. 176–8; Jeffrey H. Schwartz and Ian Tattersall, "Significance of Some Previously Unrecognized Apomorphies in the Nasal Region of Homo Neanderthalensis," *Proceedings of the National Academy of Sciences USA*, vol. 93 (1996), pp. 10852–4.

79. Wes Burrows and Oliver A. Ryder, "Y-Chromosome Variation in Great Apes," *Nature*, vol. 385 (1997), pp. 125–6.

80. Michael D. Lemonick, "Stone-Age Bombshell," *Time* (June 19, 1995), p. 49; Tim Appenzeller, "Art: Evolution or Revolution?" *Science*, vol. 282 (1998), p. 1451.

81. B. Aschenback, R. Egger, and J. Trümper, "Discovery of Explosion Fragments Outside the Vela Supernova Remnant Shock-Wave Boundary," *Nature*, vol. 373 (1995), p. 588; A. G. Lyne, R. S. Pritchard, F. Graham-Smith, and F. Camilo, "Very Low Braking Index for the Vela Pulsar," *Nature*, vol. 381 (1996), pp. 497–8.

82. Ross, *The Genesis Question*, pp. 173–6; Scott A. Elias, Susan K. Short, C. Hans Nelson, and Hilary H. Birks, "Life and Times of the Bering Land Bridge," *Nature*, vol. 382 (1996), pp. 61–3.

83. C. Simon, "Stone-Age Sanctuary, Oldest Known Shrine, Discovered in Spain," *Science News*, vol. 120 (1981), p. 357; Bruce Bower, "When the Human Spirit Soared," *Science News*, vol. 130 (1986), pp. 378–9.

84. Ross, *The Genesis Question*, pp. 151–4; Gerhard Schönknecht and Siegfried Scherer, "Too Much Coal for a Young Earth," *Creation Ex Nihilo Technical Journal*, vol. 11 (1997), pp. 279, 281.

85. Kuhn, et al., "The Effect on Earth's Surface Temperature," pp. 11, 129–31, 136; James F. Kasting and David H. Grinspoon, "The Faint Young Sun Problem," *The Sun in Time*, ed. C. P. Sonnett, M. S. Giampapa, and M. S. Matthews (Tuscon, AZ: University of Arizona, 1991), pp. 447–50; Ken Caldeira and James F. Kasting, "Susceptibility of the Early Earth to Irreversible Glaciation Caused by Carbon Dioxide Clouds," *Nature*, vol. 359 (1992), pp. 226–8.

86. Guillermo Gonzalez, "Circumstellar Habitable Zones," *Facts & Faith*, vol. 12, no. 4, p. 5.

87. S. J. Mojzsis, et al., "Evidence for Life on Earth Before 3,800 Million Years Ago," *Nature*, vol. 384 (1996), pp. 55–9; John M. Hayes, "The Earliest Memories of Life on Earth," *Nature*, vol. 384 (1996), pp. 21–2.

88. Oberbeck and Fogleman, "Impacts and the Origin of Life," p. 434; Chyba and Sagan, "Endogeneous Production," pp. 125–32.

89. Shapiro, "Origins: A Skeptics Guide," p. 128.

90. Ross, *The Genesis Question*, pp. 59–62.

91. Ross, *The Genesis Question*, pp. 19–57.

92. Archer, *Encyclopedia of Bible Difficulties*, pp. 58–65; Archer, "A Response to the Trustworthiness of Scripture," pp. 321–34; Ross, *The Fingerprint of God*, pp. 141–69; Ross, *Creation and Time*, pp. 7–165; Ross, *The Genesis Question*, pp. 13–92.

93. Archer, "A Response to the Trustworthiness of Scripture," pp. 335–48; Van Bebber and Taylor, *Creation and Time: A Report on the Progressive Creationist Book by Hugh Ross*.

94. Ross, *Beyond the Cosmos*, pp. 178–84, 186–8, 196–8.

95. Ibid., pp. 195–205.

96. Francis Brown, S. R. Driver, and Charles A. Briggs, *A Hebrew and English Lexicon of*

the Old Testament (Oxford, UK: Clarendon Press, 1968), pp. 787–8; Harris, et al., *Theological Wordbook of the Old Testament*, vol. 2, p. 694.

97. Brown, et al., pp. 133–4; Harris, et al., *Theological Wordbook of the Old Testament*, vol. 1, p. 125.

98. Wilson, *Old Testament Word Studies*, p. 109; Jean Calvin, *Commentaries on the Twelve Minor Prophets, Voume I: Hosea*, trans. John Owen (Edinburgh, UK: The Calvin Translation Society, 1846), pp. 218–9; J. J. Given, "Hosea," *The Pulpit Commentary*, vol. 13, ed. H. D. M. Spence and Joseph S. Exell (Grand Rapids, MI: Wm. B. Eerdmans Publishing Co., 1950), pp. 166–7.

99. Harris, et al., *Theological Wordbook of the Old Testament*, vol. 2, pp. 672–3; Tregelles, *Gesenius' Hebrew-Chaldee Lexicon to the Old Testament*, pp. 612–3.

100. With certainty, astrophysicists can conclude that no significant quantities of matter traveled at faster than light velocities once the universe was older than 10^{-33} seconds. Before 10^{-33} seconds, the possibility exists, but the breadth of the universe during that period of hyperinflation would never exceed the dimensions of a grapefruit (Ross, *Creation and Time*, pp. 97–9).

101. Archer, "A Response to the Trustworthiness of Scripture," p. 329.

102. Ken Ham, "Billions, Millions, or Thousands—Does It Matter?" *Back to Genesis*, no. 29 (May 1991), p. b.

103. Ken Ham, "Closing the Gap," *Back to Genesis* (February 1990), p. c.

104. Matt. 28:19; Luke 24:47.

105. Joseph H. Thayer, *Thayer's Greek-English Lexicon of the New Testament* (Grand Rapids, MI: Baker Book House, 1977), p. 168.

106. Ross, *The Genesis Question*, pp. 20–4, 189–91.

107. Gen. 2:5–6; Ross, *The Genesis Question*, pp. 69–72.

108. 1 Thess. 5:21.

109. For example, young-earth creationists interpret Genesis 1 to mean that the sun, moon, and stars are not created until after plants appear on the earth. This leads to several scientific impossibilities. The day and night cycle (creation Day 1) for Earth cannot be explained without a stabilizing body of the mass and distance from Earth as is the Moon. Nor can the day-night cycle be explained without a source as luminous, massive, and distant from Earth as is the Sun. Likewise, the heat and light for the survival of plants requires a body as luminous and as distant from Earth as is the Sun. For these and many more reasons, secular physicists and astronomers are unanimous in assessing the young-earth doctrine as having less scientific credibility than the proposition that the earth is flat.

110. On the Reasons To Believe telephone hotline, this is by far the most frequently expressed objection by secularists for accepting the Bible as the inspired word of God.

111. Our scientific research team at Reasons To Believe records 20 to 40 scientific discoveries per month that add to the weight of evidence for the accuracy of the Bible.

J. Ligon Duncan III & David W. Hall

THE 24-HOUR RESPONSE

We appreciate much of the day-age essay, especially how it interprets Scripture as providing a clearly sequential revelation that does not demand a complicated literary artifice to be understood. At the same time, however, the day-age essay sometimes misses its intended target and is rooted in a rationalistic approach that leaves little room for miracle and faith. In this response, we will explore each of these areas and respond to the day-age essay by: (1) commending its fine points and original contributions; (2) clarifying some of its misunderstandings of our 24-hour view; and (3) confuting its more significant factual and interpretative errors.

COMMENDATION

Giving Priority to Evangelism

We congratulate Ross and Archer for giving proper priority to the great mission of evangelism. Ross and Archer consistently attempt to craft a theory that will attract the lost. While we may differ about the wisdom of tailoring our theories to the mental state of unbelievers, we cannot help but thank Ross and Archer and express our fondest admiration for their effort in this regard, which is consistently driven by evangelistic sensitivity. Indeed, if adjusting our exegesis were to find evangelistic success, this kind of tailoring has more promise than excessively arcane theories that, on the one hand, call for more literary ability than normally expected and, on the other hand, unwittingly strip the historicity from the narratives. So we appreciate the Ross-Archer effort to avoid unnecessary hindrances to the gospel presentation. We would agree with them that debatable cosmological models should not be confused with, or elevated above, the nondebatable gospel of Christ. We part company with them, however, and believe that the gospel may have more inherent stumbling blocks, including its doctrine of creation.

Demonstrating Scientific Expertise

Ross and Archer have demonstrated expert knowledge of astrophysics and the hard sciences. We stand ready to run up the white flag of surrender if this debate called on us to demonstrate more scientific expertise than Ross and Archer.[1] Indeed, Ross and Archer have made many excellent contributions in their essay. First, their discussion of the improbability of whale evolution was informative and compelling. Second, their claim that "ecologists have observed several extinctions of horse and whale species during human history, *never* a significant change within a species, much less the appearance of a new one" fits well with the teaching of Genesis 1 (but may not be entirely compatible with suggesting the continuous creation of new species, as we show later). Third, their attempt to devise a testable creation theory is admirable. Fourth, they correctly remind us that naturalistic biologists face insuperable obstacles producing missing links within reasonable boundary conditions. Fifth, we appreciate their analysis of mitochondrial DNA, disproving common ancestry for humans, chimps, and other primates.[2]

Voicing Sound Theological Formulations

The Ross-Archer essay also voices several sound theological formulations. It refreshingly affirms biblical inerrancy[3] as well as the doctrine that "all humankind descended from Adam and Eve, who suddenly appeared no more than a few tens of thousands of years ago." Indeed, it seems that even on the age of man, Ross and Archer do not diverge from us to any significant degree. They affirm that the age of man is less than 60,000 years—a finding that may be incompatible, not so much with our classical view, as with other modern views. At this juncture, the authors have wisely resisted the lure to conform the biblical message to the expectations of unbelievers. In addition, they laudably emphasize the fact that the human Fall was predated by an angelic fall and that the entire human race is infected with sin—even though we would state this doctrine differently. Furthermore, they confess that even the Fall occurred for God's glory. Their essay contains several other sound theological formulations that should help clarify several important issues for many readers.

Criticizing Literary Approaches

We also agree with Ross and Archer that literary theories effectively reducing the Genesis narratives to myth neither echo the text nor prove apologetically compelling. We agree with many of their criticisms of mythological approaches and concur with them when they strongly affirm that the "prolific use of chronological terminology" in Genesis renders nonsequential interpretations impossible. Ross and Archer are correct that poetic accounts occur in the Bible, but that the language of Genesis 1–2 is not the same as that of the Psalms or Job. In short, even though we obviously disagree on the central point of the length of the days of creation, we nevertheless thank Ross and Archer for their contribution to this debate and for seeking to bring every thought captive to Christ.

CLARIFICATION

Having commended Ross and Archer for a job well done in many respects, we now must clarify what we perceive to be some of their misunderstandings of our position. Much of what Ross and Archer understand to be, and oppose as, the 24-hour day position is not *our* position. In the main, Ross and Archer react against a few variations of young-earth creationism. We do not understand young-earth creationism to be a central part of this debate, nor have we sought to be dogmatic about the age of the universe. That issue is not what this debate is about. This debate is about what Scripture teaches about the length of the creation days. While Ross and Archer certainly are free to criticize views that are not ours, unfortunately they have missed the mark with respect to our view in a number of places. Without detailed elaboration, but for the sake of clarification, we dissociate ourselves with the criticisms proffered by Ross and Archer on the following points:

- We do not hold our position because of "fear" of science or the physical universe. Ross and Archer may have interacted with some 24-hour creationists who are fearful in precisely this way, but this criticism simply does not alight with respect to our view. While we have no fear of good science or good exegesis, we are properly suspicious of compromise. To succeed in proving 24-hour proponents to be motivated by fear, Ross and Archer would have to demonstrate that pre-1800 evangelicals were similarly phobic, since they held the same view we defend in this book. One cannot simultaneously appeal to patristics and also accuse them of phobia if they held to classical exegesis. Long before the rise of modern science, the classical view of normal creation days obtained dominance. We wish Ross and Archer would produce pre-1800 exegetes who held to their view that Genesis 1 requires or permits a billions-of-years-old cosmos. This issue is important and should not be relegated to psychological affect. Our views are based on Scripture only.

- We have not launched a salvo suggesting that the day-age view necessarily buys into nature's cruelty.

- We are not among the young-earth creationists who "have invested their efforts in fighting the wrong battle." Far from being anti-scientific, we merely oppose any scientific theory that contradicts God's inspired revelation.

- We do not remotely believe "in the efficiency of natural-process biological evolution."

- We do not argue that "a huge number of new species of animal life appear" related to the Flood. Nor do we "propose an efficiency of natural biological speciation greater than the most optimistic Darwinist."

- We deny the charge that the 24-hour view tends toward gnosticism. Indeed, we call for a healthy respect for physical creation, even going as far as affirming that God can make enormously complex and immense biosystems by His word alone. Neither does our essay advocate a "gnostic notion that there is no life, truth, or substance in matter."

- We certainly never suggest that light travel is a "myth concocted and disseminated by the astrophysical community, a deliberate lie." We simply affirm the miraculous and believe that light travel may supersede normal or known scientific processes.

- We do not refer to the "differing time clock" argument, seeing it as unnecessary, and thus, we refuse to speculate about it.

- We do not deny the 1987 supernova eruptions and other events of recent history.

- We never claim that Adam's body "entered the world through the womb of a woman," and would be hard-pressed to cite any credible theologian who propounds that view. In the heat of argument, advocates may attribute certain implications to their opponents, but we have no knowledge of any leading evangelical scholar who holds to such a view. even more afield is the mistaken suggestion that to hold to classical interpretations of Genesis 1 logically implies somehow that Adam carried "memories of his nonexistent childhood." Can any commentary be produced advocating that view? It is certainly not our view.

- We never address the subject of whether there was nonhuman death prior to Adam's Fall.[4] That simply is outside the scope of our debate and distracts from the issues at hand. Nevertheless, we are confident that any view contradicting Romans 5 or 8 is incorrect.

- We certainly do not place the Genesis creation "in the category of myth."

In sum, we do not hold to our position because of fear, gnosticism, a denial of recent supernova eruptions, differing time clocks, or a belief that Adam had pre-existent memories. By making these arguments, Ross and Archer are not responding to us, and we are not guilty by association.

CONFUTATION

Now that we have commended Ross and Archer and distinguished our approach from others, we must confute several factual and interpretative errors they made in their essay.

Scientific Rationalism

Perhaps unwittingly, Ross and Archer seem to espouse a type of rationalism that is incompatible with the best of biblical Christianity. They open their essay by affirming—at least on the surface—parity between sinful observers of nature and God's infallible revelation. An equal authority seems to be awarded to nature (as observed by sinful man) as to Scripture. The result is a rationalism that persistently squeezes Scripture. If Scripture must conform to the status of scientific theory, God's word is subject to man's mind. Indeed, it appears that this view advocates reconciling God's word to man's fluctuating catalogue of observations. If that observation is true, Ross and Archer have to explain why so many earlier Christians symphonically thought the "words of the Bible and the works of creation" taught the 24-hour view. As we took great pains to demonstrate, the 24-hour view was the majority view for centuries. Were *all* those interpreters wrong? Further, what if future scientists abandon their present theories and return to more biblically compatible cosmologies? Would that agreement between revelation and nature contradict the Ross-Archer revisionary proposals? Despite their protests to the contrary, it appears that for Ross and Archer, science controls Scripture.

Historical Inaccuracies

Ross and Archer also err in their appeals to history. Besides selectively appealing to history, Ross and Archer make several claims that are not confirmed by the historical record. We are thankful that Ross and Archer do not make the early Church fathers appear to be prescient Carl Sagans, as some have attempted. Nevertheless, none of the Reformers or Church fathers espoused the view of the Ross-Archer essay. Although the Ross-Archer claim that none of the thousands of pre-Nicene pages of commentary[5] defines the length of *day* is fraught with rhetorical panache, it does not itself explain that fact. The explanation, not mentioned by Ross and Archer, is that *few, if any, of the pre-Nicene writers held anything other than a 24-hour view.* Neither did the post-Nicene writers hold the Ross-Archer view. Instead, as we have shown, orthodox commentators, prior to the modern scientific revolution, either held to the 24-hour view or followed Augustine in his nanosecond view. If, as Ross and Archer claim, "all these early scholars accepted that *yôm* could mean 'a long time period,'" perhaps Ross and Archer will produce cites from early commentaries from those who "explicitly taught that the Genesis creation days were extended time periods." Meanwhile, we are convinced that Robert Bishop more accurately summarized the historical record: "Neither the original audience of that book [Genesis] nor anyone else until about two hundred years ago would have understood a 'geological era' to be a meaningful concept."[6]

Just as Ross and Archer overstate the historical case for the day-age view, they also claim that no "Ante-Nicene Father explicitly endorsed the 24-hour interpretation." Basil did, and so did Ambrose. (Ross and Archer themselves categorize Augustine, Ambrose,[7] and Basil in this period; so we call them as witnesses, too.) None except a minority who followed Augustine's creative exegesis asserted that creation occurred over a long period before modern revisionism took root in orthodox Christian circles. If Ross and Archer cannot produce documentation, then they must cease from associating the ancients with modern views that the ancients never held. The historical record is clear, and it strongly dissents from the unsubstantiated assertions in the Ross-Archer essay. In fact, Ross and Archer nearly admit that the Church fathers wrote "long before" the scientific revolution and before "evidences" (heavily skewed by an interpretive bias) of antiquity "became available." The ancients *did* write before that bias arose, and they *did not* espouse views compatible with modernity.

Ross and Archer's claim that no pre-Nicene commentator ever defined "day" is another misfire. This claim would be roughly analogous to claiming, "No baseball player, out of the thousands of major leaguers before 1997, ever hit over 62 home runs—*not one!*" Such a claim may sound impressive at first, and may even lead an unwary reader to believe that no one has ever accomplished this feat, but the broader record of history is clear: two players exceeded that number of homers in a single season. To "forget" to mention Mark McGwire and Sammy Sosa or to define the issue in a way that excludes them leads to embarrassing factual errors. Thus, Ross and Archer have defined the issue to exclude the clear testimony of Basil, Ambrose (who contrary to the claim did not waver), Augustine, Anselm, all the major Reformers, and other preeminent theologians who clearly and uniformly endorsed views at odds with the day-age and framework views.

Many consistently misrepresent Augustine; his view is not that creation occurred over a long period, but that it happened instantaneously— the exact opposite direction in time of those who seek protection in his shadow. Aquinas and Luther are clear, as are Calvin and the consistent biblical tradition. Any Christian can consult the Nicene Fathers and see for himself what they believed and taught. Ironically, the Ross-Archer view finds no support in the historical record.

Theological Idiosyncrasies

Ross and Archer set forth several idiosyncratic[8] theological notions. One is that the seventh day continues to provide for an ongoing creation. They even contradict this notion. At one place Ross and Archer claim that God's "physical creation is complete" on the sixth day, but elsewhere, they assert that "God supernaturally introduced new species . . . replacing those that became extinct." It is not altogether clear how both propositions can be true, most likely indicating the attempted fusion of contradictory ideas.

Quite apart from *any* biblical testimony, Ross and Archer attempt to maintain a continuing creation of new species "to suit the changing environment." Yet, previous biblical interpreters did not detect or expect a continuation of creation. Indeed, the Ross-Archer claim for replacement species contradicts the Bible itself. The Church has long understood that God's creation work was completed by the original Sabbath (which should not be conveniently elongated to make room for recent theories), and we have difficulty finding any exegete who asserts that God created new species (contra Gen. 2:2–3). The Bible does *not* teach continuous creation. It teaches that the seventh day signaled the end of God's creation work.

The Ability of Fallen Man

Ross and Archer also overstate the ability of fallen man. While we agree that no needless barriers should be erected to prevent us from evangelizing the lost, we do not share the view that those who are fallen will be unbiased, make an unassisted free and rational choice, and commit their lives to Christ "when they see a creation model that successfully predicts future discoveries and withstands the assaults of skeptics." We do not find, and the Bible does not teach, that people come to a saving knowledge simply when arm-wrestled by numerous facts, scientific proofs, or predictive models. Neither are we of the opinion that "our effectiveness in fulfilling our God-given assignment on the earth" depends on reconfiguring the Bible to meet science's claims *du jour*.

According to Scripture, the minds of men are darkened (Eph. 4:18). They willfully refuse God's word unless their hearts are first melted by the Spirit. The New Testament teaches that the worldly mind cannot understand spiritual matters (Rom. 8:5; 1 Cor. 2:10–14) and that rebellious sinners—scientific or otherwise—have clouded vision and are "darkened in their understanding" (Eph. 4:18). The god of this world has even blinded them (2 Cor. 4:4). Evangelism is not designed to cater to blindness, darkness, ignorance, rebellion, or insensitivity (Eph. 4:19). The evangelist's job is to tell the truth, even if it is unpopular.

Ross and Archer sincerely expect that if scandalous barriers are removed, "the evangelistic impact of such a resolution will be enormous." That would be nice, but there is no specific biblical promise that evangelism will be more effective if we attempt to lessen the scandal of the cross.

We also think it unwise to suggest, as do Ross and Archer, that a vocational group is an *ethnos*, even figuratively. even if true, the standards and message of God are unaltered for all nations, tribes, languages, and peoples. We doubt that the Scriptures will support different gospels tailored for different professions, especially since even astrophysicists are included in the biblical teaching that common dynamics apply to all people and all subspecialties (1 Cor. 10:13). It would not, for example, be wise for us to avoid God's truth by claiming that drug-dealers, abortionists, or prostitutes had their own *ethnos* and that evangelism should not place "barriers" in their paths.

The Nature of the Miraculous

The Ross-Archer model also demonstrates a confusion about the nature of miracles. In fact, their model leaves little, if any, room for the miraculous. For them, creation involved a providential implanting. Thereafter, nature took its course over millions or billions of years. Nowhere do Ross and Archer allow for God creating quickly by His word alone; to satisfy modern scientific dogma, He must always be subordinate to nature, which, under their construction, can never be suspended. Their essay does not merely assume, but dogmatizes, the uniformity of natural processes. Indeed, Genesis is recast to fit the mold of modern science.

On the other hand, we refuse to insist that God fit creation into our rationalistic mold. There is room in our view for a miracle, even if that miracle does not fit with current scientific theory. The miraculous may be part of the scandal of the cross today.

We disagree that the Bible views things as Ross-Archer suggest: "A galaxy measured to be about 13 billion light-years away must have existed about 13 billion years ago." That is to put God in a box or to expect Him to march to our watches. Surely, the God of all eternity and Creator of time is freer and more capable than Ross and Archer posit. God can create in any fashion He wishes, and He is not bound by our paltry understanding after the fact.

Nor do we view God as inherently "deceptive" if the galaxies, *according to our understanding,* appear to be old, just because He miraculously created them as full-blown. Concluding that He is "deceptive" is our mistaken reckoning, not His. To insist that God fit in with our chronology is to subordinate the Creator of nature to nature. We deny the antisupernaturalism inherent in any attempt to manacle God and coerce Him to fit our fallible observations.

The very essence of miracles is to confound our wisdom and defy scientific law. Consider the example of Jesus turning the water into wine in John 2. At one moment, it "appeared" to observers to be water, and the next moment, after the miracle occurred, it was wine. And wine, apart from a miracle, normally takes time to ferment. When it comes to the miraculous, "appearances" do not contradict reality. The water really did turn into wine, and the essence of that miracle was that it did not take the time it normally takes to ferment. Observers may employ their normal powers of observation and categorize things normally. However, when God works a miracle, things change quickly, and man's observations must bow to the realities brought about by God. Every miracle, by definition, flies in the face of known science. But even if it defies conventional wisdom, the miraculous does not transform God into a deceiver.

Similarly, we cannot allow the facts of creation—that Adam appears fully-grown, that the Garden appears fully developed, and that the universe and its effects appear to be old—to trump God's inventive and marvelous creating ability. This obvious truth does not make God a deceiver. Creation, like any other miracle, must allow for change in substance, and we cannot allow such change to be trumped by rationalistic demands that appearances must dominate.

The most serious flaw in the Ross-Archer approach is that it gives equal ultimacy to revelation and reason. All creation, it seems, is squeezed into the mold of this presupposition, which, if unchecked, must insist that all Scripture's miracles (including walking on water, multiplying fishes and loaves, and rising from the dead) either deceive us (if truly miraculous) or can be explained only in terms of uniformitarianism.

Questionable Interpretations

At some points, the Ross-Archer essay adopts questionable biblical interpretations. When Ross and Archer assert[9] that the wording of Genesis 2 "indicates" that Eden's trees "were permitted to grow and mature from seeds," they not only contradict orthodox interpretations prior to 1800, but also impose their extraneous view on the Hebrew language itself. Contrary to their assertion, the Hebrew makes no mention of seeds, nor does the text itself vaguely suggest that such long development occurred. Ross and Archer read that proposition into the text.

Likewise, they read the following into the text concerning the sixth day: "It must have taken a good deal of study for Adam to examine each specimen thoroughly and decide on a suitable name." The claim that "many weeks', months', or even years' worth of activities took place" on the sixth day begs the question they have to prove in the first place.

even more speciously, Ross and Archer assert that Adam somehow lost "his initial excitement and thrill" after tilling the garden for a while. This assertion is based on mere speculation and finds no support in the text.

As we have discussed above, we also specifically disagree with the Ross-Archer interpretation that the seventh day of creation has not ended. While one may need to extrapolate to this conclusion to support other theological schemes, no such teaching is contained in Genesis 2:1–3. Nor do we believe that the other passages cited are correctly interpreted to create an unending seventh day (an interpretation rejected by other insightful biblical interpreters). No doctrine of a weekly Sabbath could ever be supported if such were the case. Grammar, good theology, logic, and the history of interpretation do not demand any such conclusion.

In addition, Ross and Archer misapply John 5:16–18. They attempt to claim that Jesus advocated continuous creation consistent with an ongoing Sabbath, spanning from Eve's creation until today. The context, however, suggests otherwise, and needless to say, most biblical commentators[10] would not attempt to stretch the language unless they had some other agenda to promote.

Among other objectionable biblical interpretations, we simply alert the careful reader to the following:

- The appeals to God's days being different than ours (Psa. 90) is a proof of His timelessness, not an affirmation that the Genesis record is inscrutable.

- If the miraculous is permitted, the sixth day does not require long periods.

- The reference to the "day of wrath" does not necessarily, if at all, refer to a long period.

- The language of Genesis 2:4 does not require yôm to mean a long period elsewhere in Scripture.

- Habakkuk 3:6 does not in any way support an expansive period for creation. For Ross and Archer to claim that it does is for them to read their view into the text.

- Far from proving the day-age view, references to the Hebrew words for evening and morning actually fit more naturally with our 24-hour view.

- The claim that the vast number of observable stars proves a huge, "and if huge, then old," universe is but another example of begging the question. Ross and Archer's unproven assumptions should not be confused with the Bible's objective message.

It is also dubious that secular scientists will readily agree that the scientific method is derived from Scripture, and seculars would likely join us in affirming that the Ross-Archer essay certainly does not espouse a literal view.

While we appreciate Ross and Archer's hard work to make the Scriptures fit with modern science to reach the lost, we sincerely disagree with their interpretations of many scriptural passages. We simply believe that the lost will be more impressed with the majestic God of Scripture than with the barely visible deity the Ross-Archer essay offers—the God who seldom rivals, and often is conformed to, nature or the latest scientific rendition.

CONCLUSION

Having commended Ross and Archer for their finer points, clarified some of their misunderstandings of our view, and confuted some of their errors, we think it only appropriate to conclude with Augustine and through him, with the Church through the ages until the last 200 years: "Creation, therefore, did not take place slowly in order that a slow development might be implanted . . . nor were the ages established at the plodding pace at which they now pass."[11]

Mendicant appeals to past thinkers at first do not seem helpful, but if such appeals push readers to consult the unadulterated historical record, they may do more than anything we can say to convince readers to adopt the classical view we have espoused. When we ponder the considerable "evolution" of myth regarding the subject of creation, the classical view of creation, serendipitously, becomes strengthened the more it is attacked by defective theories. In the end, the classical view of creation may survive because . . . it is the fittest.

NOTES

1. Of course, numerous other scientific professionals have expertise in these areas. Indeed, some take exception to the scientific conclusions presented by Ross and Archer. By confessing our lack of expertise in the hard sciences, we do not mean to imply that the scientific conclusions reached by Ross and Archer are beyond criticism.

2. We must admit, however, that many scientists may not agree that the Ross-Archer model is quite as compelling as our friends believe. We also note that the Ross-Archer testable model selectively affirms belief in "fiat miracles" at some times but not at others.

3. While we appreciate Ross and Archer's affirmation of biblical inerrancy, we believe that they cannot rightfully lay claim to a "literal" interpretation when their position is so clearly nonliteral. Ross and Archer really should stop describing their view as "literal." It is not credible, except as a rhetorical guise, in the present debate for them to claim the mantle of literal interpretation, especially in light of the exegetical history we have presented. While Ross and Archer attempt to gain the confidence of evangelicals by employing preferred language, it simply does not pass the test of candor for them to claim that a literal day may span millennia.

4. The New Testament seems to contradict the argument that there was pre-Fall animal death when it speaks of the *entire universe* becoming enslaved to corruption through Adam's singular act (Rom. 8:21). Earlier, the same passage affirms that death entered the cosmos—not merely the sphere of man—through that one sin (Rom. 5:12). Further, the "creation," not just man, ever since has been subjected to vanity (Rom. 8:20).

5. There also are far more pages written post-Nicea which uniformly support our view. The weight and amount of testimony is irrefutable.

6. Robert C. Bishop, "Science and Theology: A Methodological Comparison," *Journal of Interdisciplinary Studies*, vol. 5, no. 1/2 (1993), p. 155.

7. Ambrose did not vacillate; it is merely that Ross and Archer did not read far enough to allow him to clarify any perceived ambiguity. The citation in our opening essay provides the needed context. In addition, as our essay's footnotes indicate, all later interpreters of Ambrose and Basil interpreted them as we have, in contradistinction to the claims of Ross and Archer. Neither Augustine nor any other early theologian sought to correct the 24-hour views of Ambrose and Basil.

8. Though these idiosyncratic views are interesting, over time they probably will be recognized as creative attempts to fit the Bible into a scientific mold, much like flat-earth conformity centuries ago. Besides, of the 111 references given to bolster their claims, 50 are to writings of Ross or his organization and 7 are to the works of Archer.

9. Thankfully, at least Ross and Archer had the wisdom not to associate any previous commentators with these views.

10. John Calvin, among others, did not envision the Ross-Archer idea of an unending seventh day in his commentary on John 5:17.

11. Augustine, "The Literal Meaning of Genesis," bk. 4, chap. 27, *Ancient Christian Writers: The Works of the Fathers in Translation*, no. 41, *The Literal Meaning of Genesis*, p. 33.

THE
FRAMEWORK
RESPONSE

*A*s with Duncan and Hall, Ross and Archer have given much of their contribution to matters other than the specific exegetical issues at the heart of this debate, particularly to the well-known research on cosmic origins published by Ross. At least Ross and Archer present these tangential matters in an interesting fashion, and we heartily agree with many of the points they make against the young-earth position. Our own experience, for example, supports their observation that the present level of agitation over the days of the creation account is due to a fear that questioning the 24-hour view will open the door to macroevolution. Many are afraid that creationists who advocate or allow for the possibility of an old earth cannot logically avoid a slippery slope to a macroevolutionary, naturalistic worldview, in spite of their emphatic protests to the contrary. Ross and Archer are to be commended, therefore, for showing the logical coherence and stability of an old earth, non-macroevolutionary creationist position.

We also agree with Ross and Archer when they insist that we must uphold the meaningfulness and trustworthiness of natural revelation against the appearance-of-age defense forwarded by many young-earth creationists. Ross and Archer also argue correctly that young-earth advocates who reject plant and animal death before the Fall base their conclusions on faulty theological assumptions. Moreover, in general outline, we find the Ross-Archer positive cosmogony model persuasive. Although we prefer a more moderate concordism when correlating the text of Genesis with scientific models, we accept the proposed model in broad outline,[1] though such acceptance is not essential to the framework interpretation per se. The most compelling aspect of the Ross-Archer model is its use of the fossil record to argue against a macroevolutionary picture of the origin of living things in favor of one that sees God repeatedly creating new kinds to replace extinct ones during the creation period but with no new kinds after the creation of man, which marks the close of the creation period. Against the young-earth theorists, Ross and Archer also rightly maintain that a creation model allowing for a long era in no way compromises the power of God, observing that, "God would have created everything in one immeasurable instant, if time were a measure of His power." God has His own reasons for the time scale, reasons which we may never be able to fathom, but which we certainly have no right to question.

On the origin and antiquity of man, we again generally agree with Ross and Archer. Acknowledging that the incompleteness of the biblical genealogies limits their usefulness for determining precise dates, Ross and Archer correctly hold that a realistic time frame for the antiquity of man would range from 10,000 to 60,000 years. With Ross and Archer, we affirm that Adam was a historical figure, that he was the product of a special act of divine creation from the dust of the ground apart from biological ancestry, and that Eve was fashioned out of Adam's side by a subsequent act of special creation. Those who honor the authority of Scripture cannot rightly adopt evolutionary scenarios for the origin of man.[2]

HERMENEUTICAL CONCERNS

Science-Driven Approach to the Text

Despite our areas of agreement with Ross and Archer, we reject the hermeneutic they employ in arriving at their day-age interpretation. That hermeneutic may be described as an extreme form of concordism in which they interpret the text as providing a detailed, scientifically testable model of cosmic origins. In contrast to this science-driven approach, we believe it is best to set scientific questions to the side while exegeting the text. As Henri Blocher persuasively argues:

In the case of the opening chapters of Genesis, it is not plausible that the human author knew what we are taught by astronomers, geologists and other scientists. Therefore we must curb the desire to make the scientific view play a part in the actual interpretation; the interpretation must cling solely to the text and its context. The inescapable comparison with the sciences of cosmic, biological and human origins will not come until after; this will no doubt have repercussions on the work of interpretation which is never completed, but they will be of a merely external nature. . . . We conclude that the place of the sciences in the reading of the Bible is this: they have neither authority, nor even a substantial ministerial role within the actual interpretation; they act as warnings and confirmations at a later stage.[3]

Our "Scripture first, science later" methodology accords best with the nature and purpose of Scripture, which does not normally speak in scientific terms for the purpose of answering purely scientific questions. The Bible was given, rather, as the covenant revelation of God to His people that they might be made wise unto salvation through faith in Christ Jesus (2 Tim. 3:15). The creation account functions as a prologue to the book of Genesis, indeed to all the canonical Scriptures, laying the presuppositional foundations concerning the doctrine of creation and God's eschatological purpose for the cosmos with man as central to that purpose. Answering detailed scientific questions concerning the order and time frame of creation is not one of the purposes of the creation account.

But in warning against assigning priority to science in the hermeneutical process, we need to clarify that we are not endorsing an *anti*-concordist approach to the creation account.[4] Many modern scholars who are not committed to an evangelical view of Scripture argue that the Genesis account belongs to the category of myth, saga, or theological parable. Thus "whatever the significance of the [creation] record may be, it is not a revelation of physical fact which can be brought in line with the results of modern science."[5] Biblical language simply operates in a different universe of discourse, they argue. But this approach is fundamentally Kantian, since it supposes that knowledge and belief are ultimately incommensurable. The fact that the primary purpose of Genesis is covenantal and eschatological does not rule out the possibility that it includes disclosures of significance for cosmogony and cosmology. Since all realms of creation are ordained and sustained by God, we must not separate the scientific and the theological into distinct compartments.[6]

Thus, in dealing with the creation record, we must avoid the Scylla of unbridled concordism, but we also must steer clear of the Charybdis of Kantian fideism, which denies that Scripture provides any normative data in the physical sphere. Both approaches involve a faulty view of Scripture. On the one hand, Kantian fideism errs since it contradicts the claim of the Genesis cosmogony to be a historical account of events that actually transpired. Unbridled concordism, on the other hand, errs by obscuring the covenantal and eschatological thrust of the text in the process of treating it as a series of anticipations of future scientific discoveries.

Ross and Archer criticize our more moderate concordist approach as being "defeatist" because it does not set forth a testable, verifiable creation model. But this criticism begs the question. Is it proper to approach the text assuming at the outset that it will give us a lengthy list of scientifically testable propositions, and reject as defeatist those interpretations that do not yield such lists? Shouldn't we instead strive to interpret the text on its own terms, and only then draw out its scientific implications? Harmonization of Scripture with scientifically interpreted natural revelation should not drive our interpretation of the text, nor should we assume that an interpretation is viable only if it yields experimentally verifiable data. While we agree that concord between the Bible and science is achievable in principle, the engine driving the interpretive train should not be the experimental testability of a particular interpretation, but rather, how well it *exegetically* harmonizes with the whole Bible.

Moreover, in our interpretation, the creation account does yield some scientifically testable data concerning physical reality, including the following:

- The creation had an absolute beginning (Gen. 1:1).[7]
- The six days constitute a closed period initiated and punctuated by supernatural origination, after which no further acts of special creation occur (Gen. 2:1–2).
- Man was created at the end of the process of cosmos formation and population (Gen. 1:26–31).[8]

Thus, Ross and Archer's assertion that the framework interpretation "offers no model for life's history and, therefore, cannot be tested" is factually incorrect. They might still claim that their view is preferable because it purportedly boasts a longer list of verifiable events, but we challenge as hermeneutically unsound the assumption underlying such a claim—that the interpretation which yields the largest scientific or apologetic pay-off is, for that very reason, superior. Such pragmatic considerations are irrelevant in evaluating whether a given interpretation is correct.

Other Hermeneutical Questions

Predictive Prophesies? In support of their hermeneutic of maximal apologetic usefulness, Ross and Archer appeal to predictive prophecies as a biblical analogy. Although providing proof of the divine origin of the biblical message may indeed be an incidental purpose of such prophecies, the degree of apologetic evidence they afford is not a valid criterion for preferring one interpretation to another.[9] Moreover, it does not seem plausible to treat Genesis 1 as a sort of prophecy that is confirmed by modern scientific discoveries since the text contains no internal pointers suggesting the possibility of future confirmation.

Narratives as Myths? Worse still, as they strain to make a case for their extreme harmonistic hermeneutic, Ross and Archer make the blunder of asserting something about biblical narratives that utterly subverts the sound theology they normally advocate. In particular, they assert that scientifically "unverifiable narratives" belong to the genre of myth. On this definition, however, they would be forced to relegate the narratives of the virgin birth, the resurrection of Jesus, and the other miraculous events recorded in Scripture to the mythical realm since they too are scientifically unverifiable!

Literary Sequence as Actual Historical Sequence? On the related question of chronological sequence in the creation account, Ross and Archer attempt to argue, contrary to the framework interpretation, that *wherever* we find "sequence markers," the literary sequence represents the actual historical sequence. But this argument overstates the case. Examples of the nonsequential use of "sequence markers" occur throughout Scripture, including the nonsequential use of the *waw*-consecutive in Hebrew narrative,[10] the numbered openings of the seven-sealed book of Revelation 6:1–8:1 (notice the striking similarity with the use of the number seven in Genesis 1), and the use of the sequence marker "and I saw" throughout Revelation to establish a literary, but not necessarily historical, sequence.[11] But most decisively, the specific exegetical evidence we have adduced for the nonsequential nature of the days of Genesis sufficiently demonstrates that in Genesis 1, at least, the sequence markers do not reflect the actual historical sequence.

EXEGETICAL AND SCIENTIFIC CONCERNS

Mishandling Exegetical Data

As might be expected, the precommitment of the day-age view to maximal concordism results in a mishandling of the exegetical data. As Kline warns, the danger is that when "the perspectives of science [are] brought to the aid of the Biblical exegete . . . the judgment of the exegete will be influenced to espouse an interpretation of the Biblical text which the text will not properly sustain."[12] The day-age interpretation runs against the grain of the text in two primary areas.

The Meaning of the Days. The first major area where the attempt to find maximal harmony with science leads to untenable exegesis pertains to the meaning of the days of the creation week. At this point we agree with the 24-hour theorists that at the literal level, Genesis 1 speaks of seven ordinary days, and that the sixfold evening-morning formula signifies the ordinary cycle of sunset and sunrise. The day-age attempt to take *yôm* as denoting a finite but extended period cannot be sustained in this context, regardless of whether the term can have that meaning in other contexts. Genesis 1 identifies *yôm* as an evening and morning complex, that is, as an ordinary day composed of a period of daylight and a period of darkness.

Of course, we part ways with the 24-hour view when we insist that the *total picture* of the divine workweek with its days and evening-morning refrain be taken figuratively.[13] The creation history is figuratively presented as an ordinary week in which the divine Workman/Craftsman goes about His cosmos-building labors for six days with intervening pauses during the night between each day, and finally rests from His work on the seventh day. This anthropomorphic[14] interpretation of the week finds further corroboration in subsequent revelation, which explicitly draws the parallel already implicit in Genesis 2:2–3 between God's work-rest pattern and man's (Exo. 20:11; 31:17). Actually God's workweek of creation, which is revealed in Genesis 1:1–2:3 as a sabbatically structured process, was the archetype (original), while the weekly pattern of life appointed for God's human image-bearer is the ectype (copy).

Although we expound in our main essay the exegetical evidence that the author of Genesis wants us to view the picture of the creation week figuratively, we pause now to highlight the following points:

- The literary structure of the two parallel triads.

- The obvious correspondence between the first and fourth days, indicating the presence of recapitulation and thus encouraging us to take the days as picture frames in which the creative activity is narrated topically rather than sequentially.

- The argument from Genesis 2:5–6, which indicates that God so ordered the sequence of creation acts that His providential operations could proceed by ordinary rather than extraordinary means, thus reinforcing the presumption that the creation of the luminaries (Day 4) precedes and is the natural source of the daylight, whose creation is described in Day 1.

- The evidence that the Genesis cosmogony has been shaped by the employment of the Bible's two-register cosmology, thus demonstrating that the picture of the week of days is but one element of a broader pattern in which upper-register realities are described through the metaphorical use of lower-register terminology.

- And finally, the fact that the seventh day is an eternal, upper-register day—the unending day of God's own Sabbath enthronement in the upper register—demands that we take the entire picture of the week, of which the Sabbath is the concluding capstone, as an upper-register week rather than a week of literal solar days.

Thus, the attempt of day-age interpreters to show that yôm can be used in some contexts to mean a long period results in clouding, if not totally eclipsing, the picture painted in the text. The 24-hour advocates are closer to the truth in this regard, although their insistence on taking the picture literally misses the *point* of the picture.

The Luminaries and the Fourth Day. The second major area where the attempt to find maximal harmony with science leads to untenable exegesis is the approach Ross and Archer take to the statements in Genesis 1:14–19 concerning the luminaries of the fourth day. In their attempt to make the textual sequence harmonize with the scientific sequence, Ross and Archer do violence to the language of the fourth day. The text describes the events as the creation of the luminaries on that day. Because Ross and Archer believe that the luminaries were created during day-age one or before, they are forced to conclude that the events recorded on the fourth day do not describe the *creation* of the luminaries; rather, they describe the luminaries *becoming visible* to an earthbound observer by reason of the "transformation of the atmosphere from perpetually translucent to occasionally transparent." But the text explicitly says that God "made" (v. 16) the luminaries on Day 4 and employs the same fiat-fulfillment language employed on the other five days for acts of creation. If Genesis 1 were intended to provide astounding predictions of future scientific discoveries as Ross and Archer maintain, why didn't the Holy Spirit simply say that the luminaries "became visible" on Day 4? The attempt to find exact sequential harmony between Genesis 1 and science, which is essential to the day-age interpretation, founders on the insoluble difficulties raised by the fourth day.

Problems with Scientific Data

Finally, this is a good place to point out that the day-age interpretation not only leads to a mishandling of the exegetical data, but also runs into difficulty with the scientific data. As scientific experts critical of the ex-treme concordism Ross articulates have observed, the alleged "perfect fit" between the narrative sequence of Genesis 1 and the scientific record breaks down when one looks at the scientific record in detail. For example (be-sides the Day 1/Day 4 problem), scientific findings propose that reptiles (Day 6) came into existence before the earliest birds (Day 5), and fish (Day 5) before seed-bearing land plants (Day 3).[15]

SOME BIBLICAL-THEOLOGICAL ERRORS

In addition to the concerns outlined above, we also have some major biblical-theological concerns with the day-age position as formulated by Ross and Archer.

De-eschatologizing the Seventh Day

According to Ross and Archer, the seventh day is a finite period that will end when God brings about a new creation in the eternal state. We reject this reading of the seventh day on the ground that Scripture views the Sabbath as the sign of eschatological consummation.[16] Reflecting on the failure of the wilderness generation to enter the land because of unbelief, Psalm 95 and Hebrews 3–4 speak of our eschatological inheritance as a participation in God's own seventh-day rest. But on Ross and Archer's view, the seventh day ends *immediately prior* to the consummation, thus destroy-ing the eschatological significance of the seventh day of creation (Matt. 11:28; 2 Thess. 1:7; Heb. 4:1–11; Rev. 14:13).

Furthermore, this interpretation of the seventh day as terminating prior to the eternal state undercuts the eschatological aspect of creation. Ac-cording to Ross and Archer, when the seventh day is terminated, at that moment God will resume His work of creation by making a replacement cosmos to be the eternal abode of the redeemed in the eternal state. This scenario is contradicted, however, by the teaching of Scripture that the *original* creation was destined for Sabbath consummation, as the picture of the creation week as a workweek ending in the divine rest on the seventh day indicates.[17] The Fall did not negate that original hope but required the remedial work of redemption for its ultimate accomplishment in spite of sin. Thus, there will not be a new creation in the sense of a replace-ment creation totally discontinuous with the present one, but a purifying judgment, analogous to the Flood, resulting in the emergence of a renewed and transfigured creation in which the current distinction between the up-per and lower registers will be permanently removed.

Confusing Creation and Redemption

Ross and Archer also err from a biblical-theological standpoint when they assert that *creation* was the remedial process employed by God to conquer evil. This analysis logically implies that evil was present before the creation of the universe. But Satan and his demonic followers are created beings, righteous at the very beginning when God created the *heavens* and the earth (Gen. 1:1; Neh. 9:6; Col. 1:16).[18] Furthermore, as we have argued, the original creation was made with a built-in eschatological hope, and He who began this good work will complete it, despite the rebellious attempt of Satan to thwart God's purpose for creation. It is not creation, then, but *redemption* through Christ that constitutes the remedial program for dealing with evil. We must understand the work of Christ in its cosmic dimensions as the work of the Last Adam (1 Cor. 15:45), whose obedience to the covenant has reversed the effects of the Fall and ushered in the positive eschatological advancement originally held out to Adam in the Garden under the covenant of works. Christ came as the rightful heir of creation (Col. 1:15; Heb. 1:2) to redeem the entire creation, that the creation itself might be delivered from corruption into the freedom of the glory of the children of God (Rom. 8:18–23). Ross and Archer are correct in saying that God will conquer all evil. But He will do so, not by replacing this creation with a new one, but by bringing *this* fallen creation to its original consummation goal by means of the redemptive work of Christ.[19]

CONCLUSION

Though we find ourselves generally agreeing with the old-earth creation model of Ross and Archer, their interpretation of the chronology of Genesis 1:1–2:3 is not a valid option because of its serious hermeneutical, exegetical, and theological failings.

NOTES

1. As we explain in this section, we take exception to the Ross-Archer proposal that the current creation will be replaced by a totally new one in the eternal state.

2. John Murray demonstrates that Genesis 2:7 is irreconcilable with biological ancestry for man in "The Origin of Man," *Collected Writings of John Murray*, vol. 2 (Edinburgh, UK: The Banner of Truth Trust, 1977), pp. 3–13.

3. Henri Blocher, *In the Beginning: The Opening Chapters of Genesis*, trans. David G. Preston (Downers Grove, IL: InterVarsity Press, 1984), pp. 26–7.

4. Kline argues that his position is radically misinterpreted if it is taken as being anti- or even nonconcordist. See his reply to Jack Collins in *Perspectives on Science and Christian Faith*, vol. 48, no. 3 (1996), pp. 209–10.

5. John Skinner, *Genesis*, *The International Critical Commentary*, 2d edition (Edinburgh, UK: T. & T. Clark, 1930), p. 5.

6. Blocher, *In the Beginning*, p. 24.

7. We appreciate the apologetic labors of Ross in showing that the recent scientific confirmation of the Big Bang is in harmony with the teaching of Scripture.

8. Kline writes, "The implications of man's position as lord of creation, the scope of the cultural mandate, and other considerations require that the creation of man concluded the creative acts of God in the actual historical sequence as well as in the order of narration" ("Because It Had Not Rained," *Westminster Theological Journal*, vol. 20, no. 2 [May 1958], p. 154).

9. Furthermore, Ross and Archer's specific appeal to Jeremiah 31:38–40 and Daniel 9:24–7 presupposes the dispensational system of interpretation—a system we regard as being contrary to scriptural teaching.

10. E.g., Gen. 1:16; 2:15. Randall Buth, "Methodological Collision Between Source Criticism and Discourse Analysis: The Problem of 'Unmarked Temporal Overlay' and the Pluperfect/Nonsequential *wayyiqtol*," *Biblical Hebrew and Discourse Linguistics*, ed. Robert D. Bergen (Dallas: Summer Institute of Linguistics, 1994), pp. 138–54.

11. G. K. Beale, *The Book of Revelation*, *The New International Greek Testament Commentary* (Grand Rapids, MI: Wm. B. Eerdmans Publishing Co., 1999), pp. 121–41, 974–83; R. Fowler White, "Reexamining the Evidence for Recapitulation in Rev. 20:1–10," *Westminster Theological Journal*, vol. 51 (1989), pp. 319–44.

12. Meredith G. Kline, "Review of *The Christian View of Science and Scripture*, by Bernard Ramm," *Westminster Theological Journal*, vol. 18, no. 1 (1955), p. 53. In addition, the interpreter may unwittingly wed the text to a particular scientific model, which later turns out to be a misinterpretation of natural revelation.

13. "It is possible to treat the terminology of the week as figurative language, but at that moment 'day' has its ordinary meaning and *with that meaning* plays a figurative role." Blocher, *In the Beginning*, p. 45.

14. Not all metaphors used to describe God in our text are anthropomorphic (e.g., Gen. 1:2 describes the Spirit of God as a hovering bird), and not all the text's metaphors are used to describe God (e.g., some describe the upper register). Thus, the anthropomorphic picture of God as a human worker is simply one species of the broader genus of archetype-ectype language founded on two-register cosmology, as we explain more fully later in our essay, "The Framework View."

15. Reptile fossils predate both *Protoavis* and *Archaeopteryx* (primitive birds), and *Agnatha* (the earliest fossils of vertebrate fish) predate the rise of gymnosperms (primitive seed-bearing plants). While it is possible that further fossil discoveries may resolve these sequential difficulties, it also is possible on the same basis that further discoveries could throw the whole day-age model into confusion again.

16. Geerhardus Vos, *Biblical Theology* (Grand Rapids, MI: Wm. B. Eerdmans Publishing Co., 1985), pp. 138–43.

17. Meredith G. Kline, *Kingdom Prologue* (published by author, 1991), pp. 21–6.

18. For our exegetical defense of this reading of these texts, see our main essay.

19. Vos has taught us that eschatology is prior to soteriology and that soteriology is the means for the accomplishment of the original eschatology of creation.

Hugh Ross & Gleason L. Archer

THE DAY-AGE REPLY

uman interactions are wonderfully enriched—and complicated—by the interplay of intellect and emotion. As our discussion of the Genesis creation days reveals, the intricacy and
balance of these distinct yet interconnected components make
human relationships uniquely satisfying as well as uniquely challenging.

Our debate with Irons and Kline has stimulated our thinking and fueled
our determination to dig deeper into both the biblical and scientific data,
that which exists today and that which the future will bring. Our reply to
their critique of our position appears first in the following paragraphs.
Though abbreviated, it addresses the more important issues and looks forward to further dialogue.

Our debate with Duncan and Hall, by contrast, seems less promising.
Surging emotions seem to have swamped the intellectual exchange, drown-
ing out all but a flicker of hope for progress toward resolution or even for
thoughtful, respectful dialogue. Nevertheless, we offer our reply, attempting to explain why the misunderstandings and misrepresentations occur
and what can be done to calm the powerful feelings that foment them.

REPLY TO THE FRAMEWORK RESPONSE

In their opening statement, Irons and Kline commend our testable creation model, not just for its content on the origin of the universe, life, and man, but also for its fossil record analysis. This response, combined with their repudiation of theistic evolution and their affirmation of a recent, historical Adam, leads us to conclude that the gap between our two positions may be smaller than we first realized.

Irons and Kline clarify for readers that their denial of a Genesis chronology of creation events is only partial. Apparently, they interpret Genesis 1 as explicitly teaching that cosmic creation preceded primitive life's creation, which in turn preceded humanity's creation. If we understand them correctly, the only major points on which we diverge are these two: first, the risk of closely connecting the Genesis 1 chronology to the current understanding of nature's record; and second, the relative importance of the physical creation message in Genesis 1 to other doctrines.

In response to the first concern, we must point out that to establish the scientific security of our interpretation requires much more space than this volume allows. Whole books have been devoted to the task, including *The Genesis Question* and *Genesis One and the Origin of the Earth*.[1] For the past two decades, as technology has accelerated the pace of discovery, we repeatedly have been able to affirm and refine the close fit between science and Scripture. The trend favors increased security. Our trust in God's character and purpose as a truth-Revealer tells us that there is no risk in this enterprise.

Concerning the second point, we remain open. For example, we recognize that Genesis 1 hints at the doctrine of the Trinity with nouns and pronouns indicating that God is simultaneously singular and plural. Likewise, Genesis 1 establishes humanity's role and responsibility with respect to the planet and its life forms. While we view Irons and Kline's "upper-register cosmology" as a *stretch* from the Genesis 1 text alone, we do not deem it contradictory to other Scripture passages.

What Drives Our Interpretation

Like us, Irons and Kline are "concordists." What separates us is merely the degree of concordism. They suggest that we overdo it; we believe they do not go far enough. Irons and Kline raise four main hermeneutical and exegetical concerns in response to our concordism.

The first hermeneutical and exegetical concern Irons and Kline identify involves what drives our interpretation. We agree with framework scholar Henri Blocher that comparisons between Genesis 1 and the sciences of cosmic, biological, and human origins are inescapable. In quoting Blocher, however, Irons and Kline omit this significant sentence: "The sciences will stimulate the interpreter from without, driving him to verify his exegesis and test the evidence, or encouraging him by favorable convergences which bear witness to the common origin of the two Books of God."[2] Our scientific interpretation is driven by the biblical affirmation that such an interpretation is valid. We stand by the statement of the International Council on Biblical Inerrancy concerning the role of science in Bible interpretation that we cited earlier.

Irons and Kline's "Scripture first, science later" approach misses the obvious point that the "later" has arrived. Science has advanced to the point of practical certainty on the events outlined in Genesis 1. This does *not* mean that science and Scripture are equivalent. While nature's record can be considered one of God's "books," science is merely man's attempt to interpret and integrate that book's contents just as theology is man's attempt to interpret and systematize Scripture's contents.

We agree that Scripture "does not normally speak in scientific terms for the purpose of answering purely scientific questions." But the questions of Genesis 1 are *simultaneously* spiritual *and* scientific. While the passage tells us how the universe came to exist—a spiritual message—it also serves as the clearest, most specific, most detailed, and most direct Bible passage on natural history.

One of the important distinctives of the Bible compared to all other "holy books" is its extensive testability with respect to natural and historical records. Irons and Kline appear to accept Scripture's historical testability while denying its scientific testability. This imbalance seems unwarranted, especially given the declarations about nature's "message" in Psalm 19:1–4; 50:6; and Romans 1:18–22.

Irons and Kline assert that Genesis 1 lays the foundations for the doctrine of creation, and we wholeheartedly concur. We see no basis for assuming, however, that doctrinal truth necessarily excludes scientific truth about "the order and time frame of creation."

Irons and Kline at least acknowledge the possibility that Genesis 1 "includes disclosures of significance for cosmogony and cosmology." This acknowledgment would seem to allow for the possibility of developing a biblical cosmology. If that cosmology's concordism proves too extreme, ongoing scientific testing and biblical exegesis will expose it, and adjustments can be made. If the concordism proves too conservative, ongoing scientific testing and biblical exegesis will expose that, too. Again, the necessary adjustments should follow.

Since our understanding of God's revelations always will be less than perfect, it is a foregone conclusion that we will need to adjust and refine our biblical and scientific interpretations. Just as time and scholarship reassure us about the accuracy and stability of major biblical doctrines, so, too, time and scholarship attest that we run little risk of having to substantially alter our creation model, and certainly not on any point relevant to salvation or biblical inerrancy.

Of course, we agree that concordism must be bridled. Misguided enthusiasm leads some people to argue, for example, that Genesis 1 speaks of quarks, continental drift, dinosaurs, and pre-Adamic bipedal primates. While these components of nature are in no way inconsistent with the biblical creation account, no words in the passage demand or even suggest such interpretations. While we encourage scientific illustrations explaining how God might have achieved His creation results, we must insist that any interpretation of Genesis 1 stay within the boundaries of the lexical definitions of the words of Genesis 1.

Irons and Kline seem to misunderstand our response to scientifically unverifiable biblical narratives. Most biblical narratives portray human history, which can be verified using historical data. Biblical narratives for which little or no specific verification can (yet) be found may still be believed on the basis of more general proofs for biblical authority. However, we must regard any creation account or narrative of human events that clearly contradicts scientific and/or historical data as erroneous, mythical, or fictional.

What the Sequence Markers Imply

Another hermeneutical and exegetical concern Irons and Kline raise involves sequence markers. Irons and Kline seem to misunderstand our point about sequence markers. We do not claim that every sequence marker in Scripture necessarily implies an unfolding chronology. In the case of Genesis 1, however, the quantity and quality of sequence markers and of other contextual clues powerfully suggest a time-ordered series of events.

The "counter example" of Revelation 6:1–8:1 given by Irons and Kline contrasts with Genesis 1 on several counts, including the quantity and specificity of sequence markers. Furthermore, their assertion that Revelation 6 and 7 are not chronological is widely disputed. Scholars disagree over the degree to which symbols are used in the passage. They disagree over how many chronologies are given and over the possibility of overlapping chronologies. Finally, the entire passage deals with future, rather than past, events.

If Irons and Kline argue that Genesis 1 is nonsequential, consistency would demand that they rule out all biblical narratives as nonsequential.

Most students of Scripture would not go so far. Thus, Irons and Kline are on shaky ground to argue that Genesis 1 is nonsequential.

The Length of the Seventh Day

Irons and Kline also take issue with our view of the seventh day. Certainly we agree with Irons and Kline that our human Sabbath rest is not equivalent, but rather analogous, to God's. However, interpreting Day 7 as eternal implies that God will never create again. But this implication contradicts Revelation 21–22, 1 Corinthians 2:9, and 2 Corinthians 4:16–18. If the present cosmos and earth "pass away" and are replaced by new heavens and a new earth with different physical laws and different dimensionality (as discussed in *Beyond the Cosmos*[3]), the seventh day must end, and a new creation era must begin. The seventh day cannot be eternal.

The Bible declares that our future as God's children holds something far better than merely a return to Eden. While Eden provides the best possible human abode permitted by the laws of physics, the Bible portrays a new creation so splendid that no human words or images and nothing within the physical laws can adequately describe it. The present universe, including earth, is part of God's perfect plan for conquering sin and death. But according to His Word, His plans go beyond that conquest.

We do not mean to suggest that "creation was the remedial process employed by God to conquer evil." Rather, it is but the setting for that conquest, which is a spiritual victory. Our view may seem to "logically imply that evil was present before the creation of the universe," but such an implication arises *only* from a denial of divine foreknowledge or predestination. Irons and Kline quote verses proving that angels were created simultaneously with the cosmos and were righteous at that time, but their interpretation holds only if the "heavens" referred to in those verses constitute a reference to the angels as well. The one unambiguous verse referring to angels before Eden is Job 38:7. That verse simply implies that angels were created before earth's foundations were laid. It says nothing about *when* Satan's rebellion occurred, though apparently that event preceded Adam's creation.

Concordism

Taking a cue from Blocher, Irons and Kline charge that the Achilles heel of our day-age interpretation is the fourth-day appearance of the sun, moon, and stars. Note the word "appearance." The text does *not* say that these luminaries were "created" on the fourth day. In Genesis 1:14, the verb is *haya* (be or exist) not *bara* (create). From the perspective of an observer on earth's surface, the existence of the luminaries could not be known until God transformed earth's atmosphere from translucent to transparent. Verse 16, a parenthetical note, does use the verb *asa*, but the form of the verb employed indicates only that God completed manufacturing the luminaries on *or before* the fourth day. The usage of *asa* in verse 16 does not negate the possibility that God created the luminaries "in the beginning" (Genesis 1:1) and made them visible from the earth's surface for the first time on the fourth day. (A more complete defense of our fourth day interpretation can be found in previously published works.[4])

Irons and Kline dispute our claim of a "perfect fit between the narrative sequence of Genesis 1 and the scientific record" on the grounds that reptiles and seed-bearing plants are out of correct scientific sequence. As they read the passage, seed-bearing plants arrive earlier than the fossil record attests, and reptiles arrive much later than the fossil record indicates.

While we would agree with Irons and Kline that the definitions for *hayya* and *remes*, sixth-day creations, are broad enough to include reptiles, these words do not necessarily refer to reptiles. The latter portion of the fifth creation day brings the introduction of "soulish" animals, birds, and sea mammals, generically. The sixth day seems to hone in on three specialized kinds of land mammals—excluding reptiles—which God created to cohabit the earth with humans.

The word *sheres* mentioned on Day 5 might include fish. Regardless, the Hebrew words translated as "trees," "fruit," and "seeds" are defined broadly enough to include the most primitively structured plants. Any plant that produces a stiff stalk and an embryo with an accompanying food sac that together can be separated from the parent plant would qualify. Such plants date back to the Cambrian explosion (543 million years ago) or earlier. Archaeopteris, a tree combining characteristics of a conifer and a giant fern, was earth's dominant plant species as far back as 370 million years ago.[5] Recent research suggests that the split between flowering plants and other gymnosperms may have occurred much earlier than previously thought, possibly at or before 290 million years ago.[6]

A more detailed demonstration of the fit between the Genesis 1 narrative and nature's record appears in *The Genesis Question*.[7] In truth, the Genesis 1 narrative has *always* fit the established scientific record. As new discoveries have been made, the scientific record has been established more firmly and in much greater detail, and it always has agreed with the Genesis creation chronology. We have every reason to be confident that God has truthfully revealed Himself in the Bible and in nature, and we look forward to accumulating even more mutually corroborating data.

REPLY TO THE 24-HOUR RESPONSE

At the outset, Duncan and Hall dispute the way we have described their interpretation and the way Irons and Kline have done so. Whereas the four of us identify the 24-hour interpretation with a young-universe, young-earth creation model, Duncan and Hall claim that the age of the universe and earth are separate issues from the length of the Genesis creation days. Duncan and Hall never explain, however, how such a separation is possible.

Of course, they can opt for one of two ways to separate these two issues: (1) they can introduce some form of the gap theory, or (2) they can argue for age-separated creation days. Since they make no reference to the gap theory, we presume they do not hold to one, and thus, we offer no response to it, though we have commented on it in other publications.[8] The gap theory, however, cannot be reconciled with biblical inerrancy. As for age-separated creation days, we have argued on exegetical grounds that the sixth and seventh creation days must be longer than 24 hours. However, we find no fault with either the order or the descriptions of creation events as proposed by age-separated-day theorists.[9] Indeed, the order and descriptions developed by them are virtually identical to ours. This is also the case for the first of the two creation chronologies of the gap theory.

Since Duncan and Hall do not adopt the gap theory and since they clearly disagree with our proposed chronology, we can only assume that they embrace the tenets of young-earth creationism, even though they reject that label for some reason. Their comment that "light travel may supersede normal or known scientific processes," their denial of stellar burning processes, and their appeals to "the appearance of age" make sense only from a young-earth perspective.

The Seventh Day

Given the tenets of young-earth creationism, we can understand Duncan and Hall's reaction to our position. Though we state otherwise, they seem to think that we believe "the seventh day continues to provide for an ongoing creation." Apparently, when they read our assertion that "God supernaturally introduced new species . . . replacing those that became extinct," they suppose we mean that these divine replacements of extinct species occur *after* the six creation days. From their young-earth perspective, there would be no time for species to become extinct during six 24-hour creation days.

This response to our stated view makes no sense. We plainly concur that ecologists have never witnessed in real time the appearance of a new animal species, and we underscore our belief that God's physical creation ended with the close of the sixth day. Ignoring or misreading our state-

ments that all God's creation of new species occurred during the six creation days and none afterward, Duncan and Hall incorrectly charge us with
"the attempted fusion of contradictory ideas." But this charge simply doesn't
stick.

In note 10 of their response, Duncan and Hall attack our supposed
belief in an unending seventh day when, in fact, we clearly state that the
seventh day is a finite period during which God rests from His creating.
We state further our belief, based on Scripture, that the seventh day will
be followed by an "eighth day," during which God will create again. While
we see no room for such an interpretation within a young-earth paradigm,
it poses no problem for the day-age view.

Miracle and Faith

Duncan and Hall charge us with "a rationalistic approach that leaves little
room for miracle and faith." They write that we "nowhere allow for God
creating quickly by His Word alone" and accuse us of "dogmatizing the uniformity of natural processes." Worse yet, they report that we "affirm parity
between sinful observers of nature and God's infallible revelation." They
are not responding to our words and make these statements only because
they are committed to a powerful and irrational ideology.

Short-day creationism requires ultra-efficient evolution in the years
since God's creation week; otherwise, we have no explanation for how carnivores could develop from herbivores and millions of species could develop
from the thousands aboard Noah's ark. Based on the assumption of short
days, we can see how long days would *seem* to eliminate the need for miraculous interventions. With long timespans in which to work, their rapid
natural-process scenario could accomplish plenty. From our stated perspective, however, natural processes operate so inefficiently that regardless of
the duration of creation days, earth's suitability for life and rich abundance
of life can only result from countless divine interventions—that is, miracles.
We propose that the vast majority of these miracles occurred "quickly by
His Word alone."

The difference between our view and Duncan and Hall's view on this
point is as follows: we acknowledge hundreds of millions of miracles over
millions, even billions of years, while they acknowledge hundreds or perhaps thousands of miracles compressed into a 144-hour sequence. Incidentally, this sequence is so brief that time-order would be indiscernible.

While we do not "dogmatize" the ubiquity of natural processes, we do
see a secure basis for believing that the physical laws and constants are
truly constant. We are not isolated in this belief. However, because the
physical laws and constants prove God's existence, a few ardent atheists

look for reasons to alter them. And because the physical laws and constants prove that the cosmos and earth are billions of years old, young-earth creationists look for reasons to reject or alter them. But the vast majority of scientists, both Christian and non-Christian, accept the overwhelming evidence supporting their constancy. Our so-called "dogmatism" is justified both by observational affirmation and biblical revelation.

Nature and Scripture

Duncan and Hall's assertion that we "affirm parity between sinful observers of nature and God's infallible revelation" is untrue. Young-earth creationists' hostility to the billions-of-years duration of nature's record would collapse were they to concede (a) that students of the Bible may be just as sinful as students of nature, (b) that God's Holy Spirit has the same capacity and desire to spark faith in students of nature as He does in students of Scripture, or (c) that nature's "book" is as reliable as the Bible, though it is sometimes harder to read. For Duncan and Hall's creationist ideology to survive, they must ignore or discount an enormous body of scientific evidence and demean or marginalize all scholars who accept it.

Duncan and Hall are concordists, as we are, but their approach to the relationship between Scripture and nature is radically different from ours. For them, Scripture seems to offer no flexibility of interpretation, while nature provides nearly total flexibility. For us, the flexibility of interpretation is more even. We see it as limited for both Scripture and nature.

Does the Shoe Fit?

In the pages that follow, we reply to Duncan and Hall's attempt to dodge our critique and then to several significant challenges Duncan and Hall raise in opposition to our creation scenario.

We can understand why Duncan and Hall want to distance themselves from certain implications of young-earth creationism. They are mistaken, however, in thinking that the implications we list apply to just "a few variations of young-earth creationism." That whole set of slightly variant interpretations leads those who hold to them to deny objective reality, similar to gnosticism, and quietly embraces hyper-efficient Darwinian evolution. The gnostic leaning is evidenced by the fact that young-earth proponents deny most recorded astronomical events (for example, the 1987 supernova eruption in the Large Magellanic Cloud) and light-travel times. All young-earth creationists (in agreement with atheists) accept the impossibility of integrating the established record of nature with a conservative interpretation of Scripture. For these obvious reasons, Duncan and Hall declare that they are "not guilty by association" with young-earth creationists. Unfortunately, they offer no clarifications as to exactly how their views differ from their young-earth counterparts.

In maintaining our conclusions about young-earth creationists—including Duncan and Hall—we do not think that they are deliberately deceptive gnostics or Darwinists. We simply charge them for failing to consider the logical implications of their young-earth interpretation of nature and Scripture. We take them at their word when they state that they abhor gnosticism and Darwinism. The problem arises from a failure to extrapolate, to follow to its logical end, each assumption on which their position rests.[10] We long to see them address and correct this failure. Nothing less than the credibility of our Christian testimony is at stake.

Scientific Merit

In their response to our position, Duncan and Hall "run up the white flag of surrender" when the debate touches on the hard sciences. Nevertheless, they persist in questioning the validity of physical laws and constants in general and of stellar physics in particular. In a footnote, they comment that some within the scientific community take exception to our scientific conclusions and, thus, infer that our conclusions are not "beyond criticism."

While Duncan and Hall lack formal training in the hard sciences, they are not lacking in the means to test the security of our scientific conclusions. Who are the science professionals who "take exception" to our hard science conclusions? With the exception of a few dogmatic atheists, *all* are young-earth creationists. Has any scientist ever drawn the conclusion from scientific evidence alone that the universe or earth is young? The answer is no—not one. Even leaders of young-earth organizations admit that in several decades of full-time ministry, they have yet to persuade a scientist, on the basis of science, of the young age of the universe or earth.[11]

In note 8 of their response, Duncan and Hall imply that the current scientific record holds no more certainty than the flat-earth notion. However, no scientist—Christian or non-Christian—has ever made such a suggestion, apart from young-earth indoctrination. On the contrary, even the most cautious scientists accept the certainty of much of this record. One Nobel laureate, in fact, has been quoted as saying that we have more scientific evidence for a flat earth than for a universe and earth less than 50,000 years old.[12] (Incidentally, a UC Santa Barbara history professor recently debunked the story that Christians once used the Bible to argue for a flat earth.[13])

Many non-Christian scientists reject Darwinism's strictly naturalistic explanation of life's origin and the descent of man from primates. Many accept the evidence for a transcendent creation event and the meticulous design of the universe, solar system, and life. None endorse a young earth. Thus, one does not need science degrees to conclude that old-earth creationism has strong scientific support, while young-earth creationism totally lacks it.

When Duncan and Hall state that "rebellious sinners—scientific or otherwise—" suffer from "blindness, darkness, ignorance, rebellion, or insensitivity" and lump them together with "drug-dealers, abortionists, or prostitutes," they appear to be reacting to harsh words from the American Association for the Advancement of Science (AAAS). Two of that group's members have publicly stated that "adoption of [young-earth] creationist 'theory' requires, at a minimum, the abandonment of essentially all of modern astronomy, much of modern physics, and most of the earth sciences."[14] Duncan and Hall may be influenced, too, by the recent Kansas school board decision forced through by young-earth creationists. Recognizing the threat to the young-earth view posed by cosmology, stellar physics, and faraway stars and galaxies, the Kansas school board only requires that its schools instruct students on objects in the universe that are no more distant than solar system bodies.[15]

Old-Earthers and the "Scandal" of the Cross

Duncan and Hall accuse those who believe in long creation days of attempting "to lessen the scandal of the cross." To the contrary, we focus attention on the scandal of the cross, away from the scandal of false assertions, poor scholarship, and dogmatic subjectivism. The length of God's creation days is *not* a salvation issue. Who creates and why—these are the crucial questions. Over what span of time God creates is immaterial. To erect stumbling blocks other than the cross itself is the real scandal, and young-earth proponents are the ones who have to plead guilty to that charge.

Contrary to what Duncan and Hall imply, we believe the same gospel applies to people of all backgrounds and professions. We most certainly reject the idea that "those who are fallen will be unbiased, make an unassisted free and rational choice, and commit their lives to Christ" simply because of a long-day creation model. We have denied this notion repeatedly, and still do. (Only young-earth creationists accuse us of preaching this distorted gospel.) We believe that no one from any background, Christian or non-Christian, can choose Christ and receive eternal life apart from the agency of the Holy Spirit.

We reject the notion that biblical faith is blind. Biblical faith is rooted in established truth. The Holy Spirit reveals truth, encourages us to test it (1 Thess. 5:21), and empowers us to act upon it. According to the Scriptures, God wants us to test things, to sift truth from seeming truth, and to cling to that which is good.

We agree with Duncan and Hall that the gospel has inherent stumbling blocks. It challenges our sin, our pride, and our autonomy, among other things. We disagree, however, that the Bible's creation doctrine is included among those "inherent stumbling blocks." Quite the opposite is true. The Bible's teaching on creation serves to remove, not add, stumbling blocks. We see this time and again in our ministries. The Holy Spirit uses evidence of the Bible's uniquely accurate creation account to move people toward eternal salvation in Christ.

The Day-Age Interpretation as Nonliteral?

Duncan and Hall describe our claim to a literal interpretation of the Genesis days as a "rhetorical guise." We have no trouble understanding their desire to lay claim to the exegetical higher ground. However, all Hebrew lexicons cite three different literal definitions for *yôm*: (1) approximately 12 hours (the time from sunrise to sunset, variable according to season and location); (2) 24 hours (the time from one sunset to the following sunset); and (3) a long period of time (arbitrarily, but not infinitely, long). Thus, we can authoritatively state that there are three possible *literal* interpretations of the Genesis creation days: six daylight periods, six 24-hour periods, and six long timespans.

We must remember that Old Testament Hebrew contained relatively few nouns. Multiple meanings were the norm, not the exception. When vocabulary is limited, synonyms are rare. No suitable word in biblical Hebrew other than *yôm* serves to denote a long but finite timespan. (The word *olam* was later adopted to denote a long timespan, but that usage arises only after all the Hebrew Scriptures were written.[16])

Nowhere in our analysis of Genesis 1 do we rely on a figurative or metaphorical treatment of words and phrases. The "rhetorical guise," if any, seems to lie on the side of Duncan and Hall and other young-earth creationists, who insist that their interpretation of Genesis 1 is *the* only literal interpretation.

Miracles and "Apparent Age"

Duncan and Hall describe us as "anti-supernaturalists" who put "God in a box" and "expect Him to march to our watches." Our God, they say, is a "barely visible deity." We see things very differently, and so do most people who read and hear our messages. We can easily argue, as we indicated earlier, that we believe in more dramatic and more frequent miracles than they do.

Scripture suggests to us that when God performs miracles, He leaves evidence for someone to detect. God does not play tricks. Duncan and Hall, however, appeal time and again to "appearance of age," the idea that scientific measurement reveals a false age. In their view, God hides His miracles, making things appear as they are not. Ironically, we could say that at least in this respect Duncan and Hall are the ones who actually believe in a "barely visible deity."

God, of course, is free to change the march of time. We believe that if He had, however, He would have left evidence of the change for us to discover, in keeping with His character. He would not force cosmic clocks to run millions of times faster than "real" time. To do so would be deceptive and, thus, out of character. Astronomers have observed thousands of clocks ticking over the past history of the universe (Cepheid and RR Lyrae variable stars, supernovae, pulsars, etc.). These clocks are at distances ranging from a thousand to 11 billion light-years. Arguments that light speed has changed, that the light may not arise from the clocks, that light travels on different geometric paths, or that the clocks may reside in different time dimensions all have been exposed as bogus.[17] Thus, these astronomical clocks affirm that time has always run at the rate we observe on earth today. In fact, if it did not, physical life would not be possible at any time in the universe's history.

We agree with Duncan and Hall that God can create in any way He wishes, but again we hold that He does not lie about the manner in which He creates. For example, Duncan and Hall fail to understand that astronomers can look back in time and directly observe how God created galaxies and stars.

Duncan and Hall argue, "Galaxies, *according to our understanding*, appear to be old, just because He miraculously created them as full-blown" (emphasis in the original). Actually, astronomers do not see all galaxies as old or "full-blown." None of them is old enough to have experienced the demise, the total fuel consumption of all its stars. Nearby galaxies appear middle-aged. Galaxies at a distance of 6 billion light-years from Earth are seen in their youth. Galaxies some 12 billion light-years away are observed in a near new state. At a distance of 13 to 14 billion light-years from Earth, galaxies do not yet exist. At that distance astronomers observe newly formed star clusters beginning to merge into future galaxies. Astronomers even have looked back to that moment soon after the creation event, before stars existed, when light first separated from darkness.[18]

What seems to bother Duncan and Hall is that the light structure, star formation, and galaxy formation astronomers observe seem so "natural." A deeper look into the scientific literature reveals, however, that this "natural" capacity requires the exquisite fine-tuning of more than thirty cosmic characteristics.[19] The degree of fine-tuning exceeds human design capability by more than a trillion trillion trillion times.[20] In acknowledging this design evidence, astronomers recognize that ordinary galaxy, star, planet, and moon formation cannot generate even one galaxy-star-planet-moon system capable of supporting life. God must have supernaturally intervened to shape and craft the just-right galaxy, star, planet, and moon to make our existence possible.[21] We see this as a significant concession to the reality of the supernatural.

Duncan and Hall pay a huge price when they insist that the natural record astronomers observe may have no bearing on reality. They toss out all the divine design evidence astronomers have discovered in nature's record. A young-earth interpretation of Scripture demands the rejection of what secular scholars acknowledge as the strongest evidence for the biblical God, evidence indicating a transcendent Cause of the universe and of exquisite design for physical life.

Duncan and Hall take a different view of miracles than ours. They write, "The very essence of miracles is to confound our wisdom and defy scientific law." We would say miracles show God's power over the physical laws (and over us), demonstrating His capacity to create and implement those laws at will. Some miracles may be described as totally transcendent events. For example, some are: God's creating matter, energy, space, and time; God's creating Adam as a spiritual creature; and God's raising Jesus from the dead. Other miracles show God's power to create, manufacture, or orchestrate events within the natural realm. For example, Deborah and Barak's victory over Sisera came from a supernaturally timed and placed flood.[22] Similarly, planet Earth coalesced in keeping with, rather than in violation of, the physical laws, and yet the physical laws are inadequate in themselves to explain Earth's capacity to support physical life.[23] This capacity requires God's exacting control over Earth's characteristics *and* cosmic environment.[24]

Duncan and Hall's interpretation of Genesis 1 permits *only* transcendent miracles. We believe that the four different Hebrew verbs for God's creative activity in Genesis 1 (*bara, asa, haya,* and *dasha*) allow for God's exercise of both transcendent and manufacturing-type miracles. In some cases the text indicates totally transcendent miracles (e.g., the creation of the universe); in other cases, manufacturing-type miracles (e.g., the formation of land masses on Earth); and in still other cases, both types combined (e.g., the creation of human beings).

Duncan and Hall's biblical support for appearance of age unravels on other grounds, as well. Unfortunately, they seem to misunderstand our argument about Adam's size and age. We merely point out some fallacies of their reasoning; we do not assign to them strange beliefs about Adam's body and mind. Two fallacies warrant a reply. First, Adam's adult body would be evidence of age only if he were born. He was not born of woman. So his size is not an indicator of age. Second, if we accept the notion of apparent, but unreal, age, we cannot be certain that our memories reflect actual past events.

When Jesus transformed water into wine, He did not simply "accelerate" time. Duncan and Hall write, "The essence of that miracle was that it did not take the time it normally takes to ferment." No amount of time turns water to wine. Water does not ferment. Nothing in the biblical text forces us to conclude that God used the fermentation process. He did certainly add to the water whatever gives wine its unique flavor, perhaps its color, too. All we know is that the guests were amazed at its excellent taste.

Taste and age are not equivalent. For example, a Japanese distillery has found a way to make new whiskey taste like thirty-year-old scotch. Even professional whiskey-tasters could not discern the difference. Chemical analysis could, however. We believe that Jesus' transformation of the water can be described as a transcendent miracle. He supernaturally "treated" the water to give it the enjoyable qualities of wine.

The 24-Hour View before the Modern Era
In their opening and response essays, Duncan and Hall seem to give more weight to the testimonies and opinions of early church leaders than to exegetical evidence. Between these two bases of support, we would consider testimonial evidence the more subjective and, thus, the less weighty. Scholars disagree more widely about how to interpret the testimonies than they do about the text itself. But even on the basis of the testimonial evidence, Duncan and Hall's position is unfounded.

Duncan and Hall persist in claiming that "long before the rise of modern science, the classical view of normal [24-hour] creation days obtained dominance." That claim is erroneous based on our extensive research. Prior to 1650 exegetes gave little attention to the length of the creation days. Of the approximately two thousand extant pages of creation-day commentary by early Church fathers, only a total of about two pages address the duration of the creation days. Anyone who reads the original source literature will notice the difference in tone between the early Church fathers and modern 24-hour advocates. The older writings are devoid of passionate certainty and dogmatism about the length of the creation days. Rather, they evidence a tentativeness and exhibit tolerance on this point.

Many of these same Church fathers and Reformation leaders did hold firmly and passionately to our doctrine of creation. They taught that God miraculously prepared earth for life, then prepared earth and life for Adam and Eve in a systematic, discernible sequence of six creation days. There is a big difference, however, between six creation days and six consecutive 24-hour creation days.

Duncan and Hall refuse to accept our claim that many pre-1800 Bible scholars allowed for a long-day view. They demand a quotation showing that any of these scholars believed "Genesis 1 requires or permits a billions-of-years-old cosmos." Quotations *permitting* such a view abound. Quotations *requiring* it do not, for the simple reason cited—these scholars saw no reason for being dogmatic on the subject. We make no claim that Genesis 1 specifically and explicitly teaches a 15-billion-year-old universe or a 4.6-billion-year-old earth. We make no claim that biblical scholars prior to 1800 taught a billions-of-years-old universe. The validity of our interpretation is established if at least some of those scholars understood the six Genesis creation days to last longer than 144 hours. A review of the ancient literature indicates that our view stands on safe ground. In fact, it suggests that Duncan and Hall stand on shaky ground, at best. Isaac Newton and his colleagues were not, as Duncan and Hall declare, 24-hour proponents. In fact, they were very emphatic and explicit about their long-day views. Likewise, Duncan and Hall are wrong in stating that "none of the Reformers or Church fathers espoused the [long-day] view" and that *"few, if any, of the pre-Nicene writers held anything other than a 24-hour view"* (emphasis in the original).[25]

Justin Martyr and Irenaeus, for instance, used Psalm 90:4 and 2 Peter 3:8 to support their view that the creation days were each a thousand years long.[26] Describing the events of the sixth creation day, Irenaeus expresses the reason behind his interpretation:

> Thus, then, in the day they did eat, in the same did they die. . . . For it is said, "There was made in the evening, and there was made in the morning one day." Now in this same day that they did eat, in that also did they die. . . . On one and the same day on which they ate they also died (for it is one day of creation). . . . He (Adam) did not overstep the thousand years, but died within their limit . . . for since "a day of the Lord is as a thousand years," he did not overstep the thousand years, but died within them.[27]

Origen saw the six Genesis creation days as representing the time that men work on the earth (the period of human history) while the seventh day represents the time between the creation of the world and its extinction at the ascension of all the righteous:

He [Celsus] knows nothing of the day of the Sabbath and rest of God, which follows the completion of the world's creation, and which lasts during the duration of the world, and in which all those will keep festival with God who have done all their works in their six days, and who, because they have omitted none of their duties will ascend to the contemplation (of Celestial things) and to the assembly of righteous and blessed beings.[28]

Writing later in the third century, Lactantius (c. A.D. 250–325), Victorinus of Pettau, and Methodius of Olympus all concurred with Justin Martyr's and Irenaeus' view of the creation days as thousand-year epochs.[29]

In *The City of God*, Augustine wrote, "As for these 'days,' [Genesis creation days] it is difficult, perhaps impossible to think—let alone explain in words—what they mean."[30] In *The Literal Meaning of Genesis*, he added, "But at least we know that it [the Genesis creation day] is different from the ordinary day with which we are familiar."[31] Elsewhere in that book he made this comment:

Seven days by our reckoning after the model of the days of creation, make up a week. By the passage of such weeks time rolls on, and in these weeks one day is constituted by the course of the sun from its rising to its setting; but we must bear in mind that these days indeed recall the days of creation, but without in any way being really similar to them.[32]

In his *Confessions*, Augustine notes that for the seventh day Genesis makes no mention of an evening and a morning. From this omission he deduced that God sanctified the seventh day, making it an epoch extending onward into eternity.[33]

In reference to the first Genesis creation day, Basil poses the question, "Why does Scripture say 'one day' not 'the first day'?" His response:

The beginning of time is called "one day" rather than "the first day," it is because Scripture wishes to establish its relationship with eternity. It was, in reality, fit and natural to call "one" the day whose character is to be one wholly separated and isolated from all the others. If Scripture speaks to us of many ages, saying everywhere, "age of age, and ages of ages," we do not see it enumerate them as first, second, and third. It follows that we are hereby shown not so much limits, ends, and succession of ages, as distinctions between various states and modes of action.[34]

Ambrose, in his 280-page homily on the six days of creation, devotes less than a page to the discussion of the length of the creation days. Even then, he does not make an explicit statement as to their length. He appears to imply, though, that the creation days are 24-hour periods:

Scripture established a law that twenty-four hours, including both day and night, should be given the name of day only, as if one were to say the length of one day is twenty-four hours in extent. . . . The nights in this reckoning are considered to be component parts of the days that are counted. Therefore, just as there is a single revolution of time, so there is but one day.[35]

However, in the following sentence, Ambrose—perhaps thinking about Genesis 2:4 where the Hebrew word for "day," *yôm*, refers to the entire creation week—acknowledges:

There are many who call even a week one day, because it returns to itself, just as one day does, and one might say seven times revolves back on itself.[36]

One sentence later, he refers to *yôm*'s possible definition as an era or epoch: "Hence, Scripture appeals at times of an age of the world."[37] He follows this acknowledgment with the examples of the "day of the Lord" and the "eternal day of reward" in the new creation. Thus, it is not clear how old Ambrose deemed the universe and the earth to be.

A summary of the early Church fathers' teachings on creation days appears in *Creation and Time*.[38] More importantly, some 2,000 pages of commentary have been translated into English and are available in almost every seminary or Catholic library. We encourage readers to investigate for themselves what these luminaries wrote.

Duncan and Hall charge us with defining the issue "to exclude the clear testimony of Basil, Ambrose, Augustine, Anselm, all the major Reformers, and other prominent theologians who clearly and uniformly endorsed views at odds with the day-age and framework views." We neither define the issue to exclude their thoughts nor do we exclude their direct testimony. We simply disagree with Duncan and Hall that the testimony of these luminaries was clear and uniform.

More accurately, we would say that these preeminent theologians did not clearly and uniformly endorse any of the three positions in this book: the 24-hour, the day-age, or the framework view. Quite likely, these theologians were brief and lacked specificity because there was no challenge or data coming from general revelation or nature's record in their time. For these scholars, the length of the Genesis creation days simply held no special significance.

Not until Isaac Newton and his contemporaries who wrote in the late seventeenth century does any exegete take a position on the duration of the Genesis creation days that is both unambiguous and emphatic.[39] The wisest handling of the pre-1650 literature would be to remember the historical and scientific context in which it was written, a context in which the length of creation days had no special significance for faith.

Adam's Sin and the Introduction of Death

Duncan and Hall claim in their response that Romans 8 "speaks of the *entire universe* becoming enslaved to corruption through Adam's singular act." Romans 5, they say, "affirms that death entered the cosmos—not merely the sphere of man—through that one sin" (emphasis in the original). They add that "the 'creation,' not just man, ever since has been subjected to vanity." We dispute their analysis on these five counts:

1. Romans 8 does not attribute "enslavement to corruption" to Adam's singular act.

2. Sin was present in God's creation before Adam's singular act.

3. Romans 8 refers to decay, corruption, vanity, frustration, and groaning, i.e., *entropy*, as described by the second law of thermodynamics. Death of all physical life—apart from access to the tree of life—would be the inevitable consequence of cosmic entropy.

4. Subjecting the entire universe to the law of decay means that the law of decay, or thermodynamics, has operated from the cosmic creation event onward. It will cease to operate when God's purpose for the creation, the conquest of evil, has been fulfilled and He creates a new "heaven and earth" and a "new Jerusalem." All humanity, not physics, changed at Adam's Fall.

5. Whereas the English word cosmos can only refer to the entire physical universe, the Greek word *kosmos* is more broadly used. It can mean "the universe," "planet Earth," "the whole of humanity," or "a portion of the earth's surface."[40] In light of this variable usage and the context of Romans 5, no reputable translator has chosen "the universe" as a definition for *kosmos* in that passage.

We have discussed the meaning of "death through sin" in our opening essay in this volume and address it more fully in other publications.[41]

Biblical Evidences for Long Creation Days

Duncan and Hall are correct in stating that tree growth from seeds is not explicitly mentioned in Genesis 2. We offer our comment simply as a reasonable inference. Growth does imply development from one stage of life to another. Growth from *something* is implied, and that conclusion is all we need for our point. In the case of our inferences about Adam, we were wrong to imply that Adam, in time, lost his excitement for tending the magnificent garden, Eden. We would have been wiser to say that Adam probably came to recognize that life holds more than gardening.

The point on which we seek to focus is that God introduces Adam, step by step, first to the physical world, then to the soulish physical world (birds and mammals), and finally to the body-soul-spirit world of fellow humans, specifically, his life partner. Even without sin, Adam's limitations would not permit him to achieve all these tasks and experiences in just a few moments at the end of a 24-hour day. Adam, after all, was human, not divine. Duncan and Hall argue that Adam's sixth-day experiences can be squeezed into 24-hours "if the miraculous is permitted." They never explain, however, how the miraculous would make a difference, and they do not demonstrate how the text indicates such miraculous intervention.

Duncan and Hall interpret Psalm 90 as an expression of God's timelessness. We disagree. Whatever else can be drawn from Psalm 90, it certainly declares that God's perspective of time is much more expansive than is ours. Thus, our argument holds. (For an explanation of the mathematics of time implied in Psalm 90, see *Beyond the Cosmos*.[42])

The word *day* in biblical references to the "day of wrath" is not one of our biblical evidences for the length of the creation days. We would agree that the phrase "day of wrath" refers to a much shorter timespan than any of the creation days. To succeed in making our point, though, we need only establish that it refers to a time period longer than 24 hours. Likewise, we never suggest that because *yôm* in Genesis 2:4 refers to a time period longer than 24 hours, it always and only refers to a long period elsewhere in Scripture. The usage of *yôm* in Genesis 2:4 simply establishes that *yôm* possibly can refer to a timespan longer than 24 hours in Genesis 1.

In their treatment of Habakkuk 3:6, Duncan and Hall simply reject our view out of hand, without citing any relevant scholarship. All of the English translations of that passage use words such as "ancient," "age-old," "eternal," "everlasting," or "perpetual" as adjectives for the mountains and hills. Such choices are well-supported by lexical treatments of the words *'olam* and *'ad*.[43]

The evening and morning refrain that brackets the creation days does not fit with the 24-hour view as Duncan and Hall suggest. Theologian Paul Elbert raises an interesting question on this matter. He asks why, if the Genesis 1 text really intends us to understand the creation days as 24 hours, does it mention "there was evening and there was morning" rather than the scriptural norm for 24-hour days, namely, "there was evening and there was evening" or "there was morning and there was morning."[44]

Duncan and Hall dispute our deduction that the number of stars in the universe translates to a certain size and thus to a certain age. They say that our conclusion is based on "unproven assumptions." In fact, we do establish our assumptions in the text, and we offer more extensive proofs in other publications we cited.[45]

The Bible speaks explicitly of the vast number of stars, a number confirmed by astronomical observations. Recent research shows, further, that physical life in our universe would be impossible without that vast number of stars (fewer stars would result in a universe devoid of carbon, nitrogen, and oxygen). Physical life also depends on the stars' wide separation from one another (necessary for stable, low-eccentricity star and planet orbits). The fact that the stars are far apart has been adequately confirmed by astronomical observations. Thus, the biblical statement about the number of stars and the astronomical evidence for the distances separating them translate into a statement about the vastness of the universe.

Further, astronomers have proven that the light from distant bodies actually arrives here from those bodies and that the velocity of light has been constant for as long as stars have existed. Given these and an abundance of other relevant facts, we can confidently conclude that the universe is old, about 15 billion years old.[46] No plausible escape from this conclusion remains. The only possible loophole would be a recent and wholesale revision of the laws of physics. As we pointed out in our opening essay, both Scripture and nature's record refute such a revision.

The Future of Science and the Day-Age Interpretation

Duncan and Hall express their concern by asking this loaded question: "What if future scientists abandon their present theories and return to more biblically compatible cosmologies?"

From the outset, we must note that the question incorporates an incorrect assessment of current cosmology. Through time and research, cosmologists' theories have moved closer and closer to biblical truth. This movement has been vigorously opposed—thus rigorously tested—by nontheistic astronomers. However, as historians of astronomy note,[47] that movement has been forced by the data. Today, even ardent secularists concede that the Causer of the cosmos independently, transcendently brought into existence all its matter, energy, and space-time dimensions.[48] Similarly, the fingerprint of God is evident in the recent successful measurements of the universe by astronomers. Agnostic astronomer Paul Davies concludes his book, The Cosmic Blueprint, with these words: "The impression of design is overwhelming."[49]

To be sure, future discovery will alter, or more accurately, refine, cosmological theory. Indeed, cosmology has changed even during the time we have written this book.[50] This advancement of discovery does not mean, however, that we run the risk of losing scientific support for our interpretation of Genesis 1. Nor does it mean that past scientific accomplishments will be radically overturned. To the contrary, we have every reason to expect that the evidence for our position will grow stronger through time and that the scientific conclusions of the past and present will be fine-tuned, closer and closer to the truth.

This confidence arises, in part, from the track record of the past three hundred years. Newtonian mechanics established that God's creation is vastly larger than anyone dreamed, that it is well ordered, and that, in the case of the solar system and our galaxy, it is exquisitely designed for life. The discoveries of general relativity and quantum mechanics two hundred and fifty years later did not refute Newtonian mechanics. They merely adjusted it slightly for certain domains of measurement. What these adjustments yielded were many more design evidences, and in some cases, evidences so spectacular that all explanations except the biblical one were eliminated. Furthermore, general relativity's space-time theorem affirmed the necessity of a transcendent Creator.

Two years ago, physicists determined that four-dimensional general relativity must be expanded to accommodate a ten-dimensional creation scenario.[51] This development did not overthrow general relativity. It simply made the theory more powerful. It also ruled out the nearly pervasive religious (though not Christian) notion that God's existence and operations are confined to a four-dimensional box. Christianity is the only scientifically plausible survivor of that breakthrough. In June 1999, astronomers determined that general relativity must be modified slightly to account for a factor they call a "cosmological constant."[52] Again, this work represented not a repudiation of general relativity, but rather an extension of it. In fact, this particular adjustment of cosmological theory yielded what constitutes the most profound design evidence by far of any yet discovered.[53]

Fearing or hoping that Newtonian mechanics, general relativity, or the hot Big Bang theory will be overturned by future scientific advance is a waste of emotional energy. It is akin to believing geophysicists will soon prove the earth is flat. The emotional energy would be better used to promote scientific advance, for we can be certain that future discoveries, properly understood, will yield even more evidence for God and His word, the Bible. These discoveries will help us refine our knowledge of God's truth— and of His character, as expressed in His creative acts. (For example, the acceptance of Newtonian mechanics, general relativity, or the Big Bang establishes a billions-of-years-old universe and earth.[54])

Does this expectation mean that "science controls Scripture" in any way? To the contrary, science keeps showing us Who controls the cosmos. Correctly interpreted, scientific discovery will always agree with Scripture, if Scripture is correctly interpreted. Incorrectly interpreted science will always disagree with correctly interpreted Scripture, and incorrectly interpreted Scripture will always clash with correctly interpreted science.

An incorrect interpretation of Scripture may, however, agree with incorrectly interpreted science, and this incorrectness on both counts is what Duncan and Hall attribute to our position. Readers need not be stuck, however, on the horns of a "their-word-against-ours" dilemma. You can do some investigative work. It does not require an advanced degree in science or theology, but it may require that you communicate with people who have such degrees. The best people to consult would be those scholars who have no stake in our debate. Ask them for their evaluation of the relative merits of the evidence and of the logic applied to it.

FUTURE STEPS TOWARD RESOLUTION

Irons and Kline make a convincing case for the connection between our creation beliefs and other doctrines at (or near) the core of the Christian faith. Because of its bearing on such doctrines, our debate is important. Given its importance, we pray that fellow Christians will make every effort to understand, evaluate, and articulate our own and others' creation beliefs as completely and carefully as possible. We must all be prepared to make adjustments to our positions in light of new understandings, insights, and information.

Because the debate involves complex issues—and because God calls us to—we must exercise patience and charity in the process. Although open, respectful dialogue may not erase all the points of disagreement, it will give us the best opportunity, not only to bring our Genesis 1 interpretations a little closer to God's truth, but also to show unbelievers the power of God's Spirit at work in our lives.

In *Creation and Time*, Hugh Ross proposes a modern-day ecumenical council to resolve the creation-date controversy.[55] Although some significant meetings have occurred, the hoped-for series of meetings of evangelical leaders has yet to take place. The process of attempting to convene such a council has taught us some valuable lessons, including these:

1. We must focus on the right questions, and address them one at a time. For example, we would do well to consider whether or not the laws of physics have changed through time and on what basis that determination can be made. Similarly, we should consider what research reveals about the limits, narrow or broad, on possible natural biological changes for different species.

2. We must focus only on creation models that are both scientifically and theologically testable. This means identifying appropriate tools for testing, such as a model's ability to predict future
discovery. The most accurate model will be the one most successful in accurately predicting what scientists and theologians discover
in their ongoing research.

3. Council participants must not be ideologues. Ideologues are beyond rationality, so committed to their ideas that no amount of
evidence influences their thinking. Allowing ideologues to partici-
pate in the discussion will only widen the gaps and deepen the
animosities dividing people of different views.

4. Council participants must demonstrate a commitment to biblical
inerrancy as well as to sharing their Christian faith with secular
scholars and other unbelievers. Such individuals have keen awareness of secularists' questions and stumbling blocks and a commitment to uphold the truth in ways that reflect godly character.

We believe that God is more interested in Christlike character than in
argumentative skill. The process of addressing and resolving the controversy the modern church faces gives us ample opportunity to grow in both
areas, but character will always matter more. We trust that this book will
help us all grow in character. May Jesus Christ be glorified.

NOTES

1. Robert C. Newman and Herman J. Eckelmann, Jr., *Genesis One and the Origin of the Earth* (Hatfield, PA: Interdisciplinary Biblical Research Institute, 1977); *The Genesis Question* (Colorado Springs, CO: NavPress, 1998). See also Hugh Ross, *The Creator and the Cosmos*, 2d edition (Colorado Springs, CO: NavPress, 1995).

2. Henri Blocher, *In the Beginning: The Opening Chapters of Genesis*, trans. David G. Preston (Downers Grove, IL: InterVarsity Press, 1984), p. 27.

3. Hugh Ross, *Beyond the Cosmos*, 2d edition (Colorado Springs, CO: NavPress, 1999), pp. 218–23.

4. Ross, *The Genesis Question*, pp. 19–24, 42–6.

5. Brigitte Meyer-Berthaus, Stephen E. Scheckler, and Jobst Wendt, "Archaeopteris is the Earliest Known Modern Tree," *Nature*, vol. 398 (1999), pp. 700–1.

6. Paul Kenrick, "The Family Tree Flowers," *Nature*, vol. 402 (1999), pp. 358–9; Yin-Long Qiu, et al., "The Earliest Angiosperms: Evidence from Mitochondrial, Plastid, and Nuclear Genomes," *Nature*, vol. 402 (1999), pp. 404–7.

7. Ross, *The Genesis Question*, pp. 29–57.

8. Ibid., pp. 24–6.

9. Newman and Eckelmann, *Genesis One.*

10. Ross, *The Genesis Question*, pp. 37–57, 70–1, 87–92, 95–100; Hugh Ross, *Creation and Time* (Colorado Springs, CO: NavPress, 1994), pp. 53–80, 119–25, 134–8.

11. For example, talk radio host John Stewart asked John Morris, president of the Institute for Creation Research and a geological engineer, in my presence and on the air ("Bible on the Line," KKLA radio, North Hollywood, California, December 6, 1987) if he or any of his associates had ever met or heard of a scientist who became convinced that the earth or universe is only thousands of years old based on scientific evidence without any reference to a particular interpretation of the Bible. Morris answered honestly, "No." Stewart has since asked the same question of several other prominent young-universe proponents, and the answer has been consistent: No.

12. Murray Gell-Mann made this statement in his testimony in the United States Supreme Court case, *Edwards v. Aguillard*, 482 U.S. 578 (1987), concerning Louisiana's law granting equal time for creation science in schools.

13. Jeffrey Burton Russell, *Inventing the Flat Earth: Columbus and Modern Historians* (New York: Praeger, 1991).

14. Allen Hammond and Lynn Margulis, "Creationism As Science: Farewell to Newton, Einstein, Darwin . . . ," *Science*, vol. 81 (December 1981), p. 55.

15. Kansas Curriculum Standards for Science Education, final version, August 11, 1999, Grade 8, Standard 3, Benchmark 4 and Grades 9–12, Standard 4, Benchmark 3.

16. R. Laird Harris, Gleason L. Archer, and Bruce K. Waltke, *Theological Wordbook of the Old Testament*, vol. 2 (Chicago: Moody Press, 1980), p. 613.

17. Ross, *Creation and Time*, pp. 95–100.

18. The image is shown and explained in the video documentary *Journey Toward Creation* (Pasadena, CA: Reasons To Believe, 1998). The discovery paper is: George F. Smoot, et al., "Structure in the COBE Differential Microwave Radiometer First-Year Maps," *Astrophysical Journal Letters*, vol. 396 (1992), pp. L1–L6.

19. Ross, *The Creator and the Cosmos*, pp. 111–21. The latest update available from Reasons To Believe lists 35 different characteristics that must be exquisitely fine-tuned for physical life to be possible in the universe.

20. Hugh Ross, "Einstein Exonerated in Breakthrough Discovery," *Connections*, vol. 1, no. 3 (1999), pp. 2–3. The two discovery papers are: Lawrence M. Krauss, "The End of the Age Problem and the Case for a Cosmological Constant Revisited," *Astrophysical Journal*, vol. 501 (1998), pp. 461–6; and S. Perlmutter, et al., "Measurements of W and L from 42 High-Redshift Supernovae," *Astrophysical Journal*, vol. 517 (1999), pp. 565–86.

21. Ross, *The Creator and the Cosmos*, pp. 131–45. The latest update available from Reasons To Believe lists 112 different characteristics of our solar system and galaxy that must be fine-tuned for physical life to be possible on earth. The probability for a nondivine explanation for this fine-tuning is less than 10^{-117}.

22. Judges 4:1–5:21.

23. Ross, *The Genesis Question*, pp. 30–9.

24. Ross, *The Creator and the Cosmos*, pp. 131–45.

25. We have obtained permission from NavPress to include some of our previously published material concerning the early Church fathers taken from Hugh Ross, *Creation and Time*, pp. 16–24.

26. Justin Martyr, "Dialogue With Trypho," chap. 81, *Writings of Saint Justin Martyr*, in *The Fathers of the Church*, vol. 6, ed. Ludwig Schopp (New York: Christian Heritage, 1948), pp. 277–8; Irenaeus, "Against Heresies," bk. 5, chap. 23, sec. 2, *The Ante-Nicene Fathers*, vol. 1, ed. Alexander Roberts and James Donaldson (Grand Rapids, MI: Wm. B. Eerdmans Publishing Co., 1981), pp. 551–2.

27. Irenaeus, "Against Heresies," pp. 551–2.

28. Origen, "Against Celsus," bk. 6, chap. 61, *The Ante-Nicene Fathers*, vol. 4, ed. Alexander Roberts and James Donaldson (Grand Rapids, MI: Wm. B. Eerdmans Publishing Co., 1979), p. 601.

29. Lactantius, "The Divine Institutes," bk. 7, chap. 14, *The Ante-Nicene Fathers*, vol. 7, p. 211; Victorinus of Pettau, "The Created World," bk. 6, *The Ante-Nicene Fathers*, vol. 7, p. 342; Methodius of Olympus, "Fragment," *The Ante-Nicene Fathers*, vol. 6, p. 310.

30. Aurelius Augustinus, "The City of God," bk. 11, chap. 6, *The Fathers of the Church*, vol. 14, ed. Roy Joseph Defferrari (New York: Fathers of the Church, Inc., 1952), p. 196.

31. Aurelius Augustinus, "The Literal Meaning of Genesis," bk. 5, chap. 2, *Ancient Christian Writers: The Works of the Fathers in Translation*, ed. Johannes Quasten, Walter J. Burghardt, and Thomas C. Lawler, no. 41, St. Augustine, *The Literal Meaning of Genesis*, trans. John Hammond Taylor, vol. 1, books 1–6 (New York: Newman Press, 1982), p. 148.

32. Augustinus, "The Literal Meaning of Genesis," p. 135.

33. Aurelius Augustinus, "The Confessions," bk. 13, sec. 51, *The Fathers of the Church*, vol. 21, trans. Vernon J. Bourke (New York: Fathers of the Church, Inc., 1953), p. 455.

34. Basil, "The Hexaemeron," *A Select Library of Nicene and Post-Nicene Fathers of the Christian Church*, 2d edition, ed. Philip Schaff and Henry Wace, vol. 8, *St. Basil: Letters and Select Works; The Nine Homilies of the Hexaemeron and the Letters of Saint Basil the Great*, trans. Blomfield Jackson (Grand Rapids, MI: Wm. B. Eerdmans Publishing Co., 1955), p. 64.

35. Ambrose, "Saint Ambrose: Hexameron," trans. John J. Savage, *The Fathers of the Church, A New Translation*, vol. 42, ed. Roy Joseph Deferrari, et al. (New York: Fathers of the Church, Inc., 1961), p. 42.

36. Ambrose, "Hexameron," pp. 42–3.

37. Ambrose, "Hexameron," p. 43.

38. Ross, *Creation and Time*, pp. 16–24.

39. While Calvin emphatically states that the Genesis creation days are 24-hour periods, he is not clear whether those days are consecutive. He also was a strong proponent of scientific research and the value of such research in supporting good Bible interpretation and for correcting faulty Bible interpretation.

40. Joseph H. Thayer, *Thayer's Greek-English Lexicon of the New Testament* (Grand Rapids, MI: Baker Book House, 1977), pp. 365–6.

41. Ross, *Creation and Time*, pp. 60–9; *The Genesis Question*, pp. 93–100.

42. Ross, *Beyond the Cosmos*, pp. 55–6, 73–9.

43. See, especially, the discussions of these Hebrew words in Harris, Archer, and Waltke, *The Theological Wordbook of the Old Testament*, vol. 2, pp. 645–6, 672–3.

44. Paul Elbert, *The Journal of the Evangelical Theological Society* (2000). Preprints are available from the author or from Reasons To Believe, P.O. Box 5978, Pasadena, CA 91117.

45. Hugh Ross, *The Fingerprint of God*, 2d edition (Orange, CA: Promise Publishers, 1991), pp. 124–5, 127; *Creation and Time*, pp. 58–9, 95–100.

46. Ibid., pp. 95–100.

47. Robert Jastrow, *God and the Astronomers*, 2d edition (New York: W. W. Norton, 1992); Ross, *The Fingerprint of God*, pp. 39–138.

48. Ross, *Beyond the Cosmos*, pp. 27–33.

49. Paul Davies, *The Cosmic Blueprint* (New York: Simon & Schuster, 1986), p. 203.

50. Hugh Ross, "Einstein Exonerated in Breakthrough Discovery," *Connections*, vol. 1, no. 3 (1999), pp. 2–3.

51. Ross, *Beyond the Cosmos*, pp. 27–46.

52. S. Perlmutter, et al., "Measurements of W and L from 42 High-Redshift Supernovae," *Astrophysical Journal*, vol. 517 (1999), pp. 565–86.

53. Lawrence M. Krauss, "The End of the Age Problem and the Case for a Cosmological Constant Revisited," *Astrophysical Journal*, vol. 501 (1998), p. 461.

54. Ross, *Creation and Time*, pp. 91–118.

55. Ibid., pp. 159–65.

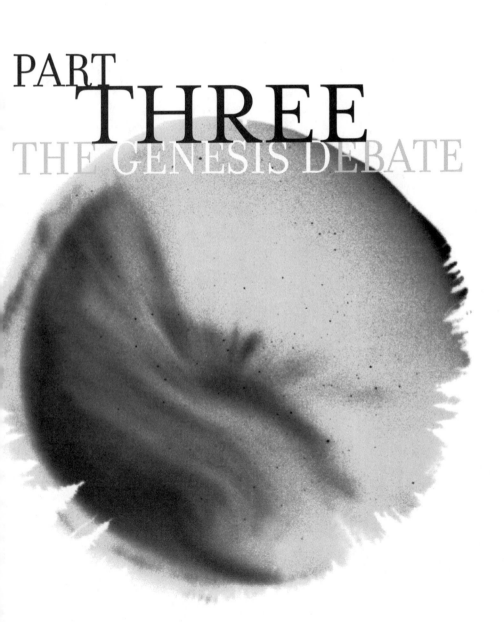

The Framework View

PART THREE

THREE

THE GENESIS DEBATE

Lee Irons with Meredith G. Kline

THE FRAMEWORK VIEW

The framework interpretation[1] strives to understand the text of Genesis 1:1–2:3 on its own terms, independently of any questions that may arise from the empirical study of origins. In contrast to the other two positions represented in this book, the framework interpretation recognizes the exegetical implications of the unique literary and theological character of this inspired record of the history of creation. The Holy Spirit has given us an inerrant historical account of the creation of the world, but that account has been shaped, not by a concern to satisfy our curiosity regarding sequence or chronology, but by predominantly theological and literary concerns.[2]

THE ADVANTAGE OF THE
FRAMEWORK INTERPRETATION

Those who accept the framework interpretation, therefore, are not bound to any particular view of the age of the earth or universe. On such matters the framework interpretation itself is silent. Careful exegesis shows that the text cannot be used to determine how much time has elapsed since the creation. Since Scripture has hermeneutical and presuppositional priority over our fallible study of general revelation, if the inspired text did teach us that creation was a recent event, we would be bound to accept this teaching as absolute truth on the basis of divine revelation. However, we believe that the inspired text, rightly interpreted, is simply silent with regard to the age of the earth and universe. That question can only be answered by examining the data of general revelation, although we must always remember that the results of such investigation are always subject to change and therefore will never have the same certainty as Scripture.

Although many who hold to the framework interpretation today are also persuaded by the current evidence for an old earth/universe, such a stance is not a necessary component of the framework interpretation itself. In fact, one may hold to the framework interpretation and affirm a more recent date for creation, should one be so convinced. What the framework interpretation does *not* allow, however, is binding the conscience of the Church to one particular view of the age of the earth/universe—whether that of "creation science" or of mainstream geology and astronomy. Teachers of God's word cannot say, "As a Bible-believing Christian, you *must* believe that the earth is young (or old). To take any other position is to fail to submit to the authority of God's word." Rather, we must speak where Scripture speaks, and be silent where Scripture is silent.

At just this point, the framework view holds a distinct advantage. Both the 24-hour and day-age views hear the text as speaking to issues about which it is silent, and consequently, they fail to have ears to hear what the Spirit *is* saying to the Church. The real theological message has been drowned out by its alleged sequential and chronological message. This fundamental misreading of the text is based on an unexamined assumption regarding the nature of biblical history. Both the 24-hour and the day-age views fail to recognize that, while Scripture inerrantly reports historical and chronological information, it always does so with a covenantal and redemptive historical purpose.

Genesis 1 was given to stimulate and strengthen our response of faith to its disclosure of the creation events. Biblical history is not video footage but theological proclamation (*kerygma*). Both alternative views misconstrue the character and purpose of the creation narrative because they read the text in such a way as to make it speak to empirical questions regarding the sequence, order, and date of creation. Consequently, adherents of those views lose sight of the covenantal and theological burden of the narrative. By contrast, the framework interpretation removes the false expectations that have muzzled the text in the past and liberates it to address the people of God kerygmatically and theologically.[3]

DEFINITION AND EXPOSITION

What then is the framework interpretation? It is that interpretation of Genesis 1:1–2:3 which regards the seven-day scheme as a figurative framework. While the six days of creation are presented as normal solar days, according to the framework interpretation the total picture of God's completing His creative work in a week of days is not to be taken literally. Instead it functions as a literary structure in which the creative works of God have been narrated in a topical order. The days are like picture frames. Within each day-frame, Moses gives us a snapshot of divine creative activity. Although the creative fiat-fulfillments (e.g., "Then God said, 'Let there be light' [fiat]; and there was light [fulfillment]") refer to actual historical events that actually occurred, they are narrated in a nonsequential order within the literary structure or framework of a seven-day week. Thus, there are two essential elements of the framework interpretation: the nonliteral element and the nonsequential element.

The Nonliteral Element
A nonliteral approach to the text is not, as many assume, a recent innovation devised to accommodate modern geological and astronomical evidence for an old earth/universe. Augustine held a nonliteral interpretation of the days, and he was followed by Anselm, Peter Lombard, and others. While these Church fathers did not teach the framework interpretation in the precise form we advocate here, no one can deny that nonliteral approaches to the creation days have a venerable place in the history of Christian interpretation.[4]

Augustine proposed his nonliteral view in his commentary on Genesis, De Genesi ad Litteram (The Literal Meaning of Genesis). He argues that the first three days cannot be normal days for the simple reason that they existed prior to the creation of the sun on the fourth day.

> Thus, in all the days of creation there is one day, and it is not to be taken in the sense of our day, which we reckon by the course of the sun; but it must have another meaning, applicable to the three days mentioned before the creation of the heavenly bodies. . . . That day in the account of creation, or those days that are numbered according to its recurrence, are beyond the experience and knowledge of us mortal earthbound men.[5]

In other words, the institution of the solar day on the fourth day, after the creation week has already begun, indicates that the days are not to be understood literally as solar days. The days "are beyond the experience and knowledge of us mortal earthbound men." Our ordinary week recalls, but is not the same as, the week of creation.

We exercise great caution so that we do not equate a nonliteral interpretation with a nonhistorical interpretation of the text. The framework interpretation does *not* teach that creation was a nonhistorical event. Jesus and the apostles attest to the historicity of the creation narrative, when they repeatedly appeal to the events recorded in the opening chapters of Genesis as an authoritative, historical revelation of God's will for mankind (Matt. 19:4–8; 1 Cor. 11:8–9; 1 Tim. 2:14). The New Testament also places tremendous weight upon Adam as a historical individual whose primal apostasy had significant ramifications for the subsequent unfolding of God's redemptive plan (Rom. 5:12–21; 1 Cor. 15:21–22). Adam's historic representative headship over all his descendants serves as the foundation for the biblical doctrine of the federal headship of Christ, the Last Adam (1 Cor. 15:45). To undermine the historicity of the first Adam by viewing him as a mythic symbol representing "everyman" is to undermine the reality of the redemption the Last Adam accomplished on behalf of His people. These New Testament allusions to the Genesis account presuppose its historicity and factuality.

Cognizant of the grave theological implications considered, the framework interpretation maintains the historicity of Genesis, which contains the presuppositional foundations for the subsequent unfolding of progressive revelation. Because of our firm commitment to the historicity of Genesis, the framework interpretation militantly resists all attempts to relegate the creation to the status of myth or saga or any category other than that of a history of events that actually transpired in space and time. In other words, by interpreting the days of creation in a nonliteral manner, we do not, in any way, deny their historicity. We affirm a historical creation, a historical Adam, and a historical Fall. Genesis 1–3 is a historical narrative of events that actually took place in space and time with the angels of God as "eyewitnesses" of everything but the initial *ex nihilo* creation event.

The Nonsequential Element

The second defining element of the framework interpretation is the conviction that the eight historical creative works of God have been arranged according to other than strictly sequential considerations. An outstanding instance of this nonsequential ordering is found in the relation of Days 1 and 4, where the narrative order does not coincide with the historical sequence. The framework interpretation maintains that the creation of the luminaries, and in particular the solar system, on Day 4 actually coincides with the creation of daylight on Day 1. Thus, the text is narrated in a topical rather than a purely sequential order. However, we cannot conclude that *nothing* in the text has been arranged sequentially. The Sabbath of the seventh day, for example, must follow the previous six days of creation, and man is created last due to his position of delegated dominion over all creation. In these cases the narrative sequence and the actual historical sequence are the same. But the order of narration alone is not sufficient in itself to determine the historical sequence; other considerations, such as theological concerns and general revelation, must be factored in as well. In most cases, the text's predominantly topical nature will preclude detailed conclusions regarding sequence.

Nonsequential narration is a common occurrence in Scripture. Many conservative scholars have noted this literary technique in commentaries and exegetical studies. O. T. Allis, for example, has done much work in this area, primarily as part of the apologetic task of defending Scripture against the claims of higher critics. In the past, higher critical arguments for the Documentary Hypothesis (the view that the Pentateuch was written by multiple authors over a long period) have consistently misconstrued nonsequential narration as evidence that the text has been redacted from multiple sources. Allis, by contrast, deals with a great number of these alleged discrepancies and shows that they can be explained much more cogently as normal and intentional features of the Hebraic literary style.[6]

Dischronologization. Biblical scholars refer to nonsequential ordering as *dischronologization* or topical arrangement, which actually is a common feature of biblical historical narrative. It occurs whenever the order in which events are narrated does not correspond to the actual chronological sequence. Allis states that in general "the sequence in which events are recorded may not be strictly chronological." He notes as well that the narrator has "the tendency to complete a topic or subject, carrying it forward to its conclusion or a logical stopping-place and then to return to the point of departure and resume the main thread of the narrative."[7]

An excellent example of dischronologized narrative is Ezra 4:1–24. This text begins (vv. 1–5) with the opposition to the rebuilding of the temple that was encountered during the reign of Cyrus in the late sixth century B.C. In verses 6–23, the narrator then describes opposition to the rebuilding of the walls of the city that occurred in the fifth century. The narrator then concludes in verse 24 by returning back to the sixth century scene: "Then work on *the house of God* in Jerusalem ceased, and it was stopped until the second year of the reign of Darius king of Persia" (i.e., in 520). Opposition to the work of rebuilding the *city walls* in the fifth century

(vv. 6–23), therefore, was inserted as an illustration of the kind of opposition encountered in the attempt to rebuild the *temple* in the sixth century. The author structures his narrative to maintain thematic unity rather than a strict chronological sequence.[8]

Similarly, the temptation accounts in Matthew (4:1–11) and in Luke (4:1–13) present the three points of our Lord's temptation by the devil in different chronological orders. D. L. Bock writes, "It is . . . clear that one of the Gospel writers has rearranged the order for literary reasons. The event shows that the Gospel writers are not averse to arranging materials for the sake of topical or theological concerns."[9] Though one of the accounts has been dischronologized, that fact in no way diminishes its historical veracity.

Temporal Recapitulation. A specific type of dischronologization commonly found in biblical historical narratives is temporal recapitulation. Allis explains: "We often find in describing an event, the biblical writer first makes a brief and comprehensive statement and then follows it with more or less elaborate details. This may involve some repetition and is at times confusing."[10] Genesis 1–2 contains some clear illustrations of temporal recapitulation. One is the account of the creation of man, which is recorded twice.[11] In Genesis 1:26–28 God creates man, male and female. This event is resumed and expanded upon in chapter 2 by an account of the creation of Adam (2:7) and then of Eve (vv. 21–25). It is obvious that the account of the creation of Adam and Eve in Genesis 2 returns to the sixth day of chapter 1, after the completion of God's work of creation (2:1–2), and offers details not included in the summary statement given in chapter 1.

Another illustration of temporal recapitulation in Genesis 2 is the twofold account of God's placement of Adam in the garden. In verse 8, we read that "the LORD God planted a garden toward the east, in Eden; and there He *placed* the man whom He had formed." A brief description of the garden's location and environment is then given in verses 9–14. In verse 15 Moses repeats the previously narrated event of God's placement of Adam in the garden: "Then the LORD God took the man and *put* him into the garden of Eden to cultivate it and keep it." This is immediately followed by additional information about the tree of the knowledge of good and evil (which had also been mentioned earlier in verse 9). In particular, the LORD now commands Adam not to eat of it upon the penalty of death (vv. 16–17). Here, then, is a clear example of temporal recapitulation. E. J. Young observes,

> Indeed, without warning, the biblical writer may deviate from a chronological order and arrange his material artificially. . . . It is obvious that a chronological order is not intended here. How many times did God place

man in the garden? . . . Clearly enough Moses here has some purpose other than that of chronology in mind.[12]

Moses recapitulates the placement of man in the garden to provide more detailed information about his covenant probation as it relates to the tree of the knowledge of good and evil.[13]

Another large-scale example of thematic arrangement involving chronological recapitulation is the overall ordering of the ten sections of the Book of Genesis. After the prologue (Gen. 1:1–2:3), Genesis is divided into ten sections, each introduced by the formula, "These are the generations of . . ." (*eleh toledoth*). Each section is an account of the subsequent historical developments of the individual named.[14]

In many instances, the *toledoth* formula picks up the thread of the historical narrative at a point earlier than the last recorded event of the previous section. For example, section one (2:4–4:26) begins the account of the subsequent history ("the generations") of the heavens and the earth by recounting the creation of man, even though that event had already been dealt with in the preceding prologue. Section two (5:1–6:8), which concerns the subsequent generations of Adam, begins at the same point, thus constituting a third narrative of man's creation. Section five (11:10–26), dealing with the generations of Shem, is a recapitulation of much of the same genealogical material given previously (10:21–31). The topic of the generations of Ishmael (25:12–18), which constitutes section seven of Genesis, goes all the way back to Ishmael's birth to Hagar, an event recorded as far back as Genesis 16 in the heart of section six. And the eighth section (25:19–35:29) similarly begins with a summary statement of Isaac's birth and marriage to Rebekah, events which had been addressed at length in section six (21:1–3; 24:1–67). Thus, temporal recapitulation for the purpose of topical arrangement appears to be a key structural device in Genesis.

These examples show that not only biblical history in general but the Genesis history in particular, which forms the context of the creation record, narrates events in an order that does not necessarily correspond to the actual historical sequence. The fact that Genesis 1:1–2:3 narrates the divine work of creation in a nonsequential order, as the framework view holds, does not detract from its historicity or veracity any more than the fact that the Gospel writers often recorded events in the ministry of Jesus in an order dictated by topical rather than sequential considerations detracts from the inerrancy or historical accuracy of the Gospel accounts. We must reject the idea that biblical narratives are neutral, video-like reports uninterpreted by the author's theological concerns. As with all biblical narratives, the Genesis account of creation presents the facts accurately and inerrantly, but in a literary form intended to convey the rich theological significance of the creation history. Biblical historical narratives normally display literary craftsmanship, and the presence of such craftsmanship in no way detracts from the inerrancy of Scripture or undermines its historical credibility.

So there are two essential criteria defining the framework interpretation: a nonliteral interpretation of the days and a nonsequential ordering of the creative events. While the framework and day-age views both hold to nonliteral interpretations of the days, they part ways over the matter of sequence. Recognition of the topical arrangement of the eight creative works is an additional element that distinguishes the framework view not only from the 24-hour view, but also from the day-age view.

The modern framework interpretation builds upon Augustine's figurative interpretation of the days and is in fundamental continuity with it. However, several exegetical features of the framework view were lacking in its patristic form. The following three exegetical arguments represent an advance upon the nonliteral interpretation of the Church fathers, each of which we will expound in depth.

THE TWO TRIADS

The first exegetical argument for the framework interpretation begins with the observation that the days form a framework consisting of two parallel triads. The first triad (Days 1–3) deals with the *creation kingdoms*, while the second triad (Days 4–6) deals with the *creature kings* who exercise dominion over those kingdoms. The fact that the first six days form a two-triadic unit highlights the uniqueness of the seventh day, which depicts the Creator King enthroned in His heavenly Sabbath rest over all creation. So strong is this parallelism that many scholars consider it to be a literary device intentionally crafted by the author.[15] This symmetry may be represented as follows:

Creation kingdoms		Creature kings	
Day 1	Light	*Day 4*	Luminaries
Day 2	Sky	*Day 5*	Sea creatures
	Seas		Winged creatures
Day 3	Dry land	*Day 6*	Land animals
	Vegetation		Man

The Creator King
Day 7   Sabbath

Based on this triadic scheme, the term "framework" has been attached to our position. Moses, under the inspiration of the Holy Spirit, seems to have intentionally arranged the creative works of God according to this framework. So impressed are certain scholars by this scheme that it has been called an artistic arrangement or a literary framework.

Dutch theologian Arie Noordtzij pioneered this approach to the creation week in 1924.[16] The substance of his work has been made available in English by N. H. Ridderbos in his book *Is There a Conflict Between Genesis 1 and Natural Science?*, published in the United States in 1957. Ridderbos presents a popular treatment of the framework interpretation and depends heavily on the work of Noordtzij, whom he cites extensively. He quotes Noordtzij as follows:

> The six days of Genesis 1 are obviously intended as the sum of two triduums which consequently reveal a clearly pronounced parallelism, while the total arrangement is intended to place in bold relief the surpassing glory of man who attains his true destiny in the Sabbath. . . . Given this plan of the creation account we may infer meanwhile that the author consciously used days and nights, evenings and mornings, as a literary framework.[17]

Noordtzij sees in this "pronounced parallelism" a clue to the authorial intent. Moses "consciously used" the conceptual scheme of a six-day workweek followed by a Sabbath rest to convey a theological point regarding the ultimate destiny of man and creation. If the creation "week" is a literary framework, then the evenings and mornings are subsidiary elements within that framework and share in its nonliteral character.

Kings and Kingdoms

The first triad deals with the forming of the creation kingdoms, while the second triad deals with the creature kings. Since the motifs of dominion and kingship are prominent in Genesis 1:1–2:3, the king/kingdom rubric nicely distills the theological significance of the two-triad structure. In each of the days of the second triad, the created entities are assigned a ruling task. The luminaries of Day 4 are established to "rule over" the day and night (1:16). The fish and birds of Day 5 are blessed with a dominion mandate that implies rule over the spheres established on Day 2: "Be fruitful and multiply, and fill the waters in the seas, and let birds multiply on the earth" (1:22). This "be fruitful and multiply" mandate closely parallels the mandate given to man (1:26, 28) and is therefore to be understood in similar terms as a *dominion* mandate. In the case of man, he too is given authority, but not one that is limited merely to the sphere of Day 3. He is to rule over the fish, the birds, the cattle, and "over all the earth" (1:26).

Finally, all the kingdoms of creation and their creature kings are subordinated as vassals of their Creator King on the seventh day. The rising chain of command does not stop at the sixth day; it ascends to the seventh day, to the supreme dominion of the Creator enthroned in His royal Sabbath rest. Just as God's human image-bearer observes an earthly Sabbath rest and thereby consecrates all the labor of the previous six days to the glory of God, so God Himself placed all the creatures of the six days of creation under His royal feet when He took His seat on the seventh day enthroned in His heavenly Sabbath rest.[18]

Sabbatical Symbolism

Deliberate schematic arrangements are a common feature of scriptural history. In this case we are particularly concerned with *sabbatical* symbolism used to structure biblical history. An illustration of sabbatical theology used to structure biblical history is also found in the seventy years of captivity. This is obviously a round number, since the actual length of time from the first deportation (605 B.C.) to Cyrus's decree of liberation (538) was 66–67 years. Scriptural commentary itself tells us that the figure of seventy years has a profound theological significance. In Leviticus 26:43, for example, Moses himself tells us, "The land will be abandoned by them, and will make up for its sabbaths while it is made desolate without them." Second Chronicles 36:21 tells us, "All the days of its desolation, it kept Sabbath to fulfill seventy years" (NASB, marginal reading). As a multiple of seven, the seventy-year period of captivity functions theologically as a sabbatical figure.

The Book of Daniel gives us another illustration of a nonliteral use of the image of a week. In Daniel 9:24–27, Gabriel reveals to Daniel the mystery of the seventy "weeks." He is told, "Seventy weeks have been decreed for your people and your holy city, to finish transgression, to make an end of sin, to make atonement for iniquity, to bring in everlasting righteousness, to seal up vision and prophecy, and to anoint the Most Holy One" (translation ours). The seventy "weeks" (literally "sevens") comprise a definite period of time until the coming of the Messiah and the destruction of Jerusalem (and probably even beyond that until the end of history), a period that is actually longer than a literal 490 years.[19]

Dispensationalists, who seek a literal fulfillment of the prophecy of the seventy weeks, fallaciously assume that each "week" translates into seven literal years. Ultimately, however, the point of the seventy weeks is not to provide a precise chronological prediction but to make the profound theological point that the coming of Christ and the abrogation of the Old Covenant order will usher in the eschatological Sabbath rest for the people of God. The fact that the Holy Spirit employs the language of "weeks" is, of course, highly significant, for it echoes the creation narrative's metaphorical use of the week. That, in turn, is highly significant for our interpretation of the "week" of creation.

Similarly, in his genealogy of Christ, Matthew employs sabbatical theology to structure history. He purposely dropped at least four names and counted David twice to construct a sabbatical structure of the history of redemption from Abraham to the Messiah. He states that from Abraham to David is 14 generations; from David to the captivity is 14 generations; and from the captivity to the Messiah, 14 generations (Matt. 1:17). This was intentional: the author purposely wanted to stress this numerical system, primarily because of its sabbatical symbolism ($3 \times 14 = 6 \times 7$); the generation of the Messiah represents the seventh seven, thereby showing that it is He who inaugurates the ultimate Sabbath rest for the people of God, the eschatological age. Matthew employs sabbatical symbolism to underscore one of his major themes: the Messiah's advent constitutes the apex and fulfillment of redemptive history.[20]

Use of the Sabbath concept to provide a literary scheme for conceptualizing redemptive history is a major feature of Scripture. Obviously, this concept has implications for the framework interpretation. If the subsequent use of the seven-day scheme in redemptive revelation is symbolic and not necessarily concerned with exact chronological calculations, then we would expect the same for the original use of the Sabbath structure in Genesis 1–2.

Eight Works in Six Days

Clearly, this structuring of the creation narrative according to a seven-day scheme is an intentional literary device. Further supporting this conclusion is the observation that there are a total of *eight* distinct creative works distributed over *six* days. The last day within each triad (i.e., Days 3 and 6) contains *two* creative acts. Critical scholars have incorrectly appealed to this distribution of eight works over six days as evidence of a hypothetical original source document that allegedly contained a record of the eight creative acts. The so-called Priestly creation account (Gen. 1:1–2:3) is thought to be a reworking of this hypothetical creation story to fit within a six-day scheme in keeping with the Priestly author's Sabbath theology. Skinner concludes "that the series of works and the series of days are fundamentally incongruous, that the latter has been superimposed on the former."[21]

Such source-critical speculations are totally unnecessary. The same data can be accounted for by simply recognizing that Moses employed a literary framework. He wanted to highlight the strong connections between Day 3 (vegetation) and Day 6 (man) to set the stage for the institution of the covenant of works in the garden, which was based upon a close relationship between man and vegetation (i.e., the two trees in Gen. 2:9). The dual thematic focus established by the parallel third and sixth day-frames sets the stage for Genesis 2:4–25, which resumes and expands upon this twofold theme of vegetation and man. Moses placed two creative acts on Day 3 and Day 6, while all the other days contain only one fiat, which strengthens the connection between vegetation and man, thus preparing for the subsequent narrative which would explain that connection in greater detail (Gen. 2:4–25).

We now can appreciate the theological significance of the literary design that brought the first triad of days to a climax in trees and the second triad to a climax in man. In this way, the design set the stage for the crucial connection of the two that would be examined in greater detail in the subsequent narrative of man's unsuccessful probation under the covenant of works (Gen. 2–3).[22]

Chiastic Relationship of Days Two and Five

Further demonstrating the presence of an artistic arrangement, the author reverses the kings/kingdoms on the middle days (Days 2 and 5). On Day 2, he narrates the creation of the sky and sea kingdoms in the following order: the sky is created first, then the seas. The parallel day-frame in the second triad (Day 5) records the creation of the corresponding kings in reverse order: the creation of the kings of the sea-kingdom is narrated first, then that of the winged creatures to rule over the sky-kingdom.[23] Thus, we have a typical Hebrew chiasm, or inverted parallelism, based on the two kingdoms dealt with in the second and fifth day-frames (sky-sea-sea-sky). This chiasm strengthens the symmetry of the two triads.

Parallelism of Days One and Four

We have seen the tight relationship between Days 3 and 6: they both contain two creative acts, and they are thematically connected in a way that sets the stage for a fuller treatment in Genesis 2:4–25. We have seen that the relationship between Days 2 and 5 is reinforced as well, but in a different manner, namely, through the artful employment of Hebrew chiasm.

The pattern of parallelism is also exhibited in the relation of Days 1 and 4, which not only deal with the same topics of light/darkness and day/night but also employ identical language of separation (Gen. 1:4, 14, 18). On the fourth day God created the sun, moon, and stars. We are told that they were created for several purposes: to give light on the earth and to separate the day from the night, the light from the darkness. "Then God said, 'Let there be lights in the expanse of the heavens *to separate the day from the night. . . .'* God placed them in the expanse of the heavens to give light on the earth, to govern the day and the night, and *to separate the light from the darkness*" (1:14, 17–18).

The problem for any sequential view is that precisely these same purposes were accomplished on Day 1 when God said, "Let there be light," and in this way "*separated the light from the darkness*" (1:4–5). This difficulty is made all the more apparent in Hebrew when one observes that the exact same verb is used in both Day 1 and Day 4 ("to separate"). In other words, the divine purposes in creating the light on Day 1 and the luminaries on Day 4 are identical. That this separation of light from darkness was satisfactorily accomplished on Day 1 is evident from God's declaring it to be "good" (Gen. 1:4). Those who insist that Day 4 chronologically follows Day 1 must ask themselves why God felt the need to discard the arrangement established on Day 1 and replace it with a new one on Day 4.

This argument assumes that Day 4 records the origination of the luminaries, an interpretation that the 24-hour view accepts. However, some of those who hold the day-age view argue that the fourth day only describes the unveiling of the luminaries which had actually been created earlier. The language of the text, though, does not allow for this argument. The same fiat language that is used for acts of divine origination on the other six days is used on Day 4 as well: "Then God said, 'Let there be lights in the expanse of the heavens . . .'" (v. 14). If one admits that this fiat language describes divine origination when used on the other days, consistency demands that the same meaning be applied to Day 4. Furthermore, the text clearly states that God "made" the luminaries and "set" them in the sky (vv. 16–17).[24]

Thus, we may properly conclude that on any sequential view the fourth day describes the creation of a new mechanism for producing light and maintaining the day/night separation. It is therefore legitimate to ask why God would create a replacement mechanism when the original system of light production (whatever it was) did a perfectly fine job of giving light to the earth and of separating the day from the night. Would an all-wise God create one physical mechanism, call it "good," and then replace it with a new mechanism three days (or ages) later?

Rather than adopting an interpretation of the text that ends up questioning God's wisdom, a more reasonable explanation consistent with the text is that Day 4 returns to the scene pictured on Day 1 to provide a more detailed explanation of *how* God produced daylight on the earth and separated the light from the darkness. This is what the framework interpretation maintains: Day 1 relates the results; Day 4 goes back and informs us regarding the physical mechanism God employed to produce those results. That physical mechanism is, of course, our solar system.

Not all who recognize the symmetry of the triads espouse the framework interpretation as we have defined it (nonliteral days, nonsequential narrative). It is certainly possible that a narrative might have striking thematic parallelisms and still be informed by a literal, sequential chronology. But in the case of the creation record, there is evidence of chronological recapitulation, not just thematic parallelism. The clearest evidence is found in the relation of Days 1 and 4. The temporal recapitulation of Day 1 on Day 4 justifies taking the whole week of seven days as a figurative framework that provides a literary and theological structure for the narrative of the divine work of creation.

"BECAUSE IT HAD NOT RAINED"

The second argument in the exegetical case for the framework interpretation takes its name from Meredith G. Kline's 1958 article, "Because It Had Not Rained."[25] In this article, Kline argues that Genesis 2:5–6 establishes the principle of continuity between the mode of providence during and after the creation period. But a sequential interpretation pits Genesis 1:1–2:3 against Genesis 2:5–6 in numerous ways. Both the 24-hour view and the day-age view must invoke *extraordinary* providence at certain points to maintain a sequential interpretation, in contradiction to Genesis 2:5–6, which teaches that God employed *ordinary* providence during the creation period. The "because it had not rained" argument depends upon the analogy of Scripture in that it brings the exegetical force of one text (Gen. 2:5–6) to bear upon the interpretation of another (Gen. 1:1–2:3).

Explanation of the Argument

Genesis 2:5 states that there was no vegetation and supplies the reason: "For the LORD God had not yet caused it to rain upon the earth." Then a parenthetical statement is added: "and there was no man to cultivate the ground." This additional statement is not intended to convey the idea that a human cultivator is necessary for vegetation to exist, but rather to explain why the absence of rain resulted in a lack of vegetation. Moses' audience knew that the absence of rain would not necessarily lead to a lack of vegetation as long as human cultivators were present to overcome drought conditions through the skillful use of irrigation. So Moses demonstrates the tightness of the causal connection (no rain; therefore, no vegetation) in this context by reminding his audience that there was as yet no human cultivator.[26]

Genesis 2:6–7 then explains how God began to deal with these deficiencies. In verse 6 God deals with the first deficiency (lack of rain) by causing the rain clouds to form. In verse 7 He deals with the second deficiency (lack of cultivator) by creating man from the very ground he is to cultivate.[27] Unfortunately, however, most English translations obscure this twofold solution by mistranslating verse 6 as if it referred to a substitute water-supply. For example, the NASB reads, "But a mist used to rise from the earth and water the whole surface of the ground." But this popular translation makes nonsense out of the flow of thought in this passage. We see two translation problems: one is with the *verb*, the other is with its *subject*. Let us examine each in turn.

First, the verb "to rise" can be translated in one of two ways, defining either durative action in the past ("used to rise") or inceptive action in the past ("began to arise"). The first option must be rejected because it makes nonsense out of the flow of thought. According to the NASB, verse 6 would be affirming the *presence* of an ample supply of water at the very time when, according to verse 5, the *lack* of such a water supply is stated as the reason for the absence of vegetation. If the past durative translation is chosen, why does verse 5 bother to go to such lengths to explain why there is no vegetation (there was no rain, and since there was no man, there was no artificial irrigation system either), only to be followed by an explanation that there was a watering mechanism in place after all ("a mist used to rise")? The context thus demands an inceptive meaning.

Second, the grammatical subject, commonly translated either "mist" (NASB) or "streams" (NIV), is a rare word that occurs only one other time in the Hebrew Bible. The difficulty with such obscure words is that scholars often disagree on their meanings. In a situation like this, students of lexical semantics determine meaning by using two complementary methods: by studying cognate languages—Semitic languages such as Ugaritic, Akkadian, and Eblaite; and by examining the context—ultimately the most important test. In this case, both methods lead to the same conclusion: the word should be translated "rain-cloud" rather than "mist" or "streams."

The evidence supporting the translation "rain-cloud" may be summarized as follows. First, Mitchell Dahood, a leading expert in cognate studies, has argued that the Hebrew word is to be identified with an Eblaite word meaning "rain-cloud."[28] Second, and more important, "rain-cloud" finds strong corroboration from Job 36:27, the only other text where the word occurs in the Hebrew Bible. Dahood translates this verse as follows: "When he draws up drops from the sea, they distill as rain from his rain cloud." The next verse then continues the thought quite nicely: "The clouds pour down their moisture and abundant showers fall on mankind" (v. 28, NIV). In fact, the "clouds" of verse 28 provide a verbal link to the "rain-cloud" of verse 27, thus forming a hinge connecting the first part of the rain cycle (evaporation) with the second part (rain).[29]

Our exegesis thus yields the following translation of Genesis 2:5–6:

> Now no shrub of the field was yet in the earth, and no plant of the field had yet sprouted, for the LORD God had not yet caused it to rain upon the earth (and there was no man to cultivate the ground). So a rain-cloud began to arise from the earth and watered the whole surface of the ground.[30]

Let us now step back and examine the implications of this crucial text for the framework interpretation. If our exegesis of Genesis 2:5–6 is correct, then it informs us that the Creator did not originate plant life on the earth before He had prepared an environment in which He might preserve it without bypassing secondary means and without having recourse to extraordinary means. As such, Genesis 2:5 contains an "unargued presupposition," namely, "that the divine providence was operating during the creation period through processes which any reader would recognize as normal in the natural world of his day."[31] If God had so decreed, there would have been no obstacle to His creating the vegetation *prior* to establishing a normal providential support system. He could have created the plants and sustained them supernaturally even before He created the soil. God in His omnipotent creative power *could* have done these things. Yet Genesis 2:5–6 tells us that in planning the order in which He would call the various creatures into existence, God did not rely upon supernatural means to maintain them once created.

With this principle in hand, we are now in a position to show still more conclusively that the two triads reflect something more radical than a mere thematic parallelism conceivably compatible with a sequential interpretation. The principle enunciated in Genesis 2:5–6 forces us to take the parallelism of Days 1 and 4 in a stricter sense. If the divinely decreed order of creative acts was dictated by a concern to avoid unnecessary supernaturalism in providence, then a sequential reading of Genesis 1 must be incorrect. For such an interpretation would require the day/night cycle to be sustained by a supernatural providence for three days until an ordinary providential means (our current solar system) was established. In other words, if the Creator was concerned to establish a natural watering system prior to creating vegetation to avoid relying unnecessarily upon extraordinary providence in His maintenance of vegetation, would we not be imputing the divine procedure with inconsistency if we suggested that the Creator was not similarly concerned to avoid unnecessarily relying upon extraordinary providence in His maintenance of daylight and the division between day and night?

Implications for the 24-Hour Interpretation

The principle of comparing Scripture with Scripture dictates that data disclosed in Genesis 2:5–6 be applied in our interpretation of the fourth day. We find that a literal, sequential interpretation results in a head-on collision with the principle that, during the creation week, God used ordinary means in His providential maintenance of the created order. Such an interpretation would imply that light and the day/night cycle were maintained by a supernatural or nonordinary providence for the first three days, since it was not until Day 4 that God put into place the current mechanism provided by the solar system to produce daylight and the day/night cycle. We therefore conclude that Day 4 is an example of temporal recapitulation: the narrator returns to events that he had previously reported but now retells in greater detail. On Day 1, the creation of light is narrated in summary fashion, and its fundamental result—the separation of day and night—is reported. On Day 4, the author returns to the same event and expands upon it in greater detail, explaining the creation of the mechanism employed by God to produce the light and maintain the day/night cycle.

The "because it had not rained" argument refutes the literal 24-hour view in other ways as well. For one thing, the literal interpretation requires the existence of vegetation prior to the sun, which is normally necessary for photosynthesis. Obviously, God *could* have sustained the photosynthesis process by some other source of light (say, some primal light of Day 1). In other words, God could have used an extraordinary method. But Genesis 2:5–6 indicates that God employed ordinary methods of the same kind in operation now. If vegetation could have been sustained without the sun, it could have survived without rain. But if the text wanted us to entertain such extraordinary possibilities, the Holy Spirit's appeal in Genesis 2:5 to completely natural causes for the absence of vegetation would appear to be quite out of place.[32]

Again, the literal interpretation requires God to have established the day-night cycle prior to establishing the earth's rotation with respect to the sun (Day 4). It is possible that the light of Day 1 may have been somehow focused to provide a temporary substitute for the sun. However, this interpretation would imply that God used an extraordinary means for sustaining the day-night cycle, thus contradicting again the principle enunciated in Genesis 2:5–6.

It becomes evident, then, that the 24-hour view cannot be correct since its literal, sequential interpretation of Genesis 1:1–2:3 repeatedly creates tension with the principle disclosed in Genesis 2:5–6. This principle states that the mode of divine providence during the creation period was

not fundamentally different from its current mode after the creation period. Because it insists on taking the *days* as very short periods of time,
the 24-hour view must repeatedly appeal to supernatural providence between creative acts to explain how events could occur in such a brief
timespan. Similarly, because the 24-hour view insists on taking the days
sequentially, it must appeal to supernatural providence to uphold and maintain the creation between creative acts.

Positing extraordinary providence between acts of supernatural origination is nothing more than an exegetical presumption. Even more, it directly contradicts the revelation of Genesis 2:5–6, which shows that the
mode of divine providence between such supernatural acts of creation was
the ordinary mode currently in effect today. If we believe that Scripture is
inspired, and therefore inerrant, we are required to adopt an interpretation of Genesis 1:1–2:3 that does not conflict with Genesis 2:5–6. The
analogy of Scripture, as applied in this context, forces the Bible-believing
interpreter to abandon a literalist reading of the creation narrative.

Implications for the Day-Age Interpretation

The "because it had not rained" argument also suggests that the sequential
interpretation of the day-age view is incorrect. Although the day-age view
does not have to appeal to extraordinary providence to explain the flurry
of divine creative activity in a short period of 144 hours, its insistence
that the textual order of the creation events corresponds to the historical
sequence does require such an appeal. The sequential approach of the day-
age view requires the existence of vegetation (day-age three) prior to that
of the luminaries (day-age four) for a whole geological era. But vegetation
ordinarily requires sunlight in order to grow, thrive, and reproduce. And
as we have seen, an appeal to extraordinary providence would be
contradicted by the teaching of Genesis 2:5–6.

One way some day-age proponents have attempted to elude the force
of this argument is to hypothesize that Day 4 only records the unveiling
of the luminaries. According to this view, the luminaries had already been
created either "in the beginning" or concurrently with the creation of light
on Day 1. Day 4, therefore, relates the unveiling of the luminaries to an
earthbound observer by means of a divine act that caused the atmosphere
to become at least intermittently transparent. (For the first three days, it
had been translucent or overcast.) We have already seen that this interpretation is exegetically untenable based on the language of the text ("Let
there be lights . . . God made . . . God placed them" [Gen. 1:14, 16, 17]).

Even if this interpretation were admitted, translucent atmospheric conditions still are not the ordinary means by which God provides the light

necessary for maintaining plant-life. Ordinarily, most vegetation needs the full, direct light of the sun at least some days of the year, and some species require direct moonlight, to grow and flourish. It is certainly possible that God could have sustained plant-life for the entirety of the third geological era (Day 3) by means of whatever light could pierce the translucent cloud-cover. But this would be an extraordinary method of sustaining plant-life, and certainly not the one that Moses' audience would have recognized as operating in its own day.

Thus, both forms of the day-age view run counter to the teaching of Genesis 2:5–6 by teaching some form of sequentialism. Insofar as Genesis 2:5–6 supports a nonsequential reading of Genesis 1:1–2:3, it also undermines the day-age view.

Clarifying a Common Misunderstanding

Before we move on to the third exegetical argument for the framework interpretation, we must clear up a common misunderstanding of the "because it had not rained" argument. E. J. Young, an early critic of Kline's argument, seems to have misunderstood the framework interpretation when he wrote: "It cannot be held that the present modus operandi of divine providence *prevailed* on the third day, nor does the appeal to Genesis 2:5 prove such a thing."[33] This implies Kline taught that the divine activity was only providential, to the exclusion of supernatural, creative activity.

However, the framework advocates teach that the "six days" of creation comprise a closed era within which God completed His work of creation. We clearly distinguish between the unique, closed era of the six days, which are marked by a series of supernatural acts of origination, and the post-creation era, which is primarily (though not exclusively) marked by ordinary providence. As a result, far from being the time when ordinary providence prevailed, the creation week was *characteristically* the era of supernatural creation.

Now all—whether literalist, day-age, or framework advocate—should be able to agree that during this closed era of creation, divine providence was at work sustaining the creatures between creative acts. The questions are: What was the mode of divine providence during the creation week? And was it ordinary or extraordinary? Or to put it another way: Was the mode of divine providence the *same* as the current mode of divine providence after the creation period or *different*?

We argue that Genesis 2:5–6 gives us a clear and direct answer. To explain the absence of vegetation within the six-day era, the text gives a very normal and ordinary reason: because it had not rained. This explanation, therefore, presupposes that the mode of providence that was in

operation during the creation period and that which is currently in operation—and which Moses' audience would have recognized—are the same.

This piece of information revealed in Genesis 2:5–6 was not a foregone conclusion. It might have been very different. Certainly, the creation
period was a time characterized by supernaturalism of the highest order.
Thus, if God had so determined, His providential upholding of the creation might *also* have been by supernatural means. Yet Genesis 2:5 tells us
that during the creation period, God chose to employ ordinary means. This
insight does not mean God used *nothing but* ordinary means. On the contrary, the creative fiat-fulfillments indicate that divine acts of supernatural origination both initiated and punctuated the creation process. Thus,
Young seriously misrepresented the framework interpretation when he asserted that it teaches that ordinary providence prevailed during the creation period, *to the exclusion of the supernatural.*

In summary, the "because it had not rained" argument challenges the
competing views of the days of Genesis by calling into question their appeal to extraordinary providence—and in some cases, to outright miraculous intervention—as the means of sustaining the creatures after they have
been brought into existence by fiat creation. The sequentialism of both
the day-age and 24-hour views (as well as the compressed timespan required
by the latter) forces their advocates to assume an extraordinary mode of
providence during the creation period in contradiction to Genesis 2:5–6.
By undermining these competing views, therefore, Genesis 2:5–6 enhances
the plausibility of the view that the work days of the creation week must
be viewed as six frames arranged in two panels, with various creative events
pictured in each day-frame according to the topical and theological concerns of the author.

TWO-REGISTER COSMOLOGY

Taken together the two triads and the "because it had not rained" argument are sufficient to show that the framework interpretation lays claim
to a solid exegetical foundation. However, questions still remain: What
exactly is the nature of the day-frames? Are they mere poetic figures of
speech? Or do they reflect an objective reality of some kind? Answers to
these questions are provided by the third exegetical argument in support
of the framework interpretation: the two-register cosmology of Scripture,
consisting of the upper (invisible) and lower (visible) registers. As we shall
see, two-register cosmology explains the significance of the nonliteral nature of the time indicators in Genesis 1 within the overall cosmological
teaching of Scripture.[34]

We will present this third argument for the framework interpretation in two stages. First, we will lay the presuppositional groundwork by attempting to show that the created cosmos comprises an upper and a lower register, that is, the invisible and the visible dimensions. Second, we will attempt to show that the two registers are related to one another analogically. This analogical relationship between the two registers provides the theological rationale for speaking of the chronological data of the creation narrative (e.g., the days, and the evening-morning formula) as referring to a heavenly, upper-register time frame.

The Two Registers

Although some critics might be tempted to dismiss two-register cosmology as a speculative construct, in reality the terms *upper register* and *lower register* are useful terms for the two realms that compose the created order. The upper register is the invisible dwelling place of God and His holy angels, that is, heaven. The lower register is called "earth," but includes the whole visible cosmos from the planet Earth to the star-studded sky (Col. 1:16). A number of scriptural texts teach this two-tiered structure of the cosmos. The psalmist, for instance, declares that "the *heavens* are the heavens of the LORD, but the *earth* He has given to the sons of men" (Psa. 115:16; see also 102:19–20). As another illustration, the Great King of all the earth declares, "*Heaven* is My throne, and the *earth* is My footstool" (Isa. 66:1; see also Matt. 5:34–35). The New Testament also teaches a two-register cosmos in a number of passages (e.g., Col. 1:16; see also 3:1–2; John 3:12–13, 31; 1 Cor. 15:47–49; 2 Cor. 5:1).

The heaven where God dwells (the upper register) is a part of creation, and therefore, it is a real place. We must ever keep the Creator-creature distinction in view. When we do, we clearly see that the invisible realm is not co-eternal with God, as if it existed in eternity past prior to creation. Rather, it belongs to the creature side of the Creator-creature distinction. This is the express point of Paul's statement that through Christ "all things were *created*, both in the heavens and on earth, visible and invisible, whether thrones or dominions or rulers or authorities" (Col. 1:16). Paul's reference to various angelic beings is appositional to, or explanatory of, "the invisible things." When the invisible heaven is opened, we invariably see God as the King of glory enthroned in the midst of myriads of heavenly beings (Isa. 6:1–3; Dan. 7:9–10; Ezek. 1:5–28; Rev. 4:1–5:14). These heavenly beings are gathered around the King as His servants, courtiers, and advisors who constitute the judicial "council of the holy ones" (Psa. 89:5–7).

While it may be difficult for us to conceive of God's heavenly dwelling place as a created realm, the angels assist us in conceptualizing a transcendent but real dimension of the creation. Although the angels are finite creatures, they are invisible, spiritual beings not limited to the earthly plane. So if the citizens of the upper register are capable of transcending the visible sphere, then the upper register itself (which is their environment) must have a similar quality. Heaven is the invisible dimension of the *created* cosmos.

Because it is invisible, believers ordinarily perceive the upper register only by faith. "The things which *are seen* are temporal, but the things which *are not seen* are eternal" (2 Cor. 4:18). In our current position in redemptive history, we can see this realm only with "the eyes of [the] heart" (Eph. 1:18; cf. 2 Cor. 5:7). However, this state of affairs has not always been the case. At times God has given His people supernatural perception to see the upper register. When God opened up that dimension to human perception, it appeared that the very ground where the angels stood was the gate of heaven (Gen. 28:16–17). Stephen "gazed intently into heaven and saw the glory of God, and Jesus standing at the right hand of God" (Acts 7:55–56). Similarly, Elisha's servant was granted a special illumination from God to see that "the mountain was full of horses and chariots of fire" (2 Kings 6:17).

Thus, the upper and lower registers relate to each other spatially, not as different locations, but as different dimensions of the one cosmos. God's heavenly habitation, therefore, exists on a mysterious, invisible, spiritual plane, a dimension permeated with created spirit-beings. We are not to conceive of heaven as a location within our universe (or even outside it), as if one could travel there via a spaceship set to certain coordinates within the space-time continuum. Although it is presently seen only with the eyes of faith, Christ is seated as our King and Priest in the upper register. From there He will come in the clouds of heaven with all His holy angels to execute judgment upon the world and to bring about a perfect and eternal union of the visible and invisible worlds. Ultimately, the upper register will become permanently visible, for the two registers will be united in the last day, removing the present distinction between the two levels. Clothed in the brilliance of the glory of God, the new Jerusalem will come down out of heaven and the dwelling place of God shall be with men (Rev. 21:2–3, 10–11).

Although two-register cosmology may seem novel or exotic at first, careful exegesis shows that it embraces the panoramic drama of redemptive history from creation to redemption to consummation. Hence, the two registers are really a fundamental component of biblical cosmology.

Application to the Framework Interpretation

So how does this two-register cosmology apply to the framework interpretation? We appeal to two-register cosmology to determine the *nature* (literal or figurative) of the seven-day temporal scheme in which the creative acts have been arranged. Specifically, if the days are figurative frames providing a literary framework for the creation narrative, what do these *days* refer to?

Critics have argued that the framework interpretation turns the days into a "mere manner of representation and hence of no significance for the essential knowledge of the divine creative activity."[35] But nothing could be further from the truth. Though not ordinary days as measured by the Earth-sun relationship, they do have genuine significance. The days of Genesis 1 belong to the upper register. If we keep in mind that the upper register is a created reality, it will be evident that in assigning the days of creation to that realm, we cannot view them as a "mere manner of representation" with no essential significance. To make this assertion would be to dismiss the upper register itself as nothing more than a figure of speech when, in fact, it is a real, created dimension of the cosmos. Our critics fallaciously assume that when we deny that the days are lower-register days, we empty them of their reality and turn them into a mere set of ideas. But the upper register to which the days belong is just as real as the lower register.

How do we arrive at the conclusion that the creation "week" belongs to the upper rather than the lower register? We must begin by examining the relationship between the upper and lower registers. That relationship is fundamentally analogical. The upper register is an archetype, and the lower register is an analogical replica of the upper register.

Because of this analogical relationship, lower-register features can be employed to describe upper-register realities. If the earth is an image of heaven, then the earth provides a rich thesaurus for describing the unseen realities of heaven above. Consider the fact that *clouds* are literally present only in the lower-register heaven, yet they routinely figure in biblical images of the upper register (e.g., Daniel's vision of the Son of Man coming "with the clouds of heaven" [Dan. 7:13]). This is also true for other features of the invisible heaven. A *rainbow* overarches the divine presence upon the throne (Ezek. 1:28; Rev. 4:3). Awesome pyrotechnic displays of *lightning* and other fearful aspects of the *thunderstorm* are connected with the upper register (Psa. 29:3, 7; Ezek. 1:4). The *wind* is said to be God's chariot (Psa. 18:9–14), on which He rides accompanied by the crushing power of the *hailstorm* (Rev. 11:19). *Stars* are frequently employed as figures for the angels (Isa. 14:13; Rev. 1:20; 12:4). The blinding brilliance of the light of the *sun* itself is a favorite image for the glorified, exalted Christ (Matt. 17:2; Acts 26:13; Rev. 1:16; 21:23).

Each relationship is an example of earthly things being used as metaphors for upper-register realities. Our argument, then, is that the language of the *days* and the "evenings and mornings" is not literal but an instance of lower-register terms being used metaphorically to describe the upper register. Just as the heaven where God dwells does not have literal clouds or a rainbow, so heavenly time is not literally measured by solar days or earthly evenings and mornings. Because of the analogical relationship between the two registers, Scripture employs the language of earthly time to speak of the progress of heavenly time.

In support of this argument, we now turn to Genesis 1:1–2:3 to exhibit the significant and determinative role played by two-register cosmology in this text. We have already shown that two-register cosmology is a scriptural construct, but we must now show that it is a salient feature of the creation narrative, and, more specifically, that the *analogical relationship* of the two registers is also evident in the text. As we will see, it turns out that two-register cosmology has, in fact, left its literary imprint upon the creation narrative—from the opening verse to the conclusion of the divine rest on the seventh day. Five major aspects of the text point to the pervasive presence of the analogical relationship between the upper and lower registers. After examining this evidence, we will argue that the figure of the creation "week" is simply another instance of this phenomenon.

The Heavens and the Earth. The very first verse of the creation narrative refers to the creation of both the upper and lower registers: "In the beginning God created the *heavens* and the *earth*." An alternative interpretation of this verse takes it to be a summary heading which the subsequent narrative then explains in greater detail. But if Genesis 1:1 is taken as a summary of the subsequent narrative, "the heavens and the earth" would then denote the *visible* heaven and *visible* earth and therefore would have *only* the lower register in view.

It is more likely that Genesis 1:1 states that at the absolute beginning, God created the heavens (upper register) and the earth (lower register), as Genesis 2:1 confirms. Thus, this proposition is an independent statement referring to the absolute beginning of the totality of the two-register cosmos. The "heavens" mentioned in Genesis 1:1 and 2:1 are the upper register, the invisible heavens and their angelic hosts, not the visible heaven (the sky). Likewise, the "earth" of Genesis 1:1 refers to the lower register, which includes both the visible heaven and the earth.

This interpretation is made clear by the subsequent unfolding of the creation narrative. "The earth" mentioned in verses 1–2 is fashioned not only into the land and seas, but into the visible heavens, for on the second day the firmament of heaven is formed by a separation that occurs *within* the "earth" of verses 1–2. Later, in verses 14 and 17, the sun, moon, and stars are placed in this firmament of the visible heavens, and are therefore placed in the "earth," or the lower register. When used in contrast with the visible heavens, "earth" denotes what we know as the planet earth, on which we earthbound creatures live. But when used in contrast with the invisible heaven of God's dwelling place, "earth" denotes the entire *visible* cosmos, both the earth and the heavens. So Genesis 1:1 states that in the beginning God created both the upper and lower registers.[36]

Not only is the cosmos defined as a two-register universe right at the beginning of the creation narrative, but the analogical relationship between the two registers is also clearly taught in the text. The Hebrew word for the *lower*-register heavens or sky (*shamayim*) is employed metaphorically to denote the upper register (Gen. 1:1; 2:1).[37] The vast expanse of the sky, with its luminous clouds and bright stars, is a visible picture of God's heaven. The text appropriately identifies the upper register by the name of its lower-register counterpart, "the heavens." In other words, the second register of the two-register cosmos is itself divided into two registers, so that "the heavens and the earth" of Genesis 1:1 are replicated in the lower register and therefore can refer as well to the two subdivisions of the visible, lower register. The following diagram explains this relationship (subscripts have been used to distinguish the twofold usage of *heaven* and *earth*):

Upper Register—Invisible Cosmos (Heaven$_1$)

Lower Register—Visible Cosmos (Earth$_1$)
    Upper: Star-studded Sky (Heaven$_2$)
    Lower: Planet (Earth$_2$)

The lower register itself was created as a replica of the total bipartite cosmos. As a result, the lower-register heaven$_2$ can be used to describe the upper-register heaven$_1$, and the lower-register Earth$_2$ can be used to describe the lower register itself (Earth$_1$). Thus, the dual usage of the terms *heaven* and *earth* throughout the creation narrative presupposes an analogical relationship between the two registers.

Spirit Hovering over the Deep. The text points to the presence of two-register cosmology in verse 2: "The earth was without form, and void; and darkness was on the face of the deep. And the Spirit of God was hovering over the face of the waters" (NKJ). The Spirit of God here is the heavenly reality that in the later unfolding of redemptive revelation found earthly expression in the Glory-cloud. Comparison of this text with Deuteronomy

32:11, which also employs the rare word "to hover" (*rachaph*), supports this identification of the Spirit of Genesis 1:2 with the Glory-cloud that led Israel in her wilderness journeys. Now this Glory-presence of God, also known as the Shekinah, filled the tabernacle and the temple—which were earthly copies of heaven (Isa. 6:1; Heb. 8:1–5; 9:23–24; Rev. 8:3–5; 9:13; 11:19; 13:6; 15:5–8; 16:17)—and thus, was an earthly local representation of the upper register. Granting these biblical theological connections, it is clear that the Spirit of Genesis 1:2 represents the upper-register dimension, while the deep over which the Spirit hovers is the lower register. The Spirit is hovering over the formless void to fashion it into an orderly cosmos, a visible replica of the invisible upper register (cf. the Spirit's transforming role as replicator in the new creation—John 20:21–22; 2 Cor. 3:18).[38]

And It Was So. The eight fiat-fulfillments that begin in verse 3 and continue throughout the six days have been shaped by a two-register cosmology. The fiats ("And God said") represent the royal creative commands being issued from on high by the King enthroned in the upper register. The fulfillments ("And it was so") represent the fulfillment of the divine fiats in earthly history in the lower register as the Spirit hovers over the world. God the Son is the divine Word of creation (John 1:1–3; Heb. 1:2). God the Spirit is the active agent through whom the Christological fiats are executed on the earth. "You send forth Your Spirit, they are created" (Psa. 104:30). Again, two-register cosmology has shaped the text and left its imprint on its literary structure.

Let Us Make Man. The two registers play an even more pronounced role on Day 6 of creation. God deliberates with the angelic council, "Let Us make man in Our image, according to Our likeness" (Gen. 1:26). The plural form here is most likely a reference to the angels, since this form is used elsewhere in the Old Testament with that meaning (Gen. 3:22; 11:7; 18:21–22; Isa. 6:8).[39] Clearly, this fiat emanates from the divine throne in the upper register. Furthermore, man himself is created in the image not only of God but also of the judicial council which is a central feature of the upper register (1 Kings 22:19–21; Psa. 89:7; Jer. 23:18, 22; Heb. 12:22–23; Rev. 4:6–9). Man is a lower-register counterpart to the judicial authority of God and His angels in the upper register. It is for this reason that men, when functioning in their judicial capacity, are called "the sons of the Most High" (Psa. 82:6), a title that also belongs to the angels (Job 1:6; 2:1; 38:7). This prepares the way for the Bible's subsequent use of anthropomorphic metaphors to represent both God (Dan. 7:9; Ezek. 1:26) and angels (Josh. 5:13; Dan. 10:5). Anthropomorphisms are but one kind of lower-register metaphor used to describe upper-register realities. The upper-register council has been replicated in the lower register in the creation of man as a being with judicial capacity. Thus, the analogical relationship between the two registers is confirmed once more.

And God Rested. We also can see the literary imprint of two-register cosmology at the conclusion of the creative week when God enters His Sabbath rest on the seventh day (Gen. 2:2–3). God's rest is an upper-register rest in the heavenly places (v. 2). But this upper-register rest has an earthly, lower-register parallel: God sanctifies the seventh day for man's weekly observance of a day of rest in lower-register time (v. 3). Just as God's keeping vigil on the first Passover night was the archetype for Israel's repeated observation of the Passover vigil (Exo. 12:42), so God's Sabbath rest became the pattern for man to follow.

Our survey of the impact of two-register cosmology on the creation narrative may be summarized in the following chart:

TWO-REGISTER COSMOLOGY IN GEN. 1:1–2:3					
	v. 1	*v. 2*	*Days 1–6*	*Day 6*	*Day 7*
Upper Register	Heaven	Spirit	Fiats	Divine Council	God's Rest
Lower Register	Earth	Deep	Fulfillments	Man as Image	Sabbath Ordinance

From beginning to end, the upper and lower registers have left their mark on the whole creation narrative. The text's literary structure is pervasively patterned on a two-register cosmology. At each point, the upper register has been replicated in a lower-register analogue, thus charging the lower register with meaning that will later be tapped in biblical images of the upper register. The use of lower-register language to describe the upper register is well established, not only in Scripture generally, but in the creation account specifically. Our contention, then, is that the days and the evenings and mornings are to be explained as further examples of lower-register language being used metaphorically in descriptions of the upper register. The temporal framework of the creation narrative belongs to the upper register, though it is linguistically clothed in the humble garb of lower-register, chronological terminology ("day," "evening and morning").

The Creation Days as Upper-Register Time

Setting forth the evidence of a pervasive pattern gives *prima facie* plausibility to our argument, but we must press still further to bring forward evidence that the seven days are a part of this pattern.

The Nonliteral and Nonsequential Nature of the Narrative. Any evidence that the days are nonliteral is evidence that they belong to the upper register. This would include, for example, the evidence that the narrative sequence of Genesis 1 does not correspond at every point to the actual historical order. As we saw, the fourth day must be interpreted as a temporal recapitulation that goes back over the previously narrated creation of light on Day 1. Particularly telling is the fact that this dischronologization of the narrative does not occur just anywhere, but at Days 1 and 4—the precise point in the narrative when lower-register time is established. The fact that the establishment of lower-register time (i.e., solar days) is narrated *within* the framework of the creation week (both in Days 1 and 4) demands that the framework of the seven days itself belongs to the upper register. This convergence of literary craftsmanship and theological disclosure is highly significant.

The Beginning of the Creation Week. Decisively demonstrating the upper-register nature of the creation week is the upper-register nature of the beginning of the creation week. The creation week begins "in the beginning" (*breshith*). We mentioned that some interpret Genesis 1:1 as a title summarizing the whole creative process narrated in Genesis 1:2–2:3. Those who hold this view take "in the beginning" as covering the entire creation week, rather than as referring to the absolute initial point that marks the interface between God's self-existent eternity prior to creation and the moment when the creation first sprang into existence.

But the latter interpretation is strongly supported by the analogy of Scripture. Proverbs 8:22–31 defines "the beginning" of Genesis 1:1 as the time prior to the progressive fashioning of the world described in the subsequent six days of creation. Wisdom says, "The LORD possessed me at *the beginning* (*reshith*) of His way, before His works of old. From everlasting I was established, from *the beginning* (*merosh*), from the earliest times of the earth" (Prov. 8:22–23). Wisdom goes on to say that this was before the LORD created the depths of water (v. 24), established the mountains and hills (v. 25), or made the earth and the fields (v. 26). For Wisdom was there "in the beginning" even before God had separated the waters above from the waters below on Day 2 of creation (vv. 27–28).

The point is that Proverbs 8:22–30 provides an inspired commentary on Genesis 1:1. According to that inspired commentary, "in the beginning" cannot be a general time-reference to the entire six-day creation period, for Wisdom explicitly places the events of the six days *after* "the beginning." "In the beginning," therefore, cannot be interpreted as an ordinary, lower-register time statement. John 1:1–3 echoes Genesis 1:1 when it speaks of the instrumental role of the second member of the Trinity at the initial point of creation. In other words, "in the beginning" belongs to the upper register. Since it is the starting point for the first day, and thus for the entire week of days, it clearly marks the whole creation week as a framework of days in the upper-register time frame.

The Conclusion of the Creation Week. Just as the initial point of the creation week is a part of the upper register, so is the conclusion of the creation week. The creation week *concludes* with an upper-register day of rest for God: "And on the seventh day God ended His work which He had done, and He rested on the seventh day from all His work which He had done" (Gen. 2:2, NKJ). This seventh day is not an earthly day of rest for man, but the heavenly rest of God Himself. Because it is synonymous with God's heavenly enthronement, the seventh day argues for the upper-register nature of the creation week, and as an eternal day, it argues for the nonliteral nature of the creation days.

One might be tempted to assume that the seventh day ended, whereas God's rest continues eternally. But the author of Hebrews *equates* the two: "For He has said somewhere concerning *the seventh day,* 'And God rested on the seventh day from all His works.' . . . So there remains a Sabbath rest for the people of God. For the one who has entered His rest has himself also rested from his works, as God did from His" (Heb. 4:4, 9–10). Hebrews interprets God's rest "on the seventh day" as an upper-register reality—an eschatological, heavenly rest to which the people of God are called to enter by faith in Christ. According to this inspired New Testament commentary on Genesis 2:2, the seventh day itself is equated with the Sabbath rest that awaits the people of God. And this Sabbath rest is an ongoing, eternal reality. It was offered to the people of God in the wilderness in Numbers 14 (Heb. 3:16–4:3). It was offered to the Israelite church in Psalm 95 (Heb. 3:7–11, 15; 4:7). It is still being offered "today" if we will hear His voice (Heb. 3:7, 13). Therefore, God's Sabbath rest is clearly eternal.[40]

If it was not an eternal day, are we to imagine that on the eighth day God returned to work? Obviously not. In fact, the absence of the evening-morning formula at the conclusion of the seventh day flags this day as unique in that it has no end. Now if the seventh day was unending and eternal, it certainly cannot be an ordinary, lower-register day. But if the seventh day is an upper-register day, the entire week of which it is an integral part must be an upper-register "week" as well.

The Intervening Six Days. With respect to the upper-register nature of the creation week, we have seen that the six days of creation are bracketed by upper-register time at the outset and at the conclusion. The six days are bounded on both sides at their starting point ("in the beginning") and at their climax (the seventh day) by upper-register realities. If both the threshold and the conclusion of the creation week have an upper-register time frame, then certainly the six days, which are part of the same temporal series, must be upper-register days. Psalm 104, a meditation on the Genesis creation account, reflects the same bracketing technique. The works of the six days of creation (vv. 5–30) are bracketed on one side by the upper-register depiction of God in heaven "clothed with splendor and majesty" (vv. 1–4), and on the other side by God taking His Sabbath rest as He looks upon the world from His heavenly abode and delights in the finished product of His hands (vv. 31–35).

Perhaps one may attempt to evade the force of this "bracket" argument by conceding that the initial threshold and the seventh day belong to the upper-register time frame, but that the intervening six days are literal lower-register days. But can the creation week be dismembered in such a fashion? Isn't it clear that God's rest on the seventh day is a rest *from His labor* of the previous six?

Thus, if the time of divine rest is heavenly, must not the time of divine work which prepares for, and leads up to, that rest be heavenly as well? Dividing the creation week into a literal lower-register component (solar Days 1 through 6) and an upper-register conclusion (the heavenly seventh day) destroys the unity of the seven-day scheme. Likewise, isn't it clear that "the beginning" is the beginning *of something*? And isn't that something the time line of the series of days which is continued throughout the text and indeed functions as its primary structural principle?

If the initial point of the creation time line is an upper-register metaphor for the mystery of the relationship between time and eternity, how can the subsequent units of time that flow from that initial point be anything other than upper-register units of time? Thus, we cannot dissect the creation week by conceding the heavenly nature of the seventh day while also insisting on the earthly, literal nature of the six preceding days.

Imagine if we treated the parables of Jesus with such an arbitrary hermeneutic. Let us take, for example, the parable of the sower and the seed. In this parable we have a series of four scenarios: (1) the seed that falls by the wayside and is devoured by birds; (2) the seed that falls into the rocky soil and perishes for lack of root; (3) the seed that falls among thorns and is choked; and, finally, (4) the seed that falls on good soil and produces a bountiful crop. Would it be a proper hermeneutic to say that the first three scenarios must be interpreted literally as instruction for farmers while the fourth scenario signifies the effectual calling of the elect? The parable is a unity. And as a unity, it demands that we apply our hermeneutic consistently throughout. If Day 7 is recognized as an upper-register day and if it is the climax of a series of days forming a unified whole (a week of seven days), then we have no right to take the seventh day figuratively while we take the first six days literally. Such selectivity would be utterly arbitrary and make nonsense of the text.[41]

Answering an Objection to Two-Register Cosmology

We have demonstrated that two-register cosmology is an important element of the framework interpretation. It explains what these nonliteral *days* refer to. It demonstrates that while the days are not ordinary solar days, neither are they simply a literary figure having no referential connection to objective reality because they are as real as the upper register of which they are a part.

Critics have alleged that the framework interpretation relegates the seven-day scheme to a mere literary structure having no referential significance to objective reality. They allege that if the days of the creation week are part of the upper register, then they are devoid of any real content and thus tell us nothing about how God actually created. Young, summarizing G. Aalders, writes, "In the text of Genesis itself . . . there is not a single allusion to suggest that the days are to be regarded as a form or mere manner of representation and hence of no significance for the essential knowledge of the divine creative activity."[42] James Jordan declares that the framework interpretation "platonizes the time sequence into a mere set of ideas."[43]

No! Whenever lower-register language is employed metaphorically for upper-register realities, it communicates genuine truth about the upper register. Just because we do not interpret such language literally, it does not follow that such language is meaningless. Analogical statements may not be interpreted univocally, but they are not therefore equivocal or devoid of content. Just as we cannot take the Bible literally when it tells us that God has hands and eyes, so we cannot take the Bible literally when it tells us that God created the cosmos in six days and rested on the seventh. However, just as we take the Bible *seriously* when it tells us that God has hands and eyes, so we take the Bible *seriously* when it tells us that God created in six days and rested on the seventh. Because man bears the image of God, the Holy Spirit correctly and meaningfully describes God and His creative activity in language that is strictly appropriate for man. Because of the reality of man's nature as the divine image-bearer, *genuine truth* about God is communicated when God is pictured in human form or performing human actions.

Just as anthropomorphic statements are not mere poetic hyperbole devoid of real content, so lower-register metaphors for upper-register phenomena are not empty or meaningless literary devices. They are part of

God's authoritative and infallible self-revelation, since God Himself has chosen to reveal analogical truth about the upper register by replicating it in lower-register form. By charging that the framework interpretation reduces the days of creation to a mere manner of representation having no significance for the essential knowledge of creation, the critic dismisses God's own revelation of the upper register via its lower-register replica as having no significance for the essential knowledge of the upper register.

The upper register is a real part of the space-time creation. Thus, all upper-register events recorded in Scripture are real, historical events. For example, each of the divine fiats "Let there be light" and "Let us make man in our image" is a divine speech-act that really occurred in the upper register with the angelic council as the audience. The fiats therefore occurred at some moment in upper-register time, just as their corresponding fulfillments occurred at some moment in lower-register time. Just because the measurement of upper-register time is not calibrated according to a lower-register chronometer (such as the rotation of the earth with respect to the Sun), that does not mean that upper-register time is imaginary. Genesis 1:1–2:3 and Exodus 20:11 teach that God created the universe in the space of six upper-register days. That upper-register "six-day" period is a real unit of time. At present we cannot translate it into its lower-register equivalent—God has not chosen to reveal that information. However, it is not therefore less real or less historical.

In conclusion, advocates of the framework interpretation argue that the six days are not literal days but frames arranged into two panels. They provide a literary structure in which the creative activity of God is topically narrated according to the theological concerns of the author. The complete seven-day framework is a metaphorical appropriation of lower-register language denoting an upper-register temporal reality. With their evenings and mornings, the six days do not mark the passage of earthly time in the lower register, but of heavenly time in the upper register.

TWO PRIMARY OBJECTIONS

We have examined the three exegetical arguments for the framework view (two triads, "because it had not rained," and two-register cosmology), and we have seen that the nonliteral and nonsequential approach of the framework view is grounded in objective exegesis of the text. However, critics have put forward two objections to the nonliteral element of the framework view. Because these objections are regarded by some as definitively refuting the framework view, we should conclude our positive exegetical case by briefly responding to them.

The Fourth Commandment

Perhaps the most frequently raised objection to the framework interpretation is that it cannot deal with the divine commandment to labor for six days and rest on the seventh (Exo. 20:8–11). Noel Weeks argues that "Exodus 20:8–11 is significant in that it gives us a clear answer to the debated question about whether the 'days' of Genesis are to be taken literally. The commandment loses completely its cogency if they are not taken literally."[44]

Far from being a devastating refutation of the framework interpretation, the Fourth Commandment actually argues very strongly *for* the framework interpretation. Why? Because Exodus 31:14–17 (a clear parallel to Exodus 20:11) demonstrates that the language of God's working and resting is profoundly anthropomorphic. This truth can be seen in the unique verb used to describe God's rest: "on the seventh day He rested and *refreshed Himself*" (our translation). This verb "to refresh oneself" (*naphash*) is used only two other times in the Hebrew Bible. The first instance reads, "Six days you are to do your work, but on the seventh day you shall cease from labor so that your ox and your donkey may rest, and the son of your female slave, as well as your stranger, may *refresh themselves*" (Exo. 23:12). Notice the context: ceasing from labor to be rejuvenated after arduous labor. The other remaining reference is even clearer, "And the king and all the people who were with him arrived weary and he *refreshed himself* there" (2 Sam. 16:14). A person only needs to rest and be refreshed if he is weary and suffering from exhaustion. However, when Exodus 31:17 says that God rested on the seventh day and refreshed Himself, we cannot take this reference to God's rest and refreshment literally, as if God were exhausted from the difficult work of the six days of creation.

Literalists are selective. They argue that the Fourth Commandment loses its cogency if the days are not taken literally. Using their reasoning, we would be compelled to conclude that the Sabbath command loses its cogency if God's resting and refreshing Himself are not taken literally. For the Fourth Commandment to be valid on their view, we would be forced to interpret each element of God's rest literally (the nature of the rest, the presupposed weariness that was the occasion of the rest, the length of time of the rest). But this interpretation is patently absurd.

Literalists must admit that the command is still valid because there is an *analogy* between God's rest and man's, even if there is not exact identity. God's rest sets the pattern for man's, even though His rest is that of "the Creator of the ends of the earth [who] will not grow tired or weary" (Isa. 40:28). But if the literalists recognize that the *nature* of the rest is not identical to man's, why not recognize the same thing with respect to the *duration* of the rest? If a nonliteral interpretation of the divine refreshment does not invalidate the Fourth Commandment, neither does a nonliteral interpretation of God's seventh day. Thus, the objection from Exodus 20:8–11 completely loses its cogency, unless literalists insist on taking the divine refreshment of Exodus 31:17 literally.

Furthermore, the seventh day is actually an eternal day (as Heb. 4:4–10 clearly teaches), and yet *as such*, it provides the pattern for man's observation of a weekly Sabbath (Exo. 20:11). The fact that God's Sabbath is an eternal rest that belongs to a transcendent realm (the upper register) and one which is not part of *our* weekly cycle does not prevent it from serving as the grounds for man's recurring Sabbath rest. God's labor for six upper-register days and His rest on the seventh is the archetype after which man's lower-register week is patterned. That is to say, the analogy between God's rest and man's remains intact, even though the seventh day is unending. Man is still held accountable to observe a weekly Sabbath, even though God's Sabbath is eternal.

The fundamental weakness of this objection, then, is that it assumes *identity* rather than *analogy* between God's rest and man's. Exodus 31:17 strongly suggests—or even requires—that the relationship is more properly characterized as analogical. This, in turn, is perfectly consistent with the framework interpretation, which sees the initial week of creation as the upper-register archetype for man's recurring week. So rather than refuting our view, the Fourth Commandment actually supports it.

The Meaning of Yôm

The second major objection to the framework interpretation is the argument that the Hebrew word *yôm* (day) ought to be taken in its normal, literal meaning due to several syntactical factors. This objection applies equally to the day-age view. Robert Grossmann speaks for many when he states:

> Nowhere in Scripture do we find a numbered series of days and nights referring to anything but a chronological sequence of days. . . . If each of them is numbered like a day, ends like a day [with the evening and morning formula] and is called a 'day,' why even think that they were really something else?[45]

Not only does the word *yôm* normally denote a normal, solar day, but Grossmann argues that the presence of these additional syntactical features makes that meaning even more certain.

How are we to respond to this objection? The day-age view defends taking *yôm* in the sense of "age" by citing other texts where *yôm* may have that meaning.[46] However, defenders of the framework interpretation prefer a different approach. Unlike day-age advocates, framework advocates give yôm its normal sense of an ordinary day. But then, unlike literalists, they take account of the fact that the *days* are part of an extended chronological metaphor. In all metaphors, words are employed to make a comparison between a literal referent and a metaphorical referent.[47] For example, the word *fox* in the sentence, "Go and tell that fox . . ." (Luke 13:32), denotes a small carnivorous mammal of the dog family. Yet in this context, *fox* is being used as a metaphor to describe something about Herod.

In saying that Herod is a fox, Jesus is not saying that he is a small carnivorous mammal, but that he has a fox-like, crafty nature. It is unnecessary and misleading to argue that this unique usage may be explained as an instance where the word *fox* has a different meaning. The metaphor succeeds in conveying meaning precisely by comparing Herod to a literal fox. To search for secondary meanings of the term *fox* is to miss the point of the comparison between Herod's and the fox's crafty natures. Likewise in Genesis 1. If we were to argue that yôm has a figurative meaning here denoting "an indefinite period of time" or some such meaning, the metaphorical element would be lost.[48]

As we saw in our study of two-register cosmology, the temporal language ("day," "evening and morning") of Genesis 1 is being used metaphorically. Terms properly used to denote lower-register units of time have been appropriated to refer to upper-register time. Because the lower register is a visible replica of the upper register, the Holy Spirit intentionally and quite fittingly employed terms with lower-register significance to describe upper-register realities beyond our ordinary experience. Thus, the word yôm in Genesis 1 denotes an ordinary, lower-register, solar day. Yet it is being used metaphorically to describe an upper-register unit of time that is not defined by the earth's rotation with respect to the Ssun. A word with a literal denotation has been employed to describe a nonliteral referent. This metaphorical usage is appropriate due to the analogical relationship between the literal denotation (solar day) and the nonliteral referent (upper-register unit of time).

So, then, the fact that the days are part of a numbered series does not turn out to be very significant. Why should the addition of ordinals ("first," "second," etc.) or placement within a series militate against a metaphorical usage of *day*? Nor does the fact that each day ends just as a normal, solar day ends—with an evening followed by a morning—demonstrate that the days are not being used figuratively. Even E. J. Young agrees: "If the word 'day' is employed figuratively . . . so also may the terms 'evening' and 'morning', inasmuch as they are component elements of the day, be employed figuratively."[49]

When critics attempt to prove that the word yôm in Genesis 1 has exclusive reference to a normal solar day by appealing to the normal usage of *yôm*, to the presence of the evening-morning formula, and to the fact that the days are numbered, the real issues have not been engaged. Proving that a particular word has a literal denotation does not decide whether it is also metaphorical in a particular context. Luke 13:32 employs the word *fox* with a literal denotation; but it is also being used metaphorically. The metaphorical usage requires the literal denotation for the comparison to work. Evidence that *yôm* has a literal, lower-register denotation is not germane to the question of whether or not it is part of an extended metaphor based on the analogy between the upper and lower registers. For if the framework interpretation is true, we would *expect* to find evidence that *yôm* normally has a literal, lower-register meaning.

The only way to determine whether a particular word is being used metaphorically is to examine the particular context in which it is being used. For example, a metaphorical usage of *fox* in Judges 15:4–5 is not possible because the context demands an exclusively literal reference. It is this kind of contextual consideration that needs to be given to Genesis 1. If the critics of the framework interpretation want to prove that *yôm* is not being used as part of an extended metaphor, they would either have to disprove the concept of two-register cosmology or show that, in this particular case, the context of Genesis 1 does not point to a metaphorical usage of lower-register language to denote upper-register time.

In other words, they would have to study either the entire canonical context of Scripture (to show that two-register cosmology per se is invalid) or the immediate context of the creation narrative (to show that two-register cosmology does not play a role in this text). But lexical research on the word *yôm*—giving statistics about the frequency of its literal usage, showing that when it occurs with a series of ordinals it always means a normal day, etc.—is irrelevant. It misses the basic point that the critical question is not the meaning of *yôm* but the nature (literal or metaphorical) of the total image of the week of days.

CONCLUSION

Hampered by the unexamined assumption that the text addresses the earthly sequence and chronology of origins, the 24-hour and day-age views fail to grasp the overriding theological message of the text. But the framework interpretation stands out among its competitors on account of its sensitivity to the literary, thematic, and theological aspects of the creation narrative. Let us gather together the various points that we have made in the course of our defense of the framework interpretation and summarize the theological message of the creation narrative.

The obvious place to begin is with the figure of the week. The creation narrative has been shaped according to the literary structure of a week of six days of divine work followed by a seventh of divine rest. The Sabbath is clearly the conclusion and goal of the creation week. It is highlighted as well by the fact that the previous six days form a unit composed of two parallel triads, thus setting off the seventh day as the capstone of the whole. The creation account has been shaped by this sabbatical symbolism to show that the Alpha-Creator who began the good work of creation will also complete it as creation's sabbatical Omega-Consummator. Creation was established from the beginning with a built-in eschatological direction and hope.

In addition, we observed that the two triads lead to a subordinate climax of their own in Days 3 and 6, which deal with the twin themes of vegetation and man. The fact that man's creation is recorded at the end of the six-day account suggests that he is the vice-regent under God and has been given a federal representative headship over all creation. Furthermore, his being made in the image of the Creator suggests that just as God worked for six days and then entered into His own rest, so man must imitate the divine pattern by working and then entering into God's rest. Here then we find the means by which the eschatological direction and hope of creation would be fulfilled. Through Adam's successful probation under the covenant of works (signified by man's relationship with the two trees—vegetation), the creation would, under man's federal headship, be enabled to enter into the eschatological Sabbath rest of God.

This eschatological thrust of the creation narrative is not only made clear through the linear symbolism of the Sabbath but is also evident in the vertical dimension of the text's eschatology, namely, the pervasive presence of the upper register. As we saw in our discussion of two-register cosmology, the text has been shaped from beginning to end by the awareness of a profound interaction between heaven and the earth. Heaven, the glorious dwelling place of God, stands above the text and intrudes into the historical process of creation at each key point. The heavenly, eschatological arena of God's glory comes down from above into the midst of the creation history and leaves its analogical imprint on the very fabric of the cosmos. By means of a process by which the upper register is replicated in lower-register form, the creation has been stamped with eschatological hope at every point and is thus marked as bound for Sabbath-consummation in the last day. Therefore, the text teaches us that the chief end of creation is to glorify God and to enjoy Him forever.

NOTES

1. Though popularly referred to as "the framework hypothesis"—a label which might give the impression that we regard the view as a tentative interpretive suggestion—we prefer "the framework interpretation" or "the framework view."

2. "The author's intention is not to supply us with a chronology of origins. . . . He wishes to bring out certain themes and provide a theology of the Sabbath." Henri Blocher, *In the Beginning: The Opening Chapters of Genesis*, trans. David G. Preston (Downers Grove, IL: InterVarsity Press, 1984), p. 50.

3. See the conclusion of this essay for a summary of the text's theological message.

4. C. J. Collins, "How Old Is the Earth? Anthropomorphic Days in Genesis 1:1–2:3," *Presbyterion*, vol. 20, no. 2 (1994), p. 125; Jack P. Lewis, "The Days of Creation: An Historical Survey of Interpretation," *Journal of the Evangelical Theological Society*, vol. 32, no. 4 (Dec. 1994), pp. 433–55; Robert Letham, "'In the Space of Six Days': The Days of Creation from Origen to the Westminster Assembly," *Westminster Theological Journal*, vol. 61, no. 2 (Fall 1999), pp. 149–74.

5. Augustine, *The Literal Meaning of Genesis*, vol. 41, *Ancient Christian Writers*, ed. J. Quasten, et al. (New York: Newman Press, 1982), pp. 134–5.

6. O. T. Allis, *The Old Testament: Its Claims and Critics* (Presbyterian & Reformed Publishing Co., 1972). For a more recent treatment of the problem, see Randall Buth, "Methodological Collision Between Source Criticism and Discourse Analysis: The Problem of 'Unmarked Temporal Overlay' and the Pluperfect/Nonsequential *wayyiqtol*," *Biblical Hebrew and Discourse Linguistics*, ed. Robert D. Bergen (Dallas: Summer Institute of Linguistics, 1994), pp. 138–54.

7. Allis, *The Old Testament: Its Claims and Critics*, p. 97.

8. Ibid., pp. 102–5.

9. D. L. Bock, *Luke 1:1–9:50*, Baker Exegetical Commentary on the New Testament (Grand Rapids, MI: Baker Book House, 1994), p. 365.

10. Allis, *The Old Testament: Its Claims and Critics*, p. 82.

11. Actually, the creation of man is recorded three times if Genesis 5:1–2 is included.

12. E. J. Young, *Studies in Genesis One* (Philadelphia, PA: Presbyterian & Reformed Publishing Co., 1964), pp. 73–4.

13. Ibid.

14. Meredith G. Kline, *Kingdom Prologue* (published by author, 1991), pp. 6–7.

15. Bernhard W. Anderson, "A Stylistic Study of the Priestly Creation Story," *Canon and Authority: Essays on the Theology and Religion of the Old Testament*, ed. G. W. Coats and B. O. Long (Philadelphia, PA: Fortress, 1977), pp. 154–9; Umberto Cassuto, *A Commentary on the Book of Genesis*, Part I, trans. I. Abrahams (Jerusalem: The Magnes Press, 1961), p. 17; Nahum M. Sarna, *Genesis*, The JPS Torah Commentary (Philadelphia, PA: The Jewish Publication Society, 1989), p. 4; Gordan J. Wenham, *Genesis 1–15*, Word Biblical Commentary (Waco, TX: Word Books, 1987), p. 7.

16. Arie Noordtzij, *Gods Woord en der Eeuwen Getuigenis* (Kampen, 1924).

17. N. H. Ridderbos, *Is There a Conflict Between Genesis 1 and Natural Science?*, trans. John Vriend (Grand Rapids, MI: Wm. B. Eerdmans Publishing Co., 1957), p. 11.

18. Kline, *Kingdom Prologue*, pp. 25–6.

19. Meredith G. Kline, "The Covenant of the Seventieth Week," *The Law and the Prophets: Old Testament Studies Prepared in Honor of O. T. Allis*, ed. J. H. Skilton (Nutley, NJ: Presbyterian & Reformed Publishing Co., 1974), pp. 452–69.

20. For more on gaps in the biblical genealogies, see William H. Green, "Primeval Chronology," *Bibliotheca Sacra* (April 1890), pp. 285–303.

21. John Skinner, *Genesis, The International Critical Commentary*, 2d edition (Edinburgh, UK: T. & T. Clark, 1930), pp. 8–10.

22. For an extensive treatment of the thematic connections between Genesis 1 and 2, see Mark D. Futato, "Because It Had Rained: A Study of Gen 2:5–7 with Implications for Gen 2:4–25 and Gen 1:1–2:3," *Westminster Theological Journal*, vol. 60, no. 1 (Spring 1998), pp. 1–21.

23. Mark Throntveit, "Are the Events in the Genesis Creation Account Set Forth in Chronological Order? No," *The Genesis Debate*, ed. R. Youngblood (Grand Rapids, MI: Baker Book House, 1990), p. 46.

24. For additional arguments against the view that Day 4 narrates the unveiling of the luminaries rather than their divine production, see the detailed discussion in Meredith G. Kline, "Space and Time in the Genesis Cosmogony," *Perspectives on Science and Christian Faith*, vol. 48, no. 1 (April 1996), pp. 8–9.

25. Meredith G. Kline, "Because It Had Not Rained," *Westminster Theological Journal*, vol. 20, no. 2 (May 1958), pp. 146–57. Forty years later Futato reinforced many of Kline's conclusions with additional argumentation in "Because It Had Rained" (cf. note 22).

26. Kline, "Because It Had Not Rained," p. 150.

27. "The . . . problem with its twofold reason will be given a twofold solution." Futato, "Because It Had Rained," p. 5.

28. Mitchell Dahood, "Eblaite *i–du* and Hebrew '*ed*, 'Rain-Cloud,'" *Catholic Biblical Quarterly*, vol. 43 (1981), pp. 534–8.

29. Futato, "Because It Had Rained," p. 7.

30. Do rain-clouds arise from the *earth*? Yes: "He makes clouds rise from the ends of the earth" (Psa. 135:7). Futato, "Because It Had Rained," p. 8.

31. Kline, "Because It Had Not Rained," pp. 149–50.

32. Ibid., p. 153.

33. Young, *Studies in Genesis One*, p. 65.

34. Kline, "Space and Time in the Genesis Cosmogony," pp. 2–15.

35. Young, *Studies in Genesis One*, p. 47.

36. Nehemiah seems to have Genesis 1:1; 2:1 in view when he speaks of the Lord as Creator of "heaven, the heaven of heavens, with all their host" (Neh. 9:6, NKJ). Nehemiah thus interprets the heavens of Genesis 1:1 and 2:1 not as the sky but the heavenly dwelling place of God. Similarly Paul equates the heavens with the invisible realm inhabited by principalities and powers (Col. 1:16). See Kline, "Space and Time in the Genesis Cosmogony," pp. 4–5.

37. The NIV obscures this connection by translating *shamayim* as "sky" in Genesis 1:8, 15, 17, 20.

38. Kline, "Space and Time in the Genesis Cosmogony," p. 5; for more on the Glory-cloud as a theophany of the Spirit, see Kline, *Images of the Spirit* (Eugene, OR: Wipf and Stock Publishers, 1998).

39. Kline, *Images of the Spirit*, pp. 22–3.

40. John Murray recognized the unending nature of the seventh day in *Principles of Conduct* (Grand Rapids, MI: Wm. B. Eerdmans Publishing Co., 1957), pp. 30–2.

41. Unlike most parables, the figure of the seven days in Genesis 1:1–2:3 was employed to narrate events that actually occurred. The analogy between the creation week and the Gospel parables is intended only to show the necessity of employing a consistent hermeneutic.

42. Young, *Studies in Genesis One*, p. 47.

43. James B. Jordan, *Through New Eyes* (Brentwood, TN: Wolgemuth and Hyatt, 1988), p. 11. Douglas Kelly makes a similar charge in *Creation and Change* (Ross-Shire, Great Brit-

ain: Mentor, 1997), pp. 116–7. For a response to Kelly, see the book review by Lee Irons, "Douglas Kelly on the Framework Interpretation of Genesis One," *Perspectives on Science and Christian Faith*, vol. 50, no. 4 (Dec. 1998), pp. 272–4.

44. Noel Weeks, "The Hermeneutic Problem of Genesis 1–11," *Themelios*, vol. 4, no. 1 (Sept. 1978), pp. 12–9.

45. Robert E. Grossmann, "The Light He Called 'Day'," *Mid-America Journal of Theology*, vol. 3, no. 1 (1987), pp. 7–34.

46. E.g., Gen. 2:5; Psa. 30:5; 49:14; 90:6; Hos. 6:2; 2 Pet. 3:8.

47. Peter Cotterell and Max Turner, *Linguistics and Biblical Interpretation* (Downers Grove, IL: InterVarsity Press, 1989), p. 300.

48. Blocher, pp. 44–5.

49. Young, *Studies in Genesis One*, p. 104.

THE 24-HOUR RESPONSE

e compliment Lee Irons, who, in consultation with Meredith G. Kline, has presented a case for the framework interpretation marked by utmost clarity and some fine statements with which we heartily agree. For example, the essay affirms that "Scripture has hermeneutical and presuppositional priority over our fallible study of general revelation" and that "the results of such [natural] investigation are always subject to change and therefore will never have the same certainty of Scripture." We also personally appreciate Kline, who has challenged and stimulated our thinking for years, and Irons, who has emerged as a gifted thinker in his own right. We do not question the orthodoxy of Kline or Irons, both of whom are committed to the inerrancy, infallibility, and authority of Scripture. Significantly, the framework essay affirms the historicity of creation, Adam, and the Fall, and provides that we are to take most aspects of the Genesis creation literally.

Except one.

The framework interpretation views the creation days as figurative and nonsequential. This view is curiously selective, and we wonder whether the Church actually can draw the line there were it to adopt fully the hermeneutic that framework advocates employ. What, for example, would be the exegetical consequences for the rest of the Genesis protology? What elements of Genesis 1–11—which, historically, have been taken literally— must we now reinterpret? What about the rest of Scripture?

The version of the framework hermeneutic presented in this volume diligently attempts to avoid being classified as liberal and non-inerrantist. It reiterates again and again that it not only is drawn from, but also is demanded by, the text itself and that it does not contradict the perspicuity of Scripture in any way. Nevertheless, evangelical audiences consistently react to the framework view with the concern that it undermines the clarity of the scriptural narratives. This concern weighs heavily on this frail view, and despite the protestations of its adherents, we contend that the view is incorrect, eccentric, and thinly supported.

FOUR SPECIFIC PROBLEMS

We begin by noting four specific problems with the framework view presented here by Irons and Kline.

Not Uniquely Agnostic on the Age of the Earth

Although the framework interpretation incorrectly claims to be uniquely agnostic on the age of the earth, the nature of the creation days is not inextricably tied to the age of the earth. Our presentation of the historic literal-day view (like Calvin before us) pressed no particular view of the age of the earth or universe. Yet the framework essay presents this agnosticism as one of its central advantages, saying, in essence, "The 24-hour view thinks that Genesis 1 speaks to cosmogony and chronology and so adopts an antiscientific posture, while the day-age view thinks Genesis 1 must be harmonized with science for apologetic purposes and thus reads it in light of Christianized scientific theory." The framework interpreter sees himself as above this fray, merely wanting to "listen to the text." In fact, the framework view attempts to slip the Gordian knot of the age-of-the-earth debate. This is itself, however, an apologetical stance and thus the idea that the framework view has an exegetical, rather than an apologetic, focus cannot withstand scrutiny. None of us can approach this passage in our current setting without apologetic concerns. (Nor should we!) The more quickly we realize that fact, the better.

Not Liberating the Church's Conscience

Furthermore, the framework view claims to uniquely liberate the conscience of the Church on the age of the earth and wrongly assumes that the age of the earth is the essence of the 24-hour view. Again, the framework view misses the mark. Nowhere in our presentation of the 24-hour view do we bind the conscience of the Church on this matter. The 24-hour view is marked by deeper exegetical and theological concerns. Moreover, the "freedom" of the framework view is purchased at a dear price—the unprecedented denial that the creation account speaks to the issues of chronology and sequence. The passage is history, they say, but says nothing whatsoever about the timing, duration, and order of the actual creation. Never before in the history of the Christian Church has this denial been so comprehensively stated. This denial is what causes some to charge the framework interpretation with nominalism, however odious that charge may seem to its proponents.

Self-Congratulatory and Condescending

The framework interpretation also is self-congratulatory. Irons and Kline state, "In contrast to the other two positions represented in this book, the framework interpretation recognizes the exegetical implications of the unique literary and theological character of this inspired record of the history of creation." Such assertions are overdrawn and self-aggrandizing—all too typical in the framework literature. Seemingly, they also propose that only when one surrenders any interest in what Genesis may have to say about cosmogony can one truly understand the text. This amounts to nothing more than chronological snobbery. ("Our new view is superior to the old views and for the first time in the history of the Church we provide serious exegesis of this passage.")

The framework interpretation is also condescending when it claims unique insights into, and understanding of, the text of Genesis 1–2. The framework essay claims that "both the 24-hour and the day-age views fail to recognize that, while Scripture inerrantly reports historical and chronological information, it always does so with a covenantal and redemptive historical purpose." Irons and Kline later write that, "by contrast, the framework interpretation removes the false expectations that have muzzled the text in the past and liberates it to address the people of God kerygmatically and theologically." One would expect the same kind of rhetoric from Bishop Spong as he "rescues the Bible from fundamentalism."

This kind of rhetoric has caused many within conservative circles to look askance at, and to be suspicious of, the framework view. When framework proponents claim to have liberated the text so that it can finally speak to us, they deny the fruit of two thousand years of competent, consensual Christian interpretation of creation. By contrast, we contend that there is not a single theological truth from the creation account that depends upon a framework reading of the text. In fact, the *only* unique theological contribution of the framework theory is that it negates the temporal duration and sequence of the creation days.

Unconvincing Exegetical Justifications

Most important, the central exegetical justifications that the framework interpretation presents for reading the creation week as figurative and nonsequential are singularly unconvincing. This is a fatal problem for the view because it markets itself as doing the best exegesis. The exegesis, however, is strained. The framework view makes the following "exegetical" arguments:

- The creation of the sun on Day 4 shows that the author did not intend for us to understand the days of the creation week as literal calendar days.

- Genesis 1 and 2 show various evidences of nonsequential narration, dischronologization, and temporal recapitulation. Therefore, there is internal warrant for reading the creation days as topically, as opposed to chronologically, arranged.

- The creation days form a framework of two parallel triads representing the creation kingdoms and the creature kings, culminating in the Sabbath day, and thus the account is theologically stylized.

- Since sabbatical symbolism is found elsewhere in Scripture, it is legitimate to read the sabbatical argument of Genesis 1 and 2 figuratively, not literally.

- Negatively, any sequential view of the narrative is unable to account adequately for the "replacement mechanism" for the "original system of light production," thus commending the framework explanation.

- Positively, more than merely displaying thematic parallelism, this passage entails temporal recapitulation of Day 1 on Day 4, showing that the whole week is a figurative framework.

- Genesis 2:5–6 proves that God employed ordinary providence during the creation period and thus, for instance, the idea that God ordered the day and night by extraordinary providence on Days 1–3 is ruled out as exegetical presumption.

- The "two-register cosmology" supplies a biblical explanation of the significance of the nonliteral nature of the time indicators in Genesis 1.

To state some of these arguments is to refute them. For example, the two-register cosmology is not evidence for the framework view but rather something that would be consistent with it if it were true. However, it could also be consistent with views other than the framework position.

The argument from the alleged presence of dischronologization in parts of the creation narrative is hardly direct evidence of a merely literary day (even if granted). Only a few are willing to grant this assumption.

The arguments regarding Days 1 and 4 and the source of light on Days 1–3 are just variations on the old "the sun wasn't created until Day 4" theme. None of those arguments takes seriously: (1) the mystery of creation (the "second greatest miracle" ever wrought by God); (2) the fact that the earliest proponent of this argument was the third-century pagan enemy of Christianity, Celsus; or (3) the unflinching response of Calvin to the mere suggestion of it.

In terms of *ad populum* appeal, the three framework arguments that seem to resonate most with audiences are: (1) the assertion that the sun's appearance on Day 4 is conclusive proof that the days of Genesis 1 cannot be understood as literal days; (2) the suggestion that Genesis 2:5–6 proves that ordinary providence operated during the creation period and thus literal days would not suffice for the events Moses said occurred on the various "days"; and (3) the appeal to thematic parallelism as justifying a nonchronological reading of the narrative. How does a historic literal day view respond to these framework arguments?

The creation of the sun on Day 4 does not prove the creation days to be nonliteral or nonsequential. Indeed, that argument has been around for several centuries, has not proved compelling to mainstream Christian exegesis, and seems to rest upon an implicit denial of the work of creation as "miracle." You simply cannot get away from sequence and extent of time if you pay attention to the language and grammar of Genesis 1: the numbered days, the refrain "evening and morning," and the use of the Hebrew *waw*-consecutive are decisive arguments against seeing the creation of the sun on Day 4 as exegetical "proof" of the nonsequential and nonchronological nature of the creation days. Interestingly, when framework advocates use this argument, they raise a question about their own claim to exegetical altruism and apologetic neutrality. Can we really believe that Moses intended to signal premodern hearers of Genesis that his account of the days was nonsequential by stating that the sun's creation was on the fourth day? Could such an "exegetical marker" have made sense to anyone in the second millennium B.C.?

The framework argument that Genesis 2:5–6 "proves" the operation of ordinary providence during the creation days is yet another instance of moderns finding a nonexistent modern argument in the Mosaic text. The fifth and sixth verses of Genesis 2 provide a context for the account of the creation of man. Far from being designed to clue us in on the mechanics of the flourishing of God's creation in Genesis 1, these verses refer to the sixth day and set the stage for explaining man's obligation to care for the garden. Genesis 1 and 2 make clear that God established certain blessings and obligations for man at the very outset of His relationship with man. For example, in each of the creation ordinances, there is blessing as well as responsibility. These verses remind us of Adam's responsibility to cultivate the garden in which God graciously placed him. Furthermore, Moses writes these verses to remind us that the world was not ordered and full in its initial form: the paradise of Eden was God's gift.

By appealing to thematic parallelism and the triads, framework advocates create more problems for themselves. Once you say that Days 4–6 refer to the same events as Days 1–3, you have a cycle of four events, not seven, in violation of the supposedly sabbatical arrangement of the text, which framework interpreters advocate. The two-register cosmology lends no assistance here, but just sinks the framework advocate deeper into the quagmire. Having dispensed with sequence and chronology, now the real events behind the literary devices are beginning to disappear.

Notice also that each of these three main arguments for the framework view serves only to attack the notion of literal days and does nothing to advance the supposedly "unique" theological insights framework advocates "discover" in the text. Thus, a 24-hour proponent may deny the framework theory at this point and still borrow every legitimate deduction that the framework advocate makes from his study of parallelism and other literary devices. This is an important point and shows that the fundamental difference between the framework view and the 24-hour view is not exegetical but theological.

Wittingly or unwittingly, the framework interpreter believes that the biggest difficulty with the 24-hour view is its preoccupation with cosmogony and its relation to current scientific opinion. He thinks that the day-age view's biggest problem is harmonization—though in a different direction. The framework view then claims to "come to the rescue" by adjusting our exegetical approach to the passage so that these matters are no longer a concern for the reader. In effect, the framework view says: "Who cares about the age of the earth or harmonizing Genesis with secular scientific cosmogony? Permit the text to speak for itself."

This stance sounds compelling, and it certainly is sincere. But it belies a vulnerable theological presupposition: namely, that the biggest problem facing the 24-hour view is its apologetical concern and that the biggest problem facing the day-age view is its harmonistic concern. These things, say framework proponents, blind those who hold these views from the real meaning of the text. All the unique exegetical positions of the framework view are thus deployed to attack this one point. The rest of their exegesis yields no unprecedented theological insight.

Irons and Kline say that their exegesis is theologically richer than the classical view because their view emphasizes the covenantal relationship between God and man, the call to covenant obedience, God's wisdom and power in the created order, the *imago Dei*, the Sabbath ordinance, and the eschatological dimension of the created order. But all these themes are found in the commentaries and theological treatises of theologians long before the framework view came on the scene. If the crowning glory of the framework view is that it "liberates" the text from apologetical and harmonistic considerations to speak to these theological matters, then its billing is more than a little disappointing. It offers a freedom that many in the evangelical tradition already enjoy. But it does so at an enormous cost.

This is the fundamental problem with the whole approach. The exegetical discussion is just a sideshow compared to the real issue. The framework hypothesis gets rid of a perceived apologetical problem by denying that the Genesis protology speaks to cosmogony or chronology. But in the end, the hypothesis buys us far more difficult and momentous theological questions about the perspicuity of Scripture, the historicity of Genesis 1–11, and most significantly, the goodness of the original creation and the causal connection between sin and death in the created order.

For example, the framework view of what it sees as ordinary providence in Genesis 2:5–6 is a *sine qua non* for the interpretation. If its advocates are wrong on that point, the whole theory fails. Yet, by insisting on their novel reading of Genesis 2:5–6 and its implications for ordinary providence in creation, framework theorists cannot easily explain why no exegete in the history of Judaism or Christianity ever remotely suggested their interpretation until circa 1958. The perspicuity of Scripture is jeopardized by this eccentric hermeneutical approach.

Or take the issue of the historicity of Genesis 1–11. If you want to establish détente with science by saying that the text does not address the length of the creation days, you haven't accomplished much. Any reading that views Genesis 1–11 as historical conflicts irreconcilably with current scientific opinion in paleontology, paleoethnology, and paleogeology. In turn, these "conflicts" force you to discover other "figurative elements" in other narratives such as Noah's Flood. Thus, many evangelicals who favor figurative interpretations of Genesis 1–2 (including many framework proponents) also argue for a limited flood that only appeared to be universal.

In this way, a framework hermeneutic forces us into an ongoing theological discussion about other potentially "figurative" elements in Genesis protology (Adam and Eve, the lifespans of Genesis 5, the *nephilim* of Genesis 6, the table of nations in Genesis 10, Babel, etc.). In the end, this approach seriously endangers our ability to honestly claim that we hold to the historicity of Scripture.

Finally, the framework interpretation tends (along with other figurative interpretations of Genesis 1–3) to restrict the effects of the Fall to humankind and emphasize pre-Fall/post-Fall continuity in all the subhuman creation (plants, animals, etc.). This dramatically and devastatingly affects the historic Christian understanding of the nature of the goodness of the original creation, the distinction between an unfallen and a fallen creation, the cosmic effects of redemption (Rom. 8; 2 Pet. 3), and the Pauline connection between sin and death. Taken to its logical conclusion, the framework hermeneutic may require a radical theological reconstruction of Christian soteriology and eschatology.

In short, by resorting to exegetical gymnastics, the framework view attempts to spare us from an apologetical conundrum, only to leave us with critical theological problems that are far more perplexing than the apologetic problem from which the theory purports to rescue us. Indeed, the "cure" is worse than the supposed "disease."

THE HIGH STAKES

We itemize below several key issues that are at stake in the debate over the framework view.

Creates Interpretive Problems
The framework essay claims to liberate the text from received interpretations and, serendipitously, to have removed "the false expectations that have muzzled the text in the past" so that the theological message may shine through. By making this claim, framework adherents disenfranchise virtually all earlier exegesis and sport an eccentric view that purportedly rescues the theological message. We, on the other hand, have presented a view that preserves both medium and message, and we disavow the claim that the sequence and chronology suffocate the theological message. Indeed, the central affirmation of the creation narratives is *the sovereignty and majesty of our Creator*, a truth that our view emphasizes, not obscures.

Moreover, the framework view requires more than anyone may credibly posit about the literary sophistication of (1) the original audience, (2) all subsequent Old Testament epexegesis, (3) New Testament commentaries on creation, and (4) the orthodox understanding of the Christian Church until relatively recent revisions. The need for readers in Moses' time to apply the hermeneutic of dischronologization was neither suspected nor asserted until recently. Indeed, the appearance of such an assertion only after the rise of modern cosmological theories and devoid of earlier exegetical precedent raises due suspicion about the legitimacy of the framework view. We suspect that the history of theology will judge this particular exegetical fad as another reactionary (if restrained) effort of our era to conform to secular cosmogony. The framework exegesis is strictly recent, contrived, and demands that virtually no one before now was able to interpret the creation account's "hidden code."

Undermines Perspicuity

The framework theory seriously undermines our confidence in the clarity of Scripture. One of the beauties of the Christian faith is that God, in His grace, reveals Himself in a way that even children and nonliterary specialists can understand His mind, at least substantively. We daresay that children and nonliterary theorists cannot easily grasp the framework interpretation. It is simply too foggy and requires too much audience imposition. The simple man and centuries of Christians—as illumined by the Spirit as moderns—would never have surmised that Genesis 1 really taught this promise: "the theological significance of the literary design that brought the first triad of days to a climax in trees and the second triad to a climax in man [and] in this way, set the stage for the crucial connection of the two that would be examined in greater detail in the subsequent narrative of man's unsuccessful probation under the covenant of works." Such extreme theorizing stretches the fabric of the text so thin that it snaps.

In addition, the framework essay converts Moses' language of "evening and morning" into mere "subsidiary elements." Thus, the entire narrative loses distinct meaning. In context, we are hard-pressed to understand why framework adherents fail to see "the fish, the birds, the cattle" as symbolic, nonliteral, or "simply subsidiary elements." Once framework advocates begin to employ excessive symbolism, they cannot easily or logically limit it.

While we ought to compare Scripture with Scripture, the framework essay fails to do so. In particular, it fails to compare the creation narratives with other creation passages, such as Psalm 104, which only support the sequential pattern. We agree with Ross and Archer when they write: "Neither of us has ever met or heard of any secular scientist who, independent of Christian influence, has ever denied that Genesis 1 is a chronology of creation events." Indeed, a certain theological agenda appears to lead framework theorists to re-engineer the text. Their goal, apparently, is to avoid the challenge of modern science. Again, we agree with Ross and Archer when they write that "such an escape hatch is bound to engender ridicule from secularists" and robs "the text of significant testable content."

Obfuscates the Sabbath

Ironically, one of the chief victims of the framework interpretation is the Sabbath's 6+1 pattern taught throughout Scripture. For the framework theory to be convincing, it must also demonstrate that the putative 3+3+1 framework is not an arbitrary artifice. For example, what is to prevent another commentator from finding another form altogether such as (3x2)+1, 6+1, or 6+0?

Despite its stated intention, the framework view actually destroys the Sabbath. If the framework interpretation were correct when it holds that "Day 4 returns to the scene pictured on Day 1," the form would be 3+1. The framework essay eliminates Days 4–6 by having them refer to Days 1–3. Where is the scriptural clue telling us that Genesis is speaking about three days that are reiterated (but not Days 4–6) followed by a fourth day (but not really the seventh)? The framework interpretation yields a quadrath instead of a Sabbath, for it sees Days 4–6 as recapitulations of Days 1–3, respectively. The pattern would be as follows: 1a-2a-3a, 1b-2b-3b. Despite the invention of an elaborate set of tables emphasizing perceived parallelisms, the framework essay never indicates why we shouldn't take the whole account as a quadratarian scheme. In the name of exalting the Sabbath, the framework interpretation completely undermines it.

Neither do we think that sound biblical interpretation views the seventh day of creation as continuing. And we are dubious that the sequentialism of Days 1–3 abruptly ceases. Putative chiasms notwithstanding, we need greater proof. At times, it appears that the framework essay uses chiasm like a nose of wax—to prove or disprove anything. Chiasm can both prove parallelisms between Days 2 and 5 and be simultaneously reversed.

Ignores Church History

The framework essay commendably admits that previous Church fathers "did not teach the framework interpretation in the precise form we advocate here." In fact, they did not teach any kind of "framework" theory at all! History indicates that the Church fathers put forth no such theory, and we would repudiate the past if we adopt this new theory. In other words, if we accept the framework theory, we must admit that all others were wrong until now.

As has become customary, the framework essay kidnaps Augustine from his context and wrongly appeals to Peter Lombard. Augustine, however, never "argues that the first three days cannot be normal days for the simple reason that they existed prior to the creation of the sun on the fourth day." In *The Literal Meaning of Genesis* (4:33), Augustine writes: "It follows, therefore, that he, who created all things together, simultaneously created these six days, or seven, or rather the one Day Six or seven times repeated." He believed creation occurred in a split second, not over long days. Thus, Augustine lends no support to the framework interpretation.

To embrace the framework interpretation, you have to believe that everybody in the history of interpretation got it wrong—badly wrong—until Kline. You also have to conclude that the best Christian exegetes and theologians of every other school during the last two hundred years seriously erred by concluding that the text speaks, at least in some rudimentary way, to the issue of cosmogony. Furthermore, you have to reject this earlier exegesis as deficient, while admitting that the framework view fails to contribute a single new, orthodox insight into the Christian theology of creation, except that the days were not days! Indeed, the framework view is much ado about nothing.

Suffocates the Miraculous

The framework interpretation adopts a view of providence that suffocates the miraculous. It presupposes "that the mode of providence that was in operation during the creation period and that which is currently in operation . . . are the same."

We rather agree with E. J. Young, who wrote: "In the text of Genesis itself . . . there is not a single allusion to suggest that the days are to be regarded as a form of mere manner of representation and hence of no significance for the essential knowledge of the divine creative activity." We certainly take strong exception to the assertion that "God's own revelation" intends to refer to "the upper register via its lower-register replica." That may be the view of the framework essay, but it can hardly be defended as "God's own revelation."

CONCLUSION

The claim that the framework interpretation is a unique literary theory that understands the creation narrative "on its own terms" may be true in a sense. However, we believe it does so only by undermining the perspicuity of Scripture, obfuscating the Sabbath, suffocating the miraculous, ignoring history, and destroying the sense of the narrative itself. Moreover, the framework view is not uniquely agnostic on the age of the earth, does not liberate the Church's conscience, is self-congratulatory and conde-scending, and does not offer convincing exegesis. In the end, the price the framework view pays for its supposed uniqueness is too high for the Church to remit.

Hugh Ross & Gleason L. Archer

THE DAY-AGE RESPONSE

*S*trong support for biblical inerrancy, Mosaic authorship of Genesis, a literal Adam and Eve, and the miraculous nature of the Genesis 1:1 creation event—these are the major issues on which we agree with the framework essay. We also agree that there is no need to bind "the conscience of the Church to one particular view of the age of the earth/universe," because age is not a salvation issue, nor is it pinpointed in Scripture. We differ chiefly on whether the Bible even addresses the age issue—or any other significant aspect of physical reality—in its creation account. Irons and Kline assert it does not, while we make a case that it does.

CREATION VERBS

In critiquing our long-day interpretation of the text, the framework essay argues that the Hebrew verb *haya* (used in Genesis 1:3, 6, 9, and 14) is essentially synonymous with *bara*, "create." While we agree that *haya* can carry the same meaning, its predominant usage in the Bible more closely parallels our English "be" verbs. The fact that *bara* appears just three times in Genesis 1 and each time in the context of something entirely new and dramatically significant—the universe, soulish animals, and humans (vv. 1, 21, and 27)—suggests to us a deliberate distinction.

We see nothing in the context of Genesis 1 that would compel any meaning other than the commonly interpreted "let be" for *haya*. When the light, the water cycle, the land masses, and the great lights appear through God's miraculous shaping of nature's (created) components, God's "creating" more closely resembles the work of a sculptor or maestro. For example, light—the wave-photon phenomenon created in the cosmic beginning— was brought to Earth's surface for the first time during Day 1 as a result of God's miraculous working with Earth's atmosphere and the interplanetary debris.[1]

As God made additional, perfectly timed changes to Earth's crust and atmosphere on Day 4, the specific objects responsible for that light become clearly visible on Earth's surface for the first time.[2] Genesis 1:16 ("God made . . .") offers a parenthetical note consistent with this interpretation. The verb *asa* ("made") appears in the form denoting past completed action, time unspecified.[3]

While the framework essay allows that our exegesis of Days 1 and 4 has at least the possibility of being correct, it rejects our exegesis on scientific grounds. Irons and Kline say that science rules out our interpretation because some plants cannot survive without the occasional visibility of the sun and moon. They have misapplied the science, however. Only certain advanced plants—those that would have been produced (as needed) on the fifth and sixth creation days—require the distinct visibility of the sun and moon. Genesis 1 tells us that land plant production began during the third creation day, but it does not necessarily imply that land plant production ended on the third creation day. Plant production after the third day seems most evident in symbiosis. We see plants, both today and in the fossil record, that depend on the existence of advanced animals (animals that were not created until the fifth and sixth creation days) for their survival.

Irons and Kline at least acknowledge that "a narrative might have striking thematic parallelisms and still be informed by a literal, sequential chronology." Their two-triad symmetry need not negate the chronology of the six creation days. We can see how one could hold to the day-age view *and* a two-triad interpretation, although not in the precise form they propose.

The degree of symmetry and parallelism the framework essay imposes on the text of Genesis 1, though not compelled by the text, may indeed have some merit. The triadic interpretation of Genesis 1 imparts a certain beauty and grandeur to the prose and, in that respect, makes the apologetics of Genesis 1 all the more compelling. However, we see nothing in the triadic view of the text that diminishes or destroys a chronological interpretation of the Genesis creation events.

BROKEN CHRONOLOGIES

The framework essay commendably documents not only biblical examples of broken or reset chronologies, but biblical reasons why biblical writers break and reset chronologies. In some cases, though, Irons and Kline seem to push their point too far. While the Gospel of Matthew lists three sets of 14 progenitors from Abraham to Jesus, sets that are obviously incomplete, the 42 generations are arranged in chronological order.

We recognize the recapitulation that appears between Genesis 2:4 and 2:5. In fact, we would expect one here, for the focus of the passage shifts from a description of physical creation events to instructions for managing all aspects of creation.[4] However, the framework case for a recapitulation between the third and fourth creation days rests on no such obvious shift, unless one insists on assigning precisely equivalent meanings to *haya* and *bara*. Our response to that issue appears earlier.

RELIABILITY OF REVELATION

The framework essay passes harsh judgment on general revelation, judgment that seems unwarranted. To say that studies of general revelation are always fallible and that studies of special revelation are consistently flawless and infallible is to deny reality. Not all conclusions about the record of nature are subject to overthrow. Can we really imagine scientists of the future overturning evidence for the composition of protons by quarks or for the nearly spherical shape of Earth? Scientific evidence for the transcendent creation of the cosmos now exceeds 99.999999999999 percent certainty.[5] We stake our lives every day on lesser certainties. Such a number comes very close indeed to describing our degree of certainty that Genesis 1:1 and Hebrews 11:3 teach a transcendent creation event.

We suspect that framework theorists deny the chronology of Genesis 1 out of caution. They seem to fear the integration of special and general revelation because, at some points in the past, the two have appeared to conflict, thereby shaking the faith of some. However, the conflicts have always been resolvable upon closer, more careful investigation and analysis—just as we can reasonably expect, since the God who created nature also inspired Scripture.

Chapters 10 and 11 of Daniel help illustrate the apologetic importance of linking objective facts with inspired words. Daniel's prophecy reaches far into the future in intricate detail and chronology. The precise fulfillment of Daniel's predictions provides convincing proof of God's foreknowledge, power, and desire to be known and trusted. Likewise, the Genesis 1 creation account matches subsequent scientific discovery in such exquisite detail and order as to establish its divine inspiration to those who might struggle with doubt. Denying the chronology of Daniel 10–11 robs the passage of its faith-building force. The same can be said, of course, for Genesis 1.

We must never lose sight of the obvious. Genesis 1 simply and eloquently records our grand beginning, the physical launch of God's unfolding plan for humanity. Nature tells the same story, perhaps vaguely at first, but through the centuries, in greater and greater detail as human technology enables and as human skepticism requires (see Rom. 1:18–20). That's the power of Genesis 1, the power of God's wisdom and love. It anticipates our need. God gives the ancient inquirer and today's secular skeptic compelling reasons to continue reading and believing past the first page of His Book.

FORCED PARALLELISM

The numbering system in the framework essay, "eight distinct creative works distributed over six days," seems subjectively overlaid on the text. We count as many as thirteen distinct creative works. Could it be that the framework essay is forcing parallelism and symmetry where it does not necessarily exist? How clear to even a careful reader is the "symbolic link" between production of vegetation on Day 3 and the creation of mankind or of the trees of life and of the knowledge of good and evil later on?

We detect forced parallelism in the way that Irons and Kline treat other creation days as well. For example, they deduce from the second day events that "the sky is created first, then the seas." This deduction contains some obvious flaws. First, the text does not employ *bara*, the Hebrew word for create. It uses *haya*. Second, the seas already existed before the six days of creation began (Gen. 1:2). Third, the sky must also have existed when the week began. Under the laws of physics, established "in the beginning" (Gen. 1:1) and preserved throughout creation (see our response to the 24-hour view earlier), planets the size of Earth must possess an atmosphere, and such an atmosphere is necessary to sustain liquid water seas. Fourth, the point of the text is not to describe the origin of the seas and sky but rather to describe the division, or balancing, of water between the sky and seas so that the efficient and abundant cycling of water can occur.[6] Scientists now have some idea what a delicate—one could reasonably say *miraculous*—balance that cycle turns out to be.[7]

The two most fundamental requirements for life on land are light for photosynthesis and a stable, abundant water cycle. The laws of physics mandate that these two events occur sequentially, the light coming first, then the water cycle.

The framework essay interprets the purpose of Day 4 as the separation of light from darkness. Again, on a common sense and scientific basis, we disagree. By sheer volume of words alone, the text emphasizes the role of the lights in marking the passage of days, nights, seasons, and years. The permanently overcast atmosphere of Days 1, 2, and 3 would make for some difficulty or vagueness in distinguishing the onset of day and night. Moreover, storms would simulate night during the day and even day during the night. At high latitudes, an observer would be unable to distinguish night from day during the heart of summer and winter, let alone tell late morning from early afternoon.

God's transformation of Earth's atmosphere on Day 4 from translucent to potentially transparent provided creatures on Earth's surface with essential time markers. The visibility of the sun, moon, and stars permits sentient creatures to differentiate not only day from night, but also among portions of day and night, seasons of the year, and recurring cycles of seasons. Before the advent of modern technology, the heavenly bodies served as the only means for tracking and, in the case of humans, recording time.

Humans are not the only creatures who need timekeeping capability. Virtually all the animals God introduced on Days 5 and 6 require heavenly markers to regulate their complex biological clocks.[8] Life forms created before the fourth day do not. The timing of this atmospheric transformation is perfect.

According to the framework essay, "the same fiat language that is used for acts of divine origination on the other six days is used on Day 4 as well." As we noted above, the verb *haya*, not *bara*, is used, and Hebrew scholars observe a significant distinction between the two words. We acknowledge that the verb *asa* does represent fiat language, and rightly so, for God did act to form the sun, moon, and stars exactly as life requires. However, the verb's form of *asa* indicates past completed action, either during the first few creation days or, more likely, before the creation days (Gen. 1:1–2).

NATURE OF MIRACLES

At least some of the controversy stirred by Genesis 1 arises when readers and commentators commit the "either-or" fallacy. They presume that *either* natural processes alone account for all the phenomena described *or* God's direct intervention from beyond matter, energy, space, and time causes all the phenomena. The Bible shows us more options, however, than just these two. On some occasions, God does act from beyond the space-time dimensions and physical laws of the universe. He certainly did so in bringing the cosmos into existence and in raising His Son, Jesus Christ, bodily from the dead. On other occasions, however, God's miracles are natural events that occur or converge with supernatural timing, supernatural placement, supernatural design, or some combination of these factors.

On this question of causation, the framework essay leans toward natural cause or "ordinary means" to explain phenomena such as those described in Genesis 2:5–6. (In our opinion, their subsequent clarification helps but does not go far enough.) While we would agree that in providing sustenance for each creature God did not necessarily intervene moment by moment from beyond space and time, we see nothing in the context that would rule out intervention of the second type. Scientific evidence strongly suggests that miracles of time, place, and fine-tuning did occur.[9]

For example, while stars readily form by gravitational condensation of gas clouds, the characteristics of the sun and its neighboring stars are so amazingly fine-tuned for life's existence, we simply cannot avoid the conclusion of design. Perfect design requires a perfect Designer, and the only credible candidate to be found is the God of the Bible.[10] Thus, the language of Genesis 2:5–6 in no way undermines the chronology of the Genesis 1:3–19 miracles we seek to defend.

TWO-REGISTER COSMOLOGY

The Bible speaks frequently of a created heavenly realm beyond the space-time manifold of our universe. However, we must be cautious about calling this realm, or "upper-register cosmos," the dwelling place of God. God fills (and thus dwells in) the entirety of both the physical realm we know as the universe and the heavenly realm. He is confined to neither one nor the other. He exists and is totally functional apart from the "geography" of either realm. This truth can be affirmed not only with "the eyes of [biblical] faith," but also with the eyes of scientific research. The space-time theorem of general relativity and ten-dimensional string theory independently demonstrate that an "upper-register cosmos" exists and that the Causer of our physical universe has the capacity to create any number or kind of space-time dimensions at will.[11]

Genesis 1:2 contradicts the notion presented in the framework essay that "Scripture employs the language of earthly time to speak of the progress of heavenly time." The frame of reference for the six-day creation account is identified as the surface of earth's waters. We can reasonably conclude, then, that the six-day creation events unfold in earthly time. We do agree, however, that in Exodus 20:11 and 31:14–17, God's workweek is presented not as identical to the human workweek but rather as analogous to it. We also agree that the "refreshment" in Exodus 31 contradicts the identity between God's and man's workweek.

Claiming that the Genesis 1 creation week "belongs to the upper rather than the lower register" stretches the contextual elements beyond reason. A more accurate statement would be that the description and chronology of Genesis 1 may *possibly* reflect a pattern of creation in the upper register, but that this possibility rests only on speculation and scriptural silence.

Few would deny that the Bible employs metaphorical constructs. The problem with the framework position is that the text offers neither internal cues nor subsequent biblical corroboration (from Jesus or others) that an allegory or extended metaphor is intended in Genesis 1. In His parables, Jesus made extensive use of earthly analogies to describe the upper register. In each case, He clearly sets up the similes ("the kingdom of God is like . . ."). Where are the simile markers in Genesis 1? We find not a single textual clue of metaphorical language anywhere in the account. Beautiful prose in no way "proves" a nonliteral message.

The framework's two-register cosmology leads to at least three exegetical errors. First, it tampers with the meaning of *eres*, translated "earth." Irons and Kline try to stretch this word to encompass all the stars, galaxies, dust, and gas of the universe. No reputable (or even disreputable) Hebrew lexicon allows such a stretch. Nowhere in the Bible does *eres* refer to stars and galaxies or even to planets. Scripture always places the stars in the heavens (*shamayim*), not in *eres*. Thus, we find no basis for concluding the "heavens" of Genesis 1:1 represent the upper-register creation, while the "earth" of Genesis 1:1 represents the lower-register creation.

Second, the framework essay tampers with the role of angels, designating them as participants in the creation of man. Scripture emphatically asserts that only God "creates" in the sense of the words used in Genesis 1:24–27. As for "the judicial council," God alone declares Himself Judge. He does not share His judicial role with the angels. (The Scripture references cited by the framework essay establish that heavenly angels exist, that a "council" exists, and that God serves as Judge. The references do not state that angels serve on a judicial council.)

Scripture explicitly and implicitly identifies God the Father, God the Son, and God the Holy Spirit as the Creator.[12] It declares that there is only one Creator and that God alone creates.[13] The mixing of singular and plural pronouns for God in Genesis 1:26–27 appropriately presages the doctrine of the Trinity. The Trinity is so foundational to the Christian faith that the account of beginnings needs to include some reference of it.

The third exegetical error seems merely an oversight. The seventh day "rest" of Genesis 1 obviously applies directly to God's earthly creative activity. The creation Sabbath is a time in which God ceases (and refrains) from creating new species of life and thus from preparing the earth for new species. The fossil record offers abundant evidence for God's creative activity before the advent of humanity: His introduction of new species and His preparation of the planet for them.[14] Since that time, we see a lack of speciation and alteration.[15]

Claiming that the seventh day of Genesis 1 is eternal in either the lower or upper register overlooks the biblical declaration that God will create again. Scripture tells us He will create a new heaven and a new earth. The description of His new creation implies that it will operate according to physical laws and dimensionality radically different from those of the present cosmos.[16] The Sabbath will end and the new creation begin when evil is permanently dealt with at the Great White Throne Judgment. In other words, an eighth day is coming when God will resume His creative work.

The absence of an "evening-and-morning" marker for the seventh day in Genesis 1 signals something different about that day—that the seventh day did not end. The ongoing seventh day, however, does not argue for "the nonliteral nature of the creation days." Long (but finite) days may be considered "literal" in ancient Hebrew, whose word count is tiny compared to English and other languages. (As we explained earlier in our opening essay, seven consecutive, long time periods are just as literal in Genesis 1 as are seven 12-hour or seven 24-hour time periods.)

The framework essay claims that Genesis 1 "communicates genuine truth about the upper register." If this interpretation were valid, we would expect to glean much (or even some) information about the upper register from the text and from the surrounding passages. We do not. The details the framework essay presents come from other Bible texts. At best, Genesis 1 gives obscure hints about the upper-register creation.

The framework essay strips Genesis 1 of its lower-register content and packs it instead with upper-register content. While this relieves Irons and Kline from providing a scientific defense of the text, it robs them of the opportunity to challenge secular society. Since the language of Genesis 1 is directed and specific to the lower register, it robs them, too, of the apologetically useful information from the text. While the framework interpretation avoids overt violation of biblical inerrancy, it does injustice to the text by sacrificing valuable content. If this same interpretative approach were applied to the rest of Scripture, one wonders how much of the Bible's message would remain to challenge secularists and to establish the truth claims of the gospel. Such a loss would be tragic, for the sacrifice is made to protect against an ally misperceived as an enemy.

NOTES

1. Hugh Ross, *The Genesis Question* (Colorado Springs, CO: NavPress, 1998), pp. 19–27, 30–6.

2. Ibid., pp. 42–6.

3. Ibid., pp. 44–5.

4. Ibid., pp. 69–77.

5. Hugh Ross, *Beyond the Cosmos*, 2d edition (Colorado Springs, CO: NavPress, 1999), pp. 28–33; Roger Penrose, *Shadows of the Mind* (New York: Oxford University Press, 1994), pp. 229–31.

6. Robert C. Newman, *The Biblical Teaching on the Firmament*, 1972, masters thesis in theology. This thesis is available as an offprint from the Theological Research Exchange Network in Portland, Oregon.

7. Ross, *The Genesis Question*, pp. 31–6.

8. Ibid., p. 47.

9. Hugh Ross, *The Creator and the Cosmos*, 2d edition (Colorado Springs, CO: NavPress, 1995), pp. 131–45.

10. Ibid., pp. 134–5.

11. Ross, *Beyond the Cosmos*, pp. 28–46.

12. Gen. 1:2; Job 26:13; 33:4; Isa. 40:12, 13, 28; John 1:3, 10; 1 Cor. 8:6; Col. 1:13–6; Heb. 1:2; James 1:17–8.

13. Gen. 1:27; Isa. 44:24; 45:18; Acts 17:24; Eph. 3:9; Col. 1:15–7; Rev. 4:11.

14. Ross, *The Genesis Question*, pp. 64–5, 150–1.

15. Ibid.

16. Ross, *Beyond the Cosmos*, pp. 218–23.

Lee Irons with Meredith G. Kline

THE FRAMEWORK REPLY

ecause the two essays critiquing the framework interpretation differ so widely in their approach and argumentation, we will respond to them separately. We are thankful for the opportunity to engage in respectful and thoughtful theological dialogue about these important matters.

REPLY TO THE 24-HOUR RESPONSE

Response to Exegetical Objections

Although we applaud Duncan and Hall for making a stronger effort to interact with our arguments than they did in their opening essay, similar problems mar their response essay as well. Their perfunctory performance in the exegetical arena suggests that, in their minds, the truly substantive issues lie elsewhere. We will turn to those issues momentarily, but we first must address their exegetical critique of our view. Duncan and Hall attempt to summarize and challenge our exegetical arguments with eight bullet points. We respond to each in turn.

The Creation of the Sun on Day Four. In their first point, Duncan and Hall contend that we believe that the creation of the sun on Day 4 shows that the author of Genesis did not intend for us to view the creation days as literal calendar days. But this contention simplifies our actual argument to the point of distorting it. The creation of the sun on Day 4 does not prove that the days are nonliteral, but the textual evidence that Day 4 is a temporal recapitulation going back over the events narrated on Day 1 does. The difference is not pedantic, because an unqualified appeal to the creation of the sun on Day 4 as evidence that the days are nonliteral falsely presumes that God could not have sustained the light and the day/night cycle for the first three days by nonordinary or miraculous means. Having distorted our argument, Duncan and Hall charge us with not taking the mystery of creation seriously—"an implicit denial of the work of creation as 'miracle.'"

But their concerns are misplaced. We do not argue as they have suggested. The sovereign, miracle-working God of Scripture could very well have sustained the light for the first three days in a supernatural manner. We object to this alternative light hypothesis, not because we reject the supernatural on *a priori* grounds, but because it contravenes what we have argued—that Moses taught that God used normal providence during the creation era (Gen. 2:5–6).

Nonsequential Narration. Their second point targets our appeal to the evidence throughout Scripture of nonsequential narration, dischronologization, and temporal recapitulation in historical narratives. Duncan and Hall argue that even if such devices were granted, they would not constitute "direct evidence" for nonliteral days.

True, but we never claimed that they did. We argued that the presence of nonsequential narration in Scripture in general and in the immediate context of Genesis in particular makes it more plausible to suggest that Day 4 is a temporal recapitulation of Day 1. This suggestion is then confirmed by *independent* exegetical evidence (e.g., the two-triad structure, the identity of language in describing the purposes of the creation of light and luminaries, and Genesis 2:5–6).

Duncan and Hall have severely weakened their case by not responding to our detailed documentation of the nonsequential narration in Ezra 4:1–24, the differing accounts of Christ's temptation, the near-context instances in Genesis 1 and 2, and the macrostructure of the book of Genesis as a whole.

In fact, the only evidence they raise against dischronologization in Genesis 1:1–2:3 is Psalm 104, which they claim supports the sequential reading. But there are several differences in the sequence of the two creation texts. For example, Psalm 104 mentions the luminaries and the establishment of the day-night cycle (vv. 19–23) *after* the "beast of the field" (v. 11), "the birds of the heavens" (v. 12), and man himself (vv. 14–15). In addition, the teeming things that dwell in the seas are the last recorded creatures of Psalm 104 (vv. 25–26). Therefore, Psalm 104 does not undermine our interpretation.

Two-Triad Literary Structure. The third point focuses on the two-triad structure we see in the creation narrative. Duncan and Hall suggest that we argue that "the account is theologically stylized" based on this two-triad structure.

Duncan and Hall badly misstate our argument. Aside from the ambiguity of the phrase "theologically stylized" (which we did not employ in describing our view), they frame the argument incorrectly. We do not argue that the week of days is figurative rather than literal on the grounds that the account has a literary structure with theological significance. Many biblical historical narratives display theologically significant literary structures without any hint that the chronological markers are to be taken in a nonordinary sense. We hold that the two topically parallel triads of Genesis 1 alert us to the possibility of a thematic, rather than sequential, narrative order. But we recognize that this possibility must be confirmed on other grounds, and we proceed to produce exegetical evidence to that effect.

Sabbatical Symbolism. In their fourth point, Duncan and Hall attribute to us the argument that because sabbatical symbolism is found elsewhere in Scripture, the sabbatical scheme of Genesis 1–2 may therefore be taken figuratively.

Again, Duncan and Hall have misidentified a contextual, plausibility argument as a direct argument. Our appeal to the usage of sabbatical symbolism elsewhere in Scripture in a nonliteral manner does not *prove* that the same symbolism in Genesis 1:1–2:3 is nonliteral. But if we can prove that sabbatical symbolism is often figurative in Scripture, we will not be surprised if we find *independent* proof that it is also figurative in Genesis 1:1–2:3. (Note that Duncan and Hall do not challenge our claim that sabbatical symbolism is used in a nonliteral manner elsewhere in Scripture.)

Replacement Mechanism. The fifth point is highly confused. Duncan and Hall summarize our argument as follows: "Negatively, any sequential view of the narrative is unable to account adequately for the 'replacement mechanism' for the 'original system of light production,' thus commending the framework explanation."

Our actual argument is that the 24-hour interpretation requires the supposition that there was an alternative, nonstellar method of light production for the first three days until the creation of the luminaries on Day 4. But this scenario calls the wisdom of God into question, for it implies some deficiency in the original light-producing mechanism, requiring its replacement by the sun and stars. Duncan and Hall do not address this objection.

Temporal Recapitulation. With the sixth point, we at last come to an argument we can begin to recognize as our own. "Positively, more than merely displaying thematic parallelism, this passage entails temporal recapitulation of Day 1 on Day 4, showing that the whole week is a figurative framework." Duncan and Hall respond: "You simply cannot get away from sequence and extent of time if you pay attention to the language and grammar of Genesis 1." They then appeal to several features of the text—the numbered days, the evening-morning refrain, and the use of the Hebrew *waw*-consecutive—as "decisive arguments" against the claim of temporal recapitulation at Day 4. But are they really so decisive?

The fact that the days are numbered need not be taken as evidence of chronological sequence any more than the numbering of the seven seals, trumpets, and bowls in Revelation. The days are numbered to call the reader's attention to the theological significance of the sabbatical structure of the creation account.

What about the evening-morning refrain? This exegetical feature can be explained just as easily in terms of the framework interpretation. The evenings and mornings are not separable from the word *yôm*, which is appositional to (explanatory of) the evening-morning refrain ("there was evening and there was morning, *yôm* x"). Thus, all evidence that the word *yôm* in its contextual usage as part of a figurative framework is to be taken as a lower-register term used metaphorically with an upper-register meaning is also evidence that the evenings and mornings are likewise employed metaphorically in the two-register cosmology of Genesis 1:1–2:3. Taken as a whole—that is, as a week of days with their constituent mornings and evenings—the creation week presents an anthropomorphic picture of God going about His creative labors in the course of six ordinary solar days and resting on the seventh.

This brings us to Duncan and Hall's appeal to the *waw*-consecutive. It is a form of the Hebrew verb frequently translated "and . . ." followed by the past tense, which often indicates chronological sequence. This final argument against temporal recapitulation is misguided. For it is well-known that the *waw*-consecutive does not always indicate chronological sequence, though that is its most common use. One defender of the 24-hour view even concedes that "it may have the effect of recapitulation."[1]

A widely accepted example of the *waw*-consecutive in a recapitulatory sense is found in the near context, where the creation of the living creatures out of the dust of the ground is narrated *after* man is already on the scene. If the *waw*-consecutive in Genesis 2:19 ("And out of the ground the LORD God formed every beast of the field . . .") denotes chronological sequence, we have an apparent discrepancy with Genesis 1:24–28, which places the creation of the living creatures *before* that of man. Another example would be the second narration of the placement of man in the garden in Genesis 2:15 (cf. v. 8).

Even within the Day 4 account, Moses employs the *waw*-consecutive in a nonsequential manner. The fiat statement in verses 14–15 ("Let there be lights") is followed by the expected fulfillment statement ("and it was so"). The *waw*-consecutive occurs in the very next verse: "And God made the two great lights" (v. 16). If the *waw*-consecutive always denotes sequence, this statement would have to refer to an event chronologically subsequent to that of verses 14–15.

Several examples of this nonsequential usage of the *waw*-consecutive occur in the immediate context. Therefore, students of the Bible cannot appeal to the presence of the *waw*-consecutive in Genesis 1 as evidence for a strictly sequential reading.

Genesis 2:5–6. In their seventh point, Duncan and Hall summarize our argument from Genesis 2:5–6 and respond by making some vague statements about the way in which these verses "provide a context for the account of the creation of man" and "set the stage for explaining man's obligation to care for the garden."

We are not at all clear how these observations—to which we do not object—present a problem for our interpretation. Duncan and Hall have merely told us that Genesis 2:5–6 has something to do with man and his obligation to care for the garden, but they have not explained why Moses provides a *natural* explanation (absence of rain) for the lack of vegetation. And they have ignored the implications of this fact for our interpretation of the sequence of the creation events in Genesis 1.

Rather than addressing the question exegetically, Duncan and Hall seek sanctuary in the safety of tradition, arguing that the framework exegesis of Genesis 2:5–6 is relatively recent in the history of Jewish and Christian interpretation. But unless one holds that no new light can ever be gained from the scholarly study of Scripture, *recent* does not necessarily spell *erroneous*.[2]

Two-Register Cosmology. The eighth and final point Duncan and Hall present deals with Kline's two-register cosmology, which Duncan and Hall dismiss as irrelevant. They claim that it provides no evidence for the framework view, since it could be incorporated into views other than the framework position.

That's news to us. We devoted nearly half of our main essay to an exegetical defense of the two-register cosmology and its implications for the
present debate. Clearly *we* think that it is evidence for the framework view,
and we do not understand how it could be incorporated into the 24-hour
view. At the end of their response, Duncan and Hall seem to recognize
the impossibility of this combination when they "take strong exception"
to Kline's thesis that Genesis 1 refers to upper-register realities using the
language proffered by their lower-register replicas. Observe that Duncan
and Hall's last point is simply an assertion without any discussion of the
exegetical or theological grounds upon which they take such strong
exception.

The Eternality of the Seventh Day. Missing from Duncan and Hall's
points is any reference to our argument that because God's seventh-day
Sabbath rest is eternal, it therefore is not literal. Duncan and Hall address this pivotal argument only in passing near the end of their response:
"Neither do we think that sound biblical interpretation views the seventh
day of creation as continuing." A discussion of their preferred exposition
of Hebrews 4:1–11 and John 5:17 would have been more helpful.

At the conclusion of their sketchy response to our exegetical arguments, Duncan and Hall state that "the exegetical discussion is just a sideshow compared to the real issue." Instead, Duncan and Hall's defense of
the 24-hour view has minimized exegesis, relegating it to a sideshow. The
stated purpose of this volume, however, is to understand what the text
teaches, making exegetical discussion "the real issue" at hand.

Response to Theological Objections

If not exegesis, then what *is* driving Duncan and Hall's criticism and concern? They argue that the framework interpretation is fatally flawed because it purchases reconciliation with natural revelation at too high a price.
The price tag is a long list of alleged threats to orthodoxy.

The Historicity of Genesis 1–11. Duncan and Hall charge that "a
framework hermeneutic forces us into an ongoing theological discussion
about other potentially 'figurative' elements in Genesis protology," thus
"endanger[ing] our ability to honestly claim that we hold to the historicity of Scripture." Some of the specific events recorded in Genesis 1–11
they alleged to be endangered by a framework hermeneutic are the existence of Adam and Eve, the lifespans of Genesis 5, the *nephilim* of Genesis
6, the table of nations in Genesis 10, and the building of the tower of
Babel.

Rather than giving our exegetical position on each of these specific
issues, which would take us too far afield, we will focus on the larger con-

cern: where are we to draw the line? If the days of Genesis may be interpreted figuratively to avoid a conflict with science, what is to prevent one from taking figuratively other elements of Genesis 1–11 that conflict with current scientific opinion?

Our position is that natural revelation and Scripture cannot contradict one another. If there is an apparent conflict between our interpretation of natural revelation and our interpretation of Scripture, the only role of natural revelation in the exegetical task is to serve as a warning that we may need to reexamine our exegesis. However, we must carry out that reexamination process objectively by interpreting the words and propositions of the text in their canonical context in accordance with the analogy of Scripture. We cannot rightly adopt any interpretation that resolves the apparent conflict, but which is not demanded by objective exegesis.

Advocates of the 24-hour view seem to take the easy way out. They want to draw the line by making an *a priori* commitment to close their eyes to the data of natural revelation and take everything in Genesis 1–11 literally, regardless of the implications. But a precommitment to maximal literalism is not the Protestant rule of interpretation. Rather, as *The Westminster Confession of Faith* states,

> The infallible rule of interpretation of Scripture is the Scripture itself; and therefore, when there is a question about the true and full sense of any Scripture (which is not manifold, but one), it must be searched and known by other places that speak more clearly. (I.9)

Where then do we draw the line? We do not arbitrarily draw it ahead of time by committing ourselves to a maximally literal hermeneutic. Instead, we commit ourselves to the principle that Scripture interprets itself. In some cases, this procedure may allow us to reconcile the text with certain aspects of scientifically interpreted natural revelation. But if and when it does not, we will steadfastly uphold the presuppositional authority of Scripture over natural revelation and argue that we must reinterpret natural revelation accordingly. For example, we uphold the special creation of man based on our exegesis of Genesis 2:7 against "scientific" claims for the evolutionary origins of man.

In theory even Duncan and Hall do not espouse a purely literal hermeneutic. They recognize that "it is not necessary to assert that God intended the biblical narratives on creation to be literal in every aspect." Thus, they too must deal with the "Where do you draw the line?" argument. But rather than drawing the line by appealing to the self-interpreting character of Scripture, they rely on Church history and tradition to determine the legitimate extent of figurative interpretation.

Before moving on to the next theological objection, we need to clear

up a misunderstanding. Implicit in the objection that the framework interpretation endangers the historicity of Genesis 1–11 is the assumption
that the framework interpretation takes the *entire* creation account
figuratively. This assumption fails to recognize the crucial distinction between the divine works of the creation week and the literary structure of
the six-fold evening-morning refrain. Genesis 1:1–2:3 is a historical account of God's work of creation, narrating observable events that transpired in space-time history at the lower register. But the scheme of
topically arranging those events within an upper-register week is figurative. Kline writes: "My position is not that Genesis 1 as a whole is figurative; it is rather that the chronological framework of the creation narrative
is figurative but the persons and episodes mentioned there are historical."[3]

Pre-Fall Animal Mortality. The next concern Duncan and Hall present
is that nonliteral interpretations of the days either allow or teach an old-
earth creation model in which much of the fossil record is conceived of as
falling within the creation era. This implies nonhuman death before the
Fall of man. Duncan and Hall argue that this position is unacceptable, for
it "dramatically and devastatingly affects the historic Christian understanding of the nature of the goodness of the original creation . . . [and] may
require a radical theological reconstruction of Christian soteriology and
eschatology."[4]

The basic question is this: Is nonhuman death a result of man's Fall,
or was it a normal feature of the prelapsarian order consistent with the
goodness of creation? Several exegetical and theological considerations suggest the latter view.[5]

First, in the context of a poetic meditation on the creation period,
Psalm 104 speaks of the predatory relationship between carnivorous animals and their prey: "The young lions roar after their prey, and seek their
food from God" (v. 21). The immediate context in which this statement
is imbedded relates the appointment of the moon and sun for seasons
(vv. 19–23). When the sun goes down and it becomes dark, the predatory
beasts creep about searching for food (vv. 20–21). In the morning when
the sun rises, they lie down in their dens (v. 22), and man goes forth to
his labor until evening (v. 23). This description of the nighttime hunting
habits of beasts of prey is contextually embedded in a paragraph which refers to the creation week, clearly *before* the Fall.

Psalm 104:21 states that the lions "seek their food from God." Such
provision is a testament to the goodness of the Creator in caring for His
creation. This theme is elaborated several verses later when the psalmist
praises God for His concern for His creatures: "These all wait for You, that
You may give them their food in due season. What You give them they

gather in; You open Your hand, and they are filled with good" (vv. 27–28). There is no suggestion in this text that we are to view the provision of prey for carnivorous beasts as anything but a blessing from the hand of a good Creator. It certainly is not pictured as an abnormality resulting from the entrance of sin into the world.

Second, Paul in 1 Timothy 4:1–5 warns Timothy against the demon-inspired prohibition of marriage and foods.[6] Paul refutes this notion by appealing to the doctrine of creation. The Jewish legalists of Paul's day were commanding abstinence from foods "which God created." In doing so, they were violating the principle that "every creature of God is good" and to be "received with thanksgiving." Paul's appeal to creation to support the notion that believers are free to partake of "every creature of God" presupposes that man's diet was not restricted in the pre-Fall situation. Note that Paul classifies dietary freedom along with marriage as a pre-Fall creation ordinance.

The familiar reply that Genesis 1:29 restricted man's diet to the plant kingdom is an argument from silence. Kline observes that this verse has the special literary purpose of providing the background information necessary to make sense of the exception enunciated in Genesis 2:16–17 in which the tree of the knowledge of good and evil was prohibited (cf. Gen. 3:1–3 where the general acceptability of all other trees is contrasted with this solitary exception). It is unwarranted to take the silence of Genesis 1:29 as a prohibition against man's use of animal flesh for food.[7]

Third, in their response to the day-age interpretation, Duncan and Hall argue that the New Testament specifically teaches that nonhuman death is a consequence of the Fall "when it speaks of the entire universe becoming enslaved to corruption through Adam's singular act (Rom. 8:21)." But Romans 8:21 does not afford any exegetical proof of pre-Fall animal immortality. The text says: ". . . in hope that the creation itself also will be set free from the bondage of corruption into the liberty of the glory of the children of God." Duncan and Hall assume that the "corruption" the text refers to is the corruption of the nonhuman realm. Rather, the context suggests that it is the corruption of believers themselves. Prior to the redemption of their bodies at the last day, believers are subject to corruption on account of their mortality and death. The word "corruption" (*phthora*) is the same word Paul uses in 1 Corinthians 15:42, 50 to refer to the physical death and mortality of believers. In both 1 Corinthians 15 and Romans 8, deliverance from the corruption of mortality is brought about by the resurrection of believers at the coming of Christ. Romans 8:21 thus teaches that the creation will be set free from the bondage of *believers'* corruption at the resurrection.

But how can the *creation* be in bondage to the corruption of believers? We can answer this question by noting that the "groaning" of creation (v. 22) clearly alludes to Isaiah 24:4–6. Kline demonstrates the textual dependence of Romans 8 on Isaiah 24–26, noting their similar interest in the resurrection of the dead (e.g., Isa. 25:6–9; 26:17–19), and draws some conclusions for our understanding of Romans 8:21:

> In the context of [Isaiah] 24:4, what makes the earth groan is that it is obliged to become the grave, to cover over the human dead. . . . From this mutually illuminative relationship of Isaiah 24–26 and Romans 8 one perceives that the "bondage of corruption" over which, says Paul, the creation groans (Rom. 8:21) is the earth's being subjected to the fate of covering the blood of the innocent and concealing the corpses of the saints. . . . And in Romans 8, as we have seen, what the earth looks forward to in hope as its deliverance from this corruption is precisely the resurrection of the righteous. . . . That event is not merely the occasion of the earth's deliverance but is itself the liberation from the corruption over which the earth groans.[8]

When one rereads Romans 8:21 against the backdrop of Isaiah, Paul's meaning becomes clear. The creation itself is earnestly looking forward to the resurrection of the righteous, because this event will deliver the creation from its bondage as the receptacle of the dead. Thus liberated, the renewed cosmos then will become the eternal abode of glorified believers.

Duncan and Hall also claim that Romans 5:12 "affirms that death entered the cosmos—not merely the sphere of man—through that one sin" of Adam. However, that is not exactly what the verse says. Romans 5:12 says, "Just as through one man sin entered the world, and death through sin, and thus death spread to all men, because all sinned." If by "world" Paul intends to include the nonhuman sphere, one must be prepared to argue that *sin* entered the nonhuman sphere as well, for Paul argues that "sin entered the world, and *death through sin*." Notice that Paul's thought is restricted to *human* death on account of Adam's sin. He rounds out the argument by saying, "and thus death spread to *all men*," not to the entire cosmos inclusive of the nonhuman sphere. Paul narrows the referent of *kosmos* (world) by using the synonymous expression "all men" later in the same verse and again in verse 18. In Paul's writings, as throughout the New Testament, *kosmos* most often refers to the world of humanity (e.g., Matt. 18:7; John 3:16; Rom. 3:6, 19; 11:12; 2 Cor. 5:19). The rare cases where the term refers specifically to the nonhuman realm of creation are identified by additional contextual factors, which are lacking in Romans 5:12. If anything, the context of Romans 5:12 exhibits an exclusive interest in the world of mankind.

In addition to these weak exegetical arguments, Duncan and Hall fear that positing pre-Fall, nonhuman death leads to a denial of the distinction between the unfallen and fallen creation. But we do not think there is any scriptural warrant for assuming that the very fabric of the physical universe underwent a radical restructuring as a result of the Fall. In its pre-eschatological state before the Fall, creation would have had the tendency (known as entropy) to "wind down" to an inert, disorganized state.[9] Does taking this stance commit us to the eschatological error of undercutting the cosmic effects of redemption as Duncan and Hall suggest? Only if one assumes that the eschatological transformation will be limited to undoing the effects of the Fall and the curse, merely restoring man and the creation to the pre-Fall condition. But if covenant theology is correct in its understanding of the covenant of works, we must assume that the unfallen Adam (and with him the entire creation) enjoyed the prospect of eschatological advancement to greater glory, on condition that he passed the probationary test of not eating the forbidden fruit.[10] Such an understanding of the eschatological potential of creation is a forceful argument against assuming that we must picture the pre-Fall condition of creation as the equivalent of the consummated, eschatological state.

Literary Sophistication. Duncan and Hall further object that the framework interpretation requires too much "literary sophistication" on the part of the original audience. The specific feature of the framework interpretation that Duncan and Hall claim requires such unexpected sophistication is the literary device of dischronologization.

First of all, we question the assumption that the hermeneutical capabilities of the original audience are a valid yardstick for evaluating the legitimacy of any given exegetical proposal. Original audiences rarely grasped the message of divine revelation addressed to them. Were we limited in our study to what "the slow of heart" could understand, we would miss the true meaning of Scripture entirely (Isa. 6:9–10; Mark 4:11–13; Luke 24:25–27; John 2:19–21; 2 Cor. 3:14–16).

Second, dischronologization may appear to be a sophisticated literary technique from our modern perspective, but we should not assume that it was recondite to the ancient near-eastern mind. The study of ancient literature shows that compositional technique and the literary/aesthetic shaping of historical materials were commonplace. It is the Enlightenment standard of "neutral" historiography that would have been incomprehensible to the ancient Hebrews. Ridderbos writes, "In Biblical historiography the artificial arrangement or grouping of material (without an explicit statement to the effect that the chronological order has been broken) played a larger role than is customary in modern historiography."[11]

But in the end, the question is moot if one grants that the literary device of dischronologization actually occurs in Scripture—a fact we have demonstrated with numerous examples. In light of Duncan and Hall's decision not to engage that exegetical evidence, speculating about the literary abilities of the original audience is beside the point.

The Perspicuity of Scripture. This objection is an extension of the preceding one. The charge is that since "children and nonliterary theorists cannot easily grasp the framework interpretation," it undermines our confidence in the clarity of Scripture.

With this statement, Duncan and Hall make a misguided appeal to the traditional Protestant claim that Scripture is perspicuous or clear. The doctrine of the perspicuity of Scripture, properly formulated, is not that all *passages* of Scripture are equally capable of being understood by the unlearned, but that all *the doctrines necessary for salvation* are so clearly taught in Scripture that even the unlearned can, through study and other ordinary means, arrive at a sufficient understanding of them. Though Duncan and Hall ignore this important distinction, Protestant theology has always recognized that not all texts of Scripture are equally plain and clear. For example, *The Westminster Confession of Faith* states:

> All things in Scripture are not alike plain in themselves, nor alike clear unto all: yet those things which are necessary to be known, believed, and observed for salvation, are so clearly propounded in some place of Scripture or other, that not only the learned, but the unlearned, in a due use of the ordinary means, may attain unto a sufficient understanding of them. (I.7)

Are Duncan and Hall prepared to argue that a correct understanding of the nature and length of the days of creation is necessary for salvation? Even granting this extravagant claim, the framework interpretation still would accord with the principle of the perspicuity of Scripture. As the Confession states, the things that are necessary for salvation are not so clearly stated in Scripture that an individual can arrive at a sufficient understanding of them without "a due use of the ordinary means," which presumably includes the kind of exegetical study we have attempted in this volume.

The Sabbath Principle. Duncan and Hall fear that the framework interpretation obscures the Sabbath principle. They argue that the two-triad framework reduces the 6+1 (sabbatical) structure to a 3+1 ("quadratarian") scheme because it eliminates Days 4–6 by having them refer to Days 1–3.

This objection is based on a simple misunderstanding. While Days 5 and 6 *thematically* parallel Days 2 and 3, respectively, they do not necessarily return to the same moment in time or describe the same creative events from a different perspective. The chronological relationship between Days 1 and 4 is unique and does not apply to the other two sets of parallel days.

In addition, this objection confuses the figurative framework of the creation week with the events topically arranged within that framework. Although some of those topically narrated events are chronologically overlapping, the literary framework of the creation week brings the 6+1 structure into bold relief.

Church History. Duncan and Hall then return to their favorite argument, Church history. They worry that the novelty of the framework interpretation sleights two millennia of historic interpretation: "To embrace the framework interpretation, you have to believe that everybody in the history of interpretation got it wrong—badly wrong—until Kline."

But if we accept the Protestant premise that Scripture, not tradition, is our ultimate authority, new interpretations cannot be ruled out simply because they are new. If Duncan and Hall's approach were applied to other debates in the history of theology, we would have to reject many biblical truths.

The framework interpretation, however, is not without historic precedent. Augustine and Church fathers influenced by him thought that the days had no reference to the actual time frame of creation. With due respect to Duncan and Hall's knowledge of Church history, their interpretation of Augustine is idiosyncratic at best. For example, Louis Berkhof's description of Augustine's view reads more like a figurative interpretation than the literal, 24-hour view:

> Some of the early Church Fathers did not regard [the days] as real indications of the time in which the work of creation was completed, but rather as literary forms in which the writer of Genesis cast the narrative of creation, in order to picture the work of creation—which was really completed in a moment of time—in an orderly fashion for human intelligence.[12]

Since Augustine did not hold that the days were indicators of ordinary time, his belief in instantaneous rather than long-period creation does not make him an ally of the 24-hour view. Of course, this does not mean that Augustine's view and the framework interpretation are identical. But since he and his followers read the days as a literary framework rather than a literal chronology, the framework interpretation can claim to be a further development and refinement of a traditional view.

Creation Miracles. Because we interpret Genesis 2:5–6 as informing us that during the creation period God's providential operations were ordinary rather than extraordinary, Duncan and Hall list as their final theological objection that the framework interpretation suffocates the miraculous.

But this argument is a non sequitur. It is not necessary to eliminate the miraculous during the creation period to posit ordinary providence, for the creation period included both types of divine activity. Surely Duncan and Hall recognize that the mode of providence in effect *after* creation is primarily ordinary; yet that does not commit them to denying the virgin birth or the miracles of Jesus. During the creation week, God repeatedly did work apart from secondary causes at each point when acts of supernatural creation intruded to interrupt the providential order. These intrusions of the miraculous were not "suffocated" by the normal operations that both preceded and succeeded them, any more than Christ's supernatural transformation of water into wine was "suffocated" by the divine employment of ordinary means to sustain both the premiracle water and the postmiracle wine.

This completes our response to Duncan and Hall's theological objections. Is the theological price tag of the framework interpretation too high? Although that is ultimately for the reader to decide, we think that Duncan and Hall's concerns are largely without merit.

Is the 24-Hour View Agnostic on the Age of the Earth?

Our final response to the 24-hour view concerns Duncan and Hall's claim that their view does not commit them to a specific age of the universe. They attempt to distance themselves from the young-earth creationists by claiming that they are agnostic concerning the age of the earth and that their primary concern is that the creation period must be a short period of six ordinary days in which God brought the world to its completed state via a rapid succession of creative events. If someone were to propose a way to find room for an old earth, without lengthening the creation period itself, that would be fine with them.

But this accommodating stance falls apart on inspection. Outside the creation week itself, there are only two places where additional chronological leeway could be found: either before the creation period or after. Since the creation week begins with the *ex nihilo* creation event, prior to which there is no temporal reality, no extra time can be inserted before the creation period.

What about after? That possibility won't work either, since it would be difficult to stretch the genealogies of Genesis 5 and 11 beyond 100,000 years.[13] Duncan and Hall, therefore, are noncommittal about the age of the earth only within very narrow limits. Although they may not identify with everything that goes by the label "young-earth creationism," their position logically disallows an old earth/universe.

REPLY TO THE DAY-AGE RESPONSE

We respond now to Ross and Archer's critique of the framework interpretation by using their own headings.

Creation Verbs

Under this heading, the primary concern of Ross and Archer is with the acute problems that Day 4 of the biblical account poses for their view. As we have contended, the nonsequential nature of the creation narrative is established by the fact that the products assigned to Day 4 duplicate items previously assigned to Day 1. Moreover, the record of Day 4 contains the most glaring contradiction of Ross and Archer's distinctive claim that there is a remarkable correspondence between the order of events as reconstructed in scientific cosmogony and as narrated in Genesis 1. The origination of the sun, moon, and stars is assigned to this fourth day and thus to what would be (on Ross and Archer's sequentialist view of Day 4) a relatively recent epoch in the development of the cosmos.

Ross and Archer join the usual attempt of sequentialists to avoid the clear meaning of what is said to have transpired on Day 4.[14] They venture a version of the notion that the Day 4 account does not state that the luminaries were brought into existence at this point but merely says that previously existing luminaries became visible. Days 1 and 4 mark two stages in a process of increasing visibility of the luminaries through a gradual reduction in the opaqueness of the atmosphere.

Ross and Archer begin their exegetical argument with a discussion of the verb *haya*, which is used in the fiat statement of Day 4 (*yehi*, "let there be," v. 14) and in the fulfillment formula (*wayehi ken*, "and it was so," v. 15). They convey the false impression that the issue in the exegesis of the Day 4 passage (Gen. 1:14–19) is whether *haya* here is precisely equivalent to *bara*, "create" (a view they wrongly attribute to the framework interpretation), or whether it means simply "be, occur, happen" (a view they falsely identify as their own). In fact they make *haya* in Day 4 mean something else, namely, "appear."[15] The real issue with respect to *haya*, however, is whether in the fiat and fulfillment sections of Day 4 it means "to be/to be brought into existence," as the framework view holds, or whether it means "appear/become visible," as Ross and Archer would have it.

The fiat *yehi* ("let there be") is found in the account of Days 1, 2, and 4, each time followed by *wayehi* ("and there/it was") in the corresponding statement of fulfillment. *Wayehi* is also found in both segments of Day 3 (dealing respectively with the dry land and vegetation) and in the first segment of Day 6 (which deals with animals). The contention of Ross and Archer that *haya* in Day 4 does not describe a coming into existence, but merely a coming into visibility, of the luminaries totally disregards the context. It is generally recognized that throughout the account of the six days, *haya* consistently means "to be/to come into existence" and signifies the producing of objects (like the dry land set over against the waters below or the land creatures) or phenomena (like day-light or the firmament vault).

Contextual evidence makes it unmistakably clear that the *wayehi* of fulfillment signifies an act of production. To demonstrate this meaning for the *wayehi* of fulfillment is, of course, to demonstrate the same for the fiat *yehi*, the counterpart component of this matching pair. For one thing, the productive sense of *wayehi* is indicated by the term that replaces it in two statements of fulfillment. In Day 5 (dealing with the production of sea creatures) and in the second segment of Day 6 (dealing with the origin of man) *wayehi* yields to *bara*, "create," in the fulfillment side of the fiat-fulfillment pattern. This does not mean that *bara* is a precise semantic equivalent of *wayehi*. But it does indicate that like *bara*, its structural alternative, *wayehi* also has to do with production, bringing into existence, not merely rendering visible something that previously existed.

Further supporting this conclusion is the fact that the outcome of the divine fiat referred to by the *wayehi* of fulfillment is spelled out by verbs denoting production, structuring, and the like: "made" and "separated" (Day 2); "sprouted" (Day 3, second segment); and "made" (Day 6, first segment).[16] The Day 4 account is itself a prime example. Elucidating *wayehi ken* ("and it was so") in Day 4 are verbs of production (*asa*, "make") and positioning (*natan*, "gave, put"). These statements of divine origination appositional to *wayehi* flatly contradict Ross and Archer's interpretation of *wayehi* in this verse. They must, therefore, try to disconnect the *wayehi* of the fulfillment formula from the following statements that God made the luminaries and set them in place. They do this by proposing to make what follows the *wayehi* a parenthesis referring to God's previous production of the luminaries before the episode referred to by *wayehi*. This involves regarding the past completed verbal forms as pluperfect (thus, *wayyaas*, "and [God] had made"). Genesis 1:16 would then be, as they put it, "consistent" with their interpretation of *haya* in verses 14–15.

With its pluperfect rendering of the verbs of production after *wayehi*, this proposed disconnect within the Day 4 paragraph is inconsistent with the uniform pattern of the fiat-fulfillment structure in all the other day-paragraphs. For throughout the creation account, all that is recorded in the section following each fiat follows the fiat temporally. That is obviously true in the case of the fulfillment statements themselves. As for the statements associated with them, they are all explications of the fulfillment and thus they too must refer to developments subsequent to the fiat.[17] Unless we are prepared to defy the consistent scheme of the context, we will not make *wayyaas* (v. 16) a pluperfect. It refers to a development following upon the fiat, "let there be luminaries." It is a detailing of the outcome declared in the summary fulfillment formula, *wayehi ken*. This clinches the identification of *haya* as a verb of production in the fulfillment (and, therefore, also in the fiat) statement (vv. 14–15).

Our examination of the creation verbs leads us to conclude that Ross and Archer's view of Day 4 and the relation of Day 4 to Day 1 is *exegetically* untenable. Apart from any additional scientific difficulties, this means that their overall hermeneutic with its extreme harmonistic approach to the days of Genesis 1 and modern science is unsound.

Broken Chronologies

Ross and Archer do not deny that dischronologized narratives occur in Scripture, but they feel that framework advocates push their point too far.[18] They argue that one would expect a temporal recapitulation between Genesis 2:4 and 2:5 because "the focus of the passage shifts." The problem with seeing a recapitulation at Day 4, they argue, is that no such obvious shift is present.

Actually, vague "shifts" in "focus" do not provide sufficient exegetical evidence. According to our more stringent criteria, nonsequential narration must be proven by specific exegetical evidence, such as the use of identical terminology ("to divide the light from the darkness"), additional chronological data (such as that supplied by Genesis 2:5–6), literary structure, comparison with parallel texts in which the same events are narrated in a different order, and so on. Ross and Archer's attempt to limit the extent of dischronologization in Scripture would, by their criteria, result in finding dischronologization where it does not exist and in missing it where it does.

Reliability of Revelation

Another area of concern is a perceived "harsh judgment on general revelation." Ross and Archer unfortunately regard us as adopting a distrustful attitude toward natural revelation. The issue is not reliability or trustworthiness—for all of God's revelation is totally trustworthy—but the hermeneutical relationship between general and special revelation in the exegetical task. Given two possible interpretations—one that conflicts with certain scientific claims but is exegetically well supported, and another that does not conflict with science but is exegetically forced—which should be adopted? We believe that presuppositional priority should be accorded to Scripture despite the potential difficulties of harmonization with science.[19]

Hence, mere apologetic caution is not what drives us to deny that the creation narrative is sequential. Even if the scientific cosmogony happened to enjoy precise sequential harmony with the Genesis account, the exegetical evidence that the text has been arranged topically rather than sequentially would remain and would determine our exegesis.

Forced Parallelism

The framework interpretation calls attention to the features of symmetry and parallelism between the members of the two triads of days. These literary features alert the reader to the possibility of thematic rather than sequential ordering of the creation narrative. Under this heading, all that Ross and Archer's comments amount to is an attempt to weaken this literary consideration by challenging the validity of certain details.

One case they question concerns the relationship between Days 3 and 6, which Ross and Archer judge to be a "forced parallelism." Let us review the strong connections between Days 3 and 6. There are eight fiat sections in Genesis 1: one each for the first two days of each triad and two each for the third day of each triad (Days 3 and 6).[20] The two fiats of Day 3 are the gathering of the seas to produce the dry land and the production of vegetation. Those of Day 6 are the creation of land animals and the creation of man. The parallel between the *land realm* of Day 3 and the *land rulers* of Day 6 is obvious. Since man and vegetation are closely linked by the covenant of works, a thematic relationship exists between the second fiat of Day 3 (vegetation) and the second fiat of Day 6 (man). In fact, this interconnection of man and vegetation is reiterated three different times. First, on Day 6 the plants are given to man and the beasts for food (1:29–30). Second, in Genesis 2 the relationship between man and vegetation becomes the focus of verses 5–6 to explain the absence of vegetation. And third, the granting of all the trees of the garden to man for his enjoyment echoes the giving of the plants to man in Genesis 1:29–30 and sets the context for establishing the tree of the knowledge of good and evil as the central element in Adam's covenant probation (2:9, 16–17). Let the reader decide whether these connections are "subjectively overlaid on the text."

A second case concerns the parallelism between Days 2 and 5. In Day 2, the author describes the origin of the phenomena we know as sky and seas (i.e., the waters below in distinction from those above and from the primal deep of Gen. 1:2) as resulting from the separation of the waters into those below and those above. Correspondingly, Day 5 describes the origin of the sea creatures and the birds to whom the realms of sea and sky were assigned as their domain. Ross and Archer would challenge this parallelism by denying that Day 2 relates to the origin of the sky and seas, arguing instead that Genesis 1:6–8 merely relates the establishment of the water cycle. Let the reader decide.

A third case is the parallelism between Days 1 and 4. Day 1 relates the production of daylight and the day/night realm, while the subject of Day 4 is the luminaries, the sources of light which God appoints to rule over the day and the night. In dealing with Days 1 and 4, Ross and Archer find themselves confronted again with the fact that beyond the thematic parallelism of these days (which they do not seem prepared to dispute) there is in Day 4 a recapitulation of the origin of daylight and the day/night cycle already attributed to Day 1. The problem this poses for sequentialists understandably haunts Ross and Archer, and they proceed to struggle with it again here, even though it does not belong strictly under the heading of Forced Parallelism. But as we point out above in our response to their section on Creation Verbs, Ross and Archer fail to interact meaningfully with contextual exegetical evidence to prove that Day 4 is a temporal recapitulation of Day 1.

Nature of Miracles

Here Ross and Archer charge us with committing the either-or fallacy, presuming "that *either* natural processes alone account for all the phenomena described *or* God's direct intervention from beyond matter, energy, space, and time causes all the phenomena." They think that on this question of causation, we lean too heavily toward natural processes. They would like to see a more miraculous intervention than we allow since "scientific evidence strongly suggests that miracles of time, place, and fine-tuning did occur."

Ross and Archer do not seem to view the various creative events in which plants, animals, and man were formed.[21] Rather, their focus is on the development of the expanding universe after the Big Bang, especially the formation of the sun and solar system. "The characteristics of the sun and its neighboring stars are so amazingly fine-tuned for life's existence, we simply cannot avoid the conclusion of design." Ross and Archer do not want to lose the argument from design ("Perfect design requires a perfect Designer") by overemphasizing ordinary providence and natural processes during this period of cosmos formation.

By arguing that the many evidences of design (e.g., intentional fine-tuning necessary for life, improbable spatio-temporal convergences, etc.) necessarily imply miraculous intervention, Ross and Archer ironically commit the either-or fallacy: either certain features of the natural world are designed and thus demonstrate the supernatural intervention of an intelligent Designer, or these features arose by natural processes alone and thus

are not designed. This dilemma is unbiblical, for all events within the created realm are the result of God's eternal decree, and therefore no event
or fact in the universe fails to demonstrate the hand of an intelligent
Designer. God's wise, purposeful, and intentional activity is present not
only when He intervenes miraculously, but also when He sovereignly and
secretly directs secondary causes to effect His perfect will (Eph. 1:11).[22]
Therefore, arguing that the features of the natural world which display design and fine-tuning can only be explained by an appeal to supernatural
divine activity is unsound since providential employment of secondary
causes could produce the same remarkable results. As those who subscribe
to the Reformed doctrine of providence, we are not persuaded that evidence of design by itself constitutes evidence of miracle.[23]

Two-Register Cosmology

Finally, Ross and Archer raise several objections to the two-register cosmology we set forth in our main essay. We take this opportunity to clarify
our position.

Is God Confined to the Upper Register? Ross and Archer mistakenly
assume that when the Bible speaks of the upper register as God's dwelling
place, it implies His confinement to that dimension of the cosmos. But
the biblical imagery of the divine dwelling place is not intended to convey
confinement. Scripture teaches two seemingly discordant truths: (1) God's
throne is in heaven above (Psa. 11:4; Isa. 6:1; 66:1; Matt. 5:34; Rev. 4:2),
and (2) the omnipresent God fills both heaven and earth (Psa. 139:7–10;
Jer. 23:23–24). This apparent tension in the biblical data is easily reconciled if we recognize that the upper-register throne site of YHWH is not a
physical location confined within cosmic space, but an omnipresent (though
presently veiled) dimension of the created cosmos.[24]

The Temporal Frame of Reference. Does Genesis 1:2 contradict our
thesis that the language of the days refers to the progression of celestial
time? Ross and Archer believe that this text fixes the temporal frame of
reference for the entire creation account to the surface of earth's waters.
This argument is valid only if we assume that the "clock" starts ticking at
Genesis 1:2 rather than "in the beginning" (Gen. 1:1). Contrary to those
who take Genesis 1:1 as a banner statement summarizing the result of the
six days' work, Genesis 1:1 actually narrates the original *ex nihilo* event, as
subsequent canonical commentary demonstrates (Prov. 8:22–31; John 1:1–
3; Col. 1:16). But if the identification of the temporal frame of reference
of the creation narrative occurs at Genesis 1:1 rather than 1:2, we cannot
assume that the days of creation unfold on earth time. According to John's
inspired commentary, we are to understand the "beginning" (*reshit; arche*)

referred to in Genesis 1:1 and Proverbs 8:22 within the frame of reference of the relationships among the members of the Trinity (John 1:1–3). Further supporting a celestial frame of reference is the endpoint of the creation week—the Creator's heavenly Sabbath-enthronement on the seventh day.

In addition, Ross and Archer seem to think that the framework interpretation regards the creation events themselves as transpiring outside the earthly space-time dimension. This misunderstanding, shared by Duncan and Hall, needs to be cleared up. We have argued that while the fulfillment segment of each of the eight creative fiat-fulfillment pairs refers to events occurring in lower-register history, the literary framework of the sixfold "evening-morning, day x" refrain refers to the upper register, as indicated by the upper-register identity of both the starting point ("the beginning") and the endpoint (the seventh day), which anchor that framework in the celestial sphere.

Simile Markers. While Ross and Archer do not deny that the temporal literary framework of the creation week could be metaphorical, they desire more explicit evidence in the text itself, such as the "simile markers" employed by Jesus in His parables ("the kingdom of God is *like* . . ."). But this criterion is too narrow. If applied consistently, we would have to believe that God is literally a shepherd (Psa. 23), is a mother bird who protects her young (Exo. 19:4; Psa. 57:1), has feathers (Psa. 91:4), has literal eyes (2 Chron. 16:9; Psa. 11:4), and so on, since none of these texts employs simile markers.

In addition, Ross and Archer recognize that the divine workweek and Sabbath provide the analogical basis for the human workweek and Sabbath, as subsequent Mosaic commentary on the creation narrative shows (Exo. 20:11; 31:14–17). Granting this obvious analogical relationship between God's week and man's—and in view of Scripture's routine use of lower-register terms as metaphors for describing divine attributes and actions—the interpreter does not need explicit simile markers to perceive that the picture of God's performing His creative work in six days and resting on the seventh is yet another instance of metaphorical or anthropomorphic language.

The "Heavens and the Earth" in Genesis 1:1. Ross and Archer continue their critique of two-register cosmology by maintaining that it leads to three exegetical errors. Their first complaint is with our interpretation of "the heavens and the earth" in Genesis 1:1 as referring, respectively, to the invisible upper-register and the visible lower-register realms. They prefer to take these terms as referring to the visible heavens (sky and stars) and the planet Earth.

But it is quite clear that *shamayim* (heavens) cannot be identified with the visible heavens. Subsequent inspired commentary on Genesis 1:1 and 2:1 demands the upper-register interpretation of *shamayim*. In Colossians 1:16, we read that God through the agency of Christ "created all things— things in heaven and on earth, things visible and invisible." The chiastic structure of the verse suggests that Paul equates "things in heaven" with the invisible realm and "things on earth" with the visible:

A   things in heaven

   B   and on earth;

   B' things visible

A' and invisible[25]

Paul thus interprets Genesis 1:1 as teaching that in the beginning God created both the invisible and visible realms.[26]

Ross and Archer object to this reading on the ground that it allegedly implies that *erets* (earth) encompasses all the stars, galaxies, dust, and gas of the universe, a meaning that is not attested in any of the standard Hebrew lexica. Ross and Archer are partially on the right track: In scriptural usage *erets* does not include the sun, moon, or stars. On the other hand, *erets* in Genesis 1:1 does not mean the *planet* Earth. Rather, it denotes the visible world in an anthropocentrically limited sense. To which category, then, do the luminaries belong? In biblical cosmology, the sun, moon, and stars are not components of the visible heavens or the firmament (both of which, according to Gen. 1:6–8, are formed from the *erets* mentioned in Gen. 1:1–2). Rather they are "the hosts of heaven" (Deut. 4:19), the luminaries that God "placed" in the firmament vault (Gen. 1:17), the lamps, as it were, that God hung in the heavenly ceiling. Galaxies and cosmic dust and gas are not referred to specifically in biblical cosmology.

The Role of Angels in Creation. The second perceived exegetical error is that "the framework essay tampers with the role of angels, designating them as participants in the creation of man." Ross and Archer prefer the trinitarian interpretation of the plural in Genesis 1:26 ("Let us make man in our image, according to our likeness").

While we respect this traditional approach held by many Church fathers, we feel that it is exegetically unsupported and appears to read too much into the text. Kline has argued elsewhere in greater detail[27] that the divine "Let us" formula must be interpreted in light of its usage elsewhere in the Hebrew Bible. Repeatedly in these texts, angels are contextually present, thus supporting the view that God is addressing the heavenly council. Interpreted in this manner, Genesis 1:26 does not teach that angels were co-Creators with God (which would be theologically erroneous), but that man's identity as the image of God has special reference to the royal/judicial function so clearly highlighted by the angels in their role as members of the heavenly council.[28]

The Nature of the Seventh Day. We direct the reader to our response to the day-age essay earlier in this volume where we outline the biblical-theological difficulties with the view that God's Sabbath rest will end when, according to the day-age view of Ross and Archer, He resumes the work of creation at the day of judgment. Ross and Archer incorrectly define God's rest on the seventh day as a mere cessation of creative activity. Rather, it is an upper-register enthronement of the Creator King over all the creation kingdoms and their creature kings.

CONCLUSION

While we appreciate the efforts of the 24-hour and day-age teams to interact with the framework interpretation we have presented, their critiques are impaired by their preoccupation with other than strictly exegetical concerns. The 24-hour critique is motivated largely by perceived theological dangers allegedly inherent in the framework interpretation, dangers we have addressed in this reply. While the day-age critique interacts more closely with the exegetical issues, it too appears to be driven by an outside concern, namely, the desire to fit the text into a certain scientific mold for apologetic purposes, a desire that does not accord with the best exegesis.

In the end, the framework interpretation withstands the scrutiny of the 24-hour and day-age interpretations and best accords with the biblical evidence.

NOTES

1. Joseph A. Pipa, Jr. and David W. Hall, "From Chaos to Cosmos: A Critique of the Nonliteral Interpretations of Genesis 1:1–2:3," *Did God Create in Six Days?* (Taylors, SC: Southern Presbyterian Press, Greenville Presbyterian Theological Seminary; and Oak Ridge, TN: The Covenant Foundation, 1999), p. 156.

2. The Protestant exegesis of the Pauline doctrine of justification in terms of a forensic imputation of Christ's alien righteousness, rather than an ontological infusion of inherent righteousness as Roman Catholicism teaches, is relatively recent (sixteenth century). Does the recent origin of Reformed exegesis automatically settle the debate in Rome's favor?

3. Meredith G. Kline, *Perspectives on Science and Christian Faith*, vol. 48, no. 3 (Sept. 1996), p. 210.

4. In view of Duncan and Hall's statement (made in their response to the day-age interpretation) that the issue of pre-Fall animal mortality "simply is outside the scope of our debate and distracts from the issues at hand," it is puzzling to see them raise the issue here.

5. As a figurative interpretation of the days of creation, the framework interpretation

does not speak to this particular issue. Therefore, our response is not the position of the framework interpretation per se, but the views of two individuals who hold to the framework interpretation.

6. Although the word *broma* is generic for food, it is used in Romans 14:15, 20 and 1 Corinthians 8:8, 13 in the context of the controversy between Jews and Gentiles regarding meat.

7. Meredith G. Kline, *Kingdom Prologue* (published by author, 1991), p. 36.

8. Meredith G. Kline, "Death, Leviathan, and the Martyrs: Isaiah 24:1–27:1," *A Tribute to Gleason Archer*, ed. Ronald F. Youngblood (Chicago: Moody Press, 1986), p. 234.

9. For a response to the view that the law of entropy was a consequence of the Fall, see John C. Munday, Jr., "Creature Mortality: From Creation or Fall?" *Journal of the Evangelical Theological Society*, vol. 35, no. 1 (March 1992), pp. 51–68, esp. pp. 56–8.

10. Geerhardus Vos, "The Doctrine of the Covenant in Reformed Theology," *Redemptive History and Biblical Interpretation*, ed. Richard B. Gaffin, Jr. (Phillipsburg, NJ: Presbyterian & Reformed Publishing Co., 1980), pp. 234–67; Kline, *Kingdom Prologue*, pp. 1–73; Lee Irons, "The Case for Merit in the Covenant of Works," *Always Reformed*, ed. David G. Hagopian (Phillipsburg, NJ: Presbyterian & Reformed Publishing Co., forthcoming).

11. N. H. Ridderbos, *Is There a Conflict Between Genesis 1 and Natural Science?* (Grand Rapids, MI: Wm. B. Eerdmans Publishing Co., 1957), p. 38.

12. Louis Berkhof, *Systematic Theology* (Grand Rapids, MI: Wm. B. Eerdmans Publishing Co., 1941), p. 153. After summarizing the framework interpretation, Berkhof states: "This view reminds us rather strongly of the position of some of the early Church fathers" (p. 154).

13. Old Princeton scholar William Henry Green convincingly argued that there are in all likelihood significant gaps in the early genealogical records. "Primeval Chronology," *Bibliotheca Sacra* (April 1890), pp. 285–303.

14. For a survey and critique of these attempts, see Meredith G. Kline, "Space and Time in the Genesis Cosmogony," *Perspectives on Science and Christian Faith*, vol. 48, no. 1 (April 1996), pp. 8–9.

15. While arguing that *haya* is not to be treated as an equivalent of *bara*, the verb of miraculous creation, Ross and Archer confusingly speak of the action referred to by *haya* as a "miraculous working."

16. These verbs associated with *wayehi* may precede it (as in Day 2) or follow it (as in Day 3, second segment; Day 4; and Day 6, first segment).

17. Also included in the account are actions subsequent even to the specific fulfillment of the fiat, such as a divine word of approbation, God's seeing that what He made was good.

18. Ross and Archer misunderstand our appeal to Matthew's genealogy when they include it here under "broken chronologies." Our purpose in citing that text was to illustrate Scripture's use of sabbatical symbolism to structure history in a nonliteral manner, not to demonstrate dischronologization.

19. This is obviously not to say—and we do not say, as Ross and Archer allege—that "studies of special revelation are consistently flawless and infallible."

20. Ross and Archer apparently confuse fiat sections with smaller units of some kind when they object that they "count as many as thirteen distinct creative works."

21. Apparently, Ross-Archer agree that the basic "kinds" of flora and fauna were formed by supernatural acts of creation while permitting microevolution (variation) within the "kinds." However, the framework interpretation itself, as a nonliteral interpretation of the creation week, does not logically commit one to any position on the question of macroevolution. The exegetical, theological, and scientific debate over macroevolution is a separate issue.

22. "Although, in relation to the foreknowledge and decree of God, the first Cause, all things come to pass immutably, and infallibly, yet, by the same providence, he ordereth them to fall out, according to the nature of second causes, either necessarily, freely, or contingently. God, in his ordinary providence, maketh use of means, yet is free to work without, above, or against them, at this pleasure" (*The Westminster Confession of Faith*, 5.2–3).

23. This questionable assumption is a recurring tendency in the Intelligent design movement. For example, see Michael Behe, *Darwin's Black Box* (New York: Free Press, 1996); *Mere Creation: Science, Faith and Intelligent Design*, ed. William A. Dembski (Downers Grove, IL: InterVarsity Press, 1998); Phillip E. Johnson, *Reason in the Balance* (Downers Grove, IL: InterVarsity Press, 1995); *The Creation Hypothesis*, ed. J. P. Moreland (Downers Grove, IL: InterVarsity Press, 1994).

24. The cosmological theories of contemporary physics (e.g., ten -dimensional string theory) may be compatible with this biblical teaching, but they hardly constitute independent apologetic confirmation since they just as easily could be incorporated within a non-theistic/naturalistic worldview.

25. Paul goes on in Colossians 1:16 to clarify what the invisible heavenly realm includes by citing some specific examples: ". . . whether thrones or dominions or principalities or powers." Most commentators agree that these are titles for the various ranks of angels, beings whose presence is always associated with the upper register. E.g., James D. G. Dunn, *The Epistles to the Colossians and to Philemon*, The New International Greek Testament Commentary (Grand Rapids, MI: Wm. B. Eerdmans Publishing Co., 1996), pp. 92. Dunn cites the Testament of Levi 3:8 ("thrones and authorities") and the Apocalypse of Elijah 1:10–11 ("thrones") as parallels from inter-testamental Jewish literature where some of these ranks of angelic beings are mentioned.

26. Paul's interpretation of Genesis 1:1 was possibly suggested to him by Nehemiah 9:6, which alludes to Genesis 1:1; 2:1. Nehemiah interprets "the host of heaven," not as the stars (which would be expected if the heavens in view were the visible, lower-register heavens or sky), but as the angelic hosts who ceaselessly worship the Lord. To make this clear Nehemiah adds a precising phrase, ". . . heaven, even the heaven of heavens," to distinguish the invisible, upper-register heaven from its visible, lower-register replica (the star-filled sky). Old Testament usage of "the heaven(s) of heavens" confirms its upper-register denotation in Nehemiah 9:6 (Deut. 10:14; 1 Kings 8:27; 2 Chron. 2:6; 6:18; Psa. 68:33; 148:4, though the last reference is ambiguous).

27. Meredith G. Kline, *Images of the Spirit* (Eugene, OR: Wipf and Stock Publishers, 1998), pp. 13–34.

28. Contrary to Ross and Archer, angels are indeed members of the heavenly assembly or council (Job 1:6–12; 2:1–7; Psa. 89:5–7 [holy ones = sons of the mighty]; Isa. 6:1–8; 14:13; Heb. 12:22–3; Rev. 4–5), as are human prophets (Jer. 23:18, 22; Amos 3:7). In the analogy of a typical royal court in the ancient world, the angels are the attendants, courtiers, servants, and advisors of YHWH, the Great King (1 Kings 22:19–23; Psa. 103:20; Dan. 7:10; Heb. 1:7). A king without a court would be unthinkable.

David G. Hagopian

CONCLUSION
THE GENESIS DEBATE

*A*s our debate about the Genesis creation days draws to a close, we would be remiss if we failed to extend our heartfelt appreciation to each of the author teams for presenting their respective views.

We thank J. Ligon Duncan III and David W. Hall for reminding us of the clarity of Scripture and cautioning us against being quick to accommodate our Christian faith to the spirit of the age, noting that he who marries the spirit of the age often makes himself a widower in the next. "Let God be found true," they shout at the top of their lungs, a message we need to recapture and proclaim to the ho-hum, postmodern culture all about us. Duncan and Hall help us to understand what C. S. Lewis called our *chronological snobbery*, the mistaken assumption that the new-fangled is necessarily truer. Creativity is not necessarily a virtue in theology, and we need to heed Duncan and Hall's invitation to walk the ancient paths and sit at the feet of our elders in the faith. In a day when we may be tempted to strike out on our own, Duncan and Hall are to be thanked for bringing us face to face with how our forebears wrestled with the Genesis creation account and spoke with such a clarion voice about the grand miracle of creation.

If the 24-hour team should be thanked for pointing us to the ancient paths and the glory of the miraculous, then we owe an equal debt of gratitude to the day-age team of Hugh Ross and Gleason L. Archer for reminding us that the God of the *Word* is the God of this *World*. God has revealed Himself in Scripture and in nature, and He never contradicts Himself in either. If an apparent incongruity exists between the two, that incongruity necessarily results from a misunderstanding of Scripture, nature, or both. No other choices exist. Ross and Archer also commendably exhort us not only to critique opposing worldviews, but also to be about our positive task of building a distinctively Christian response to the challenge presented by opposing belief systems. While Ross and Archer would be the first to remind us that the finite can never grasp the Infinite, they admirably point the finite to the Infinite. The heavens, as the psalmist reminds us, declare the glory of their Maker, and the firmament, the work of His hands. We thank Ross and Archer for directing our thoughts—and eyes—heavenward.

We also express our fond appreciation to Lee Irons and Meredith G. Kline for turning over the marvelous tapestry of the Genesis creation account to show us the intricate pattern of the weave below the surface. That pattern is truly something to behold. The parallel triads of creation kingdoms on Days 1, 2, and 3 and creature kings on Days 4, 5, and 6 seem hard to miss now that Irons and Kline have pointed them out. The intentional Sabbatical structure of the text also surfaces. God's creative work culminates in a Sabbath rest, which is woven into the very fabric of creation and which will be celebrated throughout eternity. Irons and Kline also commendably remind us to marvel at the most holy, wise, and powerful way God creates all things, and then both preserves and governs them, thereby revealing His intelligent design. Miracle and providence speak of Him.

Creation is no dry and crusty doctrine. It truly is a cause to rejoice! It causes us to look to God as more than simply our Creator. He also is our Redeemer. As with the Genesis creation account, so it is with the rest of Scripture—a seamless web. The first Adam failed to keep covenant with his Creator by not doing what he was commanded to do and by doing what he was commanded not to do, thereby plunging himself and all his posterity into sin and misery. At that horrific moment of darkness and despair, the Creator bowed low and kissed His fallen son. He then graciously promised a risen Son. In the fullness of time, the Creator became that risen Son, our Redeemer. As the last Adam, He came to do what the first Adam failed to do and came to undo what the first Adam did. The last Adam perfectly fulfilled all righteousness, died in the place of the unrighteous, and rose again to glory for our justification. The One who knew no sin became sin for us that we might become the righteousness of God in Him.

Indeed, Christ is our Alpha and Omega, the First and the Last. The protology of Genesis points us to the eschatology of Revelation. The One who created the heavens and the earth will one day unveil a new heavens and a new earth. Once again the tree of life will be planted in our midst, and this time, the Light that shines will never be eclipsed.

In that glorious day, there will be no more debates. We will fall at His feet to render the only thing a fallen yet redeemed humanity can offer its Creator and Redeemer—true worship. We will join the heavenly chorus and eternally sing, "Worthy art Thou, our Lord and our God, to receive glory and honor and power; for Thou didst create all things, and because of Thy will they existed, and were created" (Rev. 4:11, NASB).

THE GENESIS DEBATE

J. Ligon Duncan III, B.A., Furman University; M.A. and M.Div., Covenant Theological Seminary; Ph.D., University of Edinburgh, is ordained as a teaching elder in the Presbyterian Church in America, is the Senior Minister of the historic First Presbyterian Church in Jackson, Mississippi, and is Adjunct Professor of Systematic Theology at Reformed Theological Seminary in Jackson, Mississippi. He has written several books, including *Covenant in the New Testament* (forthcoming, Crossway) and *The Westminster Assembly: A Guide to Basic Bibliography* (with David W. Hall, Reformed Academic Press). He also has edited several volumes, including *The Westminster Confession into the 2lst Century: Essays in Remembrance of the 350th Anniversary of the Publication of the Westminster Confession of Faith* (with Duncan Rankin, John Muether, et al., Reformed Academic Press), and *Ancient Christian Commentary on Scripture: The Historical Books*, vol. 2 (Thomas C. Oden, general editor, InterVarsity Press). He also has written articles for publications such as the *Scottish Bulletin of Evangelical Theology*, *Journal of the Evangelical Theological Society*, *Christian Observer*, *Tabletalk*, *Modern Reformation*, *Premise*, and *The Presbyterian Witness*. He is a member of the Scottish Evangelical Theology Society, Rutherford House Fellowship, the Evangelical Theological Society, and the North American Patristic Society. He also is a Fellow in the Center for the Advancement of Paleo-Orthodoxy (CAPO), as well as the Carl F. H. Henry Institute for Evangelical Engagement (Southern Baptist Theological Seminary).

David W. Hall, B.A., University of Memphis and M.Div., Covenant Theological Seminary, is ordained as a teaching elder in the Presbyterian Church in America and is Pastor of The Covenant Presbyterian Church in Oak Ridge, Tennessee. He has written several books, including *Savior or Ser-*

vant? Putting Government in Its Place (Kuyper Institute); The Millennium of Jesus Christ: An Exposition of the Revelation for All Ages (Covenant Foundation); The Arrogance of the Modern: Historical Theology Held in Contempt (Covenant Foundation); Paradigms in Polity (with Joseph H. Hall, Eerdmans); The Westminster Assembly: A Guide to Basic Bibliography (with J. Ligon Duncan III, Reformed Academic Press); and The Swiss Reformation and the American Founding (forthcoming). He also has edited a number of volumes, including Did God Create in Six Days? (with Joseph A. Pipa, Southern Presbyterian Press/Covenant Foundation); Evangelical Hermeneutics (Covenant Foundation); Evangelical Apologetics (Covenant Foundation); To Glorify and Enjoy God: A Commemoration of the Westminster Assembly (Reformed Academic Press); Election Day Sermons (Kuyper Institute); and The Practice of Confessional Subscription (Covenant Foundation). He also has written articles for publications such as The Presbyter's Review, Premise, Antithesis, and The Journal of Biblical Ethics in Medicine.

Hugh Ross, B.Sc., University of British Columbia; M.Sc., and Ph.D., University of Toronto, is President and Director of Research with Reasons To Believe, an international, interdenominational organization dedicated to proving that science and faith are allies and to establishing the veracity of Scripture. He has written several best-selling books, including The Fingerprint of God: Recent Scientific Discoveries Reveal the Unmistakable Identity of the Creator (Promise Publishing) and several NavPress titles, including Creation and Time: A Biblical and Scientific Perspective on the Creation-Date Controversy; The Creator and the Cosmos: How the Greatest Scientific Discoveries of the Century Reveal God; Beyond the Cosmos: What Recent Discoveries in Astronomy and Physics Reveal About the Nature of God; and The Genesis Question: Scientific Advances and the Accuracy of Genesis. He also has contributed essays to other volumes, including The Creation Hypothesis: Scientific Evidence for an Intelligent Designer (edited by J. P. Moreland, InterVarsity) and Mere Creation: Science, Faith and Intelligent Design (edited by William A. Dembski, InterVarsity). He also has written articles for publications such as Nature, The Astrophysical Journal, Die Sterne, World Magazine, Christianity Today, Moody Monthly, Eternity, Decision, and Philosophia Christi. In addition to lecturing worldwide at more than 200 colleges, universities, and seminaries, he has produced or appeared on numerous television programs and videos and has given hundreds of radio interviews on the relationship between science and faith. He is a member of the American Association for the Advancement of Science, the American Astronomical Society, the American Institute of Physics, the American Scientific Affiliation, and the Evangelical Theological Society.

Gleason L. Archer, B.A., A.M., Ph.D., Harvard University; B.D., Princeton Theological Seminary, and L.L.B., Suffolk University Law School, is an ordained minister in the Presbyterian Church USA. He served as Professor of Biblical Languages and Acting Dean at Fuller Seminary (Pasadena, California), Professor of Old Testament and Semitics and Chair of the Old Testament Department at Trinity Evangelical Divinity School (Deerfield, Illinois), Visiting Professor in Old Testament at Tyndale Theological Seminary (Netherlands), and is Professor Emeritus of Old Testament and Semitic Studies at Trinity Evangelical Seminary (Deerfield, Illinois). He translated the Old Testament of the *New American Standard Bible*, is the co-author of *A Theological Wordbook of the Old Testament* (with R. Laird Harris and Bruce Waltke, Moody), and is the author of several other books, including *Old Testament Quotations in the New Testament: A Complete Survey* (Moody); *A Survey of Old Testament Introduction* (Baker); *Encyclopedia of Bible Difficulties* (Zondervan); *In the Shadow of the Cross* (Zondervan); *The Epistle to the Romans* (Baker); and *The Epistle to the Hebrews* (Baker). He has contributed to several other volumes, including *The Bible Expositor* (edited by C. F. H. Henry, A. J. Holman); *Baker's Dictionary of Theology* (edited by E. F. Harrison, G. W. Bromiley, and C. F. H. Henry, Baker); *World Book Encyclopedia*, commentary on Isaiah in the *Wycliffe Bible Commentary* (edited by C. F. Pfeifer and E. F. Harrison, Moody); *The Pictorial Bible Dictionary* (edited by Merrill C. Tenney, Zondervan); *New Perspectives on the Old Testament* (edited by J. Barton Payne, Word); *Baker's Dictionary of Christian Ethics* (edited by C. F. H. Henry, Baker); *The Law and the Prophets: Old Testament Studies Prepared in Honor of O. T. Allis* (edited by John H. Skilton, Presbyterian & Reformed); *The Foundation of Biblical Authority* (edited by James M. Boice, Zondervan); and *Inerrancy* (edited by Norman L. Geisler, Zondervan). He also has written articles for publications such as *The Westminster Theological Journal*, *Bibliotheca Sacra*, *Journal of the Evangelical Theological Society*, *Journal of the American Scientific Affiliation*, *Christianity Today*, *Moody Monthly*, *Eternity*, and *Decisions*. He is a member of the National Association of Biblical Instructors, the Society of Biblical Literature and Exegesis, the Evangelical Theological Society (President, 1986), and the International Council on Biblical Inerrancy.

Lee Irons, B.A., University of California, Los Angeles, M.Div., Westminster Theological Seminary in California, is an ordained minister in the Orthodox Presbyterian Church and is currently Pastor of Redeemer OPC in the San Fernando Valley, California. He has authored essays for *Always Reformed* (edited by David G. Hagopian, Presbyterian & Reformed) and *Creator, Redeemer, Consummator: A Festschrift for Meredith G. Kline*, ed.

Howard Griffith and John R. Muether (Greenville, SC: Reformed Academic Press; Jackson, MS: Reformed Theological Seminary, 2000)). He also has written articles for publications such as *Modern Reformation*, *Reformation and Revival*, *Kerux*, *Perspectives on Science and Christian Faith*, and *Ordained Servant*.

Meredith G. Kline, A.B., Gordon College, Th.B. and Th.M., Westminster Theological Seminary (Philadelphia, Pennsylvania) and Ph.D., Dropsie University, is an ordained minister in the Orthodox Presbyterian Church. He served as Professor of Old Testament Languages and Literature at Westminster Theological Seminary in Philadelphia; Professor of Old Testament at Gordon Conwell Theological Seminary (South Hamilton, Massachusetts); Visiting Professor at Claremont School of Theology and Reformed Theological Seminary; and currently is Emeritus Professor of Old Testament at Gordon Conwell and Professor of Old Testament at Westminster Theological Seminary in California. He has written several books, including *Treaty of the Great King* (Eerdmans); *By Oath Consigned: A Reinterpretation of the Covenant Signs of Circumcision and Baptism* (Eerdmans); *The Structure of Biblical Authority* (Wipf and Stock); *Images of the Spirit* (Wipf and Stock); and *Kingdom Prologue* (published by author). He has authored commentaries on Deuteronomy and Job in the *Wycliffe Bible Commentary* (edited by C. F. Pfeifer and E. F. Harrison) and on Genesis in *The New Bible Commentary*, 2nd rev. ed. (edited by D. Guthrie). In addition, he has contributed essays to other books, including *Can I Trust the Bible?* (edited by Howard F. Vos, Moody); *The New Bible Dictionary* (edited by D. Guthrie, Eerdmans); *The Law and the Prophets: Old Testament Studies Prepared in Honor of O. T. Allis* (edited by J. H. Skilton, Presbyterian & Reformed); *A Tribute to Gleason Archer* (edited by Ronald F. Youngblood, Moody); *Through Christ's Word* (edited by W. R. Godfrey and J. H. Boyd III, Presbyterian & Reformed); and *Biblical and Near Eastern Studies* (edited by G. A. Tuttle, Eerdmans). He has written two seminal articles on the framework interpretation of the days of creation—"Because It Had Not Rained" in the *Westminster Theological Journal* and "Space and Time in the Genesis Cosmogony" in *Perspectives on Science and Christian Faith*—as well as articles for publications such as *Journal of the Evangelical Theological Society* and *Kerux*.

9/06

Start Your Own

RESTAURANT AND FIVE OTHER FOOD BUSINESSES

W9-BXZ-055

Additional titles in *Entrepreneur's **Startup Series***

Start Your Own

Bar and Tavern

Bed & Breakfast

Business on eBay

Business Support Service

Car Wash

Child Care Service

Cleaning Service

Clothing Store

Coin-Operated Laundry

Consulting

Crafts Business

e-Business

e-Learning Business

Event Planning Business

Executive Recruiting Service

Freight Brokerage Business

Gift Basket Service

Growing and Selling Herbs and Herbal
    Products

Home Inspection Service

Import/Export Business

Information Consultant Business

Law Practice

Lawn Care Business

Mail Order Business

Medical Claims Billing Service

Personal Concierge Service

Personal Training Business

Pet-Sitting Business

Self-Publishing Business

Seminar Production Business

Specialty Travel & Tour Business

Staffing Service

Successful Retail Business

Vending Business

Wedding Consultant Business

Wholesale Distribution Business

Entrepreneur MAGAZINE'S
startup

Start Your Own

RESTAURANT AND FIVE OTHER FOOD BUSINESSES,

Your Step-by-Step Guide to Success

Entrepreneur Press and Jacquelyn Lynn

EP
Entrepreneur Press

Editorial Director: Jere L. Calmes
Managing Editor: Marla Markman
Cover Design: Beth Hansen-Winter
Production: Eliot House Productions
Composition: Patricia Miller

This publication is designed to provide accurate and authoritative information in regard
to the subject matter covered. It is sold with the understanding that the publisher is not
engaged in rendering legal, accounting or other professional services. If legal advice or
other expert assistance is required, the services of a competent professional person
should be sought.

Library of Congress Cataloging-in-Publication Data

Lynn, Jacquelyn.
    Start your own restaurant and five other food businesses 2/e/by Entrepreneur Press and
Jacquelyn Lynn.
        p.   cm.
    ISBN 1-59918-020-0 (alk. paper)
        1. Restaurant management. 2. Food service management. 3. New business enter-
prises. I. Entrepreneur Press. II. Title.
TX911.3.M27L9775 2006
647.95068—dc22   2006011749

Printed in Canada

12 11 10 09 08 07 06   10 9 8 7 6 5 4 3 2 1

Contents

Chapter 18

Financial Management **221**

Chapter 19

Tales from the Trenches. **233**

Appendix

▲

Preface

Food is a basic need. Though tastes and trends will change, technology will advance and demographics will shift, people will always need to eat.

Now that doesn't mean that starting and running a profitable food-service business will be a proverbial piece of cake. Quite the contrary: This will probably be the hardest work you've ever done. But it has the potential to be tremendously rewarding—both financially and emotionally—and it can be lots of fun.

There are many ways you can enter the food-service industry, from buying a small coffee cart to building a high-end restaurant from the ground up. In this book, we examine six basic food-service businesses: a generic restaurant, a pizzeria, a sandwich shop/delicatessen, a coffeehouse, a bakery, and a catering business. It's important to remember that these are not mutually exclusive businesses; they can be customized and combined to create the specific business you have in mind.

Perhaps you know exactly what type of food-service business you want to start, or perhaps you haven't made a final decision yet. Either way, it's a good idea to read all the chapters in this book—even those that pertain to businesses you think you aren't interested in. If you read with an open mind, you may get ideas from one type of operation that you can apply to another.

This book will give you the basic information you need to start a food-service business. You'll learn how to develop a business plan; what the day-to-day operation is like; how to set up your kitchen and dining area; how to buy and maintain equipment and inventory; how to deal with administrative, financial, personnel, and regulatory issues; and how to market your venture.

Because the best information about business comes from the people who are already in the trenches, we interviewed successful food-service business owners who were happy to share their stories. Their experience spans all types of food-service operations, and several of them illustrate in practice that you can successfully blend more than one type of operation. Throughout the book, you'll read about what works—and doesn't work—for these folks and how you can use their techniques in your own business.

You'll also learn what the food-service business is really like. The hours can be flexible, but they're usually long. The profit margins are good, but only if you're paying attention to detail. The market is tremendous, but you'll have a substantial amount of competition, which means you'll need a plan to set yourself apart. The opportunity to express yourself creatively is virtually limitless, but sometimes you'll have to do what the market demands—even if it's not your preference.

Like anything else, there's no magic formula, no quick path to success. Thriving in the food-service business takes hard work, dedication, and commitment. But it can be well worth the investment of your time, energy, and resources. After all, everybody's got to eat—including you.

1

Introduction

As increasing numbers of consumers want to dine out or take prepared food home, the number of food-service operations has skyrocketed from 155,000 about 30 years ago to nearly 900,000 today. But there's still room in the market for your food-service business.

Beware!
The three primary reasons why food-service businesses fail:

- undercapitalization
- poor inventory control
- poor payroll management

Shifting demographics and changing lifestyles are driving the surge in food-service businesses. Busy consumers don't have the time or inclination to cook. They want the flavor of fresh bread without the hassle of baking. They want tasty, nutritious meals without dishes to wash. In fact, the rise in popularity of to-go operations underscores some clear trends in the food-service industry. More and more singles, working parents and elderly people are demanding greater convenience when it comes to buying their meals.

Though the future looks bright for the food-service industry overall, there are no guarantees in this business. Even the most successful operators will tell you this isn't a "get rich quick" industry. It's more like a "work hard and make a living" industry.

A hard reality is that many restaurants fail during their first year, frequently due to a lack of planning. But that doesn't mean your food-service business has to be an extremely complex operation. In fact, the more streamlined you can make it, the better your chances for success. Robert V. Owens, owner of RV's Seafood Restaurant, a casual seafood restaurant in Nags Head, North Carolina, observes, "The restaurant business is a simple business that people make complicated." His formula for success is quality food, good service, and great people—an approach that's worked for him for nearly a quarter century.

Who Are the Diners?

No single food-service operation has universal appeal. This is a fact that many newer entrepreneurs have trouble accepting, but the reality is that you will never capture 100 percent of the market. When you try to please everyone, you end up pleasing no one. So focus on the 5 or 10 percent of the market that you can get, and forget about the rest.

With that said, who is eating at restaurants? Let's take a look at the main market categories of food-service business customers.

Generation Y

This generation, also tagged the "millennial generation," the "echo," or the "boomlet" generation, includes those born between 1980 and 2000. Generation Y is the most ethnically diverse generation yet and is more than three times the

Stat Fact
More than 50 billion meals are eaten in restaurants and school and work cafeterias each year.

size of Generation X. Generation Y teenagers have an average of $100 per week of disposable income, and 40 percent of them hold at least a part-time job. One in four lives in a single-parent household, and three out of four have working mothers. They are a prime market for food-service businesses.

Members of Generation Y go for fast-food and quick-service items. About 25 percent of their restaurant visits are to burger franchises, followed by pizza restaurants at 12 percent. This group's food-consumption behavior is not significantly different than previous generations at the same age.

Stat Fact

According to the National Restaurant Association, by 2010, the restaurant industry's share of the food dollar is expected to rise from its present 46 to 53 percent; that's up from 25 percent in 1955.

Generation X

Generation X is a label applied to those who were born between 1965 and 1977. This group is known for strong family values. While earlier generations strove to do better financially than their parents, Gen Xers are more likely to focus on their relationship with their children. They are concerned with value, and they favor quick-service restaurants and midscale operations that offer all-you-can-eat salad bars and buffets. To appeal to this group, offer a comfortable atmosphere that focuses on value and ambience.

Baby Boomers

Born between 1946 and 1964, baby boomers make up the largest segment of the U.S. population. Prominent in this generation are affluent professionals who can afford to visit upscale restaurants and spend money freely. During the 1980s, they were the main consumer group for upscale, trendy restaurants. In the 1990s, many baby boomer families were two-income households with children. Today, those on the leading edge of the boomer generation are becoming grandparents, making them a target of both restaurants that offer a family-friendly atmosphere and those that provide an upscale, formal dining experience.

Empty Nesters

This group consists of people in the age range between the high end of the baby boomers and seniors (people in their early 50s to about age 64). Empty nesters typically have grown children who no longer live at home, and their ranks will continue to increase as the baby boomers grow older and their children leave home. With the most discretionary income and the highest per-capita income of all the generations, this group typically visits upscale restaurants. They are less concerned with price and are focused on excellent service and outstanding food. Appeal to this group with elegant surroundings and a sophisticated ambience.

Seniors

The senior market covers the large age group of those who are 65 and older. Generally, the majority of seniors are on fixed incomes and may not be able to afford upscale restaurants often, so they tend to visit family-style restaurants that offer good service and reasonable prices. "Younger" seniors are likely to be more active and have more disposable income than "older" seniors, whose health may be declining. Seniors typically appreciate restaurants that offer early-bird specials and senior menus with lower prices and smaller portions, since their appetites tend to be less hearty than those of younger people.

Stat Fact
More than 65 percent of restaurant customers agree that food served at their favorite restaurant provides flavor and taste sensations they cannot easily duplicate at home.

Industry Trends

In the 1980s—by many accounts the decade of greed—new restaurants were typically upscale establishments that centered on unique and creative dishes by famous chefs. Young, professional baby boomers, often with liberal expense accounts, supported these concepts. The 1990s brought a trend to the restaurant industry that is continuing into

Behind the Angel-Hair Curtain

The typical American food-service business owner began his or her career in an entry-level position such as busperson, dishwasher or cook; works long hours; is energetic and entrepreneurial; is usually more involved in charitable, civic, and political activities than the average American.

Although these traits are characteristic of restaurateurs, they are not required attributes. For example, some food-service business owners have entered their fields without any previous experience. They hire employees who have the experience they lack and who can help guide their operation to success. There is, however, no substitute for energy and a desire to succeed. Successful restaurateurs know they've chosen an industry where hard work is the norm, and they're willing to do what it takes to turn their dreams into reality.

the 21st century: an appreciation of value. There's no question that family-minded Generation Xers and baby boomers are concentrating on stretching their dollars.

Stat Fact
An estimated 75 percent of restaurant-goers ask for alternative preparation methods, off-the-menu orders, and substitutions.

Some other industry trends include:

- *Carts and kiosks.* Eating establishments no longer require customers to come to them. In many cases, the restaurant goes to the customer in the form of a cart or kiosk. Many limited-service mobile facilities are operating at locations that attract large numbers of people, such as malls, universities, airports, sports stadiums, and arenas. These restaurants typically offer very limited menus but attract customers with their recognizable names.

- *Co-branded operations.* Especially popular in the fast-food market, "co-branding" or "dual-branding" is when two or more well-known restaurants combine their menus in one location to offer customers a wider selection of items. The concept of co-branding began in the 1990s and continues to be a strong trend.

- *Nutrition-conscious customers.* Restaurant-goers are showing a heightened interest in health and nutrition. Many are looking for low-fat dishes and fresh foods.

- *Popular menu items.* Barbecued foods and appetizers remain two of the most popular menu groups. Barbecue appears to satisfy customers seeking spicy foods and regional cuisines. Appetizer orders are increasing thanks to customers who omit entrees and choose starters instead. Customers are also increasingly looking for menu items that are compatible with weight-loss trends such as the low-carb, high-protein diets and Weight Watchers.

- *A focus on children.* Because many baby boomers still have children living at home and an increasing number of them are dining out with grandchildren, the majority of their restaurant experiences are family-oriented. Food-service operations wanting to reach this market are offering children's menus and children's value meals with smaller portions. Some offer child-friendly environments with booster seats, toys, balloons, crayons, menus featuring games on them and even free table-side entertainment in the form of magicians and clowns.

Menu Trends

As you put together a plan for your food-service business, be aware of some of the trends in menu content and design. These factors could—and, in fact, should—influence the type of food-service business you open.

Restaurant operators report that vegetarian items, tortillas, locally grown produce, organic items, fusion dishes (combining two or more ethnic cuisines in one dish or on one plate), and microbrewed or local beers are gaining in popularity. Pita dishes and wraps continue to be in high demand, too, as an easy-to-consume alternative to sandwiches. You will also see a strong demand for bagels, espresso and specialty coffees, and "real meals," which are typically an entree with a side order. Consumers are also eating more chicken, seafood, and beef dishes than they have in recent years. At the same time, people expect to see meatless alternatives on the menu.

Customers also are demanding "comfort food": the dishes that take them back to their childhoods, when mothers baked from scratch, and meat and potatoes were at the center of each plate. Creative chefs are looking for ways to redefine and reinvigorate comfort food favorites. Instead of the traditional version of shepherd's pie, for example, you might see one made with mushrooms, spinach, carrots, and lobster sauce.

Menus are also showing a number of ethnic dishes and spice-infused offerings. It's not surprising to find Thai, Vietnamese, Creole, Tuscan, and even classic French cuisines on the same menu and even on the same plate.

At the same time, be sure to keep the kids in mind as you plan your selections. If families are a key part of your target market, you'll want to offer a range of four or five items in smaller portions that youngsters will enjoy, such as a half portion of pasta or small hamburger. If you serve snack items as well as entrees, note that kids are choosing healthier snacks more often than they did a few years ago, thanks to concerned parents. For example, while salty snacks remain popular, yogurt is the fastest-growing snack food based on consumption frequency among kids under 13. The average child in that age group eats yogurt 11 times more in a year today than five years ago. Fruit cups and applesauce cups are also growing in popularity among children and teens. While most restaurants still offer fixed kids' meals, you might consider allowing your young diners to choose among a selection of nutritious options.

Stat Fact

The most popular items on children's menus are:

1. Chicken nuggets or strips
2. French fries
3. Hamburgers
4. Pasta
5. Grilled cheese sandwiches
6. Hot dogs
7. Pizza
8. Fish sticks
9. Cookies
10. Shrimp
11. Pancakes
12. Milkshakes

Though menu variety has increased over the years, menus themselves are growing shorter. Busy consumers don't want to read a lengthy menu before dinner; dining out is a recreational activity, so they're in the restaurant to relax. Keep the number of items you offer in check, and keep menu descriptions simple and straightforward, providing customers with a variety of choices in a concise format.

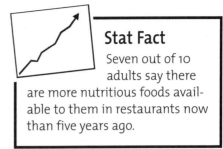

Stat Fact

Seven out of 10 adults say there are more nutritious foods available to them in restaurants now than five years ago.

Your menu should also indicate whether dishes can be prepared to meet special dietary requirements. Items low in fat, sodium, and cholesterol should also be marked as such.

Most large chains do a significant amount of market research before adding new items to their menus. Occasional visits to popular chain outlets (or just paying attention to their ads or visiting their web sites) can help you benefit from their investment. For example, Applebee's has teamed up with Weight Watchers International to develop menu items for diners who are counting "points." T.G.I. Friday's has partnered with Atkins Nutritionals Inc. to offer Atkins-approved, low-carb menu items. The newest concept in the Darden Restaurants chain (Olive Garden, Red Lobster, Smokey Bones) is Seasons 52, which offers nutritionally balanced, lower-calorie menu items and desserts in bite-sized portions. When P.F. Chang's China Bistro sponsored a marathon, it also created special high-carb, high-protein entrees for participating athletes. Even the fast-food outlets, which aren't known for nutritious fare, are offering healthier options. Pay attention to these trends, and make adjustments to your own menu when the market demands it.

"We took successful items from a lot of the major chains and incorporated them into our menu," says Bill Ellison, co-owner of Frasier's, a sports bar and restaurant in Apopka, Florida. But he and partner Frank Perez also came up with some of their own dishes. "Every restaurant should add their own signature items," Ellison says, "things you can't get anywhere else."

Understanding Takeout Customers

Research conducted by the National Restaurant Association indicates off-premises consumption of restaurant food is on the rise. Of respondents to a survey conducted by the organization, 21 percent who use off-premises restaurant services purchase one or more such meals a day; 26 percent purchase off-premises meals every other day; 22 percent purchase them about twice a week; and 31 percent buy them less than once a week.

Fast-food restaurants (operations that prepare food quickly) represent the largest share of off-premises dining, followed by carryout restaurants (operations that target the off-premises diner either in part or exclusively). However, full-service establishments are increasing their takeout services. A growing number are allowing diners to call in their order and a description of their car, and then deliver the food to them in a designated parking area. What motivates consumers to buy prepared food to consume elsewhere? Mainly, they are in a hurry and want easy access, fast service and reasonable prices. Another reason is that they're just too tired to shop for and prepare food themselves. Often, consumers looking for a special treat are inclined to buy takeout food, particularly ice cream, snacks, and gourmet coffees. Another strong motivator of takeout customers is the desire to eat something that is good for them. These people tend to order takeout from full-service restaurants. They also get takeout items from grocery stores and cafeterias or buffets for tasty, fresh foods. Interestingly, studies show that consumption of takeout food increases during times of national crisis, when people are hungry for information and want to get home to their TVs as quickly as possible.

Where Is the Competition?

Competition in the food-service industry is widespread, varied, and significant. When you open a restaurant, you'll be competing not only with other similarly themed restaurants, but also with every restaurant in the area you serve. In addition, your customers themselves are a form of competition, because they can make their own meals at home if they choose. Take a closer look at the primary competition categories.

Chains

Chain restaurants may be the biggest threat to independent operators. Chains are growing as private companies and franchises take over a greater portion of the market. With well-known names and large advertising budgets, chains enjoy significant consumer recognition.

What these restaurants do not offer is the personalized attention that many small, independent operations provide—this is where independent restaurants have an advantage. Many restaurateurs become acquainted with their regular customers and build relationships with them. This is not to say that chains do not offer personalized service—indeed, many of them excel in this area. But there is a difference when customers know they are dealing directly with the owner.

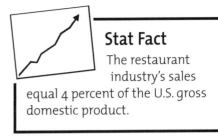

Stat Fact
The restaurant industry's sales equal 4 percent of the U.S. gross domestic product.

Independent restaurants have several other competitive advantages over chains. For one thing, independently-owned fine-dining establishments are often willing to take reservations, while chains usually are not. Independents may also offer live music, experienced chefs (rather than just basic cooks) and creative foods and beverages. While chains have the advantage of a well-known name, many independents offer the atmosphere customers prefer.

Supermarkets and Convenience Stores

Supermarkets and convenience stores are fairly recent competitors for restaurants. These businesses offer customers food that is freshly prepared and ready to go—although not always healthy. Their menus typically include fried chicken, sandwiches, side dishes, salads, and desserts. The primary concern of customers who visit these establishments is convenience, so supermarkets and convenience stores offer serious competition to quick-service restaurants that also compete on the basis of convenience and value.

Eating at Home

Dining out is not a necessity for most people. Restaurants, like other service businesses, sell convenience: They perform a task that consumers could otherwise handle themselves. Some consumers perceive dining out as something to do only on special occasions, which may be the attitude of a large portion of upscale restaurant customers. Quick-service and midscale restaurants must appeal to value- and time-conscious consumers. They must stress how eating out can save customers the time and trouble of cooking and how customers can relax while they eat and not worry about cleaning up afterward.

Operations

Owning a food-service business may seem like an entrepreneurial dream come true. Even the smallest operations have an element of glamour: On the surface, it looks like the owners make their living greeting guests and serving meals while becoming recognizable figures in the community.

Stat Fact

Lunch is the most popular meal for people to eat away from home. Popular lunch items include hamburgers, wraps, salads, soups, and ethnic foods.

And as more and more celebrities enter the food-service industry, they enhance the restaurant business's image as an exciting, lucrative opportunity.

But dealing graciously with customers and playing the role of elegant host is only part of a restaurateur's many duties. Food-service business operators spend most of their time developing menus; ordering inventory and supplies; managing personnel; creating and implementing marketing campaigns; making sure their operation is in compliance with a myriad of local, state, and federal regulations; completing a wide range of paperwork; and doing other administrative chores. Certainly the financial opportunities are there—as are the fun aspects of the business. But starting, running, and growing a food-service business is also hard work.

Regardless of the type of food-service business you intend to start, the best way to learn is to work for a similar operation for a while before striking out on your own. Doing so will give you significant insight into the realities and logistics of the business.

Jim Amaral, founder of Borealis Breads in Portland, Maine, started working in bakeries when he was 15. "I worked my way up from washing pots and pans to frying doughnuts to doing the basic . . . retail bakery stuff," he recalls. Today, he owns a bakery that specializes in sourdough breads and brings in more than $2 million a year in both wholesale and retail business out of three locations in Maine.

Michael Greene was also 15 when he got his first restaurant job, washing dishes on Friday nights. Later, he attended Cornell University in Ithaca, New York, and worked in all types of restaurants and private clubs before opening River City Billiards, a pizzeria in Haverhill, Massachusetts. Greene's partner, Anthony Allen, didn't have any food-service experience when he opened his first restaurant—a small, 300-square-foot takeout pizza shop—and he says now that some practical experience would have helped tremendously. "Even though I was just doing pizza, and it was a very narrow menu, there were many things I needed to learn [about] making the dough. It took us [several months] to achieve the dough I felt comfortable with. Not having any background in that area was a definite liability." However, Allen didn't go into the business blind; he did some serious research. He went to Rome, where he observed and interviewed pizza-makers. When he returned to the United States, he visited numerous pizza parlors to watch how they operated, and he talked at length with equipment sellers. "I put together what I thought was reasonable," he says.

Still another restaurateur who started in the business at the age of 15 is Scott Redler. "As soon as I started working in a restaurant, I realized this was my passion," he says. "The energy level of a restaurant—there's nothing like it in the world. When you have a busy restaurant, and you're watching everything happen as it should, it's just a wonderful feeling of satisfaction. You're making people smile." After working in various restaurants for 11 years, he opened a Chinese fast-food place at the age of 26. That venture failed within eight months, then Redler went to work for a large restaurant company, where he eventually advanced to the position of senior vice-president, overseeing 15 operations. But he still yearned for his own place, so he developed the concept that became Timberline Steakhouse & Grill, which now has five locations in Kansas. He later created Freddy's Frozen Custard, which offers hot dogs, hamburgers, and (as you might expect) frozen custard. Today, Redler is franchising the operation.

Ann Crane took a more direct path to restaurant entrepreneurship. For 15 years, she worked for Meyerhof's & Cuisine M, a catering business in Irvine, California. When the owner passed away, Crane bought the company from his heirs.

Bill Ellison and Frank Perez were working together managing a sports bar-style restaurant when they decided to go into business for themselves. In 2002, they found an existing operation that was doing enough business to stay open but not enough to be profitable. "We figured if it had enough business to stay open the way it was, if we added the [right] attitude, our concept and our customer service, we would increase sales

Closed for Business

If you have a retail food-service business, you may find you don't have time to spruce up your facility during the year. For this reason, many independent restaurants close for one to two weeks every year so the owners can look over their facilities and make any necessary changes. They may add a fresh coat of paint, repair ripped upholstery and inspect all the equipment. Since there are no customers or employees in the facility, repair people can work quickly and without interruption. This annual closing period also allows employees to take vacations.

To maintain good relations with your customers, give them advance notice of your upcoming closure. Post a sign on your door stating the dates during which you will be closed and the date you will reopen. Record an outgoing message on your answering machine or voice mail with the same information. While you're closed, check your answering machine or voice mail regularly in case a supplier or anyone else needs to get in touch with you or someone on your staff.

Generally, restaurants close during the slowest time of the year, when the closing will have the least impact on revenue and customers. Of course, if you're a seasonal operation, such as Robert Owen's seafood restaurant in the resort area of Nags Head, North Carolina, you can take care of major maintenance and updates when you're closed during the off-season.

and make a profit," Ellison says. They changed the name of the place, redecorated the interior and created their own menu. Frasier's, in Apopka, Florida, has been thriving ever since.

Rebecca Swartz began partnering with her mother in a small retail gourmet pasta shop in West Des Moines, Iowa. Today, Viva La Pasta has grown to include a restaurant, a cooking school, a catering operation, private-label foods, gift baskets, and wholesale distribution—in addition to the retail shop.

> **Tip...**
>
> **Smart Tip**
>
> Be sure each square foot in your restaurant generates income. You'll pay the same rent for the kitchen and the closets as you do for the dining area, so you should have absolutely no wasted space.

As you can see, there are several ways to get started in the food-service business. You can purchase a franchise, build an independent operation from the ground up, buy an existing operation, or lease space in an existing structure. Each approach has its advantages and disadvantages, which you need to consider carefully before making a final decision (Chapter 13 discusses these options in greater detail). But regardless of how you get started, there are some things you need to know about operations that are common to virtually all types of food-service businesses.

Setting Hours of Operation

Your hours of operation will vary depending on the particular type of food-service business you have. Ultimately, it is up to you to determine the hours for your business.

Most quick-service restaurants are open for lunch, dinner, and the post-dinner crowd. Typically, they open at 10:30 or 11 A.M. and close anywhere between 9 and 11 P.M. Some national fast-food franchises and chains also serve breakfast and open as early as 6 A.M. Others stay open until well past midnight on weekends, and some are open 24 hours a day.

The hours of midscale and upscale restaurants vary depending on the concept. A restaurant that offers only a buffet will, most likely, not serve breakfast and may only be open from 11 A.M. to 9 P.M. Many family-style restaurants, on the other hand, specialize in serving breakfast and typically open at 6 A.M. They continue serving meals until after dinnertime, closing around 9 P.M.

Casual-dining restaurants tend to cater to the lunch and dinner crowds. These establishments open around 11 A.M. and stay open late, especially on weekends, to appeal to the post-dinner crowd. During the week, they tend to close at 10 or 11 P.M. On Fridays and Saturdays, they may stay open until midnight or 1 A.M.

Often, upscale restaurants that just serve dinner are only open from 4:30 or 5 P.M. to 9 or 10 P.M. These businesses are able to survive on dinner sales alone because they have found a concept that works, and they're sticking with it. Most full-service restaurants, however, are open for both lunch and dinner, six or seven days a week. Those that are only open six days a week usually close on either Sunday or Monday.

Hours vary somewhat among full-service restaurants. If you open such a restaurant and do not plan on offering cocktail service, start off with a split-shift operation: Open for lunch from 11 A.M. to 2 P.M. and then open for dinner from 4:30 to 9 P.M. each day. If you decide to serve cocktails, you could keep the same dinner hours but serve appetizers and drinks at all hours, say from 11 A.M. to 11 P.M. If you have just a beer-and-wine bar, as opposed to a full bar, the split-shift system can work well.

Sandwich shops, delicatessens, and pizzerias are typically open for lunch and dinner six or seven days a week. Hours vary depending on location and market, but most open from 10 or 11 A.M. to 6 or 8 P.M. (for sandwich shops) or as late as 11 P.M. or midnight (for pizzerias and full-service delis).

Commercial bakeries begin baking the day's products as early as 2 or 3 A.M.; some even operate 24 hours a day. Retail bakeries and coffeehouses tend to open early enough to capture the breakfast crowd.

Caterers typically have an office staffed during normal business hours, perhaps 8 or 9 A.M. to 5 P.M. The actual hours people work depend, of course, on their particular jobs and span all hours of the day and all days of the week.

Scheduling Employees

When you'll need employees to report to work depends a great deal on the type of food-service business you have. As a general guide for restaurants, the first person to arrive in the morning should be your head cook or chef—the person responsible for the kitchen. He or she should arrive a few hours before the restaurant opens to begin preparing the side dishes that you will serve throughout the day. These items can include soups, vegetables, sauces, homemade breads or biscuits, rice, and generally anything else you might serve in large quantities over a span of several hours. The preparation of side dishes should be completed 30 minutes before the doors open for business.

The head chef or cook might also be responsible for accepting and inspecting deliveries, or, if you prefer, your manager or assistant manager can arrive at the same time to take care of paperwork and deliveries. If your chief cook comes in before opening, he or she should be able to

Smart Tip

Be around and visible. Of course, large chain restaurants are run by managers, and you may want to hire managers to help you run your operation. But most successful independent food-service operations have an owner who works in the business every day. They're in touch with their customers and their employees, they know what's going on in the day-to-day operation, and they're available to make decisions as needed.

leave after the lunch or dinner crowd has been served, with the second cook carrying on until closing. The second cook will be responsible for cleaning the kitchen so it is ready for the next morning.

Your dining-room manager, maitre d', or chief host or hostess should arrive 30 minutes to an hour before opening to make sure that everything in the front of the house is in order. This will allow time for him or her to check the dining-room table settings, napkins, salt and pepper shakers, and any other elements that will make the front room more presentable to the public.

The person in charge of these front-of-the-house pre-opening chores can work through the lunch hour and dinner hour—if you serve both meals—or from the dinner hour through closing if you only serve dinner. This employee can also close out the cash register.

The bar manager should come in 30 minutes before the restaurant opens for business. He or she will be responsible for the appearance of the lounge area, stocking the bar and keeping track of liquor inventory, making sure free bar snacks are out, and preparing to open the bar.

The bar manager will also likely be your chief bartender. This person will continue working through the early-evening shift, and your second bartender will usually handle the late-evening crowds. Because weekend evenings are the busiest for both bars and restaurants, schedule your bar manager to work Tuesday through Saturday to cover the most hectic times. In addition to the bar manager, one or two part-time bartenders can assist with the weekend crowd.

Service Procedures

Regardless of how formal or casual your operation is, your goal should be to treat customers like royalty, and you can meet this goal by providing strong, professional service from the moment your customers walk in the door. Because your team of employees will be responsible for how well your customers are treated, they should reflect the policies you've established as the owner.

Uniforms will help develop a sense of identity and pride among your staff, as well as project a professional image. All employees who work at the same level should wear an identical uniform. For example, all buspersons should wear the same uniform, and everyone on your waitstaff should wear the same uniform.

Set standards for your business's appearance. Everything from the restrooms to your plates and utensils should receive the same careful consideration. If you find spots on your glassware or

> **Smart Tip** Tip...
>
> To build a profitable food-service business, you need systems. Approach your operation with the understanding that, regardless of how creative or fun it might be, it is a business, and successful businesses are built on systems that produce consistent, reliable results.

plates, then you have failed to meet high standards. If toilet tissue and towels are strewn about the restrooms, then you have failed to meet high standards. If you want to create a dining experience that people will remember, make it a good one.

The actual service should range from polite to ingratiating. The host or hostess should greet customers with a cheerful hello and ask how many people are in the party and whether they prefer smoking or nonsmoking (unless you're located in an area that prohibits smoking in public places). If a line forms, or if all the tables are full, the host or hostess should take customers' names and let them know how long they should expect to wait. Unless you take reservations, customers should be seated on a first-come, first-served basis. If you have a bar, give customers the option of waiting there. Make menus available to people who are waiting so they can be thinking ahead about what they'd like to order.

Once customers are seated, promptly present them with a menu and inform them that their server will be with them in a moment. The busperson should fill their water glasses immediately (unless you are in an area with water restrictions). When the server arrives, the first thing he or she should do is inquire if the customers would like anything before ordering their meals, such as a beverage or an appetizer.

After giving the customers time to review the menu, the server should come back to answer any questions and take meal orders. The server should be thoroughly familiar with the menu and any specials so he or she can answer any questions. All orders should be recorded on a check and should be repeated back to customers to make sure they are correct.

Servers should remove food from the left and beverages from the right and should never reach in front of a customer to serve or remove anything.

The waitstaff and buspersons should always be in their stations checking to make sure customers have everything they need for a satisfying meal. They should refill water glasses regularly, supply the necessary condiments and ask if the food is satisfactory after customers have had time to start eating. After the guests have finished their entrees, servers should ask if they would like dessert or coffee. Only when the server is sure the customer is finished with the meal should the check be presented.

If there has been a service failure of any sort, even an unavoidable one, do your best to make amends, perhaps with a free dessert or after-dinner drink. If a customer complains about a particular dish, offer to replace the item at no charge. Above all, never argue with a customer. When you do, even if you win, you lose, because chances are that customer will never return, and you will have created negative word-of-mouth advertising that might prevent other customers from visiting your establishment.

When They Don't Come In

More and more restaurants are offering drive-thru service. Lunch is the most frequently purchased meal in the drive-thru lane, and 53 percent of meals purchased at drive-thru windows are typically eaten at home, not in the car. In general, households with children use drive-thrus more than those without.

There's more to creating an efficient drive-thru than just setting up a window in your building and a lane in your parking lot. Consider this: For every 10 seconds saved serving drive-thru customers, you can add $1,000 in incremental sales.

Stat Fact
Eating and drinking establishments are mostly small businesses. Seven out of 10 have fewer than 20 employees.

To keep the line moving quickly, have a clear, easy-to-read menu board positioned before the ordering station. Assure accuracy by having employees confirm each order before the customer proceeds to the payment/pickup window. To speed up payment, have the customer's change ready before he or she gets to the payment window.

Cleaning Your Facility

At the end of every business day, you must clean your facility. You can either have your staff or an outside commercial cleaning service handle this task. Your cooks can clean the grill and mop the floor after closing. The waitstaff and buspersons can refill condiments and clean the tables, booths, and floors in the dining area. The dishwasher should finish the day's dishes and restock dishes for the cooks and waitstaff.

If you cannot afford to pay your employees to complete all these duties or would simply prefer not to, a commercial cleaning service can take care of them. For a set fee, a cleaning service will visit your restaurant every night after the employees have left. They can clean the entire restaurant, including the kitchen, wait stations, dining area, and restrooms. If you decide to use a cleaning service, ask for references and check the company out before making a final decision. It's also a good idea to find out what cleaning products they use. You wouldn't want someone to clean the grills with the same product they use to clean the restrooms. A growing number of janitorial and commercial cleaning services are expanding to target the restaurant market. Ask other restaurant owners for recommendations, or check your telephone directory for companies.

Details on operational issues relating to specific types of food-service businesses will be explained in later chapters.

Developing
Your Plan

Whether you've got years of food-service

experience behind you or you're a novice in the industry, you

need a plan for your business—and you need to have it in place

before you buy the first spoon or crack the first egg. This chapter

will focus on a few issues particular to planning food-service

businesses, but they are by no means all you need to consider when writing your business plan. *Start Your Own Business* by Rieva Lesonsky (Entrepreneur Press) has complete guidelines on how to put together a general business plan.

Many entrepreneurs view writing a business plan with even less enthusiasm than they had for homework when they were in school. But if you're excited about your business, creating a business plan should be an exciting process. It will help you define and evaluate the overall feasibility of your concept, clarify your goals, and determine what you'll need for start-up and long-term operations.

This is a living, breathing document that will provide you with a road map for your company. You'll use it as a guide, referring to it regularly as you work through the start-up process and then during the operation of your business. And if you're going to be seeking outside financing—either in the form of loans or investors—your business plan will be the tool that convinces funding sources of the worthiness of your venture.

Beware!

When you make a change to one part of your business plan, be sure you think through how that change will affect the rest of your operation. For example, if you decide to add more items to your menu, do you need to change your kitchen setup to accommodate them? Or if your original plan was to offer limited service where customers ordered and picked up their food at a counter, but you have now decided to take the food to the tables, how will that affect your staffing plans?

Putting together a business plan is not a linear process—although looking at the final product may make it seem that way. As you work through it, you'll likely find yourself jumping from menu development to cash-flow forecasts to staffing, then back to cash flow, on to marketing, and back to menu development. Take your time developing your plan. Whether you want to start a coffee-and-snack cart or a gourmet restaurant, you're making a serious commitment, and you shouldn't rush into it.

Carving Your Niche

Before you can begin any serious business planning, you must first decide what specific segment of the food-service industry you want to enter. While there are many commonalities among the various types of food-service businesses, there are also many differences. And while there is much overlap in the knowledge and skills necessary to be successful, your own personality and preferences will dictate whether you choose to open a commercial bakery, a coffee cart, a fine-dining restaurant, or another type of operation. Then, once you have decided what business best suits you, you must figure out the niche you'll occupy in the marketplace.

Chances are you already have a pretty good idea of the type of food-service business that appeals to you. Before you take the actual plunge, read through the chapters that describe the various operations and see how they suit your particular working style.

For example, are you an early riser, or do you prefer to stay up late and sleep late? If you like—or at least don't mind—getting up before dawn, your niche may be a bakery or a casual breakfast-and-lunch operation. Night owls are going to be drawn to the hours required for bar-and-grill types of restaurants, fine-dining establishments, and even pizzerias.

Do you like dealing with the public, or are you happier in the kitchen? If you're a people person, choose a food-service business that gives you plenty of opportunity to connect with your customers. If you're not especially gregarious, you'll probably lean more toward a commercial type of business, perhaps a bakery or even a catering service, where you can deal more with operational issues than with people.

Some other types of questions to ask yourself include: Do you have a passion for a particular type of cuisine? Do you enjoy a predictable routine, or do you prefer something different every day? Are you willing to deal with the responsibilities and liabilities that come with serving alcoholic beverages?

As you do this self-analysis, think about your ideal day. If you could be doing exactly what you wanted to do, what would it be? Now compare your preferences with the requirements of each type of food-service business (as described in Chapters 5 through 10) and come up with the best match for yourself.

Once you have decided on the right niche for you as an individual, it's time to determine if you can develop a niche in the market for your food-service business.

Researching Your Market

You must do an in-depth examination of your market. Market research will provide you with data that allows you to identify and reach particular market segments and to solve or avoid marketing problems. A thorough market survey forms the foundation of any successful business. Without market research, it would be impossible to develop marketing strategies or an effective product line. The point of doing market research is to identify your market, find out where that market is, and develop a strategy to communicate with prospective customers in a way that will convince them to patronize your business.

Market research will also give you important information about your competitors. You'll need to find out what they're doing and how that approach meets—or doesn't meet—the needs of the market.

One of the most basic elements of effective marketing is differentiating your business from the competition. One marketing consultant calls it "eliminating the competition," because if you set yourself apart by doing something no one else does, then you essentially have no competition. However, before you can differentiate yourself, you need to understand who your competitors are and why your customers might patronize their businesses.

Are You on a Mission?

Your mission statement is the foundation of your business plan. Most food-service business owners have a reasonably clear understanding of the mission of their company. They know what they are doing, how and where it's being done, and who their customers are. Problems can arise, however, when that mission is not clearly articulated into a statement, written down, and communicated to others.

A mission statement defines what an organization is and its reason for being. Writing down your mission and communicating it to others creates a sense of commonality and a more coherent approach to what you're trying to do.

Even in a very small company, a written mission statement helps everyone involved see the big picture and keeps them focused on the true goals of the business. At a minimum, your mission statement should define who your primary customers are, identify the products and services you offer, and describe the geographical location in which you operate. For example, a caterer's mission statement might read "Our mission is to provide businesses and individuals in the Raleigh area with delicious food delivered to their location and set up and served according to their instructions." A coffeehouse's mission statement might read "Our mission is to serve the downtown business community by providing the highest-quality coffees, espresso, baked goods, and sandwiches in an atmosphere that meets the needs of customers who are in a hurry as well as those who want a place to relax and enjoy their beverages and food."

A mission statement should be short—usually just one sentence and certainly no more than two. A good idea is to cap it at 100 words. Anything longer than that isn't a mission statement and will probably confuse your employees.

Once you have articulated your message, communicate it as often as possible to everyone in the company, along with customers. Post it on the wall, hold meetings to talk about it, and include a reminder of the statement in employee correspondence.

Bright Idea

Update your business plan every year. Choose an annual date when you sit down with your plan, compare how closely your actual operation and results followed your forecasts, and decide if your plans for the coming year need adjusting. You will also need to take your financial forecasts out for another year, based on current and expected market conditions.

Bright Idea

Your business plan should include worst-case scenarios, both for your own benefit and for your funding sources. You'll benefit from thinking ahead about what you'll do if things don't go as you want them to. You'll also increase the comfort level of your lenders/ investors by demonstrating your ability to deal with the unexpected and potentially negative situations.

You should also make it clear to your suppliers. If they understand what you're all about, it will help them serve you better. It's more important to adequately communicate the mission statement to employees than to customers. It's not uncommon for an organization to use a mission statement for promotion by including it in brochures and on invoices, but the most effective mission statements are developed strictly for internal communication and discussion. Your mission statement doesn't have to be clever or catchy—just motivating and accurate.

Although your mission statement may never win an advertising or creativity award, it can still be a very effective customer-relations tool. For instance, you could print your mission statement on a poster-sized panel, have every employee sign it and hang it in a prominent place so customers can see it.

A critical part of your plan to open a food-service establishment will involve setting up your facility. In the next chapter, we'll take a look at the fundamentals of setting up a kitchen and dining area.

Kitchen and Dining Room Basics

The two key parts of your facility are the production area, where the food is prepared, and the public area, where your customers either dine or make their carryout purchases. How you design and equip these areas depends, of course, on the particular type of operation you want to have.

This chapter will take a look at the basics that apply to most operations, and the following six chapters will go into more detail regarding specific types of food-service businesses.

As you begin planning your facility, you might want to consider hiring an experienced, reputable consultant to assist with the layout of your dining and production areas. Consultants can also help you link all the elements—menu content and design, pricing, décor, kitchen layout, staffing, training, and other support services. To find a good consultant, network with restaurateurs who have businesses similar to the one you want to open, read trade publications, talk with equipment dealers, and perhaps even ask restaurant brokers for referrals.

Dining Room and Waiting Area

Much of your dining-room design will depend on your concept. It might help you to know that studies indicate that 40 to 50 percent of all sit-down customers arrive in pairs, 30 percent come alone or in parties of three, and 20 percent come in groups of four or more.

To accommodate the various party sizes, use tables for two that can be pushed together in areas where there is ample floor space. This gives you flexibility in accommodating both small and large parties. Place booths for four to six people along the walls.

Develop a uniform decorating concept that will establish a single atmosphere throughout your restaurant. That means whatever décor or theme you choose for the dining area should also be reflected in the waiting area. Also, be sure your waiting area is welcoming and comfortable. Whether your customers are seated immediately or have to wait a while for their tables, they will gain their first impression of your operation from the waiting area, and you want that impression to be a positive one.

Regardless of the type of operation you choose, the quality of your chairs is critical. Chairs are expensive, and how comfortable they are—or aren't—is the second most common source of environmental complaints in restaurants (the first is noise). But while your seats should be comfortable, they shouldn't be too soft, either—you don't want customers falling asleep. They should also allow for ease of movement. Diners should be able to get up and down easily and slide across surfaces without tearing clothing or hosiery. And seats need to be sturdy. When an overweight customer sits down or even tips a chair back on one or two legs, the chair shouldn't break. Also, the appearance of your seating—including chairs, benches, stools, and sofas—should match your overall ambience. Choose materials that can tolerate abrasive cleaning products as well as the abuse of being stacked and unstacked.

Bright Idea

Produce a concise paper version of your menu that your customers can take with them to make placing carryout or delivery orders easier.

Production Area

Generally, you'll need to allow approximately 35 percent of your total space for your production area. Include space for food preparation, cooking, dishwashing, trash disposal, receiving, inventory storage, and employee facilities and an area for a small office where daily management duties can be performed.

Smart Tip

All restrooms should be supplied with hand soap, paper towels or a hand-drying device, toilet tissue, and easily cleanable waste receptacles.

Allow about 12 percent of your total space for food preparation and cooking areas. If you want to entertain your customers with "exhibition cooking," design a protective barrier that allows the cooking to be seen but limits physical access by customers.

To make your production area as efficient as possible, keep the following tips in mind:

- Plan the shortest route from entrance to exit for ingredients and baked goods.
- Minimize handling by having as many duties as possible performed at each stop—that is, at each point the item or dish stops in the production process.
- Eliminate bottlenecks in the production process caused by delays at strategic locations. When things aren't flowing smoothly, figure out why. Be sure your equipment is adequate, well-maintained and located in the proper place for the task.
- Recognize that the misuse of space is as damaging to your operation as the misuse of machinery and labor.
- Eliminate backtracking, the overlapping of work, and unnecessary inspection by constantly considering possibilities for new sequences and combinations of steps in food preparation.

Set up the dishwashing area so the washer can develop a production line. The person responsible for washing dishes should rinse them in a double sink, then place them

These Mats Were Made for Standin'

An important piece of equipment in every food-service operation is matting. Rubber mats help reduce employee fatigue and prevent falls from spills. Place quality mats in all areas where employees such as cooks, dishwashers, preparation staff, and bartenders will be standing for long periods of time. Also place mats wherever spills may occur, such as at wait stations, near storage areas, and in walk-in refrigerators and freezers. A good 3-by-5-foot anti-fatigue mat will range in price from $37 to $55.

Bright Idea

Check the dirty dishes when they are returned to the kitchen to evaluate waste and determine whether you're serving too much. You may be able to increase profits by reducing portion sizes.

into racks on a small landing area next to the sink. From the landing area, the racks full of dishes are put through the commercial dishwasher, then placed on a table for drying. The size and capacity of your dishwasher will depend on the needs of your particular operation.

Receiving and inventory storage will take up to about 8 percent of your total space. These areas should be located so they are accessible to shipping vans. Use double doors at your receiving port, and keep a dolly or hand truck available at all times. Locate your dry-storage area and walk-in refrigerator and freezer adjacent to the receiving area.

Most food-service businesses require employees, and if you have them, you should also have a private room for them that includes a table, a few chairs, a closet or garment rack (to hang coats and street clothes after staffers have changed into their work clothes), lockers for safe storage of personal belongings and valuables, and a restroom. The staff facility should not take up more than 5 percent of your total space.

You'll also need a small area where you or your manager can perform administrative tasks, such as general paperwork, bank deposits, and counting out cash drawers. This space is essential even if you have another office at home where you do the majority of your administrative work.

Ventilation

Pollution control is tightening across the country, and new regulations are being introduced every year. This has had a significant impact on ventilation requirements

---

Shedding Light on the Subject

Throughout your facility, be sure you have adequate and appropriate lighting. The kitchen and work areas should be brightly lit to assure productivity, accuracy, and safety. Your dining and waiting areas and other customer spots should be lit in a way that is compatible with your theme and overall décor. Keep safety in mind at all times. A candlelight dinner is certainly romantic, but not if your patrons trip and fall on their way in or out because they can't see where they are going.

---

for restaurants. New, more efficient systems that meet the stringent requirements have increased the cost of starting a food-service business. Expect to pay $150 to $400 per linear foot for the hood and grease filter, and $18 to $48 per linear foot for the ductwork. While ventilation systems are expensive to install, they offer a tremendous opportunity for energy conservation. The more efficient systems are worth their extra cost because they result in substantially lower monthly utility expenses. Check with prominent HVAC (heating, ventilation, and air conditioning) system manufacturers and installers to find the best options for your particular facility.

You have three basic ventilation-system options. The first is reducing the quantity of exhaust air, which will decrease the exhaust fan size and ultimately lower your purchasing and operating costs. In conjunction with this option, you can also reduce the amount of makeup (fresh) air you have to introduce to compensate for the amount of exhaust air you release. This, in turn, will reduce the size of the makeup air fan you need and result in lower purchasing and operating costs. Finally, you can change the method of introducing makeup air so it doesn't have to be conditioned. This will significantly reduce the air-handling costs.

One of the best ways to achieve a reduction in exhaust and makeup air is to install a high-velocity, low-volume system, which reduces the exhaust air output by 40 percent. This directly affects the makeup air quantities—since makeup and exhaust must be in balance—and results in savings in processing the makeup air. A key benefit of such a system is that it introduces raw, unconditioned air directly into the exhaust ventilator, a process that eliminates the cost of heating or cooling a portion of the makeup air.

Merchandising

How you present your food and beverages is as important to sales as how those offerings taste. You can have the most delicious sirloin steak in town, but if you don't present it to the customer properly, it won't be as enjoyable as it could be. Presenting food in an attractive manner is called "merchandising," and is a powerful marketing tool that successful restaurateurs take advantage of to improve sales.

Merchandising is an art that requires a creative mind that can anticipate public likes and dislikes. Your concept, for instance, is a form of merchandising. So is how you present the dishes on your menu and the drinks in your bar. Arranging each of your dishes so the food looks appealing will not only please the customer who ordered the dish, but will also attract the attention of other customers.

Bright Idea
Food doesn't have to be served on traditional plates or in an expected setting. One California barbecue chain, for example, serves a full meal family style in a wooden wagon. It's different, memorable, fun, and keeps the customers coming back.

Many restaurants use parsley as a basic garnish, but an increasing number of establishments are turning to more creative options ranging from fresh fruits and herbs to little ornaments and even edible flowers.

Just as important as the garnish you use is selecting the right plate or glass for your food and beverages. For instance, you can serve a regular cut of prime rib on one type of plate and a deluxe cut on a different plate. This also applies to drinks. You might have one type of glass for regular beer and a better glass for premium beer and imported classics. You could, for example, serve a German beer in a stein.

Good merchandising is a great way to increase your sales. It is also a way to enhance your image and develop that all-important word-of-mouth advertising.

Pricing Menu Items

Before pricing each item on your menu, you must first account for how much it costs to purchase the ingredients. Then you should incorporate your overhead and the labor costs for preparing and serving the food into the price of each item. Finally, you can add your profit. The net profit restaurants expect on food ranges from 8 to 20 percent, depending on the item. In many cases, the menu price is about three times the food cost. But Anthony Allen of River City Billiards points out that this is just a general guideline. There will be many situations when the market will allow you to charge more. For example, the first few years his first pizzeria was in operation, Allen set his prices based on food costs alone, but he was delivering a product of significantly higher quality that people would have been willing to pay more for. Finally, a friend persuaded him to increase prices beyond the basic "cost-times-three" formula. After making the change, sales stayed steady, and profits increased. "[I had] two or three years of lost revenue from not doing more scientific research on pricing," he says.

Your net profit before taxes on drinks can be quite high: as much as 60 percent—or even more—of your total selling price. You should generally charge anywhere from 1,500 percent to 4,000 percent of your cost for drinks, depending on the particular drink and your location.

Setting prices can be tedious and time-consuming, especially if you don't have a knack for juggling numbers. Make it your business to learn how to estimate labor time accurately and how to calculate your overhead properly so that when you price your menu, you can be competitive and still make the profit you require.

Restaurant

The mainstay of the food-service industry is the general-category restaurant. The popularity of restaurants stems primarily from the fact that people have to eat. But there's more to it than just that.

The rise in single-parent families, dual-income couples, and individuals working more than one job are all factors driving customers who don't have the time or desire to cook for themselves into restaurants. Of course, time issues aren't the only reason people dine out. Restaurant customers also benefit from the relatively low inflation of menu prices; competition in the industry in recent years has kept menu prices at fairly reasonable levels.

Bright Idea

Choose a site for your restaurant that is near a well-known landmark. It will be easier for customers to find you if they can use a local landmark as a reference point.

Restaurants are also great places to entertain or conduct business. Going to a restaurant with friends or associates takes the pressure off people who want to concentrate on interacting rather than on preparing a meal. Many restaurants offer private rooms, large tables, and banquet facilities for these customers.

Many restaurants also cater to customers who want a certain dish but for whatever reason—perhaps a lack of culinary skill or the inability to find ingredients—are unable to prepare it for themselves. Ethnic restaurants or restaurants that serve exotic desserts often attract customers with such strong cravings.

Finally, beyond the food itself, many customers want to enjoy the atmosphere of the restaurants they visit. Ethnic restaurants and specialty-themed restaurants are examples of operations that meet this particular market need.

Before starting any type of restaurant, you must know who your customers are and where they are located. With that information, you can decide on the best site and move forward with your plans. However, restaurateurs don't always agree on the best approach to concept development and site selection.

Some restaurateurs believe you must determine your concept and market before choosing a location. For example, you may want to start an Italian restaurant, so you research the market for this type of cuisine, and then, based on what you find out, choose a general area and later a precise location for the restaurant.

Smart Tip

Tip...

Dine out often. Knowing what other restaurants are doing will help you maintain your competitive position, as well as give you ideas to improve your own operation.

Others believe that finding the location is the most important task and place secondary emphasis on concept and market. For instance, an entrepreneur may find a great building in a downtown business district, decide that it is perfect for a restaurant, and then determine the best concept for the location.

When it comes to restaurants, it does not really matter whether you research your market or your location first; what's critical is that you take the time to research both thoroughly.

Choosing Your Concept

Restaurant patrons want to be delighted with their dining experience, but they don't necessarily want to be surprised. If you're anticipating a family-style steakhouse (based on the name or the décor of the establishment), but you find yourself in a more formal environment with a bewildering—and pricey—gourmet menu, the surprise may keep you from enjoying the restaurant. Concepts give restaurateurs a way to let patrons know in advance what to expect and also to provide some structure for their operation. Here are some of the more popular restaurant concepts:

Seafood Restaurants

Quick-service seafood restaurants generally offer a limited range of choices, often restricted to fried seafood. Midscale and upscale seafood restaurants offer a wider selection, prepared in ways other than fried, such as baked, broiled, and grilled. Most seafood restaurants also offer a limited number of additional menu items, such as steak and chicken.

Seafood can be a risky area on which to focus, as prices are always changing, and many kinds of seafood are seasonal. Also, quality can vary tremendously. When shopping for seafood, make sure that the items are fresh and meet your standards of quality. If you are not happy with what a distributor offers, you can be sure your customers won't be, either.

The decor of a typical casual seafood restaurant consists of marine-related décor, such as fishing nets, buoys, and aquariums. Finer seafood restaurants will usually have minimal marine-related furnishings. Seafood restaurants are often located on or near a waterfront, which adds to the nautical ambience.

Beware!

Consider your options carefully before deciding to open a themed restaurant. Some theme operations—especially those owned by celebrities—have enjoyed popularity, but the allure of theme operations appears to be on the wane. One restaurant analyst says the problem with theme restaurants is that most people visit them once, twice or maybe three times but don't go back. It doesn't matter how good the food is if you can't pull in repeat customers because they take a "been there, done that" attitude toward your operation.

Steakhouses

Steakhouses are part of the midscale and upscale markets. Midscale steakhouses are typically family-oriented and offer a casual environment with meals perceived as good value. In terms of décor, comfort is emphasized, and Western themes are popular.

Upscale steakhouses offer a more formal atmosphere and may serve larger cuts of meat that are of

The Three Food Groups

Restaurants are classified into three primary categories: quick-service, midscale, and upscale. Quick-service restaurants are also known as fast-food restaurants. These establishments offer limited menus of items that are prepared quickly and sold for a relatively low price. In addition to very casual dining areas, they typically offer drive-thru windows and takeout service.

When people think of fast-food restaurants, they often envision hamburgers and french fries, but establishments in this category may also serve chicken, hot dogs, sandwiches, pizza, seafood, and ethnic foods.

Midscale restaurants, as the name implies, occupy the middle ground between quick-service and upscale restaurants. They offer full meals but charge prices that customers perceive as providing good value. Midscale restaurants offer a range of limited- and full-service options. In a full-service restaurant, patrons place and receive their orders at their tables; in a limited-service operation, patrons order their food at a counter and then receive their meals at their tables. Many limited-service restaurants offer salad bars and buffets.

Midscale restaurants embrace a variety of concepts, including steakhouses; casual dining; family dining; and ethnic restaurants such as Italian, Mexican, Asian, Mediterranean, and others. Even in full-service midscale operations, the ambience tends to be casual.

Upscale restaurants offer full table service and do not necessarily promote their meals as offering great value. Instead, they focus on the quality of their cuisine and the ambience of their facilities. Fine-dining establishments are at the highest end of the upscale restaurant category and charge the highest prices.

better quality than those served in midscale restaurants. Upscale establishments also charge higher prices, and their décor may be similar to that of other fine-dining establishments, offering guests more privacy and focusing more on adult patrons than families.

Although red meat is the primary focus of steakhouses, many offer additional items, such as poultry, seafood, and pasta selections. Ssare popular at midscale steakhouses.

Family-Style Restaurants

As the name implies, these establishments are geared toward families. Since they charge reasonable prices, they also appeal to seniors. They offer speedy service that falls somewhere between that of quick-service places and full-service restaurants. Their menus offer a variety of selections to appeal to the interests of a broad range of customers, from children to seniors. Family-style restaurant prices may be higher than those at fast-food restaurants, but these establishments provide table service to compensate.

The décor of family-style restaurants is generally comfortable, with muted tones, unremarkable artwork and plenty of booths and wide chairs. Booster seats and high chairs for children are readily available.

Stat Fact
According to the National Restaurant Association, by 2010, the restaurant industry is expected to have more than 1 million individual locations throughout the United States.

Casual-Dining Restaurants

These establishments appeal to a wide audience, ranging from members of Generation Y to Generation X to baby boomers with families, to seniors, and they provide a variety of food items, from appetizers and salads to main dishes and desserts. Casual-dining restaurants offer comfortable atmospheres with midrange prices. Many center on a theme that is incorporated into their menus and décor.

Ethnic Restaurants

Ethnic restaurants enjoy a significant share of the U.S. restaurant market. They range from quick-service places with limited menu selections to upscale eateries with a wide variety of menu items. Their menus typically include Americanized versions of ethnic dishes, as well as more authentic food. Most ethnic restaurants also include a few American cuisine dishes.

In the United States, the three most popular kinds of ethnic restaurants are Italian, Chinese, and Mexican. Other popular types include Indian, Thai, Caribbean, English, French, German, Japanese, Korean, Mediterranean, and Vietnamese. An even wider variety of ethnic restaurants can thrive in areas with a culturally diverse population, such as large metropolitan areas.

Setting Up Your Facility

The major factors to think about in terms of a restaurant's design are the size and layout of the dining room, kitchen space, storage areas, and office. Dining space will occupy most of your facility, followed by the kitchen and preparation area and then by storage. If you have an office on the premises—and you should—it will most likely take up the smallest percentage of your space.

You may want to hire a food-service consultant or designer to help you plan your layout, or you can do it yourself. Anthony Allen—co-owner of River City Billiards in Haverhill, Massachusetts—has done it both ways, and he recommends using a consultant. "I'd recommend using a consultant for dining room design, kitchen design, menu design,"

What's on the Menu?

Your restaurant's menu is an important sales and communication tool. It must portray your restaurant's theme clearly and consistently. It also must clearly describe the dishes you offer and their prices. Some restaurant owners also use the menu to describe the history of their operation or to provide other information that customers may find interesting. Be sure to make your menu attractive and easy to read.

If you run an upscale, fine-dining establishment, use a paper menu with a cloth binder. Many midscale and upscale restaurants use paper or laminated menus. If you plan to make changes to your menu throughout the year, a cost-effective method is to use plastic menu covers and insert paper menus that can be changed whenever necessary. The plastic covers are easy to clean and preserve paper menus for extended use.

If you offer takeout service or delivery, consider a smaller version of your standard menu printed on inexpensive paper for customers to take with them.

---

he says. "All those components have to work together. If you have one weak link, it can break up your whole system."

The design of your restaurant should promote an efficient operation. The kitchen should be close to the dining room so that the waitstaff can serve meals while they are still hot—or cold, as the case may be. The office is the least important factor in the design. You can locate it in the back of the restaurant or even in the basement, along with the storage area. Consider which personnel will need access to which items, then try to locate these items as conveniently as possible to the appropriate workstations.

Customer Service Area

This area is important because it determines the first impression your restaurant will make on your guests. It must accurately convey the atmosphere of the restaurant in a way that takes advantage of the space available. Your customer service area should include a waiting area for customers, a cashier's station, public restrooms, and a bar, if you choose to have one.

The waiting area and cashier's station should be located near the entrance. The cashier's station can be designed as a small counter with a cash register, or you can use more space

> **Smart Tip** *Tip...*
>
> Before hiring a consultant, determine exactly what you want help with, then get a complete proposal in writing, including the scope of the work, a timetable, and a fee schedule.

to display merchandise or any baked goods you might sell.

If you decide to set up a small retail center, your cashier's station will take up a little more room, and you'll have to invest in a counter with a glass casing or shelves. This is a small investment, however, when you consider the potential return on the additional sales.

You can use your cashier's station as the host or hostess station, or you can set up a separate station at the threshold between the customer service area and the dining area. A host or hostess stand usually consists of a small wooden podium with a ledger for recording the names of waiting guests.

The waiting area itself should have a few

Bright Idea

A popular and effective marketing technique used by quick-service restaurants is offering value meals. These meals typically include a main item, side dish, and beverage, all packaged at a price lower than a customer would pay to buy each item separately. For example, a hamburger restaurant may offer a value meal of a burger, fries, and soft drink. A Mexican restaurant might offer a burrito, side salad, and beverage. Like fast food in general, value meals offer convenience and savings to the customer.

benches lining its walls. Don't skimp on these seats. They should be cushioned, unless your theme dictates otherwise, so your customers are comfortable during their wait. If the wait turns out to be long, and your seats are hard and uncomfortable, chances are you will lose customers and generate some bad word of mouth.

In some restaurants, a bar will generate a good portion of the operation's revenue. Profit margins on beverage sales are much higher than on food sales, so a bar will help improve your bottom line. Generally speaking, you should have one bar seat for every three dining seats. For example, if you have 150 dining seats, your bar should have about 50 seats, including bar stools and seats at tables. Allow about 2 square feet of floor space per stool. Your tables should have about 10 to 12 square feet per customer.

A bar also provides an additional waiting area for your restaurant. It's a good place for your customers to relax and enjoy themselves while their table is being prepared.

Dining Area

This is where you'll be making the bulk of your money, so don't cut corners when designing and decorating your dining room.

Visit restaurants in your area and analyze the décor. Watch the diners. Do they react positively to the décor? Is it comfortable, or do people appear to be shifting in their seats throughout their meals? Make notes of what works well and what does not, and apply this to your own décor plans.

The space required per seat varies according to the type of restaurant. For a small casual-dining restaurant, you'll need to provide about 15 to 18 square feet per seat to assure comfortable seating and enough aisle space so servers have room to move between the tables.

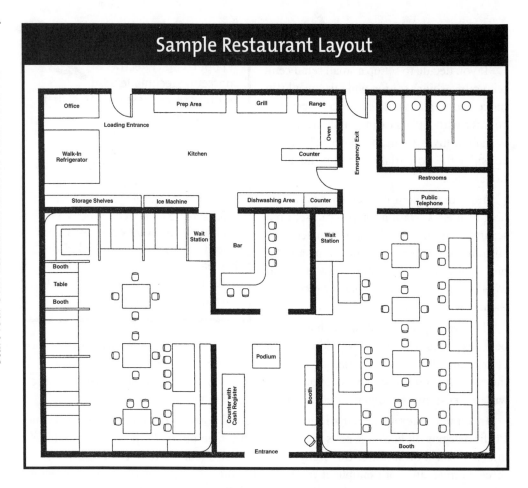

Sample Restaurant Layout

Production Area

Too often, the production area in a restaurant is inefficiently designed, and the result is a poorly organized kitchen and less-than-top-notch service. Your floor plan should be streamlined to provide the most efficient delivery of food to the dining area.

Keep your menu in mind as you determine each element in the production area. You'll need to include space for food preparation, cooking, dishwashing, trash disposal, receiving, inventory storage, and employee facilities and an area for a small office where daily management duties can be performed.

The food preparation, cooking, and baking areas are where the actual production of food will take place. Allow about 12 percent of your total space for food production. You'll need room for prep and steam tables, fryers, a cooking range with griddle top, small refrigerators that you will place under the prep and steam tables, a freezer for storing perishable goods, soft drink and milk dispensers, an ice bin, a broiler, exhaust fans for the ventilation system, and other items, depending on your particular operation.

Arrange this area so everything is only a couple of steps away from the cook. You should also design it in such a way that two or more cooks can work side by side during your busiest hours.

You'll want to devote about 4 percent of your total space to the dishwashing and trash areas. Place your dishwashing area toward the rear of the kitchen. You can usually set this up in a corner so it doesn't get in the way of the cooks and servers. Set up the dishwashing area so the washer can develop a production line.

Customer Areas

The areas that have the greatest impact on your customers are the dining area, waiting area, and restrooms. Essential items for your dining area include china or dishware, glasses, napkins (either cloth or paper), flatware, and an assortment of containers for foods not served on plates. Make sure all your tableware is compatible with your overall concept. Plan to pay about $2,000 to $3,500 for a complete set of dinnerware.

The furniture and fixtures in your dining area should match your concept and be appropriate to the market you are trying to attract. For example, a family-style restaurant needs to have tables and booths that are comfortable and can accommodate children's booster seats and highchairs. A fine-dining establishment should be more elegant, with tables situated to provide your patrons with privacy.

Develop a uniform atmosphere throughout the public areas of your restaurant. That means the décor of your waiting area, dining room, bar, and even restrooms should match.

Equipment

Getting your restaurant properly furnished and equipped requires a substantial investment, both financially and in terms of taking the time to make the best choices. It's important not to skimp when it comes to developing a customized plan for your particular operation. You can use the information in this section as a guide.

Production Equipment

Regardless of the type of restaurant you're opening, you're going to need production equipment. While specific equipment needs will vary from one restaurant to another, most establishments serving hot meals will have to equip a service and preparation kitchen.

If you're entering a facility that already has a kitchen, it may have much of the equipment you need. You can modify what's there to meet your needs and add any additional pieces.

Outfitting your preparation kitchen requires a substantial amount of equipment. Plan to budget anywhere from $27,000 to $40,000 for your heavy-production equipment.

Restaurant Major Equipment and Fixtures

- ❏ Bakers' bins and tables
- ❏ Bar
- ❏ Beverage dispensing system
- ❏ Blender
- ❏ Broiler
- ❏ Can openers
- ❏ Cash register
- ❏ Cheese melter
- ❏ Coffee maker
- ❏ Convection oven
- ❏ Dishwasher
- ❏ Food cutter
- ❏ Freezer
- ❏ Fryer
- ❏ Garbage disposal
- ❏ Griddle-top range with an oven
- ❏ Hand truck (dolly)
- ❏ Heat lamps
- ❏ Ice-cream cabinet
- ❏ Ice machine
- ❏ Ladles
- ❏ Meat grinder
- ❏ Microwave oven
- ❏ Mixer
- ❏ Pans
- ❏ Portion scale
- ❏ Pot holders
- ❏ Prep and steam table
- ❏ Preparation sinks
- ❏ Pressureless steamer
- ❏ Refrigerator
- ❏ Roll warmer
- ❏ Sandwich table
- ❏ Security system
- ❏ Signage
- ❏ Slicer
- ❏ Soap dispensers
- ❏ Soda system
- ❏ Spatulas
- ❏ Spoons
- ❏ Steam kettle
- ❏ Storage shelves
- ❏ Three-compartment sink
- ❏ Toaster
- ❏ Tongs
- ❏ Utensil rack
- ❏ Ventilation system

Before you buy anything, study all the developments that have taken place in the industry and look for versatile, cost-effective equipment.

Most full-service restaurants will have a mixer, a slicer, preparation sinks, a portion scale, a food cutter, baker's bins and tables, a meat grinder, a blender, a griddle-top range with an oven, a convection oven, a fryer, a cheese melter, a broiler, a pressureless steamer, a steam kettle, and a refrigerator and freezer in their preparation kitchens.

Figure on spending another $1,000 to $2,500 for small-production items like ladles, tongs, spoons, pans, potholders, spatulas, can openers, and other items.

The service area of the kitchen is typically where the final touches are put on the plate and where side orders like salad, soup, sandwiches, and so forth are prepared. A kitchen helper or the server will generally be responsible for food preparation in the service kitchen.

A complete service kitchen should consist of a prep and steam table, a toaster, heat lamps, a microwave oven, a utensil rack, a roll warmer and a sandwich table. You'll also

want to place your beverage center in or near your service kitchen. You'll need a coffee-maker, an ice machine, a beverage stand, a soda system, an ice-cream cabinet, and a water station. You'll end up spending from about $10,000 to $18,000 to equip this area.

Dishwashing Equipment

A three-stage dishwashing machine is probably the best way to tackle your dishwashing needs. The machine will cost from $3,000 to $9,000. Installing the equipment, complete with landing area, dish table, garbage disposal, and three-compartment sink, will run you anywhere from $4,000 to $20,000.

Receiving and Storage Equipment

The largest and most costly piece of equipment in your receiving and storage area will be your walk-in refrigerator/freezer, which will cost between $2,000 and $6,000. This will be your main storage area and one of your most important pieces of equipment, because it will preserve your food and keep it fresh. Don't cut corners here.

Your receiving area will also need a scale, a breakdown table, and shelving for the walk-in refrigerator/freezer. You should be able to pick these items up for $1,500 to $3,000.

How Much Do You Need?

Use the following chart to determine how much tableware and how many dishes and glasses to buy for your restaurant. Simply multiply the quantity needed by your restaurant's seating capacity.

- O 2 spoons and knives
- O 1 iced-tea spoon
- O 1 soup spoon
- O 3 forks

- O 2 salad plates
- O 2 cups, saucers, and plates
- O 1 12-oz. soda and iced-tea glass
- O 1 ice cream/salsa dish

Bar Equipment

Outfitting a lounge area in a restaurant can be almost as taxing as buying equipment for the restaurant. The first thing you'll need, of course, is the bar. You can buy a standard bar with a refrigerator underneath from an equipment dealer, or you can have one custom made. Either way, plan to spend about $4,000 to $7,000 for the bar.

Equipping the bar will require a cash register, a three-compartment sink with drain board, an ice bin, an ice machine, a beverage-dispensing system, a beer-dispensing system, glasses, mixers, blenders, ice crushers, bottle openers, and other miscellaneous tools. Altogether, the bar equipment will cost between $10,000 and $18,000.

One of the most important pieces of equipment for your bar is your beverage-dispensing system. You'll want one that performs a variety of functions. Two types of automatic beverage dispensers are available: one for mixes and one for liquor. A seven-valve dispensing system that can calibrate the amount of mix served will be sufficient when you start out. You can lease this piece of equipment for $150 to $300 per month, and leasing makes it easier to upgrade the equipment if demand warrants.

You can also pour liquor by hand. To help with portion control, you can attach pre-pour plastic spouts to each open bottle. These prevent overpouring by dispensing a measured amount of liquor into a drink. Bar equipment manufacturers usually sell these spouts for $28 and up apiece.

Tableware and Miscellaneous Supplies

Purchase your tableware, dishes, and glasses based on the seating capacity of your operation. (See "How Much Do You Need?" on page 41, for quantity guidelines.) In addition, you'll need salt, pepper, and sugar containers for each table, plus about a dozen sets for backup. Don't forget about a dozen sets of tongs and a dozen large pans.

You will also need paper products such as napkins, doggie bags, to-go containers with covers, place mats, towels, and tissues. Suppliers can advise you on how large an order you should place based on your seating capacity and anticipated volume.

Other important items are ashtrays, potholders, spatulas, a wire whisk, a can opener, towel dispensers, garbage cans, a first-aid kit, a mop, a bucket, a broom, a dustpan, and bus boxes.

Uniforms

Most restaurants require their staff to wear uniforms, giving employees and the restaurant a more professional appearance. Your cooking staff may need aprons, chef's hats, hairnets, and other items. Uniforms for serving personnel are available in a wide range of styles and colors. Choose attractive uniforms and, if possible, pick uniforms that reflect the theme of your establishment.

Inventory

A restaurant's inventory consists of items used in the preparation of meals and other restaurant fare. This includes fresh food items such as milk, produce, and meat and preserved items such as canned vegetables and frozen sauces. Nonfood items, which also make up part of a restaurant's inventory, may include garnishes, miniature umbrellas for drinks, and disposable bibs for customers who order messy dishes like ribs or lobster. Restaurant supplies such as napkins, paper towels, cups, plates, and flatware are considered equipment rather than inventory because they are not actually food.

Your basic stock must fulfill two functions: First, it should provide customers with a reasonable assortment of food products. Second, it should cover the normal sales demands of your business. To calculate basic stock accurately, you must review sales during a set time period, such as a full year of business. Of course, during your start-up phase, you will have no previous sales and stocking figures to guide you, so you'll project your first year's stock requirements based on your business plan.

Depending on the size and type of your restaurant, during your first year, you can expect to spend anywhere from $9,000 to $65,000 on food, $2,500 to $17,000 on beverages, and $400 to $1,200 on paper products.

Staffing

There are several categories of personnel in the restaurant business: managers, cooks, servers, buspersons, dishwashers, hosts, and bartenders. Each has a specific function and contributes to the operation of the restaurant. When your restaurant is still new, you may find that some of the duties will cross over from one category to another. For example, the manager may double as the host, and servers may also bus tables. Because of this, be sure to hire people who express a willingness to be flexible in their duties.

Your payroll costs, including your own salary and that of your managers, should be about 24 to 35 percent of your total gross sales. If payroll costs are more than 35 percent of gross sales, you should look for ways to either cut those costs or increase sales.

Most restaurant employees typically work shifts from 10 A.M. to 4 P.M. or 4 P.M. to closing. One lead cook may need to arrive at your restaurant early in the morning to begin preparing soups, bread, and other items to be served that day.

Manager

The most important employee in most restaurants is the manager. He or she can help you with your duties or handle them entirely if you plan to be an absentee owner.

Your best candidate for the job will have already managed a restaurant in your area and will be familiar with local buying sources, suppliers, and methods. A manager should be able to open and close the restaurant; purchase food and beverages; open the cash register(s); track inventory; train and manage the staff; deal with suppliers; develop and implement a marketing strategy; handle other miscellaneous duties. Beyond these responsibilities, the manager must reflect the style and character of your restaurant. Don't hire a cowboy to manage your fine-dining establishment.

A good manager should have at least three years of nonmanagement restaurant experience in addition to two years of managerial experience. It's often best to hire a manager with a background in small restaurants because this type of person will know how to run a noncorporate eatery. As a rule, restaurant chains buy in mass quantities from central suppliers, which means chain managers probably won't have the buying experience your operation requires.

You'll also want a manager who has leadership skills and the ability to supervise personnel in the kitchen, service area, hospitality entrance, bar, lounge, and restrooms, and who can also make customers feel welcome and comfortable.

Restaurant managers typically work long hours—as many as 50 to 60 hours a week—which can contribute to a high burnout rate. To combat this potential and to reduce turnover, be careful not to overwork your manager, and be sure he or she has adequate time off to relax.

To get the quality of manager you want, you'll have to pay well. Depending on your location, expect to pay a seasoned manager $30,000 to $42,000 a year, plus a percentage of sales. An entry-level manager will earn $22,000 to $26,000 but will not have the skills of a more experienced candidate. If you can't offer a high salary, work out a profit-sharing arrangement; this is an excellent way to hire good people and to motivate them to help you build a successful restaurant.

You should hire your manager a month before you open so that the person can help you with setting up your restaurant. Once the business is up and running, the manager will be able to anticipate the slowest times of the day or week and schedule his or her off-hours during those periods. Depending on your level of hands-on work and the size of your operation, the manager should hire and train one or two assistant managers so the restaurant will run smoothly in his or her—and your—absence.

A good manager can make you, and a poor manager can break you, so take your time finding the right person for the job.

Tip...

Smart Tip

Be sure your entire wait-staff is familiar with everything on the menu. They should know how items are prepared, how they taste, and if special requests can be accommodated. Spend at least 15 minutes with your entire crew every day before the restaurant opens going over the menu, the specials, and any special events that will be occurring that day.

Chefs

At some restaurants, the star attraction is the chef. A chef creates his or her own culinary masterpieces for you to serve. Chefs command salaries significantly higher than cooks, averaging $650 to $750 a week, and often more. You may also find chefs who are willing to work under profit-sharing plans.

Cooks

When you start out, you'll probably need three cooks—two full time and one part time. One of the full-time cooks should work days, and the other should work evenings. The part-time cook will help during peak hours—such as weekend rushes—and can work as a line cook, doing simple preparation, during slower periods. The full-time cooks can also take care of food preparation before the restaurant opens, during slow times, and after the restaurant closes.

Hire your cooks according to the type of restaurant you want. If your goal is a four-star, fine-dining establishment, you'll want to hire a chef instead of a short-order cook. If you plan to have an exciting and extensive dessert menu, you may want to hire a pastry chef. Cooking schools can usually provide you with the best in the business, but look around and place ads in the paper before you hire. Customers will become regulars only if they know they can expect the best every time they dine at your restaurant—and to provide that, you need top-notch cooks and chefs.

Salaries for cooks vary according to their level of experience and your menu. If you have a fairly complex menu that requires a cook with a great deal of experience, you may have to pay anywhere from $450 to $550 a week. You can pay part-time cooks on an hourly basis; check around to see what the going rate in your area is. College students can make good part-time cooks.

Smart Tip

Tip...

If you want your food prepared according to basic recipes you have developed, hire a cook rather than a chef. Cooks will follow your instructions, whereas chefs typically want to create their own dishes in addition to preparing standard fare. Chefs generally have more extensive training and command significantly higher salaries than cooks.

Dishwashers

As the job title implies, dishwashers keep clean dishes available in your restaurant. You can probably get by with two part-time dishwashers: one working the lunch shift and the second covering the dinner shift. If you're open for breakfast, you can go with either one full-time and one part-time person or three part-time dishwashers. Expect to pay minimum wage to minimum wage plus $1.50 an hour.

Bright Idea

When training servers, give them an opportunity to work in every department of your operation. Let them take reservations, greet and seat guests, bus tables, and even work in the kitchen. With this experience, they'll not only be able to provide superior service once they're out on the floor waiting tables, but they will also be better team players because they'll have a firsthand understanding of everyone else's role in the process of satisfying the customer.

Serving Staff

Finding the right serving staff is just as important as finding the right manager. The servers are the people your customers will have the most interaction with, so they must make a favorable impression to keep customers coming back. Servers must be able to work well under pressure, meeting the demands of customers at several tables while maintaining a positive and pleasant demeanor.

In general, there are only two times of day for waitstaff: very slow and very busy. Schedule your employees accordingly. The lunch rush, for example, usually starts around 11:30 A.M. and continues until 1:30 or 2 P.M. Restaurants are often slow again until the dinner crowd begins arriving around 5:30 to 6 P.M. Volume will typically begin to slow at about 8 P.M. This is why some restaurants are only open for peak lunch and dinner times. During slow periods, your waitstaff can take care of other duties, such as refilling condiment containers.

Because servers in most types of establishments earn a good portion of their income from tips, they are usually paid the minimum wage for tipped employees (which is lower than the standard minimum wage) or slightly above. It's also customary for the waitstaff to share their tips with the buspersons who clean the tables at their stations. In fact, some restaurants require their servers to pay the buspersons assigned to their sections 10 percent of their tips.

When your restaurant is new, you may want to hire only experienced servers so you don't have to provide extensive training. But as you become established, you should develop a training program to help your employees understand your philosophy and the image you want to project.

As part of your serving staff, you may want to hire runners who are responsible only for delivering food from the kitchen, freeing up the servers to focus on the customers.

Hosting Staff

Depending on the size and style of your restaurant, you may need someone to seat guests, take reservations and act as cashier. You may want to hire someone part time to cover the busy periods and have the waitstaff or manager handle these duties during slower times. Hire people-oriented, organized individuals for host positions; after all,

How Many Servers Does it Take . . .

The number of servers you need depends on the type of service you want to offer, your table turnover rate, the size of your restaurant and the type of technology you're using. In the past, when everything was done by hand, there were two forms of service. In the first, the server worked alone with maybe 15 seats to handle. A single server took the order, got the drinks, served the food, and wrote the check with just the help of a busboy. The other form was more elaborate, with a captain, a front and back waiter and a busboy for each station. A team could handle 25 to 30 seats.

But technology has changed the way many restaurants approach staffing and service. Computers are streamlining the ordering and serving processes, with one server taking the order and entering it into the computer, where it is transferred to the kitchen, and then, when the food is ready, it's delivered by a runner who may have no further contact with the guests. A restaurant may have one or two runners whose sole job is to deliver food as it comes out of the kitchen.

Try to design a floor plan that will let you create flexible stations that can be adjusted based on your volume and staffing. If you're using runners to support the servers, and the server is doing everything else except delivering the food and busing the tables, limit each server to 25 seats, or "covers." If you're not using runners, limit it to no more than 15 seats per server.

they will determine the first impression your customers form of your service staff. Students often make great hosts. Pay for this position typically ranges from minimum wage to minimum wage plus $1.50 an hour.

Buspersons

Buspersons are responsible for setting up and clearing tables and filling water glasses after customers are seated. Your buspersons should be assigned to stations, just like your waitstaff; in fact, buspersons and servers should work together as a team. Buspersons should be trained to pay attention to their stations, refilling water glasses as necessary, making sure condiment containers are clean and full when the table is turned, and generally supporting the server.

Typically, buspersons will be part-timers who work during peak periods. Servers can handle busing tables during slow times. Consider hiring high school and college students as buspersons. These positions usually earn minimum wage plus a portion of the tips received by the servers they assist.

Bartenders

If you have a small bar in your restaurant and it is only open at night, one bartender will probably be sufficient. Of course, if you expect to earn a good portion of your business from the bar, you'll need two bartenders—one full- and one part-time person to assist during peak periods. If your bar attracts customers during both the lunch and dinner periods, you'll need two or three bartenders, or you might try a combination of a full-time bartender or bar manager, plus two or three part-time helpers.

The bartender begins his or her day by prepping the bar, which includes preparing the condiments and mixers for the entire day as well as ordering supplies. The bartender also needs to check the liquor requisition sheet and inventory, and restock the bar. If you use a computerized beverage-dispensing and inventory-management system, the bartender will check the meters and hook up the necessary bottles.

The night bartender will close the bar. Last call for drinks should occur 30 minutes before the legally required closing time. The closing process usually includes packaging the garnishes and placing them in the refrigerator, wiping down the bar area and stools, and restocking the bar.

It's important to look for a bartender who knows how to pour regular well drinks and prepare special requests. Experienced bartenders can make small talk and relate to people individually while juggling several drink orders in their heads. They also know when to stop pouring drinks for intoxicated customers and call a taxi or other transportation to take the customer home. Bartenders are usually paid an hourly wage—often $6 to $9 an hour—plus tips.

6

Pizzeria

The first pizza restaurants appeared in the United States during the 1930s. In the decades that followed, pizza went from novelty to fad to habit. Originally an Italian dish, pizza is now one of the most popular American fast foods. It's enjoyed as lunch, dinner, and even snacks by consumers of all age groups and socioeconomic backgrounds. People flock to try new varieties, such as Chicago style or Sicilian style, stuffed crusts, double crusts, and creative topping combinations. But as popular as pizza is, the competition is intense—and a successful pizzeria is much more than a great pie.

You have two primary choices when starting a pizzeria. One is a to-go restaurant in a modest facility with a specialized menu highlighted by pizza and beer, limited seating, and a self-service atmosphere. The other is a full-service pizza restaurant with a menu that features not only a variety of pizzas and beer and wine, but also Italian entrees like spaghetti, ravioli, and lasagna; side dishes such as salads (or even a salad bar), and a few desserts.

Stat Fact
Pizza is a $33 billion industry. There are more than 75,000 Italian and pizza restaurants in the United States, and approximately 3 billion pizzas are sold in the United States each year.

Within these generalities, specialization is the key to success for any pizzeria. A to-go pizzeria will specialize in pizza and beverages, perhaps with a limited selection of salads and simple sandwiches. Of course, even a full-service pizzeria will specialize in pizza, though you may offer a wider range of sandwiches, pasta dishes, garlic bread, and salads. If your goal is to open a pizzeria, don't try to grow your operation into a full-service Italian restaurant. This will detract from your image as a pizzeria and will probably reduce your profits.

Stat Fact
October is National Pizza Month. It was so designated in 1987.

An operation that usually works well by itself and can easily be multiplied into a chain is the to-go concept, with anywhere from 30 to 55 seats for a small section of sit-down customer dining but without any table service.

If you don't have the extra money necessary for the sit-down portion of the business when you start, you'll be able to grow into it after things are rolling. Just be sure to plan for that growth, and be sure your facility has the space to accommodate it.

Many to-go pizza stores also deliver and find the revenue from this portion of their market substantial. With a little advertising and two or three licensed drivers from a local high school or college, you can offer the convenience and reap the profits of home and office delivery.

The Pizza

The foundation of a pizzeria is, of course, the pizza. If you don't know how to make a good pizza, hire a good pizza cook who does. Without a good product, you are sure to fail, regardless of what else you do. Invest in top-quality ingredients and preparation

The Art of the Pie

Here's the key to it all: how to make the pizza. Roll out the dough about two inches larger than the pan. Press it into the curves of the pan, then pull some slack dough into the center to compensate for shrinkage, and trim the edges around the pan. Spread sauce with a ladle over the entire surface to the edges. Use more cheese on the plain cheese pizzas and less on those with other toppings. Add the toppings chosen by the customer, spreading them evenly. Never overload the pie—it will take so long to cook through to the middle that the bottom will burn.

The oven should be set from 500 to 550 degrees Fahrenheit—hotter if you are busy and opening the oven door often. If you are using fresh dough, cook the pizza in the pan until the top is golden brown, then slide the pie off the pan to brown the bottom.

Remove the pizza from the oven with the peel (the long-handled wooden spatula), slide it onto a cool pizza pan, cut and serve.

methods, and make every pizza as if you were going to eat it yourself. Do that, and your customers will keep coming back.

Should you offer thick or thin crust? It depends on your market. A thick, doughy crust tends to be popular in the Eastern United States, while in the West, the crust of choice is generally thin and crisp. However, you'd be wise to provide customers a choice and offer both types. For thinner crusts, you can use preformed shells, but make the thick ones yourself.

You might also want to offer a choice of crust flavors. For instance, you could try to sprinkle special toppings or spices—such as garlic, Parmesan cheese, or poppy seeds—on the crust before baking. The market response to these "specialty" crusts has been tremendous, and you can offer them for free or for a nominal extra charge, because they cost you practically nothing extra, yet they make your pizzas much more flavorful. If you offer a variety of crusts, be sure to promote them on your menu and other marketing materials.

Stat Fact
While total food service is growing annually at 1.3 percent, pizza and Italian operations are growing by an average of 6.3 percent.

Beyond the basic crust is the style of pizza. Sicilian- and Chicago-style pizzas are varieties with thick, chewy crusts. Chicago-style pies are baked in a deep dish, while Sicilian is baked on a flat pan. But the ingredients are essentially the

And to Top it Off

What do Americans want on their pizzas? Their favorite topping is pepperoni. Other popular toppings are mushrooms, extra cheese, sausage, green peppers, and onions. Anchovies rank last on the list of favorite toppings.

In some parts of the country, gourmet toppings are gaining in popularity. Pizza lovers are experimenting with such toppings as chicken, oysters, crayfish, dandelions, sprouts, eggplant, shrimp, artichoke hearts, and tuna. Approximately two-thirds of Americans prefer meat toppings, while the remaining one-third prefer vegetarian toppings. Women are twice as likely as men to order vegetarian toppings on their pizza.

same, so you can try experimenting with both traditional and other styles to see what sells best in your market. But don't get carried away with variety: You don't want to overburden your cook with too many shapes and sizes that have different cooking times, require customized pans or need special dough-rolling procedures.

Setting Up Your Facility

A to-go pizzeria has minimal space requirements. Most range in size from small take-out and home-delivery operations of only 800 square feet to larger limited seating-capacity operations of 1,500 square feet. For a full-service pizzeria, you'll need a facility between 2,500 and 4,000 square feet. Depending on the type of facility you want to open and your own resources, expect to spend $70,000 to $1.5 million to get your pizzeria ready for your grand opening.

There are no textbook ratios for distribution of space in a pizzeria, but a good formula is to allocate 20 percent for your customer service area (25 percent in a strictly to-go/home-delivery operation), 45 percent for the dining area, and 35 percent for your production area. Of course, if you do not provide a dining area, your production area will be adjusted upward to 75 percent.

For dine-in pizzerias, allotting 60 to 65 percent of the space for dining and customer service allows adequate room for quality food production. If you let the production area fall

> **Stat Fact**
> As if we didn't know already: Kids between the ages of 3 and 11 prefer pizza for lunch and dinner above all other foods.

below 35 percent, you run the risk of limiting yourself in a way that could result in poor-quality food.

Customer Service Area

Your customer service area determines the first impression your customers will have of your pizzeria's atmosphere. Use this space to create an appropriate ambience that takes maximum advantage of the available space. The customer service area should include a waiting area for customers, a cashier's station, and public restrooms.

The exact layout will depend on whether your operation is a to-go or full-service pizzeria. With both types, the waiting area and cashier's station will be located directly at the entrance to the facility, but this is where the similarities end.

In addition to the waiting area and cashier's station, a to-go pizzeria will have an order/pickup counter that serves both the takeout and sit-down customers. This counter will usually stretch wall-to-wall across the facility to separate the production area from the customer service and dining areas. The cashier's station should be incorporated into the order/pickup counter so customers can pay when they order.

Line the walls of the waiting area for takeout customers with bench seats. Don't skimp on quality here; provide cushioned seating so your customers are comfortable during their wait. Think about it: Even a short wait seems like a long time when someone needs

Location Is Everything

Most pizzerias are located near business sections of cities and towns. The industry leaders—Domino's, Pizza Hut, and Papa John's—look for strong lunch business, as well as early dinner, dinner, and post-dinner business. Your best location choice is one with a strong day and night-time population, easy access for both cars and pedestrians, and a consistent traffic flow.

In the past, most pizzerias were in freestanding buildings, but that trend has shifted. Now pizzerias are springing up in all sorts of locations, including shopping centers and mall food courts. You may find it profitable to locate your business either in a mall or a freestanding building next to a mall, which will let you share the mall's traffic. Another good location would be one that is convenient to commercial office developments. You can turn almost any space into a thriving pizzeria if you have the customer base, the knowledge, and the capital to make it happen. Just be sure your market research supports your final location decision.

Stat Fact

Collectively, Americans eat approximately 100 acres of pizza each day, or 350 slices per second. People across America eat an average of 46 slices (23 pounds) of pizza a year, and 93 percent of Americans eat at least one single-serving pizza per month.

to get back to the office at lunchtime or is tired, hungry, and in a hurry to get home in the evening. Hard seats or no seats in an uncomfortable waiting area can generate unfavorable word-of-mouth advertising and may send customers to your competition.

In a full-service pizzeria, make the cashier's station a small counter that parallels one wall at the entrance. To conserve space, the cashier's station can double as the host stand, or you can set up a separate host stand at the threshold between the customer service area and the dining area. A small wooden lectern with a ledger-type book to record the names of waiting guests, and perhaps a storage area underneath for menus, is usually sufficient for a host stand. As in a to-go pizzeria, the waiting area should have a few bench-style seats lining its walls.

Locate your beverage center behind the customer service counter toward the end. If you choose to have customers serve themselves beverages—as many fast-food and self-service restaurants are doing these days—place the dispenser near the front counter so your employees can keep an eye on it. You need to make sure it is clean and functioning properly at all times.

If you have sit-down customers, you will need to provide public restrooms, which are usually located close to the dining area.

Dining Area

Whether your pizzeria is self-service or full-service, a sit-down dining area increases your profit potential. That's why it's imperative that you don't cut corners when designing and decorating your dining room. This is, after all, the area that has the most impact on your customers.

The space required per seat will vary depending on your type of operation. In a to-go, self-service pizzeria, the amount of space per seat should range between 12 and 15 square feet. A full-service pizzeria will need between 15 and 18 square feet per seat. This ensures comfortable seating and enough aisle space so servers have room to move between tables.

Essential service items for your dining area include dishware, glasses, flatware, and an assortment of containers to hold foods not served on plates. Salt and pepper shakers and napkin holders for each table are optional. If you decide to present them on request, be sure you have enough for at least half the tables at any given time. If your menu includes bread with most meals, you'll need as many bread baskets as you have tables.

Keep your overall concept in mind when choosing your dinnerware. Many to-go pizzerias place paper plates and plastic forks, spoons, and knives on a self-service table

Sample To-Go Pizzeria Layout

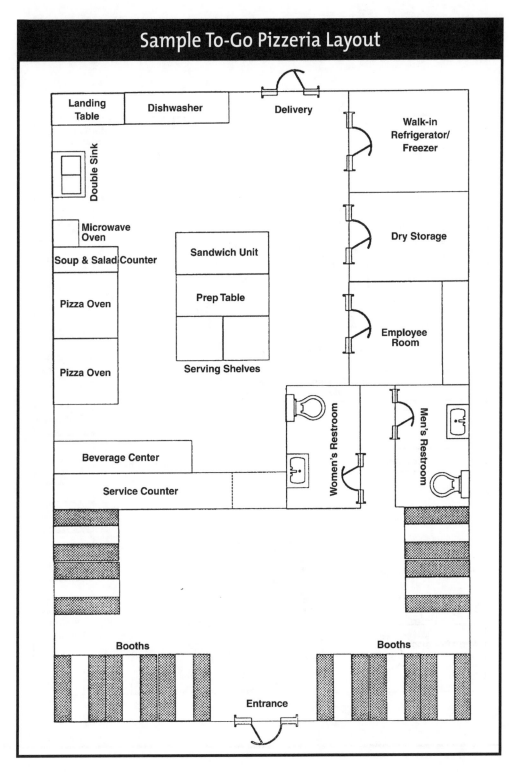

Sample Full-Service Pizzeria Layout

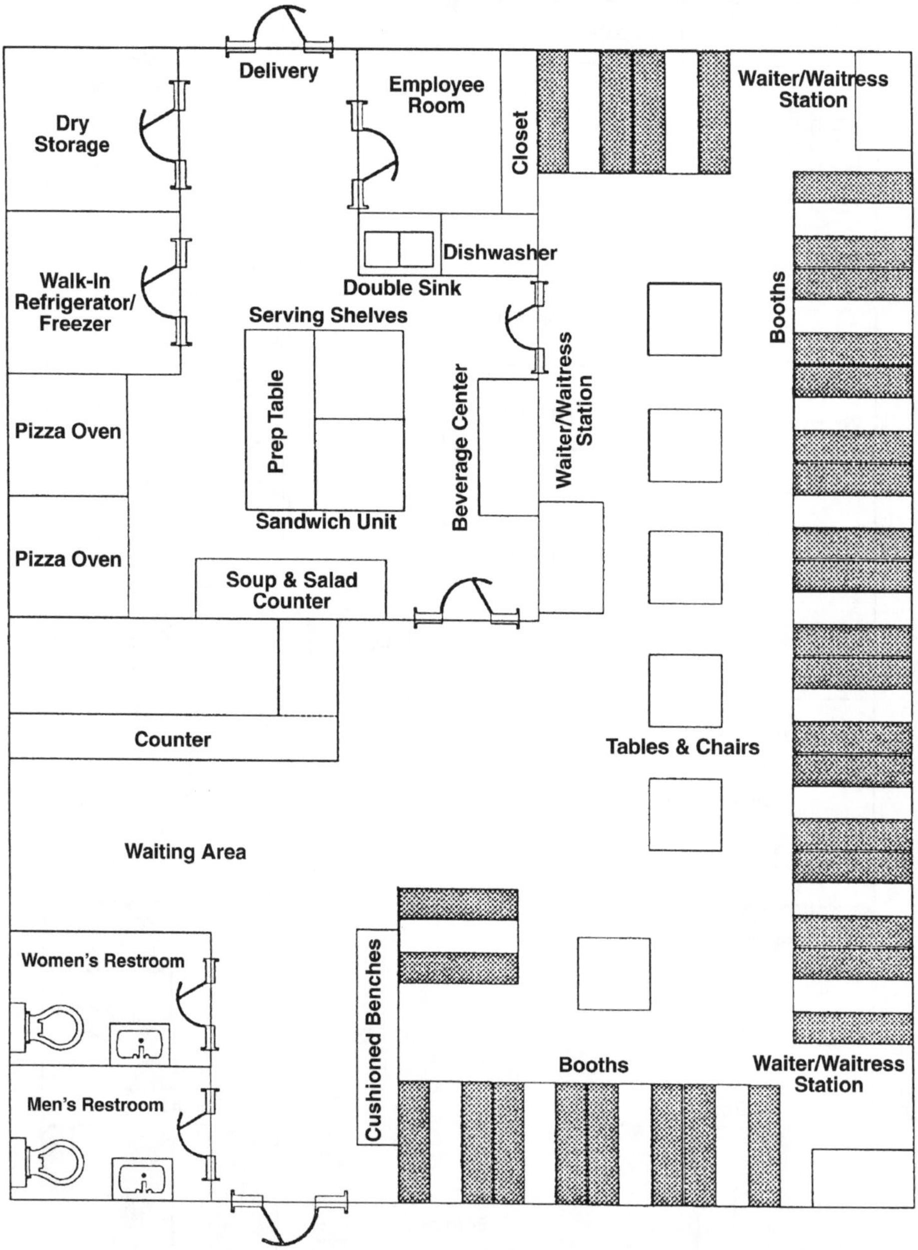

Delivery

Employee Room

Closet

Waiter/Waitress Station

Dry Storage

Walk-In Refrigerator/ Freezer

Dishwasher

Double Sink

Serving Shelves

Prep Table

Sandwich Unit

Beverage Center

Waiter/Waitress Station

Booths

Pizza Oven

Pizza Oven

Soup & Salad Counter

Counter

Tables & Chairs

Waiting Area

Women's Restroom

Men's Restroom

Cushioned Benches

Booths

Waiter/Waitress Station

and serve the beverages in mugs. A full-service pizzeria can't get away with this cost-cutting approach. For a full-service pizzeria, plan to spend about $2,000 to $3,500 for a complete set of dinnerware.

Production Area

You need enough room in the food preparation area to accommodate prep tables, pizza oven(s), a range, microwave oven(s), a small refrigerator with a freezer, an exhaust fan for the ventilation system, utensils and smallware, and other food-production equipment. To-go pizzerias might require less food-prep space than full-service operations, depending on menu offerings and specific equipment needs. In any case, arrange this area so everything is positioned within a few steps of the cook. It should also be designed so that two or more cooks can work side by side during rush periods.

Dishwashing and trash areas should be located toward the rear of your operation, near the receiving port. Allow about 4 percent of your total space for these areas. Dishwashing equipment can usually be situated in a corner so it doesn't get in the way of food-service personnel. A to-go pizzeria may not need a commercial dishwasher, but you will need a three-compartment sink as well as adjacent counter space and racks for washing cooking utensils and the small amount of tableware you use.

Your production area will also need receiving and inventory storage facilities, an employee room, and a small office or administrative area. (See Chapters 4 and 5 for more on setting up your facility.)

Equipment

Aside from building preparation, equipment will be one of your biggest start-up expenses. New equipment to run your pizzeria will cost anywhere from $50,000 to $100,000, depending on the type of operation you choose. The good news is that you don't have to buy everything new. This section will explain the process of deciding what you need, how and where to find it, and how to acquire it for as little as possible.

Equipment selection for a pizzeria is a complex process and will require some time and research beyond the scope of this guide. For example, some ovens can perform a multitude of cooking procedures, from baking pizza and cooking meats to reheating entrees and melting cheese on appetizers. Ice machines, on the other hand, have only one use: They make ice. Some equipment is basic to every food-service operation; other items are unique to pizzerias. The prerequisite to purchasing equipment is knowing exactly what you need to prepare the foods on your menu. It will also help you to know how other pizzerias are equipped. Before Anthony Allen started his pizzeria in Massachusetts, he visited other pizzerias, observed as much as he could and asked as many questions as possible. "I tried to find people to interview, people who worked in pizza places and people

▲

Where the Ovens Are

You have three choices when it comes to pizza ovens: electric, gas, or wood fired. Electric is the least desirable because it doesn't generate enough heat to cook the pizza crust properly. Pizzeria owner Anthony Allen says gas generates a good hot, dry heat, which can produce a consistently good product. But, he adds, "Wood fire beats gas and electric hands down because you can get the temperature almost twice as hot as you can with a gas oven. In my opinion, the rate of that heat is what really makes the dough: deliciously crunchy on the outside and chewy on the inside. Wood-fire heat is the way to go." He insists that even the nonconnoisseurs who routinely order pizza from takeout chains can tell the difference between a conventionally-cooked pizza and a wood-fired pizza.

Though wood-fired ovens may be best, they're not cheap. Anthony and his business partner, Michael Greene, installed two wood-fired ovens imported from Italy in their restaurant at approximately $12,000 each. "They give us a superior product," he says.

who sold the equipment," he says. "I found out as much as I could, then I put together what I thought was reasonable."

You may want to spend some time talking with a restaurant consultant before making your final purchase decisions. Don't rush into choosing your furniture, fixtures, and equipment—especially if you're not sure exactly what you want or require or how it will all blend together.

Food-Production Equipment

While the equipment needs of a to-go pizzeria and a full-service facility will vary, one piece of equipment essential to both is a pizza oven. Your oven should be able to heat to 650 degrees Fahrenheit and have a minimum deck space of 32 inches deep and 42 inches wide, with a 7-inch mouth. A new single-deck oven can be purchased for $2,500 to $4,000. If you anticipate a sales volume of $1,500 or more per week, buy a double unit for $4,000 to $7,500. Because gas ovens heat more intensely than electric ovens, most pizza chefs prefer them.

In addition to the oven, you'll need a range or hot plate for cooking sauces and pastas. You can buy a used household range for about $125 or a used commercial gas hot plate for about $100. Whichever you choose, set it up next to the pizza oven for the cook's convenience. Other necessary items include a toaster oven for preparing garlic bread and a microwave oven for reheating pasta.

Pizzeria Major Equipment and Fixtures Checklist

- ❏ 45-gallon bakers' bins on wheels (2)
- ❏ Beer/wine serving equipment
- ❏ Breakdown table
- ❏ Cash register
- ❏ Coffee maker
- ❏ Company vehicle
- ❏ Dinnerware
- ❏ Dishwasher
- ❏ Dolly/hand truck
- ❏ Dough mixer/blender
- ❏ Dough roller
- ❏ Dry storage shelving
- ❏ Fixtures (booths/tables)
- ❏ Gas hot plate/range
- ❏ Grinder
- ❏ Hand slicer/electric slicer

- ❏ Hot boxes
- ❏ Ice machine
- ❏ Microwave oven
- ❏ Office equipment
- ❏ Office furniture
- ❏ Pasta machine
- ❏ Pizza oven(s)
- ❏ Portion scale
- ❏ Prep table
- ❏ Production-area refrigeration units
- ❏ Scale for receiving area
- ❏ Security system
- ❏ Service counter
- ❏ Signage
- ❏ Soft-drink system
- ❏ Three-compartment sink

The service area of the kitchen is typically where the pizza will be made and side orders (such as salads and bread sticks) prepared. The cook should be in charge of preparing the pizza, and a kitchen helper or the servers (if you have them) can handle side orders.

A complete service area for a pizza kitchen usually contains a prep table, a slicer or grinder, a portion scale, a dough mixer/blender, a dough roller, production hardware, and a utensil rack.

Your health department may require a stainless-steel top on the prep table. If so, a 6-foot table will cost about $100 used and up to $400 new. Otherwise, you can buy a Formica top or work counter for about $50 used. It's a good idea to have an inexpensive second table to use for cutting and boxing orders.

Some pizzerias grind their toppings; others slice them. It doesn't seem to make a lot of difference to customers, so the choice is yours. A slicer is a must, however, if your menu will include Italian sandwiches. A new electric slicer will cost $800 to $3,000 and should last for several years. You may consider a hand slicer with various attachments for smaller jobs; you can expect to pay $250 to $650.

You'll need a small grinder or cheese grater to grate the cheese for your pizzas. You should invest in a good professional grinder, which will range in price from $3,000 to

$4,000. Don't try to "make do" by grating cheese by hand; you'll wear yourself out and probably won't be able to keep up with the demand.

To maintain consistency in quality and give your inventory control procedures a fighting chance, you will need a portion scale. It's not enough to buy the scale—make sure your employees use it. This will help you estimate the amount of each ingredient required to prepare each dish efficiently and with accuracy. If your chefs are "guesstimating" on portions, they'll probably use too much inventory, and you'll be serving your profits rather than taking them to the bank. Dollar for dollar, the $30 to $150 you'll spend on a portion scale may well be the wisest investment you make in your pizzeria.

Assuming you are going to make your own pizza dough but don't want the upper-body workout mixing dough by hand provides, you will need a dough mixer/blender. This is not a necessity when starting, but will probably become crucial as your business grows. A new heavy-duty dough mixer/blender will cost about $1,200, and used ones can be found for as low as $350.

Smart Tip

Budget between $27,000 and $40,000 for the heavy production equipment in your pizza kitchen. Before you buy, study all the new developments in the industry, as new technologies and methods are being developed constantly, and you need to know what's out there so you can make the best choice for your operation. Read trade magazines and industry newspapers to keep up on the latest equipment advances and design innovations.

Bright Idea

Consider using manufactured pizza shells. While pizza connoisseurs say premade crusts don't have the taste of those made with fresh dough, manufactured shells simplify a pizza operation. Try some and see for yourself. There might be a manufacturer in your area who uses a formula that surpasses the run-of-the-mill recipes. You can expect to pay 25 to 30 cents wholesale for a 12-inch (small) pizza shell and more for larger sizes. To find a supplier, look under "Food Products" and "Restaurant Supplies" in the Yellow Pages.

For rolling out your pizza shells, you can either work by hand or purchase a mechanical roller. The speed and efficiency of a mechanical roller lets you prepare shells as you need them. If you're going to do it by hand, however, you can roll the shells in advance and refrigerate them until you're ready to use them. Don't roll more than you can use in two or three hours, though, as shells get tough and gummy if left sitting around too long.

If you are planning on a full-service restaurant and your menu will include a variety of pasta dishes in addition to pizzas, consider investing in a pasta machine. This is a purely optional investment that lets you make your own noodles from scratch rather than buying premade pasta from grocery wholesalers. Because your main menu focus is pizza, a home-kitchen-style pasta machine should be sufficient. You can expect to pay about $200 for a high-quality machine.

Bakers' bins are especially useful in a full-service operation. These will make preparing your pizza crusts, pasta, and other products much easier. Your prep table should have enough space underneath for these large containers. Also, the bins should be on rollers so they can be moved around easily. You'll spend $175 to $350 for bakers' bins.

Utensils and Miscellaneous Equipment

The cost of the small stuff can add up, so pay close attention to what you really need in this area. In a typical pizzeria, you'll need 12 plastic or stainless-steel bins (about $2 each) for pizza ingredients; four 12-inch, four 15-inch, and four 18-inch pizza pans (about $4 each, used) for baking pizzas and sorting dough; and one peel ($7 used to $35 new), which is the large, long-handled wooden spatula that is used to lift the pizzas from the oven. You will also require a large pot (20- to 40-gallon variety for cooking sauce; two four-quart pots (for weighing dough ingredients, etc.); one rolling pin; one can opener; one pizza cutter; one large ladle (for spooning sauce); and knives. Plan to spend $800 to $1,200 on these items.

You may or may not want to insist on uniforms for your cooking staff, but your employees will at least need aprons, chef's hats, and hairnets. Uniforms for servers are available in a variety of styles, colors, and price ranges.

Beverage Center

Your beverage center can be located completely in the service kitchen or split between the service kitchen and the customer service area if you offer self-service drink machines. The typical beverage center will include a coffee machine, an ice machine, a water station, and a soft drink-dispensing system. If you sell beer, the tap should be behind the counter under your employees' control. Bottled beer and wine should also be stored in coolers out of the reach of customers. Expect to spend $6,000 to $11,000 on beverage equipment.

Inventory

Your menu will determine your inventory, but there are some specialty items you must purchase for your pizzeria. Here are some of the more typical inventory categories you'll be dealing with:

- *Meats.* You'll need sliced and processed meats as part of your pizza toppings selection. Some of the more common meats are pepperoni, sausage, and Canadian bacon. You may also need ground beef if you will be offering dishes with meatballs or pasta shells filled with meat (such as ravioli).

- *Dairy products.* Pizzerias use great quantities of cheese as a primary pizza topping. If you are going to make your own pizza crust, garlic bread, or pasta, you may also be using milk and eggs in large quantities.

- *Sauces.* You'll need a variety of sauces, both for pizzas and for other Italian dishes. Sauces can be purchased by the can in bulk quantities or made from scratch. Most restaurateurs buy canned sauces and add various herbs to spice them to taste and give them a unique flavor.

Stat Fact
Pizza Hut is the largest pizza seller in the world, with nearly 13,000 restaurants and combination delivery and takeout units in the United States and more than 90 other countries. Domino's is the world leader in pizza delivery. Papa John's is considered the fastest-growing pizzeria chain in the United States.

- *Fresh produce.* You'll use fresh vegetables as pizza toppings, in salads, and as side dishes.

- *Pastas and breads.* If you make your own pizza dough, pastas, and breads, you'll use a great deal of flour. Some of these products are available either premade or partially prepared, which can speed up your production process.

- *Condiments and dressings.* You will need salt, pepper, cooking oil, garlic, oregano, red pepper flakes, Parmesan cheese, and many other items that help finish off your dishes. If you offer salads, you'll want to stock canned and packaged items like olives, pickles, kidney beans, and garbanzo beans. Unless you are serving only antipasto salads, you'll need a selection of dressings, such as Italian (of course), bleu cheese, French, Thousand Island, and perhaps an herb or honey-mustard flavor. At least one dressing should be low fat.

The Ongoing Battle: Price vs. Quality

Pizzeria owners tend to vacillate between price promotions and focusing on quality in their marketing efforts. A recent Pizza Hut survey asked customers what they ranked as most and least important when choosing a restaurant. More than half—57 percent—ranked the quality of the food as the most important consideration. Meanwhile, 20 percent said the cleanliness of the restaurant was most important, 11 percent ranked the price of the food as most important, 4 percent said their chief concern was speed of service, and 3 percent said it was the courtesy of the employees. Only 4 percent of respondents named quality as their least important concern, while 20 percent said price was least important.

- *Beverages.* Soft drinks are considered necessary beverages for a pizzeria. You will also need to serve coffee, tea, and milk. Beer and wine are very profitable, but state and local licenses may be expensive and are not always easy to obtain.

- *Paper and plastic products.* You will need a variety of paper and plastic products for your takeout and delivery orders, as well as for your dining room service. The list includes straws, napkins, paper cups, bags, plastic tableware, pizza boxes, spaghetti/pasta cartons, and salad containers. Most of these are available from paper products distributors. Check the Yellow Pages for distributors in your area.

- *Hot-food bags.* If you offer delivery, you'll need insulated food bags to keep the pizza and other food warm during transit. Hot-food bags run $25 to $35 each, and you'll need three or four for each driver.

Staffing

How you staff your pizzeria will depend, of course, on the size and scope of your operation. You'll definitely need a cook to make the pizzas and other menu items and a cashier. If you offer sit-down dining, you'll need a host or hostess and waitstaff. If you offer delivery, you'll need drivers. You may also need buspersons and other cleaning staff.

Keep security in mind when planning your staffing. Even a small to-go operation should have at least two people on duty at all times.

Pay scales will vary depending on region and whether or not the position is likely to earn tips. A glance through the help-wanted section of your local newspaper will give you a fairly accurate idea of what you can expect to pay.

Sandwich Shop/
Delicatessen

The wide appeal of sandwiches, both nationally and internationally, ensures the stability of sandwich shops and delicatessens. Sandwiches, after all, have been around for a long time. In fact, the sandwich is named for the fourth Earl of Sandwich, John Montagu. This English nobleman of the 1700s is said to have eaten sandwiches while at the gaming table so he didn't have to take time out for a formal meal.

For centuries, sandwich shops have lined the streets of Europe. One cannot walk down a street in Paris, for instance, without passing a sandwich shop or a bakery that sells baguettes (French long bread) and sandwiches. The croque monsieur (melted ham and cheese on bread) is a very popular sandwich in France. Italians, on the other hand, often make their sandwiches with focaccia (a spiced bread), vegetables, salami, and mozzarella cheese. Sandwiches are no less popular in the United States. Philadelphia, for example, is well known for its "Philly cheesesteak" sandwiches.

One reason sandwich shops are so successful is that they enjoy high profit margins. Sandwich shops and delicatessens can also change their menus quickly and easily to adapt to the current tastes. For example, with the growing interest in health and nutrition in the United States, sandwich shops and delicatessens have started offering more low-fat, healthy ingredients in their sandwiches, salads and other menu items. They've also added a range of low-carb items. In addition, many sandwich shops and delis have been able to keep up with American workers who eat at their workplaces by adding delivery and catering to their sit-down and takeout operations.

Sandwich shops and delicatessens can be differentiated by the foods they serve. Most sandwich shops serve only sandwiches, possibly with some side dishes or desserts. A delicatessen, meanwhile, usually serves a more extensive menu, including sandwiches, prepared meats, smoked fish, cheeses, salads, relishes, and various hot entrees. The word "delicatessen" comes from the French délicatesse, meaning "delicacy."

A full-scale delicatessen will usually have a dining area and offer sit-down service as well as takeout, while a sandwich shop may only offer takeout. This chapter will discuss both types of businesses, and you'll need to decide whether you want to open a sandwich shop, a deli, or a combination of the two.

Factors that contribute to the fast growth of sandwich shops and delis are their start-up costs and operating costs, which tend to be lower than those of other fast-food enterprises. Many sandwich-shop franchises promise start-up packages for as low as $150,000, and some are only $40,000. Low-end independent establishments have started their businesses for as little as $36,500. The average start-up cost for a sandwich shop is $91,800.

Competition

Your competition in most locations will consist of other quick-service outlets (such as fast-food, specialty, and ethnic restaurants, and other sandwich shops and delis), grocery store deli departments, national sandwich shop chains and some sit-down restaurants.

- *Quick-service/fast-food restaurants.* One major advantage a sandwich shop or deli has over many fast-food restaurants is the ability to provide both quick service and healthier food choices. You can promote this as a strong selling point.

You should also be able to compete easily against fast-food restaurant prices. You may not be able to match a 59-cent burger, but you should be able to come close to matching prices for chicken or steak sandwiches, which usually sell for $2.50 or more. If you offer a pickle or coleslaw with your sandwiches, you can sell a more satisfying meal to your customers than some of the fast-food chains, which usually sell just the sandwich.

> **Bright Idea**
>
> If your sandwich shop/or deli will offer party platters or catering as a service, be sure to ask if prospective customers ever buy party platters or use caterers when you conduct your initial market research.

- *Grocery store deli departments.* Because they buy in volume and appear to have a captive audience, an in-store deli may seem like strong competition, but don't let it scare you. Many people just don't think of going to the grocery store for lunch, and they will find your easy-in, easy-out shop preferable to going into a supermarket.
- *National sandwich shop chains.* National chains may have huge advertising budgets, but you have a number of competitive advantages. For one thing, you can offer an innovative menu that's customized to local preferences, and you can provide high-quality food. Personalized service is another plus for an independent operator, and it pays to get to know your customers by name and greet them when they come through the door. Eye contact, good service and a smile go a long way toward building customer loyalty, whether you're competing against a national chain or another independent business.

Setting Up Your Facility

Whether you plan on opening a takeout sandwich shop with a limited menu or a full-scale sit-down delicatessen, you will need enough space for a production area (a kitchen or sandwich preparation area), a customer-service area, a receiving and storage area, and at least one employee restroom. You will also need some kind of office, though some sandwich shop and deli owners use a homebased office to keep commercial space requirements to a minimum. A dining area and public restrooms may also be included in your facility. You will probably need a space with somewhere between 500 and 3,000 square feet.

Converting an existing food-service operation (such as a bakery, deli, or small restaurant) can lower your initial investment. In any case, if you will specialize in serving customers on the go, you can probably get by with 500 to 750 square feet, including kitchen

Catering to Their Every Whim

Offering delivery services and small-scale catering can generate additional revenue for your sandwich shop or deli. You can provide delivery of standard menu items to a specified geographic area around your shop for no charge or a small charge, depending on the market demand.

A catering operation could consist of sandwich and party platters or more elaborate menus. Include both of these options in your market research to determine demand. You'll also need to consider whether your start-up budget allows for the equipment you'll need to provide these additional services. You may want to start out with a small shop and expand your service offerings later. However, knowing your eventual goals will help you make better choices on your initial equipment purchases. Maxine Turner, owner of Cuisine Unlimited in Salt Lake City, started with a catering operation and added three delicatessens. Today, each deli has a catering menu prominently displayed.

See Chapter 10 for more information on starting a catering service.

space. If you want to offer a more extensive menu and allow space for customer seating, you'll want a facility as large as 3,000 square feet.

In a strictly takeout operation, allow 75 percent of your space for your production area, 15 percent for customer service, and 10 percent for storage, restrooms, and a lounge. If you plan to have a combination takeout/sit-down operation, allow about 35 percent of your space for the production area, 5 percent for customer service, 50 percent for the dining area and 10 percent for storage, restrooms, and the lounge.

Production Area

The production area will include space for sandwich and salad preparation. Depending on your menu, it may require space for preparing hot items as well. If you decide to offer sit-down service and a full menu, you will probably want to set up both a service kitchen and a preparation kitchen. (A service kitchen is simpler than a preparation kitchen; it's used to prepare sandwiches and basic items such as soups. A preparation kitchen is more elaborate, allowing you to prepare a wide variety of hot items.) Many sandwich shops and delis can get by with a relatively simple setup.

Bright Idea

When researching where to locate your business, consider a nontraditional site, such as a mobile kitchen or a cart. This will allow you to take your food to where your customers are.

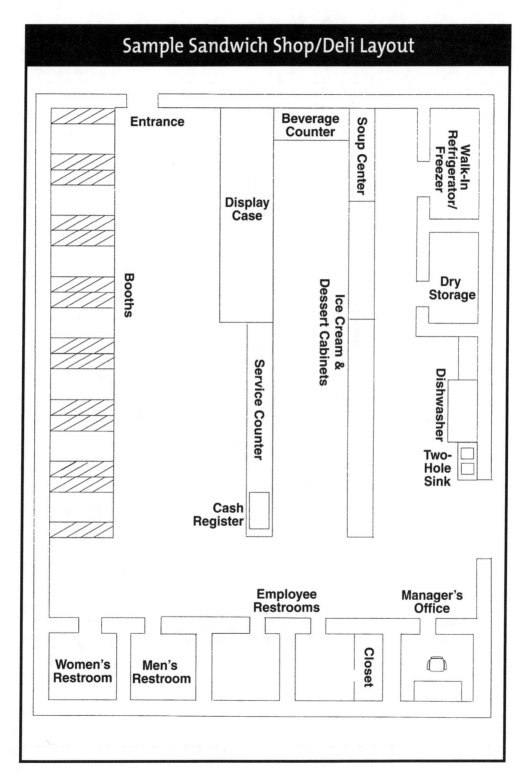

Sample Sandwich Shop/Deli Layout

Entrance

Beverage Counter

Soup Center

Walk-In Refrigerator/ Freezer

Dry Storage

Display Case

Booths

Ice Cream & Dessert Cabinets

Dishwasher

Service Counter

Two-Hole Sink

Cash Register

Employee Restrooms

Manager's Office

Women's Restroom

Men's Restroom

Closet

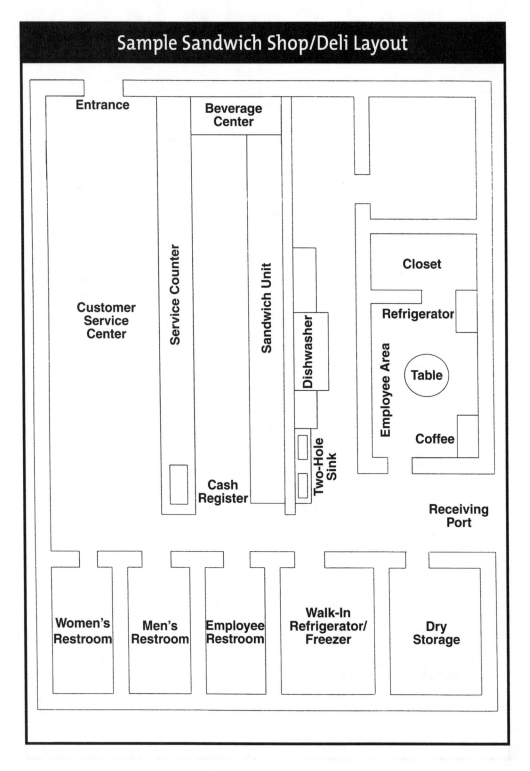

Sample Sandwich Shop/Deli Layout

Entrance

Beverage Center

Customer Service Center

Service Counter

Sandwich Unit

Dishwasher

Closet

Refrigerator

Employee Area

Table

Two-Hole Sink

Coffee

Cash Register

Receiving Port

Women's Restroom

Men's Restroom

Employee Restroom

Walk-In Refrigerator/ Freezer

Dry Storage

For example, in a sandwich shop, the customer service and production areas are usually separated by a simple service counter. A deli should have a three-tiered, refrigerated, glass-fronted case (instead of a counter) to display the wider variety of cheeses, salads and various types of fish.

Against the wall behind either the service counter or display case could be your sandwich preparation area. This section can contain bread boards on which sandwiches will be made, a meat slicer and shelving for frequently used ingredients. Toward the rear of the production area, on the same side of the wall, you could have a sandwich warmer, a double sink unit, and a refrigerator. On the other side of the sandwich-preparation area, nearest the entrance, you could place your soft drink-dispensing system and coffeemaker.

Whether you use this layout or a more traditional layout with both service and preparation kitchens, your primary concern is to make sure the production area is as streamlined as possible to ensure the efficient delivery of food to waiting customers. A poorly designed area reduces the effectiveness of both equipment and personnel.

Customer Service Area

A principal requirement for the customer service area is that it be large enough to accommodate customers, display case(s), or service counter(s), and at least one cashier station. In a strictly takeout operation, you may want to devote as much as 15 percent of your space to this area to accommodate several waiting customers during busy periods. If you plan to offer sit-down service, the customer service area should only occupy about 5 percent of your space, which is just enough for takeout customers to place orders and for sit-down customers to wait to be seated (if need be).

In a deli, your refrigerated display cases will be important marketing tools, as they'll be displaying and thus advertising much of your menu. The salads and ingredients should be attractively displayed, and the case should be well-lit. The glass should be spotless, and the chrome should be shiny and clean.

Likewise, the counter area in a sandwich shop should always be clean. Since the customer service area will be the first thing patrons see upon entering your shop, cleanliness will make a good first impression.

As for the cashier's station, all you need is enough space for the cash register at the end of the counter nearest the entrance.

Dining Area

Dining areas in delis and sandwich shops range from small self-service sections set aside almost as a courtesy to customers (with perhaps

---

Tip...

Smart Tip

Be sure to keep the front of your display cases clean and clear. As customers make their selections, they are likely to touch the cases and will naturally leave fingerprints behind. After every meal period, wipe off the sides and tops of your counters and cases.

three to five tables, each with two to four chairs) to full-scale dining rooms with booths lining the walls, tables and chairs in the center of the area, and a waitstaff to serve patrons. The latter borders on being a full-scale restaurant; if that's your goal, use the information in Chapter 5 to guide you in setting up and managing your operation.

For a typical sandwich shop or deli in a small facility of 500 square feet, consider having six to eight small tables with a total of 12 to 18 chairs. For a larger facility of, say, 1,200 square feet, consider having 10 to 12 tables with 20 to 36 chairs. You don't want the chairs to be overly comfortable; look for chairs that discourage lingering. Turnover is key in this business, which must capitalize on a few peak periods—or even one period, namely lunch—per day.

Receiving and Storage, Office and Restrooms

About 5 to 10 percent of your total space will be used for receiving and storing food. Your receiving area should be accessible to delivery vans. It should also have double doors and a dolly for the easy transport of goods. Your dry-storage area should be located next to your receiving area. This section might include a second freezer and an employee restroom. Contact your county or state health department for area regulations that govern how many employee restrooms are required.

For a sit-down shop, you'll probably want to provide at least one, if not two, public restrooms, each fully equipped for handicapped access. Contact your city or county building

How Much Do You Need?

If you're going to offer sit-down dining, use the following guide to determine the amount of tableware you'll need. Simply multiply the quantity listed below by your facility's seating capacity:

❏ 2.5 spoons and knives

❏ 1.5 iced-tea spoons

❏ 1 soup spoon

❏ 3 forks

❏ 2.5 cups, saucers, and plates

❏ 2 salad plates

❏ 1.5 12-ounce soda and iced-tea glasses

❏ 1 ice cream or salsa dish

In addition, you'll need salt, pepper, and sugar containers for each table, plus a dozen sets as a backup.

department for the building and plumbing codes that apply. Your restrooms don't need to be fancy or elegant, but patrons will expect them to be attractive and clean.

A large storage room can double as your back office. You'll need enough space for a desk, a phone, a small filing cabinet, and shelves. If you have the room, you may also want to provide some lockers in the storage area for your employees to use.

Image

The image of any food-service operation is important to attracting and keeping customers. Always balance professionalism and cleanliness with a comfortable atmosphere.

Research shows that you have less than 10 seconds to attract the attention of a passerby, so your signs and the exterior of your facility must have high impact. There is a variety of decorating ideas and thematic treatments you can use to set your operation apart from the sterile look of fast-food restaurants.

In shopping center takeout operations, proprietors often use eye-catching displays with large, high-quality product photos and unique logos. Be sure to replace photos regularly; a tattered or limp picture of a faded sandwich is not especially appetizing.

A clever attention-getting device used by many sandwich shops is having the production process clearly visible to passersby. Displaying the ingredients and showing the sandwiches being made has proved an effective technique for drawing customers.

Inside, create a warm, inviting setting with inexpensive hanging plants (live, not artificial), posters, photographs, and so on. Paintings, murals, wall plaques, and pictures can effectively establish a theme, but you don't need to spend too much money on decorations. Creativity and cleanliness are much more important than spending thousands of dollars on themed decorations.

Because spotlessness is essential, choose surfaces that are durable and easy to clean, such as washable wall coverings, tile floors, and walls covered in enamel-based paints.

Equipment

A key advantage of starting a simple sandwich shop is that your equipment needs will be minimal compared with those of a full-scale restaurant. Many sandwich shops serve only cold sandwiches and don't do any on-site cooking, so their equipment costs are comparatively low. A deli or sandwich shop serving hot entrees requires a larger investment.

There is some equipment that all restaurants need, such as preparation tables, slicers, cutlery, pots and pans, ovens, refrigerators, and freezers. Whether you decide to bake your own bread, how extensive a menu you offer and whether you offer sit-down service will determine what further investment you will need to make in equipment and fixtures. Most likely, it will be somewhat lower than for the typical dine-in restaurant.

Production Equipment

A service kitchen, which you'll use for fairly simple tasks such as preparing sandwiches, requires a preparation and steam table, a toaster, heat lamps, a microwave oven, a utensil rack, a roll warmer, and a sandwich table. You'll also need to install your beverage center near your service kitchen, where you should have a coffeemaker, an ice machine, a beverage stand, a soda system, an ice-cream cabinet, and a water station. In all, you'll end up spending from $10,000 to $18,000 to equip the service kitchen.

Setting up your preparation kitchen will require a lot more equipment and a lot more capital, so you should budget anywhere from $27,000 to $40,000 for your heavy production equipment. Most sandwich shops and delicatessens have some or all of the following: a slicer, preparation sinks, a portion scale, a food cutter, bakers' bins and tables, a meat grinder, a blender, a griddle-top range with oven, a convection oven, a fryer, a cheese melter, a broiler, a pressureless steamer, a kettle, and a refrigerator with a freezer. Your cooking staff may need aprons, chef's hats, hairnets, and other items, and if you have serving personnel, you'll want to provide them with uniforms.

You'll also need a variety of kitchen cookware, such as measuring cups and spoons, ladles of various sizes, spatulas, wire whisks, a can opener, tongs, and large kitchen spoons. Other miscellaneous items will include ashtrays (if you will allow smoking), potholders, towel dispensers, garbage cans, first-aid kits, a mop and bucket, a broom and a dustpan, and dish containers for busing tables. Plan to spend from $1,000 to $2,000 for cookware and miscellaneous items.

Retail/Service Area Equipment

The specific equipment you will need for this area depends on the type of shop you plan to open. For many sandwich shops, a 6- to 10-foot service counter or display case can also serve as the customer service area. Customers order their sandwiches and pay for them at one end of the counter. Your staff makes the sandwiches and calls customers' numbers when they are ready, and the customers pick up their order at the other end of the counter.

As mentioned earlier, a deli will probably display cheeses, salads, meats, and fish in three-tiered, refrigerated, glass-fronted cases, which can range in cost from about $1,200

> **Tip...**
>
> **Smart Tip**
>
> If you use plants as part of your décor, be sure they are healthy and well-maintained. Droopy or brown leaves or plants infested with insects are not likely to contribute to a positive dining experience.

(for used equipment) to $8,000 or more (for new equipment). At Cuisine Unlimited in Salt Lake City, caterer/deli owner Maxine Turner uses two refrigerated delicatessen cases: one for salads—including green salads, fruit salads, specialty pastas, and natural grains—and one for what she calls "savory" items, such as chicken tortes, quiches, stuffed manicotti, and lasagna rolls.

Whether you place it on your service counter or have a separate stand for it, you'll also need a cash register in this area.

Sandwich Shop/Deli
Major Equipment and Fixtures Checklist

❏ Bakers' bins and tables	❏ Ice machine
❏ Beverage center	❏ Kettle
❏ Blender	❏ Lighting
❏ Breakdown table	❏ Meat grinder
❏ Broiler	❏ Microwave oven
❏ Cappuccino maker	❏ Portion scale (for food)
❏ Cheese melter	❏ Preparation and steam table
❏ Coffee maker	❏ Preparation sinks
❏ Convection oven	❏ Pressureless steamer
❏ Dinnerware	❏ Refrigerator
❏ Dishwashing machine	❏ Roll warmer
❏ Display case(s)	❏ Sandwich table
❏ Equipment for dishwashing	❏ Scale (for receiving area)
❏ Fax machine	❏ Service counter
❏ Food cutter	❏ Shelving
❏ Freezer	❏ Slicer
❏ Fryer	❏ Tables and chairs
❏ Griddle-top range with oven	❏ Toaster
❏ Heat lamps	❏ Utensil racks
❏ Hot water machine	❏ Ventilation system
❏ Ice-cream cabinet	❏ Water station

Know the Locals

Some owners buy for their restaurants the same way their customers buy for themselves—on impulse. This is not necessarily a bad practice, as long as your tastes coincide with a sound knowledge of your patrons' preferences and your estimates closely resemble your actual inventory requirements. In general, a wide array of foods will attract a diversified clientele. With practice and diligent market research, you can identify your strongest menu items and order inventory accordingly.

Dining Area Equipment

Preparing your dining area (if you have one) will be another expense. You can expect to spend as little as $300 for tables and chairs for a small sandwich shop and up to $5,000 for tables, chairs, and booths for a larger establishment.

Other necessary items for the dining area include dishware, glasses, flatware, and an assortment of containers to hold foods not served on plates. These items should match your overall theme or image. A very casual sandwich shop or deli may use paper or plastic plates and cups. For a more formal establishment, you will need flatware and dishware. Figure on your dinnerware costing up to $2,500.

Dishwashing Equipment

If you're going to use disposable tableware, flatware, and cups, you'll only need to wash pots, pans, and preparation utensils. A dishwashing machine would be easiest, but you can make do with a three-compartment sink and do the washing by hand. You'll spend $1,300 to $1,800 for a sink.

If you're going to be using regular dishes, flatware, and glasses, you'll need a small, three-stage dishwashing machine. Your dishwashing area, complete with landing area, drying table, garbage disposal, three-compartment sink, and small machine will run you anywhere from $6,500 to $20,000.

Receiving and Storage Area Equipment

If your volume warrants, you may want to purchase a walk-in refrigerator and freezer for your storage area. This will cost between $4,500 and $7,500, but is not necessary for most smaller shops. Most sandwich shops and delis can get by with just a scale, a breakdown table, and shelving in their receiving and storage area. If your operation is on the small side, you can probably equip this area for less than $1,000.

Inventory

Your specific inventory will, of course, depend on your menu. Caterer/deli owner Turner says one of the challenges she faces is offering enough variety to keep nearby businesspeople returning for lunch on a daily basis while maintaining an efficient inventory system. When you're starting out, keep your inventory low until you can work out a suitable ordering pattern. You'll probably open with about $8,000 to $10,000 in inventory, and your full food and beverage inventory should turn over about once every two weeks.

Let's take a look at the basic food categories you will probably be dealing with:

- *Bread.* The basic ingredient of every sandwich, bread can make or break your sandwich shop/deli. You may be tempted to buy packaged breads and rolls from distributors, but the most successful sandwich shops and delis purchase freshly baked bread daily from a local baker or bake their own breads on-site. While "home baking" your breads can be an excellent marketing tool, you may not have the budget to invest in the necessary equipment and labor. The equipment alone will cost between $15,000 and $150,000, depending on the quantities of bread you plan to bake each day. If you can't afford to make the investment, don't worry. Virtually all cities and towns have bakeries known for their delicious

The Paper Chase

In addition to your food and beverage supplies, you'll need a wide array of paper and plastic products, as well as miscellaneous items unique to your type of restaurant.

Paper goods will be a significant monthly expense. Disposable plastic or paper plates, napkins, and cups range from 8 to 16 cents per setting, depending on your business volume. Negotiate with several paper-products distributors (they're listed in the Yellow Pages) to get the best prices.

It's not necessary to order paper products with your shop name and logo printed on them. This adds considerably to the cost and doesn't do very much to advertise your business or boost your bottom line. It may work for large chains that order in huge quantities, but it doesn't make sense for the owner of a single shop just starting up.

products. Make arrangements with them to buy the bread and rolls you need at wholesale prices. You'll also want to have wraps as an alternative to bread. Plain tortillas work well, or you can offer flavored wraps such as spinach or tomato basil.

Dollar Stretcher

Portion control is a key element in preventing waste and preserving profits. Standardize everything, from the appropriate amount (by weight) of meat and the number of slices of cheese you will use per sandwich to the number of garnishes, such as pickles, you will serve with each order.

- *Meats.* Your meats must be of the highest quality—and fresh—so plan to reorder at least every other day. High-volume shop owners use 150 to 300 pounds of roast beef, ham, and salami each week as well as about 75 to 100 pounds of pastrami, turkey, and other meats. Shop carefully to find the best quality at the best prices.

- *Additional deli items.* Delis usually offer a complete selection of salads (such as potato, three-bean, coleslaw, cucumber, pasta, green, and others), various types of fish (including cod, salmon, herring, sturgeon) and an extensive selection of cheeses. Sandwich shops may have a more limited menu.

  Both sandwich shops and delis may serve hot entrees, such as soup, chili, stew, quiche, barbecued ribs, and chicken, and so on. Dessert items may also be included to round out a sandwich shop or deli's menu. Purchase these extras in limited quantities at first, until you can determine demand.

- *Beverages.* Some delis and sandwich shops offer canned soda; pints of milk; and glasses of iced tea, lemonade, or carbonated drinks. Virtually all serve coffee, and some serve hot chocolate during the winter. You might also want to invest in an espresso or cappuccino machine, and provide a variety of hot teas. Some beverage suppliers provide the beverage-dispensing systems for free or at a reduced cost to high-volume operations, provided you buy your beverages from those companies. Check with a variety of beverage suppliers, and negotiate for the best deal possible.

  If you decide to include shakes, malts, frozen yogurt, floats, and ice-cream sodas (or soft-serve ice cream), all the ingredients you'll need should be available from the same distributor that supplies your milk. These ice cream items can dramatically increase your dollar-per-customer sales figures.

  Many sandwich shops and delis serve beer by the bottle and wine by the glass or bottle. Most do not serve hard liquor; a limited beer-and-wine license meets their needs and is easier to obtain than a full liquor license.

- *Fresh produce.* It's easiest to order your fruits and vegetables through a fresh-produce supplier, although some shop owners like to visit a farmer's market themselves. Although vegetables are available year-round, they are seasonal and subject to climatic conditions. Be flexible in your buying, and look for items in plentiful supply. Take advantage of price swings by modifying the makeup of your salads or sandwiches according to the season and produce availability. But regardless of the season, you'll use several cases of lettuce and tomatoes and several pounds of cheese each week.

Stat Fact
Males tend to consume more sandwiches (51.6 percent) than females (48.4 percent), and people with incomes of $100,000 or more consume 20 percent of all sandwiches (excluding burgers).

- *Canned, frozen, and packaged foods.* If you offer soups and salads, you'll need canned and packaged items like soups, olives, pickles, kidney beans, garbanzo beans, and some canned condiments. Purchase these items from a processed-foods distributor, and start with their minimum order, which is usually a case of each.

You'll also need several different dressings for salads, such as bleu cheese, French, Thousand Island, Italian, and honey mustard. Make sure you provide low-fat options. You'll probably want to buy them commercially since home-made dressings generally require too much time and labor. Offer a variety of salad toppings, including olives, chopped vegetables, nuts, bacon bits, grated cheese, soybeans, raisins, and sunflower seeds.

Condiments for sandwiches and other menu items (mustard, ketchup, salt, pepper, cooking oil, relish, etc.) can be purchased through a processed-foods distributor.

If you include french fries on your menu, you can either buy potatoes from a fresh produce supplier and cut them yourself (which may be too time-consuming) or buy precut, precooked frozen french fries by the pound. You might also want to offer onion rings, which can be purchased precooked and frozen.

Staffing

Your staffing needs will vary depending on the size of your operation. If you're planning to work full time in your sandwich shop or deli, you could probably open with just one additional full-time employee: an experienced sandwich maker. As your business grows, you'll probably want to cover busy periods with part-time workers. For security reasons, try to have at least two employees in the shop at all times. Of course, if you're planning a full-service deli with a dining area, you'll need to staff more along the lines of a typical restaurant.

▲

Look for employees who are pleasant, people-oriented, and well-groomed. Food prepared by sloppy employees won't be appealing to your customers.

Most sandwich shop and deli positions do not earn significant tips, although some shops have a tip jar by the cash register. Wage scales vary by region, but you can expect to pay 50 cents to $2 above minimum wage. A glance through your local newspaper's help-wanted section will give you an idea of the going rates in your area.

Coffeehouse

Coffee connoisseur or neophyte, aficionado or abstainer, you've probably noticed the tremendous growth in the specialty-coffee industry. New incarnations of this previously background beverage have taken center stage in restaurants and shops around the world. Coffee has become a culture, complete with its own language and accessories that offers a wide-open retail opportunity.

Coffee is a global industry that employs more than 20 million people worldwide and ranks second only to petroleum in terms of dollars traded. With more than 400 billion cups of the drink consumed every year, coffee is the world's most popular beverage.

The first coffeehouses opened in Constantinople nearly 450 years ago and did so well that by the 1630s, European coffeehouses had become the center of cultural and social activities. Coffeehouses also enjoyed some popularity in colonial New England, but Americans did not accept the coffeehouse as a place for social or cultural gatherings until well into the second half of the 20th century. Before the 1970s, Americans either drank their coffee at home or in a restaurant and settled for the canned variety that was brewed in a percolator.

In the 1960s, coffeehouses and folk musicians appeared on the scene. Although the coffeehouses seemed to focus on the counterculture, they managed to create a demand for fresh coffee beans that people could grind and thus brew their own coffee at home. However, starting in the late 1960s, the number of people who consumed coffee declined sharply. "In 1962, 75 percent of the population drank coffee on a typical day," says Robert F. Nelson, president of the National Coffee Association (NCA). "In 1997, it was 49 percent." He blames that decline on dwindling social support for coffee, negative publicity about the effects of coffee and caffeine on health, and competition from other beverages, such as soft drinks. In the late 1990s, that trend started to reverse. By 2001, 52 percent of the U.S. adult population drank coffee every day, representing some 107 million daily drinkers. Of those, 29 million drink gourmet coffee beverages such as specialty coffee, espresso-based beverages, and frozen and iced coffee beverages.

While most of the statistics on coffee consumption focus on adults, teenagers represent a growing market for coffee. Many don't care for the taste of coffee, but enjoy frothy, sweet, milkshake-like frozen coffee drinks. "In the past, coffee was a commodity, and there was very little innovation [in the industry]," Nelson says. "It was seen as an old-fashioned beverage for older folks. In the '90s, the social supports [re-emerged] for coffee. [Now] it's seen as a relevant, contemporary beverage." About coffee's impact on health, he observes that "today, the consumer takes a much more pragmatic approach to healthy eating and living." It's possible and common for a healthy lifestyle to include coffee.

In many situations, coffee is replacing alcohol as the social beverage of choice, with people meeting for coffee instead of cocktails. "Here in Portland, you go to the bigger coffeehouses, and they're real [hot spots]," says Ward Barbee, pub-

> ### Smart Tip
> **Tip...**
>
> Although just about every business guru advises choosing a business where the owner can combine profitability with passion, the requirement to love the product is especially true in the coffee industry. Learn everything you can about the culture of coffee and about how to identify and produce quality beverages.

lisher of *Fresh Cup* magazine, a Portland, Oregon, trade publication for the gourmet coffee and beverage industry.

Beyond the beverage itself, people frequent coffeehouses and espresso bars for a variety of reasons. Some go to meet with friends, socialize, and perhaps enjoy some live music or conversation; some are looking for a quick lunch and a drink that will help them weather the afternoon doldrums; others simply want a great cup of coffee to start off each morning. Coffeehouse patrons tend to be sophisticated, and they often want unusual, exotic coffees that are expertly prepared.

These days, coffeehouses are meeting a strong social need. They give people a place where they feel like they belong, where they see the same faces regularly. It's often called the "third-place phenomenon": People have home and work, and they need a third place to go. That place needs to be somewhere they can go very regularly so they can form relationships with other people—in this case, with other customers and staff. While most people don't go to their favorite restaurant every day, they will go to a coffeehouse every day. Today's coffee cafes cater to a marketplace as varied as the coffee flavors themselves. Some target the breakfast and lunch-on-the-go market, others operate as evening destinations, with food items and perhaps entertainment, and there's a wide range of styles in between.

"There continues to be innovation, and there continues to be expansion in the whole gourmet and specialty shop area. That will continue to have a positive impact on the consumption of coffee," the NCA's Nelson says.

Another plus for the industry is the growing sophistication of the American coffee drinker. "As more and more [types of] coffee are introduced to consumers and more and more coffee beverages are available, the consumer is developing a more educated palate and becoming more educated about the beverage itself," says Nelson. He points out that coffee drinkers are consuming different types of coffee beverages at different times of the day. "You may have one type of coffee at home for breakfast, a different type at lunch, and maybe an espresso after dinner. What the industry has tried to do is respond to consumers by providing them with different varieties so people can choose what they like."

Most successful coffeehouses have heavy foot traffic and high-volume sales. The majority will serve up to 500 customers per day and manage up to five customer turnovers during the lunch hour, despite having limited floor space and modest seating capacity. Profit margins for coffee and espresso drinks are extremely high—after all, you're dealing with a product that is more than 95 percent water. At the same time, customers' average purchase amount is $2 to $3, so you need volume to reach and maintain profitability.

Though most restaurants try to have either very fast turnover and low prices with basic food or slower turnover and higher prices with fancy food, coffeehouses break those rules. People will hang around a coffeehouse for an hour or more, sipping a $1 cup of coffee, but because of the huge profit margins coffee drinks can bring, even relatively low-volume operations can turn a profit if the business is run correctly.

Besides specialty roasted coffee by the cup, most coffeehouses also have espresso-based drinks (such as cappuccinos and lattes), assorted teas, bottled water and fruit juices, along with an inviting assortment of baked goods such as biscotti (Italian dipping cookies), bagels, croissants, muffins, and a selection of desserts. Many also sell beans by the pound so customers can enjoy their favorite brews at home. A hot trend is adding flavors to coffee drinks. Customers are ordering varieties ranging from simple chocolate and vanilla to raspberry and fudge ripple. Flavorings can be roasted into the beans or added in the form of syrups at the time the coffee is served.

Competition

You may find the competition from large chains such as Starbucks intimidating, but industry experts insist there's a place for everyone in the business. In fact, *Fresh Cup* magazine's Barbee says the independent retailer probably has the potential to be most profitable because it can ride on the marketing coat tails of giants like Starbucks, yet its size provides a level of flexibility that larger organizations simply don't have.

Many smaller operators don't see the giant chains as a threat but rather as a marketing engine that can help educate the public about specialty coffee. Each individual shop then competes on its own—and you need to know what the other shops are doing. Small operations may not be able to compete in terms of marketing dollars spent, but they can compete with top-quality products, people, and presentation. You can get coffee just about anywhere you go—restaurants, bars, nightclubs, department stores, boutiques, gift shops, hair salons, automotive repair shops, even hardware stores. It's a universal drink that appeals to the majority of the population, and it's inexpensive to prepare. But not all these locations should be considered competitors.

Your four primary competitor groups are other coffeehouses, bakeries and doughnut shops, retail coffee and tea stores, and mobile coffee/espresso carts. Study what they're doing, and then put together a product, service, and ambience package that your target market will prefer.

Industry Trends

If you're going to operate a coffeehouse, you'll be interested in the following trends and predictions.

- *Product categories are solidifying their niches.* According to industry experts, straight (unblended) coffees will continue to move toward "estate marks," in which the specific geographic location—not simply the country—of the coffee's origin will play a key role in product marketing. Dark-roast coffees will remain popular for espresso-based beverages, and product quality will improve as the roasting community achieves greater sophistication. Though blends do not demonstrate the same strength as other categories, local roasters will blend coffees that sell well in their marketing area because of regional taste preferences or local water conditions that may affect taste. In the future, we can expect to see a broader range of decaffeinated coffees, and flavored coffees will continue to be popular. We'll also see a significant increase in the market for organically grown coffees.

• *Coffee cafes will set the pace for new outlet creation.* The fastest-growing distribution channel will be coffee cafes, including espresso bars and espresso carts. This rapid growth will be fueled by three factors: the high gross-profit margin of selling coffee by the cup; the fact that espresso-based beverages are difficult for consumers to prepare correctly at home; the fact that existing food-service outlets will be slow to upgrade their product quality to the level of specialty coffee operations.

• *Retail roasters are a driving force in product lines and marketing.* "Microroasteries" are growing, opening at the impressive rate of approximately 100 per year, with the principal limitation being the availability of equipment.

• *Consumers will continue their two-tier system of shopping.* Consumers patronize both establishments that sell bulk items, typically at a discount, and specialty stores, which consumers are visiting with greater frequency. The specialty coffee product category is expanding rapidly.

Setting Up Your Facility

Just as coffeehouses are not restricted to serving a particular market group, neither are they limited to occupying a certain kind of facility to be profitable. Given the markets you are going to target, your hours of operation, the volume of coffee you expect to sell, and the geographical locations under consideration, you can choose from freestanding buildings, downtown or center-of-town storefronts, and mall spaces. A typical coffeehouse is 800 to 3,000 square feet. If coffee and espresso on the go will be your specialty, you won't need as large a facility as someone who intends to run a coffeehouse and bookstore. Likewise, starting up in a large facility of 2,500 square feet or more is ideal for an entrepreneur who wants neighborhood regulars to be able to lounge around drinking coffee for hours and not feel rushed or crowded.

When allocating space, a good formula to follow is to allow 55 percent of your space for the seating area, 25 percent for your production area, and 20 percent for your customer service area, including the bar. If you let the production area fall below 25 percent, you run the risk of having problems with service.

Depending on the amount of cash you have to invest, you can spend $20,000 to $200,000—or more—on your facility. This depends on whether you are starting from scratch or converting an existing food-service business and what you plan for a theme and décor.

Smart Tip

Coffee experts advocate storing beans so they will be protected from light and air. To let your clients know your beans are properly stored and therefore of high quality, display only beans that are not going to be sold in transparent containers.

Customer Service and Seating Area

This area must convey the atmosphere you have chosen in a manner that takes advantage of the available space. Large coffeehouses use a waiting area and cashier's station

---

Grab 'Em by the Nose

Since location, high-volume foot traffic, and repeat business are the real keys to success, don't spend more than 5 percent of your advertising budget on conventional advertising. Instead, you can do several inexpensive promotions to help get the traffic started and keep it coming.

When you walk into a coffeehouse, you are immediately struck by the distinctive aroma of fresh-roasted coffee beans. This is what entices many people to go inside and linger over a hot cup of coffee, a delicious cappuccino, or a shot of espresso. People passing by can't resist slowing down a bit to see what's brewing inside.

Take a tip from cookie shops and bakeries: Grab customers by the nose. Savvy owners help nature along by having an open setup that will push aromas out the door with the help of strategically placed fans and vents. A fan mounted in a door transom is one of your best bets.

The smell of coffee will permeate the store even if you lock the beans in airtight bins. It is crucial that you make sure the smell—and the beans themselves—always stays fresh, which is why it's so important to use the correct display and storage equipment.

located at or near the entrance to avoid causing traffic jams at the service counter. The cashier's station is usually parallel to a wall. You can design it as just a small counter with a cash register or use the space to display specialty items such as coffee grinders and mugs, bags of coffee beans, and perhaps some of the baked goods you offer. As an alternative, you can set up your cashier's station at the threshold between the counter and the seating area.

If you are tight on space, you can skip the display areas. Any accessories you sell can go on shelves within customers' reach. More expensive items, such as espresso and cappuccino makers, can go behind and above service counters.

When considering the layout of your service area, keep this in mind: While long lines out the door generally convey the fact that quality goods are inside, they can also deter busy shoppers or commuters who want to pop in and out. Try to leave space to allow for a two- or three-line service approach, with enough room for those who have ordered to stand off to the side if necessary. Also, be sure your coffee production equipment is placed near the service counter, not away from it, so that efficiency in serving beverages is maximized.

Assuming you want to have a coffee bar, you will generally want to have one bar seat for every three table seats. A coffeehouse with 75 table seats, for example, should have about 25 seats at the bar. For bar stools, allow about 2 square feet per stool, while tables should have about 10 to 12 square feet per seated customer.

A bar is a good idea because it also serves as an additional waiting area for people looking to grab a table when one opens up. You'll also need to provide public restrooms, which should be located close to the dining area.

Bright Idea

Set aside some room for coffee tasting. This can consist of a simple setup of thermoses of the coffees you sell at the end of the counter. Provide small tasting cups, stirrers, cream, and sugar, and encourage customers to sample coffee before they place their orders.

Production Area

Your coffee- and food-production area should promote the efficient delivery of food and coffee to the customer area. Your menu should be your prime consideration when you design your the production area. By taking what you serve into consideration, you'll be able to cut down on the amount of space and equipment needed to run an efficient operation. Generally, you'll need to allow approximately 25 to 35 percent of your total space for your production area. This includes room for receiving, storage, food

Stat Fact

Coffee drinkers consume an average of 3.3 cups of coffee per day, and the average coffee cup size is 9 ounces.

▲

and drink preparation, cooking, baking, trash, dishwashing, an employee-only area, and a small office. Receiving and food storage will take up about 8 percent of your total space. These areas should be strategically located as close to the front or rear door as possible. Your dry storage area should be adjacent to the receiving area.

If you have decided to serve food as well as coffee, you'll need about 12 percent of your total space for food preparation—cooking and baking (depending on what you plan to serve). Your equipment might include prep tables, fryers, a cooking range with a griddle top, a refrigerator with a freezer, soft drink and milk dispensers, an ice bin, a broiler, and exhaust fans for the ventilation system. Arrange this area so everything is positioned within reach and two or more people can comfortably work side by side when you are at maximum production. You can center the prep area in the middle of the kitchen or, for smaller cafes and bars, below or behind the counter. For more on setting up prep or full-service kitchens, study the chapters on sandwich shops/delicatessens, bakeries, and restaurants, and adapt that information to the size and scope of your menu.

Most coffeehouses use interesting-looking and sometimes ornate espresso machines, so they locate their beverage centers directly behind the counter in full view of the customers. Customers want to be able to smell the aromas, watch you prepare drinks, and make sure they're getting exactly what they want. This also allows employees to get the order to the customer quickly.

Arrange your dishwashing area toward the rear of the kitchen, perhaps in a corner, so it doesn't interrupt the flow of employees in the prep area. Your dishwashing equipment needs will depend on whether you use traditional tableware or disposable products.

Your facility must make it as easy as possible for you and your employees to serve a large number of customers quickly. By allowing customers to seat themselves and approach the counter when they want to order, you can eliminate most of the problems traditional restaurants and other labor-intensive food-service operations face.

Equipment

For an average-sized coffeehouse, equipment costs range from $10,000 to $60,000 or more, depending on the number of coffee and espresso machines purchased and the extent of food-service operations.

Coffee and Espresso Machines

Coffee and espresso machines are the heart of a coffeehouse. You can operate profitably without a convection oven or a walk-in refrigerator, but good coffeemakers and espresso machines are absolutely mandatory.

Coffeemakers are used for brewing straight coffee, and espresso machines are used for brewing espresso and for making espresso-based drinks that require steamed or frothed

Sample Coffeehouse Layout

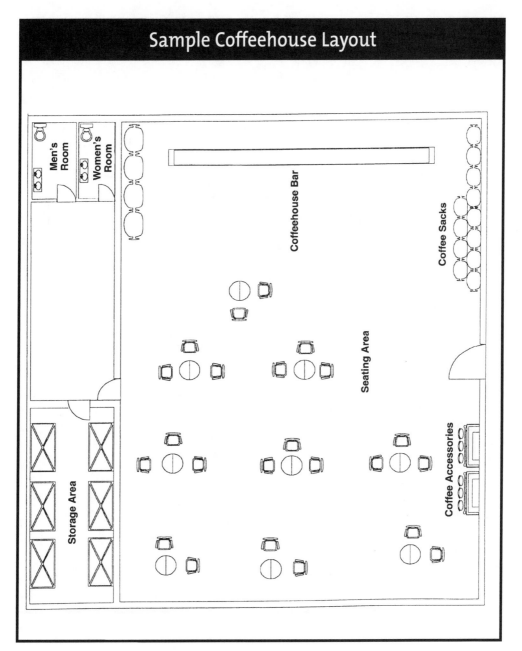

Sample Coffeehouse Layout

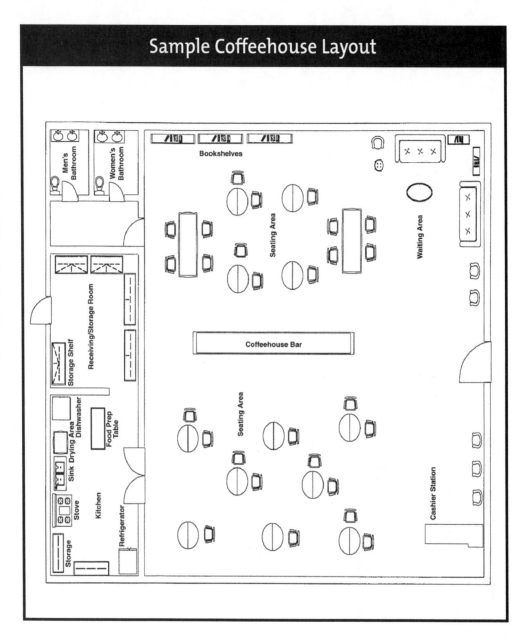

milk. Although they are notoriously expensive and temperamental, industrial espresso machines have come down in price over the years, and their reliability has improved. Still, the most frequent and costly problems coffeehouse and espresso-bar owners face are usually with their espresso machines. Sales either stop when the machines go down, or owners have to do what they can with a backup system, which annoys customers who expect prompt service. Daily cleaning and regular maintenance of these machines is a must. Many parts of the machine can be quickly rinsed with hot water and/or wiped down after each drink. You may want to have your machines completely serviced on a monthly or semimonthly basis.

There are four key features to look for in an espresso machine:

1. *Volume.* How much espresso can the machine make each day? Here's how to tell: Espresso machines differ chiefly in the number of "groups" they have. The group is the part of the machine that acts as a stationary lock to fix the removable handle or "head" to the machine. The finely ground coffee is placed in a perforated metal cup known as a "portafilter." The filter is placed into the head, and the head

Coffeehouse Major Equipment and Fixtures Checklist

❑ Bakers' bins and tables	❑ Ice-cream cabinet
❑ Beverage center	❑ Ice machine
❑ Blender	❑ Kettle
❑ Breakdown table	❑ Lighting
❑ Broiler	❑ Preparation and steam table
❑ Cappuccino maker	❑ Preparation sinks
❑ Cheese melter	❑ Pressureless steamer
❑ Coffee grinder(s)	❑ Refrigerator
❑ Coffee machines	❑ Roll warmer
❑ Convection oven	❑ Sandwich table
❑ Dishwashing machine	❑ Scale (for receiving area)
❑ Display cases	❑ Service counter
❑ Equipment for dishwashing	❑ Shelving
❑ Espresso machine(s)	❑ Tables and chairs
❑ Food cutter	❑ Tableware
❑ Freezer	❑ Toaster
❑ Fryer	❑ Utensil racks
❑ Griddle-top range with oven	❑ Ventilation system
❑ Heat lamps	❑ Water station
❑ Hot-water machine	

Coffee on Ice

One way to add some variety to your menu is to serve iced coffee drinks. Making delicious iced coffee takes a special knack. It's not enough to just brew coffee and chill it. One coffeehouse owner we spoke with uses a "cold drip" method. She combines the ground coffee with cold water for an extended period of time, and the process extracts the flavor and aromatics but not the acidity from the coffee. It then forms a concentrate, which can be diluted to make iced coffee drinks.

Because the resulting beverage has no acidity, it is very creamy and works better as a cold beverage. However, keep in mind that acidity is a very important part of the coffee profile. If you were drinking a cup of hot coffee that didn't have acidity, you would find it bland or flat. But using a cold drip process and no acidity for iced coffees makes for a much better cold drink.

locks into the espresso machine at the group. Most of today's machines are single-group or two-group, with one group and one corresponding head that locks into place or two groups and two corresponding heads, respectively. Heated water comes out of the espresso machine's tank at the group and is forced, at ten atmospheres (a unit of pressure equal to the air pressure at sea level) of pressure, through the coffee grounds.

Most coffeehouses and espresso bars that do any volume of business have two-group machines, which range in price from $4,000 to $8,000. You will probably never need anything larger. Using a single-group machine with a twin head (having two spouts at the bottom of the head instead of one, which doubles your capacity), you can make 100 to 200 espresso-based drinks a day. However, keep in mind that a busy coffeehouse can sell upwards of 300 espresso drinks a day.

In the beginning, to save on your initial cash outlay, a single-group machine may provide sufficient capacity. After you're established and your business begins to grow, you may find that you need to buy a second single-group machine.

2. *Warranty.* Any machine you buy should come with some kind of warranty—at least 90 days and preferably a year. Warranties vary tremendously among espresso-machine manufacturers. If you buy a

> ## Smart Tip
> *Tip...*
>
> High-volume coffee sales help offset the high cost of food preparation. That means at least 30 percent of your total sales should be in coffee.

foreign machine, there's no guarantee that you will be able to find someone who can fix it for you unless you buy it through an American distributor.

3. *In-line filters.* If you use an outside water source to provide water for your espresso machine, you won't know much about the water's chemical com-

position. If the water in your area is high in minerals and other compounds, those substances will begin to collect in your water line much like they do in your reservoir. Espresso machines that come with simple in-line filters will slow the rate at which deposits begin to collect in the machine, allowing it to run better and require less maintenance.

4. *Reservoir or tank.* Look for machines with reservoirs made of stainless steel rather than copper. Stainless steel is better at retarding the buildup of calcium and other mineral deposits along the tank walls.

Coffeemakers are far more readily available than espresso machines, and they are relatively easy to operate. With a few exceptions, they all work the same way: Heated water is forced at 10 atmospheres of pressure through finely ground coffee beans to infuse them. Regular coffee has about 7 percent soluble solids, while espresso contains roughly 25 percent.

Your expected business volume will determine the number and kind of coffeemakers you should purchase. Coffee machines are fairly standard. Most use paper filters (some use metal) to hold the coffee grounds as the water filters through, and each pot holds 50 to 70 ounces of coffee. Prices for commercial coffeemakers range from $250 to $600. You may want equipment that looks good sitting behind the counter, but reliability and quality output should be the two factors that influence your purchasing decision the most.

Inventory

Your initial inventory will depend largely on how much start-up capital you have available. For a 600- to 1,000-square foot coffeehouse or espresso bar, plan to spend $3,000 to $8,000 on coffee and $1,500 to $5,000 on accessories (if you sell them) to get started.

Your inventory costs will probably fluctuate during the year. If you serve food, you'll likely buy more produce during the summer when you're serving lunches with fresh vegetables. In the winter, coffee sales will soar because of the cold weather and gift-giving holidays.

Order coffee beans once or twice a week from local suppliers to ensure freshness. Most roasters do their best to accommodate clients and deliver in whatever quantities are needed. Remember that coffee beans begin to go stale the moment they're roasted and will keep for only one to three weeks if stored properly.

Your inventory should include coffees from several countries. To start, offer at least five decaffeinated coffees, plus at least a dozen regular coffees (your wholesaler can give you suggestions about the bestselling types). For the sake of variety, do not focus strictly on blended coffees or devote your entire inventory budget to select estate-grown beans. Create as much diversity as you can with the amount of start-up capital you have. You should begin with a coffee inventory of 400 to 700 pounds.

Here is a list of the different kinds of coffee, decaffeinated coffee, tea, and accessory items that can be used to stock your coffeehouse:

- *Coffee.* House blend (your choice), Espresso Roast, French Roast, Italian Roast, Vienna Roast, Colombian Supremo, Colombian Popayan, Brazilian Santos, Moka Java, Mexican, Guatemalan High-Grown, Java Estate, Costa Rican Terrazu, Royal Hawaiian Kona, El Salvadorian, Kenya Nairobi AA, Antiguan, Arabian Moka (Yemen), Yirgacheffe, Ethiopian Sidamo, Bolivian, Honduran, Nicaraguan, Panamanian, Paraguayan, Venezuelan, Tobago, Celabese, Ecuadorian, Peruvian, Haitian, Madagascar (Malagasy), Indonesian, Jamaica Blue Mountain, Tanzanian, Ugandan, Ivory Coast, Rwanda/Burundi, Sierra Leone, Zaire, Singaporian, Philippino, Liberian, Sumatra Mandehling, Sumatra Linton, and Zimbabwe Code 53.

- *Decaffeinated coffee.* Espresso, Colombian, Costa Rican, El Salvadorian, Brazilian Santos, Sumatran, Moka Java, Vienna Roast, and French Roast.

- *Tea.* Earl Grey, chamomile, English Breakfast, oolong (Taiwanese jasmine), black jasmine (from mainland China), Lapsang, pingsun, Congou, Keemun, Darjeeling, Assam, Ceylon, rose hips, Russian, spearmint, peppermint, lemon mist, lemon lime, orange pekoe, golden-tipped pekoe, lemon, apple cinnamon, cherry, orange nutmeg, and cinnamon.

- *Miscellaneous.* Sugar, artificial sweetener, cream, nondairy creamer, ground cinnamon, vanilla and chocolate powder, flavored syrup and lemon slices.

- *Accessories.* Consumer coffee mills (electric), filter coffeemakers (various sizes and styles), tea eggs and filters, coffee filters (various), insulated carafes, tea kettles (include copper), espresso makers (nonelectric), mugs, cups, creamers, sugar bowls, and tea services.

- *Retail and other supplies.* Sealable bags (for selling coffee beans by the pound), labels (for coffee bags), plastic or metal scoops, paper cups and lids, stirrers, and napkins.

Bright Idea

An essential element of success in the coffee business is to remember that the anchor is coffee, but it pays to explore options that will enhance the primary product, such as pastries and other baked goods, additional beverages, gift baskets, and so on.

Staffing

It's not enough to have the right equipment and properly roasted coffee. You also need people who understand coffee and know how to make the beverages with skill.

A key member of a coffeehouse staff is the *barista*, the person who prepares espresso. Baristas are extremely well versed in the language of coffee, and espresso-based drinks are their specialty.

If you expect to stay open more than 12 hours a day, you'll need two baristas, one working full time and one part time. The part-time person can help tend the counter during peak hours or work the early-morning or late-evening shifts. Baristas are usually paid an hourly wage and keep whatever tips they generate, which can be substantial if they make exceptionally good espresso. As with a good bartender, you can hire a qualified barista at a very reasonable $6 to $8 per hour, depending on your location. The best place to find talent is at your competitors—espresso bars, restaurants, and other establishments that sell espresso drinks.

Bright Idea

During peak periods, consider adding an express line to accommodate customers who just want a basic hot or iced coffee and a simple pastry or snack so they can get in and out quickly. The customer who wants the cappuccino, the latte, the double iced mocha, or other more labor-intensive beverage can go through the regular line and get full service.

Look for someone who knows how to make all the standard espresso drinks as well as concoct their own creations and fill customers' exotic drink requests. Your espresso expert should be quick pouring, consistent, and especially personable—more so than any other server in the house. Just like good bartenders, experienced baristas possess the ability to make small talk with people while juggling several drink orders in their heads.

The remainder of your staff will depend on the size and style of your establishment and the range of your menu. The chapters on sandwich shops/delicatessens and restaurants can serve as a guide to help you determine how many people to hire based on the kind of establishment you want to open.

The Coffeehouse Market

Even chain coffeehouses vary in style, design, and menu offerings depending on the particular market they serve. For an independent operator, it's critical that you understand your target market and tailor your operation to meet its needs.

Just about everyone over the age of 15 is a potential coffeehouse/espresso-bar patron. But such a vague market description will not help you build a successful coffeehouse. Consider targeting one or more of the following customer groups:

- *Local consumers.* Area residents are clearly a prime market for most coffeehouses. Those who live in the neighborhood are in close proximity for all or part of the day and therefore constitute a substantial group of potential customers. If you plan to set up shop in a rural area, a suburban neighborhood

---

You've Got to Know Beans about Beans

When it comes to storing and displaying your beans, you may be tempted to go with something attractive, such as natural wood cases, barrels and bins, instead of something practical, such as nonporous wood or plastic. Wood is the worst type of material for coffee bean storage, because it can promote staleness and bad taste. It is notorious for absorbing coffee oils, which penetrate the wood grain and then go rancid. When you add fresh coffee beans, they absorb the rancid oils and are ruined.

If you go with a wood décor, get a guarantee from the manufacturer that the wood is nonporous, or line the bins with heavy-duty nonporous plastic. Replace the plastic routinely to ensure freshness. Remember, coffee is best stored away from light and air.

For displaying limited quantities of beans, your best option is to use nonporous display bins made of acrylic, glass, or plastic. Be sure to wash them on a regular basis.

Add It Up

When it comes to extenders and additives, such as chicory and other spices, the best route is to sell them selectively. Many spices such as cinnamon, orange, chocolate, and anise go well with coffee, but if you routinely order coffee spiced with these flavors, you will probably run into a serious inventory problem. The same holds true for chicory, which is not roasted with coffee but added afterward.

Offer spices and coffee extenders (available through coffee suppliers) for consumers to add to their own beverages or that they can purchase and take home. Spiced teas are another matter, since many teas are at their best and most popular with certain spices. Let a good tea supplier put you on the right track on that front.

---

area, or an urban area with a large residential population nearby, this is the first market to target.

- *Commuters.* A coffeehouse offers precisely what most morning commuters are looking for: a good cup of coffee and a bite to eat. Coffee is the universal breakfast drink, and a muffin, croissant, or pastry is the perfect accompaniment. While competition for the breakfast market among doughnut shops, fast-food chains and traditional coffee shops is fierce, a business that specializes in coffee has a competitive advantage over the more generic breakfast places that serve low-grade coffee. The only substitute for good coffee—as far as coffee drinkers are concerned—is better coffee. Coffeehouses can offer quick breakfast foods and often serve the best coffee in town.

   At the end of the day, coffeehouses in urban areas can target customers who work in the area but live elsewhere and don't have time to go home before meeting up with people for dinner or evening entertainment. Given the choice between battling other drivers on the highway or spending a relaxing hour in a cafe until traffic dies down, many commuters will choose your cafe. The evening is ideal for promoting "happy hour" coffee specials.

- *Campus folk.* Some of the most profitable coffeehouses in the country are located near schools and universities. High school and college students, as well as faculty members, are a strong market. Despite apparently limited spending power, students have embraced coffeehouses and are putting in long hours drinking coffee, studying and talking within their walls. Coffeehouses near campuses are typically open well into the night. In addition, the coffee and foods they serve are inexpensive, and, unlike bars, both the atmosphere and menu are conducive to industrious behavior. Because coffeehouses don't serve alcohol, they don't enforce age limits, and that means students under 21 who cannot go to bars have a place to gather.

- *Entertainment crowd.* Those who travel to shopping districts and commercial centers seeking entertainment are also usually in search of some food or refreshment. A coffeehouse located near an entertainment venue is a convenient place for a snack, a quick meal, or just a cup of coffee before or after the main event.

- *At-home gourmets.* Many people who call themselves gourmets also enjoy experimenting with new coffee flavors and espresso drinks at home. You can encourage these individuals to try different varieties and expand their awareness of unblended or "straight" coffees and espressos. One of the big appeals of a specialty coffee operation is that customers can pick and choose their own coffee beans to take home or to the office.

About Beans

Many coffeehouse patrons are well-heeled in the language of coffee, which means they understand the difference between arabica and robusta beans, and they know how an espresso, cappuccino, or latte is supposed to taste. Coffeehouse patrons are usually acutely aware of the consumer choices they make, buying food products for prestige, nutritional value, and distinct taste. For instance, they are most likely to buy estate coffee, which is labeled with the name of the estate on which it is grown and carries the same status and appeal of fine wines. Having become accustomed to the taste of high-quality coffee, coffee connoisseurs don't consume the low-grade, mass-produced coffee brands that are found in supermarkets.

As a coffeehouse owner, you must at least match, if not surpass, the coffee knowledge of your patrons. While this book will provide you with valuable information on the mechanics of starting and running a successful coffeehouse, you should dedicate yourself to in-depth research on your product before you invest your time, energy, and financial resources in opening a shop of your own. Despite its apparent abundance, only a small amount of the total coffee harvested each year is true

Beware!
Coffee roasting is a complicated process and shouldn't be undertaken lightly or without a great deal of study. Roasting is truly an art—it is what transforms the beans into a flavorful brew. Though there are numerous advantages to roasting your own beans (lower cost and quality control, for example), don't move into this area until you have sufficient industry experience and capital to support the required investment.

gourmet coffee, which is made with premium arabica beans instead of low-grade robusta beans.

You'll need to decide what types of beans you'll offer and use in your beverages. Some people love dark-roasted coffee; others believe it kills the natural taste of the drink. Will you offer one or the other, or will you offer the full spectrum? How many types of whole beans will you make available?

Starting Each Day

At the beginning of the day, you should inspect your facility to be sure everything is as you or your manager left it the night before. The next step is to make a working plan of the day's events.

By the time your doors open in the morning, all your preparation work should be done. The better your setup routine, the easier it will be for you and your staff to focus on serving customers and the less you will have to worry about whether you're going to run out of inventory and supplies in the middle of a rush. For heavy coffee and espresso production, you need to be prepared. If you are going to have a slightly different menu each day—which is a good idea as customers will appreciate the change—all the ingredients that go into the day's menu items—certain coffee beans, milk, sugar, cream, flavorings, toppings, ice, condiments, etc.—must be ready. Give yourself enough time to make sure you have everything you need.

Grinding It Up

A key piece of equipment will be your coffee grinder. Grinding coffee to the right consistency has a lot to do with the quality of the finished product. Electric mills have dials indicating the kind of coffee grind that's right for various coffeemakers.

You can buy a new coffee grinder with several grind selections for $700 to $1,200, or you can lease one for $20 to $35 per month. Your coffee supplier will either have them on hand or know where you can get one.

Most coffee mills are 24 to 36 inches high. Place the mill on your rear display counter, and position it so your clerks can use it easily. When customer traffic increases, add a second grinder. As with your espresso machine, cleaning and maintaining your grinder is crucial.

A Matter of Taste

The language of coffee is complex, and you'll need to do some in-depth studying to be able to communicate comfortably with true coffee aficionados. Professional coffee bean tasters use a process called cupping to determine the quality, acidity, and aroma of beans for selection in their blends. Here are some basic tasting terms you'll need to be familiar with:

○ *Acidity.* This is the sensation of dryness that the coffee produces under the edges of your tongue and on the back of your palate. Without sufficient acidity, coffee tends to taste flat, so this is a desirable characteristic. Don't confuse acidity with sour, which is an unpleasant, negative flavor characteristic.

○ *Aroma.* Smell is a very powerful sense, and fragrances contribute to the flavors we discern on our palates. The aroma of brewed coffee has a wide range of subtle nuances.

○ *Body.* The feeling, or the texture, of the coffee in your mouth is its body. An example of body is the difference between the way whole milk and water feel in your mouth. Coffee body is related to the oils and solids extracted during brewing.

○ *Flavor.* Acidity, aroma, and body combine to create the overall perception of the coffee in your mouth, and that is its flavor. General flavor characteristics are richness, which refers to body and fullness; complexity, which is the perception of multiple flavors; and balance, which is the satisfying presence of all the basic taste characteristics.

Most coffeehouses have about five different varieties of coffee brewed and ready at the bar. It's important to keep the coffee fresh and warm. Some shops use the warmers that come with coffee machines or hot pads to help maintain heat, while others prefer to take the coffee immediately from the machine and pour it into insulated dispensers or carafes. Because of their high temperatures, warming plates tend to keep coffee so hot that it loses freshness and develops a burned flavor after 30 minutes or so. That means you don't want to serve coffee that's been kept on a burner for more than a half hour.

You will need to grind beans every morning and at intervals throughout the day. To ensure the freshest coffee, you should grind beans for each pot of coffee you make. For espresso, the rules are a little different. Because it is made by the cup, you are better off grinding perhaps half a pound or a pound at a time to accelerate the process. Your customer traffic and menu will determine what you need to grind and how many pots should be ready.

An over-the-counter coffee bar that seats 35 people may need to keep five varieties of coffee (four regular roasts and one decaf) brewing in five pots at any given time, while operating a single-capacity espresso machine. A popular 100-seat coffeehouse may have 15 different coffees ready to drink throughout the day (perhaps 11 regular and four decaf) and have a barista working a double-capacity espresso machine constantly.

Bakery

Bread: Its role in our lives is larger than simple nourishment. Bread has always been a fundamental part of our world. Thousands of years ago, people learned to soak wheat kernels, beat them to a pulp, shape them into cakes, and cook them over a fire. Crushed cereal grains—a precursor to

Bright Idea

You can sell more bread and increase profits by selling hot, buttered rolls or bread by the slice. This is an attractive concept to customers, especially if you're located in a shopping area and also offer a selection of beverages. The taste of a fresh slice of warm, buttered cinnamon bread will keep shoppers coming back. Most bakers charge at least 50 cents per slice.

flour—have been found in the 8,000-year-old remains of Swiss lake dwellers. By 1680 B.C., the Egyptians had invented leavened bread as well as the bakery. They established a hierarchy of breads: wheat for the rich, barley for the middle class, and sorghum for the poor. Centuries later, the British parliament enacted a series of laws that limited the profits bakers could make from bread and required that every baker put his mark on his loaves; it was the beginning of the trademark.

As colonists settled in the New World, their wheat crops flourished and so did bread innovation. The first successful threshing machine was invented, and milling processes were refined, creating better-quality flour. By 1850 there were more than 2,000 commercial bakeries in the United States.

With the emergence of strip malls and competition from supermarkets with in-store bakeries, "bread only" retail bakeries have almost disappeared from the United States. In addition to selling bread, bakeries today offer cakes, scones, bagels, and coffee drinks and sometimes even offer full menus, including sandwiches, hot entrees, beer, and wine. Consumers love fresh bakery goods, but the market is extremely competitive. As you develop your particular bakery concept, keep in mind that you'll need something to differentiate yourself from other bakeries in town.

Before you start, survey the market. People strongly prefer some breads over others. The age, income level, and ethnic background of your market are important considerations when

Easy Bake

Staggering baking schedules throughout the day guarantees fresh product for the customer. To set up your daily baking schedule efficiently, start by baking breads with high yeast levels or shorter proofing times. Get these first batches in the oven so they can bake while you're mixing breads with longer proofing times. You'll be ready to take a batch out of the oven at the same time another batch finishes the final proofing stage.

The average batch of bread takes about an hour and 45 minutes to bake. However, you can bake 15 to 20 varieties a day by baking all the whole wheat–based breads together, for example.

deciding what breads and other items to offer. Begin by checking area supermarket shelves to see which breads are fast movers and which end up on the day-old rack. Don't be afraid to ask grocery-chain buyers what the bestsellers are.

In the Western United States, exotic breads remain popular. In the South, soft white bread is the bestseller, and cakes make up a significant portion of bakery sales. People in the Midwest seem to favor white bread as well, and sales of cakes, muffins, and cookies are strong in this area. The preferred bread in the Northeast is the traditional Italian loaf; cakes, doughnuts, and bagels are also popular.

You'll need to decide whether you're going to bake hearth or pan breads or both. Hearth breads are made directly on a shelf or oven bottom, while pan breads are made in loaf pans. French, rye, and Italian varieties are leaders of the "hearth" breads. Your product mix will depend, in part, on how much of a purist you want to be and how much your customers like natural foods.

The best location for a bakery is a middle- to upper-middle income area with a population of at least 100,000. In less affluent neighborhoods, buyers might not want to pay the extra money for a loaf of specialty raisin bread when they can get plain white bread for substantially less at the supermarket.

Keep in mind that breads are low-margin items. It's possible but not likely that you would be able to make a living on high-volume bread sales alone. It's better to offer a wide variety of products.

Once you get your systems in place, producing at high volume shouldn't be a problem. After about four months in business, you should easily be able to produce 35,000 loaves of bread a month. That said, baking thousands of loaves a day is one thing, but selling them is another. Set realistic production and sales goals based on customer flow and projected growth. Also, become familiar with your customers' buying patterns. Demand for certain products will be different on different days of the week.

You can get formula recipes from suppliers, some flour mills and, of course, from cookbooks. Many people who start bakeries are already avid bakers and spend a lot of time baking at home. Even many large multimillion-dollar wholesale bakeries began with a person who baked as a hobby. Tried-and-true home recipes can be adapted for large-scale baking.

Smart Tip

Tip...

If you are going to sell wholesale, don't try to serve the commercial supermarkets. Most buy in huge volume, drive hard pricing bargains, and can change suppliers with no notice. Find wholesale customers who appreciate the quality you provide. Portland, Maine, bakery owner Jim Amaral, for example, sells to independent groceries, sandwich shops and delis, health food stores, schools, corporate cafeterias, and restaurants. "We stay away from big stores because they treat the product like a commodity," he says. "We've had them come to us, and we've turned them down."

Competition

The key to combating your competitors is knowing their business as well as you know your own. Here are some of the places where you can expect competition:

- *Supermarket bakeries.* In-store bakeries at supermarkets offer shoppers the convenience of one-stop shopping. What these bakeries usually lack, however, are high-quality baked goods and personal service. Many supermarkets use mixes or even buy ready-to-sell baked products rather than baking them from scratch. The items they do bake fresh are usually made early in the morning, so the store doesn't have that bakery-fresh aroma throughout the day.

  Supermarket bakers may not market their services as aggressively as independent bakeries might. While supermarkets may mention these departments in their weekly ads and announce in-store bakery specials over the intercom, they generally do not focus strongly on this segment of their business. With aggressive promotion, you should be able to compete successfully with such bakeries.

- *Chain bakeries.* These have the advantage of strong advertising campaigns to promote the chain name so it's recognizable. By purchasing a franchise, the franchisee automatically gets the benefit of the franchisor's marketing skills and ad budget. Chain bakeries also usually sell high-quality food at competitive prices. They should provide good service, but depending on how busy they are, might not always do so. They don't always get to know their customers as independent bakeries do. This is where you have an advantage.

Not by Bread Alone

Bread may be the staff of life, but it is certainly far from the only item produced by bakeries. For example, a baker may also bake pies, cakes, cheesecakes, cookies, doughnuts, rolls, pretzels, croissants, bagels, muffins—the list goes on. You may want to offer a range of items, as does Jim Amaral, owner of Borealis Breads in Portland, Maine, or you may want to specialize in a very narrow product line, which is how Kenny Burts built Key Lime Inc. in Smyrna, Georgia. (Burts makes key lime pies exclusively—more than 1,500 of them every day.)

If you choose to focus on a narrow product line, it needs to be outstanding. "We had people tell us early on, 'You can't survive on this one product,'" Burts recalls. "But I knew it was so special and so good that we could. Where we were able to excel was that we have something very unique and something nobody else was doing."

Your product line will be guided by a variety of factors. Amaral, for example, loves sourdough bread, and that's what he started his bakery with. Burts loves key lime pie and was making it as a hobby when friends urged him to go into business.

In addition to your own personal preferences, consider the demands of your market. Who will your customers be, and what type of baked goods do they buy? This information should have been revealed by your initial market research.

Consider your available space and equipment. Be sure they are adequate for the product line you choose. Can your equipment do double or even triple duty? Will you have to spend a lot of time cleaning equipment and work areas to switch from making one product to another? How will that affect your productivity and profitability?

Think about how your products work together and about the collective image they project. For example, if you bake a variety of breads and have only one dessert or sweet item, that product doesn't really fit in with your primary image. Or, if you're promoting your business as a whole-grain or natural-foods bakery, you don't want to have items that include highly processed or artificial ingredients.

Setting Up Your Facility

You have several options when selecting your facility. If you will specialize in serving customers on the go, you probably won't need a very large facility: 1,000 to 1,500 square feet, including kitchen space, should suffice. On the other hand, if you choose to offer a full menu and allow space for customer seating, you may want a space as large

---

Credit Where Credit Is Due

Most of your retail sales will be paid in cash, check, or credit card. You'll want to get a deposit or full payment in advance for special orders. But if you are selling wholesale, your customers will likely expect you to extend credit. Accurate record keeping is critical to maintaining your profitability.

Create a permanent record of credit sales, and maintain it separately from your sales slips and invoices. This record should show the date, the invoice number, the amount of any new charges, a running balance of the total amount owed, the date and amount of each payment received, and a record of any invoices, collection letters, and collection phone calls made to this customer.

Make sure your invoices are clear, accurate, and timely. Send them to the right address and correct person. The prices on invoices should agree with the quotes on purchase orders or contracts, and disputes should be handled promptly. Your invoice and contracts should also clearly state the terms of sale (such as "net 30 days").

as 3,000 square feet. Keep in mind that having more square footage doesn't necessarily mean higher sales, so you may want to start small and expand or move if business warrants.

Plan on spending anywhere from $20,000 to $200,000 or more on the facility, depending on whether you are converting an existing facility or building from the ground up.

There is no one-size-fits-all bakery layout, which is why we haven't provided a sample layout in this chapter. If you will be starting a retail bakery, your front setup will be similar to the layout of the sandwich shop/deli (see Chapter 7 for information on setting up this type of facility). The back will depend on what you're baking. It's best to check out similar operations for guidance. This advice also applies to setting up a wholesale bakery.

Kitchen/Production Area

The kitchen is usually located in the back of the store and includes all your bread-baking equipment, such as a mixer, divider, roller, proof box (a device that maintains the right temperature and humidity for dough to rise), oven and walk-in refrigerator or cooler. You will also need counter space for baking and decorating activities, and enough space for your employees to move around comfortably. Arrange production equipment according to the sequence of operations so you eliminate backtracking, reduce materials handling, and streamline the flow of work. Most bakeries allot at least 40 percent of their space to the kitchen.

Front Retail/Display Area

In the front of your operation, you will have a retail area that includes such things as pastry display cases, a checkout counter, at least one cash register, and maybe a few pieces of equipment behind the counter, such as a cappuccino machine, coffee machine, soft drink dispensers, or other refreshment machines. The presentation of your storefront should be appealing and draw customers in.

You may also want to provide tables and chairs for customers, either inside or on a patio, so they can eat on the premises. Devote about 35 to 40 percent of your space to this area.

Bakery Major Equipment and Fixtures Checklist

- ❏ Bench scrapers
- ❏ Cash register
- ❏ Counters/display cases
- ❏ Dishwashing machine
- ❏ Dough divider
- ❏ Dough thermometers
- ❏ Lighting
- ❏ Mixer
- ❏ Molder (rounder)
- ❏ Oven
- ❏ Pans

- ❏ Proofer
- ❏ Racks
- ❏ Refrigerator
- ❏ Scales
- ❏ Showcases
- ❏ Sinks
- ❏ Slicer
- ❏ Tables and chairs
- ❏ Utensils
- ❏ Ventilation

Restrooms

You will need at least one restroom that is accessible to employees and possibly to customers. You may want to have two—one for men and one for women—especially if you offer a sit-down eating area. Your local health department can advise you on any legal requirements that may apply for restrooms.

Office/Shipping/Receiving Area

See the guidelines in the chapters on opening a pizzeria (Chapter 6) and a sandwich shop/delicatessen (Chapter 7) for details on setting up this area.

Other Areas

Your bakery may also feature a hot case in the sandwich area for prepared hot foods such as lasagna; a dimmed area with spotlights at each decorator station; some successful supermarket-style presentations, such as self-service racks for bread and rolls and half-sized or quarter-sized cakes.

Equipment

The only way you'll meet high-volume production goals is with ultramodern automated equipment, such as Jet Air ovens that move air for faster baking; rotating rack ovens; a drum grater/shredder that allows for continuous loading; high-speed bun lines and molders (for pan breads, baguettes, rolls, soft pretzels, and other items); conveyor

Going to Sell in a Bread Basket

Your bakery can sell its wares either wholesale or retail, or both. Jim Amaral, owner of Borealis Breads in Portland, Maine, says it's easier for a wholesale baker to transition to the retail side than the other way around. Wholesale bakeries are generally larger and organized differently than retail operations. Wholesalers need to line up their commercial accounts, develop a sales strategy and be able to service those accounts with fresh, delicious products delivered on a timely basis. Retailers need to be more concerned about generating foot traffic and attracting walk-in customers.

Retailers who try to expand into the wholesale market often find their retail facilities are inadequate in terms of space, capacity, and logistics. Amaral believes a retailer who understands this issue and is willing to open a separate wholesale location has a better chance of success.

Wholesalers who decide to expand into retail need to take the time to understand merchandising and displays and create an attractive environment for retail shoppers.

---

belts designed for high-volume operations; belt washers that reduce downtime. To reach this level of automation, figure on a minimum of $45,000 in total equipment costs. Of course, this equipment can be financed or leased with minimal down payments.

If you're starting on a small budget, you can buy used equipment packages that start at less than $20,000. Look for ads in the newspaper or in trade publications for bakeries for sale. Also keep an eye out for bankruptcy sales and special equipment auctions, as these are opportunities for substantial savings on good used equipment. However, while this equipment can get you started, you should plan to add the up-to-date items later.

Your main fixtures and equipment will be a refrigerator, sinks, display cases, a mixer, a dough divider, a molder (rounder), a proofer, a slicer, and a double-rack rotary or revolving oven.

A rounder is a device that smoothes the dough into the correct shape for baking. Look for a system with adjustable rounding tracks for more accurate results. New rounders range in price from $4,000 to $9,000.

Dividers cut a large mass of dough, dividing it into individual pieces. Models vary in the pieces of dough per hour they can process. Make certain the divider you purchase is capable of operating at the volume you anticipate for your bakery. Dough dividers can cost as little as $3,000 or as much as $10,000.

Dough is damaged somewhat by the dividing and rounding process, and the proofer gives the dough time to "relax" before the final baking stages. Inside the proofer are pockets where the dough rests. These pockets, which are typically mesh, are about the size of half a watermelon. Ranging in price from $5,000 to $60,000, proofers are available in many models.

Mixers usually come in various sizes and range in capacity from 40 quarts to about 160 quarts. For high-volume bread baking, use a spiral mixer, which holds from 100 to 200 pounds of flour. A spiral dough mixer is best.

Stat Fact

The commercial bread slicer was perfected in 1928 by Otto Rohwedder, but it was not popular with consumers. Sliced bread grew stale faster than a whole loaf. It took packaging and improved storage techniques for sliced bread to become a truly great thing.

The oven will be one of your most expensive items, at $15,000 to $26,000 or more, depending on its capacity and whether you choose a revolving oven or a pricier rack oven. In a revolving oven, the bread trays go in a revolving container, and the tray rotates, exposing the bread to all parts of the oven for even baking. Rack ovens work in a similar fashion, except vertically. You will probably be baking many types of breads,

Mixing It Up

Ingredient suppliers or flour companies will provide you with bread bases, blended mixes, and plenty of advice. A premix includes ingredients like flour, shortening, milk, and salt. You only have to add water and yeast. This cuts the number of scalings (ingredient weighings) from seven or eight to three (mix, yeast, water), making it easier to produce a finished loaf quickly.

Bases require flour, yeast, and water. To make bread dough, you add three parts flour to one part base. Once you gain experience, you'll be able to cut back on some expensive mixes and experiment with your own specialties. With mixes for only three types of bread (white, wheat, and rye), you can create an enormous variety of breads by adding ingredients according to quantity recipes (known as formulas) or to your own taste. The difference between your bread and the ordinary loaf will be in these added ingredients.

The type and amount of ingredients you order will depend on the products you offer. You'll need molasses to bake a lot of sweet breads. For "healthy" breads, you'll use products such as wheat flour, honey, and organically grown fruits.

cakes and pastries, so buy an oven with a combustion system that easily converts from direct to indirect heat. This provides flexible control of bottom and top heat, allowing you to use different baking methods for different products. For superior-quality hearth breads, the oven should have a steam-distribution system. Steam keeps breads like pumpernickel, French, and Italian from drying out and ensures a crisp crust on the outside.

Besides the major pieces of baking equipment, you'll need a wide assortment of small kitchenware items like pans, racks, scales, and utensils. Depending on the volume and type of goods you make, you may need as many as 200 pans. Half of these will be bread or sandwich pans of different sizes. The remainder may be used for rolls, pastries, and other items baked on a regular basis. One set of five pans can cost $50 or more. Expect to pay from $2,500 to more than $5,000 for pans, depending on whether you buy them used or new.

Inventory

When you're getting started, it's best to order your inventory conservatively until you know what will sell best. Your basic larder will include sugar, yeast, salt, dried fruits, shortening, nuts, cheese, and garlic powder. The premixed flours represent the largest single category of ingredient you will need. At least in the beginning, you'll be relying on premixes and won't need many additional ingredients.

Bright Idea
Use day-old bread creatively by dicing or grinding it into croutons, stuffing mix, and bread crumbs. You could also set up a thrift counter and sell day-old bread for one-third or half off the price of fresh bread. This will allow you to at least recover the cost of the raw materials on the products you aren't able to sell fresh.

You should budget 35 percent of your weekly gross income for inventory, and more than half of this outlay will go toward flour. Your monthly outlay will increase if you use a lot of special flours, like rice flour, which costs considerably more than white flour.

It's best to order flour every week or two from a nearby mill or supplier. This way, you can ensure quality control and freshness. These suppliers can also provide the paper goods you need. Polyurethane wrappings and bags represent about 3 percent of gross revenue, a surprising chunk of your business.

You Don't Have to Bake It All

Even though you operate a bakery, not every product you sell has to be baked on the premises. You have a range of options when it comes to buying baked goods from wholesale bakers.

You can buy other bakers' goods for your bakery but not advertise their name. Some companies sell fully baked products, which can be put right on the shelf as well as frozen, fully baked products, and frozen dough that has to be scooped, shaped, proofed, baked, cooled, packaged, and sold. The last choice lets you advertise your products as being "fresh baked."

Another option is to use the wholesaler's products and advertise the name of the supplier. This may require a licensing agreement so the supplier knows you are presenting its products in a good light. Some suppliers will also require a licensing fee.

Alternatively, you could become a franchisee, operating your business according to an agreement with a franchise operation.

Staffing

If you are going to be a hands-on owner, you need to be prepared to work long hours and be comfortable working on a set schedule. "There's a lot of routine to running most bakeries," says Amaral. "You make onion bread every Tuesday, you make baguettes every day of the week." At the same time, he says, "You need some artistic sense about the food you are creating, where it's coming from, and how you are going about making it."

Unless you have baking experience, you will need to hire a baker. The most efficient approach is to hire a baker/manager and an assistant baker. Although the equipment does most of the work, machinery isn't entirely reliable. Many things can go wrong that only a baker would know how to correct. Dough can be overmixed, undermixed, overproofed, and so on. It takes a lot of experience and practice to develop baker's intuition.

In addition, bakers know the inventory requirements, and they are usually well-acquainted with suppliers and manufacturers. Your baker/manager can buy the inventory, deal with suppliers, and supervise production. The assistant baker will work the night or early-morning shift, depending on shop hours and volume requirements.

Experienced bakers are paid $450 to $700 or more per week, depending on their background and your local market conditions. Bakers' assistants will sometimes work as apprentices and can be paid less. Depending on your shop hours and volume, it's usually a good idea to have an assistant manager, too.

You'll also need salespeople to work the counter, ring up customer sales, take orders for cakes and other specialty items, and keep the front area clean and orderly. Whether or not you will need cooks and servers depends, of course, on the scope of your menu. If you sell wholesale, you'll need delivery people.

How much you'll pay in wages will depend on where you're located and the specific skill and experience level of the workers.

Food and
Party Catering

Does working hard in the kitchen while everyone else is eating, drinking, and socializing in the living room sound like your idea of a good time? If your goal is to be in the catering business, the answer should be an emphatic yes. Americans' love of dining and entertaining has created a

Bright Idea

Catering is a great way to expand an existing food-service operation without investing a significant amount of capital. If you have a restaurant, deli, sandwich shop, pizzeria, or bakery, you can easily add a catering division. For example, Viva La Pasta, Rebecca Swartz's pasta shop and restaurant in West Des Moines, Iowa, also offers drop-off catering. The food is prepared and arranged on attractive platters and trays that are all disposable. Everything is dropped off ready to be set up on a buffet, and the containers can be thrown away after the event.

tremendous market for off-premises caterers across the country. A wide range of social and business events are providing the opportunity for caterers to cook up tasty dishes and delicious profits. In fact, social catering has seen some of the strongest growth in the overall food-service industry in recent years, and that trend is expected to continue.

Successful caterers are organized, consistent, and creative. They enjoy working in an environment that changes every day. "Most restaurateurs hate catering for the exact reason that I love it: It's different every day," says Ann Crane, owner of Meyerhof's & Cuisine M, a catering service in Irvine, California. "A restaurateur is happy in a completely confined space where they're in control and they don't have to worry about anything leaving the building. With catering, you can get your inside operations down to the wire, but then you have to put it all in a truck and take it someplace to set it up, and you could lose control." Another appeal

Site Seeking

Unlike a retail food-service operation, the location of your catering business is not critical from a sales perspective. You'll be going to your clients' homes or offices to discuss the event and inspect their facilities; they will have little or no need to visit your kitchen. Even so, be sure your operation does not violate any zoning ordinances or rental agreements or pose any threat to the community welfare.

Your location should be reasonably accessible by main thoroughfares, both for your employees to get to work and for you to get to various event sites. Be sure the parking lot is adequate and well-lit, as your employees may frequently be returning to their cars late at night.

Your facility needs to be able to accommodate the regular food deliveries a successful caterer will get; having standard loading docks makes this significantly easier.

Niche Hunt

Before you start your catering business, advises Salt Lake City caterer Maxine Turner, know your market from both the competition and customer perspectives, and find a niche no other caterer is serving. "Know every catering company and what they do," Turner says. "Find something someone else is not providing, and focus your attention there in the beginning. Start out small. The diversity will happen as your company grows."

She advises targeting areas near office parks, because if you do a good job for a company's breakfasts, lunches, and business parties, the employees may also hire you to handle their personal social events. Ask businesspeople you know what they look for in a caterer and what they would like to have that they can't find.

You also need to know what the other caterers in town are doing. Call them up and ask for their menus. Find out what services they offer, who works for them and who their clients are. Use that information to develop your own service package and marketing strategy. "It's much easier to get started," Turner says, "when you're providing a service people want but that no one else is offering."

of catering, she says, is the strong relationship that tends to develop with clients. "This is something that's really personal. Food is a personal reflection of the host, whether it's in a corporate environment or someone's home."

From a cost-of-entry perspective, catering is probably the most flexible of all the foodservice businesses. While you need a commercial location, you can start small and build your equipment inventory as you need to. You may even find an existing commercial kitchen that you can rent, as Maxine Turner did when she started Cuisine Unlimited, her Salt Lake City catering operation. She operated in a school cafeteria for ten years before moving into her own commercial facility.

In the beginning, if you need something unusual, such as a champagne fountain for a wedding reception, you can usually rent it rather than buy it. And your food inventory is easy to control, because in most cases you know well in advance exactly how many people you're cooking for.

Off-premises caterers—those who take the food to the customers rather than a catering department that operates on-site in a hotel or convention center—may offer everything from a gourmet breakfast in bed for two to elegant dinners for 20 to charity galas for more than 1,000. Some caterers specialize in one kind of food—cakes and breads, for example—while others offer a wide range of services, including floral arrangements, specialized props, and costumes for theme parties, and wedding coordination.

The three major markets for off-premises caterers are:

- *Corporate clients.* The primary need of this market is food for breakfast and lunch meetings, although there will be some demand for cocktail parties and dinners. Service can range from simply preparing a platter of food that is picked up by the client to cooking an elaborate meal and arranging it at the site of the meeting.
- *Social events.* Millions of dollars are spent each year on wedding receptions—most of them on food. Other special events that are commonly catered include bar and bat mitzvahs, anniversary dinners, birthday parties, and graduations.
- *Cultural organizations.* Opera houses, museums, symphonies, and other cultural and community organizations frequently have catered events ranging from light hors d'oeuvres to formal dinners, sometimes for as many as several thousand people.

You will see a tremendous amount of crossover between these market groups. Turner started out with a primarily corporate clientele, serving continental breakfasts and boxed lunches. As her business grew, the corporate customers began hiring her to handle their personal social events, such as weddings and parties. And while she still does simple breakfasts and lunches, she's also catered such events as the celebration for the 100th episode of the hit TV series, *Touched by an Angel*, which was filmed in Salt Lake City.

Of course, there is a wide range of additional markets and specialties. You might cook for people with very specific dietary restrictions, such as kosher, macrobiotic, or other special food-preparation requirements. You might focus on afternoon teas, celebration breakfasts, or even picnic baskets. Another popular niche market is cooking health-conscious meals for dual-career couples who don't have time to cook for themselves. You can either go to their home and prepare the meal there or cook at your own facility and deliver the food ready to be served. Another option is to offer several days' or a week's worth of meals prepared in advance that your customers can simply heat and serve. Let your imagination run wild with possible market ideas, then do some basic market research to see what's likely to work.

First-rate caterers can demand and get top dollar for their services—but you and your food must be top rate. You should also keep in mind some general market trends. For the most part, extravagant meals and rich foods are a thing of the past. These days, people are eating less beef and more poultry and fish, and they are drinking less hard liquor and more wine. They are also more concerned about the bottom line than they once were. Many caterers say these trends have forced them to be more creative chefs, working with spices and ethnic dishes rather than rich sauces.

Setting Up Your Facility

The foundation of your catering business is your commercial kitchen. Reserve at least 75 percent of the area for food production, 15 percent for receiving and storage, and the remaining 10 percent for the office, where administrative activities take place. If you provide a lot of props and accessories for events, you may need additional storage.

The main thing to keep in mind when laying out your facility is to set up an efficient food preparation area. Organize your appliances, work surfaces and equipment systematically so you're not trotting ten feet to the sink to wash a handful of vegetables or carrying hot pots across the room to drain pasta.

Organize your kitchen around the major appliances and work areas for easy accessibility. For example, everything you need for cooking should be in close proximity to the stove, and all necessary peeling and cutting tools should be stored near the vegetable prep counter.

Give yourself plenty of clear work space. Ideally, your counters should be stainless steel for both maintenance reasons and sanitary reasons. Wooden counters are illegal in many areas because they increase the risk of food contamination. "We have a lot of linear table space," says Crane. "A lot of our business will be 500 box lunches or 20,000 pieces of hors d'oeuvres for a party, and we'll need a lot of flat counter space, rolling racks, and movable pieces to put them together."

Locate your dishwasher next to the sink so you can prerinse dishes and utensils. If you plan to handwash your dishes, a triple-sink arrangement (one sink for soaking, one for

Don't Try this at Home

Although some successful caterers start their businesses from home, most industry experts caution that the potential risks involved outweigh the economic advantages. Operating without health and fire department approval immediately opens you up to liability risks. Most insurance companies won't insure your business without compliance with state regulations and licensing requirements. In addition, you won't get wholesale price breaks from reputable food distributors who refuse to sell to operators without a resale license. Without adequate insurance, licensing, and payment of workers' compensation, some operators have lost their homes in lawsuits filed either by clients or injured workers. Bite the bullet and do it right from the start.

Of course, even when they are properly licensed and located, legitimate caterers often face stiff competition from cooks operating illegally from their homes in violation of health codes. It's difficult for a caterer working out of a commercial kitchen to price competitively against such adversaries, who don't have the same overhead expenses. Even so, don't let these illegal operators drive your prices down to an unprofitable level. Focus on professional service and quality food, and you'll be around long after the home-based cooks have given up.

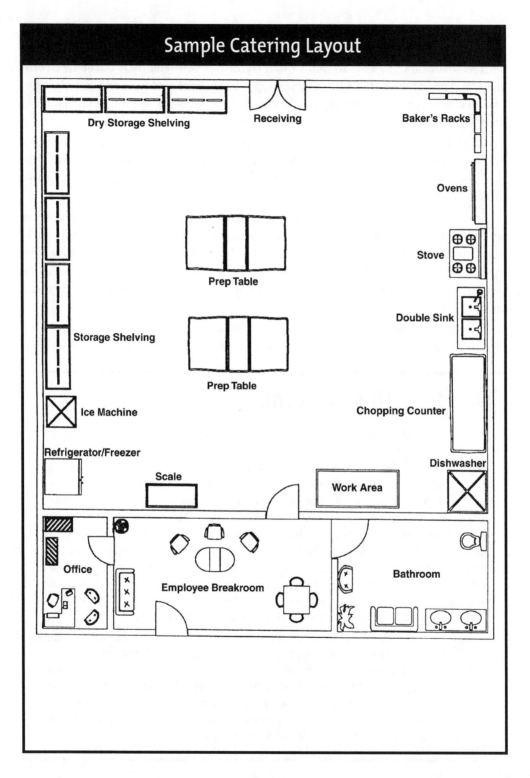

Sample Catering Layout

Dry Storage Shelving

Receiving

Baker's Racks

Ovens

Stove

Prep Table

Double Sink

Storage Shelving

Prep Table

Chopping Counter

Ice Machine

Refrigerator/Freezer

Scale

Work Area

Dishwasher

Office

Employee Breakroom

Bathroom

washing, and one for rinsing) is best. Keep racks on the counter next to the rinsing sink for drying the dishes, and store clean dish towels near the sink. A garbage disposal is a must for disposing of food scraps. Some municipalities require a separate sink for hand washing, so check your local health codes to be sure you set up right the first time.

The receiving area should be separate from the food preparation area and needs to be accessible to delivery vans. Ideally, it should have double doors and a hand truck for the easy transport of goods. You should also have a weighing scale to ensure that your deliveries are correct.

Your office area does not need to be elaborate. A simple desk, chair, phone, and computer should be sufficient.

If you have room, set up a small area where employees can hang their street clothes and store their personal belongings. You will also want to put your restrooms in this space. A table and chairs for employees to use while on their breaks is a nice touch.

There is no one-size-fits-all layout for a catering operation. The best research you can do is to check out other operations and adapt them to your needs.

Kitchen Equipment

As you look at all the possibilities for equipping your commercial kitchen, you may find yourself overwhelmed by the quantity and potential cost of what you need. Just keep in mind that you don't need everything listed in this chapter to get started—and you may never need some of the items. It all depends on your volume and the type of food you are interested in preparing. Also, the price estimates listed here are for new equipment. Smart shopping for used items can save you a bundle.

Your major equipment purchases are likely to include:

- *Two commercial ovens.* One should be a hot top (an oven with a solid metal top that heats evenly) and the other should be a range top (an oven with the ringed metal burners you see in consumer kitchens). Expect to pay anywhere from $900 to $2,200 per oven, depending on size and number of burners.

- *Two convection ovens.* These ovens cook by circulating heated air and allow for very efficient cooking that uses all the available oven space. A double convection unit, with two ovens stacked on top of each other, will run $4,500 to $5,000.

- *Refrigerator.* A three-door commercial refrigerator will cost $2,000 to $3,000.

- *Freezer.* A two-door commercial freezer will cost $2,200 to $2,400.

- *Dishwasher.* A commercial dishwasher will be about $2,500.

- *Commercial-grade mixer.* This item can range from $450 to $2,200, depending on capacity.

- *Scale.* A 300-pound scale will ensure that items you purchase by weight are delivered in the correct amount. The price of $1,500 to $2,000 you will pay for a good scale is well worth the investment in inventory control.

- *Ice machine.* Ice storage capacity should range from 45 to 400 pounds, depending on your needs. Prices increase with capacity, but you can expect to pay $800 to $1,800.

- *Food processor.* This item will cost $400 to $850.

- *Slicer.* This product is needed for meats and cheeses for sandwiches and deli trays. Cost is $500 to $2,000.

- *Sink.* You will need either two or three compartments. A sink will cost between $400 and $700.

- *Stainless-steel worktables.* You'll pay about $120 each for tables.

- *Baking equipment.* You will need a proofing box (about $1,400) and a baker's rack (about $150) if you plan to do your own baking.

- *Pizza oven.* If you plan to make pizzas, expect to pay $750 to $2,000 for a pizza oven.

- *Two heat lamps.* You need these for keeping hot hors d'oeuvres warm at buffets. You will pay $100 to $250 each.

- *Two hotboxes.* Hotboxes are necessary for transporting hot food. Expect to pay $300 to $600 each.

- *Carrying units.* Four to six fiberglass carrying units are needed for transporting both hot and cold food. These run $100 to $400 each.

- *Two to four coffeemakers.* Commercial coffeemakers run $200 to $550 each.

- *Six stainless-steel chafing dishes.* These cost $60 to $120 each.

Miss Manners

An extremely valuable piece of "equipment" is a good book on etiquette. Amy Vanderbilt, Charlotte Ford, and others have written informative etiquette guides. You can check out these books from your local library, then purchase the one that best suits your needs. It will help clear up any questions you might have about table display, serving protocol, proper attire, and other issues that you may encounter from time to time. Your clients will expect you to know the answers to questions they may have about throwing their party in the most appropriate way, so brush up on your knowledge of etiquette.

- *Miscellaneous serving items.* You will need assorted trays, sauce bowls, vegetable platters, meat platters, salad bowls, and punch bowls.

Cooking and Serving Equipment

In addition to major appliances and event accessories, you'll need an assortment of utensils for preparing and serving a variety of hors d'oeuvres and full meals. If you're an experienced cook, chances are you already own most of the cooking equipment you need. "The first mixing bowls I had were from my own kitchen," Turner says. "My first trays were wedding gifts I hadn't used in 10 years. My first inventory was my own personal things." Later, she began a wish list of items her chefs said they wanted or needed. When a particular item was repeatedly requested, she would budget for the purchase.

The point is that it's not necessary to go out and buy everything at once. Get the most frequently used items, of course, but give yourself some time to see what you really need before you buy an assortment of special equipment. You could easily spend $500 to $2,500 or more on miscellaneous cooking utensils such as flatware, spatulas, garlic presses, cutting boards, and so on—but you don't have to. Don't buy needlessly. And remember: If your rate of use doesn't justify the cost of purchasing, you can always rent.

As you go along, you'll also learn to use whatever the client has for decoration, preparation and serving. You can combine your items with theirs, particularly if you are catering an event in someone's home.

Use the following equipment list as a guide, and accept or discard the suggestions as seems appropriate for your particular operation.

- *Utensils.* You will need small and large ladles, tongs, kitchen spoons, measuring spoons (metal and plastic), measuring cups (metal and plastic), carving boards, cutting boards, spatulas, wire whisks, pastry brushes, a potato peeler, a flour sifter, a can opener, a knife sharpener, an aluminum colander, funnels, a cheese grater, a radish rose, a melon ball maker, a garlic press, a pastry bag with assorted tips, a portion scale, meat and candy thermometers, an egg slicer, heavy-duty plastic food warmers, a citrus knife, sterno setup(s), wicker bread baskets, wicker cracker baskets, and three-prong plug adapters.
- *Knives.* A quality set of kitchen knives (with three brads holding the blade to the handle) can be bought for $200 to $300. The types of knives you need are carving, cheese, bread, paring, boning, and chef's cleaver.
- *Pots and pans.* You need frying pans; pots in 1/2-, 1-, 2-, 3-, 4-, 5-, 6-, and 10-quart capacities; a double boiler; a spaghetti pot; a fondue pot with warmer; omelet pans; roasting pans.
- *Mixing bowls.* You'll need an assortment of ceramic, stainless-steel, and glass bowls in varying sizes.

- *Baking dishes.* Depending on whether you'll be doing your own baking or buying breads and pastries from a bakery, you'll need nine-inch pie pans, nine-inch cake pans, rectangular cake pans, cookie sheets, muffin pans, angel-food cake pans, bundt cake pans, spring-side pans, loaf pans, tart tins, and quiche dishes.

- *Hors d'oeuvres trays.* You should have small and large pizza pans, silver serving trays (round, square and oblong), a coffee urn, and a candle warmer.

- *Chinaware.* Cups and saucers, soup bowls, salad bowls, salad plates, bread plates, dinner plates, base plates, and dessert plates are a necessity. White porcelain is a good choice, since it's durable, dishwasher safe, and goes well with a variety of foods and decorating themes.

- *Glassware.* You'll need water goblets, red-wine glasses (10-ounce), white-wine glasses (6-ounce), champagne flutes, martini glasses, highball glasses, old-fashioned glasses, cordial glasses, and brandy snifters.

- *Flatware.* Dinner knives, butter knives, dinner forks, fish forks, salad forks, soup spoons, iced-tea spoons, and teaspoons are essential. High-quality stainless-steel flatware will wear better than silverware and will require much less maintenance (in terms of polishing).

- *Linens.* You will probably need napkins, round tablecloths, and rectangular tablecloths.

- *Cocktail accessories.* Pitchers, serving cart(s), strainers, shakers, stirrers, toothpicks, cocktail napkins, corkscrew(s), and ice bucket(s) are a requirement.

- *Miscellaneous.* You might also need cream and sugar sets, ashtrays, salt and pepper mills, a wheeled serving cart, scissors, candles, ribbons, matches, masking tape, paper napkins, transparent tape, garbage bags, garbage cans, paper doilies, mops, buckets, brooms, dustpans, and a first-aid kit.

Company Vehicle

For most catered events, you'll be transporting food and equipment. You can either use your personal vehicle if the amount of required supplies is small enough, or you'll have to lease or purchase a vehicle that will meet your needs.

It's possible to spend $30,000 or more outfitting a new van with all the inventory and equipment a caterer might need. Some caterers have elaborate vans equipped with virtually everything but running water. Some outfit their vehicles with propane tanks to cook on-site for outdoor events where electricity is unavailable, and mobile warmers and refrigerators for locations where the facility is limited. But these are very expensive extras that are not necessary for someone just starting out. Your best bet is a no-frills approach: Invest in a good late-model used van; you should be able to find one for $8,000 to $12,000 if you shop carefully.

Inventory

The advantage of catering over other food-service businesses is that you always know how many people you will have to feed. There's no guesswork, no waste and no inventory needed in the traditional sense—at least in the beginning.

Certainly staples such as flour, sugar, grains, spices, canned goods, and frozen foods can be purchased in bulk and stocked on a long-term basis. But you won't be stocking food inventory the same way a restaurant does. Typically, you won't purchase foods until you have agreed on an exact menu with a client and determined the number of guests. Of course, as your business grows, you'll be able to stock more inventory and take advantage of the savings of volume purchasing.

The key to good shopping is organization. Sit down with your menu and make a list of everything you will need to produce the party. If the preparation is going to require any new equipment you don't yet own, be sure to include that on your shopping list.

Once you have determined everything you'll need, organize your list by store and department. Then figure out the most efficient order in which to visit each store. A single shopping excursion may take you to a farmer's market, a wholesale outlet, a general grocery store, a delicatessen, a bakery and a gourmet shop. Most of your shopping should be done the day before the party, although some fresh items (such as lettuce and bread) should be purchased the day of the event.

Wholesale or Retail?

Depending on the size of your jobs, it may or may not be worth it to buy wholesale goods. There are dealers in every major city who can supply you with fresh produce, meat, and other items in large quantities at low prices. This can mean significant savings when you're buying for large jobs or for several events at a time. Also, a big advantage of wholesalers is that most of them will deliver to your kitchen. But if you just need eight chicken breasts for a small dinner party, most wholesale dealers probably wouldn't be interested in making the sale. It would probably be easier to visit your nearby supermarket.

Staffing

Most catering operations have a core permanent staff that is supplemented by part-timers on a per-project basis. To provide quality service, you need to understand the basic structure and division of labor at a catered affair.

The three basic kinds of catered social affairs are the formal, sit-down dinner; the informal buffet dinner; and the cocktail party. Naturally, as individual events develop personalities of their own, these three definitions often vary or converge.

The majority of business affairs will require little or no service and will mainly involve preparing platters of food for business luncheons that are either picked up at your facility or delivered to your clients. However, some business events—such as office holiday parties or formal dinners for major clients—will be run the same way as social affairs.

Typically, it takes two days to prepare food for any party. If all your ingredients are fresh and prepared from scratch at the last possible minute, those days will be full. An average party serving 50 to 125 people requires one chef plus one or two kitchen helpers, depending on the complexity of the setup.

Managers and Other Employees

The key employee at any catered affair (and this is going to be you in the beginning) is the project manager. This person organizes the food preparation and serving, hires the temporary help, and oversees the entire affair. The project manager must also be able to pitch in and prepare food in an emergency if the chef or one of the kitchen assistants fails to show up.

If you supply bartenders for an event, a good ratio is one bartender for every 50 people. You will either employ these specialists yourself or subcontract their services, depending on your volume.

Waiters, buspersons, drivers, and warehouse personnel may be hired on either a temporary or permanent basis. Temporary means on a per-project basis; permanent means an employee who is paid regularly on a full- or part-time schedule. If you have 10 servers you can call to work as needed, they are typically paid as temporary workers.

Serving and food preparation personnel should be considered separate categories. A server might double as a driver and even as a busperson, but cooking and serving are two different areas of labor. Even with that in mind, you should look for employees who are flexible and won't mind pitching in as needed in an emergency.

Clients who are trying to save money will frequently try to cut down on the number of service personnel for an event. Be firm and clear as you explain why this is not a good idea. Guests who can't get their dirty plates taken away, get another hors d'oeuvre, or get a fresh drink are unhappy guests. Nothing will ruin a party quicker than insufficient serving personnel.

Event Staffing Guidelines

There is no better teacher than experience when it comes to knowing how to staff various events. To help you get started, let's look at what experienced caterers would do when catering a party for about 100 people.

For a formal sit-down dinner with many courses, there will be 8 or 10 people per table and 10 to 12 tables. You'll need two cooks or one cook plus one or two assistants. For most parties, one server per table will be sufficient, but this can also vary. Some caterers will have one server for every 15 people; others will put two at each table to keep everything running smoothly. Another option would be to have one server for each table, plus an extra server for every two tables to remove dirty dishes and glasses. The project manager will oversee the service to all tables.

An informal buffet dinner will require three or four serving people and one cook, plus the manager. All people on the job should be versatile enough to double on tasks after the job is completed—for example, clearing tables, storing food and loading equipment.

Now Presenting...

In addition to preparing delicious food, you must also be concerned with how your meals look. Your clients hire you to create a special experience for them, to use your professional expertise and abilities to design a meal they couldn't produce themselves.

This doesn't mean simply plopping a sprig of parsley or a tomato rosette on each plate before it goes out the kitchen door. It does mean planning your garnishes and arranging your plates so that your food looks as good as it tastes. You have only two rules when it comes to garnishing: Everything should be edible, and the garnish should taste good with the food. Beyond these rules, the only limit is your imagination.

For both formal and informal dinners, if there is cocktail service, two bartenders will be required.

For a cocktail party for 100 people, have at least one bartender on hand, plus two service personnel. If both hot and cold hors d'oeuvres will be offered, upgrade to three or four servers. If a lot of blended drinks will be served, your best bet is to have two bartenders. For a party of this size, some caterers routinely have two bartenders, two servers, and a busperson, regardless of the types of drinks being served. Still other operations have servers double as buspersons. Staffing requirements vary greatly depending on the type of cocktail party desired.

Some caterers don't provide the bartender or liquor for a cocktail party but will refer the client to reputable sources for this. Some provide ice, glasses, and bar setups, while others do not. Some provide beer and wine but no hard liquor or mixers.

These guidelines will help you plan your staffing until you are comfortable estimating your labor needs. No matter what kind of event you cater, having enough help on hand is crucial. Service can make or break a catered affair—and lack of it will surely kill your business.

> ## Bright Idea
> If you have a steady client who hires you for several events each year, change your catering menus monthly to offer variety and a new look.

Developing Menus and Setting Prices

Even though your clients will tell you what they want you to serve, you still need menus. Of course, none of those menus should be carved in stone; they must be flexible enough to accommodate your clients' preferences.

Providing sample menus will give you a solid base for meeting with clients, and they may give your clients some ideas about food combinations they would not have otherwise had. Also, you can cost out your sample menus beforehand, which will make figuring prices much easier. This will also allow you to give your clients a more accurate estimate.

Nutritionally, you should strive to produce balanced meals with a good blend of the basic food groups. Each meal should contain about 1,000 calories.

You should also balance ingredients, textures and tastes. If you serve leek and garlic soup as the opener, for example, you should not serve garlic chicken as the main course. Similarly, if the main course is chicken mousse, chocolate mousse would be out of place as a dessert.

> ## Smart Tip
> *Tip...*
> Coordinate menus with the season. Serve lighter foods in the summer (such as lobster and rice, Cobb salad) and heavier in the winter (such as beef Wellington and cassoulet).

Bright Idea

To check out the competition when you're doing your initial market research, give a few catered parties of your own. Hire the caterers you expect to be your strongest competitors so you can see exactly how they operate and what level of service they provide. It's a worthwhile investment in the future of your company.

When creating sample menus, include a variety of dishes and price ranges. If you specialize in Southern cooking or spectacular desserts, organize your menus to make these elements the focal point of your meals.

If you are planning to focus on the wedding market, you will need a wide range of menus for hot buffets, cold buffets, sit-down dinners, and other arrangements. A buffet table with a combination of hot and cold hors d'oeuvres, sliced meats and bread, fruit, and cheese and crackers is a very popular choice. If you go this route, you should put together a list of hors d'oeuvres that your clients can choose from. You will also need a wide range of wedding cakes (you can contract out to a local baker if cake decorating is not one of your talents). A photo album showing pictures of the kinds of cakes you can offer will help your clients select the cake they want. Punches—both with champagne and nonalcoholic—are also a staple at weddings.

The corporate market leans more toward platters of food that are suitable for business breakfasts and lunches. Middle management and below will tend to want deli plates with sandwiches, cookies, vegetables and dips, fresh fruit, and similar items. If you are working with the upper echelons, you may be called on to produce something more elaborate, perhaps even cooking part of the meal at their office and supplying a server. Develop several different menus based on these levels of formality.

Figuring out how much to charge is probably the most difficult thing you'll need to learn. When you're new, you may not have a solid feel for how much you can charge in your marketplace, how much ingredients for a particular dish will cost, or how much labor it will take to prepare a meal. You'll get better at this over time, but when you're starting out, it's important to cost out your menus carefully so you can make a respectable profit.

To cost out a menu, first sit down with the full menu. For each dish, break out the cost of the food by ingredients. Some dishes will be easier to price than others. For example, if a recipe calls for a boneless breast of chicken, a quick trip to the store can tell you exactly how much this item will cost. It's much harder to figure out the cost of a teaspoon of salt or other seasonings. Estimate the cost of smaller quantities and staples (such as flour, sugar, salt) as best you can.

Once you've determined the prices of all your ingredients, add them up. This is the total cost of the food you will need to prepare the full menu. Multiply this figure by three to get the price you will charge the client. Dividing this figure by the number of guests will give you the price per head for the meal.

Bright Idea

Offer to provide gifts for event attendees. You can help your clients choose a memento to be placed at each setting, perhaps something imprinted with a corporate logo, or help them choose special gifts for the guest of honor or committee members. You can purchase and wrap the gifts to provide a special service for your clients and increase your own revenue.

This is the most basic method of figuring prices, and most of the time it should cover your food costs, labor, and overhead and still leave you a net profit margin of between 10 and 20 percent.

You should check your prices to make sure they are acceptable in your market by calling other caterers to find out what they charge for a comparable menu. If your prices seem to be in line with your competition, you're probably figuring correctly.

There are, of course, instances where this method won't work entirely. For example, if you are preparing a menu that is very labor-intensive, even if the ingredients aren't particularly expensive, you won't be able to pull a profit simply by multiplying your food costs, because your time and employees' wages won't be adequately covered. In these cases, you should increase your prices so you and your employees are earning a decent hourly wage, based on the number of hours it's going to take to prepare the meal. Conversely, if you're making something like filet mignon, for which the main ingredient is quite expensive but easy to prepare, you'll have difficulty justifying high prices. In this case, you might consider multiplying the cost of the steak by two and the other ingredients by three to arrive at a fair price.

The cost per person, arrived at by multiplying the cost of the food price by three and dividing by the number of guests, is the cost for the food, labor, and overhead only. It does not include the cost of liquor, rental equipment, serving staff, or anything else. Be sure the final price you quote the client takes these expenses into consideration. Use the "Catering Price Quote Worksheet" on page 131 to figure out your price quote.

When the Customer Calls

When a client calls, you must be prepared to answer all his or her questions, make suggestions and generally handle yourself in a pleasant and professional manner. The first phone call will rarely result in a sale for a number of reasons. First, the customer may be shopping several caterers. Second, you probably won't decide during that conversation exactly what is going to be served, so you won't be able to give a specific quote. Third, you'll want to inspect the site of the event before putting together your final proposal.

Catering Price Quote Worksheet

Food Costs

Item	Cost
_____	_____
_____	_____
_____	_____
_____	_____
_____	_____
_____	_____
_____	_____

Total food costs _____

Food price to client[1] _____

Liquor[2] _____

Rental equipment[3] _____

Serving staff[4] _____

Miscellaneous _____

Total price[5] _____

1. When quoting to the client, use a per-person figure; divide the worksheet number by the total number of guests to arrive at this figure.

2. You need a liquor license to provide alcohol; it is common for clients to purchase their own liquor and for you to provide the setups. The mark-up on setups can be substantial; call around to other caterers to find out what the market will bear in your area.

3. Quote your client the "retail" cost of rental equipment without a mark-up; the rental company should give you a discount, which you can include in your profit for the event.

4. Use a standard gratuity to cover the cost of serving staff; clients may also offer an additional gratuity if the service was exceptional.

5. This is the sum of the food price to client, liquor and setups, rental equipment, serving staff, and miscellaneous.

Many clients will pressure you for an exact price quote during the first phone call. Resist the temptation to do this. Even if the client knows exactly what he or she wants served, you won't know what the cost of food and labor is going to be until you've had a chance to do your own calculations. If you make up a quote on the spot, it may either be too high, in which case you'll lose

the job, or too low, in which case you'll lose money—or you'll have to raise your quote later, which is not good for customer relations. Instead, try to satisfy the client with a general price range and promise a full written proposal later.

Use the "Initial Client Contact" worksheet on page 133 as a guide for taking notes during your first conversation. Many clients will be reluctant to tell you their budget for an event, but you should try to get a fairly good idea of how much money they have to spend. You should be able to adjust your menus to suit their budget, but you'll have to know what that budget is first. There are many cost-cutting methods you can use if the client seems uncomfortable with your more-expensive-sounding suggestions. For example, you can substitute lower-cost ingredients with a similar flavor or use dishes that are easy to prepare rather than more labor-intensive ones.

After the first telephone conversation, your next meeting will likely be in person, preferably at the site where the event will be held. Bring your menus so the customer can review them and determine exactly what to serve. Get a firm number of guests and put it in writing; let the customer know that you will be planning your quote based on that number and that any changes will affect the final price. Determine the style of the event (sit-down, buffet, cocktail) and any particular equipment or service needs the client will have.

Take a tour of the site to see what equipment is available for your use and what you'll need to bring. Decide where the buffet will be, if there is one, and where the bar setup will go. Discuss staffing needs, and be very specific about who will provide what to prevent any misunderstandings later. This information should also be included in your price proposal.

Take a day or two to calculate the final price, and be sure it includes everything, then call the customer with your quote. If it's acceptable, send out a detailed contract that itemizes the prices, outlines mutual responsibilities, and requires a deposit (typically 25 to 50 percent of the total amount) upon signing.

Once you've received the signed contract and deposit, you're ready to start arranging for staff and purchasing food. A few days before the event, call the customer to confirm the number of guests and other details. If the customer wants to make changes to the contract, be as accommodating as possible, but don't let it cause you to lose money.

Checklist for Initial Client Contact

Name: _____

Address: _____

_____

Business phone: _____ Home phone: _____

Date of event: _____

Time of event: _____

Beginning: _____ Ending: _____

Location of event: _____

Type of occasion: _____

_____

Number of guests: _____

General age group of guests: _____

General mix of guests: _____

Type of service (cocktail, buffet, sit-down): _____

Foods client would like to have: _____

_____

_____

_____

Dishes to avoid: _____

_____

General budget of client: _____

Special services needed: _____

_____

_____

Timing Is Everything

You should have at least a week's notice for a catered event. A month's notice is quite common and not too much for an established caterer to ask. In fact, some catered affairs are booked as many as 10 months in advance. Of course, if a client is in a bind—for example, a business needs a deli-style luncheon for six people at the last minute—and you can handle the work, you'll build customer loyalty by doing so.

Make a Packing List

Once the food for an event is prepared and ready to go, you'll need to pack it along with the serving dishes, utensils, linens and other necessary equipment. To be sure you don't forget or lose anything, you'll need to prepare a packing list (see the "Sample Packing List" on page 135 and 136).

A day or so before the event, sit down with your menu. List the equipment you will need to finish preparing each dish on-site and to serve it. When you are finished, double-check your figures, taking care to properly count multiple units of items, such as when different dishes require the same serving equipment. Don't forget miscellaneous supplies such as cocktail napkins, toothpicks, salt and pepper shakers, and so on. If you are taking care of rental furniture or flowers, make sure these are either going to be delivered to the event site or to your kitchen or will be available for you to pick up. With your completed packing list, you can start assembling the food and supplies. Pack the items you'll need first on top so you don't have to dig through several boxes to find them. Place items close together so nothing has room to shift and break. Use common sense: Don't put sacks of crushed ice on top of the bread. Make sure all containers of food are covered tightly so they won't spill if you have to turn or stop your vehicle suddenly.

The packing list will also serve as a checklist to help you collect all your items when the party is over. Leaving items behind can quickly eat up your profits. Caterer Turner puts waterproof labels on trays and other items that identify each piece of equipment for inventory-control purposes. "If something is missing, we go back through the inventory sheets to see what party it was used at last and contact the person who ordered the catering," she says. "It's amazing what we have found. One lady had coffee pots, trays, and serving pieces from a year before. It was a drop off, and we forgot to go back and pick it up. She put it in a cupboard and forgot about it."

Sample Packing List

Client: _____

Date of event: _____

Address: _____

Item	Amount Needed	In	Out	Item	Amount Needed	In	Out
Glassware				*Accessories*			
Wine (10 oz.)				Blender			
Wine (6 oz.)				Stirrers			
Champagne/ martini				Corkscrew			
				Strainers			
Old-fashioned				Toothpicks			
Highball				Paper umbrellas			
Brandy				Ice tongs			
Liqueur				Cork coasters			
Water goblets							
Water pitchers				*Dinnerware*			
				Cups			
Bar Mixes				Saucers			
Whiskey sour				Salad plates			
Bloody mary				Dinner plates			
Orange juice				Base plates			
Grapefruit juice				Dessert plates			
Piña colada							
Collins				*Flatware*			
Heavy cream				Teaspoons			
Bitter lemon				Salad forks			
Tonic				Dinner forks			
Diet tonic				Dinner knives			
Club soda				Soup spoons			
Perrier				Serving forks			
Coke				Serving spoons			
7 UP				Butter knives			
				Cheese knives			
Food Mixes							
Lemon twists				*Table Accessories*			
Olives				Creamer			
Onions				Sugar bowl			
Pineapple wedges				Salt shaker			
Red cherries				Pepper mill			
Green cherries				Bread basket			
Celery stalks				Cracker basket			

Sample Packing List, continued

Item	Amount Needed	In	Out	Item	Amount Needed	In	Out
Punch bowl set				*Linens and Papers*			
Candles				Cocktail napkins			
Candle holders				Dinner napkins			
Ash trays				(paper)			
Toothpick holders				Toothpicks			
				Garbage bags			
Pots and Pans				Paper doilies			
Omelette pans				Dinner napkins			
Small chafing dish				(linen)			
Large chafing dish				Hand towels			
Rectangular				Tin foil			
chafing dish				Matches			
				Disinfectant			
Trays				Dishwashing			
Pizza pans				detergent			
Cookie sheets				Straight pins			
Silver trays (round)				Safety pins			
Silver trays (oblong)				Masking tape			
Silver trays (square)				Scotch tape			
				Stapler			
Utility Equipment				Ribbons			
Coffee maker							
Coffee mill				*Staple Food Items*			
3-prong adaptors				Coffee (ground)			
Sterno setup				Coffee (beans)			
Heat lamp				Decaff coffee			
Coffee pitcher				Milk			
Serving tables				Instant milk			
Ice buckets				Cream			
Bus boxes				Artificial sweetener			
Salad bowls				Sugar			
Coffee urn/burner				Tea bags			
Serving carts				Saltines			
Cheese boards				Sesame crackers			
				Pretzels			
				Breadsticks			

Beginning packer: _____ Double-checked by: _____

Time of delivery: _____

Ending packer: _____ Double-checked by: _____

Smart Tip

After you've billed each event, evaluate how things went. Collect all your receipts and figure out your total expenses. Were the costs close to the assumptions you made when you priced the event? If not, you may need to revise your menu prices or your method of estimating costs for a bid.

How smoothly did the event itself go? Did you have adequate staffing? Were the guests satisfied? What comments did you get from the guests and your client? Make notes of things that went well, so you can be sure to repeat them, and of areas where you need improvement.

At the Party

Once you've arrived at the event site, unpack everything and organize your service area. You'll want to arrive an average of 60 to 90 minutes in advance to make sure the food will be ready and available at precisely the right time.

If you are taking care of rental furniture, flowers or the bar setup, make sure everything is in place and arranged attractively. Start reheating or cooking anything that needs to be served hot. Make sure every tray that leaves the kitchen has been attractively garnished and arranged. Some caterers work with tweezers in the kitchen to arrange garnishes so that all platters look like pictures. It's an extra touch that will enhance your reputation.

As the party gets under way, keep an eye on what food is being consumed, and have more trays ready to go out as the empty ones are returned. If you are serving from a buffet table, continually replenish the trays so they don't look picked over.

Throughout the event, your serving staff should be collecting dirty dishes, emptying used ashtrays, returning empty glasses to the bar, and taking care of other things so the party site does not look cluttered and untidy.

As your servers return the dirty dishes to you, rinse and pack them for later washing. After the event is over, clean any of the client's dishes or utensils that have been used. Get out your packing list to make sure you retrieve all your own glassware, tableware, cookware, and other equipment. Also, take care that you don't accidentally take any of the client's property. Check off each item on your packing list as you load it into your vehicle.

Leftover food should be wrapped and left with the client. Floors and counters should be clean, but you shouldn't be expected to function as a maid service. Just leave the facility as you found it. You are only responsible for your own messes.

Some caterers demand payment of the balance due immediately after the event; others will send the client a bill the day after the party. Whichever you choose, be sure the client knows in advance what to expect, and make it clear that the bill does not include gratuities for the serving staff. If the client decides to tip, the money should be divided among the staff after the party.

While you should always be on the alert for ways to promote your business, you should never promote yourself at an event you're catering. "I never market myself at events,"

Turner agrees. "We're there as a support to whatever event we're doing, and that is not the proper time for us to advertise." Her company name is on the aprons the staff wears but not on anything else. And while she'll provide a business card if asked, she does not put her cards on display. A truly professional caterer, she believes, is virtually invisible at the event, where the focus should be on the occasion itself. "We don't intrude. We are not guests; we are there to provide a service. I tell this to my service staff. Also, I don't allow [my staff] to talk to each other when they're in front of the client, other than to take care of business. Even if they have friends who are attending the event, I discourage them from stopping to talk. They are there for a purpose, and that purpose is to serve the client."

11

Inventory
Buying, Storing, and Tracking Supplies

Food and beverage inventory purchasing is one of the most mismanaged areas in the food-service industry, neglected by most due to lack of knowledge. Business owners who never learned to implement proper inventory—purchasing and control—techniques can still be successful, but they will usually pay for this lack of knowledge with reduced profits, constant frustration, and years of repeated inventory-ordering mistakes.

There are two key components to inventory: acquisition and management. You must know how to find distributors you can count on to deliver quality products on time; you must be able to place accurate orders with them so you have enough of what you need when you need it; you must be able to estimate how much inventory you will consume during any given period of time—daily, weekly, monthly, or yearly.

Poor inventory management is one of the main reasons food-service businesses fail. Every shortfall or excess affects your bottom line. To succeed in this industry, you need good purchasing procedures and a system that will help you accurately control your inventory from acquisition through preparation.

Quality, prices, and availability often fluctuate in the seesaw food and beverage market. You need to study the market, pay attention to what's going on in the world and track conditions so you can buy with confidence. With practice and diligent market research, you can identify your strongest menu items and order inventory accordingly.

When you calculate basic stock, you must also factor in lead time—the length of time between ordering and receiving a product. For instance, if your lead time is four weeks and a particular menu item requires 10 units a week in inventory, then you must reorder before the basic inventory level falls below 40 units. If you do not reorder until you actually need the stock, the basic inventory will be depleted, and you'll lose sales—and probably some customers, too.

One of the ways many small-business owners protect themselves from such shortfalls is by incorporating a safety margin into basic inventory figures. The right safety margin for your particular operation depends on the external factors that can contribute to delays. You must determine your safety margin based on past experience and anticipated delays.

Caterer Ann Crane says she works closely with her kitchen manager on inventory issues and discusses the challenge with other caterers. At one point, she discovered that another caterer stocked about a quarter of the amount of dry goods that she stocks. "She told me that most of her business had a week or two of lead time, so she has plenty of time to order goods. I know another caterer who does small dinners for 10 or 20 people, and she just goes to the market that morning and picks up what she needs. But a lot of my business has just 24 to 48 hours' lead time, and we can't afford the time or money to go to the store and buy all that last-minute product. For our day-to-day breakfast and lunch business, we keep an enormous amount of goods on the shelf."

Beverage Systems

Soft drinks, milk, coffee, and hot and iced tea are necessary beverages for most food-service operations. For soft drinks, you can either offer canned beverages or buy a dispensing system. Unless you expect an extremely low sales volume in this area, the

> ## Bright Idea
>
> If you have the demand, invest in an espresso and cappuccino machine. Even though these devices are fairly expensive and time-consuming to run, coffee drinks are extremely popular. Your coffee supplier probably has both new and used machines available.

dispensing system will be more profitable. You will typically pay 50 to 60 cents a can for soft drinks, which you can then sell for about 90 cents. While that's certainly an acceptable profit, a soft-drink system will generate 10 to 15 cents more profit per drink. Syrups for colas, root beer, diet drinks, and other beverages can be obtained from your local beverage distributor.

Check with your local health department to see if you must serve milk in individual cartons or if it may be poured into glasses from a larger container. You'll make more money using the latter method.

Buy your coffee from a coffee wholesaler, which can also provide burners, coffee-brewing systems, coffee-bean grinders, and all the other equipment you need to make fresh-brewed coffee. These vendors are listed in the Yellow Pages under "Coffee Break Service and Supplies." Be sure to let the company know you run a restaurant; you'll get a better price. Also, the coffee service can supply you with individual packets of sugar and artificial sweetener, nondairy creamer, stirrers, and other coffee-related items.

Avoid freeze-dried-coffee dispensers. Although they reduce waste, they'll hurt sales; they do not offer the aroma and taste of freshly brewed coffees. Also, freeze-dried-coffee systems use much hotter water, which means customers can't drink the beverage right away. Finally, these systems often produce a bitter final product because operators put too much coffee in their machines. It's worth the money to go for fresh-brewed coffee.

Iced tea should be made at the start of the day and placed in its own stainless-steel dispenser (aluminum containers can alter the taste). Tea is remarkably cost-efficient. You can buy premeasured bags to make any specified amount. Just as with coffee, remember individual packets of sugar, artificial sweetener, stirrers, and lemon slices.

Where to Buy

You can purchase meats from a meat jobber who specializes in portion-controlled supplies for restaurants. A meat jobber will usually deliver five days a week, so, except for weekends and holidays, you won't need to stock a large quantity on-site. Though prices from this type of specialized distributor may be slightly higher than from wholesale distributors, the quality of the meat is usually excellent, and you can benefit from their expertise.

For dairy products, try to find a wholesale distributor who can handle many of your needs and negotiate a volume discount. If you purchase a great deal of cheese, milk, and eggs—as a pizzeria would—consider a daily trip to the local farmer's market to haggle with growers face to face. Often, this type of direct buying gives you the lowest price and the best quality available.

Smart Tip

Tip...

Smart Tip

Pay attention to world events. Weather, natural disasters, and politics can all impact the price and availability of various food items, which affect what you can serve and how much you must charge for it to make a profit.

Canned foods can be purchased from a processed-food distributor. These vendors function as wholesale grocers that specialize in packaged products. They can be found under "Grocers—Wholesale" in your local Yellow Pages.

Dealing with Suppliers

Regardless of what kinds of foods you offer, developing good relations with local food distributors is essential. They will be able to pass along vital information that will aid you in your purchasing activities. If you have a good rapport with your suppliers, they will also work harder on your behalf to provide you with quality products at competitive prices.

This doesn't mean wining and dining your suppliers' sales reps. Good relations simply mean paying your bills on time and being upfront with your suppliers about your needs and capabilities. You'll be pleasantly surprised at what adhering to the terms of your contract will do for you, especially in an environment where so many businesses fail to live up to their part of the bargain.

Reliable suppliers are an asset to your operation. They can bail you out when your customers make difficult demands of you, but they will do so only as long as your business is profitable for them. Like you, suppliers are in business to make money. If you argue about every bill, ask them to shave prices on every item, fail to pay promptly after goods or services have been delivered, don't be surprised when they stop calling and leave you dangling.

Of course, the food-service business is competitive on all levels, and you must look for the best deal you can get on a consistent basis from your suppliers. No business arrangement can continue for long unless something of value is rendered and received by everyone involved. The lesson is this: Don't be a doormat, but don't be excessively demanding. Tell your suppliers what you need and when you need it. Have a specific understanding about costs, delivery schedules, and payment terms. Build a relationship based on fairness, integrity and trust, and both you and your suppliers will profit.

Receiving Procedures

Only you or one of your most trusted employees should receive inventory. Compare all goods received with your purchase specifications and completed price quote

Bright Idea

Always deal with the same person at each of your wholesalers. They will quickly learn what is acceptable to you and what is not, what you mean by "ripe," and how you like things handled. This will increase your chances of getting consistent quality and service.

sheets. Weigh all products (that are sold by weight), and count all products (that are sold by count). You should also break down all the cases to check for broken or deformed containers, a full count, and spoilage. Containers of fresh produce and similar goods should be inspected thoroughly.

If you discover any shortages, spoilage, or damaged goods during the receiving process, make immediate adjustments to the invoice, which both you and the delivery person should initial. Check all mathematical calculations on the invoice, and when you're satisfied that everything is acceptable, stamp the invoice "received."

Goods should be placed immediately into their proper storage places. If you leave products strewn all over the floor, you'll find that they'll disappear. Effective storage will help you maintain adequate stocks of goods with minimum loss and pilferage. As stock is being put into storage, check it once again against your delivery report. As with receiving, this is a task only you or a trusted employee should do.

Label all items, and place them in the appropriately marked areas for easy retrieval. Make sure your inventory is constantly rotated. Goods that come in first should be used first.

Enough Is Enough

The ideal in inventory control is to always have enough product on hand to meet customer demand while avoiding both shortage and excess. Unavoidably, in the course of operating a business, both of these situations will occur. Rather than viewing them as mistakes, however, the smart restaurateur will use a shortage or an excess as an indicator of sales trends and alter the inventory control system accordingly.

If a shortage occurs, you can:

○ review the preparation and cooking processes to locate any problems

○ place a rush order

○ employ another supplier

○ use substitute ingredients

○ remove an item from the menu if key ingredients are difficult or exceptionally expensive to acquire

You can address overstocking by returning excess stock to suppliers or creating a promotion to stimulate demand. But don't just deal with the fallout of excess stock; analyze your ordering system to understand why the excesses occurred. If you conduct purchasing and reordering correctly, you should be able to keep both excesses and shortages to a minimum.

▲

Hidden Inventory Costs

Excess inventory creates additional overhead, and that costs you money. In fact, it can cost a restaurateur anywhere from 20 to 30 percent of the original investment in inventory just to maintain it. Inventory that sits in your storeroom does not generate sales or profits. Rather, it generates losses in the form of:

- food spoilage from excess shelf life
- debt service on loans used to purchase the excess inventory
- increased insurance costs on the greater value of the inventory in stock

The natural reaction of many restaurateurs to excess inventory is to move it out. While that may solve your overstocking problem, it will reduce your return on investment. In your financial projections, you based your figures on using specific ingredients in dishes that would be sold at full retail price. If you opt to clear out excess inventory by reducing menu prices and offering specials and one-time-only meal discounts, you're ultimately taking money out of your own pocket.

Responding to spoilage and inventory excesses with overly cautious reordering is understandable. The problem there is that, when you reduce your reordering, you run the significant risk of creating a stock shortage. We didn't say this would be easy.

You need to plan carefully, establish a realistic safety margin, and do your best to order only what you're sure you'll use to prepare your foods.

> ### Smart Tip   Tip...
>
> Follow your receiving procedures consistently, without exception, no matter how well you get to know a vendor or delivery person or how much you trust him or her. Finding damage or a shortage after the driver has left can create an awkward situation as you try to determine who is actually at fault. Avoid potential problems by inspecting, weighing, and counting all deliveries at the time they arrive.

Tracking Inventory

A critical part of managing inventory is tracking it—that means knowing what you have on hand, what's on order and when it will arrive, and what you have sold. This information allows you to plan your purchases intelligently, quickly recognize fast-moving items that need to be reordered, and identify slow-moving merchandise that should be marked down and moved out.

There are a variety of inventory-tracking methods you can use, from basic handwritten records to computerized bar code systems. The food-service business owners we talked to use simple systems, most on basic computer databases. Your accountant can help you develop a system that will work for your particular situation.

Controlling Bar Losses

Managing liquor inventory is one of the most challenging aspects of having a bar. Losses from spillage, theft, and honest mistakes can cost a single outlet thousands of dollars per week—dollars that fall straight to the bottom line in the form of lost profits.

One popular solution is a computerized inventory-auditing system. Bevinco, a Canadian-based company with franchises in the United States and 11 other countries, provides this service using portable electronic scales and a notebook computer. "When I started the business, we conducted a study, and I was amazed to learn that the accepted loss level in alcoholic beverages in the restaurant and bar business is 20 percent," says Barry Driedger, Bevinco's founder and president. "When you look at the volume most places do—even the smaller bars and restaurants—that's a lot of money."

Driedger is quick to point out that bar losses are not exclusively related to deliberate and calculated theft by employees. A significant amount of shrinkage can be traced to spills and carelessness in preparation, misdirected "good intentions" of bartenders who over-pour drinks for regular customers, and external fraud or theft. He also notes that although the primary reason for liquor-loss control is profitability, staff morale is likely to rise when control methods are implemented. "Most bars and restaurants have fairly large staffs, and it's usually only a small number of people who are causing the problem," he says. "The honest, hardworking people on the staff will appreciate having the dishonest people weeded out."

Bevinco's service starts with a baseline audit. After that, audits are conducted regularly—usually weekly or biweekly. All open liquor bottles, wine bottles, and beer kegs are weighed; other inventory is counted; sales and purchase figures are factored in. The auditor is then able to generate a report identifying the source and volume of losses. With that information, a plan can be developed and implemented to correct the problem. Bevinco's audits typically range from $150 to $250, depending on the size of the inventory and the frequency of the audit. Although the Bevinco system is proprietary, if you want to audit yourself, you can purchase the necessary equipment through other companies.

There are a variety of liquor inventory management systems on the market, and the choices increase as technology advances. Check the Appendix of this book for resources, or search the internet for "liquor inventory management."

Critics of auditing systems say using them is like closing the proverbial barn door after the cow has escaped. An alternative is liquor control systems, which are designed to prevent rather than simply identify losses and which use a variety of techniques to measure and track product use. If you're shopping for a liquor control system, consider these points:

- *Flexibility.* The bartenders should be able to move around comfortably while they're working and be able to pour more than one drink at a time.

- *Compatibility with other systems.* Be sure the liquor control system can communicate data to your cash register and inventory system.

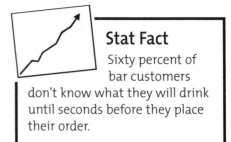

Stat Fact

Sixty percent of bar customers don't know what they will drink until seconds before they place their order.

- *Reliability.* Check the vendor's references carefully to evaluate the performance record of the system.

- *Training.* Be sure the vendor will provide thorough training on the system.

- *Warranty and ongoing support.* Find out the details of the warranty, and make sure the company will answer questions and respond to problems after the sale.

While technology can go a long way toward reducing bar area losses, it can't replace common sense. Here are some simple, easy-to-implement suggestions that can improve profits and customer service.

- *Restrict access to the bar.* Allow only bartenders behind the bar, and be sure that they are the only personnel making drinks.

- *Require drink purchases to be entered into the register before they are made.*

- *Watch backdoor security.* Check in and put away deliveries promptly; never allow inventory to sit unsupervised in loading areas. Install an alarm on the back door that will alert you if an unauthorized person attempts to leave the facility.

- *Provide lockers for employees to store their personal belongings in.* Do not allow them to bring bags or containers into the bar or serving area.

- *Make people accountable for mistakes.* Require mistakes, such as mixing the wrong drink and causing spills, to be logged in and signed off on by the manager on duty. Such accountability increases awareness and leads to a reduction in these types of losses.

- *Cushion surfaces to reduce breakage.* Quality floor mats not only prevent slipping and ease back and leg stress on bartenders, but also they can provide a cushion that reduces breakage if bottles or glasses are dropped.

- *Be sure spouts fit securely.* Sometimes spouts can loosen and leak, especially when used on odd-shaped bottles.

- *Check the ice.* Be sure the ice is free from debris that would cause the drink to be refused.

- *Provide incentives for loss reduction.* Come up with ways to reward employees for positive performance in this area.

- *Encourage employees to report theft.* Consider setting up a system where such reports can be made either anonymously or, at the very least, in strict confidence.
- *Hire carefully.* Screen prospective employees thoroughly. Conduct complete background checks and contact references.

Structuring
Your Business

No doubt you're attracted to the food-service business because you enjoy food preparation and service. And while that is a big part of the business, there are plenty of other mundane issues you'll have to address both in the start-up phase and in the long run.

Legal Structure

One of the first decisions you will need to make about your new food-service business is what type of legal structure the company should have. This is an important decision, and it can affect your financial liability, the amount of taxes you pay, and the degree of ultimate control you have over the company, as well as your ability to raise money, attract investors, and ultimately, sell the business. However, legal structure shouldn't be confused with operating structure. Attorney Robert S. Bernstein of Bernstein Law Firm P.C. in Pittsburgh explains the difference: "The legal structure is the ownership structure: who actually owns the company. The operating structure defines who makes management decisions and [who] runs the company."

A sole proprietorship is a business that is owned by the proprietor; a partnership is owned by the partners; and a corporation is owned by its shareholders. Sole proprietorships and partnerships can be operated however the owners choose. In a corporation, the shareholders typically elect directors, who in turn elect officers, who then employ other people to run the company and work there. But it's entirely possible for a corporation to have only one shareholder and to essentially function as a sole proprietorship. In any case, how you plan to operate the company should not be a major factor in your choice of legal structures.

So what goes into choosing a legal structure? The first thing to consider, says Bernstein, is who is actually making the decision about the legal structure. If you're starting the company by yourself, you don't need to take anyone else's preferences into consideration. "But if there are multiple people involved, you need to consider how you're going to relate to each other in the business," he says. "You also need to consider the issue of asset protection and limiting your liability in the event things don't go well."

Something else to think about is your target customers and what their perception will be of your structure. While it's not necessarily true, Bernstein says, "There is a tendency to believe that the legal form of a business has some relationship to the sophistication of the owners, with the sole proprietorship as the least [sophisticated] and the corporation as the most sophisticated." So if your target market is going to be other businesses, it might enhance your image if you incorporate.

Your image notwithstanding, the biggest advantage of forming a corporation is asset protection, which, says Bernstein, means ensuring that the assets you don't want to put into the business aren't liable for business debt. However, to take advantage of the protection a corporation offers, you must respect the corporation's identity. That means you must maintain the corporation as a separate entity, keeping your corporate and personal funds separate, even if you are the sole shareholder, and following your state's rules regarding holding annual meetings and other record-keeping requirements.

Is any one structure better than another? Not really. We found food-service businesses operating as sole proprietorships, partnerships, and corporations, and their owners made their choices based on what was best for their particular situation. Choose the

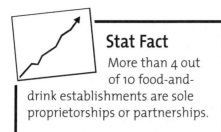

form that is most appropriate for your particular needs.

Do you need an attorney to set up your business's legal structure? Again, no. Bernstein says there are plenty of good do-it-yourself books and kits on the market, and most of the state agencies that oversee corporations have guidelines you can use. Even so, it's always a good idea to have a lawyer at least look over your documents before you file them, just to make sure they are complete and will allow your business to function the way you want to.

Finally, remember that your choice of legal structure is not an irrevocable decision, although if you're going to make a switch, it's easier to go from the simpler forms to the more sophisticated ones than the other way around. Bernstein says the typical pattern is to start as a sole proprietor, then to switch to a corporation as the business grows. But if you need the asset protection of a corporation from the beginning, start out that way. Says Bernstein: "If you're going to the trouble to start a business, decide on a structure and put it all together, it's worth the extra effort to make sure it's really going to work."

Naming Your Company

One of the most important marketing tools you will ever have is your company's name. A well-chosen name can work very hard for you; an ineffective name means you will have to work much harder at marketing your company.

There is no surefire formula for naming a food-service business. Names range from the name of the owner to the name of a place to the wildest name the owner could think of. You should pick a name in keeping with the theme of your restaurant, so that it is compatible with the food and atmosphere. A dramatic example of this is the Rainforest Cafe at Walt Disney World in Florida. The entire restaurant is designed to create the atmosphere of a jungle, complete with lush vegetation, animals, volcanoes, and sound effects. You probably won't go to such an extreme, but if your goal is a fine-dining restaurant, you don't want to name it something like Road Kill Cafe.

Your company name should also very clearly identify what you do in a way that will appeal to your target market. If you're going to use your own name, add a description. For example, instead of just Angelo's, call your pizzeria Angelo's Pizza and Pasta. As you become known in the community, people will likely drop the description when they refer to you, but until that time, it will pay to avoid confusing the public.

The name should be short, catchy, and memorable—and it doesn't hurt to make it fun. It should also be easy to pronounce and spell. People who can't say your restaurant's name may patronize your business, but they probably won't tell anyone else about you.

▲

Though naming your food-service business is without a doubt a creative process, it helps to take a systematic approach. Once you've decided on two or three name possibilities, take the following steps:

- *Check the name for effectiveness and functionality.* Does it quickly and easily convey what you do? Is it easy to say and spell? Is it memorable in a positive way? Ask several of your friends and associates to serve as a focus group to help you evaluate the name's impact.

- *Search for potential conflicts in your local market.* Find out if any other local or regional food-service business serving your market area has a name so similar that yours might confuse the public.

- *Check for legal availability.* Exactly how you do this depends on the legal structure you choose. Typically, sole proprietorships and partnerships operating under a name other than that of the owner(s) are required by the county, city, or state to register their fictitious name. Even if it's not required, it's a good idea, because that means no one else can use that name. Your attorney can help you file the paperwork for your business's fictitious name, or your "doing business as" name. Corporations usually operate under their corporate name. But no matter which route you choose, you need to check with the appropriate regulatory agency to be sure the name you choose is available. Bakery owner Jim Amaral says one of his biggest mistakes was in not checking the availability of the name he initially chose for his company, Bodacious Breads. He used that name for two years and then had to change it when he was challenged by the trademark owner.

- *Check for use on the internet.* If someone else is already using your name as a domain site on the web, consider coming up with something else. Even if you have no intention of developing a website of your own, the fact that someone else is using it online could be confusing to your customers.

- *Check to see if the name conflicts with any name listed on your state's trademark register.* Your state department of commerce can either help you or direct you to the correct agency. You should also check with the trademark registry maintained by the U.S. Patent and Trademark Office (PTO). Visit the PTO's web site at www.uspto.gov.

> **Bright Idea**
>
> Once you've narrowed down your name search to three or four choices, test-market your ideas by asking a small group of people who fit the profile of your potential customer what they think of the names you're considering. Find out what kind of company the name makes them think of and if they'd feel comfortable patronizing a food-service business with that name. Get them to explain the reasoning behind their answers.

Once the name you've chosen passes these tests, you'll need to protect it by registering it with the appropriate state agency. Again, your state department of commerce can help you with this. If you expect to be doing business on a national level—for example, if you'll be handling mail orders or operating on the web—you should also register the name with the PTO.

Business Insurance

It takes a lot to start a business, even a small one, so protect your investment with adequate insurance. If you maintain your office at home—as many food-service business operators do—don't assume your homeowner's or renter's policy covers your business equipment. Chances are, it doesn't. If you're located in a commercial facility, be prepared for your landlord to require proof of certain levels of liability insurance when you sign the lease. And in either case, you'll need coverage for your inventory, equipment, fixtures and other valuables.

A smart approach to insurance is to find an agent who works with businesses similar to yours. The agent should be willing to help you analyze your needs, evaluate what risks you're willing to accept and what risks you need to insure against, and work with you to keep your insurance costs down.

Once your business is up and running, consider business interruption insurance to replace lost revenue and cover related costs if you are ever unable to operate due to covered circumstances.

If the Unthinkable Happens

You buy insurance hoping you'll never need it, but if you do, take the appropriate steps to make sure you get the full benefit from your coverage. Notify your agent or carrier immediately if you suffer a property loss or if something happens that could turn into a liability claim. In the case of a property claim, be prepared to provide the appropriate documentation and proof of loss.

In the case of potential liability, there doesn't have to be an actual loss before you get your insurance company involved. For example, if a customer slips and falls on your premises, even if he or she says there is no injury, get the person's name, address, and telephone number as well as contact information for any witnesses, and pass this information on to your insurance company. Don't wait until you are served with legal papers.

Professional Services

As a business owner, you may be the boss, but you can't be expected to know everything. You'll occasionally need to turn to other professionals for information and assistance. It's a good idea to establish a relationship with these people before you get into a crisis situation.

Pizzeria owner Anthony Allen says his first experience in the food-service business, a pizzeria, proved the value of quality professional advice. He was inadequately protected by his first lease, and when that lease expired, the landlord refused to renew the lease and opened his own successful pizzeria in that location. "I simply wasn't protected," he says. "When you're setting up, it pays to spend the money on an attorney. And make sure you use one who has experience in the type of thing you are doing."

To shop for a professional service provider, ask friends and associates for recommendations. You might also check with your local chamber of commerce or trade association for referrals. Find someone who understands your industry and specific business and who appears eager to work with you. Check the person out with the Better Business Bureau and the appropriate state licensing agency before committing yourself.

As a food-service business owner, the professional service providers you're likely to need include:

- *Attorney*. You'll need a lawyer who understands and practices in the area of business law, who is honest, and who appreciates your patronage. In most parts of the United States, there is an abundance of lawyers willing to compete fiercely for the privilege of serving you. Interview several, and choose one you feel comfortable with. Be sure to clarify the fee schedule ahead of time, and get your agreement in writing. Keep in mind that good commercial lawyers don't come cheap. If you want good advice, you must be willing to pay for it. Your attorney should review all contracts, leases, letters of intent, and other legal documents before you sign them. They can also help you with collecting bad debts and establishing personnel policies and procedures. Of course, if you are unsure of the legal ramifications of any situation, call your attorney immediately.

- *Accountant*. Of all your outside advisors, your accountant is likely to have the greatest impact on the success or failure of your business. If you are forming a corporation, your accountant should counsel you on tax issues during start-up. On an ongoing basis, your accountant

> **Tip...**
>
> **Smart Tip**
> When you purchase insurance on your equipment and inventory, ask what documentation the insurance company requires for filing a claim. That way, you'll be sure to maintain appropriate records, and the claims process will be easier if it is ever necessary.

can help you organize the statistical data concerning your business, assist in charting future actions based on past performance, and advise you on your overall financial strategy regarding purchasing, capital investment and other matters related to your business goals. A good accountant will also serve as a tax advisor, making sure you are in compliance with all applicable regulations but also that you don't overpay any taxes.

▲ 12 / Structuring Your Business

Smart Tip — Tip...

Sit down with your insurance agent every year to review your insurance needs. As your company grows, your needs are sure to change. Also, insurance companies are always developing new products for the growing small-business market, and it's possible that one of these new policies will be appropriate for you.

- *Insurance agent.* A good independent insurance agent can assist you with all aspects of your business insurance, from general liability to employee benefits, and probably even handle your personal policies as well. Look for an agent who works with a wide range of insurers and understands your particular business. This agent should be willing to explain the details of various types of coverage, consult with you to determine the most appropriate coverage, help you understand the degree of risk you are taking, work with you to develop risk-reduction programs, and assist in expediting any claims.

- *Banker.* You will need a business bank account and a relationship with a banker. Don't just choose the bank that you have always done your personal banking with; it may not be the best bank for your business. You'll definitely want to interview several bankers before making a decision on where to place your business funds. Once your account is opened, maintain a relationship with the banker. Periodically sit down with the person and review your accounts and the services you use to make sure you are getting the package that is most appropriate for your situation. Ask for advice if you have financial questions or problems. When you need a loan or you need a bank reference to provide to creditors, the relationship you have established will work in your favor.

- *Consultants.* The consulting industry is booming—and for good reason. Consultants can provide valuable, objective input on all aspects of your business. Consider hiring an HR consultant to evaluate your business plan, a marketing consultant to help you promote your new business, and a restaurant consultant to help you design your facility. When you are ready to hire employees, an HR consultant may help you avoid some costly mistakes. Consulting fees vary widely, depending on the individual's experience, location, and field of expertise. If you can't afford to hire a consultant, consider contacting the business school at the nearest college or university and hiring an MBA student to help you.

- *Computer expert.* If you don't know much about computers, find someone who can help you select a system and the appropriate software, and who will be available to help you maintain, troubleshoot, and expand your system as necessary. If you're going to pursue internet sales, use a professional web-page designer to set up and maintain your website. Just as you wouldn't serve sloppily prepared food, you shouldn't put up an unprofessional web page.

Create Your Own Advisory Board

Not even the president of the United States is expected to know everything. That's why he surrounds himself with advisors—experts in particular areas who provide knowledge and information to help him make decisions. Savvy small-business owners use a similar strategy.

When Maxine Turner decided to expand her Salt Lake City catering company, Cuisine Unlimited, to include a delicatessen, she made some serious mistakes and nearly bankrupted her company. In the middle of her crisis, she realized that the way to get a handle on her own company was to get help from other business owners. She formed an advisory board of successful small-business owners, offering them nothing but good food at the meetings and her personal commitment to return the kindness by helping them in the future. "We met once a month, and the first meeting was about the biggest jolt I had ever had in my life," she recalls. At her request, her advisors were completely candid. She realized how much she was doing wrong that she thought she had been doing right and came up with a strategy to correct her problems. Today, she believes that if she had started her company with an advisory board in place, she would never have had the problems she did. "I think it's a great idea to have an advisory board before you open your doors, while you're still putting together your business plan," she says. And if you're seeking financing, having such a support network will likely weigh heavily in your favor with potential lenders.

You can assemble a team of volunteer advisors to meet with you periodically to offer advice and direction. Because this isn't an official or legal entity, you have a great deal of latitude in how you set it up. Advisory boards can be structured to help with the operation of your company as well as keep you informed on various business, legal and financial trends that may affect you. Use these tips to set up your board:

- *Structure a board that meets your needs.* Generally, you will want a legal advisor, an accountant, a marketing expert, an HR person, and perhaps, a financial advisor. You may also want successful entrepreneurs from other industries who understand the basics of business and will view your operation with a fresh eye.
- *Ask the most successful people you can find, even if you don't know them well.* You will be surprised how willing people are to help other businesses succeed.

- *Be clear about what you are trying to do.* Let your prospective advisors know what your goals are and that you don't expect them to take on an active management role or to assume any liability for your company or for the advice they offer.

- *Don't worry about compensation.* Advisory board members are rarely compensated with more than lunch or dinner—something you can easily provide. Of course, if a member of your board provides a direct service—for example, if an attorney reviews a contract or an accountant prepares a financial statement—then they should be paid at their normal rate. But that's not part of their job as an advisory board member. Keep in mind that even though you don't write them a check, your advisory board members will likely benefit in a variety of tangible and intangible ways. Being on your board will expose them to ideas and perspectives they may not otherwise have encountered and will also expand their own network of contacts.

- *Consider the group dynamics when holding meetings.* You may want to meet with all the members together or in small groups of one or two. It all depends on how the individuals relate to one another and what you need to accomplish.

- *Ask for honesty, and don't be offended when you get it.* Your pride might be hurt when someone points out something you're doing wrong, but the awareness will be beneficial in the long run.

- *Learn from failure as well as success.* Encourage board members to tell you about their mistakes so you can avoid making them yourself.

- *Respect the contribution your board members are making.* Let them know you appreciate how busy they are, and don't abuse or waste their time.

- *Make it fun.* Create a pleasant atmosphere. You are, after all, asking these people to donate their time.

- *Listen to every piece of advice.* Stop talking, and listen. You don't have to follow every piece of advice, but you do need to hear it.

- *Provide feedback to the board.* Good or bad, let the board know what you did and what the results were.

13

Locating and Setting Up
Your Business

Successful food-service businesses can occupy a wide array of facilities, from free-standing buildings constructed especially to house a specific operation to existing buildings converted to suit the particular operation. Train stations, retail stores, and even banks are among the numerous structures that have been successfully converted to food-service businesses.

With most restaurants, the owner begins by coming up with the concept, then determines the market for that concept, and finally finds a location for the restaurant. After determining the general location, the next step is to find a specific facility in the area. This is when you must decide whether you will convert an existing structure or build an entirely new facility. Typically, converting will cost less than building. Even if you gut an entire building and install completely new fixtures, it will be cheaper than buying the vacant land, building the structure, and adding the fixtures you need.

Of course, a little bit of creativity can go a long way toward saving start-up capital. When Maxine Turner started Cuisine Unlimited in Salt Lake City, she was working out of a school cafeteria. She leased the space, provided lunches for the school, and used the kitchen to prepare foods for her corporate clients. That setup worked successfully for ten years, until she decided to open a retail deli and moved her commercial kitchen there.

Depending on how much money you have to invest in your food-service business and the particular type of business you choose, you can spend anywhere from $30,000 to $1.5 million on a facility.

Retail Locations

Not every food-service operation needs to be in a retail location, but for those that depend on retail traffic, here are some factors to consider when deciding on a location:

- *Anticipated sales volume.* How will the location contribute to your sales volume? Consider the presence or potential presence of other food-service businesses that will compete with you, and be sure the market is strong enough to support both of you.

- *Accessibility to potential customers.* Consider how easy it will be for customers to get into your business. If vehicle traffic is often heavy, or if the speed limit nearby is more than 35 mph, drivers may have difficulty entering or leaving your site. Narrow entrances and exits, turns that are hard to negotiate, and parking lots that are always full can prevent would-be customers from patronizing your business.

If you are relying on strong pedestrian traffic, consider whether

Bright Idea

If you're opening an independent operation in a food-service business with a lot of national competition, take a look at where the national chains are locating. They invest in a tremendous amount of market research. Study the characteristics of their sites, and then look for a site for your own business that is similar, perhaps even nearby, and offer a better product or service.

or not nearby businesses will generate foot traffic for you. Large department stores will draw shoppers who may then stop in your restaurant for a meal or snack, and shopping centers in busy office districts might attract pedestrian customers, particularly during weekday lunch hours. By contrast, a strip mall anchored by a supermarket may not be the best location, as grocery shoppers typically go directly to the store and back to their cars.

Consider the entrance to the site. Is it on the street level or an upper floor? Can it be reached from a main street, or is it difficult to find?

Analyze the site. Monitor foot and auto traffic patterns at different times of the day. See if those patterns fit the hours when you want to do business. Visit the prospective site on several different days to assess any changes in the pattern.

- *The rent-paying capacity of your business.* The best locations will usually command the highest rents. If you have done a sales-and-profit projection for your first year of operation, you will know approximately how much revenue you can expect to generate, and you can use that information to decide how much rent you can afford to pay.

And the Answer Is . . .

As you analyze the pedestrian traffic at a retail location you're considering, use this as a model for your interviews:

Begin by dressing professionally and carrying a clipboard on which you can make notes. Approach people very courteously and say, "Excuse me, I'm considering opening a restaurant in this shopping center, and I'm trying to decide if this is a good location for my type of operation. May I have two minutes of your time to ask a few questions?"

If they refuse, thank them anyway, and move on to the next person. However, most people will agree. When they do, quickly ask your questions, and let them get on with their day. Make your survey very simple. The following questions should give you an idea of what to ask:

- ○ What is your primary purpose for being at this shopping center today?
- ○ Which store or stores have you visited or will you visit?
- ○ Do you think this shopping center needs a [name the specific type of food-service business you intend to open]?
- ○ If a [name the specific type of food-service business you intend to open] opened in this location, would you patronize it?

161

- *Restrictive ordinances.* You may encounter unusually restrictive ordinances that make an otherwise strong site less than ideal, such as limitations on the hours of the day when trucks can legally load or unload. Cities and towns are composed of areas—from a few blocks to many acres in size—that are zoned only for commercial, industrial, or residential development. Each zone may have further restrictions. For example, a commercial zone may permit one type of business but not another, so check the zoning codes of any potential location before pursuing a specific site or spending a lot of time and money on a market survey.

> **Smart Tip** Tip...
>
> In addition to finding the right location, it's important to negotiate the right deal on the real estate. You may find the best spot on a main street, but if you're paying too much rent, your business won't be profitable.

- *Traffic density.* Modern site analysis distinguishes between automobile and pedestrian traffic. If only auto traffic were important, most businesses would be located near highways or main roads. With careful examination of foot traffic, you can determine the approximate sales potential of each pedestrian passing a given location. Two factors are especially important in this analysis: total pedestrian traffic during business hours and the percentage of it that is likely to patronize your food-service business.

  To count pedestrian traffic, select a few half-hour periods during busy hours of the day. You should only count potential customers for your business; total numbers of passersby are not the most significant factor. To determine whether people are potential customers or not, you need to know if they are dining out or picking up prepared food to take home. Why are they at the location at this time? To find out, conduct a brief interview. Ask them if they feel there is a need for a food-service business of the type you want to start at that location and if they would patronize the business if it existed.

  Take your sample periods, and multiply the results out over a week, month, and quarter, and use those figures in your financial forecasts. Certainly this process involves some guesswork in your calculations, but if you are careful with your questions and honest in your analysis, you should get a reasonably accurate picture of what to expect.

- *Customer parking facilities.* The site should provide convenient, adequate parking as well as easy access for customers. Storefront parking is always better than a rear lot; people like to be able to see the parking lot before they turn off the main thoroughfare. The lot should be well-lit and secure, with adequate spaces for patrons with disabilities. Consider whether the parking area will need expansion, resurfacing, or striping—possibly at an additional cost. If you are looking at a free-standing location, think big and envision how you will accommodate the hordes of customers your restaurant will eventually attract. Generally speaking, you should have one parking spot for every three seats in your restaurant. If you do a substantial amount of takeout business, you may want to reserve two or three places near the entrance for takeout customers to park briefly while they pick up their orders.

If construction costs and acquiring land for parking are a problem, consider offering valet parking. Once reserved for elegant, fine-dining establishments, this service is becoming more common at casual-dining and even family-oriented operations. Check out nearby parking facilities and research the costs involved; then compare that to the cost of constructing and maintaining your own lot and make a decision on what is most efficient and effective for your particular circumstances.

- *Proximity to other businesses.* Neighboring businesses may influence your store's volume, and their presence can work for you or against you. Studies of the natural clustering of businesses show that certain types of companies do well when located close to one another. For example, men's and women's apparel and variety stores are commonly located near department stores. Florists are often grouped with shoe stores and women's clothing stores. Restaurants, barbershops, and candy, tobacco, and jewelry stores are often found near theaters.

- *History of the site.* Find out the recent history of each site under consideration before you make a final selection. Who were the previous tenants, and why are they no longer there? There are sites—in malls and shopping centers as well as free-standing locations—that have been occupied by numerous business failures. The reasons for the failures may be completely unrelated to the success potential of your food-service operation, or they could mean your business will meet the same fate. You need to understand why previous tenants failed so you can avoid making the same mistakes.

- *Terms of the lease.* Be sure you understand all the details of the lease, because it's possible an excellent site may have unacceptable leasing terms. The time to negotiate terms is before you sign the lease; don't wait until you've moved in to try to change the terms.

- *The rent-advertising relationship.* You may need to account for up to six months of advertising and promotion expenditures in your working capital. Few businesses can succeed without any sales promotion, and the larger the sum you can afford for well-placed, well-targeted advertising and promotions, the greater your chances of success.

> **Bright Idea**
>
> Let your location complement your concept. Robert Owens' RV's Seafood Restaurant in Nags Head, North Carolina, is located on the water—literally; it sits on 10-foot pilings. "I've got great sunsets, crab pots in the water, all kinds of wildlife—herrings, turtles, muskrats, you name it," he says. "I've got a great location."

The amount you plan to spend on advertising may be closely related to your choice of site and the proposed rent. If you locate in a shopping center or mall that is supported by huge ad budgets and the presence of large, popular chain and department stores, you will most likely generate revenue from the first day you open your doors—with no individual advertising at all. Of course, your rental expenses will be proportionately higher than those for an independent location.

- *Future development.* Check with the local planning board to see if anything is planned for the future that could affect your business, such as additional buildings nearby or road construction.

If you do not locate in an area that attracts high foot traffic, you will experience a slower growth rate, even if your business fronts a high-traffic street. Your real profits will come as you develop a clientele—and this will require advertising and promotion.

Additional Retail Options

An alternative to a traditional retail store is a cart or kiosk. Carts and kiosks are a great way to test your business before moving into a regular store, and in some cases, they could be a permanent part of your operating strategy. One of the hottest trends in mall retailing is the temporary tenant—a retailer that comes into a mall, sometimes in a store but often with a cart or kiosk, for a specified period, usually to capture holiday or seasonal sales.

Streetwise

The sunny side of the street is generally less desirable for retail operations than the shady side, especially in warm climates. Research shows rents to be higher on the shady side in high-priced shopping areas. Merchants acknowledge the sunny-side-of-the-street principle by installing expensive awnings to combat the sun and make customers more comfortable.

Marketing research has also demonstrated that the going-home side of the street is usually preferable to the going-to-work side. People have more time to stop at your food-service business on the way home than when they are rushing to work—unless, of course, you offer coffee and breakfast foods, in which case even the busiest person may take time to stop.

If you have a retail store, such as a bakery or coffeehouse, a temporary cart at another location can generate immediate sales and serve as a marketing tool for your year-round location.

Renting cart or kiosk space usually costs significantly less than renting an in-line store, but rates vary dramatically depending on the location and season. Mall space in particular can be pricey. For example, a class-C mall may charge as little as $400 a month for cart space during off-peak season, but a class-A mall in December might charge $4,000 to $5,000 per month for the same cart space.

Carts can either be leased or purchased. New carts can be purchased for $3,000 to $5,000 and up, depending on how they are equipped. Monthly lease fees will typically run 8 to 12 percent of the new price. You can probably get a good deal on a used cart; just be sure it will suit your needs. If a used cart needs significant modifications to work for you, it may be better to buy new and get exactly what you need.

Though kiosks are often occupied by temporary tenants, they have a greater sense of permanency than carts. They typically offer more space and more design flexibility. They're also more expensive: You can expect to pay $10,000 or more to purchase a new kiosk. As with carts, you may be able to lease a kiosk or find a used one to purchase for less money.

Carts and kiosks are available from a variety of sources. Check out manufacturers' and brokers' ads in retail trade publications, such as *Specialty Retail Report*; you can also contact the equipment suppliers listed in this book's appendix. But before you invest in a cart or kiosk, decide where you're going to put it. Many malls have restrictions on the size and design of temporary tenant facilities, or they want all such fixtures to look alike.

Signage

When you are ready to order signs for your food-service business, keep this in mind: A 1-inch letter can easily be seen from 10 feet away, 2-inch letters can be seen from 20 feet away, and so on. A common mistake is creating a sign with letters so small that your customers can't easily read them.

It's also important to have a professional proofreader check your sign for errors. Don't spend a lot of money just to make a poor impression.

If you're going to put up banner-type signs outside, don't hang them with rope, nails and hooks—rope doesn't hold on a windy day, which means your sign will double as a sail and quickly become tattered. Instead, use bungee cords, which will allow your sign to flex in the wind and retain its original shape.

Mail Order

Setting up a mail-order operation makes the entire world your market. If you have food products that are appropriate for shipping, you can take orders over the phone, by mail, by fax, or on the internet, and send items virtually anywhere.

The All-Important Mailing List

You'll develop your customer base by mailing your catalog or brochure to people who fit your target market profile. How do you find these folks? The easiest way is by buying mailing lists. As you probably know from the amount of marketing mail you receive yourself, developing, maintaining, and selling mailing lists is big business. And the list companies can provide you with names and addresses of potential customers who meet your desired demographics.

Buying a list can be expensive, so take the time to do it right. Contact several list brokers before making a decision about which lists to buy. Find out what guarantees the

---

Holding Court

A food court is a congregation of six to 20 restaurants, usually quick-service establishments, in one location. The primary attraction of the concept is the wide assortment of menus from which to choose. In addition, food courts are appealing due to their convenience, atmosphere, and value.

Food courts are often located in large shopping malls, but they are also found in office buildings, sports arenas, universities, and other places where large numbers of people congregate. Food courts can also serve as anchors for strip malls. Some food courts insist that all restaurant tenants operate from in-line stores. Others allow some to operate from kiosks or carts. Popular food court restaurants include those specializing in pizza and Italian food, Chinese food, ice cream, Mexican food, soups and salads, baked potatoes, and hamburgers and hot dogs.

Food court rents tend to be on the high end of retail locations. But even though most food courts are in heavy-traffic areas, that's no guarantee you'll get enough business to justify the cost of the location. Do careful market research before signing a lease.

companies offer. Ask how they acquire data and what techniques are in place to assure the accuracy and currency of the information. In today's mobile society, a list that is even one year old will likely contain a sizable percentage of names of people who have moved. Ask for the list broker's references and check them before making a final selection.

Once you've found a good list broker, stick with him or her. A good broker is a valuable partner in developing a mail order business, because you'll always be trying new lists, even after you're established and profitable.

Your most valuable list will be your in-house list—the people who have become your customers. Build your list by asking people to sign a guest book or by collecting business cards for a drawing. You need to mail to this list frequently and be creative in developing ideas for ways they can purchase your products. As the list grows, you'll find maintaining it a complex, time-consuming, and critical task. Consider hiring an outside company to take over your database management.

Selling on the Internet

As e-commerce grows in popularity and acceptance, you may want to set up a website to market your food-service business and even sell specific products. For example, one bakery in Louisiana offers Creole fruitcake on its website and ships the famous holiday treat and other baked goods—formerly available only through select retail outlets—worldwide.

Packing and Shipping Tips

Get your orders out the door and on their way as quickly as possible. People want immediate gratification, and the faster you deliver, the more orders you'll get. Package your products with extreme care, and be sure the exterior of the box can take a serious beating without damaging the contents. No matter how many "fragile" and "handle with care" stamps you put on the outside, you can be sure that while it's in transit, the box will be shaken, turned upside down, tossed, and have things stacked on top of it. That's simply the nature of the shipping business.

Be Creative

Look for ways to add revenue without substantially increasing your overhead. If you make a unique sauce, for example, have it bottled and available for sale in your restaurant.

Caterer Ann Crane only has to stock a few extra items to offer a gift basket service. She

> **Tip...**
>
> **Smart Tip**
> Whenever you try a new list, test the potential response by mailing to a small segment before you spend the money on mailing to the entire list.

already has the food contents—fresh bakery items, fruit, cheeses, and crackers—and just keeps baskets and brightly colored seasonal ribbons on hand. (For more information on gift baskets, see Entrepreneur's *Start Your Own a Gift Basket Service*.)

When Rebecca Swartz and her mother started their retail gourmet pasta shop, Viva La Pasta, they listened to customer requests and began to add services. Over the years, their operation has grown to include a restaurant, a cooking school, a catering business, a private-label line, special product development, and wholesale distribution. Their primary criterion is that any new business idea be linked to pasta.

Should You Buy an Existing Operation?

If you find the start-up process a bit overwhelming, you may think taking over an existing food-service operation seems like a simple shortcut to getting your own business up and running. It can be, but you must proceed with extreme caution.

You can find various types of food-service businesses for sale advertised in trade publications, shopping-center publications, and your local newspaper. You might also want to check with a business broker—they are listed in the Yellow Pages—to see what they have available.

Buyers frequently purchase food-service businesses "lock, stock, and barrel," including store fixtures, equipment, inventory, and supplies. Others negotiate for portions of these items, preferring to remain free to create their own inventory and image.

Be careful not to select a business that is already doomed, perhaps due to poor location or the unfavorable reputation of the former owner. Especially in the case of the latter, it's much easier to start with a clean slate than to try to clean up after someone else. Before buying an existing business, take the following steps:

- *Find out why the business is for sale.* Many entrepreneurs sell thriving businesses because they are ready to do something else or they want to retire. Others will try to sell a declining business in the hopes of cutting their business losses.

- *Do a thorough site analysis to determine if the location is suitable for your*

> **Bright Idea**
>
> Want to offer delivery without having to buy or lease a vehicle and hire a driver? Set up an arrangement with an independent delivery service. In many communities, delivery services that focus on restaurant food are springing up. These services distribute menus from a variety of quick-service and midrange restaurants. The consumer places an order with the service, which sends a driver to the restaurant to pick up the food and deliver it to the customer for the menu price of the food plus a small service charge.

type of food-service business. Has damaging competition moved in since the business originally opened?

- *Examine the store's financial records for the past three years and for the current year to date.* Compare sales tax records with the owner's claims.

- *Sit in on the store's operation for a few days.* Observe daily business volume and clientele.

- *Evaluate the worth of existing store fixtures.* They must be in good condition and consistent with your plans for image and food products.

- *Determine the costs of remodeling and redecorating if you want to change the store's décor.* Will these costs negate the advantage of buying?

Be sure any business you're considering buying is worth the price. If you're going to make substantial changes, it may make more sense to start from scratch. But if you do decide to buy, include a noncompete clause in your contract so the seller can't go out and start a competing operation in your service area. And remember that no seller can guarantee that the customers they have when they sell you the business will stick around.

Franchise

Another alternative to starting from scratch is to purchase a franchise. Many people do very well with this option, but there are significant risks involved.

Franchising is a method of marketing a product or service within a structure dictated by the franchisor. When you buy a franchise, you are entering into an agreement either to distribute products or to operate under a format identified with and structured by the parent company. One major advantage of franchising is that you have the opportunity to buy into a product or system that is established rather than having to create everything yourself. There is, of course, a price for this: In addition to your start-up equipment and inventory, you'll have to pay a franchise fee. Also, most franchise companies collect ongoing royalties, usually a percentage of your gross sales. They do, however, provide you with ongoing support.

Franchises are regulated by the Federat Trade Commission (FTC) and also by a number of states. There are many food-service franchises available, and it's likely that you'll be able to find one that meets your vision of the type of operation you want to open. Thoroughly research any franchise you are considering, and expect the franchisor to want to know a lot about you, too. After all, if you're going to be responsible for operating under the franchisor's name, they'll want to be sure you'll do it right.

The bottom line: Make sure you investigate any franchise or business opportunity carefully before you invest any money.

Is Two Better than One?

One of the hottest trends in the food-service industry is dual-branding, or dual-concepting. The basic idea is to pair two restaurants that offer complementary menu items, which maximizes the use of the facility and increases customer satisfaction. Such pairings can also help companies deal with seasonal fluctuations and provide a vehicle for menu expansion. For example, frozen-treat companies and quick-service chains have benefited from this trend. The then-named Florida-based Miami Subs Corp. (which has since been acquired by Nathan's Famous) was one of the first restaurant chains to experiment with dual-branding. In the late 1980s, the company was searching for a new strategy to boost sales and strengthen some of the weaker dayparts (an industry term that refers to various meal cycles that occur throughout the day). Rather than investing time and capital into menu research and development, the chain decided to add a familiar product that customers enjoyed but could not previously purchase at Miami Subs: Baskin-Robbins ice cream and frozen yogurt. Baskin-Robbins filled the afternoon and early-evening dayparts that account for Miami Subs' downtime, and the dual-brand arrangement dovetailed with the frozen-treat chain's expansion plans. So, if dual-branding is good, does that mean multibranding is better? The popularity of food courts would indicate that consumers will not only accept but enthusiastically embrace the idea.

Dynamic Duos

More and more convenience stores and gas stations are incorporating various food-service businesses into their operations, often by partnering with a franchise or leasing space to an independent restaurateur. A relatively new configuration worth considering for a pizzeria, deli/sandwich shop, or limited menu restaurant is known as a bump-out. Similar to a porch or sunroom on a house, a bump-out is an extension of the existing floor space so the restaurant is adjacent to, rather than housed within, the convenience store or gas station.

Such partnering creates a win-win situation because the restaurant and the store can benefit from each other's traffic and combine marketing efforts. The bump-out configuration gives the restaurant greater visibility and more of its own identity, even though it's under the same roof as the convenience store or gas station.

While its benefits are numerous, dual-branding does have its risks. Here are some guidelines to keep in mind before you join forces with another company:

- *Make sure you're ready for the expansion.* Be sure the base operation is solid enough to function on its own before taking on a partner. Adding another concept to an already-foundering operation can cause both to fail.

- *Complement, don't compete.* Look for a partner that won't undercut your existing sales. You want to dual-brand with a product line that won't force customers to choose. If you're selling burgers, you can dual-brand with a line of vegetarian items or desserts. But if you're selling ice cream, don't dual-brand with a frozen-yogurt company.

- *Seek comparable quality.* Any dual-branding partner should offer the same quality that you do.

- *Consider company culture.* The corporate culture of any dual-branding partner must be compatible with your own for the relationship to work.

Human Resources

One of the biggest challenges businesses in all industries face is a lack of qualified labor. As the food-service industry in general continues to grow and thrive, the demand for workers in an already-diminished labor pool is also increasing. Finding qualified workers and dealing with rising labor costs are two key concerns for food-service business owners.

Guests will remember—and talk about—poor service long after they've forgotten how good the food was. That's why managing your HR must be a top priority.

Stat Fact
Approximately 12 million people are employed in the restaurant industry in the United States. By 2012, that figure is expected to reach 13.3 million.

"I tell employees that we work for them, they don't work for us," says Bill Ellison, co-owner of Frasier's, a sports bar and restaurant in Apopka, Florida. "It's our responsibility to make sure they have the training, the equipment, the food, and the beverage to get their job done. It's our job to get the customers in the door so employees can do their jobs."

According to research conducted by the National Restaurant Association, the typical person working in a food-service occupation has no higher than a high school degree (65 percent), is female (58 percent), under 30 years of age (52 percent), single (67 percent), living in a household with relatives (80 percent), and living in a household with two or more wage earners (80 percent). The typical supervisor is female (68 percent) and under age 35 (69 percent).

The typical food-service employee has less tenure than the average employed person in the United States. Food-service employees were with their current employer a median of 1.4 years, compared with four years for all employed persons.

The first step in developing a comprehensive HR program is to decide exactly what you want someone to do. The job description doesn't have to be as formal as one you might expect from a large corporation, but it needs to clearly outline the person's duties and responsibilities. It should also list any special skills or other required credentials, such as a valid driver's license and clean driving record for someone who is going to make deliveries for you.

Next you need to establish a pay scale. In previous chapters, we've indicated the pay ranges for many of the positions you're going to need to fill. You should also do some research on your own to find out what the pay rates are in your area. You'll want to establish a minimum and maximum rate for each position. Remember that you'll pay more even at the start for better qualified and more experienced workers. Of course, the pay scale will be affected by whether or not the position is one that regularly receives tips.

Stat Fact
The restaurant industry provides work for nearly 9 percent of those employed in the United States.

You'll also need a job application form. You can get a basic form at most office supply stores, or you can create your own. Have your attorney review the form you'll be using to ensure it complies with the most current employment laws.

Every prospective employee should fill out an application—even if it's someone you already know, and even if that person has submitted a detailed resume. A resume is not a signed, sworn statement acknowledging that you can fire the person if he or she lies about his or her background; the application, which includes a truth affidavit, is. The application will also help you verify the applicants' resumes, so you should compare the two and make sure the information is consistent.

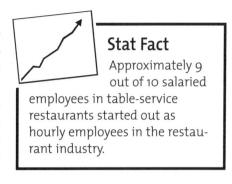

Stat Fact
Approximately 9 out of 10 salaried employees in table-service restaurants started out as hourly employees in the restaurant industry.

Now you're ready to start looking for candidates.

Look in the Right Places

Picture the ideal candidate in your mind. Is this person likely to be unemployed and reading the classified ads? It's possible, but you'll probably improve your chances for a successful hire if you are more creative in your searching techniques than simply writing a help-wanted ad.

Sources for prospective employees include vendors, customers, and professional associations. Check with nearby colleges and perhaps even high schools for part-time help. Put the word out among your social contacts as well—you never know who might know the perfect person for your food-service business.

According to a National Restaurant Association survey, roughly 80 percent of food-service business operators say that the most common resources for hourly employees are walk-in inquiries, word-of-mouth, and newspaper ads. Restaurants with average check amounts of $25 or higher are more likely to recruit hourly employees from vocational schools, while operators of establishments with average check amounts of $8 or less are more likely to use signage in their businesses to attract employees.

Consider using a temporary help or an employment agency to fill open positions. Many small businesses shy away from agencies because they think they can't afford the fee—but if the agency handles the advertising, initial screening, and background checks, their fee may be well worth paying.

Use caution if you decide to hire friends and relatives. Many personal relationships are not strong enough to survive an employee-employer relationship. Small-business owners in all industries tell of nightmarish experiences when a friend or relative refused to accept direction or otherwise abused a personal relationship in the course of business.

The key to success as an employer is making it clear from the start that you are the one in charge. You don't need to act like a dictator, of course. Be diplomatic, but set the ground rules in advance, and stick to them.

Recruiting Young People

If current recruiting initiatives and educational programs continue to grow, the food-service industry should see a sizable influx of young people. And the timing couldn't be better. Though the population of 16- to 24-year-olds declined by 3 percent during the first half of the 1990s, that group is expected to increase by 15 percent between 2000 and 2010. However, fewer members of this age group are working, so just because this anticipated demographic shift will increase the size of a targeted labor group it doesn't mean restaurateurs can afford to relax their recruitment efforts.

Too often, young people see food-service jobs as a way to work toward their "real" career without realizing the tremendous potential and varied opportunities the industry offers. The solution is a combination of awareness and educational programs that will introduce high school and middle school students to hospitality careers and provide them with training that will allow them to move smoothly from school to the workplace.

Across the country, restaurateurs and educators are joining forces to attract and train young people for food-service careers. At the national level, there are two key players in developing such programs: the Hospitality Business Alliance (HBA) and the National Academy Foundation (NAF). (See this book's appendix for contact information.)

In addition to developing school-based curricula, the HBA is aggressively working to introduce young people to opportunities in the food-service industry. The organization is a key participant in Groundhog Job Shadow Day, which was started by Gen. Colin Powell's volunteer organization, America's Promise, the National School-to-Work Opportunities Office, the American Society of Association Executives, Junior Achievement and the National Employer Leadership Council. The HBA and participating organizations, use Groundhog Day to focus on providing young people with job-shadowing experience in restaurants and other hospitality venues.

The HBA has also developed a toolkit to help restaurateurs be more effective in marketing careers in the industry. The kit includes a booklet with suggestions for ways restaurateurs can get involved with young people, a brochure outlining available opportunities, and posters and/or videos for operators and teachers to use when communicating with students.

Hiring Seniors

Changing demographics and the lifting of the Social Security earnings cap have strengthened the senior labor pool and provided restaurants of all kinds with an excellent source of staffing. Seniors tend to provide a higher level of customer service than their younger counterparts and often have experience that will help with the overall management of your operation. Also, seniors—whether they are first-time jobholders or returning to work after retirement—are more likely to stay with you longer than the worker who is just beginning a career. Another benefit of hiring seniors is that many have their health insurance and retirement plans in place, which saves you the cost of providing those benefits.

Most older workers can handle the demands of just about all front-of-the-house jobs and many back-of-the-house positions as well. Accommodate whatever physical limitations senior employees have as much as possible. If you notice a physical deterioration, communicate your concerns before it becomes a serious problem, and work with the employee to make adjustments in their duties if appropriate. Focus on specific performance issues to avoid the possibility of an age discrimination charge.

If it becomes necessary to terminate a senior worker because of a declining physical condition, try to maintain the relationship. You might, for example, offer dinner on the house once a week. It won't cost you much, but it keeps the worker feeling like a part of the team and provides you with continued access to his or her knowledge base.

Evaluating Applicants

What kinds of people make good employees for food-service businesses? It depends on what you want them to do. If you're hiring a delivery person, you need someone with a good driving record who knows the city. If you're hiring someone to help with administrative tasks, you need someone who is computer literate and who can learn your systems. If you're hiring someone to wait tables, he or she needs to be friendly, people-oriented, and able to handle the physical demands of the job. Bartenders need to know how to make drinks, cooks need to know how to cook, and managers need to know how to manage. What is really important is that the people you hire are committed to giving you their best effort while they're working so that your customers receive the best service.

When you actually begin the hiring process, don't be surprised if you're as nervous at the prospect of interviewing potential employees as they are about being interviewed.

Hire Education

Foreign-born workers account for an increasing percentage of the restaurant work force. Under the Immigration Reform and Control Act of 1986, you may only hire people who may legally work in the United States, which means citizens and nationals of the United States and aliens authorized to work in the United States. As an employer, you must verify the identity and employment eligibility of everyone you hire. You must complete and retain the Employment *Eligibility Verification Form* (I-9) on file for at least three years, or one year after employment ends, whichever period of time is longer.

▲

Bright Idea

Post the duties of all positions so new people can quickly see what they are supposed to do each day and also have a clear picture as to how their positions interact with others.

After all, they may need a job—but the future of your company is at stake.

It's a good idea to prepare your interview questions in advance. Develop open-ended questions that encourage the candidates to talk. In addition to knowing what they've done, you want to find out how they did it. Ask each candidate applying for a particular position the same set of questions, and make notes as each responds so you can make an accurate assessment and comparison later.

When the interview is over, let the candidate know what to expect. Is it going to take you several weeks to interview other candidates, check references, and make a decision? Will you want the top candidates to return for a second interview? Will you call the candidate, or should he or she call you? This is not only good business practice; it's also common courtesy.

Always check former employers and personal references. For legal reasons many companies restrict the information they'll verify, but you may be surprised at what you can find out. You should at least confirm that the applicant told the truth about dates and positions held. Personal references are likely to give you some additional insight into the general character and personality of the candidate; this will help you decide if they'll fit into your operation.

Be sure to document every step of the interview and reference-checking process. Even small companies are finding themselves targets of employment discrimination suits; good records are your best defense if it happens to you.

Once They're on Board

The hiring process is only the beginning of the challenge of having employees. The next thing you need to do is train them.

Many small businesses conduct their "training" just by throwing someone into the job, but that's not fair to the employee, and it's certainly not good for your business. If you think you can't afford to spend time on training, think again: Can you afford not to adequately train your employees? Do you really want them preparing food or interacting with your customers when you haven't told them how you want things done?

In an ideal world, employees could be hired already knowing everything they need to know. But this isn't an ideal world, and if you want the job done right, you have to teach your people how to do it. Bakery owner Jim Amaral says he looks for people with food-service experience because they're used to being on their feet in a fast-paced environment, but he expects to have to train people in the art of sourdough bread making.

"Because we do so much training, we really look for people who we think are going to be around for a couple of years or more," he says.

Virtually all table-service restaurant operators provide employees with some sort of on-the-job training, with about 90 percent providing ongoing training and 80 percent offering formal job training.

Whether done in a formal classroom setting or on the job, effective training begins with a clear goal and a plan for reaching it. Training will fall into one of three major categories: orientation, which includes explaining company policies and procedures; job skills, which focuses on how to do specific tasks; and ongoing development, which enhances the basic job skills and grooms employees for future challenges and opportunities. These tips will help maximize your training efforts.

- *Find out how people learn best.* Delivering training is not a one-size-fits-all proposition. People absorb and process information differently, and your training method needs to be compatible with their individual preferences. Some people can read a manual, others prefer a verbal explanation, and still others need to see a demonstration. In a group-training situation, your best strategy is to use a combination of methods. When you're working one-on-one, tailor your delivery to fit the needs of the person you're training.

  Figuring out how employees learn best can be as simple as asking them. But some people may not be able to tell you how they learn best because they don't know themselves. In those cases, experiment with various training styles, and see what works for the specific employee.

- *Use simulation and role-playing to train, practice, and reinforce.* One of the most effective training techniques is simulation, which involves showing an employee how to do something, then allowing him or her to practice it in a safe, controlled environment. If the task includes interpersonal skills, let the employee role-play with a co-worker to practice what he or she should say and do in various situations.

- *Be a strong role model.* Don't expect more from your employees than you are willing to do yourself.

You're a good role model when you do things the way they should be done, all the time. Don't take shortcuts you don't want your employees to take or behave in any way that you don't want them to behave. On the other hand, don't assume that simply doing things the right way is enough to teach others how to do things. Role modeling is not a substitute for training; it reinforces training. If you only use role modeling but never train, employees aren't likely to get the message.

- *Look for training opportunities.* Once you get beyond basic orientation and job skills training, you'll need to constantly be on the lookout for opportunities to enhance the skills and performance levels of your people.

Stat Fact
Average earnings for employees in the restaurant industry are similar to the U.S. average for all household incomes. Of those employed in food preparation and service occupations, 31 percent have household incomes of $50,000 or more, 32 percent have household incomes between $25,000 and $49,999, 19 percent have incomes between $15,000 and $24,999, and 18 percent have incomes of $15,000 or less.

- *Make it real.* Whenever possible, use real-life situations to train—but avoid letting customers know they have become a training exercise for employees.

- *Anticipate questions.* Don't assume that employees know what to ask. In a new situation, people often don't understand enough to formulate questions. Anticipate their questions and answer them in advance.

- *Ask for feedback.* Finally, encourage employees to let you know how you're doing as a trainer. Just as you evaluate their performance, convince them that it's OK to tell you the truth. Ask them what they thought of the training and your techniques, and use that information to improve your own skills.

Employee Benefits

The actual wages you pay may be only part of your employees' total compensation. While many very small companies do not offer a formal benefits program, more and more business owners have recognized that benefits—particularly in the area of health and life insurance—are extremely important when it comes to attracting and retaining quality employees. In most parts of the country, the employment rate is higher than it has been in decades, which means competition for good people is very stiff.

Typical benefit packages include group insurance (your employees may pay all or a portion of their premiums), paid holidays, and vacations. You can build employee loyalty by seeking additional benefits that may be somewhat unusual—and they don't have to cost much. For example, if you're in a retail location, talk to other business owners in your shopping center to see if they're interested in providing reciprocal employee discounts. You'll not only provide your own employees with a benefit, but you may also get some new customers out of the arrangement.

Beyond tangible benefits, look for ways to provide positive working conditions. "We're not just about making bread; we're about creating a good work environment where people feel like they are making some progress in their own lives in terms of developing skills and becoming better people," says Amaral. "We don't just look at the financial bottom line, we look at what the employees are doing and the value being added for the employees and the customers." Amaral's bakery provides a strong benefits package that includes health insurance, paid vacations, and holidays. He also pays employees for doing volunteer work at their regular hourly rate for up to three hours a month.

Caterer Ann Crane sends her full-time staffers to seminars to help sharpen their skills. She also provides extras, such as the time she bought tickets to Disneyland for the staff and their families. And, periodically, she brings lunch in from another restaurant (since staff members cook their own lunches every day, ordering out is a treat).

Got It Covered

In most states, if you have three or more employees, you are required by law to carry workers' compensation insurance. This coverage pays medical expenses and replaces a portion of the employee's wages if he or she is injured on the job. Even if you have only one or two employees, you may want to consider investing in this coverage to protect both your staff and you in the event of an accident.

Details and requirements vary by state, so contact your state's insurance office or your own insurance agent for information so you can be sure to be in compliance.

Same-Sex Marriages and Domestic Partnership Benefits

One of the hottest political topics these days is the issue of same-sex marriages. While many people are quick to offer an opinion on the subject, what is not clear is the impact of a state allowing same-sex marriages in the areas of employment and employee benefits.

At the present, federal law, which dominates the area of employee benefits, does not recognize same-sex marriage. This means employers do not need to treat same-sex spouses in the same manner as opposite-sex spouses for purposes of benefits governed by the Employee Retirement Income Security Act (ERISA).

However, there are areas in which state law and the recognition of same-sex marriage may have an impact. For example, an employer generally may extend benefits to same-sex spouses, even where not required by law.

Your best strategy is to understand the issues related to same-sex marriage and employee benefits and to decide on an overall approach to dealing with the issue. Be sure that this approach is clearly defined in your policies and consistently applied, and review and revise your benefit plans and employment practices as necessary.

Child Labor Issues

Teenagers make up a significant portion of the food-service industry's labor force, and it's important that you understand the child labor laws that apply to your particular operation. The Fair Labor Standards Act has set four provisions designed to protect

You Deserve a Break

No matter how much you enjoy your work, you need an occasional break from it. This is a challenge for small-business owners, but it's critical. You need to be able to be away from your operation occasionally, not only for vacations, but for business reasons, such as attending conferences and trade shows. Also, you need a plan in place in case of illness, accidents or other emergencies. Be sure your people are well-trained and committed to maintaining your service levels when you aren't there.

the educational opportunities of youths and prohibit their employment in jobs and under conditions that are detrimental to their health and well-being.

The minimum age for most nonfarm workers is 16; however, 14- and 15-year-olds may be employed outside of school hours in certain occupations under certain conditions. At any age, youths may work for their parents in their solely owned nonfarm businesses (except in mining, manufacturing, or any other occupation declared hazardous by the Secretary of Labor). This means your minor children can work in your food-service business if you are the sole owner, as long as they are not violating other age-related laws, such as serving alcohol.

The basic age-related guidelines of the Fair Labor Standards Act are:

- Youths 18 years or older may perform any job for an unlimited number of hours.
- Youths aged 16 and 17 may perform any job that is not declared hazardous by the Secretary of Labor for an unlimited number of hours.
- Youths aged 14 and 15 may work outside of school hours in various nonmanufacturing, nonmining, nonhazardous jobs under the following conditions: No more than 3 hours on a school day, 18 hours in a school week, 8 hours on a nonschool day or 40 hours in a nonschool week. In addition, they may not begin work before 7 A.M. or work after 7 P.M., except from June 1 through Labor Day, when evening work hours are extended until 9 P.M.
- Youths aged 14 and 15 who are enrolled in an approved Work Experience and Career Exploration Program (WECEP) may be employed for up to 23 hours during school weeks and 3 hours on school days, including during school hours.

Department of Labor regulations require employers to keep records of the date of birth of employees under age 19, their daily starting and quitting times, daily, and weekly hours worked, and their occupation. Protect yourself from unintentional violation of the child labor provisions by keeping an employment or age certificate on file for each youth employed to show that they are of the required minimum age for the job.

Keep in mind that in addition to the federal statutes, most states also have child labor laws. Check with your own state labor department to see what regulations apply to your business. When both federal and state laws apply, the law setting the higher standards must be observed.

Minimum Wage

The Fair Labor Standards Act also establishes minimum wage, overtime pay, and record-keeping standards. The act requires employers of covered employees who are not otherwise exempt to pay these employees a minimum wage. Youths under 20 years of age may be paid a youth minimum wage that is lower than the standard minimum wage during the first 90 consecutive calendar days of employment. Employers may not displace any employee to hire someone else at the youth minimum wage. Because minimum wage laws change, be sure to check with your state labor board or the U.S. Department of Labor Wage and Hour Division for the current minimum wage amounts.

Employers of tipped employees, which are defined as employees who customarily and regularly receive more than $30 a month in tips, may consider those tips part of their employees' wages but must pay a direct wage of at least $2.13 per hour if they claim a tip credit. Certain other conditions also must be met. Check with your accountant or the appropriate agency to be sure you're in compliance.

The act also permits the employment of certain individuals at wage rates below the statutory minimum wage, but they must be working under certificates issued by the Department of Labor. Those individuals include student learners (vocational education students), full-time students in retail or service establishments, and individuals whose earning or productive capacity is impaired by a physical or mental disability, including those related to age or injury.

Tips and Taxes

Tips received by your employees are generally subject to withholding. Your employees must report to you all cash tips they've received by the 10th of the month after the month the tips are received. This report should include tips employees receive directly in cash as well as tips you paid from charge receipts. Also include the tips employees receive from other employees and through tip-splitting.

Employees should report their tips on IRS Form 4070, Employee's Report of Tips to Employer, or on form 4070-A, Employee's Daily Record of Tips, or on a similar statement. The statement must be signed by the employee and include the employee's name, address, and Social Security number; your name and address; the month or period the report covers; and the total tips received. No report is required when tips are less than $20 a month.

As an employer, you must collect income tax, employee Social Security tax and employee Medicare tax on employees' tips. You can collect these taxes from wages or from other funds the employee makes available. You are also responsible for paying employer Social Security tax on wages and tips.

You must file Form 941 to report withholding on tips. Your accountant can help you set up a system to be sure you are in compliance with IRS reporting and payment requirements.

Certain establishments are required to report allocated tips under certain circumstances. The IRS requires that large food and beverage establishments, which are defined as providing "food or beverages for consumption on the premises, where tipping is customary and where there are normally more than ten employees on a typical business day during the preceding year," report allocated tips (which can be calculated by hours worked, gross receipts, or good-faith agreement). But you do not withhold income, Social Security or Medicare taxes on allocated tips. Check with your accountant or the IRS for more information.

Stat Fact
Total annual wages and benefits equal $35 billion for full-service restaurants and $29 billion for limited-service establishments.

When You Suspect an Employee of Stealing

Employee theft can have a serious impact on your bottom line as well as on the morale of other employees who may be aware of what's going on. When you become aware of actual or suspected employee theft, you need to act quickly—but carefully—to resolve the situation.

"Treat the complaint as valid until it is established otherwise, and treat the accused as innocent until proven guilty," says Michael P. O'Brien, a labor and employment attorney with Jones Waldo Holbrook & McDonough PC in Salt Lake City. "Also, treat the matter confidentially to the greatest extent possible." In today's litigious world, protecting the privacy of a suspect is essential; failing to do so can leave you vulnerable if that individual decides to sue later—regardless of whether or not the person was actually guilty.

The first step is to conduct a thorough investigation, including a review of all relevant documents, such as personnel files, time sheets, performance evaluations of the people involved, inventory and delivery records, and any applicable financial records. If your security system includes video surveillance, you will want to review the tapes. You may also want to interview witnesses and others who may have knowledge of the situation. Of course, you should also interview the accused—without making an accusation. When conducting interviews, be very clear that the issue under investigation is not to be discussed with unconcerned parties. "If a witness can't be trusted, think carefully about involving that person [in the investigation] in order to avoid possible defamation problems," says O'Brien.

Regardless of how much you trust a particular witness, avoid disclosing information unnecessarily, and don't ask questions that indicate the direction of your inquiry. Document every step of the investigation, and maintain those records in a secure place separate from your personnel records. Do not make details of an investigation part of an employee's personnel file unless and until the results are in and misconduct has been proven.

If your investigation confirms misconduct of any sort, take immediate and appropriate disciplinary action that is consistent with your general policies. "The worst thing you can do is nothing," O'Brien says. "You need to take some sort of disciplinary action against the individual you've concluded has done an inappropriate act." Certainly you'll want to consider the severity, frequency and pervasiveness of the conduct—for example, occasionally overpouring drinks for regular customers is certainly less severe than skimming cash out of the register—but whatever remedy you apply must end the offensive behavior. Keep in mind that whatever you do may eventually wind up in court, so maintain good records, and be sure you can always justify your actions.

You must also decide whether or not to involve law enforcement. Weigh the potential for negative publicity against the potential good, which could include restitution and the fact that the perpetrator may receive some much-needed rehabilitation.

Regulatory Issues

Because of the significant impact food-service businesses can have on the health and safety of their patrons, these establishments are subject to a wide range of regulatory requirements, which often vary by city and state. You are responsible for knowing what specific regulations apply to your particular operation and complying with them. Don't try to bend or break the regulations; if you get caught, you'll be subject to civil and perhaps even criminal liability, along with the potential of negative publicity that could put you out of business.

In addition to enforcing health and safety regulations, many agencies offer resources to help new and existing restaurateurs stay in compliance. Bill Ellison of Frasier's, a sports bar and restaurant in Apopka, Florida, notes that Florida's Department of Business and Professional Regulation will conduct what they call a "helpful inspection," where, says Ellison, "they're not actually writing you up, they're just pointing out that you need to do this, this, and that. They told us that they want [restaurant owners] to be proactive instead of reactive. So if you're calling and asking questions, that's showing your concern about the issues, that you want to know the right way to do it." Check with your local health department and licensing agencies to find out how they can help you avoid problems.

Licenses and Permits

Most cities and counties require food-service business operators to obtain various licenses and permits. Requirements vary by municipality, so do your own research to make sure your business is in full compliance with local regulations.

Business License

City business license departments operate as tax-collecting bureaus and do not perform any public service. You simply pay a fee to operate your business in that city. Some cities also claim a percentage of your gross sales.

The planning or zoning department will process your license application and check to make sure applicable zoning laws allow the proposed use and that there are enough parking spaces to meet the code.

Health Department Permit

To purvey and distribute food, you will need a food-establishment permit from your state or county health department. All food-service operations, including temporary food-service establishments and mobile units such as carts, must obtain this permit before beginning operation. The health department will inspect your facility before issuing your initial permit and will perform inspections on an ongoing basis as long as you are in business.

Health inspectors will want to make sure all areas of your operation meet legal standards. They will be concerned with food storage, food preparation, food display, employee health and cleanliness, the design and installation of equipment, the cleaning and storage of equipment and utensils, sanitary facilities, and the construction and maintenance of the facility. The type of food your restaurant specializes in is not an issue; what is important is how you store and prepare that food. Your local or state health department can provide you with guidelines.

Smart Tip

While you're still in the planning stages, contact your local health department for information about its requirements. It'll be happy to give you the information you need so you'll qualify for all the necessary permits.

Liquor and Beer and Wine Licenses

Most states require you to obtain one type of license to serve beer and wine and another to serve hard liquor. A liquor license is more difficult to obtain than a beer-and-wine license. In some areas, no new liquor licenses are being issued at all, which means you can only obtain one by buying it from an existing license holder.

One advantage of buying an existing restaurant is that if it served liquor, you may be able to acquire the license as part of the deal. Typically, you will have to file an application with the state beverage control board, then post notice on the premises of your intent to serve liquor.

In some states, the beverage control board requires holders of liquor licenses to keep all purchase records for a specific number of years, during which time they are subject to inspection by the control board and/or the IRS.

Under most circumstances, it's much easier to obtain a license to serve beer and wine than a hard-liquor license. Beer-and-wine licenses are usually issued for an annual period and are easy to renew if you haven't committed any offenses, such as selling alcoholic drinks to minors. The government section of your telephone directory will have the number for the nearest beverage control agency, which can provide you with the information you need.

Fire Department Permit

Your fire department may require you to obtain a permit if your business will use any flammable materials or if your premises will be open to the public. In some cities, you must secure a permit before you open for business. Other jurisdictions don't require permits. Instead, they schedule periodic inspections to see that your facility meets the regulations. Restaurants, theaters, clubs, bars, retirement homes, day-care centers, and schools are subject to especially close and frequent scrutiny by the fire department.

Sign Permit

Many municipalities have sign ordinances that restrict the size, location, and sometimes the lighting and type of sign you can use in front of your business. Landlords may also impose their own restrictions. You'll likely find sign restrictions most stringent in malls and upscale shopping areas. Avoid costly mistakes by checking regulations and securing the written approval of your landlord before you invest in a sign.

County Permit

County governments often require the same types of permits and licenses as cities. These permits apply to commercial enterprises located outside city limits.

State Licenses

Many states require persons engaged in certain occupations, such as hairdressers, contractors, medical-care providers, teachers, child-care

Beware!

Regardless of what the laws say about your liability, just about anyone can sue anyone else in civil court for just about any reason. And, although you may win the verdict in a lawsuit where the plaintiff had insufficient grounds, fighting a lawsuit is still expensive and time-consuming. Your best strategy is to avoid situations that could result in potential liability of any kind.

providers, and others to hold licenses or occupational permits. Food-service employees generally are not required to hold licenses, but to make sure you are in compliance, you should check with your state government for a complete list of occupations that require licensing.

Zoning Laws

In most cases, if you locate your food-service business in a structure that was previously used for commercial purposes, zoning regulations will not be a problem. However, if you intend to construct a new facility, use an existing building for a different purpose or perform extensive remodeling, you should carefully check local building and zoning codes. If zoning regulations do not allow for the operation of the type of food-service business you wish to open, you may file for a zoning variance, a conditional-use permit, or a zone change.

Music Licenses

If you plan to play music in your restaurant—whether you hire a live performer or just play on-hold music on your telephone—you will need to obtain the appropriate licenses. Federal copyright laws require that any business that plays copyrighted music pay a fee. Fees are collected by the American Society of Composers, Authors and Publishers; Broadcast Music Inc.; and SESAC Inc. (formerly the Society of European Stage Authors and Composers). (See this book's appendix for contact information.)

U.S. copyright law requires you to obtain permission from, and negotiate a fee with, the composer and publisher of a musical piece before you can reproduce or perform the material. Since contacting each composer and publisher is impossible—especially if the composer is deceased—the previously listed organizations work on behalf of their members. They require business owners who play music in their establishments to obtain licenses through them instead of directly from the composers and publishers. The fees for these licenses are used to pay composers and publishers royalties for the performance of their material. By going through these performance rights organizations, you will pay a general fee that will cover the performance of all their members' songs. You must obtain a license from each of these organizations because they represent different artists. If you play copyrighted music without having a license to do so, the appropriate agency could levy a $5,000 to $20,000 fine.

The organizations base their fees on a number of factors, including the seating capacity in your establishment, the number of days or evenings each week you play music, whether you charge patrons for admission, and whether the music is performed live or by mechanical means.

The Legalities of Liquor Vending

Most food-service businesses find that serving alcoholic beverages can help improve their profit margins and offset the costs associated with some of the less profitable aspects of the business. Over the past decade or so, however, there has been a marked increase in the sociopolitical pressure and legal trouble facing businesses that sell alcoholic beverages. Some are calling this the "new temperance era" and "a time of neoprohibitionism." On both the state and federal levels, legislators, public health officials, and special-interest groups are warring against alcohol abuse and bringing to light the fatalities and injuries caused by drunk driving. The effect on those who serve liquor—regardless of their personal beliefs—has been profound.

As a part of this movement, old statutes are being dusted off and new laws promulgated to place pressure on not just the alcohol abuser but also on the supplier. It has always been incumbent upon the owners of liquor-vending establishments to observe state liquor laws or face criminal penalties. However, these days, businesses selling liquor also face the threat of increased popular and legal support for those filing civil suits against liquor vendors.

It used to be that the average bartender or liquor-store owner just had to worry about getting caught serving minors or those who were obviously already intoxicated. Proprietors would buy special liquor-liability insurance for

Stat Fact

A dramshop is a shop or bar where spirits are sold by the dram, which is one-eighth of an ounce. The term "dramshop laws" has evolved to mean liquor liability laws.

coverage in the event of a lawsuit from a drunken patron. Lately, the liquor vendor has become potentially liable financially when a third party is injured.

Simply stated, dramshop laws and other types of third-party liability work this way: If you, the server of alcoholic beverages, act irresponsibly and over serve a patron who is later involved in an automobile crash, then the individual server, as well as the establishment, can be held financially liable for the death or injury of not only an innocent third party but of the intoxicated patron as well.

Laws regarding liquor liability vary by state and can change quickly. Your state's liquor board or alcoholic beverage commission should be able to tell you what the current laws in your particular state are.

Whether your state exposes you to high or low risks of liability, or whether your type of establishment puts you in jeopardy of civil suits or not, you must be cognizant of, and take precautions against, legal action. Progressive owners and managers take steps to minimize the risk of criminal charges and civil litigation.

One step is learning to perceive intoxication and cutting off customers as soon as it becomes necessary. Most liquor vendors (and drinkers) are familiar with the warning signs, but all sellers and servers should be acquainted with them. Among the more common indicators are staggering, slurred speech, impaired thinking, heavy eyelids, silence, talking too much or too loudly, tearfulness, hostility, acting out, nausea or vomiting, sudden mood changes, physical imbalance, and forcing verbal or physical confrontations.

Steps You Can Take

Most liquor vendors could use some reform to protect customers and themselves from accidents that can turn into lawsuits. The general idea is to control the quantity of alcohol consumed by individual patrons and the ways in which drinking is encouraged. Though it may appear counterproductive for a liquor vendor to restrict the sale of alcoholic beverages, the trouble caused by not doing so will cost more in the long run than any negligible decrease in liquor sales.

Here's one way to think of the situation: For every drunk you throw out of your place, consider how many customers are made more relaxed by his or her absence and are likely to return.

Preventive measures employed by many liquor vendors include:

- *Not serving minors.* Drunk driving is a primary killer of teenagers in this country. Observe the legal drinking age, and check ID on any patron who appears to be under 30. Everyone on your staff, whether their duties include serving alcohol or not, should know the minimum drinking age in your state and which state laws apply regarding proof of age and other alcohol service issues. Check with your state's liquor board or alcoholic beverage commission to find out what programs are available to help you train your staff and stay in compliance with the law.

- *Dealing with intoxicated patrons.* You should develop and implement consistent, diplomatic procedures for denying alcohol to customers who arrive drunk or are becoming so, and for making last calls. Each employee, from the busperson to the manager, should be familiar with these procedures and the philosophy behind them.

- *Bar layout.* Your bar cannot become so crowded that bartenders can't keep track of who and how much they have served. You cannot allow customers in inconspicuous areas of your establishment to drink all night without being monitored at least casually. Adding bartenders and servers or changing the layout of your bar can help you avoid this situation.

- *Controlling the flow.* Free pouring (as opposed to measuring) drinks is not economical, makes it difficult to control inventory, and hampers your servers' abilities to monitor alcohol consumption. Also, a free-pour bar may be in a difficult spot if you must legally account for the quantity of alcohol consumed by a particular customer. Consider cutting back on the happy-hour specials and closing time two-for-one or all-you-can-drink specials.

> **Bright Idea**
>
> Consider a program that offers free nonalcoholic beverages to the designated driver in groups of patrons. Your investment will be minimal, but the impact on your potential liability, as well as the marketing benefit, will be significant.

Instead, promote your nonalcoholic bar drinks. Your bartender can create these beverages inexpensively, with an even greater profit margin than for alcoholic beverages. Try putting more emphasis on food items, and encourage the safe consumption of alcohol by selling snacks or providing complimentary hors d'oeuvres so people aren't drinking on an empty stomach.

- *Alternative transportation.* Serving liquor responsibly may include ensuring that inebriated customers get home safely. Some establishments provide complimentary taxi service or will call a cab for intoxicated customers. Many bars and restaurants band together to provide carpool service. Cab companies and community organizations may be willing to help provide transportation for free or at a nominal cost.

Despite your best precautions, any time alcohol and people mix in your establishment, you will have the potential for danger to the public and liability to you. An important step in self-protection is to become familiar with the liquor-liability laws in your state and purchase adequate insurance. Your lawyer or insurer should be able to inform you of the relevant state laws and evaluate your risk.

Sanitation

Sanitation is extremely important to a successful food-service operation, not only for health and safety reasons, but also for image reasons. Your storage area, kitchen preparation area, serving areas, waiting area, lounge, restrooms, and dining area should be clean and in good repair from floor to ceiling.

Set standards for all employees and reinforce them with charts, labels, and placards in areas where the staff will be reminded of sanitation issues. (Certain sanitation-related signs are required by law. Your health department can inform you of the necessary requirements.) The National Restaurant Association produces a wide range of training materials that deal with various aspects of sanitation; contact the association (listed in this book's Appendix) for more information.

You or your manager should also perform thorough sanitation inspections at least once every six months. This inspection should focus on the storage of food; employees' personal hygiene; the cleanliness of all equipment and utensils; all floors, walls, and ceilings; lighting; ventilation; the dishwashing facility; water, sewage, and plumbing; restrooms; garbage and refuse disposal; insect and animal control; and linens.

Proper food storage is vitally important. A single case of food poisoning can put a restaurant out of business. Nothing should be placed directly on the floor, whether it's food in dry storage or frozen or refrigerated food. Use pallets, racks, or anything else that will raise your inventory off the floor. This makes it easier to clean the floors and protects the food from vermin and from being splashed by chemicals or dirty water.

To keep food free from contamination, place it in an area where you can maintain the proper temperature: Keep hot food hot and cold food cold. Cover all refrigerated food. Don't leave anything out longer than necessary during the preparation period.

Whether you serve fruits and vegetables raw or cooked, wash them all thoroughly. Use proper utensils and plastic gloves when appropriate during preparation so human contact with food is kept to a minimum.

Your employees' personal hygiene is also important. Employees with cuts, abrasions, dirty fingernails, any type of skin disease or a communicable disease should certainly not be preparing or serving food. Employees involved in food preparation or serving should have clean uniforms, clean hair, and clean hands and fingernails. Employees with long hair should either wear a hairnet or at least pull their hair back away from their faces to prevent hairs from falling into the food.

Smart Tip

Tip...

Too many incidences of food contamination that lead to illness can be traced to workers failing to wash their hands after using the restroom. Stress to all employees who handle or serve food the importance of thorough hand washing.

Preventive Medicine

The possibility that someone could get sick from eating food you served is a food-service business owner's worst nightmare. First, there's the fact that you—however unintentionally—caused someone to suffer. Then there's the potential liability, in terms of both paying direct medical costs and additional punitive damages. Finally, there's the bottom-line damage, because when word gets out—and it will—your business will suffer, and sales can plummet.

Preventing food-borne illnesses begins with awareness. Everyone in your operation needs to understand how to prevent problems and the consequences of failing to do so. It's not enough just to tell workers that salads need to be kept at a certain temperature and that they need to wash their hands thoroughly after using the restroom. Your employees need to know what can happen if they fail to follow these health and safety regulations.

The National Restaurant Association (NRA) offers a number of training programs and educational materials—such as signs and posters—that can help you maintain an operation that is safe for both your employees and your customers.

You might also consider providing inoculations for employees. For example, many restaurants in high-risk areas require employees to be vaccinated against hepatitis A (contact your local health department for information on whether your restaurant is located in a high-risk area). Exposure can result when an infected person uses the restroom, does not wash his or her hands, then handles food that others will eat. It can also be waterborne and spread through bodily fluids such as saliva and blood. While seldom fatal, the virus can cause diarrhea, nausea, cramping, fatigue, and jaundice. The cost of the vaccine is about $80 per person, but it may be available for less through the NRA or some local public health programs.

Emphasize to the dishwasher and all of your servers that pots, pans, preparation utensils, plates, silverware, glassware, and serving utensils should be spotless before they are used. All production equipment should be checked and cleaned regularly by your cooks. Maintain proper hot water temperatures, and make sure your water source is safe.

Your floors, walls, and ceilings should be cleaned regularly. Check them to make sure that all surfaces are smooth and free of dust, grease, and cobwebs. Set up a service contract with a local exterminator to ensure that your facility is free of insects and rodents. Clean drains often. Rubber mats should be easy to move for cleaning.

Don't neglect your garbage area. All trash containers should be leak proof and nonabsorbent and have tight-fitting covers. Wash your containers thoroughly, inside and out, when you empty them.

Equipment

For most food-service businesses, the focus is on the food preparation and service equipment. For your office, as we've said in previous chapters, chances are a small desk, a chair, a couple of locking filing cabinets, and a few bookshelves for catalogs and pricing guides will be sufficient in the beginning. Your office furnishings should be comfortable and efficient, but don't worry about how they look. Your customers aren't going to see your office, so don't waste money in this area that could be more effectively spent on the front of the house. Speaking of the front of the house, keep the following information in mind when purchasing major equipment for your food-service business.

Major Equipment

While each of the food-service operations discussed in this guide has specific equipment requirements, there are many items that are basic to just about any type of food-service business. Food-service equipment dealers are often good sources for finding out what you need and what particular piece of equipment will do it best. A good salesperson will also function as a consultant, helping you make a wise decision. After all, if you're satisfied, you're likely to come back when you need more equipment—and you'll refer others. However, you still need to be cautious when accepting advice and guidance from a salesperson. Get several opinions and price quotes before making a final decision.

Careful and thoughtful equipment selection will mean a cost-effective and productive operation over the long run. Don't buy based on price alone. You can cut down on labor costs by purchasing equipment that is fully automatic and self-cleaning, even though it may cost more upfront. Install as much modern, energy-efficient equipment as possible. That way, when gas and electricity costs rise, your energy-saving equipment will help keep your utility bills reasonable.

Buy from a well-known manufacturer who has reliable equipment and a network of repair facilities. Look for standard lines of equipment that are both versatile and mobile.

To Lease or Not to Lease?

If your initial equipment investment will be significant, you may want to consider leasing rather than purchasing. Leasing is an excellent alternative when start-up capital is limited. You should also check with your tax advisor to determine what type of tax advantages leasing offers.

The disadvantage to leasing is that if you have a tax-deductible lease, you do not build equity in your equipment and therefore do not build up your balance sheet. A financial statement showing a strong net worth is important to any business. In addition, the total cost of leasing over a period of years is going to be higher than if the same items were purchased. Consult with your accountant to make the best choice based on your tax status and cash situation.

Avoid custom-designed lines whenever possible. Standard equipment is generally lower priced and less expensive to install. It's also easier and less expensive to replace at the end of its service life.

Most food-service operations will need a walk-in refrigerator/freezer for primary food storage at the rear of the facility near the receiving door. You will also need a smaller reach-in refrigerator/freezer in your production area to keep the food supplies you need that day or for that meal period fresh and easily accessible.

Your receiving area should also include a scale to verify weights of deliveries, a breakdown table, at least one dolly or hand truck, dry shelving, and shelving for the walk-in refrigerator/freezer. You may find wheeled carts a convenient tool for managing your inventory.

Buying Used Equipment

Heavy-duty restaurant hardware does not wear out quickly, so why buy brand-new when "seasoned" used merchandise can be as good or even better? You can buy second-hand equipment for a fraction of what it would cost new. And there's plenty available from other food-service businesses that have failed, merged, or grown to the point where they require larger or more modern equipment.

Since Ann Crane bought her catering company, she's been expanding at a healthy pace. When she needed additional gear to support her growing business, she says, "I couldn't afford to go out and buy all new equipment. The only thing I bought new was my walk-in refrigerator and the overhead hood for the cooking line. Everything else was used."

Caterer Maxine Turner also buys used equipment. She used to go to auctions but got burned a few times when she bought equipment that wasn't as good as she thought. Now she only buys at auction if she knows who she's working with and is extremely familiar with the equipment being sold. She also learned how to work with equipment dealers, particularly new-equipment dealers who sell used items that have come in through trade-ins.

Buying used equipment is normally a good cost-cutting measure, but there are some pitfalls. Consider that some major equipment has

a useful lifetime of only ten years. If you buy a used walk-in refrigerator/freezer that is near the end of its useful life, you run the risk of repeated breakdowns, resulting in costly maintenance and food spoilage. Also, newer equipment will generally be more cost-efficient to operate.

Before buying a piece of used equipment, perform a cost analysis of the item you're considering over its expected lifetime versus that of a comparable new item. When you factor in maintenance and operating costs, it's possible new equipment may actually be less expensive in the long run.

Look for standard lines of equipment that are both versatile and mobile so you won't have to duplicate hardware. Try to avoid custom-designed lines. Standard equipment is generally less expensive to buy, install and replace. Also, try to install as much energy-efficient equipment as possible, as long as it's affordable.

When shopping for used equipment, carefully check it for wear, and buy only from reputable dealers. Judicious shopping may turn up some excellent bargains. Check the classified section of your local newspaper for a wide range of used furniture and equipment for sale. Also look under the "Business Opportunities" classification because businesses that are being liquidated or sold may have fixtures or equipment for sale at substantial savings.

Basic Office Equipment

Many entrepreneurs find a trip to the local office supply store more exciting than any mall. It's easy to get carried away when you're surrounded with an abundance of clever gadgets, all designed to make your working life easier and more fun. But if, like most new business owners, you're starting on a budget, discipline yourself and buy only what you need. Consider these primary basic items:

- *Typewriter.* You may think most typewriters are in museums these days, but they actually remain quite useful to businesses that deal frequently with preprinted and multipart forms, such as order forms and shipping documents. Whether or not you'll need a typewriter is a decision only you can make based on your specific operation. A good electric typewriter can be purchased for $100 to $150.

- *Computer and printer.* A computer can help you manage complex bookkeeping and inventory control tasks, maintain customer records, and produce marketing materials. A computer is an extremely valuable management and marketing tool and an essential element for developing a strong and profitable business—especially in today's technology-dependent world. At a minimum, you'll need a computer with a Pentium-class processor, the most current version of Windows, 64MB RAM, an 8GB to 10GB hard drive (or larger), a CD-ROM drive, a 56Kbps modem or broadband connection, and a video card. Printer technology is advancing rapidly; an office supply dealer can help you decide what type of printer(s) you'll need based on what you expect your output to be.

• *Software.* Think of software as your computer's "brain," the instructions that tell your computer how to accomplish the functions you need. There are a myriad of programs on the market that will handle your accounting, inventory, customer-information management, word-processing needs and other administrative requirements. Software can be a significant investment, though, so do a careful analysis of your own needs, and then study the market and examine a variety of products before making a final decision. Many new computers come bundled with software, so be sure you know what you have before buying additional software.

• *Modem.* Modems are necessary to access the internet and online services, and have become a standard component of most computers. Depending on your needs and preferences, you'll have to decide whether you want a basic telephone line modem (that probably comes standard with your computer), a cable modem (about $200 for the hardware and $100 to install), a DSL modem (about $200 to $500 for the hardware and $100 to install), or an ISDN modem (about $250 for the hardware and $200 for setup). Consider investing in DSL or a cable modem for quicker, more efficient operations.

Beware of extremely low prices, as-is deals and closeouts when it comes to purchasing computer equipment. Deals like these often hide problems you wouldn't want, even for free.

• *Photocopier.* A photocopier is a fixture of the modern office, but whether or not you need one will depend on the specific type of food-service operation you are starting. Chances are a deli or pizzeria can do without a copier, but a wholesale bakery or a catering service will likely

> **Beware!**
> Although multifunction devices—such as a copier/printer/ fax machine or a fax/telephone/ answering machine—may be cost- and space-efficient, you risk losing all these functions simultaneously if the equipment fails. Also, weigh your anticipated volume against the machine's efficiency rating and cost to operate, and compare that with stand-alone items before making a decision. However, these machines are more reliable than ever before, so one might work for your business.

find one useful. You can get a basic, no-frills personal copier for less than $400 in just about any office supply store. More elaborate models increase proportionately in price. If you anticipate a heavy volume, you should consider leasing.

- *Fax machine.* For most food-service businesses, fax capability is essential. You'll want to be able to fax orders to your suppliers, and you may want to be able to receive faxed orders from your customers. You can either add a fax card to your computer or buy a stand-alone machine. If you use your computer, it must be switched on to send or receive faxes, and the transmission may interrupt other work. For most businesses, a stand-alone machine on a dedicated telephone line is a wise investment. Expect to pay around $200 for a high-quality fax machine or $400 for a multifunctional device. When assessing the cost of a fax machine, don't just consider the cost of the machine itself. Also take into account how much the cartridges cost and how often you will need to change them.

- *Postage scale.* Unless all your mail is identical, a postage scale is a valuable investment. An accurate scale takes the guesswork out of applying postage and will quickly pay for itself. The U.S. Postal Service estimates accurate weighing can save customers up to 20 percent on mailings. It's a good idea to weigh every piece of mail to eliminate the risk of items being returned for insufficient postage or overpaying when you're unsure of the weight. If you send out an average of 12 to 24 items per day, consider a digital scale, which generally costs $50 to $200. If you send more than 24 items per day or use priority or expedited services frequently, invest in an electronic computing scale, which weighs the item and then calculates the rate via the carrier of your choice, making it easy for you to make comparisons. Programmable electronic scales cost $80 to $250.

- *Postage meter.* A postage meter allows you to pay for postage in advance and print the exact amount on the mailing piece when it is used.

> **Stat Fact**
> Food-service business owners use computers for a range of operational needs, including accounting, payroll records, sales analysis, inventory control, menu planning, employee scheduling, and online services. More than 80 percent of table-service operators use a computer to some degree, and 98 percent of operators with five or more establishments use computers.

> **Smart Tip** *Tip...*
> If you're going to accept orders via fax, be sure the fax machine is visible and that someone checks it at least every five minutes. You don't want someone arriving to pick up a faxed order that you haven't even started to prepare.

Many postage meters can print in increments of one-tenth of a cent, which can add up to big savings for bulk-mail users. Meters also provide a "big company" professional image and are more convenient than stamps. Postage meters are leased, not sold, with rates starting at about $30 per month. They require a license, which is available from your local post office. Only four manufacturers are licensed by the USPS to build and lease postage meters. Your local post office can provide you with contact information.

> **Bright Idea**
>
> Postage stamps come in a variety of sizes, designs, and themes and can add an element of color, whimsy, and thoughtfulness to your mail. Some people prefer stamps because they look personal; others prefer metered mail because it looks "corporate." Here's a suggestion: Use metered mail for invoices, statements, and other "official" business, and use stamps for thank-you notes and marketing correspondence that could use a personal touch.

- *Paper shredder.* In response to both a growing concern for privacy and the need to recycle and conserve space in landfills, shredders are becoming increasingly common in both homes and offices. They allow you to efficiently destroy incoming unsolicited direct mail, as well as sensitive internal documents. Shredded paper can be compacted much tighter than paper tossed in a wastebasket, and it can also be used as packing material. Light-duty shredders start at about $25, and heavier-capacity shredders run $150 to $500.

Telecommunications

The ability to communicate quickly with your customers and suppliers is essential to any business, but especially for a food-service business, where customers often have last-minute needs and questions. Advancing technology gives you a wide range of telecommunications options. Most telephone companies have created departments dedicated to helping small and homebased businesses. Contact your local service provider, and ask to speak with someone who can review your needs and help you put together a service and equipment package that will work for you. Specific elements to keep in mind include:

- *Telephone.* You should start with two telephone lines. As you grow and your call volume increases, you may want to add more lines.

  The telephone itself can be a tremendous productivity tool, and most of the models on the market today are rich in features you will find useful, such as automatic redial, which redials the last number called at regular intervals until the call is completed; programmable memory, for storing frequently called numbers; and a speakerphone function, for hands-free use. You may also want call forwarding, which allows you to forward calls to another number when you're not at your desk, and call waiting, which signals that another call is coming in while you are on the phone. These services are typically available through your telephone company for a monthly fee.

If you're going to be spending a great deal of time on the phone, perhaps doing marketing or handling customer service, consider purchasing a headset for comfort and efficiency. Another option is a cordless phone, which lets you move around freely while talking. However, these units vary widely in price and quality, so research them thoroughly before making a purchase. As a rule of thumb, you should have one business phone line for every five employees.

- *Answering machine/voice mail.* Because your business phone should never go unanswered, you will need some sort of reliable answering device to take calls when you can't do it yourself. Whether to buy an answering machine (which

> ### Bright Idea
> Be sure the announcement on your answering machine or voice mail includes your business name, location, hours of operation, and fax number. If a caller wants just that basic information, he or she won't have to call back when you're open to get it.

Get with the Program

The birth of online communications has been one of the most significant technological breakthroughs in history. The ability to link millions (and potentially billions) of computers allows individuals and businesses to communicate in ways never before possible and gain access to unlimited information.

You can use online services for research about your specific type of food-service business or to find out more about small business and entrepreneurship in general. Most professional associations, equipment manufacturers, and other industry suppliers have websites that provide a wealth of information about how they can help you. Take the time to visit these sites, and study the information they contain. You can also network online with food-service business owners across the country and around the world through electronic mailing lists, bulletin board services, message boards, and chat rooms.

It's well worth your time to get comfortable with the electronic world. Doing so will give you a distinct advantage over those who are not.

Meals on Wheels

If you plan to offer delivery services, you'll need a company vehicle. The type and style you need depends on the food-service business you have and exactly what you're delivering. A pizzeria, for example, can have employees use their own personal cars to make deliveries. But a wholesale bakery or a catering service will likely need commercial vehicles with greater capacity than that of the typical passenger car.

Whether you lease or buy depends on exactly what you need, your cash flow and your tax situation. Do a needs analysis, research the costs of buying both new and used vehicles, check out lease deals and consult with your tax advisor before making a final decision. For example, caterer Ann Crane owns six vehicles, including a refrigerated lift-gate truck, and does not feel she's overloaded with equipment.

costs $40 to $150 for a model that is suitable for a business) or use a voice-mail service provided by your telephone company is a choice you must make depending on your personal choice, work style preferences, and needs.

- *Cellular phone.* Once considered a luxury, cellular phones have become standard equipment for most business owners. Most can be outfitted with features similar to an office phone—such as caller ID, call waiting, and voice mail—and many equipment and service packages are very reasonably priced. You may want a cell phone so that your staff can reach you at any time. You may also want your delivery personnel or catering crews to have cellular phones. On the other hand, if you have a small family-style restaurant and are not out of the store often, a cellular phone may not be necessary. If you choose to give your employees cellular phones, work out a policy regulating their use and appropriate call-return times.

- *Pager.* A pager lets you know that someone is trying to reach you and gives you the option of choosing when to return the call. Many people use pagers in conjunction with cellular phones to conserve the cost of airtime—although with cellular service prices dropping, this option is not as popular as it used to

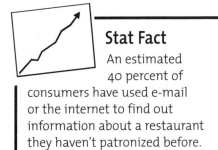

Stat Fact
An estimated
40 percent of
consumers have used e-mail
or the internet to find out
information about a restaurant
they haven't patronized before.

be. As with cellular phones, the pager industry is very competitive, so shop around for the best deal.

- *Toll-free number.* If you are targeting a customer base outside your local calling area, you'll want to provide a toll-free number so they can reach you without having to make a long-distance call. Most long-distance service providers offer toll-free numbers and have a wide range of service and price packages. Shop around to find the best deal for you.

- *E-mail.* E-mail allows for fast, efficient, 24-hour communication. If you plan to have an e-mail account for your business, be sure to check your messages regularly, and reply to them promptly.

Other Equipment

In addition to the basics just mentioned, there are other items you may need, depending on your particular operation. They include:

- *Cash register.* For a retail operation, you need a way to track sales, collect money, and make change. You can do this with something as simple as a divided cash drawer and a printing calculator, or you can purchase a sophisticated, state-of-the-art point-of-sale system that is networked with your computer. This type of register is ideally suited for a multiregister operation, with a bar and main dining area, or a multiunit chain. Of course, a high-end register will cost somewhere between $1,200 and $5,000 per terminal and may not be a practical investment for a start-up operation.

  A preferable option is an electronic cash register (ECR), which ranges in price from $600 to $3,000 and can be purchased outright, leased, or acquired under a lease-to-purchase agreement. Many ECRs offer such options as payment records to designate whether a customer paid by cash, check, or credit card; department price groupings; sign-in keys to help managers monitor cashiers; and product price groupings for tracking inventory more effectively. To free capital in the early stages of your business, check on a lease-to-purchase arrangement, which will run about $100 to $150 per month, or consider leasing a mechanical cash register in the early stages, and make your purchasing decision later. You may be able to justify the investment in an ECR because it can perform several bookkeeping functions and track inventory and customer preferences. A word of caution: Many business owners believe any cash register is a highly visible invitation to thieves, so you should consider security options not only for your cash receipts, but also for the safety of your employees and customers.

- *Credit- and debit-card-processing equipment.* This could range from a simple imprint machine to an online terminal. Consult with several merchant status providers to determine the most appropriate and cost-effective equipment for your business.

Security

Small merchandise, office equipment, and cash attract burglars and shoplifters. Not only do you need to protect your inventory and equipment with alarms and lighting and by selecting your employees carefully, but you also need to ensure your personal safety as well as that of your staff.

Begin by investigating your area's crime history to determine what kind of measures you will need to take (this is something you'll want to look into before you choose a location for your business). To learn whether your proposed or existing location has a high crime rate, check with the local police department's community-relations division or with a crime-prevention officer. Most will gladly provide free information on safeguarding your business and may even visit your site to discuss specific crime-prevention strategies. Many also offer training seminars for small retailers and their employees on workplace safety and crime prevention.

Common techniques that merchants use to enhance security and reduce shoplifting include installing mirrors, alarms, and video cameras. Technology is bringing the cost of these items down rapidly, and installing them may earn you the fringe benefit of discounts on your insurance. You can also increase the effectiveness of your security system by posting signs in your store window and discreetly around the store announcing the presence of the equipment.

Marketing

Every business needs a marketing plan, and your food-service business is no exception. But even as you consider various marketing vehicles, keep this in mind: Research conducted by the National Restaurant Association (NRA) reveals that word of mouth is still the best method of advertising. More than four out of five consumers are likely to choose a table-service restaurant they have not patronized before on the basis of a recommendation from a family member or friend. So, make the foundation of your marketing program an absolutely dazzling dining experience that customers will want to talk about and repeat. Timberline Steakhouse & Grill and Freddy's Frozen Custard owner Scott Redler says, "I truly believe people are going to try you, and if you take care of them when they come in the door, that's your best marketing. It has proven to be true for us."

Ask every new customer how they found out about you, and make a note of this information so you know how well your various marketing efforts are working. You can then decide to increase certain programs and eliminate those that aren't working.

You will need to create a basic marketing plan. Check out *Start Your Own Business* by Rieva Lesonsky (Entrepreneur Press, 2005) for help in making a plan. But there are issues and ideas specific to various types of food-service businesses that you should know about as you develop your plan.

A key question for restaurant owners is this: Do your marketing materials—menus, signs, table tents, ads, and other items—send an accurate message about who you are and what you do? Or are they confusing and misleading?

Marketing is the process of communicating with your existing and prospective customers. A key component of successful restaurant marketing is being sure your message is consistent with what you really are about. Certainly a fine-dining establishment isn't going to put its menus in clear vinyl sleeves and illustrate them with photographs of children enjoying burgers and fries. But the same restaurateur who chuckles at the absurdity of that image may well be guilty of a variety of other more subtle marketing sins.

For example, if senior citizens are a key segment of your market, do your menus and signs consider the physical changes—such as declining vision—that come with age? If you are trying to attract families, are your photographs and illustrations contemporary and relative to your market? Does each element of your marketing package—from décor to menu selections to printed materials—reflect a consistent marketing message?

Bright Idea

Entertainment enhances the dining experience, which increases customer loyalty and repeat business. Consider incorporating entertainment into your marketing plan. Some popular options include live music, display kitchens, video or board games, cooking classes, and cigar rooms.

Have you taken societal changes into account when designing your marketing materials? It's possible that what worked well for you a few years ago may be having a negative impact on your business today.

The first step in creating a complete marketing package is to know your market, and it's not enough to gather demographic information once. Markets change and food-service businesses that don't change their marketing strategies with population shifts are missing out on a lot of opportunities.

Next, step back and take a look at each element in your facility. Everything from the parking lot to the interior décor to the printed items contributes to your marketing message—and each should be an accurate reflection of what that message is.

It's not enough for each marketing component to be relevant to the audience. Rather, the elements must create a sense of continuity. Colors and textures should blend comfortably. Your printed materials should have enough common elements so there is no question that they represent the same restaurant.

Keep Up with the Trends

Staying in step with market trends is standard business advice. Restaurants can do this in a variety of subtle ways. Certainly an increasing number of diners are looking for healthy, low-fat fare, but you can take advantage of trends that go beyond food selection.

Many people are concerned about the environment. You can let them know you share their feelings by using recycled stock for all your printed items. Include a small line of type that says, "Because we care about the environment, this menu [or whatever] has been printed on recycled paper." Expressing support for a particular charity is a popular business trend; choose one that is consistent with your image and not controversial.

To appeal to parents, a family restaurant may want to provide crayons, coloring books, balloons, or toys for children. If you choose to do this, be sure each item carries your logo and basic marketing message and has been chosen with safety in mind.

Other notable trends include ornate menus and thank-you gifts such as golf tees and key chains.

Make Your Grand Opening Truly Grand

You should plan to open for business a few weeks before your grand opening. This "soft opening" gives you a chance to get things arranged properly in your facility and train your employees. At the time of your soft opening, you should have your business sign(s) up and most or all of your inventory in stock. Customers will wander in, and if they are pleased with your business, they will start spreading the word. As both a soft-opening exercise and a marketing technique, one pizzeria distributed coupons for free pizzas in its target delivery area, explaining on the coupon that the restaurant was in the soft-opening phase and that the coupons were good for a specific day and time only.

Use every possible method available to attract customers during your grand opening. Have daily drawings for door prizes such as free meals or a free dessert with a meal purchase. Keep liberal supplies of promotional fliers (perhaps with coupons for discounts on first purchases), business cards, gift certificates, and specialty advertising items in the restaurant. Complimentary coffee, refreshments, and food samples will add to the excitement. You might even consider throwing a party and inviting local dignitaries and celebrities. Whatever you do, open your food-service business with a huge splash.

Look for Marketing Opportunities

Marketing opportunities are often where you least expect them, and it pays to pay attention. Maxine Turner saw her deli business decrease sharply when the road in front of her building was under construction one summer. "It was very hot, so we put out a flier to all of the businesses here in our own complex and all around us, targeting all the people who come into our deli but who were frustrated because the construction made it difficult for them to get here," she recalls. "We did a 'beat the heat, beat the con-struction, bring a friend and have lunch on us' campaign. It was a two-for-one promotion—just a reminder that we were there and serving the community. Our business increased by 30 percent immediately, and it was amazing to see how many people came in without the two-for-one card."

Turner also pays close attention to what's going on in the offices around her store. "If someone is moving in, we send them a little complimentary lunch to introduce ourselves and to welcome them to our business community," she says. "We try to do anything we can to put our name in front of people."

> ## Bright Idea
> Check your paper's business section for announcements of staff appointments and promotions at local companies. Send a congratulatory letter to the people listed and include a coupon for a free drink or dessert.

Rebecca Swartz looks for ways to tie other events into dinner at her restaurant, Viva La Pasta. For example, she offers a Theater Plus Dinner package that includes a multi-course gourmet dinner, tickets to a show, and transportation—typically in a small bus or van—from her restaurant to the civic center or downtown theater and back. "Parking is always a problem downtown, and dining there is also a problem," she says. "We always

Remember the Tourists

More than two-thirds of table-service restaurant operators say that tourists are important to their business. At table-service restaurants with average check sizes of $25 or more, an estimated 40 percent of revenue comes from tourists. Where the check sizes are less than $25, spending by travelers and visitors accounts for about 15 to 30 percent. According to the Travel Industry Association of America, approximately half of all travelers dine out when they travel and say that dining out is the most popular activity they have planned after they arrive at their destination. Be sure to consider this lucrative market in your marketing plan.

get great seats for the show, they have a wonderful meal with us, and they meet other people and make new friends. It's a fabulous package."

Public Relations and Promotions

An easy way to promote your food-service business is by giving away gift certificates, such as for dinner for two, coffee and bagels for ten, or a free pizza. Call local radio stations that reach the demographics of your target market and ask to speak to their promotions manager. Offer to provide gift certificates or coupons to use as prizes for on-air contests and promotions. Your company name and location will probably be announced several times on the air during the contest, providing you with valuable free exposure, and it's always possible that the winner will become a paying customer.

You can also donate coupons and gift certificates to be used as door prizes at professional meetings or for nonprofit organizations to use as raffle prizes. Just be sure every coupon or gift certificate clearly identifies your business name, location, hours of operation, and any restrictions on the prize.

Make being active in the community part of your overall marketing strategy. "You have to leave your store to bring people in," says Swartz. Get out and be visible, and people will follow you back to your business.

Some other promotional methods to try include:

- *Gift certificates.* Gift certificates are convenient for gift giving, especially around holidays. Current customers may give gift certificates to friends or relatives who have never tried your restaurant. Employers may give gift certificates as employee incentives. Many people will gladly try a new eating establishment for a free meal. If you give them good food and service, they'll happily return as paying customers.

- *Sponsorships.* By sponsoring a local event or sports team, you can put your restaurant's name in front of a whole new group of customers. Your name will appear on advertisements promoting the event or on team members' uniforms. This constant exposure will keep your name in customers' minds. Because people

▲

are typically drawn to establishments they are familiar with, you may attract customers who have never visited your restaurant but feel familiar with it due to the exposure from your sponsorship.

- *Discount coupon books.* Many communities have companies that produce books of coupons for participating businesses that schools and nonprofit organizations sell as fund-raisers. As with gift certificates, many people will try a new establishment if they know they're getting a significant discount, and they'll return as full-paying customers if you give them good food and service.

- *Frequent-dining clubs.* Reward your regular customers with free food. For example, you can issue a card with 12 spaces so you can mark off each visit. When the customer has purchased 12 entrées, give him or her a free entrée.

- *Menu promotions.* By offering regular lunch or dinner specials, you can appeal to those who are on a limited budget or just like saving money. You can also offer early-bird specials (dinner at discounted prices, usually from 4 to 6 P.M.) or two-for-one specials during certain periods. These promotions not only attract customers, but can also help you reduce your inventory of overstocked items.

Crazy for Coupons

Coupons are among the most popular marketing tools food-service businesses use. You can include coupons with any print media or direct-mail advertisements you produce. Direct-mail advertising uses computer-selected mailing lists and blanket mailings to entire ZIP codes to distribute fliers, coupon mailers and other advertisements. Special mailing rates make this a highly effective, low-cost medium.

If you use coupons, track them carefully, and make sure they are having the impact you want—which is to introduce your operation to people who will come back and pay the full price. "A lot of people think coupons are the best way to get customers in the door," says sports bar owner Bill Ellison. "I've found that the people you get with coupons are [those] who only come in when they have a coupon. I don't think you have to give coupons away to get the right people in the door. What you have to give is good quality food at a good price, and good service." He notes that if people don't come in unless they can get a few dollars off their meal, you may be charging too much to begin with. Consider your particular style of food-service operation, what is customary (pizza coupons are very common; coupons are rarely used in fine-dining establishments), and what you want to accomplish with the coupon, and then try this marketing technique.

- *Contests.* The most common restaurant contest involves placing a fishbowl (or other glass container) near the cash register where patrons can drop their business card for a drawing for a free lunch or dinner. The winners may bring along friends when they come in for their free meal. Also, the cards give you a list of customers to use for direct mail campaigns.

Plan for Community Involvement

Your community-relations activities are an important part of your overall marketing campaign, and they should be carefully planned. In a recent NRA survey, restaurant owners said they received an average of 75 requests for help each year from community groups or nonprofits and chose to donate time or money to about 35 projects. The respondents said the most important reason for participating in these activities was to give back to the community, but about half cited boosting their restaurant's image and 2 out of 5 said aiding in the recruitment of new employees were "very important" reasons for being involved in civic efforts.

Be sure the organization or event you agree to sponsor is compatible with your image and won't offend prospective customers. Avoid political and controversial issues and events; you can support those privately, but it's better to stay neutral when it comes to your business.

Include the amount of your cash, food, or other donations in your annual financial forecasts, and don't feel bad if you have to say no to a worthwhile cause because you've reached your budget limit.

Be Media Savvy

When your name is mentioned in the newspaper and on local radio and TV broadcasts, it means one of two things: Either you have done something wrong and gotten caught, or you have a strong, positive relationship with the local media. Assuming that you're going to work hard to avoid the former, here are some tips for achieving the latter:

- *Build a media list.* Find out the names of local journalists who might include you in a story, including food and business editors and reporters at your local newspaper, as well as the feature editors and reporters at TV stations. Make a list of these people, and then call them and find out how they would like to receive information from you. Be brief and professional. Simply say, "I have a [description] business, and I'd like to send you periodic news releases. How do you prefer to receive that information?" Typically, they'll want it by regular mail, e-mail, or fax.

- *Make your news releases newsworthy.* Avoid news releases that are obvious bids for self-promotion. Your releases should have a news "hook." The person reading the release should have a clear answer to the question, "So what?" You can tie your releases in to a national event or a holiday to provide a local connection.

▲

A Guaranteed Gamble

Let your customers gamble for a free meal. Keep a set of dice by the cash register, and put up a few signs that read:

Win a FREE meal today! Roll the dice and win!

Two sixes—your meal is free!	*Two threes—take 33% off*
Two fives—take 55% off	*Two twos—take 22% off*
Two fours—take 44% off	*Two ones—take 11% off*

If you calculate the odds, the total discounts work out to an average of 1.2 percent on each order. But the contest produces excitement. When someone wins a free meal, your cost is minimal, but the word-of-mouth advertising is priceless. Besides, the winner is likely to come in with at least one friend to claim his or her prize.

- *Be available as a local expert.* Let your media contacts know you can be counted on as a local expert. For example, if a national wholesale food supplier has a problem with contaminated products, offer to be a resource for a feature on what local food-service operations can do to protect the health and safety of their customers.

- *Take media calls immediately, and return them promptly.* Reporters are usually on tight deadlines. When they call, they need to talk to you right away. If you are not available, they will find someone who is—and that's who they'll call next time.

- *Only give away compliments.* If a reporter does a particularly good story, either about your operation or the industry in general, write the person a brief note letting him or her know you appreciate his or her work. But never send gifts or food; most reporters are not allowed to accept them, and you'll only create an awkward situation.

Trade Shows

In addition to attending trade shows to find merchandise and learn more about running your business, consider exhibiting

Bright Idea

Take professional photos of yourself and your operation so you have them available for publications that may write articles about your establishment. That way you can control the quality and image that goes into print. Also, many local publications are on limited budgets and cannot afford to send out a photographer but will use photos you provide.

Time for a Makeover

Maintaining a consistent marketing message is an ongoing effort. In the craziness of dealing with deliveries that don't arrive on time, cooks who don't show up, and servers who drop trays of food on their way out of the kitchen, it's easy to overlook a messy parking lot or a faded poster. It's important to schedule a regular checkup of your facility. At least once a year step back and look at your restaurant through the eyes of someone who has never eaten there.

Answer these questions during your annual image overhaul:

O What are the most recent demographic trends of your trading area?

O What is the profile of your target market?

O Is your parking lot clean, easily accessible, well-marked, and well-lit for safety and comfort?

O Are your exterior signs in good condition and easy to read?

O Is your waste-disposal equipment visible, and if so, how does the area look and smell?

O Is your flooring clean and in good condition?

O Are your restrooms clean and functioning properly?

O Do your restrooms provide adequate accommodations for your target market—such as diaper-changing stations, lighted vanities, telephones, and vending machines with personal products?

O Are your menus clean, attractive, readable, and designed for your target market?

O Do all your promotional materials—including banners, in-house signs, table tents, menu inserts and other items—clearly identify your restaurant and share a common theme?

O Do the photographs on your walls, your menu boards, and your carryout menus reflect what you are offering?

O Do your posters and signs look fresh, new, and appealing?

O Are your ads easily recognizable with art and copy that appeal to your target market?

in trade shows to market your business. Local trade shows can provide a tremendous amount of exposure at a very affordable cost.

There are two types of shows—consumer (which focus on home and garden and other consumer themes) and business-to-business (where exhibitors market their products and services to other companies). Both can work for a food-service business.

"When you go to a show, you're tapping into an audience that is typically outside your network," says trade show consultant Allen Konopacki. "The other important thing is that the individuals who are going to shows are usually driven by a need. In fact, 76 percent of the people who go to a show are looking to make some kind of a decision on a purchase in the near future."

To find out about shows in your area, call your local chamber of commerce or convention center and ask for a calendar. You can also check out *Tradeshow Week's Tradeshow Directory*, which should be available in your public library, or do an internet search. (See "Trade Secrets" below.)

When you have identified a potential show, contact the sponsors for details. Find out who will attend (show sponsors should be able to estimate the total number of attendees and give you their demographics so you can tell if they fit your target market profile).

Give as much thought to the setup of your booth as you did to the design of your facility. Your exhibit does not need to be elaborate or expensive, but it does need to be professional and inviting. Avoid trying to cram so much into your booth that it looks cluttered. If possible and appropriate, bring food samples, but be sure they can be properly stored at correct temperatures to avoid the risk of contamination.

Your signage should focus on what you do for clients and then include your company name. For example, if you operate a coffeehouse, the prominent words on your booth signage might be "Great Coffee and Entertainment," followed by your establishment's name.

Trade Secrets

Trade shows and conventions are valuable business tools, whether you're attending them to shop and learn, or exhibiting to get more business. For more information on how to get more out of trade shows and to find show schedules, visit these trade show web sites: Incomm Research Center, www.tradeshowresearch.com; Trade Show Central, www.tscentral.com; Trade Show News Network, www.tsnn.com; and Tradeshow Week On-Line, www.tradeshowweek.com.

Samples Sell

Provide diners with samples of menu items to encourage them to order those items. One restaurant sends servers into the bar area with platters of bite-sized bits of main dishes. This allows people waiting in the bar for tables to have a chance to sample several different entrées ahead of time. Another restaurant owner places small portions of desserts on the table when patrons are seated (they get to eat dessert first—and last!). Tasting a bit of a delicious dessert at the beginning of the meal seems to whet customers' appetites for a full-size portion afterward.

If you purchase your food products wholesale, help your customers promote certain items with a sampling program. Baker Jim Amaral sends his employees to new wholesale accounts to conduct a sampling promotion. Generally, two or three times during the first month a new retailer is carrying his bread, Amaral sends his own people into the store to pass out samples. "We know we've got a good product," he says. "If we get it into people's hands and mouths in a no-risk situation, we'll see a return in sales."

Even though the show sponsors may provide a table for you, do not put one across the front of your exhibit space. Doing so creates a visual and psychological barrier and will discourage visitors from coming in.

Be sure not to leave your booth unattended during exhibit hours. For one thing, it's a security risk: During a busy show, it would be easy for someone to walk off with valuable merchandise. More important, you could miss a tremendous sales opportunity.

Consider offering some sort of giveaway item such as a pen, mug, or notepad imprinted with your company name. But, cautions Konopacki, do not display these items openly, as that will only crowd your booth with "trade show tourists" who are not really prospective customers. Instead, store them discreetly out of sight, and present them individually as appropriate. You should also have a stock of brochures, business cards and perhaps discount coupons available.

Financial
Management

There are two key things you need to think about in terms of money: How much do you need to start and operate your business, and how much can you expect to take in? Doing this analysis is often extremely difficult for small-business owners who would rather be in the trenches getting the work done than bound to a desk dealing with tiresome numbers. But force yourself to do it anyway.

One of the primary indicators of the overall health of your business is its financial status, and it's important that you monitor your financial progress closely. The only way you can do that is to keep good records. There are a number of excellent computer accounting programs on the market; another option is to handle the process manually. You might want to ask your accountant for assistance with getting your system set up. The key is to do that from the very beginning and to keep your records current and accurate throughout the life of your company.

Keeping good records helps generate the financial statements that tell you exactly where you stand and what you need to do next. The key financial statements you need to understand and use regularly are:

- *Profit and loss statement.* Also called the income statement, a P&L illustrates how much your company is making or losing over a designated period—monthly, quarterly, or annually—by subtracting expenses from revenue to arrive at a net result, which is either a profit or a loss.

- *Balance sheet.* This statement is a table that shows your assets, liabilities, and capital at a specific point. A balance sheet is typically generated monthly, quarterly, or annually after the books are closed.

- *Cash-flow statement.* The cash-flow statement is a summary of the operating, investing, and financing activities of your business as they relate to the inflow and outflow of cash. As with the P&L statement, a cash-flow statement is prepared to reflect a specific accounting period, such as monthly, quarterly, or annually.

Successful food-service business owners review these reports regularly, at least monthly, so they always know where they stand and can quickly correct minor difficulties before they become major financial problems. If you wait until November to figure out whether or not you made a profit last February, you will not be in business long.

Sources of Start-Up Funds

How much money you need to start depends on the type of business, the facility, how much equipment you need, whether you buy new or used, your inventory, marketing, and necessary operating capital (the amount of cash you need on hand to carry you until your business starts generating cash). It's easy to spend hundreds of thousands of dollars starting a restaurant, but it's not essential. For instance, when Borealis Breads owner Jim Amaral started his first bakery in Maine, he rented a space that had been a commercial bakery and came complete with mixers, benches, ovens, and other equipment. He was able to start with just $10,000, which he borrowed from family and friends and used that primarily for inventory.

Regardless of how much you need, you will need some cash to start your food-service business. Here are some suggestions of where to go to raise your start-up funds:

Beware!
Don't even think about inflating your financial statements to cover a lack of references. This is a felony, and is easily detected by most credit managers.

- *Your own resources.* Do a thorough inventory of your assets. People generally have more assets than they realize, including savings accounts, retirement accounts, equity in real estate, recreation equipment, vehicles, collections, and other investments. You may also opt to sell assets for cash or use them as collateral for a loan. Also, look at your personal line of credit. Many a successful business has been started with credit cards.

- *Family and friends.* The logical next step after gathering your own resources is to approach friends and relatives who believe in you and want to help you succeed. Be cautious with these arrangements; no matter how close you are with the person, present yourself professionally, put everything in writing, and be sure the individual you approach can afford to take the risk of investing in your business.

- *Partners.* Using the "strength in numbers" principle, look around for someone who may want to team up with you in your venture. You may choose someone who has financial resources and wants to work side by side with you in the business. Or you may find someone who has money to invest but no interest in doing the actual work. Be sure to create a written partnership agreement that clearly defines your respective responsibilities and obligations. And choose your partners carefully—especially when it comes to family members.

- *Government programs.* Take advantage of the abundance of local, state, and federal programs designed to support small businesses. Make your first stop the SBA, but be sure to investigate various other programs. Women, minorities, and veterans should check out special financing programs designed to help them get into business. The business section of your local library is a good place to begin your research.

Regardless of which sources of financing you go after, you should know that you'll still need to put up some of your own cash to get your business started. Most investors will want to see that you're willing to risk your own money along with theirs before they'll feel comfortable helping to fund your venture. When Scott Redler opened his first Timberline Steakhouse & Grill in Wichita, Kansas, he put up $24,000 of his own money and raised the rest through investors. He says the cash he invested was, to him, "a very significant amount of money. I also walked away from a job as a senior vice-president of a local restaurant company, and everyone knew at that point: this guy has experience, he's risking a lot, he's giving up that salary. And if it doesn't work, he's going to be out as much as anybody else."

Cold, Hard Cash

If you think finding start-up funds is difficult, be prepared: Finding money to fund expansion after you're up and running can be even more challenging. "As hard as it is to open, it's almost harder to get second-tier financing," says Rebecca Swartz, owner of Viva La Pasta in West Des Moines, Iowa.

The real difficulty will come when you're trying to make the first expansion. That's a time when your personal resources are most likely stretched to the limit, and most of your assets are already pledged as collateral. But, says Swartz, if you can hang in there and continue building a profitable operation, "you'll reach a point where people are throwing money at you."

But just because lenders want you to borrow from them doesn't mean you should. "There's always a price to money," Swartz points out. Sometimes it's simply the interest you'll have to pay; sometimes it's something else. For example, you may find someone who wants to invest in your business, but the money will come with strings attached, such as the person wanting to take an active role in managing the operation, even though you don't agree on his strategies and methods. His daughter may have just graduated from culinary school, or maybe his wife has always wanted to run a bakery, and suddenly you end up with employees you didn't bargain for and are having trouble working with.

If someone expresses an interest in investing in his or her business, find out what his or her motives are. Is the person looking for a job for his or her spouse or kids? Is he or she looking for a place to bring friends to eat for free? Or does he or she simply see a good investment opportunity? Warns Swartz: "Make sure you understand what you're getting into."

Billing

If you're extending credit to your customers—and it's likely you will if you have corporate accounts, especially if you start a bakery or go into the catering business—you need to establish and follow sound billing procedures.

Coordinate your billing system with your customers' payable procedures. Candidly ask what you can do to ensure prompt payment. That may include confirming the correct billing address and finding out what documentation may be required to help the customer determine the validity of the invoice. Keep in mind that many large companies pay certain types of invoices on certain days of the month. Find out if your customers do that, and schedule your invoices to arrive in time for the nearest payment cycle.

Most computer bookkeeping software programs include basic invoice templates. If you design your own invoices and statements, be sure they're clear and easy to understand. Detail each item, and indicate the amount due in bold with the words "Please pay" in front of the total. A confusing invoice may be set aside for later clarification, and your payment will be delayed.

Finally, use your invoices as marketing tools. Print reminders of upcoming specials or new products on them. Add a flier or brochure to the envelope. Even though the invoice is going to an existing customer, you never know where your brochures will end up.

Setting Credit Policies

When you extend credit to a customer, you are essentially providing them with an interest-free loan. You wouldn't expect someone to lend you money without getting information from you about where you live and work and your ability to repay the loan. It just makes sense to get this information from someone you are lending money to.

Reputable companies will not object to providing you with credit information or even paying a deposit on large orders. If you don't feel comfortable asking for at least part of the money upfront, just think how uncomfortable you'll feel if you deliver an expensive order and don't get paid at all. The business owners we talked to all agreed they felt awkward asking for deposits—until they got burned the first time.

Extending credit involves some risk, but the advantages of judiciously granted credit far outweigh the potential losses. Extending credit promotes customer loyalty. People will call you before a competitor because they already have an account set up, so it's easy for them. Customers also often spend money more easily when they don't have to pay cash. Finally, if you ever decide to sell your business, it will have a greater value because you can show steady accounts.

Typically, you will only extend credit to commercial accounts. Individuals will likely pay with cash (or check) at the time of purchase, or they'll use a credit card. You need to decide how much risk you are willing to take by setting limits on how much credit you will extend to each account.

Your credit policy should include a clear collection strategy. Do not ignore overdue bills. The

▲

Tip...

Smart Tip

When you take an order from a customer on open credit, be sure to check his or her account status. If the account is past due or the balance is unusually high, you may want to negotiate different terms before increasing the amount owed.

older a bill gets, the less likely it will ever be paid. Be prepared to take action on past-due accounts as soon as they become late.

Red Flags

Just because a customer passed your first credit check with flying colors doesn't mean you should never re-evaluate his or her credit status—in fact, you should do it on a regular basis.

Tell customers when you initially grant them credit that you have a policy of periodically reviewing accounts. That way, when you do another check it won't be a surprise. Remember, things can change very quickly in the business world, and a company that is on a sound financial footing this year may be quite wobbly next year.

An annual re-evaluation of all customers who have open accounts is a good idea. But if you start to see trouble in the interim, don't wait to take action. Another time to re-evaluate your customers' credit is when they request an increase in their credit line.

Some key trouble signs are a slowdown in payments, increased returns, and difficulty getting answers to your payment inquiries. Even a sharp increase in ordering could signal trouble. Companies concerned that they may lose their credit privileges may try to stock up while they can. Pay attention to what your customers are doing. A major change in their customer base or product line is something you may want to monitor.

Take the same approach to a credit review as you would to a new credit application. Most of the time, you can use what you have on file to conduct the check. But if you're concerned for any reason, you may want to ask the customer for updated information.

Most customers will understand routine credit reviews and accept them as a sound business practice. A customer who objects may well have something to hide—and that's something you need to know.

Accepting Credit and Debit Cards

Unless you are exclusively a wholesale operation, you will need to be able to accept credit and debit cards. It's much easier now to get merchant status than it was in the past. In fact, these days, merchant status providers are competing aggressively for your business.

To get a credit card merchant account, start with your own bank. Also check with various professional associations that offer merchant status as a member benefit. Shop around; this is a competitive industry, and it's worth taking the time to get the best deal.

Accepting Checks

Because losses for retailers from bad checks amount to more than $1 billion annually, many restaurants do not accept checks.

If you do choose to accept checks, look for several key items. First, make sure the check is drawn on a local bank. Second, check the date for accuracy. Third, do not accept a check that is undated, postdated, or more than 30 days old. Fourth, be sure the written amount and numerical amount agree.

Post your check-cashing procedures in a highly visible place. Most customers are aware of the bad-check problem and are willing to follow your rules. If your customers don't know what your rules are until they reach the cash register, however, you may annoy them when, for example, you ask for two forms of identification before accepting a check.

Your main reason for asking for identification is so you can locate the customer in case you have a problem with the check. The most valid and valuable piece of identification is a driver's license. In most states, this will include the driver's picture, signature, and address. If the signature, address, and name agree with what is printed on the check, you are probably safe. If the information does not agree, ask which is accurate and record that information on the check.

You can get insurance against bad checks. Typically, a check-reporting service charges a fee for check verification, usually 4 to 6 percent of the face value of the check, depending on the volume of checks you send through the system. If you called in a $60 check, for example, the service would cost you $2.40. If you weigh that charge against the possibility of losing the entire $60, the service has merit.

If you do not use a check verification system, you should ask for a second piece of identification, such as a check guarantee card, a bank card, or other documentation. Retail merchants' associations often provide lists of stolen driver's licenses and credit cards. If you are dealing with a customer you don't know, you should check the list.

The Tax Man Cometh

Businesses are required to pay a wide range of taxes, and food-service-business owners are no exception. Keep good records so you can offset your local, state, and federal income taxes with the expenses of operating your company. If you sell retail, you'll probably be required by your state to charge and collect sales tax. If you have employees, you'll be responsible for payroll taxes. If you operate as a corporation, you'll have to pay payroll taxes for yourself; as a sole proprietor, you'll pay self-employment tax. Then there are property taxes, taxes on your equipment and inventory, fees and taxes to maintain your corporate status, your business license fee (which is really a tax), and other lesser-known taxes. Take the time to review all your tax liabilities with your accountant.

You might want to look into the latest in point-of-sale check readers, which can significantly speed up the amount of time it takes to accept a check from a customer.

Dealing with Your Creditors

Most business startup advice focuses on dealing with your customers, but you're also going to become a customer for your suppliers. That means you'll have to pay for what you buy. Find out in advance what your suppliers' credit policies are. Most will accept credit cards but will not put you on an open account until they've had a chance to run a credit check on you. If you open an account with a supplier, be sure you understand their terms, and preserve your credit standing by paying on time. Typically, you'll have 30 days to pay, but many companies offer a discount if you pay early.

Dollar Stretcher

Ask suppliers if payment terms can be part of your price negotiation. For example, can you get a discount for paying cash in advance?

Hold the Line on Costs

When you think about how to improve your bottom-line profit, your first thought is probably to increase sales. An equally important and often easier route to greater profitability comes from reducing costs. David Cohen, president of Expense Reduction Group in Boca Raton, Florida, offers this illustration: Your restaurant generates $1 million a year in sales at a net profit margin of 10 percent. If you reduce expenses by $5,000, you will have accomplished the same bottom-line result as you would have if you had increased sales by $50,000. Cohen asks, "What is easier—finding $50,000 worth of new business or trimming costs by $5,000?"

The first step in a cost-reduction program is to identify the purchases that represent the greatest opportunity for savings. Typically, Cohen says, these are the items that are purchased repetitively in sizable quantities.

"Run a vendor report to identify the larger suppliers and to see whether there is any correlation in product purchases from one supplier to another," Cohen advises. Though many business owners believe using multiple sources for the same item keeps vendors honest, he disagrees. "If you're buying the same product from more than one supplier, consolidating those purchases with a single source will give you the opportunity to take advantage of quantity discounts and also earn you more negotiating strength with the vendor you choose."

Keep seasonal price fluctuations and availability in mind. A restaurant owner in North Carolina buys seafood in bulk when prices are down and freezes it for later use. She also buys dry goods in bulk and stores them.

If you are buying multiple products from a single source, consider whether or not you would be better off getting some of those purchases from a specialty vendor, which may offer better pricing. Cohen says segregating specific paper products and purchasing them at lower prices from specialty paper companies is a good example of how this can work.

Be sure the products you buy are the most appropriate and cost-effective items for your needs. It's often worthwhile to spend more money for a higher-quality cleaning or paper product if it does a better job or lasts longer. You may spend more per unit but less overall.

Regardless of how good your vendor relationships are, Cohen recommends an annual review of your overall purchasing process. "Put your major product purchases out for bid every year," he says. "Let two or three companies, plus your current vendor, bid on your business. If your current vendor is giving you good service and pricing, they should have nothing to fear. If they're treating you fairly, stay with them—don't change for the sake of change. But if they've gotten greedy or

Beware!
Including fliers or brochures with your invoices is a great marketing tool, but remember that adding an insert may cause the envelope to require extra postage. Getting out the marketing message is probably well worth the extra few cents in mailing costs. Just be sure you check the total weight before you mail so your invoices aren't returned to you for insufficient postage—or worse, delivered "postage due."

careless, they're going to get caught." The idea is to build loyalty but keep vendors on their toes. The best way to keep vendors from becoming complacent about your business is to not be complacent yourself.

Set an internal system to stay on top of rebates and manufacturer promotions. A lot of items have rebates with deadlines that are easy to overlook. Also, manufacturers might have end-of-year surpluses that will let you pick up a little extra quantity at substantial savings.

Throughout the year, look to your vendors for co-op promotional support, which means that you share the cost of a promotion. If you're going to run a special of some sort, you can generally get co-op funds through a price reduction on the item, rebates, or even free products.

Once you reach an agreement on a purchase, follow up to make sure your invoices actually reflect the stipulated terms and that the arithmetic is accurate. Beyond the actual dollars involved, check the product itself. Weigh what is sold by weight; count what is sold by unit.

Be aware of the details of your contracts. Some business owners automatically renew when a contract is up, but this isn't always smart. You should review the terms, and consider renegotiating before the contract ends. Many have escalator clauses that increase prices after a certain amount of time, and this is a point for serious negotiation.

Shopping for Vendors

The process of putting purchases out for bid is not complicated, but it does take some thought. Use a written request for proposal (RFP) or request for quote (RFQ) that clearly defines your parameters. The RFP forces you to document your criteria and address all your needs, while also allowing you to make a more accurate comparison of vendors because everyone is responding to the same information. Formalizing your purchasing process in this manner also strengthens your own negotiating position because it lets vendors know you understand and are committed to using professional procurement procedures.

Evaluate each vendor on quality, service, and price. Look at the product itself, as well as the supplementary services and support the company provides. Confirm that the vendor has the resources to meet your needs from both a production and delivery standpoint. Remember, a great product at a good price doesn't mean anything if the vendor can't produce enough of it or is unable to get it to you on time.

Verify the company's claims before making a purchase commitment. Ask for references, and do a credit check on the vendor—just as the vendor will probably do on you. Product and service claims can be verified through references. You can confirm the company's reputation and financial stability by calling the Better Business Bureau, appropriate licensing agencies, trade associations, or D&B.

A credit check will tell you how well the supplier you're going to be using pays their vendors. This is important because it could ultimately affect you. If your vendor is not paying its own suppliers, it may have trouble getting raw materials, and that may delay delivery on your order. Or it may simply go out of business without any advance notice, leaving you in the lurch.

Know Your Negotiating Points

As you negotiate your vendor agreements, consider the cost of the item itself, the quantity discounts, add-ons such as freight and insurance, and the payment terms. To determine the true value of a quantity discount, calculate how long you can expect to have the material on hand and what your cost of carrying that inventory is. Quantity discounts are often available if you make a long-term purchase commitment, which may also allow you to lock in prices on volatile commodities.

In many cases, payment terms are an important consideration. Some vendors offer substantial discounts for early payment. Others will extend what amounts to an interest-free, short-term loan by offering lengthier terms.

Freight is an excellent and often overlooked negotiating point. If you're paying the freight charges, you should be selecting the carrier and negotiating the rates. If the vendor is delivering on its own trucks, you can negotiate the delivery fee as part of your overall price.

Every element of the sale is open for negotiation. At all stages of the process, leave room for some give and take. For example, if you are asking for a lower price or more liberal payment terms, can you agree to a more relaxed delivery schedule?

Finalize the Deal in Writing

Contracts are an excellent way to make sure both you and the vendor are clear on the details of the sale. This is not "just a formality" that can be brushed aside. Read all agreements and support documents carefully, and consider having them reviewed by an attorney. Make sure everything that's important to you is in writing. Remember, if it's not part of the contract, it's not part of the deal—no matter what the salesperson says. And if it's in the contract, it's probably enforceable.

Any contract the vendor writes is naturally going to favor the vendor, but you don't have to agree to all the boilerplate terms. In addition, you can demand the inclusion of details that are appropriate to your specific situation. Here's some advice on contracts:

- *Make standard provisions apply to both parties.* If, for example, the contract exempts the supplier from specific liabilities, request that the language be revised to exempt you, too.
- *Use precise language.* It's difficult to enforce vague language, so be specific. A clause that states the vendor is not responsible for failures due to causes "beyond the vendor's control" leaves a lot of room for interpretation. More precise language forces a greater level of accountability.

▲

- *Include a "vendor default" provision.* The vendor's contract probably describes the circumstances under which you would be considered in default. Include the same protection for yourself.

- *Be wary of supplier representatives who have to get any contract changes approved by "corporate" or some other higher authority.* This is a negotiating technique that generally works against the customer. Insist that the vendor make personnel available who have the authority to negotiate.

Cohen advises including an escape clause. "If you are not pleased with the quality and service levels, you want a way to get out of the contract," he says. "You also need to know if there are any other circumstances that could release either party from the agreement and what the liability is." In any case, don't substitute an escape clause for thorough and careful vendor selection.

Tales from
the Trenches

By now, you should know how to get started
and have a good idea of what to do—and not to do—in your own
food-service business. But nothing teaches as well as the voice of
experience. So we asked established food-service business operators to tell us what has contributed to their success and what
they think causes some companies to fail. Here are their stories.

Start with a Job

The best preparation for starting your own restaurant is to work in someone else's establishment first. While you should certainly read books and take courses, you should also plan to work in a restaurant for at least a couple of years, doing as many different jobs as possible. Pay attention to people who are doing different jobs in the restaurant as well so you can understand the various positions. Think of it as getting paid to learn.

But just because you worked in a McDonald's doesn't mean you're ready to open a fine-dining restaurant. You need to work in a restaurant that's similar to the one you plan to start.

Scott Redler, owner of Timberline Steakhouse & Grill, agrees. "Before you open your own restaurant," he says, "you need to work for a good operator for a couple of years."

Do Basic Market Research

When Jim Amaral decided to start Borealis Breads, a wholesale bakery specializing in sourdough bread, no one else was doing anything similar in Maine. To find out if there was a market for the breads he wanted to bake, he called restaurants and retailers, explained his idea, and asked if they'd be interested in buying his breads. "I came up with about 15 accounts that said they would be interested," he says. And that was enough to get him started.

Test Your Real Market

When Anthony Allen opened his first pizzeria, he did some market testing of various dough recipes. "One of my test batches was a Portuguese sweetbread recipe, and I happened to do my test marketing on a night that all of the high school kids were coming out of a basketball game," he recalls. "They all loved the sweet dough, so I made that my dough." But high school kids were not his primary market, and his older patrons did not care for the sweet dough at all.

When you are test marketing, be sure that you conduct your tests on sample groups that truly represent the market you plan to target. And remember that many people will compliment free food because they think it's the polite thing to do. So, ask questions that will get you information you can work with. It's not enough for people to say they like something. Find out why they like it, if there's anything they don't like, if there's anything they would change, and if they'd be willing to buy it.

Find Your Market Niche, and Stay Focused

Amaral says one of the key things he's done that has contributed to his success is finding a market niche that no other baker occupies. "We've positioned ourselves as having a unique product. We don't have a lot of competitors, and that has allowed us to maintain fairly high wholesale prices."

Though Rebecca Swartz's company, Viva La Pasta, provides a wide range of food-related products and services, they are all focused on pasta. "We have been asked to do a lot of things that are very far off of our path," Swartz says. "We think the way to survive is to become an expert in something. We've seen places that go too far out on a limb from their core business and get lost, and then they can't be distinguished from others in the marketplace."

Choose Your Partners Carefully

Because of the financial investment most food-service businesses require, many people opt to form partnerships to raise the capital. Be very cautious, however, if these partners are friends or family members. "When you go into business with a friend or family member, it really changes the relationship," says pizzeria operator Michael Greene. "Sometimes you find out that you can't stay friends." Don't assume that just because you like someone, you can run a business together. Draw up a detailed partnership agreement, and be sure you're clear on your mutual goals and working styles.

Similarly, be careful when you hire friends and family to work for you. Draw a clear line between your professional and personal relationships, and understand that you may be risking the relationship if the job doesn't work out.

Build Relationships with Your Suppliers

Create a bond with your suppliers so that when you're in a bind, they're willing to do something extra to help you out. Be loyal to them; don't make unreasonable demands, pay your bills on time, and respect everyone on their staff—including the delivery drivers. Sports bar owner Bill Ellison always feeds the drivers. "It's amazing what that does," he says. "They give you their cell phone number, so instead of having to call the office, you can call the driver and say, 'Hey, I need this by 12 o'clock,' and he'll put you in front of other people to get the product to you in time."

Get It in Writing

If you're in the catering or wholesale food business, never assume you have an order until you have a signed contract or purchase order. Caterer Ann Crane recalls making a bid on a very upscale party. It was a new client, and she had taken her art director and florist with her to meet with the person—and they all left with the impression that they had the job. But the client was accepting bids from three other caterers. The lesson is clear: Don't take anything for granted. Find out who you're competing against and when you can expect a final decision. And don't buy any supplies or materials until you have a signed contract and a deposit.

Give Back to the Community

Amaral encourages his employees to do volunteer work in the community by paying them for up to three hours of volunteer work (at their regular pay rate) each month. Crane is a strong believer in giving back to the community and serves on a variety of non-profit boards. She says it opens her up to being asked to provide food at a discount, but it also exposes her to potential customers. "One of the more positive things that has come from volunteering is when I have underwritten a party for a nonprofit organization, the people who attend are the same people I want to taste my food, and the word-of-mouth benefit from that has been substantial."

At Swartz's gourmet pasta shop and restaurant, all tips are donated to charity. The business does not provide table service, and employees are not dependent on tips for income, but customers frequently leave gratuities behind. The tips are collected, and at the end of each month, the employees choose which organization gets the money.

Keep Customer Requests in Perspective

Providing outstanding customer service is certainly a worthwhile goal, but you won't be able to meet every single customer request. Trying to do so will stretch your resources to an unmanageable point. For example, if a few people want you to extend your hours, you have to be able to generate enough business to cover the additional overhead and make a profit, or it's not worth doing. If a few customers ask for certain products, be sure the overall demand is strong enough to make purchasing those items worthwhile. One coffeehouse operator says a few people have asked her to carry goat's milk and soy milk, but in her market, stocking those items would not be profitable. However, years ago, when customers began asking for skim milk, she realized that the market was strong enough to justify adjusting her inventory.

Flexibility is key, says Ellison. "You don't provide a service and say, 'This is what I have to offer, take it or leave it.'" You open with an idea, and then you have to evolve to what the customers want."

Provide Employees with Feedback and Recognition

Employees need to know how they're doing—both good and bad—and that their contributions are appreciated. "Our employees know they are coming to a job where a certain level of professionalism is expected, and in return, they are treated as professionals," says Amaral. Good managers provide regular verbal feedback, both for a job well done and when improvement is necessary. "We also do a lot of off-the-cuff stuff," Amaral says. "If somebody has done a really good job at something, we might give them a gift certificate to go out to dinner or something like that. We also have company events where we all go bowling or sailing."

Crane says she makes it a point to pass along customer compliments immediately. When a customer calls to praise a staff member, she immediately contacts that staff person and relays the comments. When customers write positive letters, they are also shared with staffers.

It's often just a matter of treating your employees the way you'd like to be treated, says seafood-restaurant owner Robert Owens. "Most people don't even say 'thank you' in today's world. They take the simplest things for granted. You've got to pay people competitively, but you also have to tell them you appreciate them," he says. "If you treat people how you want to be treated, most of them will treat you the same way."

Viva La Pasta's Swartz sees employees as another market you have to please. "In a way, employees are like customers," she says. "There has to be mutual respect."

Greene says that in addition to individual feedback, it helps to give your staff the opportunity to discuss problems and possible solutions as a group. Even after a situation has been resolved, you can use those circumstances as a training tool, letting employees talk about how a better resolution could have been achieved and what can be done to prevent a reoccurrence of a problem.

Watch What You Say—and Whom You Say It To

Food service is a stressful business, and it's easy to get frustrated with customers who are overly demanding or who want you to do things their way. But no matter how you feel, be careful what you say and who can hear it.

Greene relates the importance of this in a story about his own experience. Years ago, he was running a private club and dealing with a particularly difficult client who was planning a private party. The client represented a significant amount of business, but the contact person was asking for a physical layout that was not efficient or effective, refusing to listen to advice, making extensive menu revisions and in general being extraordinarily irritating.

One day, a messenger arrived with an envelope from the client. Thinking that the delivery person was with an independent service, Greene muttered, "What is she bothering me with now?" when he accepted the envelope. It turned out the messenger was an employee of the client, and Greene's remarks and attitude were promptly conveyed back to the decision maker. To make matters worse, the envelope contained a check. He apologized, the account was saved, and a valuable lesson was learned.

No Negatives

Greene points out that a basic rule of salesmanship is to never ask a question the prospect can answer with "No." He likes to take this technique a step further. "We don't want a customer to ask a question we have to say 'no' to," he says. "Even if they are asking for something they cannot get, don't tell them 'I can't do that.' Instead, tell them what you can do."

Get In with an Out

"Planning from beginning to end is the most important thing," says Ellison. "You need not just a startup plan, but an exit plan. Know how you're going to get out of it if things are going bad—as well as how you're going to get out of the business if things are going well. Don't start without an exit strategy." For example, if you have to close the operation because of a lack of business, how will you handle that process? Or, if your restaurant is a rousing success, would you entertain an offer from someone to buy it? If you're 40 when you start your restaurant, will you still want to be running it 25 years later?

Appendix
Restaurant
Resources

They say you can never be too rich or too thin. While those points could be argued, we believe you can never have too many resources. Therefore, we present for your consideration a wealth of sources for you to check into, check out, and harness for your own personal information blitz.

These sources are tidbits, ideas to get you started on your research. They are by no means the only sources out there, and they should not be taken as the Ultimate Answer. We have done our research, but businesses tend to move, change, fold, and expand. As we have repeatedly stressed, do your homework. Get out and start investigating.

As an additional tidbit to get you going, we strongly suggest the following: If you haven't yet joined the internet age, do it! Surfing the net is like waltzing through a library, with a breathtaking array of resources literally at your fingertips.

Associations

Bakery-Net (the professional baker's online magazine)
www.bakery-net.com

Coffee Science Source (web site created by the National Coffee Association), www.coffeescience.org

Coffee Universe, (800) 655-3955 www.coffeeuniverse.com

Hospitality Business Alliance, National Restaurant Association Educational Foundation, 175 W. Jackson Blvd., 1500 Chicago, IL 60604-2702, (800) 765-2122, www.nraef.org

International Dairy-Deli-Bakery Association, 313 Price Pl., 202 Madison, WI 53705-3262, (608) 238-7908, fax: (608) 238-6330, www.iddba.org

International Guild of Hospitality and Restaurant Managers, www.hospitalityguild.com

National Academy Foundation, 235 Park Ave. S., 7th Fl., New York, NY 10003, (212) 420-8400, fax: (212) 475-7375, www.naf.org

National Association of Catering Executives, 9881 Broken Land Pkwy., 101 Columbia, MD 21046, (410) 997-9055, fax: (410) 997-8834, www.nace.net

National Association of Pizzeria Operators, 908 S. Eighth St., 200 Louisville, KY 40203, (800) 489-8324, fax: (502) 736-9531, www.napo.com

National Barbecue Association, 8317 Cross Park Dr., 150 P.O. Box 14067, Austin, TX 78714-0647, (888) 909-2121, www.nbbqa.org

National Coffee Association of U.S.A., 15 Maiden Ln., 1405 New York, NY 10038, (212) 766-4007, fax: (212) 766-5815, www.ncausa.org

National Pasta Association, 1156 15th St. NW, 900 Washington, DC 20005, (202) 637-5888, fax: (202) 223-9741, www.ilovepasta.org

National Restaurant Association, 1200 17th St. NW, Washington, DC 20036-3097, (800) 424-5156, (202) 331-5900, fax: (202) 331-5950, www.restaurant.org

Specialty Coffee Association of America, 330 Golden Short, 50 Long Beach, CA 90802, (562) 624-4100, fax: (562) 624-4101, www.scaa.org

Consultants and Other Experts

Robert S. Bernstein, Esq., Bernstein Law Firm P.C., 2200 Gulf Tower, Pittsburgh, PA 15219, (412) 456-8100, fax: (412) 456-8135, www.bernsteinlaw.com

David Cohen, president, Expense Reduction Group Inc., 7777 Glades Rd., 317 Boca Raton, FL 33434, (561) 852-1099, ext. 20

Allen Konopacki, Ph.D., trade show consultant, Incomm Research Center 5574 N. Northwest Hwy., Chicago, IL 60630, (312) 642-9377, fax: (312) 642-8598, www.tradeshowresearch.com

Michael P. O'Brien, Esq. Jones Waldo Holbrook & McDonough PC, 170 S. Main St., 1500 Salt Lake City, UT 84101-1644, (801) 521-3200, fax: (801) 328-0537, www.joneswaldo.com

The NPD Group Inc., market research and consulting, 900 West Shore Rd., Port Washington, NY 11050, (516) 625-0700, www.npd.com

Credit Card Services

American Express Merchant Services, (888) 829-7302, www.americanexpress.com

Discover Card Merchant Services, (800) 347-6673, www.discovercard.com

MasterCard, (914) 249-4843, www.mastercard.com

Visa, (800) VISA-311, ext. 96, www.visa.com

Equipment Suppliers

AccuBar, liquor inventory management systems, 9457 S. University Blvd., 261 Highlands Ranch, CO 80126, (800) 806-3922, www.accubar.com

Alcohol Controls Inc., 1023 Haven Ridge Ln. NE, Atlanta, GA 30319-2692, (800) 285-BEER, fax: (404) 262-2327, www.alcoholcontrols.com

All A Cart Manufacturing Inc., custom-designed and manufactured carts kiosks and other custom vending vehicles, 1450 Universal Rd,. Columbus, OH 43207, (800) 695-CART, (614) 443-5544, fax: (614) 443-4248, e-mail: jjmorris@allacart.com, www.allacart.com

BarVision, liquor inventory management systems, Nuvo Technologies Inc., 6060 E. Thomas Rd., Scottsdale, AZ 85251, (480) 222-6000, fax: (480) 222-6001, www.barvision.com

Bevinco Liquor Inventory Systems, 250 Consumers Rd., 1103 Toronto, ON CAN M2J 4V6, (888) 238-4626, (416) 490-6266, fax: (416) 490-6899, e-mail: barry @bevinco.com, www.bevinco.com

Bunn Commercial Products, coffeemaking equipment, P.O. Box 3227, Springfield, IL 62708, (800) 637-8606, www.bunnomatic.com

CBL, carts, kiosks and RMUs, P.O. Box 404, Medford, MA 02155, (617) 292-6499, www.cblpushcarts.com

Consolidated Plastics Co. Inc. commercial matting, bags and other plastic items, 8181 Darrow Rd., Twinsburg, OH 44087, (800) 362-1000, fax: (330) 425-3333, www.consolidatedplastics.com

DMX Music, music services, sound and video systems, 11400 W. Olympic Blvd, 1100 Los Angeles, CA 90064-1507, (800) 700-4412, fax: (310) 444-1717, www.dmxmusic.com

Fetco Corp., beverage service equipment, 640 Heathrow Dr., Lincolnshire, IL 60069-0199, (800) FETCO-99, (847) 719-3000, fax: (847) 821-1178, www.fetco.com

Globe Food Equipment Co., food slicers, processors, mixers and scales 2268 N. Moraine Dr., Dayton, OH 45439, (800) 347-5423, (937) 299-5493, fax: (937) 299-4147, www.globeslicers.com

Grindmaster Corp., beverage systems, coffeemakers, espresso machines, tea equipment and grinders, 4003 Collins Ln., Louisville, KY 40245, (800) 695-4500, (502) 425-4776, fax: (502) 425-4664, (502) 425-4776, www.grindmaster.com

Hollowick Inc., liquid candle lamps and lamp fuel, 316 Fayette St., Manlius, NY 13104, (800) 367-3015, (315) 682-2163, fax: (315) 682-6948, www.hollowick.com

The Howard Company, menu systems, point-of-purchase displays and visual merchandising systems, 1375 N. Barker Rd., Brookfield, WI 53045, (800) 782-6222, (414) 782-6000, fax: (414) 782-6515, www.mainstreetmenus.com

Liquor Control Solutions, liquor inventory management systems, 58 Beach St. Staten Island, NY 10304, (866) 803-3000, fax: (718) 447-8610, www.liquorcontrolsolutions.com

Plymold Seating, food-service furniture, 615 Centennial Dr., Kenyon, MN 55946, (800) 759-6653, www.plymold.com

Rapids Wholesale Equipment Co., restaurant and bar equipment; commercial food-service supplies, 6201 S. Gateway Dr., Marion, IA 52302, (319) 447-1670, www.4rapid1.com

Renato Specialty Products Inc., display-cooking equipment including brick ovens and rotisseries, 2775 W. Kingsley Rd., Garland, TX 75040, (800) 876-9731, (972) 864-8800, fax: (972) 864-8900, www.renatos.com

SerVend International, ice and beverage systems, 2100 Future Dr., Sellersburg, IN 47172, (800) 367-4233, www.servend.com

Sicom Systems Inc., PC point-of-sale equipment, 4140 Skyron Dr., Doylestown, PA 18901, (800) 547-4266, fax: (215) 489-2769, www.sicompos.com

The Trane Company, heating, ventilation and air-conditioning equipment, 2550 Corporate Exchange Dr., 200 Columbus, OH 43231, (614) 899-5100, fax: (614) 882-5456, www.trane.com

Franchises and Business Opportunities

Atlanta Bread Co. International Inc., upscale bakery and cafe, 1955 Lake Park Dr., 400 Smyrna, GA 30080, (800) 398-3728, fax: (770) 444-1991, www.atlantabread.com

Cousins Subs, N83 W13400 Leon Rd., Menomonee Falls, WI 53051, (800) 238-9736, (414) 253-7700, fax: (414) 253-7705, www.cousinssubs.com

Freddy's Frozen Custard, 1445 N. Rock Rd., 210 Wichita, KS 67206, (316) 260-8282, fax: (316) 260-8283, e-mail: sredler@cox.net, www.freddysfrozencustard.com

Manchu Wok, quick-service Chinese restaurant, 85 Citizen Ct., Unit 9 Markham, ON, CAN L6G 1A8, (800) 361-8864, (561) 798-7800, www.manchuwok.com

Orion Food Systems Inc., various franchised brands, including a bakery, pizzeria, sandwich shop, and others, 2930 W. Maple St., Sioux Falls, SD 57107, (800) 648-6227, fax: (605) 336-0141, www.orionfoodsys.com

Inventory and Supply Sources

Great American Stock, food photography, 5200 Pasadena Ave. NE, Ste. C, Albuquerque, NM 87113, (800) 624-5834, (505) 892-7747, www.greatamerican stock.com

Insulair Inc., insulated paper cups, 35275 Welty Rd., Vernalis, CA 95385, (800) 343-3402, (209) 839-0911, fax: (209) 839-1353, www.insulair.com

McCain Foods, USA french fries and appetizers, 905 Butterfield Rd., Oak Brook, IL 60523, (800) 952-4432, www.mccainusa.com

Neighbors Coffee, specialty coffees, gourmet hot chocolate, instant cappuccino mixes and gourmet teas, P.O. Box 54527, Oklahoma City, OK 73154, (800) 299-9016, (405) 236-3932, fax: (405) 232-3729, www.neighborscoffee.com

Rich Products Corp., food products, including meats, desserts, toppings, rolls, and breads, 1 Robert Rich Wy., Buffalo, NY 14213, (800) 356-7094, (716) 878-8000, www.richs.com

StockPot, fresh refrigerated soups, sauces, entrees, gravies and side dishes, 22505 State Route 9, Woodinville, WA 98072-6010, (800) 468-1611, (425) 415-2000, fax: (425) 415-2004, www.stockpot.com

Sweet Street Desserts frozen gourmet desserts, 722 Hiesters Ln., Reading, PA 19605, (800) SWEET-97, www.sweetstreet.com

SYSCO Corp., national distributor of food-service products, 1390 Enclave Pkwy., Houston, TX 77077-2099, (281) 584-1390, fax: (281) 584-4070, www.sysco.com

Magazines, Books, and Publications

Atlantic Publishing, books, videos, training materials, tools, and software for the food-service and hospitality industries, 1210 SW 23 Pl., Ocala, FL 34474 orders: (800) 541-1336, fax: (352) 622- 5836, www.atlantic-publishing.com

Beverage World, VNU Business Publications USA, 770 Broadway, New York, NY 10003, (847) 763-9050, www.beverageworld.com

Complete Idiot's Guide to Starting a Restaurant, by Howard Cannon and Brian Tracy, Alpha Communications

Cooking for Profit, CP Publishing Inc., P.O. Box 267, Fond du Lac, WI 54936-0267, (920) 923-3700, fax: (920) 923-6805, www.cookingforprofit.com

Cornell Hotel & Restaurant Administration, Quarterly Center for Hospitality Research Cornell University, (607) 255-9780, fax: (607) 254-2922, www.hotelschool.cornell.edu/publications

The Food Service Professional's Guide to Food Service Menus: Pricing and Managing the Food Service Menu for Maximum Profit: 365 Secrets Revealed, by Lora Arduser, Atlantic Publishing Group

Entrepreneur Magazine's Ultimate Book of Restaurant and Food-Service Franchises, Rieva Lesonsky and Maria Anton Conley, Entrepreneur Press, www.smallbizbooks.com

Fresh Cup magazine, P.O. Box 14827, Portland, OR 97293-0827, (800) 868-5866, (503) 236-2587, fax: (503) 236-3165, www.freshcup.com

Menu Pricing & Strategy, by Jack E. Miller, Wiley

Nation's Restaurant News, (800) 944-4676, www.nrn.com

The New Restaurant Entrepreneur: An Inside Look at Restaurant Deal-Making and Other Tales from the Culinary Trenches by Kep Sweeney, Dearborn Trade Publishing

Penton Media publications include *Restaurant Management* and *Restaurant Hospitality*, www.penton.com

Pizza Today, 908 S. Eighth St., 200 Louisville, KY 40203, (800) 489-8324, (502) 736-9500, fax: (502) 736-9502, www.pizzatoday.com

QSR: The Magazine of Quick Service Restaurant Success, 4905 Pine Cone Dr., 2 Durham, NC 27727, (800) 662-4834, (919) 489-1916, www.qsrmagazine.com

Restaurant Business, (847) 763-9050, www.restaurantbiz.com

The Restaurant Business Start-up Guide, by Paul Daniels, Venture Marketing 2002
Restaurant Report, www.restaurantreport.com

Restaurant Start-up & Growth, (281) 545-9230, www.restaurantowner.com

Restaurants and Institutions

Reed Business Information, 2000 Clearwater Dr., Oak Brook, IL 60523, (630) 288-8242, fax: (630) 288-8225, www.rimag.com

Special Events Magazine, 23815 Stuart Ranch Rd., Malibu, CA 90265, (800) 543-4116, (310) 317-4522, www.specialevents.com

Specialty Retail Report, 195 Hanover St., Hanover, MA 02339, (800) 936-6297, (781) 312-1055, fax: (888) 213-1857, www.specialtyretail.com

Trademark: Legal Care for Your Business and Product Name, by Kate McGrath and Stephen Elias, Nolo Press, (800) 992-6656

Music Licensing Agencies

American Society of Composers Authors and Publishers (ASCAP), 1 Lincoln Plaza, New York, NY 10023, (212) 621-6000, fax: (212) 724-9064, www.ascap.com

Broadcast Music Inc., 320 West 57 St., New York, NY 10019-3790, (212) 586-2000, www.bmi.com

SESAC Inc., 55 Music Square E., Nashville, TN 37203, (615) 320-0055, fax: (615) 329-9627, www.sesac.com

Successful Food-Service Business Owners

Borealis Breads, Jim Amaral, Portland Public Market, Portland, ME 04101, (800) 541-9114, www.borealisbreads.com

Cuisine Unlimited, Maxine Turner, 4641 S. Cherry St., Salt Lake City, UT 84123, (801) 268-2332, fax: (801) 268-2992, www.cuisineunlimited.com

Frasier's, Bill Ellison and Frank Perez, 2189 E. Semoran Blvd., Apopka, FL 32746, (407) 889-9999, www.frasierssportsbar.com

Key Lime Inc., Kenny Burts, P.O. Box 2002, Smyrna, GA 30081, (707) 333-0043, fax: (770) 436-4280, www.keylimeworld.com

Meyerhof's & Cuisine M, Ann Crane, 17805 Sky Park Cir., Ste. A, Irvine, CA 92614, (949) 261-6178, fax: (949) 833-2833, www.meyerhofs.com

River City Billiards, Anthony Allen and Michael Greene, 87 Washington S., Haverhill, MA 01832, (978) 372-6988

RV's Seafood Restaurant, Robert V. Owens, III, P.O. Box 935, Nags Head, NC 27959, (252) 441-4963

Timberline Steakhouse & Grill, Scott Redler, 9422 Cross Creek Ct., Wichita, KS 67206, (316) 393-4430, www.timberlinesteakhouse.com

Viva La Pasta, Rebecca Swartz, owner, 4100 University, 104 West, Des Moines, IA 50266, (515) 222-944

Glossary

Arabica beans: a kind of coffee bean that produces superior-quality coffees that possess the greatest flavor and aromatic characteristics.

BAC: blood alcohol content.

Barista: a master espresso maker; a barista is an expert in both coffees and brewing.

Bump-out: a term describing the addition of a food-service area to a gas station or convenience store in a configuration that resembles a sunroom or porch on a house.

Comps: free drinks authorized by management.

Comp sheet: a form on which bartenders record drinks that are given away.

Corrosion-resistant materials: materials that maintain their original surface characteristics under prolonged influence of the food they're in contact with; the normal use of cleaning compounds and bactericidal solutions; and other conditions.

Cupping: Professional coffee-bean tasters use this process to determine the quality, acidity, and aroma of beans for selection in their blends; process involves steeping the coffee beans, as with tea leaves, then smelling and tasting the brew at different temperatures as it cools.

Dayparts: a restaurant-industry term that refers to various meal cycles that occur throughout the day—typically breakfast, lunch, dinner, and early evening.

Dramshop laws: statutes that impose a special liability on those in the business of producing, distributing, and selling or serving alcoholic beverages to the public.

Dual-branding: when two or more brand-name operations are located in the same retail space, working cooperatively; also called dual-concepting.

Food-contact surfaces: surfaces of equipment and utensils with which food normally comes into contact and surfaces from which food may drain, drip, or splash back onto other surfaces normally in contact with food.

Free pour: pouring alcohol without a measuring device.

Front of the house: the parts of a restaurant the customer visits, including the customer service area, bar, and dining room.

HVAC: an acronym for heating, ventilation, and air conditioning.

Kitchenware: all multiuse utensils other than tableware.

Meat jobber: a distributor that specializes in portion-controlled meat supplies for restaurants.

Peel: a long-handled, shovel-like implement used by bakers to move bread, pizza, and other items around in (or out of) an oven.

Robusta beans: supermarket-grade coffee beans that can be grown in any tropical or subtropical climate and are cultivated for their ease as opposed to their taste.

Safe materials: articles (including metal, plastic, and ceramic utensils; dishes; food storage containers; pots and pans) manufactured from or composed of materials that aren't expected to affect, directly or indirectly, the characteristics of any food.

Shrinkage: a term for inventory losses.

Single-service articles: any tableware, carryout utensils, or other items that are designed for one-time use.

Tableware: eating, drinking, and serving utensils for table use such as flatware (forks, knives, and spoons), bowls, cups, serving dishes, and plates.

Utensil: any item used in the storage, preparation, conveying, or serving of food.

Index